A Captain's Diary

MY FIRST YEAR

A Captain's Diary

MY FIRST YEAR

RICKY PONTING

& BRIAN MURGATROYD

HarperSports
An imprint of HarperCollins*Publishers*

Harper*Sports*
An imprint of HarperCollins*Publishers* Australia

First published in Australia in 2004
by HarperCollins*Publishers* Pty Limited
ABN 36 009 913 517
A member of the HarperCollins*Publishers* (Australia) Pty Limited Group
www.harpercollins.com.au

HarperCollins*Publishers*
25 Ryde Road, Pymble, Sydney, NSW 2073, Australia
31 View Road, Glenfield, Auckland 10, New Zealand
77–85 Fulham Palace Road, London, W6 8JB, United Kingdom
2 Bloor Street East, 20th floor, Toronto, Ontario M4W 1A8, Canada
10 East 53rd Street, New York NY 10022, USA

National Library of Australia Cataloguing-in-Publication data:

Ponting, Ricky.
A captain's diary.
ISBN 0 7322 7848 1.
1. Pointing, Ricky. 2. Cricket captains - Australia -
Biography. 3. Cricket players - Australia - Biography.
4. Cricket - Australia. 5. Cricket. I. Murgatroyd, Brian.
II. Title.
796.358092.

Cover photography by Phil Hillyard/© News Limited
Cover design by Stuart Horton-Stevens, Geeza Design
Internal design adapted from design by Christa Edmonds, HarperCollins Design Studio
Statistics designed by Judi Rowe, Agave Creative Group
Typeset in Sabon 11/17 by HarperCollins Design Studio
Printed and bound in Australia by Griffin Press on 79gsm Bulky Book

5 4 3 2 1 04 05 06 07

Acknowledgments

Putting together this book, which covers more than a year of intense international cricket both at home and overseas, has been a major undertaking and there are many people who deserve thanks for making it possible.

My beautiful wife Rianna has continued to be an amazing source of strength for me. You have been there for me every step of the way and it is thanks to you that I have enjoyed the successful period in my career documented in this book. I owe you more than you can ever know.

Thanks to Brian Murgatroyd for once again assisting in getting my thoughts, theories and memories down on paper, and also to Cricket Australia's media manager, Jonathan Rose, whose ongoing help and advice through the period covered in this diary has been priceless.

To my team-mates, the team's support staff and the staff at Cricket Australia, thank-you for helping to make my transition from player to Test captain so smooth. It is a joy to play cricket in an environment where everyone is always offering up ideas and suggestions and continues to challenge themselves to be better. The attitude of you all has helped to ensure we remain the side every other team measures itself against. And to Stephen Waugh, thank-you for giving us a legacy to be proud of.

To Phil Hillyard and other contributing photographers from News Limited, a big thanks for your superb pictures contained in this book, and to Ross Dundas for supplying such a comprehensive package of stats. And to everyone at HarperCollins, especially Ali Orman, Alison Urquhart, Jenny Grigg, Tracey Gibson, Helen Beard, Judi Rowe and Mel Cain, thanks once again for your professionalism and excellence in ensuring this book has gone from an idea to reality. Thanks also to Sarah Shrubb and Nicola O'Shea for their eagle-eye editing.

Thanks, too, to Brian's family and friends, and to the Gayleard family — John, Jennifer, Jessica and Jack — as well as Stephanie Beltrame, Garry Rainford and the Catherine Hill Bay Bowling Club. All of you can take pride in this book because your efforts have helped ensure it came about.

Lastly, thank-you to my family, Rianna's family and my manager Sam Halvorsen for always putting me ahead of everything else. You are always there for me. One day I hope I can do the same for you.

Contents

FOREWORD

BY STEPHEN WAUGH

Ricky Ponting was destined to lead his country — I couldn't have handed Australian cricket's ultimate individual honour to a more capable and deserving man.

A leader must earn respect and lead from the front, and on both of these counts Punter has undoubtedly excelled. When the one-day leadership duties were passed over to Ricky in South Africa, my main piece of advice to him was, 'Make sure you take care of your own game and maintain your form, because everything else will follow from that.' Since assuming the mantle, Punter has shown himself to be among the top three batsmen in the world in both forms of the game, and has elevated his hunger and desire for runs to a level most can only aspire to.

The team has enjoyed remarkable success in recent times, culminating in a 3–0 series victory over Sri Lanka on their home turf. This was a great team achievement, especially considering that they faced a first innings deficit on each occasion, something which has been extremely rare in recent years. The win was a triumph for team unity, excellent planning and strong direction, and augurs well for the team in its quest for a series win against India, Australia's main contender for the number one position in world cricket.

It's always difficult to reach the top in your chosen profession; staying there and continuing to improve and widen the gap is perhaps an even more challenging task. Right now the Aussies, under Ricky, have done that, and that is a credit to their determination and commitment to create a place for themselves in cricket's history as a great team. I for one am rapt that the boys are continuing to raise the bar, and I am sure that the foot won't come off the accelerator under Ricky's confident and astute leadership.

The only downside for Ricky, being a full-time captain now, is an increase in the number of meetings he has to attend and a lack of spare time — which might hinder his progress to the pro golf circuit after he retires from cricket ... but knowing his fierce determination and natural ability, I wouldn't bet against him making it if he wanted to.

Let's hope his next diary is one that tells of Australia's victory on the subcontinent against India.

Part 1: Australia in the West Indies

RUNS SCORED AND RUNS ENDING

Monday 17 March, 2003

Australia names a 15-man squad for the Test tour of the West Indies. It is: Stephen Waugh (captain), Ricky Ponting (vice-captain), Andrew Bichel, Adam Gilchrist, Jason Gillespie, Matthew Hayden, Brad Hogg, Justin Langer, Brett Lee, Martin Love, Darren Lehmann, Stuart MacGill, Damien Martyn, Glenn McGrath and Ashley Noffke.

Jason Gillespie's inclusion is subject to his passing a fitness test on the heel injury that forced his early return home from the World Cup.

The tour is Ricky Ponting's first as vice-captain of the Test side; he takes over the role from Adam Gilchrist.

Saturday 29 March

Damien Martyn is withdrawn from the early stages of the Caribbean tour to allow further scans and assessments of his fractured right index finger. A decision on whether or not he will join the tour at a later date will be made after the assessments. Martyn fractured the finger during the World Cup Super Six match against Kenya on 15 March but played in the World Cup final eight days later, scoring 88 not out from 84 balls.

Monday 31 March

Brian Lara is reappointed West Indies captain for the upcoming home series against Australia and Sri Lanka. Lara replaces Carl Hooper, who led the West Indies during the World Cup.

Bennett King, the head coach of the Commonwealth Bank Cricket Academy, is named as the new West Indies coach. King, who also coached Queensland, later decides to withdraw his application.

The Australia squad departs for the Caribbean.

Wednesday 2 April

Glenn McGrath is to return home to be with his wife, Jane, who has a secondary cancer infection in her hip. It is not known how long McGrath will be absent from the tour and no immediate decision is made on a replacement player.

Thursday 3 April

Western Australia fast bowler Brad Williams is drafted into the squad to replace McGrath. Williams is replaced in the Australia A squad, currently playing against South Africa A, by Damien Wright, the Tasmania fast bowler.

Damien Martyn is ruled out of the Test series against the West Indies. After visiting a hand specialist in Perth it was discovered that the fracture in his right index finger was more serious than hoped. No decision is made yet on his fitness to play in the one-day series that follows the four Tests in the Caribbean.

Friday 4 April

New South Wales batsman Michael Clarke is named as Martyn's replacement in the Test squad to the Caribbean. Currently playing for Australia A against South Africa A, his place in that squad is taken by Queensland's Clinton Perren.

Saturday 5–Monday 7 April

Everest Cricket Club, Georgetown, Guyana: The Australians 3–377 declared (Waugh 106 not out, Hayden 102, Langer 60, Love 56) and 196 (Love 59) drew with the Carib Beer XI 132 and 6–402 (Deonarine 141 not out, Baugh 115 not out, Hogg 5–112).

Australia open their Caribbean tour with a three-day fixture. Ricky Ponting and Brett Lee are both rested from the match.

Sunday 6 April

The West Indies name a 14-man squad for the first Test. It is: Brian Lara (captain), Carlton Baugh, Dave Bernard Junior, Shivnarine Chanderpaul, Pedro Collins, Vasbert Drakes, Mervyn Dillon, Daren Ganga, Wavell Hinds, Carl Hooper, Ridley Jacobs, Jermaine Lawson, Marlon Samuels and Devon Smith.

Opener Chris Gayle is omitted after opting to play in a double-wicket tournament instead of playing for Jamaica in the Carib Beer Series final against Barbados; Ramnaresh Sarwan is absent with a finger injury.

Monday 7 April

Hooper withdraws from the West Indies squad after announcing that he has reconsidered his decision to make himself available.

Tuesday 8 April

Glenn McGrath confirms that he is set to resume his place on tour in time to take part in the third Test, subject to his wife's positive response to cancer treatment.

Wednesday 9 April

The day before the first Test of the series — and my first Test as vice-captain to Stephen Waugh.

I have been Test vice-captain before, when Gilly took charge of the side against the West Indies at Adelaide in December 2000 and in England, at Headingley in August 2001, but both times were because of injuries to Stephen. Now I have been appointed to the role in my own right.

I was a bit uneasy about the elevation when I first heard about it, in Durban during the recent World Cup, because I could not see the need to change — Gilly had held the role without any problems since 2000. But Trevor Hohns explained to me that if anything happens to Stephen the selectors want me to take charge of the side and that can only happen if I am vice-captain.

Gilly has been great about it, putting aside any ambitions he may have to be captain, but although there are a couple of words after my name in the squad announcement, in reality my role has not changed very much at all.

It may seem like a cliché, but this Australia team has always considered itself a team of leaders, not a group with just one or two blokes in charge, and I cannot see that changing. Stephen has always asked everyone for ideas, and he has always sought my opinions on the game — and I have been happy to offer any suggestions I can. That will not change just because I have the title 'vice-captain' after my name.

This is my third tour of the Caribbean, and if Guyana is any guide to how the pitches will play in this series, the days of the ball flying through to the wicketkeeper have long gone. I was rested from the warm-up game to allow some of the players who did not take part in the World Cup the chance for a hit, but I could still see how the pitch behaved in that match. It was slow and low — the type of surface where you could bat all day if you wanted to. We made a low score in our second innings purely because we reversed the batting order, to give everyone a chance of time in the middle. Then, when we bowled a second time, they made a large score: we had set ultra-attacking fields because the home side needed 442 to win, which meant we had no chance of losing the game. If the pitches for the Test series resemble that one, it will be tough work to pick up 20 wickets.

Our main plan for the series is to try to bat just once in each match. We expect the pitches will be easy paced, so we want to give ourselves the maximum time to bowl them out twice — the best way to do that is to avoid taking up time by batting twice ourselves.

That might sound arrogant, but it is a realistic assessment of how we can best win. Rest assured there is no complacency in this squad. Quite a few of us were here in 1999 when we won the first Test easily, bowling West Indies out for 51, but then had to win the last match of the series to retain the Frank Worrell Trophy. The Caribbean has been a tough place for sides to come and win series in recent times, and although we know we should win if we play to the best of our ability, none of us thinks that all we have to do to win is turn up.

We discussed their squad and how we will try to play against them.

Batting

- Devon Smith — young opening batsman, likes room to play his shots outside the off-stump; in that sense is not unlike Sri Lanka's opener, Jayasuriya. Bowl a tight line to restrict him through the off-side, and short of a length to stop him driving.
- Wavell Hinds and Chris Gayle — both left-handers, both at the top of the order, so we can use similar tactics for both, although Gayle is not included as yet. Neither player moves his feet much, but both will take full toll of anything outside off-stump. Bowl a full length and swinging in, especially early on, because both are lbw candidates.
- Brian Lara — has a big jump back and across his stumps, especially early in his innings, so fast bowlers should go full and straight for a chance of lbws. Can look vulnerable to the short ball in at the body; Glenn McGrath has troubled him there in the past.
- Shivnarine Chanderpaul — well organised, and not too many weaknesses. Stay patient around off-stump: he has been dismissed edging into the slip cordon in the past.
- Ramnaresh Sarwan — like Gayle, not playing in the first match, although we expect him to figure later on. Vulnerable around off-stump, so get him feeling for the ball in that area. Was hit on the head during the World Cup and looks unsure when faced with short-pitched bowling.
- Marlon Samuels — has lots of talent and lots of shots but be

patient against him; we are not sure he always has a plan in mind. Frustrating him could cause a reckless shot.

- Ridley Jacobs — a fighter who likes width and also a chance to play the pull shot. Push the ball across him: he was caught behind a number of times on the tour of Australia two years ago.
- Daren Ganga — on the tour of Australia two years ago, he always looked vulnerable around off-stump. Keep it there and be patient.

Bowling

- Mervyn Dillon — has an awkward, funny action that is all arms and legs. Angles the ball in from wide of the crease but the odd ball may hold its line or even go away from the right-hander. Very inconsistent and will bowl you a bad ball, so be patient.
- Vasbert Drakes — good competitor, very experienced from his time in first-class cricket in South Africa and England; the most consistent member of the attack. Will be accurate and will try to force you to make a mistake, but he is only just over medium pace, so just wait for the right ball to hit. Deserves respect.
- Pedro Collins — played against us in 1999 and was quite inconsistent, but can swing the ball back into the right-handers and also make the old ball go the other way with reverse swing. Will be used as their go-to bowler to keep things quiet, along with Drakes.
- Jermaine Lawson — very quick, and has a real competitive edge, but tends to bang the ball in too short and will bowl you a bad ball. Be patient.
- Tino Best — a player we have heard could figure in the series, although we do not know much about him. Reports suggest he is just like Lawson — quick and really likes the short ball.

Thursday 10 April

First Test, day one: Australia 1–120 (Langer 55 not out) trail West Indies 237 (Chanderpaul 100, Jacobs 54 not out) by 117 runs.

An excellent day for us, which would have been even better but for one of the best innings I have ever seen. Even allowing for a pitch which did not offer the bowlers very much, Shivnarine Chanderpaul's innings was as close to flawless as you will see, and without it the West Indies would be out of the match already.

He played shots all around the wicket, pulls, drives, punches down the ground, you name it. And with the outfield like glass, with everything that beat the field pretty much guaranteed to go for four, it meant he rattled along at an amazing rate, much to the delight of the crowd — this Test is being played on his home ground. The noise levels got quite high at various stages, which was an added complication for us. Communication on the field is not always easy in those circumstances — it involves a lot of hand signals by the captain, and you need to keep an eye on him at all times.

I think Chanderpaul's hundred came up in just 69 balls; standing at slip, it was like watching a highlights tape.

Until we got Chanderpaul out to his first false shot, lbw to Andy Bichel as he tried to pull a ball that was not quite short enough for the shot, we never looked like dismissing him, even though he was scoring so quickly. All he did was play high-quality cricket shots; there was no slogging at all despite his rate of scoring.

What could we have done? Hindsight is a great thing: maybe we could have put a deep point on the fence and looked to bowl a little wider to him, cutting off his flow of boundaries and drying up his momentum that way. But his innings happened so quickly it was almost over before we knew what hit us and I think we all believed he could not keep playing so well forever.

Brett Lee bowled beautifully with the new ball, with pace, swinging the ball into all the left-handers they have in their top order. But once the hardness and shine started to fade from the ball it became hard work, especially with Chanderpaul and Ridley Jacobs playing so well; with the pitch offering our bowlers very little, our decision to go into the match with a five-man attack justified itself.

It is a shift in policy for us — I am struggling to think of another occasion in the recent past when we did not go into a Test with just four frontline bowlers. In the past, in their younger years, either Mark or Stephen Waugh filled a role as a fifth bowler, and there is an element of looking to make up for the absence of Warne and McGrath in the decision — it is pretty difficult to replace around 900 Test wickets at the drop of a hat. But on a flat pitch like this, having five bowlers will also give us plenty of different options through their differing styles.

It means Gilchrist will bat at number six with, on paper at least, a long tail to follow, but Brad Hogg, Bichel, Lee, Jason Gillespie and

Stuart MacGill are all capable of supporting a top-order player. And it is up to the batsmen to make sure we do our jobs.

Bichel was our most successful bowler picking up three wickets. One of them was the prized scalp of Brian Lara, a success that is the latest episode in a fiery contest between the two that began on the West Indies' last tour of Australia, in 2000.

On that tour Lara had a lean time in the Test series. His one big score came in Adelaide, when he made 182 in a match where we picked two spinners, MacGill and Colin Miller.

Lara is a brilliant player of spin, one of the best I have ever seen, but in the next Test, in Melbourne, we played just one spinner, Colin Miller; the conditions were pace-friendly, so it was our quick bowlers who did the bulk of the bowling.

When Lara came in to bat at the MCG, Mark Waugh, fielding at slip, tried to wind him up by shouting: 'No spinners for you to get after now, mate.' But Lara, who thrives on a bit of chat out in the middle to get his adrenaline and concentration going, looked around the field, pointed to Bichel and said: 'He'll do.'

Lara had thrashed Bichel all around Hobart two weeks earlier when the West Indies played Australia A, hitting six fours off him in one over on the way to 231. This time, all his comment did was fire Bichel up, and sure enough, Lara was out shortly afterwards — caught by Mark Waugh off Bichel.

Ever since then, Andy seems to find an extra bit of pace whenever Lara is batting and, needless to say, he takes massive pleasure in getting Lara out. When we got back to the dressing room at lunch today we heard that there was some suggestion Lara may have got an inside edge onto his pad before being given out lbw. Bichel's answer to that was simple: 'just look in tomorrow's newspapers — they will say "Lara lbw Bichel 26".' That is good enough for him, and for the rest of us.

Hayden, who struggled for his timing on the slow pitch, ran himself out when we replied, but Justin Langer and I got through to the close without any real alarms. It is now up to us to make sure we take advantage of a good pitch, a fast outfield and the West Indies' low first innings score.

Friday 11 April

First Test, day two: West Indies 237 and 0–16 trail Australia 489 (Langer 146, Ponting 117, Gilchrist 77, Drakes 5–93) by 236 runs.

We built up the type of lead we wanted today, but the job is only half-done. The pitch has shown some signs of wear, with the ball that bowled Jason Gillespie late in the day keeping so low it almost went under the stumps — there is little pace in the surface, so we know it may be hard work to bowl them out a second time if they bat with some discipline.

We showed that discipline today, with Justin Langer and I leading the way in hot conditions and Adam Gilchrist taking on their tiring attack as we pressed for a declaration. Our approach early on was not quite in keeping with the way we have played in recent years but it was very necessary, because we did not want to give them any chance of getting back into the match.

On a pitch like this, with the ball not bouncing much over stump height, the key is to play straight. That was what we tried to do, even though Langer and I both usually favour cross-batted strokes like the pull and the hook.

Those shots were only possible if the ball was banged in very short; I looked for more back-foot punches down the ground instead. They were safer shots than hitting across the line, and with the outfield so fast, you still got a boundary if you were able to beat the field.

Langer adopted much the same method, keeping the scoreboard ticking over with nudges and deflections and waiting for an over-pitched ball he could drive. The only time he really struggled was during a spell from Jermaine Lawson, the West Indies new quick bowler. At the end of one over he came down the pitch to me and said: 'I can't believe how quick this guy is bowling.' Lawson was certainly getting the ball through better than any other bowler in the match: he was managing to get the ball to bounce head-high through to the wicketkeeper — and on some occasions, over him, which was an impressive feat on this pitch. That made life especially tough for Wavell Hinds, who was filling in behind the stumps after Ridley Jacobs damaged a groin muscle when he was batting yesterday. Hinds could barely catch a ball from Lawson.

The West Indies bowlers tried hard, but they lacked the discipline to make us struggle. On a pitch like this there is no point having three or four slips once the hardness goes out of the ball, because an edge will usually not carry far; a better option is maybe two slips, a midwicket and a square leg, with the bowler trying to bowl straight in an attempt to take advantage of the low bounce.

But apart from the experienced Vasbert Drakes, the West Indies had no one who could maintain pressure by bowling straight ball after ball. It meant we were eventually able to get away from them, and although I got out playing a loose drive away from my body, we were already in the lead by then.

I felt I hit the ball pretty well, and was also pleased at the way I adjusted to Test cricket after a long period of nothing but one-day internationals. Of course I was disappointed not to go on with the job, but Drakes bowled well at me and deserved his success. He got a delivery to move away off the seam and, drawn into the drive, I edged the ball low to first slip.

My hundred showed me the value of rest as well as the value of practice. I did little but rest and see family and friends during the week I was back in Australia after the World Cup, and although I have had some solid net sessions here in Guyana, I sat out the warm-up game. I was happy with the way I was hitting the ball at the end of the World Cup, and after years of working on my game I have now reached the point where I can say that if it is not broken there is no need to fix it.

Other players, such as Langer, love to have long sessions in the nets; for me it is just a case of feeling bat on ball when we practise. As long as I know in my own mind that I am doing the basics, that is enough. It is a case of personal preference. Langer's method works for him, but for me there is no point in practising for the sake of it.

We were in danger of falling away a little after my dismissal, but a couple of players in the lower order, Andy Bichel and Brett Lee, did just what we hoped they would and offered good support to a top-order player. Gilchrist played with his usual freedom until Lawson deceived him with a slower ball, which Gilchrist chipped back for a caught and bowled.

By the time we were bowled out the light was starting to close in, so Stephen Waugh opted to use Stuart MacGill and Brad Hogg with the new ball. In the end we got five overs at their openers before the close of play. Encouragingly, though we could not get a breakthrough, both spinners turned the ball quite sharply. They may have a major role to play tomorrow.

Justin Langer

If ever you wanted an example of why Australia has been successful over the past decade or so, you could do a lot worse than look at the case of Justin Langer.

He struggled at first in Test cricket, then came to terms with it, then got a little over-ambitious, and finally, when given another chance, became one of our all-time greats.

The message with Langer, as with so many of our players, is that the more they have played at the highest level the better they have become. His history reminds us that players are not the finished article when they start playing Test cricket; providing they have the talent, though, they will get there if they are given time. Giving that time is something that England, for example, has not always done in the past, and the team has suffered as a result.

Like his great mate Matthew Hayden, Langer's major strength is his self-belief: he is another illustration of how important the mental side of cricket is. For the first five years of his international career I do not think he believed that he belonged at that level; it took a hundred against Pakistan and Shoaib Akhtar in Peshawar in 1998 to convince him he was up to the task. That Test is remembered primarily for Mark Taylor's 334 not out, but it was equally significant in the development of Justin Langer as an international cricketer.

For the next two years he grew in confidence, to such an extent that I think he eventually became overconfident and tried to dominate the bowling too much. He very rarely got out cheaply, but at the same time he did not capitalise on the starts he got, and in the end the selectors ran out of patience with him.

Although Damien Martyn came into the side instead of Langer, I was the one to take over his spot at number three, and when I scored a hundred in the fourth Test of that series, against England in 2001, Langer must have thought his Test career was over. But the fact that we were away on tour helped him: it meant that when the selectors wanted to make another change, by dropping Michael Slater, Langer was on hand, even though he was not regarded as an opening batsman.

It seems amazing to write that now, but at the time his selection was seen as nothing more than a stop-gap measure: the selectors were slotting in a player who normally batted at number three, and would probably give a regular opener the call for the first Test of the home summer that followed.

Langer's response was emphatic. He went out and scored a brilliant hundred — and has not missed a Test since. He has also set a record for most double-century opening stands with his partner, Matthew Hayden. He has been given a new lease of life, and has made the most of it.

Langer is an example of how differing approaches work for different people. While Hayden spends very little time in the nets these days, Langer still spends a long time honing his shots in the practice area. And while Langer is all shadow shots and stretching in the dressing room once he has his pads on before he goes out to bat, Hayden prefers to go outside and sit quietly on his own, composing himself before the two of them walk out together.

As they walk to the wicket they appear to be the little and large of batting, a mountain of a man next to his smaller partner, but Langer is deceptively strong and not someone you would ever want to mess with. He is a pocket battleship of a man with his shirt off, and is a black belt in a martial art, though I have never seen him put his skills into action.

I have known JL for many years — he was a scholarship coach at the Commonwealth Bank Cricket Academy during my second year in Adelaide. We also played Australia A together, toured the West Indies as reserve batsmen in 1995, and went to England together in 1997. I broke into the side halfway through that trip, while he had to bide his time as a reserve.

One thing I have learnt from all my time in his company is that he is a real gym junkie, and that has obviously stood him in good stead through his career. Also, he is desperate to play one-day cricket for Australia again, not having achieved a spot in the side since 1997. Whether he will get a chance to fulfil that ambition remains to be seen; it has been pure bad luck that he is playing in an era when we have been blessed with so many talented one-day players.

With Adam Gilchrist locked in as opener alongside Hayden, and the rest of the top order basically picking itself, it is difficult to see where Langer can slot in, especially as he cannot offer another string to his bow through bowling. But in a way, his absence from the one-day side is a bonus for us — it means he maintains his freshness for Test cricket.

That freshness is vital, because those of us who play both forms of the game can become jaded with the day-in, day-out grind, especially when we are on tour for a couple of months. Fresh faces, full of enthusiasm, coming in to join the squad can often lift everyone. Langer, always one of the best trainers around, usually has that effect — as he did in Sri Lanka in early 2004.

That enthusiasm, allied with his real passion for playing for Australia — something he seems to have inherited from his mentor, Stephen Waugh — made him the obvious choice to take over the leadership of the team song when I became Test captain.

Langer's heart-on-the-sleeve attitude to playing for his country, together with the fact that he plays with a smile on his face, is a symbol of all that is good about representing Australia. I hope he maintains his form so that he can keep doing just that for a while yet.

Saturday 12 April

First Test, day three: West Indies 237 and 5–381 (Ganga 113, Lara 110, Smith 62) lead Australia 489 by 129 runs.

A tough day, but by the end of it we could see some light at the end of the tunnel. They have a long tail, and with Ridley Jacobs injured we may be just one wicket away from wrapping up their innings reasonably quickly.

We will settle for our position, after Brian Lara and Daren Ganga batted the West Indies into a position of equality during the day. They added 185, and at 2–295 we were desperate for any sort of breakthrough. Brad Hogg got one in a bizarre way.

Lara, looking to sweep, lost his grip of the bat and his left hand came off the handle. He still followed through with the shot, but all he succeeded in doing was swinging his bat around his back and into his stumps, to be dismissed hit wicket.

It was an odd way to go, but Lara still deserves credit for the way he played. When he came in he was subjected to a fair amount of barracking from the crowd — the issue was that he had replaced the local favourite, Carl Hooper, as captain — but he put all that out of his mind and stroked the ball around beautifully. His response to the situation seems to confirm what we believe: that he thrives on some needle in a match; it gets him going and playing well. For that reason we tend not to say much to him out in the middle, although Glenn McGrath cannot always help himself.

The nature of the pitch — low and slow — blunted our plans against Lara and helped him succeed. It was difficult for the quick bowlers to inconvenience him with the short ball, and with Brett Lee, who normally swings the ball into left-handers, struggling for rhythm, we relied on a lot of overs from the spinners.

Lara's innings was full of flowing drives, but Ganga was happy just to occupy the crease. He played with the discipline the West Indies lacked in their first innings. He has a pretty simple method and did not do anything extravagant; he just tried to get forward whenever he could and play with a straight bat.

After playing like that he will be kicking himself for getting out in the way he did, falling to Darren Lehmann's gentle left-arm spin. He decided that Lehmann cannot bowl, and tried to prove it by hitting him out of the ground. Unfortunately, he miscued the ball to Lee at midwicket instead.

I took over as captain at one point during the day, when Stephen Waugh left the field to have some stitches put in the webbing on his left hand after he misfielded a drive off Devon Smith, the opening batsman. Smith survived what we all thought was a plumb lbw shout from Lee at the start of day, and was driving the ball powerfully until Gillespie had him caught behind. Like his opening partner, Wavell Hinds, Smith does not move his feet much, but on a pitch with little or no seam movement you can get away with that, especially if the ball is not swinging, and when he gets bat on ball he times it sweetly.

Sunday 13 April

First Test, day four: Australia 489 and 1–147 (Langer 78 not out) beat West Indies 237 and 398 (Ganga 113, Lara 110, Smith 62, Gillespie 5–39) by 9 wickets.

Jimmy Maher is called into the Australia squad and will arrive in time to play as wicketkeeper in the tour match against the University of West Indies XI in Barbados starting on 26 April. The decision is made to give Adam Gilchrist the chance of a break between the second and third Test matches, and comes in the light of Maher's likely selection for Australia's squad for the seven-match one-day series that follows the four Tests.

Maher's call-up means he will step down from captaining Australia A in its series against South Africa A. Simon Katich takes on that role.

Just as we hoped, we got into their tail early on today, took their last five wickets quickly and then knocked off the required runs with the minimum of fuss to go 1–0 up in the series.

It sounds simple, and in the end it was. Jason Gillespie gave the West Indies fast bowlers a lesson in how to bowl on the surface, getting close to the stumps, running in hard and bowling straight; he was the main reason we took the home side's last five wickets for just 17 runs in 45 minutes.

Then Justin Langer completed an excellent double by following his hundred with an unbeaten 78. We did have some minor concerns when it began to rain just after lunch — bad weather has been known to hang around these parts for days. The ground has a reputation for draining badly — the city of Georgetown is below sea level — and whole Test matches have been washed away, but luckily the rain did not hang about and we knocked off the runs in just over 3 hours.

We celebrated the win back at the hotel, where we sang the team song. Everyone is delighted that we have made such an emphatic start to the series. But no one is taking anything for granted after the events of four years ago. Everyone who was part of that tour is keen to avoid a similar turnaround this time.

We have no reason to be complacent, despite winning this match with a day and a half in hand. We were stretched by their batting — hundreds by Shivnarine Chanderpaul, Brian Lara and Daren Ganga — and it could have been a lot tougher for us if we had not got Lara out when we did. They will only get stronger, because Ramnaresh Sarwan and Chris Gayle should come back into their line-up at some point. We know the job is far from done.

Even though it was time to relax after the match was over, in one sense we had to stay completely alert, thanks to our social committee of Stuart MacGill, Adam Gilchrist and Martin Love. They have bought everyone a book from the children's *Mr Men* series, and each book relates to its owner's character. For example, Langer is Mr Strong, because of his love of the gym, Stephen Waugh is Mr Perfect, Gillespie is Mr Dizzy (after his nickname) and I am Mr Mischief, a throwback to my larrikin past. We are expected to carry these books at all times, even during this afternoon's get-together after the Test — anyone without their book cops a fine. Sabotage of other squad members' books — hiding them, for example — is encouraged, but anyone who gets caught also cops a fine. It might seem childish, but it is a bit of fun and gives us something else to have a laugh about.

Tuesday 15 April

The West Indies name a 15-man squad for the second Test in Trinidad. It is: Brian Lara (captain), Omari Banks, David Bernard Junior, Shivnarine Chanderpaul, Pedro Collins, Mervyn Dillon, Vasbert Drakes, Daren Ganga, Wavell Hinds, Ridley Jacobs or Carlton Baugh, Jermaine Lawson, Marlon Samuels, Ramnaresh Sarwan and Devon Smith.

Sarwan returns to the squad after missing the first Test with a finger injury; the groin injury Jacobs sustained in Guyana means Baugh is on standby to make his Test debut. Chris Gayle is still omitted, while Banks, an off-spinning all-rounder from Anguilla, is included for the first time.

Wednesday 16 April

Both Ridley Jacobs and Jermaine Lawson are ruled out of the second Test. Jacobs' groin is said to need more time to heal, and Lawson has been diagnosed with chickenpox. Fast bowler Tino Best is drafted into the West Indies squad.

Friday 18 April

Australia names a 15-man squad for the seven-match one-day series against the West Indies that follows the four Test matches. It is: Ricky Ponting (captain), Adam Gilchrist (vice-captain), Michael Bevan, Andrew Bichel, Jason Gillespie, Nathan Hauritz, Ian Harvey, Matthew Hayden, Brad Hogg, Brett Lee, Darren Lehmann, Jimmy Maher, Damien Martyn, Glenn McGrath and Andrew Symonds.

Martyn's inclusion is subject to fitness, with his fractured right index finger to be assessed in Perth next week.

Saturday 19 April

Second Test, day one: Australia 3–391 (Lehmann 160, Ponting 146 not out) v West Indies.

From a personal point of view, I could not have timed things better, either with the bat or as a husband. My wife Rianna's arrival last night coincided with my scoring a Test hundred that has helped put us in a powerful position after just one day of this match.

I got a lot of pleasure out of today's effort, and not just because Rianna was there to see it. Another major plus was having Darren Lehmann at the other end for most of the day. He scored his first Test hundred in emphatic style, almost 14 years after first being part of an Australian squad.

Lehmann has never been under pressure to succeed from inside the dressing room. His value to the side goes beyond runs: he is a great thinker about the game, someone I trust for tactical judgements and assessments of opposition players, and he is always likely to come up with a wicket with his left-arm spinners, as he showed in the last Test by getting rid of Daren Ganga. On top of that, because everyone knows through his many years of domestic cricket what a brilliant player he is, we have all expected him to make the breakthrough at Test level at some point.

On the other side of the coin, with the depth of batting talent Australia has, as illustrated by Michael Clarke and Martin Love kicking their heels on the sidelines in this match, Lehmann knew he was under pressure to perform. Today he did just that, getting a massive monkey off his back in the process.

We added an Australian record of 315 for the third wicket and I was delighted to share a beer with him over that milestone as we posed for photographers after play.

In one sense we were fortunate, because the West Indies' team selection helped our cause enormously: they were already without Ridley Jacobs and Jermaine Lawson, they lost Shivnarine Chanderpaul before the start of play when he pulled out with a knee injury picked up in the first Test, and then they chose just three frontline bowlers — Mervyn Dillon, Pedro Collins and Vasbert Drakes.

Those three are useful performers, but on a decent pitch they needed more backup than they had. The backup came from Marlon Samuels' off-spin, some medium-pace from Dave Bernard Junior and Wavell Hinds, and leg-spin from Ramnaresh Sarwan. It meant that once the new ball lost its hardness we had every chance of making a very big score.

The pitch was quicker and bouncier than Guyana but it played in a similar way. Both Lehmann and I concentrated on playing straight and being patient; cross-bat shots were difficult, and there was every chance, as the day went on and the West Indies' less experienced bowlers were exposed, that a bad ball would come along.

Lehmann survived a pretty hostile examination from Dillon at the start of his innings: the quick bowler went around the wicket and tested him with some short-pitched deliveries. Dillon was also unlucky in that he had both of us dropped.

Lehmann's chance was a looping nick to the wicketkeeper, who leapt high to try to grasp what was a tough chance — he got a hand to it but could not hold on. I was more fortunate. I'd gone looking for a big drive but only succeeded in edging to first slip, where Samuels grassed a low but straightforward chance.

That helped me focus on the job at hand; I did not offer the West Indies bowlers any more opportunities. Lehmann had some more good fortune before reaching his hundred: he tried to glide Drakes to third man but instead ran the ball straight off the face of the bat to Carlton Baugh behind the stumps. At the non-striker's end I could see and hear the nick, but umpire Rudi Koertzen somehow missed it and Lehmann was allowed to plough on.

Maybe that was justice, in a way, because the two wickets we lost before Lehmann and I joined forces were both thanks to decisions that went against us. Justin Langer and Matthew Hayden were both given out lbw by Asoka de Silva, even though both balls pitched well outside leg-stump. Perhaps Lehmann's good fortune was an example of how things can even themselves up.

After play I spoke to the media, and the inevitable question about a Test double hundred came up again. I have never made one, so the question always is, 'Can you do it this time?' I have answered that one so often in the past and then failed to get there that this time I said I did not want to talk about it. The closest I have come is 197 against Pakistan in Perth in 1999 — and I would have got there then but for a loose shot. Perhaps tomorrow I will have the chance to get that monkey off my back.

Darren Lehmann

Boof. Shrek. Darrell. All nicknames for Darren Lehmann, one of the most popular players in the side. Two are for fairly obvious reasons: Boof comes from Boofhead, referring to his lack of hair, and Shrek is from his resemblance to the cartoon character. The reason for Darrell is a bit more obscure. It comes from Andrew Symonds, who used it because he said it sounded like Darren. As you can tell from that, it takes all sorts to make up an Australian cricket team.

Lehmann is popular with his team-mates for many reasons. He is rarely without a smile on his face or a wisecrack, and someone like that, in the high-pressure atmosphere of international sport, is a priceless asset in any dressing room. But allied to that are his excellence as a player and his willingness to share knowledge with his team-mates.

Lehmann understands the game well, having acquired a vast knowledge through all the years he has played for South Australia and Victoria, and Yorkshire in the UK. That understanding alone, even without his talent as a batsman and a more than useful left-arm spinner, makes him one of the first players I want alongside me.

When I started out as Australia's one-day captain he was a huge help as I came to terms with what was required of me. He was always coming up with suggestions for fields to set and bowlers to bowl, as well as ways we could combat opposition bowlers, and was always great value in a team meeting.

He has an unshakeable belief in his own ability to play against any bowler in the world, and that was illustrated by the way he handled Muttiah Muralitharan and the rest of Sri Lanka's spinners during our series there in early 2004. At various stages he would move around the crease while batting — he even took up his stance outside leg-stump at one point, showing all three stumps to the bowler. His idea there was to put the pressure back on the bowler: rather than worrying about what he is bowling, he is suddenly wondering why Lehmann is giving himself room to play. Lehmann, meanwhile, will always back himself to counter whatever the bowler sends down, and his figures in the Test series — 375 runs, including two hundreds — suggest that he manages that pretty well.

Lehmann also enjoys proving people wrong, as he showed during the Caribbean tour in 2003. After the first Test of that series he and I had a drink with Brian Lara, and the West Indies captain said he did not believe Lehmann could play short-pitched bowling. Lehmann's answer was to score his maiden Test hundred in the next match, at Lara's home ground in Trinidad.

Lehmann is renowned as someone who likes a drink and a smoke, but I have never seen him overstep the mark when he is on duty for Australia. I think his reputation as a knockabout bloke has helped make him more popular with the public: they relate well to someone who enjoys life but is still very good at his job. He does not take himself too seriously either, a fact illustrated by the way he laughs at his nicknames, and I think people like that about him too.

Plenty is made of his shape, and he would be the first to admit that he does not fit the mould of the stereotypical 21st-century athlete. Maybe that has counted against him in the past, when the choice has been between him and another player, though I would like to think it has not. I know Lehmann has struggled with an Achilles injury in recent years, but I have never had cause to question his fitness to play at the highest level. His hundreds in baking hot conditions in Galle and Colombo are all the proof you need that he is fit enough.

Lehmann is rarely without a smile but there have been two occasions in the past year or so when he has been down in the dumps. The first was when he was banned for five matches for a racist outburst after he was dismissed in a VB Series match against Sri Lanka in Brisbane. I know it is something that he will regret for the rest of his career, and if he could take it back he would. It came at the end of a really frustrating period for him when, after breaking back into the Test side when Mark Waugh retired, he was sidelined with an infection that left him hospitalised over Christmas and debilitated afterwards. He was in the process of trying to fight his way back to form and fitness when he was dismissed, run out, in Brisbane at a crucial stage of the match. His outburst slipped out when he got back to the dressing room, but was heard outside. It meant he was sidelined again, and that left him low. But he came through it and played a major part in our World Cup win that followed.

Lehmann's other low point was the period following the death of his mentor at South Australia, David Hookes. The death of someone he thought so highly of would have been bad enough, but this was worse because Lehmann was there and witnessed the whole tragedy unfold. It shook him badly; the tour of Sri Lanka that followed was just what he needed to get him focused on playing again.

Lehmann's performances on the tour reflected his desire to make the most of the chance he was given; Hookes' death reminded all of us how fragile life is. But even though he played well and enjoyed his cricket on the trip, he was not quite the same person as usual. He did not go out in the evenings after play, and Adam Gilchrist and I had to work hard to get him out for a beer and a meal after his brilliant hundred in Colombo during the final Test of the tour. He said that was the first time he had been to a pub since the night of Hookes' death.

Lehmann has been quoted as saying that he does not expect to be around by the time of the 2007 World Cup. I know he is keen to spend more time with his four children, but as long as he is playing well, is fit enough and still has an appetite for cricket at the highest level, I would have no hesitation in having him in my side for the tournament.

Sunday 20 April

Second Test, day two: West Indies 3–186 (Lara 91, Ganga 69 not out) trail Australia 4–576 declared (Ponting 206, Lehmann 160, Gilchrist 101 not out) by 390 runs.

I got rid of the monkey by scoring 206 and we had a pretty good day as a team. It was made better late on when we got rid of Brian Lara, stopping him getting a Test hundred on his home ground in the process. But at the same time, I am not satisfied personally, because I got out in a bizarre way that took just a little of the gloss off my innings.

Adam Gilchrist and I were going along at 4 runs an over and we were heading towards 550. I tried to paddle Marlon Samuels on the leg-side and missed. But as I swivelled around and completed the shot I thought for a split second that the ball had got past the wicketkeeper, Carlton Baugh, so I set off for a run.

In fact, the ball was in the keeper's gloves, and as I moved out of my ground he made to whip the bails off. Realising what was happening I threw myself back towards my crease, but according to umpire Asoka de Silva at square leg I did not make it back in time — he sent me on my way without reference to the third umpire.

It was a soft dismissal, and meant I left the ground with a frown on my face, shaking my head, rather than celebrating my first Test double hundred. I was frustrated when I got back to the dressing room, and I became even more annoyed when I saw the replay on the television. Not only was it too close for de Silva to have given out with the naked eye, I felt, but the replay also suggested that the umpire, like me, had thought the ball had beaten the keeper and was heading to fine leg — he appeared to be facing that way at the moment Baugh whipped off the bails. On top of that, the replay seemed to show that Baugh was obscuring the umpire's view of the stumps being broken, making his decision to give me out even more mystifying.

I was so annoyed at being given out in that way that I went to see de Silva after we declared and asked him how he had made the decision. His simple answer was, of course, that he thought it was out, but on the evidence of what I had seen I could not see how he could come to that conclusion.

In one sense I can take my reaction as a positive sign: rather than feeling satisfied with myself for finally cracking the 200 barrier, I wanted more runs. I hope I can take that hunger for really big scores into future innings.

Conditions through my innings were hot and humid, and although the West Indies attack in this match is not the most testing in history, I am still delighted to get 206. I felt comfortable, and apart from the chance I gave yesterday, I never felt as if I was about to get out. At the same time, I also felt that I maintained my concentration and didn't get complacent.

Today I had the pleasure of batting with Gilchrist, who made a very controlled hundred. The pitch had something to do with that — it is not the type of surface where you can easily bludgeon the ball about. He realised that as soon as he came into bat yesterday, when Darren Lehmann was out, so he set out his stall, knowing that the runs would come.

The West Indies chose not to take the new ball, even though it was due straight away. In one sense I could understand Lara's decision: he may have thought that on a slow pitch, the harder, new ball would have helped us get off to a flying start. However, his decision also meant that we were fully accustomed to conditions by the time he did take the new ball, after 25 minutes, and it caused us few alarms.

We added 126 in the first session of play. Gilchrist was severe on Mervyn Dillon's attempts to rough him up with some short-pitched bowling, playing a couple of meaty pulls. When he eventually reached his hundred, Stephen Waugh declared. We were left with 45 overs to bowl at them.

Brett Lee and Jason Gillespie bowled aggressive opening spells to account for the West Indies openers, but Lara and Daren Ganga, the two who had made centuries in Guyana, set about turning the tables. They were particularly severe on Stuart MacGill, whose seven overs cost 50, and with Waugh happy to set attacking fields — we had so many runs on the board and so much time left in the match — the West Indies rattled along at 4 runs an over.

We were all aware that Lara had not yet made a Test hundred on his home ground. It looked as if this innings would be the one; the only question was whether it would be this evening or tomorrow. But then Gilchrist came up with a plan.

He was keen to exploit Lara's love of the sweep shot, and suggested to Brad Hogg that he should go around the wicket and bowl Lara a flipper, to see if he could bowl him around his legs. Hogg tried it, got the ball just right, and it brushed the side of the leg-stump as Lara swept over the top of it.

Lara was shocked, and couldn't believe the ball had hit the stumps: he thought it may have ricocheted there off Gilchrist's pads. It took a television replay to prove Hogg had his man. It is not every day a plan like that comes off so quickly! So although the West Indies made a spirited reply to our batting effort, it was us who left the field with a spring in our step tonight.

Monday 21 April

Second Test, day three: Australia 4–576 declared and 1–31 lead West Indies 408 (Ganga 117, Lara 91, Samuels 68) by 199 runs.

The West Indies avoided the follow-on — we would not have enforced it anyway — and after a solid day's work we are in a strong position to ram home the advantage of our sizeable first innings lead.

At tea, when Stuart MacGill got rid of Carlton Baugh, the West Indies still required 10 to reach the follow-on mark of 377 and had just three wickets in hand, but we have learnt from our recent past that there is no point in driving the bowlers into the dust.

That might go against our plan of trying, wherever possible, to bat just once in any match, but we bought ourselves time in this match by scoring our first innings runs so quickly. Also, it has been hot and humid and the pitch will only get harder to bat on as the match goes on, so rather than risk facing a small target, maybe up against the clock in the last innings, we were always going to bat again.

Their main batsman today has been Daren Ganga again. He has been a revelation on the tour so far. He may only be playing because Chris Gayle is out of favour with the selectors, but he has shown the right way to play. He has been very selective about what to play and what to leave alone, has played very straight, which is a key to success on the two pitches we have seen so far, and has played the spin of Brad Hogg and MacGill very well. He did not make an impact in Australia in 2000, but he is a much-improved player now and his powers of concentration have really impressed me. He has also benefited in this series from playing on pitches that are nowhere near as fast as the pitches were in Australia in 2000/01.

MacGill's dismissal of Baugh was bizarre. The batsman went back to cut but lost his bearings, went too far back in his crease, and instead of hitting the ball, smashed his own stumps down. It was MacGill's 100th Test wicket, gathered at a rate of better than four wickets per match, and he celebrated by saying: '100 — that will do me.' I actually hope it will not: there is the promise of more to come for him in the second innings.

The pitch provided the spinners with some turn, though it has been fairly slow apart from the odd ball that has kicked out of the bowlers' footmarks. Our hope is that in this very hot weather the pitch will get drier, crumble a bit and become uneven.

A sign of uneven bounce came late in the day when Justin Langer was trapped lbw by a ball that kept low. It really has been a case of two major disappointments for Langer after his success in Guyana, as this was the second of two poor lbw decisions he has had in this match. This evening he was struck outside the line of off-stump but the finger still went up.

Tuesday 22 April

Second Test, day four: West Indies 408 and 3–107 (Lara 52 not out) require another 300 runs to beat Australia 4–576 declared and 3–238 declared (Hayden 100 not out, Lehmann 66).

Another solid day has left us in prime position to win this Test — but Brian Lara still stands in our way.

Lara is 52 not out, and as long as he is at the crease you cannot rule out the West Indies saving the match, or even winning it, even though the pitch is offering our spinners more and more turn and the bounce continues to play the odd trick or two.

We did have a chance to get rid of him early in his innings this afternoon, but Brett Lee grassed a low return catch — and of course was totally crestfallen.

Our plan is to test Lara out with short-pitched bowling, especially early in his innings, and Lee got the plan just right. Lara pulled a short ball for four once, but when Lee followed it up with a quicker one next delivery, Lara was late on another intended pull, got the ball somewhere near the splice of the bat and lobbed it back down the pitch.

Lee was following through off the cut strip, so had to change direction to get to the ball. He flung himself to his right and got his hand to it, but after a couple of goes at hanging on, the ball went to ground and Lara had a let-off.

Let's hope that will not be too expensive. The way Stuart MacGill bowled Wavell Hinds in the last but one over of the day suggests it might not be. MacGill ripped a ball out of the rough through Hinds' defence to bowl him; if our spinners can do that sort of thing consistently tomorrow, we should win comfortably.

Matthew Hayden returned to form with a solid hundred that

was all about occupation of the crease. He eased the ball around while first I, then Darren Lehmann, played around him. We moved towards a declaration in the late afternoon, as soon as he reached three figures.

By then I had been dismissed. There was a bit of edge surrounding my departure, in more ways than one. Mervyn Dillon got a leg-cutter to bounce and Carlton Baugh took a low catch behind the stumps as I followed the delivery and got a thick edge as it left me.

I turned to walk off as the umpire's finger went up, but as I did so I felt a thump to the peak of my helmet. I turned back and discovered it was Dillon's fist as he lifted his arm to celebrate my departure.

I was not impressed. There was no way he should have been anywhere near me as he ran to congratulate Baugh over the catch and I told him so before I marched off the ground. And even though it looked accidental enough when I saw it on television, it still left a nasty taste in my mouth.

Hayden did not look in his best touch, but then it was not the type of pitch to show off his batting: the ball is not coming onto the bat to allow flowing strokes. It is the mark of how good a player he is that he can graft his way to hundred even when he is not playing especially well. Lehmann, meanwhile, carried the confidence he gained from his first innings hundred into the second innings. He made most of the running for us — a couple of meaty sixes over long-on off Marlon Samuels and some flat-bat clubs down the ground off Dillon were the pick of his shots.

After we declared, Jason Gillespie gave their bowlers another lesson in getting the ball in the right areas, plucking out Devon Smith and Daren Ganga in double-quick time. We had to settle for just one more wicket before the close, but we finished the day feeling pretty confident that we can finish the job.

Wednesday 23 April

Kenya's leg-spinner, Collins Obuya, who took 13 wickets in his side's progress to the World Cup semi-finals, is named in the University of West Indies Vice Chancellor's XI side to play in a three-day match against the Australians in Barbados starting on 26 April.

Also included is Chris Gayle, back in favour after being left out of the first two Tests because of having opted to play in a double-wicket tournament instead of representing Jamaica.

Second Test, day five: Australia 4–576 declared and 3–238 declared beat West Indies 408 and 288 (Lara 122) by 118 runs.

We have retained the Frank Worrell Trophy after just two matches of the series. This was a great win in testing conditions, and called for some major celebrations after the match.

We kept our cool despite failing to take a wicket in the first session, and although Brian Lara scored his first Test hundred at his home ground, we were comfortable winners — we had plenty of runs, time and overs in hand when Jason Gillespie took their final wicket, around tea-time.

Lara's innings was a beauty, and was made on a pitch that offered the bowlers, especially our spinners, plenty. It was a real education to watch the way he tried to manoeuvre the ball around into the gaps against slow bowling. There is no one better at doing it in world cricket, and he gave a master-class for us all.

The key to Lara's success against spin is that he has a plan, and a full range of options, against that style of bowling. He is an excellent sweeper of the ball and is never afraid to run down the pitch and drive if the bowler flights the ball, as he did today to Brad Hogg, drilling him straight for six.

Lara is also prepared to be patient, waiting for the right ball to hit, is not afraid to use his pad when necessary, and plays the ball later in defence against slow bowling than just about anyone else I have seen. That means he does not commit himself early to a shot and then make a hurried adjustment as the ball turns; instead, he waits, usually reads which way the ball is going to turn and responds accordingly.

His battle with Stuart MacGill was a classic. MacGill won in the end, when he had Lara caught by Matthew Hayden at slip, after edging a drive out of the rough. MacGill has the perfect temperament for a battle like the one today: he does not react or lose his cool when he is hit for four or six. He just trots back to his mark and gets ready for the next ball, trying to spin it as hard as he can. On a pitch like this one, with the ball turning a long way by the end of the match, that is a recipe for success.

Despite all that, it was the quick bowlers who looked just as likely to break through, first when Brett Lee produced a crackerjack spell before lunch, and then when Andy Bichel started the West Indies' slide after the interval.

Lee's spell was a beauty, and on another day he may well have picked up a five-wicket haul from it. He got the ball to reverse-swing and all but bowled Ramnaresh Sarwan with a brilliant yorker before firing a short ball past Lara then pinning him on the back foot to prompt a massive shout for lbw — it must have been close. Umpire Rudi Koertzen decided to give the batsman the benefit of the doubt.

There was no breakthrough in the first session but we were never overly concerned that we would lose the match. The fact that they still required 200 runs on a fifth-day pitch against our five-man attack gave us plenty of confidence, and that confidence was reinforced when Bichel took three wickets in a top-class spell soon after the break.

He caused Sarwan to miscue a hook to mid-on, trapped Marlon Samuels lbw and then had Bernard Junior well caught by Hayden at slip. It meant Lara was left with Carlton Baugh and the tail for company, and although he fought on for a while, we knew it was just a matter of time before we got him — and we were right. When MacGill struck it was the beginning of the end for them.

To take 20 wickets and win the match on such an easy-paced pitch is a fantastic achievement, and that was reflected in our full-on celebrations afterwards. Coach John Buchanan suffered a little more than the rest of us during our three-hour stay in the dressing room. At one point MacGill tried to pull down the bike shorts Buchanan wears under his running shorts, but that caused the coach to lose balance. He hit his head on a nearby bench and was out cold briefly. He came around, but was clearly groggy, so Bichel took him back to the hotel and put him to bed.

Despite the pleasure we took in this win there was no talk of the prospect of a whitewash. That would smack of complacency. It may seem like a cliché, but we really are happy to take it one Test at a time.

After our celebrations at the ground we moved on to Lara's house for a party he threw for both teams. He has a fantastic place that overlooks Trinidad's capital city, Port-of-Spain. Unfortunately, we could not stay very late, because we had to be up at 5 o'clock the next morning for our flight to Barbados.

The constant island-hopping involved a Caribbean tour can be hard work. Unlike flying around Australia, each flight here is an international one, involving customs and immigration. And that can be doubly tough after a big night of celebration following a Test match win.

Saturday 26–Monday 28 April

Three Ws Oval, Barbados: the Australians 6–358 declared (Maher 142, Langer 96) and 4–95 beat the University of West Indies Vice-Chancellor's XI 290 (Gayle 129, Haynes 58, MacGill 5–40) and 162 (Wallace 53, MacGill 5–45) by 6 wickets.

This match marks the return to action of Glenn McGrath, recently arrived from Australia after spending time with his wife, Jane, while she underwent treatment for cancer. Ricky Ponting, Matthew Hayden, Darren Lehmann, Brett Lee and Jason Gillespie are rested.

Thursday 1 May

Third Test, day one: Australia 3–320 (Ponting 113, Lehmann 89 not out, Langer 78) v West Indies.

Another excellent day for us, but although I am pleased to score another hundred, I am also kicking myself for throwing away the chance to make a really big score.

On an easy-paced pitch and against a raw attack I felt better than at any time in the series. I hit the ball well, picked up the length each bowler was bowling very quickly and could see no way any bowler could get me out.

I was right about that, but I managed to run myself out looking for a second run that was always going to be tight. I played the ball to fine leg and turned for the second instinctively, prepared to take on the fielder on the boundary, Test debutant Tino Best.

Unluckily for me, Best came up with the perfect throw, millimetres from the bails. Carlton Baugh did the rest. I was centimetres short of my ground, a fact confirmed by the third official after a television replay.

To say I was very angry when I got back to the dressing room is an understatement. I shouted out my frustrations for a minute or two, just to let off some steam. I'd done the hard work, got myself in and then threw it all away through a poor decision.

Even my wicket, late in the day, could not change the fact that it had been a tough day for the West Indies. They decided to put us into bat, which seemed an amazing decision given the easy-paced nature of the pitch; they may have been banking on their young fast bowlers getting more out of the surface in the first session, and they did have early chances to get at least one or two breakthroughs. They did not take them, though, and the scoreboard at the end of the day shows how tough Test cricket can be in those circumstances.

Brian Lara's decision may also have been based on the fact that Glenn McGrath has returned to our line-up. He came in for Brad Hogg, giving us a four-pronged seam attack, and maybe the West Indies shied away from facing that attack on the first morning.

My dismissal was revenge of sorts for Best after I scored heavily off him when his enthusiasm got the better of him. We had heard a bit about him, and even got the chance to watch him bowl before the match, when our team bus happened to go past the West Indies' net session at a nearby club ground.

Best is a small man, but he charges in, arms and legs pumping, and gets the ball through at a decent pace. However, as he discovered today, you need a bit more than that to succeed at the highest level.

The pitch at the Kensington Oval is slow, and when you bang the ball in short it dies in the surface, giving batsmen plenty of time to get onto the back foot and clobber it away, as I did on one occasion, hitting him onto the top of the Kensington Stand at square leg.

Best might be short in stature but he is not short of a word or three out in the middle. None of his chat is malicious; it's just an attempt to give out some advice — advice which I happily ignore. He was quite a sight today: he had zinc cream on his cheeks, applied like war paint. It also turns out he idolises Bing Lee: he even asked if he could use Lee's wicket celebration, the one where he makes a sawing motion at the end of his follow-through. I am not sure Lee has a copyright on the celebration just yet, but he did not mind Best adopting it — now it is up to all of us to make sure he does not get a chance to try it out in this match.

Best was not the only debutant for the West Indies; they also introduced an off-spinner called Omari Banks. I wanted to make sure he did not get the chance to settle in either, so I tried to disrupt his line and length by getting down the pitch and hitting him over the top of the in-field at every opportunity.

I was dropped once, by Shivnarine Chanderpaul in the gully as I sliced a drive at a Best full toss, and the West Indies missed other chances too. Justin Langer was let off twice: he edged the first ball of the match through the slips, and when he was on four he was missed by Jermaine Lawson off his own bowling.

Langer did not go on to make the West Indies pay as much as he might have done. He was out for 78, after miscuing an attempt to hit Banks for six and instead slicing the ball straight up in the air. However, Darren Lehmann was once again looking solid, and we had made it a day of hard labour for the West Indies.

There was work for me at the close of play, because it was confirmed that Damien Martyn will not be fit enough to take part in the one-day series that follows the Tests. We have a readymade replacement on hand in Michael Clarke, and I was happy to back the selectors' judgement that he is the man to step into Martyn's shoes.

Michael Clarke is announced as the replacement for Damien Martyn in Australia's one-day squad to face the West Indies in seven one-day internationals following the current Test series. Martyn has failed to recover from a fractured right index finger sustained during the World Cup in March. Clarke, who made his one-day international debut against England in January, has already replaced Martyn in the Test squad on the Caribbean tour.

Third Test, day two: West Indies 0–89 trail Australia 9–605 declared (Waugh 115, Ponting 113, Lehmann 96, Langer 78, Bichel 71, Gilchrist 65) by 516 runs.

We ground the West Indies down with our 605, and that number looks nice on the scoreboard, but the hard work for us has only just started.

The pitch is showing less and less life. Stephen Waugh, who made his 30th Test hundred in this innings — and so went past Sir Donald Bradman's record — described it as the slowest surface he had ever played on. The West Indies openers survived without too many alarms tonight, and if they bat in a disciplined way it may take a lot of sweat and toil for us to take 20 wickets.

One factor in our favour is that Brian Lara may not be able to bat; he spent most of the day in the dressing room feeling unwell. However, we cannot pin too many hopes on something like that. Much more important is the massive amount of time left in the match. We have given ourselves plenty of time to bowl them out twice. Scoring quickly to give ourselves that time was the prime consideration today, and everything went pretty much according to plan from that point of view.

What did not go according to plan was Darren Lehmann's failure to make a second Test hundred: he was trapped lbw by Vasbert Drakes for 96. It was a rough decision from umpire David Shepherd, as the ball pitched outside leg-stump, but it was another example of how things even themselves out — let us not forget Lehmann's let-off with the caught behind appeal in the last Test. Not that anyone said that to him when he came off.

I do not think of myself as especially superstitious, but 96 is not one of my favourite numbers, so I was not surprised when Lehmann was dismissed. It was the total I made on my Test debut against Sri Lanka, and that innings was also ended by a debatable lbw decision. Ever since then I have disliked that number.

Waugh did go on to make a century, which he can add to the

199 he made here in 1999, and while it was not a pretty innings, it was exactly what we required — he pushed the ball around while first Adam Gilchrist and then Andy Bichel got into their attack.

For Bichel it was a maiden Test 50, and it helped justify our decision to play him as a fifth bowler rather than use Brad Hogg or go for a four-man attack with Glenn McGrath back in the side.

McGrath could not force a breakthrough in the last session, but I'm hoping that tonight's bowl, together with the workout he got in the warm-up match, will have done him some good. He is the type of bowler who thrives on lots of bowling, and considering the state of the pitch, he may well have plenty to do if we are going to win this match.

Saturday 3 May

Third Test, day three: West Indies 8–291 (Gayle 71, Smith 59) trail Australia 9–605 declared by 314 runs.

Even though the West Indies are still in their first innings, we are pretty happy with the way things have gone so far. We have restricted them with really disciplined bowling, and as a result there is only one side that can win this Test — us.

A couple of their batsmen threw away their wickets — Daren Ganga drove a full toss from Darren Lehmann straight to mid-on, and Shivnarine Chanderpaul clobbered a long-hop from Stuart MacGill to midwicket — but I do not think there was much that could be called bad luck about those losses; we earned them by building up pressure on the batsmen until they cracked.

Bowling and fielding on this type of pitch can be very tough, and require a different approach from the one we normally adopt. There is no point in having three or four slips, because edges will simply not carry, so we settled for two slips (at most), with the other catchers in front of the wicket on either side. They are there for a mistimed drive, which is always possible with the ball not coming onto the bat; we also hope that the fielders being so close will play on a batsman's mind, as they are in his eye-line.

For those fielders left at slip, and I was one of them, it can be very difficult: the chances that do come along are almost always low because there is little bounce in the pitch. That means you end up standing much closer than you would normally, and with the fast bowlers still operating at more than 140 kilometres per hour you have precious little reaction time.

I discovered that first-hand today as I pouched one of my best-ever catches and then dropped the potentially vital wicket of Brian Lara. The catch I took was off Omari Banks, when Jason Gillespie found his edge. I was in my crouching stance with Gillespie running in, and felt I was standing ridiculously close, especially when Banks nicked a big, slashing drive. The ball travelled fast, and as it came towards me the seam became upright, causing the ball to swing away from me at the last second. On top of that, the edge went to my weaker side, my left. However, I was able to adjust and cling on for a truly satisfying catch. If I can give one lesson to slip catchers it is always to stay low rather than come up out of your stance as the bowler delivers the ball. I did that today with the Banks catch and got my reward.

The chance from Lara was similar in that it went low and fast, but this time I could not hang on to it. I expect to catch all chances that come my way, so it was annoying and frustrating, especially considering who the batsman was. Lara came out at number eight, which seems to confirm that he is not feeling well, but he did not look too bad out on the field. Like everyone else on this pitch, though, he struggled to time the ball. He did not last long after my miss, thank heavens: Andy Bichel got him lbw soon afterwards, though replays we saw in the dressing room after play suggested that he got some bat on the ball as well.

Lara batting so low in the order allowed us to dictate terms for much of the day. Our plan was simply to bowl straight to defensive fields, denying them run-scoring opportunities. That way we hoped they would lose patience, and a couple of their players did. Now we have the chance to wrap up their first innings quickly and press for victory.

Sunday 4 May

Third Test, day four: West Indies 328 (Gayle 71, Smith 59) and 3–187 (Sarwan 58, Gayle 56) trail Australia 9–605 declared by 90 runs.

I had a bowl today. That should tell you all you need to know about how little is on offer to our frontline bowlers on this pitch.

Bowling some gentle off-spin, I was one of eight bowlers we have used so far in the West Indies' second innings as we've tried to get a breakthrough on a pitch that has gone from bad to worse.

During the day Adam Gilchrist resorted to standing up to the stumps to Glenn McGrath — given the situation, it was a sensible thing to do, because very few balls were carrying through to him in his normal position. Collecting a ball awkwardly, which is what was likely to happen, is a recipe for a broken finger. Rather than take that risk, Gilchrist, complete with helmet, came up to the stumps.

Doing that also gave us a better chance of getting an lbw appeal upheld, as it forced the batsmen back into the crease. Before Gilchrist stood up at the stumps their players were trying to bat a long way down the pitch to counteract the increasingly low bounce. If a batsman is well down the pitch, even on this surface, an umpire will always be reluctant to give him out lbw.

During the day we had an additional problem with the state of the ball. The pitch's abrasive surface was roughing up the ball, stopping us getting any shine on it and generating some swing. We showed it to the umpires plenty of times in the hope of getting it changed but they would not agree — they felt it was just natural wear and tear.

With problems like that, together with some stubborn batting by Ramnaresh Sarwan and Brian Lara, up off his sickbed and batting at number five, it was no wonder I bowled.

When someone like me has a bowl at this level, the hope is that batsmen relax and try to play a shot they might not attempt against a frontline member of the attack. Darren Lehmann has had that effect twice in the series, getting rid of Daren Ganga both times, but this time neither Lara nor Sarwan fell into the trap. They showed that survival is not impossible on this surface.

Our main hopes tomorrow are the new ball, which is due after eight overs of play, and Stuart MacGill. He took four wickets in the first innings, and though there is precious little bounce to encourage him, his style of bowling does allow him to get the ball to deviate, something our fast bowlers cannot manage.

Given all these problems, there is a question about whether or not we should have enforced the follow-on when we took the last two wickets in their first innings after an hour's play. Their second innings has pretty much answered that question with a big 'yes' — because of the way the pitch is playing, we needed to give ourselves as long as possible to bowl them out a second time. I hope we can complete the job tomorrow.

Monday 5 May

Third Test, day five: Australia 9–605 declared and 1–8 beat West Indies 328 and 284 (Sarwan 58, Gayle 56, MacGill 5–75) by 9 wickets.

We have achieved one of the most satisfying Test victories an Australian side has enjoyed in the last few years, but by the time the winning runs were struck in late afternoon I was in no position to enjoy it properly.

I have come down with some sort of virus, and after singing the team song I felt shocking. I stayed around at the ground for the first part of the celebrations but could not enjoy a drink; I headed back to the hotel and some rest as soon as I had enough energy to get there.

My problems started last night during dinner with Rianna, my manager Sam Halvorsen, his wife and a couple of friends. As soon as we arrived at the restaurant I started to ache — usually a sign that I am coming down with some sort of illness. I stuck it out for as long as I could, but as the evening wore on I developed a sore throat. When I got back to the hotel I could not sleep properly, first feeling so hot the sweat was pouring off me, then so cold my teeth started chattering and I needed extra blankets. All in all it wasn't a nice night for Rianna.

Errol Alcott, our physiotherapist, came to see me during the night, and when he looked in on me again first thing in the morning it was quickly decided that I was not well enough to go to the ground with the rest of the squad. That meant I had to follow the match in my hotel room on the radio.

We took a wicket with the first ball of the day, with Stuart MacGill getting rid of Ramnaresh Sarwan, and then Andy Bichel picked up Brian Lara again — all this was before we got the chance to take the new ball. And although Shivnarine Chanderpaul and Omari Banks held us up either side of lunch, wickets started going down with a clatter again after the break.

I was determined to be at the ground when we won, so I jumped in a taxi when we took the sixth wicket. It seemed to take forever to get there, and at one point I thought I would not make it in time.

In the end I did make it, thanks to a spirited last-wicket stand between Tino Best and Jermaine Lawson that took the West Indies past our total and meant we had to bat again. And there was one final piece of drama, when Lawson claimed an unlikely hat-trick: after removing Brett Lee and Stuart MacGill with his last two deliveries in our first innings, he trapped Justin Langer with a grass-cutter with the first ball of the second innings.

I would have loved to be there playing at the end, but there was no way I was up to putting my pads on, let alone going out to bat, so Darren Lehmann took my spot at number three and finished off the match in company with Matthew Hayden. And when the winning runs were scored, the whole squad rushed onto the field and got together in a mass huddle.

For us, this is a fantastic victory considering the state of the pitch and the effort required to take 20 wickets. It also means we have regained our place at the top of the International Cricket Council's (ICC) Test championship ladder. We lost the top spot to South Africa at the turn of the year when they beat Pakistan, and although we all felt that was a nonsense — we have beaten South Africa consistently over recent years — we also knew we had to win this series outright to get back the trophy that comes with first place.

So this victory was a special one that left everyone on a high. Because of that, we decided we would sing the team song out on the ground straight after the match. I walked out to join the rest of the touring party and we let rip, but the effort involved hit me for six, and at the end of it I almost passed out. Luckily, I made it back to the sanctuary of the dressing room, and sat down quietly while the celebrations started around me. I headed back to the hotel at the first opportunity.

There was a team dinner involving partners and wives once everyone got back from the ground, but I was not up to going, so Rianna went on her own. All I wanted to do was sleep. It was not the way I would have chosen to spend the night we wrapped up the Test series, but I was incapable of doing anything else.

Tuesday 6–Tuesday 13 May

Friday 9–Tuesday 13 May, fourth Test: West Indies 240 (Lara 68) and 7–418 (Sarwan 105, Chanderpaul 104, Lara 60) beat Australia 240 (Lawson 7–78) and 417 (Hayden 177, Langer 111) by 3 wickets.

6 May — Brad Williams is allowed to return home having deputised for Glenn McGrath while McGrath was in Australia spending time with his wife, Jane.

8 May — West Indies name a 15-man squad for the one-day international series against Australia. It is: Brian Lara (captain), Ramnaresh Sarwan (vice-captain), Omari Banks, David Bernard Junior, Ricardo Powell, Shivnarine Chanderpaul, Corey Collymore, Mervyn Dillon, Vasbert Drakes, Chris Gayle, Ryan Hurley, Ridley Jacobs, Jermaine Lawson, Marlon Samuels and Devon Smith.

11 May — West Indies fast bowler Jermaine Lawson is reported to the ICC for having a suspect bowling action.

13 May — Jacobs is stood down from the West Indies' one-day squad to allow the groin injury that kept him out of the second and third Tests more time to heal.

This was one of the most dramatic Test matches in history, but I missed most of it because of a debilitating virus that made me feel as ill as any time I can remember.

Although I travelled with the rest of the squad to Antigua I was in no position to do anything when we got there, and for most of the Test I was either resting or seeing doctors, trying to get to the bottom of what was wrong with me.

On the day we left for Antigua I got up, still not feeling great, and decided that as I had some time to kill before the bus left for the airport I would go to the business centre in the hotel and check my emails. When I got there I felt hot, and pretty quickly I was a bath of perspiration. I had to take off my shirt as the sweat started pouring off me. I was able to sweep it off me — it was as if I had just walked out of the shower.

In Antigua I had more rest, but all the time I felt worse and worse. I was alternating between feeling boiling hot and freezing cold. In the space of one night I sweated so much my side of the bed was drenched and I had to have an ice-cold shower. Then I became so cold I needed to have a boiling hot shower.

On top of that my throat was swollen, and every time I lay back in bed I felt I was going to choke because I could not swallow properly. But I was little better standing or sitting up: then I felt dizzy and light-headed. It was a worrying time, not only for me but also for Rianna; and it hardly made for the perfect Caribbean vacation she'd had in mind.

Errol Alcott kept a close eye on me, and most of my time out of bed was spent visiting doctors, although I tried to make it to the ground for a period of play on most days of the Test.

As for what the problem was, or what caused it, even now, after the event, no one is quite sure. One theory that seems to make sense to me is that after all the batting I did in the first three Tests, which were played in pretty hot conditions, I became run down and susceptible to illness, so when I picked up an infection it really knocked me down. Whatever it was, there was no way I could play in the Test.

Despite the series having already been decided, there was still plenty of pressure. The West Indies had never been whitewashed in a home series before and we were keen to become the first side to do that. The clean sweep was not spoken of before the last match, because we try to focus on one game at a time; it can be dangerous to look too far ahead. All we try to do as individuals and as a team is the job in front of us each session, whether that is batting or bowling. Everything else will then look after itself. But with the final match of the series upon us, everyone knew the prize of the clean sweep was there if we could string together a final, consistent performance.

The drama really started to kick in on day two, when Brian Lara came to the crease. His record against us always makes him a big wicket, and we thought we had him when Jason Gillespie had an appeal for caught behind, but umpire David Shepherd turned it down.

Most players in international cricket wait for the umpire's decision but Lara has established a reputation as a walker: someone who gives himself out by heading to the dressing room without the umpire's say-so if he knows he has nicked a catch.

Lara stayed put on this occasion, when our players were convinced he had edged the ball, so as Matthew Hayden walked past the West Indies captain at the end of the over he chimed in with: 'Are you going to walk today, Brian?' Apparently that really upset Lara and he started trying to make a big deal out of Hayden's remark, to the point where he was toe to toe with Stephen Waugh complaining about it.

Waugh has seen enough of Lara to know he may have been attempting to fire himself up, so he did not bite back. But it made for a tense atmosphere on the ground, in the dressing room and in the stands.

After being bowled out cheaply on day one, we fought back well on day two to bowl them out for the same score. Then Hayden and Justin Langer did what they do best and put together a massive partnership that seemed to swing the match heavily in our direction. I saw little of that stand but Langer said to me after play that night that Jermaine Lawson had bowled like the wind to him.

Lawson took seven wickets in the first innings but was then off the field with a back injury on day three, and at the end of that day we found out he had been reported to the ICC for having a suspect bowling action. It would be unfair and unwise of me to comment on Lawson's action, but Langer's remarks throughout the series, and replays we saw, meant none of us was too surprised by the news.

Lawson was allowed to bowl again in the match but his back problem meant he did not, which left the West Indies one bowler down. However, they fought back bravely.

We went from 0–242 to all out for 417, and with the series already won we were again vulnerable to suggestions that our second innings batting was complacent and that we had succumbed to dead-rubber syndrome. All I can say is that when I was at the ground I saw no sign of anyone easing up on intensity. The reaction of Glenn

McGrath later in the match should tell everyone how caught up in it he was, and Hayden and Langer both scored hundreds so they certainly cannot be accused of falling into that trap. Unfortunately, if we lose a match after a series has been decided, no matter how well we play we will be accused of taking our foot off the throat of the opposition; conversely, if we win, we sometimes do not get the credit we deserve, because winning is almost expected of us.

It was obviously disappointing to be bowled out relatively cheaply after the good start we got, but it still meant the West Indies required more runs than any side in history has ever scored to win a Test match. From our point of view, our failure to win the match just shows how hard it is to win any Test match — and the fact that the home side beat us when we were desperate to complete the clean sweep should earn them some credit.

The West Indies' run chase was a dramatic affair, with the match swinging first one way then the other. We were on top early, then they fought back through a brilliant innings from Lara, then Stuart MacGill got rid of him with a beautifully flighted leg-break that spun sharply out of the rough and we hoped to be back in the box-seat — but Ramnaresh Sarwan and Shivnarine Chanderpaul wrenched the initiative back from us.

This was the period of play that ended up attracting most attention. Sarwan and McGrath went toe to toe in a stand-up row that made headlines all over the cricketing world. I did not see it live — I was on the way to see another doctor at the time — but I heard the action on the car radio in my taxi and it sounded a pretty ugly incident.

When I got back to the ground and play had finished for the day, I heard what happened. It turned out McGrath had been needling Sarwan throughout his innings. Sarwan bit back, and McGrath, who thought Sarwan had insulted his wife, flew into a rage. That is a pretty touchy subject for Glenn, because he had just spent the best part of three weeks with Jane as she battled cancer in her hip; it is no wonder he flew off the handle. However, no matter what was or was not said, the players were involved in a game of cricket, and by losing his cool McGrath helped hand the initiative to the batsmen, who took full advantage. The West Indies plundered 143 in the final session of the day, and I know John Buchanan was very upset — he felt the incident detracted from McGrath's bowling and the team's focus as a whole.

There was a lot of criticism directed at Waugh for not acting to defuse the incident before it became really ugly, with McGrath shouting and pointing his finger at Sarwan. But Waugh was not standing next to McGrath at the time, and quite often in situations like this the damage is done before the captain gets a chance to react. If the situation could have been foreseen, surely the umpires would have stepped in to calm things down.

Although it is difficult for me to comment without having seen the last session of that fourth day, one look at the statistics tells me the incident affected the whole team's performance — we clearly got nothing out of it. I think by the end of the day Buchanan was happy to get the players off the ground while the match was still alive; he, the captain and everyone else needed a chance to refocus.

The West Indies began the final day wanting just 47 runs to win with four wickets in hand. I made it down to the ground for a team meeting before the start of the day. Waugh stressed that the night's sleep would have benefited us; all it did for them was give them time to realise how close they were to making history. But although we managed to get their last recognised batsman, Chanderpaul, very early on, we could not finish them off and they won a deserved victory, thanks to calm play from Omari Banks and Vasbert Drakes.

It was a Test we should have won, but we could still take something positive from it. Most Test defeats we have suffered in the past four or five years have come about thanks to superb individual performances from opposition players; this was no exception, with Sarwan and Chanderpaul both scoring brilliant hundreds when the odds were stacked heavily against them. As long as we are constantly asking opposing teams to do extraordinary things, like chasing world record scores in order to beat us, we can be confident that we will win many more matches than we lose.

I hung around for a short while after the match — I was to receive the man of the series award, a Suzuki car which Andy Bichel took for a spin around the outfield. It would be nice to be able to bring something like that home, but with tax issues to sort out it all becomes too hard, so I decided to accept a cash prize instead once the formalities were finished with.

The West Indies players came into our dressing room after the ceremony and they were obviously ecstatic at chasing down the record score. I did not stay very long; I was ready for another lie-down, because although I was feeling a little better I was still nowhere near fit and well. With the one-day series just four days away, getting myself right for the first match was my major priority.

Friday 16 May

Shivnarine Chanderpaul is ruled out of the one-day series against Australia after fracturing the middle finger of his left hand during the fourth Test, in Antigua.

There was a lot to cover in today's team meeting before the one-day series, and not all of it was pleasant.

Over the past five days, the volume of newspaper clippings sent from Australia has shown us that the events on the fourth evening in Antigua have been of huge interest back home. Almost every single clipping shows that the Glenn McGrath incident has been received extremely badly in the media and among the public. If we did not know it already, we can now see clearly that how we conduct ourselves as a team and as individuals has a massive effect on the public.

Without wanting to distract us from our discussion of tomorrow's match, I said I hoped we had all learnt lessons from what had happened and would not allow anything like this to happen again. Everyone agreed with that sentiment.

On the cricket side of the ledger the meeting had a couple of themes. Chief among them was maintaining the momentum we'd built up in the World Cup. This is basically the same group of players, with just Michael Clarke added to the mix, and we will try to do things exactly as we did in southern Africa. The keys to our success there were:

- partnerships (we aimed for at least one of 100 runs or more per innings);
- strike rotation (one scoring shot every two balls);
- maintaining wickets in hand (batting for the full 50 overs when we bat first, to maximise our scoring opportunities);
- bowling dot balls to build up pressure (looking to concede less than 80 in the first 15 overs and less than 60 in the final 10 overs); and
- fielding excellence (catch, contain and control with minimum requirements at a 90% success rate for straightforward catches, 70% for tougher ones, at least one in three throws hitting the stumps and 15 runs saved in the field).

Improving on all that would be good, but that is our benchmark.

Our ability to execute those plans will depend on the intensity of the playing group. A few of us have been in action almost non-stop since the one-day tour to Kenya in August 2002, but we have been helped by a few fresh faces coming into the squad for this one-day series — they will liven up the mix and inject some fresh enthusiasm if necessary.

Although we have been on the road for a while, I made a point of not mentioning that when I spoke, and no one else brought it up, which was a relief. It can be easy to get into the habit of ticking off the days until we go home for a well-deserved break; but that is counterproductive, because everyone starts to focus on that rather than on the matches still to be played. I hope we can keep that sort of chat off the agenda — although I know that in the last few days before departure it may be inevitable.

The West Indies may, in theory, have some momentum after the Test win in Antigua, but that is not a theory I agree with. I believe individual players can carry momentum from one form of the game to another, but for teams it is a whole new ball game. I believe the slate will be clean when we walk out tomorrow. It will be up to us to impose ourselves on them as we have done for most of the Test series. If we can do that we will be tough to beat. It sounds simple, but most successful things are in my book.

The match referee's meeting, which took place at the West Indies team's hotel, just up the street from ours, was a straightforward one. The referee is Ranjan Madugalle, the former Sri Lanka batsman. He has arrived for the one-day series, to take over from South Africa's Mike Procter, who looked after the Tests. Much of the meeting was taken up with chat about fines for slow over rates. There was no mention of the McGrath–Sarwan incident in Antigua. Maybe Madugalle knew how many press cuttings we had received from Australia, and that almost every question we had faced had been about those events — and that we are bound to be on our best behaviour now.

I am concerned about my fitness after my recent viral infection. I have not trained much since we arrived in Jamaica three days ago; I have concentrated on getting some strength back after being laid so low. I had a net session today but it only lasted about 5 minutes, and at the end of it I felt a bit dizzy and light-headed, maybe because I have done so little over the past couple of weeks. I want to play, but if I still feel this way tomorrow I may have to rest for another day.

Saturday 17 May

First one-day international, Jamaica: Australia 5–270 (Ponting 59, Lehmann 55) beat West Indies 8–205 by 2 runs (Duckworth–Lewis method).

When I woke up this morning I had second thoughts about playing. I felt weak and a bit dizzy, but I decided to bite the bullet — and I am glad I did, because I was able to play a part in a hard-fought and well-deserved win to kick off the series.

After we made a decent score on the fastest, bounciest pitch of the tour, rain arrived to make their target much more achievable. But our bowling and fielding stood up to the challenge, and although the final margin was only two runs, we were more comfortable than that because the West Indies required 16 from the final over.

I scored 59 from 66 balls to confirm my view that practice for the sake of it is not really necessary. I have barely batted at all for two weeks, but having been in pretty good touch before my lay-off I quickly got back into the groove after adjusting to the extra pace of the Sabina Park surface.

My main problem was not a lack of touch but a lack of fitness. It was hot and humid in the middle before the storm that arrived in the afternoon, and by the end of my innings I was out on my feet, short of breath and in need of water after most overs.

During the changeover I had a sit-down in the dressing room and the chance to rehydrate, and I did not have problems when we took the field. This was partly because of that rest, partly because the West Indies' innings was split into two parts by the rain break, partly because the intensity of batting and running between the wickets in a one-day game is greater than that in a Test and greater than that of fielding, and partly because, as captain, I had plenty to think about other than myself.

My failure to go on and make a big score was not as costly as it might have been, thanks to a great late surge from Ian Harvey and Michael Bevan who added 87 from the final 62 balls of the innings. They made a good combination, with Bevan scampering singles, picking the gaps and rotating the strike while Harvey played most of the big shots.

Harvey was also our key man with the ball, shutting down the West Indies' innings after the rain delay. The break left them requiring 94 from 82 balls, with eight wickets in hand, something they should probably have managed to do. But Harvey bowled intelligently, mixing up his pace, and he proved difficult to hit, as well as getting the crucial wicket of Brian Lara, caught behind cutting.

No matter how well Harvey bowled, we may still not have won if not for our fielding. I call it the barometer of how we are going as a side: if we are sharp, catching well, looking for run-outs and closing down their batsmen in the 30-yard circle and in the outfield, we are rarely beaten. That was how it was today. If we can maintain that sort of hunger we will be tough to beat.

Brett Lee took the last over, and although his control was not great, they were never going to get the runs they needed. It was a satisfying win for us all — and I was delighted to get through the match in one piece after my spell on the sidelines.

The West Indies' reduced target does raise a question about whether or not the Duckworth–Lewis method was fair on this occasion. Most international sides would have fancied their chances chasing that revised score over a shortened number of overs; the fact that we won shows that the score could be defended.

We were fortunate in that the ball did swing a little after the rain, although that effect was reduced as time went on because the ball got wet when it was struck into the outfield. We don't play many games under the Duckworth–Lewis method so I have not had the chance to study it in real depth, but I would say it is an improvement on basing target scores on each side's run rate or their best overs. No one I speak to seems to have a clue how it is worked out, but it seems to be a fairer system, and that is all that matters.

Ian Harvey

Although he has achieved a great deal in the game, being part of the World Cup-winning squad of 2003 and enjoying countless successes as an overseas player in county cricket in the UK, it is difficult not to look at Ian Harvey and wonder if we have ever seen the best of him, especially at international level.

Harvey is a natural ball-player and seems to be top of the class at whatever sport he turns his hand to. Football, tennis, you name it, he is a very skilful person and, unlike most of us, he is almost as adept with his left hand as he is with his right. His ability to throw and bowl with both hands earned him the nickname Freak during his early days with Victoria and it has stuck through his career.

His gifts on the cricket field are wide-ranging. He is an orthodox batsman who can destroy any attack as he has every shot in the book at his disposal; as a bowler, he has revolutionised one-day cricket with his range of slower balls, and when he was younger he was capable of delivering a really quick ball as well as finding late outswing. In English county cricket he established himself as the best bowler at the end of a one-day innings and helped Gloucestershire to a host of one-day titles as a result. In the field, his ability to throw down the stumps with either hand makes him lethal, especially inside the fielding circle.

Despite all those gifts, it is possible to wonder whether he has truly fulfilled himself at international level. In one-day cricket his figures do not do justice to his great talent, and he has not been able to force his way into the Test side in an era when we have been short of a genuine all-rounder.

The late David Hookes, who coached him at Victoria, always maintained that Harvey's time playing county cricket in the UK reduced his overall effectiveness, and perhaps there is some truth in that. Playing as much cricket as they do over there, especially as an all-rounder, makes it difficult to function at full tilt all the time, and if you try to do so you can become jaded or injured, both of which will affect your output as a player.

Some players, such as Glenn McGrath and Andy Bichel, do best with a heavy workload, but Harvey, with his dual responsibilities as batsman and bowler, may have suffered; there is no doubt in my mind that his effectiveness as a wicket-taking bowler has suffered as a result of playing year-round cricket. It has taken the edge off his pace, and that may have counted against him when the time came for him to be considered for higher honours.

Despite that, he was an excellent addition to the World Cup squad in southern Africa, as a late replacement for the injured Shane Watson, and he did not let us down. He stepped up in every match he played, and leaving him out of the starting eleven on the morning of the final against India was one of the hardest decisions I have ever had to make.

Harvey had been part of our provisional squad in 1999 but did not make the final cut then, and as he is unlikely to still be around at international level in 2007, it made the task of leaving him out even harder. Harvey handled that disappointment brilliantly, and that is typical of him — he is a great team man, and a nice bloke too. He also has a lively sense of humour, and his is usually one of the loudest voices in the dressing room when there is a joke to be told or some celebrating to be done.

He is also able to laugh at himself, which is important in the Australian dressing room where there are always sharp one-liners and put-downs flying all over the place. In Harvey's case the joke is often about his eyesight, as he has had laser treatment to correct a slight impairment. The treatment seems to have worked well — I don't think he wears contact lenses to play any more. But sometimes in team meetings there may be the odd comment about how successful the treatment has been, especially if he has been dismissed in a previous match playing an especially poor shot. I remember that being the joke after he was bowled by Shane Bond of New Zealand in the World Cup match in Port Elizabeth in 2003. Harvey was on the end of a brilliant, hostile spell but seemed to spend most of his brief stay at the crease in an unsuccessful attempt to locate the ball.

Although he is nearer the end of his career than the beginning, I believe we are yet to see the best of Ian Harvey. I hope he will produce the type of form he is capable of on a consistent basis at international level before it is too late.

Sunday 18 May

Second one-day international, Jamaica: Australia 2–166 (Ponting 57 not out, Hayden 51) beat West Indies 163 by 8 wickets.

This was just about the perfect game of one-day cricket from us. We put them under pressure from ball one, not letting them get free at any stage, and then stamped on them when we batted. We won with almost 15 overs in hand — that will give them plenty to think about for the rest of the series.

One of the keys to the West Indies' chances in this series is whether or not Chris Gayle can get them off to a flying start. Yesterday he and Ricardo Powell added 75 from 14 overs; today we gave him far less to hit, and the pitch may have been a little slower. By the time he was out in the 17th over, he had scored just 28.

I was a little surprised that they dropped Powell down the order after he and Gayle clicked yesterday, but we saw during the Test series that Devon Smith was capable of playing some shots and they are clearly looking for their best combination at this stage. I think they also fancy Powell as a finisher at the end of the innings when boundaries are needed, like Harvey on Saturday, but after the start they got today it was just a case of damage limitation for them.

Andy Bichel removed not only Gayle but also Brian Lara; that contest is one people are starting to notice — he has got the West Indies captain out a few times on this trip. They lost their way completely at that point — 6–103 — and from there on we were in total control. Omari Banks and Carlton Baugh kept the board ticking over against Brad Hogg and Andrew Symonds but they never got away from us, and with Glenn McGrath back to somewhere near his best the target was straightforward.

I was happy to spend more time in the middle and felt better physically than I did on Saturday. All in all, it was a crushing win, and a weekend that has set us up for the rest of the series.

Monday 19 May

West Indies fast bowler Jermaine Lawson will miss the entire one-day series against Australia because of bulging discs in his lower back.

Wednesday 21 May

ICC Chief Executive Malcolm Speed says he believes umpires David Shepherd and Srinivas Venkataraghavan should have laid Code of Conduct charges after the McGrath–Sarwan incident during the fourth Test in Antigua. ICC President Malcolm Gray echoes those thoughts, saying: '... greater action and sterner action should have been taken'.

Third one-day international, St Lucia: Australia 4–258 (Clarke 75 not out, Symonds 75) beat West Indies 9–233 by 25 runs.

A new venue for me but the same result: another convincing win. It was a pleasing one, too, because some players who have not played a major part in the series so far put their hands up and made match-winning contributions.

Andrew Symonds, Michael Bevan and Michael Clarke did well to get us up to a defendable score, mixing sensible accumulation with some power hitting and excellent running between the wickets. It was not an easy pitch to score quickly on, especially once the ball had gone soft, but the trio assessed the conditions quickly.

Clarke is not a classically orthodox player, but what he has got in his favour is exceptionally quick hands that allow him to generate great power; he also has a wide range of shots at his disposal. He is a brilliant hitter over cover, hits well down the ground, is able to play the slog-sweep well and also has a short-arm pull where he jumps back in his crease in a flash and gets the ball through midwicket even when it does not appear to be especially short. He played one of those shots today off Omari Banks and it raced to the boundary.

It is early days for him at the highest level and he does need to work on his fitness: he's a young player, but at the moment he tires and gets bad cramps. If he can solve that issue he has a bright future.

Clarke and Bevan produced the late push in our innings after Symonds steadied the ship when we lost three cheap wickets. One of them was me, out in a frustrating way — I was run out by millimetres as Symonds and I looked for a quick single.

There was no real call from either of us when he dropped the ball out on the off-side looking for a single: we just looked at each other and decided to go; but pretty quickly I realised I was in trouble.

Rather than travel a few yards out on the off-side, the ball appeared to spin off his bat and almost stopped dead, in a perfect position for Corey Collymore, the bowler, to get to it as he followed through.

He made good ground forward, picked up and flicked the ball at the stumps as I stretched for my ground — a TV replay showed that his direct hit had found me just short.

It was particularly frustrating because I felt much better today than over the weekend, almost back to full fitness, and I'd been doubly keen to spend some quality time at the crease.

Luckily Symonds made up for my absence, showing us yet again how much he has developed as a player over the past few months. He pushed the ball around sensibly, and without ever really breaking into a sweat, and made 75 from 82 balls before Chris Gayle beat him with an excellent yorker.

Nathan Hauritz was another man who made a telling contribution for us today. He has been unlucky over the past few months: by spending time with us in Kenya, Sri Lanka and Sharjah at the start of the summer he found he'd slipped down the pecking order through lack of cricket. You need players with you as cover when you are on tour, but if those players don't get any opportunities to step in, other players back home can jump ahead of them; that is what happened to Hauritz, with Brad Hogg leapfrogging him in selection.

With Shane Warne out of the picture Hauritz has come back into contention here, and he did a superb job after Gayle got the West Indies off to a flying start. They were going so well I had to introduce him inside the first 15 overs, and straight away he made the breakthrough, with Ramnaresh Sarwan caught at mid-off. Next over he got rid of Gayle, cutting straight to Clarke at point. Suddenly we were in charge of the game — and we never really let go from that point on.

The killer blow for them was when Brian Lara fell — to Andy Bichel again. It is now almost a case of putting Bichel on as soon as Lara comes to the crease; I am sure the West Indies captain's record against the bowler is starting to play on his mind. He is always keen to dominate bowlers and that instinct will come out even more if he feels a bowler has an edge on him. That can also mean that if Bichel holds his nerve and gives him nothing to hit, there is every chance Lara will get himself out.

When Lara was out they were 4–85, which meant their batsmen had to just consolidate for a while. That in turn meant their required run rate went up. As it did, so did the pressure on them to increase the tempo. In the end they cracked, giving us a comfortable win.

It was an enjoyable first trip to this new facility, which is a decent size and has a good playing surface. The practice and dressing room amenities need to be developed, but it is certainly one of the best venues we have played at in the Caribbean.

Saturday 24 May

Fourth one-day international, Trinidad: Australia 5–286 (Gilchrist 84, Clarke 55 not out) beat West Indies 219 (Gayle 84) by 67 runs.

The way everyone roared out our team song this evening was the perfect illustration of our delight at wrapping up the series after just four matches. This was a clinical performance, perhaps our best of the series so far.

I hope that the relief everyone is feeling at winning the series does not mean we switch to autopilot for the final three matches. After a long tour, and with our objective of winning the series secured, that could happen, and we have done it before — in South Africa last year. Let's hope we can maintain our focus for the remainder of the series; I know it will not be easy.

Just about everything about today's performance was right. Adam Gilchrist led the way with a barnstorming effort at the top of the innings, Matthew Hayden and I played around him, and Andrew Symonds and Michael Clarke supplied some late impetus.

I have now fully recovered from my illness, and I felt in pretty good touch. I proved that when I belted Ricardo Powell's off-spin onto the grandstand at deep midwicket — but then I got out two balls later trying to do the same thing. I was playing well, so in one sense it was a soft dismissal, but I had already said to Gilchrist that as he was going so well it was up to me and players to come to push the tempo at the other end, and that was what I got out trying to do. I felt the shot was a risk worth taking because I was hitting with the wind — I just did not hit it well enough.

I need not have worried, because Clarke kept up the momentum with a really good innings at the death. In successive matches he has shown me that he is an excellent finisher: he is a good runner between the wickets and is also capable of hitting fours and sixes even at that stage of the innings, which makes him tough to bowl at. That was the role he filled again today, and it helped give us an intimidating total.

I found out afterwards that there had been some surprise among the media when I opted to use Brett Lee and Jason Gillespie with the new ball ahead of Glenn McGrath; in humid conditions I thought the ball would swing rather than seam, and with Lee in the side I wanted him to have the chance to exploit those conditions, especially to the left-handers at the top of the West Indies order, while the ball was still new.

My tactic worked pretty well, unlike the West Indies' decision to drop Brian Lara down to number five. I could see the idea behind that change: he obviously wanted to add stability to a middle order that was otherwise pretty inexperienced. But on the other hand, he is their best player, so he needs to bat for as many overs as possible in a long run chase, and today, by the time he came in, they were already up against the clock, with almost half their overs gone and the asking rate starting to get towards 8 runs per over. Lara played well, but with our attack maintaining its discipline it would have taken a once-in-a-lifetime effort for him to get them over the line and that did not happen.

Despite the series win there were no major celebrations tonight. We will save those for the end of the series — when, I hope, we can celebrate our continued run of good form.

Sunday 25 May

Fifth one-day international, Trinidad: West Indies 5–290 (Lara 80, W. Hinds 79) beat Australia 9–251 (Symonds 77) by 39 runs.

Although we gave a solid account of ourselves in this match, today was an example of exactly what I feared last night. We just lacked that certain something, especially when we bowled. And to give the West Indies credit, they responded by jumping all over us and securing a convincing win.

It has brought our winning run to an end, at 21 successive matches; more importantly, I called this a 'wake-up call' when the media asked me about it afterwards. The streak is a nice record to have and I would have liked us to keep it going all the way to the end of the tour. The key issue now is how we respond to this loss in the final two matches of the series.

The West Indies have already laid their cards on the table: after Saturday's loss, Brian Lara said he wanted his side to look at the last three matches as a three-match series. That is a good suggestion, because it allows them to have a new focus, instead of thinking that they have already lost the seven-match series. It is now up to us to bounce back from this loss.

There were two elements to this West Indies win. First, there was the promotion of Lara to number three. He came in to bat in the second over, and with so much time left to bat he dictated the course of the innings. He may have been out — to Andy Bichel again — with 15 overs still left, but by the time he departed they were rattling along at almost 6 runs an over and it was the perfect platform for Marlon Samuels and Ricardo Powell to play big shots in the closing overs. They looked like a different side from the one we had thumped in the first four matches.

The second element to their win was the way we batted in the first 15 overs of our chase. They had a large score on the board but it was achievable for us if we kept wickets in hand. Instead we lost three wickets to careless shots — Adam Gilchrist, Jimmy Maher and me — and that set us back too far to make a run for home.

Andrew Symonds and Michael Clarke did their best but it was difficult for them to stabilise the innings and press on at the same time, and that meant we fell behind the asking rate. This was exactly the same problem we had left the West Indies with in the previous match, of course. The pitch also began to offer some spin, and the ball no longer came onto the bat, which made forcing the pace even more difficult. In the end we were a long way from a win.

Monday 26 May

The Australian team have items stolen from their luggage at Trinidad airport. Items include bats belonging to Matthew Hayden, Michael Bevan and Andy Bichel; Bichel's bat is the one he used during the World Cup in South Africa.

Other items to go missing include shirts, shoes, sunglasses, pads and gloves. Ricky Ponting loses his one-day sweater. 'It is not the worst thing I could have lost given conditions in the Caribbean,' he said.

Friday 30 May

Sixth one-day international, Grenada: West Indies 7–254 (Hinds 125 not out, Sarwan 50) beat Australia 252 (Gilchrist 64) by 3 wickets.

We tried hard today, but again a little bit of intensity and attention to detail were missing, and the West Indies sneaked home, thanks to a brilliant innings from Wavell Hinds.

With the bat, no one went on to make the big score that would almost certainly have got us over the line for a win, and with the ball, the little things that went wrong added up to quite a lot in the end. We conceded almost two extra overs of wides and no-balls, and in a tight match like this, that became the difference between winning and losing.

In some ways I was happy we reached 250 when we batted, but it was way short of where we should have finished. Matthew Hayden and Adam Gilchrist added 90 inside the first 15 overs, and from there we should have been looking at 300, but they got out in quick succession, and when I was needlessly run out we needed to start again, almost from scratch.

I am still kicking myself over my dismissal. I turned the ball to square leg and set off, but the act of playing the ball had put spin on it and it seemed to turn straight to Brian Lara, who was a metre or two behind the umpire. He gathered the ball and sent the return to the bowler's end with me hopelessly short of my ground. It was poor cricket, as was Gilchrist's dismissal next ball, cutting a short ball straight to the same fielder. A key part of every chat we have as a team is about not losing wickets in clusters, but now we had two batsmen on nought, and both yet to face a ball.

With the ball we needed early wickets to put them under pressure, and we thought Brett Lee had provided us with one when he bowled Chris Gayle — but it was a no-ball. I am not sure what else we can do as a side to combat this problem; we seem to run up against it at least once or twice in a series, and that is once or twice too often.

I do have some sympathy for the bowlers, because it is not always possible to operate off full runs in the nets, but when you see them overstepping in warm-ups on the ground before play and ask them why they do it, they say that all they are doing is loosening up and looking for rhythm. That is not good enough, and when they then overstep in the match they know it too. It is sloppy and lets the whole side down.

It is all well and good to say we should fine them for overstepping or get an umpire in for net sessions, but it should not have to come to that. Everyone on the team is a professional, and avoiding no-balls should be something that each bowler takes responsibility for.

Luckily, that no-ball did not cost us too much — Gayle fell soon afterwards — but his opening partner Hinds ploughed on and produced a great knock. He looked out of sorts in the Test series, and was dropped, only coming into the one-day squad because of injuries to others. Today, though, he looked outstanding.

Hinds' main flaw is lack of foot movement, but if he is able to get past the new ball, as he did today, he can be devastating. He has very loose wrists, which means he can manoeuvre the ball into gaps, and he thumps the ball down the ground with real power off both the spinners and faster bowlers. The highlight of his innings was an on-drive off Gillespie that went all the way for six. Today he also showed an excellent temperament, maintaining his composure while we took wickets at the other end.

We did show that if we can get into their middle order and put them under pressure they are vulnerable, but Hinds was still able to do enough to get them over the line. What we need now is one final effort to make sure we finish the tour on the right note.

Sunday 1 June

Seventh one-day international, Grenada: West Indies 1–249 (Hinds 103 not out, Lara 75 not out, Gayle 60) beat Australia 8–247 (Lehmann 107, Gayle 5–46) by 9 wickets.

Far from finishing the tour on the right note, we were thrashed today. And to make matters worse, I had to watch most of the thrashing from the sidelines after I took a painful blow from the ball on the point of my right hip. It left me with little movement in my right leg, so I was a frustrated spectator when we fielded. The West Indies batsmen did as they liked against our bowlers, winning by a crushing margin with more than six overs to spare.

Whether I admit it or not, we have gone: mental fatigue has finally caught up with the squad. In many ways that is not surprising. We have played a lot of cricket in the past nine months, and now the players are desperate to get home for a break.

Even though everyone was trying, it was impossible to escape the conclusion that there was not much petrol left in some players' tanks, and that was reflected in today's result. The West Indies clearly wanted the victory more than we did and they got their just reward.

The incident that sidelined me happened just after I came into bat. I tried to pull a ball from Mervyn Dillon that did not bounce as much as I expected. It beat the bat and thumped straight onto my hip bone. It was very painful, but after taking a little time to compose myself I faced up to the next ball and glanced it to fine leg. I set off for a run but found I could not lift my right leg. I went down, and in the end I had to be chaired off the ground.

Physiotherapist Errol Alcott said I had been hit where the hip flexor attaches to the pelvis and that the nerves had been squashed and separated. I got some movement back in my leg as the day went on, but I was nowhere near mobile enough to field, and it would have been foolish to try — I would have been risking further injury.

I did face one more ball in the match, because I limped out for the final delivery of our innings, at number ten. It was either me or McGrath to bat, and I figured that even on one leg, I would have more chance than him of slapping a boundary — in the end I had to be content with a single.

The final result was a severe disappointment, but at least Darren Lehmann was able to hold his head up at the end of it all. Not because of his bowling — Brian Lara thumped him for three sixes in a row to win the match in emphatic fashion — but for his batting: he held our innings together with 107, at almost a run a ball.

It was a typical, intelligent one-day innings from Lehmann: he worked the ball into gaps, used his feet to the spinners and thumped the ball down the ground and through midwicket in his uncomplicated fashion. He has had a great tour of the Caribbean and has now finally established himself in both forms of the game, something that really pleases me. The end of the tour gave me a chance for a beer and chat with Lara, and he explained some of the plans they'd had during the series. He said the reason the West Indies picked just three bowlers for the Trinidad Test and then bowled first on a flat pitch in Barbados was to try to maximise their strength in batting. They believed the only way they could beat us would be to bat last, with us setting them a target to chase. It is a novel idea, and it was shown to have some merit when they chased 418 to win in Antigua.

Lara also told me his policy in one-day cricket in the Caribbean when his side is playing back-to-back matches. He said he always tries to bowl first in the first game and bat first in the second. He said if pitches were being prepared for two games they would usually have some moisture left in them for the first day, to make sure they held together, and that could be exploited by the seam bowlers early on. Then, in game two, the pitch would generally be at its best for batting at the start of the match, before losing its pace and turning more later on. That is exactly what happened in the fifth match of the series, in Trinidad, where their spinners strangled the life out of our middle order just when we needed to accelerate.

I hope it did not sound like sour grapes, but when I spoke to the media afterwards I said seven games was far too many to play against the same side, especially at the end of a long tour. We were tired, and it showed in the last week of this trip. The mood was the same as it was at the end of my first tour as one-day captain, in South Africa last year: when you win a series early on it is very difficult to stop players drifting off with thoughts of home.

I can understand people who are critical of players doing this — we do earn good salaries and are playing for our country. But at the same time we are spending more and more time away from home, travelling more and playing more, and there is a real danger of burn-out among players if we maintain the current volume of cricket.

International cricket is meant to be the top of the tree. To make sure it stays that way we have to look for quality over quantity. If we do not, two results are likely, in my opinion. First, we may find players get injured more often because of the demands made on their bodies. Second, players may decide to take part in just one form of the game, either Tests or one-day games, to ensure that they get some balance in their lives. They may even try to do that while also playing county cricket in the UK, which can offer big pay cheques and help cement a player's financial future.

Whether or not there will be a move to fewer matches remains to be seen, but in the short term, at least, the prospects do not look good. With the ICC having Test and one-day championships already in place through their ten-year programs, each country has obligations to play every other side at regular intervals; the demands are now so high that we are about to embark on winter cricket in Australia so that we can cope. We have what are called our icon series, the big-money earners for Cricket Australia against the likes of England, India, South Africa and the West Indies, but we also have to fit in home and away Tests against all the other countries too, and all our commitments have to be met every four years. That is a lot of cricket.

That is another month away, though. I will be keeping fit ahead of that time, but I do not expect to pick up my bat very often.

Nathan Hauritz, Jimmy Maher and Ashley Noffke

This Queensland trio have been on the fringe of the squad throughout the period covered by this diary, and although none of them has been able to secure a permanent spot in the side, they have ensured that there is pressure for places, which is vital for the continuing success of Australian cricket.

Hauritz has been especially unfortunate in two ways. First of all, as a reserve finger-spinner through much of 2002 and 2003 he toured with us to Sri Lanka and Sharjah without much hope of playing, and then slipped down the pecking order behind Brad Hogg's wrist-spin because his touring commitments meant he missed the chance to get overs under his belt in match conditions.

On top of that, he has experienced the problem many orthodox finger-spinners have encountered: pitches are not breaking up the way they did a generation or so ago. These days, surfaces tend to become uneven rather than crumbly or powdery, and sides tend to favour fast bowlers to exploit that uneven bounce in the fourth innings of a match rather than finger-spinners, unless, like Muttiah Muralitharan or Harbhajan Singh, they have extra tricks in their lockers.

As yet Haurie — or Finch, as Jason Gillespie calls him, because he thinks he looks like the character of that name from the *American Pie* movies — does not have those tricks, but he does have two advantages: he is level-headed and has plenty of time in the game because he is still in his early 20s. And we know that in him we have a player who has an excellent temperament and has not let us down whenever he has been picked.

Jimmy Maher has been an effective addition to our one-day squad over the past three years because he can fill several roles. When he first played for Australia, in 1997/98, he was just seen as a top-order player, but when he came back into the side, for the one-day tour of South Africa in 2002, he had developed as a player and was able to slot in as an opener, at number three or as a finisher in the middle order. On top of that, he also worked on his keeping, and has filled that role to give Adam Gilchrist a break during several tours and one-day series.

Mabo may have suffered like Hauritz from being on tour and not playing a lot of cricket — his output at domestic level has not been as high in the past couple of years as it was in the period immediately before that. I hope he can regain his touch, because his versatility gives us extra options when the selectors name a squad. And he is great value to have on tour.

Mabo is one of the funniest blokes I have ever met. He is a great impersonator, and his effort on the 2002 South Africa tour had to be heard to be believed. He put together a mock race night, with horses named after each member of the tour party. He went through the form of each horse, based on the characteristics of each person, and then called the race, right down to a dramatic finish. It had everyone in tears — if he still has the tape it will be a collector's item.

Stephen Waugh described Ashley Noffke as a 'mini McGrath' when he was called up as replacement for Nathan Bracken on the 2001 Ashes tour. The two bowlers do have plenty in common: they both try to bowl a nagging length and hit the seam. And Noffke is a little bit quicker than he looks.

That 2001 trip was cut short for Noffke when he rolled his ankle in a county match against Sussex, but he showed signs of progress in the summer of 2002/03, helping Queensland to the Pura Cup final and playing for Australia A. The England batsmen he came up against said he was the best bowler they faced outside the Test squad.

On the strength of that display he secured a spot on the West Indies tour that followed the World Cup, but with the likes of Brad Williams and Bracken around and Shaun Tait emerging, he will have to continue to impress if he is to take the next step to international honours.

Part 2:
Bangladesh home series

NEW VENUES, NEW OPPONENTS, SAME HIGH

Thursday 12 June

Bangladesh name a 15-man squad for the tour of Australia. It is: Khaled Mahud (captain), Javed Omar, Khaled Mashud, Habibul Bashar, Mohammad Rafique, Hannan Sarkar, Mohammad Ashraful, Al-Sahariar, Manjural Islam, Alok Kapali, Sanwar Hossain, Tareq Aziz, Tapash Baisya, Anwar Hossain Monir and Mashrafe Mortaza. Tushar Imran and Habibul Hossain will join the squad for the VB Series that follows the two Test matches.

Friday 20 June

Australia names 13-man squads for the Top End 3 Test series and VB Series against Bangladesh.

The Test squad is: Stephen Waugh (captain), Ricky Ponting (vice-captain), Andrew Bichel, Adam Gilchrist, Jason Gillespie, Matthew Hayden, Brad Hogg, Justin Langer, Brett Lee, Darren Lehmann, Martin Love, Stuart MacGill and Glenn McGrath.

The one-day international squad is: Ricky Ponting (captain), Adam Gilchrist (vice-captain), Michael Bevan, Andrew Bichel, Jason Gillespie, Ian Harvey, Matthew Hayden, Brad Hogg, Brett Lee, Darren Lehmann, Damien Martyn, Glenn McGrath and Andrew Symonds. Martyn is included subject to fitness following surgery to his fractured right index finger.

Thursday 17 July

Our Test and one-day series against Bangladesh starts tomorrow, and for most of us it is a trip into the unknown — in more ways than one.

To start with, we know next to nothing about any of the players we are going to face. We played them last year in one match, in the Champions Trophy in Sri Lanka, but we won so easily that there was little chance to study the opposition in depth. John Buchanan and Tim Nielsen tried to get some video footage of them, but were not able to do so.

It means our team meeting before this match is not as detailed as is normally the case at the start of a series, but in some ways I think that is a good thing. I always hark back to Shane Warne's view that you can easily overcomplicate the game. There is always scope for planning, but, as he says, the basic idea is that bowlers should be looking to hit the top of off-stump and batsmen should be looking to block or leave good balls and hit bad ones for four or six. It sounds ridiculously simple, but when you break it down, that is the game.

I am feeling very good: fresh and ready to go again, a month and a half after our last action in the Caribbean. After recovering from the hip injury I suffered at the end of the tour I kept myself ticking over with some gym work, as well as occasional nets with my brother-in-law at Sutherland, in the south of Sydney.

Those practices have been occasional, maybe once a week, and I have purposely avoided doing much more than that because I am happy with my game. All I want to do is keep feeling bat on ball; I'm not looking to tinker unnecessarily. Also, there is an air of unreality about sessions with a bowling machine. They are only useful in small doses and if you want to work on specific aspects of play.

Most of my work towards this series has been done in the gym, maintaining my fitness levels. We all have programs of weights work and cardiovascular exercises provided by the Australian team's fitness trainer, Jock Campbell, and that has taken me to my local gym in Wollongong four times a week.

My weights sessions have involved using free weights to strengthen my chest, shoulders, wrists and forearms. Additional exercises for me include pull-ups for my upper body, squat-thrusts or work on the leg-press to increase power in my leg muscles and hamstrings, and calf raises. Jock has mapped it all out for me, as he has done with every other player in the squad. My program usually involves one set to warm up then two sets of full-on work.

The weights I work with tend not to be very heavy, as I am after strength and endurance rather than massive bulk. And, of course, once I have done the sets, there is also the question of stretching and warming down — the last thing I need is a pulled muscle or stiffness.

Even though cricket involves a long time on my feet and running about, I tend not to do too much of that, especially since 2001, when I suffered a stress fracture in my left foot during the Ashes tour. Instead, most of the aerobic work I do is on an exercise bike, although I will sometimes have a jog or a walk on a treadmill just to break up any monotony.

Once we get into the season or a playing routine I just do what Jock tells me, like the other players. Much of that involves stretching and recovery work, because match programs can be intense and don't allow a lot of time outside the playing arena. I do some weights work, but it is usually pretty light stuff. I tend not to do it the day before a match, to avoid any danger of stiffness during the game.

As he does with the rest of the squad, Jock will ring me to see how I am going with my program, and the fact that we live relatively close to each other means he may occasionally pop along to see me, but the emphasis is on players taking responsibility to do the work required of them. The culture we have is that if players do not want to work they will get found out — it will show in their performances — and a lazy player lets down not only himself but also his team-mates. This means we don't see an awful lot of laziness.

The other unknown aspect of this series is the venues: the matches are in Darwin and Cairns, both of which are new to Test cricket. Here in Darwin, the oval at Marrara has had $3 million spent on it to bring it up to international standards. It has staged a warm-up game — Bangladesh playing a local select XI — ahead of this Test.

Nathan Hauritz and Michael Clarke played in that match and they have been able to pass on some information about the opposition, but it was a low-scoring affair and I am not sure how much we can learn from it in our build-up to a Test. What we do know is that the outfield is likely to be slow as the grass is quite thick. But the weather is pretty much perfect for cricket, with temperatures around 27°C (80°F). When we have not been getting ready for action, I have taken the chance to have a look around Darwin — I even did some fishing with Matthew Hayden and Andy Bichel. It is a lovely spot, and it is amazing to remember that it was basically levelled 30 years ago by Cyclone Tracy ripping through the city. There is no trace of that devastation now.

There is a degree of excitement, with people milling around our hotel looking for autographs and also dozens of people watching our practice sessions, but the interest is not out of control, despite the fact this will be the Northern Territory's first Test match. I wonder if that has something to do with the fact that we are playing in the winter, which means it is the football season. In terms of sport, the Australian Football League (AFL) is king here; that, coupled with Bangladesh's poor past record, may be combining to keep interest levels under control.

Within our squad there is still a level of excitement, though, as there was when we started playing under the roof in Melbourne's Telstra Stadium in 2000. This is not only the beginning of a Test series; it is also the beginning of something new and fresh. And given the records of the two sides, it is possible to argue that the pressure is on us, not them. Bangladesh have been so poor since they began playing Tests that no one expects them to do anything other than get soundly beaten here; so if we do not do just that, you can be sure there will be an element of the media and public who will be highly critical — and maybe rightly so.

So, despite Bangladesh's perceived lack of quality, there is no complacency in our squad. There is more a desire to get started and get the job of winning done as professionally as possible. That is our theme for this series: to crush them as quickly and efficiently as possible. That attitude will prevent us falling into the trap of coasting. It all starts tomorrow.

Friday 18 July

First Test, day one: Australia 2–121 (Lehmann 51 not out) lead Bangladesh 97 by 24 runs.

Today we wore black armbands in memory of former Victoria batsman and coach John Scholes, who passed away last Monday.

Our performance may not have been pretty, especially when we batted, but we did exactly what we set out to do: take total control through a thoroughly professional display.

We scored slowly in the second half of the day, but that was due to a slow outfield and a lack of pace in the pitch. That may have contributed to my downfall — I tried an overambitious shot — but with Justin Langer and Darren Lehmann showing the patience I lacked, we are already well placed.

For the West Indies series, we fielded five bowlers, but this time we reverted to the four-man attack that has served us pretty well over the past few years. This means we left Andy Bichel out of the squad. No disrespect to Bangladesh, but we felt that if four bowlers of the class of Glenn McGrath, Jason Gillespie, Brett Lee and Stuart MacGill could not take 20 wickets against them, a fifth member of the attack would not make too much difference. They have proved us half-right already.

Our idea this morning was to hit the Bangladesh batsmen with pace, because they have not played against too many bowlers of the quality of our fast attack, and that worked out well, even allowing for the slowness of the pitch. That, according to the curator, was down to a lack of preparation time. The pitch was grown off-site and dropped into the middle of the oval, and while that is not unusual in Australia — I can think of it happening in Melbourne and Brisbane — he had wanted more time to roll it once it was in place; time that was not available. That is something to bear in mind if we come back here next year.

The fast bowlers did not show too many signs of rustiness, despite their lack of match practice coming into this Test. For McGrath, Lee and Gillespie it is their first action in six weeks, and the fact that they were so effective today is down to a couple of reasons. They tend to be the fittest among us at the start of a season because, as their job is physically tougher than most of the rest of us, they work harder and longer in the gym. On top of that, Errol Alcott, the team's physiotherapist, makes sure they bowl at least once a week during any break in our schedule. Errol, who has been with the team for 20 years now, believes that players are more likely to suffer strains and injuries if they start to bowl again after a long break; fast bowling is not only tough on the body, it is also a pretty unusual set of movements, unlike walking or even running. So he asks the bowlers to turn their arms over regularly during the off-season so that pre-season preparation is not too much of a shock to the body.

The wickets were shared by our attack, with MacGill, who has been playing county cricket for Nottinghamshire in England since the end of the Test series in the Caribbean, also claiming a couple of successes. It was a straightforward exercise to take the 10 wickets, because, technically, Bangladesh were found wanting.

The crowd was over 6000, but for the first day of cricket at a new venue, and the first Test played in the Northern Territory, it was a little disappointing. The quality of the opposition may have had something to do with that; it may take a year or so, plus better, more well-known teams coming here, for that to change. Only time will tell.

When we batted, we quickly found out that the pitch, together with the slow outfield, played into Bangladesh's hands. It allowed them to restrict us more than we would have liked. They did not have any fast bowlers, so they were relying on medium-pacers and spinners; their main plan of attack was to try and bowl line and length. On a pitch like this, with little pace, they could do just that, and because they maintained their discipline it was very difficult for us to get them away for runs, as Langer found — he was scoring at less than a run per over.

I ran out of patience after scoring 10 in 45 minutes. I was looking to drive a ball through cover off the medium pace of Tapash Baisya, but the ball was not quite there for the shot. I went through with it and still managed to hit it pretty well, but the ball did go uppishly into the covers and the fielder dived forward to take a good, low catch.

Lehmann replaced me and gave everyone else a lesson in how to accumulate runs on a pitch like this, bringing all his years of experience in South Australia, Victoria and county cricket with Yorkshire to bear. He is relishing his chance to play Test cricket after so many years in the wilderness, and having finally broken through with a hundred in the Caribbean, I would not be surprised to see him add to that tally here.

Saturday 19 July

First Test, day two: Bangladesh 97 and 1–70 trail Australia 7–407 declared (Lehmann 110, Waugh 100 not out, Langer 71) by 240 runs.

The plan today was to get quick runs, and get Bangladesh back into bat before the close. We achieved that, thanks to the foundations laid by Darren Lehmann and Justin Langer and an increase in the tempo from Stephen Waugh and the lower order. And although Bangladesh batted with some real spirit this evening, we are still set to win in three days.

Waugh's hundred was a significant one, and not just for the team. It means he joins Gary Kirsten of South Africa as one of only two players to score hundreds against all opposition Test countries. All of us were aware that he was likely to break that record — it is an amazing achievement, as is the fact it takes his batting average back above 50 in Tests. To average that sort of figure over a career that spans almost 18 years is a phenomenal effort, and an inspiration to all of us.

Lehmann has not made anywhere near Waugh's number of hundreds, but as I suspected yesterday, he has the taste for more now. He continued to demonstrate how to put a decent score together on this pitch: he waited for the right ball to go after, pushed the ball around into the gaps — especially off his hip — off the spinners, and thumped anything with width through the covers whenever he was given the chance. From being a player who has been in and out of the side for almost a decade, he has now become a key figure in our middle order.

The downside of today's display was a failure for Martin Love. No one is naïve enough to think that every one of our batsmen is going to score a hundred, but with so much pressure on places in the middle order it was a failure that he could well have done without. Love was bowled first ball by Bangladesh's impressive young quick bowler, Mashrafe Mortaza. Let's hope that will not be the end of him in this series. The selectors have shown in the past that they are happy to back players they feel have talent, rather than chop and change, and Love should benefit from that policy now, especially as he has waited so long for his chance — he had played more than 100 first-class matches before he was finally picked last summer.

Bangladesh scored freely in the final session but that was not a major concern for us, because Waugh posted ultra-attacking fields to support our bowlers. On such a slow, easy-paced pitch, occupation of the crease is not very tough, but if we leave gaps that encourage them to play their shots, we are more likely to reap the rewards by having catchers in place to accept any mistakes. That will be the plan again tomorrow. We are all confident we can wrap the match up with two days left unused.

Sunday 20 July

First Test, day three: Australia 7–407 declared beat Bangladesh 97 and 178 (Bashar 54, MacGill 5–65) by an innings and 132 runs.

We did indeed wrap up the match with a minimum of fuss, about half an hour after lunch, which gives us a couple of days off before we head to Cairns. It was straightforward: none of their batsmen held us up for long, and we played with the type of professionalism we have shown to be one of our trademarks.

Stuart MacGill was the star for us, taking five wickets. We could see how much he has benefited from his spell of county cricket. The Bangladesh batsmen really struggled to pick his variations.

The inability of the visitors to read what MacGill was bowling surprised me a little: I would have expected players brought up on the slow pitches found in their country to be used to facing wrist-spin. But struggle they did, for whatever reason. However, given that MacGill has a strike-rate of around five wickets per match in his Test career, the Bangladesh batsmen are not the first to have problems reading him.

We sang the team song in the dressing room at the ground and there were special mentions for Waugh's record of hundreds against every other Test-playing country, as well as for his 37th Test win as captain. The win makes him the most successful Test captain of all time, an amazing record considering he has only been doing the job for four years. It sums up not just the way he leads the team, but also the aggressive way we play. I would be hard pushed to think of too many draws in those four years, and that period also includes our

16-match streak of successive wins, a record I do not believe will ever be broken. As we lost the last Test in the Caribbean, this new streak stands at one; I would like to think it will stand at two in a week's time.

Before we sang the team song there was the chance to have a chat with some of the Bangladesh players, who came into our dressing room at the end of the match. Much of what was said was small talk — their English is not great — but they seem a decent bunch of blokes who are genuinely pleased to be here playing against us.

They are obviously trying hard, and maybe they will prove me wrong by being more competitive in the second Test in Cairns, but I cannot help thinking that mismatches like this do not do an awful lot of good for cricket. I realise that every new Test-playing country has to start somewhere, but Bangladesh have barely even hinted at being competitive for almost three years now, and when that happens there has to be something wrong.

Stuart MacGill

Stuart MacGill manages to be two contradictory things: a captain's dream and a player who sets you real challenges as the leader of a side. The dream element of having MacGill in your team is that his philosophy is a simple one: he is there to get wickets. On the other hand, he does not mind how many runs he concedes to get them.

In that sense he is a bit like Brett Lee: both are pure attacking bowlers. It is my challenge as a captain to work with a player like MacGill to ensure that we get the best out of him — success with wickets, without too many runs.

That might give the impression that he is a wayward bowler; in fact he is anything but that, as his figures show. His aim is to try to spin the ball as hard as he can, but in doing that he is likely to throw in the odd loose delivery along the way. As a captain you have to accept that, because if he finds that exaggerated turn, he can get you wickets against any player through an unplayable delivery.

In the past, MacGill has had a reputation as a hothead, but I have never been on the end of any such problems from him. He is an individual and a thinker — and not just about cricket, as he showed with his decision to pull out of the tour of Zimbabwe. On the contrary, I have found him a pretty even-tempered bloke. MacGill kept his cool unbelievably well when Sanath Jayasuriya got after him during the Kandy Test against Sri Lanka. Instead of reacting when Jayasuriya hit him for four or six, MacGill simply strolled back to his mark, composed himself and ran in again, still with the idea of spinning the ball hard, convinced he would induce a mistake from the batsman sooner or later.

It is that type of conviction that has earned MacGill his amazing record at Test match level: he has a record of almost five wickets per Test, one of the best strike-rates in history. It is so good that even Muttiah Muralitharan, himself a prolific striker, commented on how impressive it was when we chatted in Sri Lanka in 2004.

MacGill has needed that conviction, given that he has spent much of his career in the shadow of Shane Warne. When the choice has been between the two of them, the selectors have almost always gone for Warne, but that is no reflection on MacGill — Warne is one of the all-time greats.

When the two of them have played together it has not always worked — as in the West Indies in 1999, when Warne was coming back from a shoulder injury— but I still firmly believe that they can play successfully in the same side. They showed that by bowling us to victory in the Galle Test in 2004, and before that they spearheaded our success against South Africa in Sydney in 2002. When both are fit and firing and conditions dictate that they should both play, they are an irresistible combination.

The fact that MacGill has had to play second fiddle to Warne, when in another era he would have had close to 100 Test caps by now, has maybe forced him to look outside cricket for other interests. He has become a real wine buff, even taking a degree in the subject, and he is also a very good talker and comes across impressively in the media, so he has plenty of options away from the game.

Less well known is MacGill's thoughtfulness and generosity. I remember that he marked Adam Gilchrist's first Test as captain — in Adelaide in 2000, when Stephen Waugh was injured — by buying a very expensive bottle of wine and getting the whole squad to sign it, then presenting it to Gilchrist in the dressing room. A gesture like that is priceless in a team environment.

MacGill is a valuable asset to Australian cricket. Warne has shown that he has the ability and desire to continue for a few years yet, and I hope MacGill also retains his enthusiasm and skill levels, because he still has a major part to play in the game at international level.

Friday 25 July

Second Test, day one: Bangladesh 8–289 (Sarkar 76, MacGill 5–77) v Australia.

Bangladesh did their best today to prove they are worthy of Test cricket, with a spirited batting effort on a pitch about as far removed from the surface at Darwin as it would be possible to find.

The Cairns pitch was hard and well grassed. We expected it be quick and bouncy, and that was exactly what it was. But we tended to bowl a bit too short and, thanks to a really impressive innings from opening batsman Hannan Sarkar, plus some other supporting contributions, they kept us in the field all day.

There were a couple of suggestions after play about why our faster bowlers were a little too short with their length today. One reason may be that they are still searching for their best rhythm; they have played only one three-day Test since the long lay-off after the Caribbean series. Another is they may have got carried away seeing a pitch with so much pace and bounce.

Whatever the reason — and each suggestion had its supporters — we were not quite as good as we could have been today. However, I do not want to take anything away from Sarkar's innings — he played Brett Lee, in particular, as well as anyone I have seen in recent times. Sarkar used his height — or lack of it, as he is not a tall man — to maximum effect, by getting under Lee's bouncers pretty comfortably, forcing the bowler to pitch the ball up. When Lee did so, Sarkar was quick to pounce, driving through the covers even when the ball was not a half-volley.

Sarkar's ability to cope with Lee's short balls shows how frustrated fast bowlers can get when they are bowling to small batsmen. A short ball that might trouble a batsman of average height will sail harmlessly over the head of a smaller player if he chooses not to play it, so the bowler has to pitch the ball further up to compensate. If he over-pitches, as Lee did on a couple of occasions today, he will get punished. It is difficult to get that length right.

Although the Bangladesh players deserve some credit for the way they played, it would also be fair to say that they had a fair amount of luck, especially against Lee. His first spell was a beauty: he bowled with pace and swung the ball away, but time and again the batsmen were not good enough to get a touch. That is the way it goes sometimes.

Looking at the positive side of things, conditions meant it was a thoroughly pleasant ground to spend the day on. The outfield was lush and a joy to field on and the weather was pretty good too, with a nice breeze off the sea in the afternoon to keep everyone cool. And with more than 5000 fans in the ground there was a decent atmosphere too.

Although Bangladesh have a few more runs than we wanted, we are still happy enough with our position. If we can wrap up their innings quickly tomorrow there is no reason why we cannot pile on the runs and put them under pressure again — the outfield is fast and the pitch is a beauty.

Saturday 26 July

Second Test, day two: Australia 3–351 (Lehmann 156 not out, Waugh 74 not out, Ponting 59, Hayden 50) lead Bangladesh 295 by 56 runs.

This was an excellent day for us. We took full advantage of the conditions and Bangladesh's limited attack to set up a position of strength. If we can go on with the job tomorrow, lifting the tempo to secure a big lead before having another bowl at them, we may even be able to win the match in three days. Mind you, that could be wishful thinking, because the pitch is still a beauty.

Lehmann again led the way for us, making his second hundred in successive innings after we took the last two Bangladesh wickets in only 13 balls today. He did much as he pleased during his innings, except against the young fast bowler Mashrafe Mortaza, and was especially severe on the gentle medium-pace of the visitors' captain, Khaled Mahmud, and the off-spin of Sanwar Hossain.

Hossain was the man who picked me up when I really should have scored a hundred. I felt in great touch, well settled, and having passed 50, I was starting to look to lift the tempo.

One of my favourite shots against an off-spinner is to get down the pitch to hit him over wide midwicket, and that was what I attempted to do today. But the ball did not turn, and as a result, it took a thick outside edge rather than the full face of the bat. That meant the ball went towards long-on rather than where I intended and I was fairly comfortably caught. To say I was frustrated at getting out would be a major understatement.

I was very impressed with Mortaza. He bowled a lively spell in the first Test and today he repeated the dose. He bowls at a good pace, in the mid-130 kilometres per hour bracket, and he also swings the ball away from the right-hander. That type of delivery will always get good players out if he can maintain a high level of consistency, and as he is just 20 years old, he clearly has the potential to get better.

The innings of Stephen Waugh and, in particular, Lehmann show the value of concentration at Test level, especially when things are already going your way. Matthew Hayden, who was bowled around his legs by Hossain as he missed a paddle sweep, and I perhaps tried to get a bit too cute; Waugh and Lehmann showed what can happen if you truly occupy the crease.

They did not initially take many risks, but as the bowlers tired they put their foot on the accelerator, scoring at close to five runs per over after the tea break, with Lehmann scoring 105 in the final session. He really is making up for lost time in his international career now. And it would be a brave man to back Waugh *not* completing another hundred tomorrow.

Sunday 27 July

Second Test, day three: Bangladesh 295 and 4–106 (Sarkar 55) trail Australia 4–556 declared (Lehmann 177, Waugh 156 not out, Love 100 not out) by 155 runs.

After another day of total domination we are well placed to wrap up the match, and with it the series, early on tomorrow. There were hundreds for Stephen Waugh and Martin Love, to go with the one Darren Lehmann made on Saturday, and when we bowled again we showed more discipline than in the first innings and reaped some immediate rewards.

Everyone is delighted for Love, who had to endure a first-ball duck in the opening Test. He is a top-class player who has waited a long time for his chance, but with Damien Martyn and Michael Clarke breathing down his neck he knew he had to score heavily today to make a case for retaining his place in the side. He did that in emphatic fashion and has given the selectors a real headache, although it is one they like to have.

One of Love's skills is his ability to time the ball pretty effortlessly, especially when driving. And with the ball coming onto the bat nicely today he was able to show that skill to full effect. He and Waugh complemented each other well, and it was good of the captain to wait until Love got to his hundred before deciding to declare.

Waugh is now just 653 runs away from Allan Border's record for Test runs, and on this evidence he looks well capable of passing that mark, although he will have to face far better attacks to do it. All his trademark shots were there today: the slog-sweep from the off-spin of Sanwar Hossain, as well as the clips to leg and the punches through the covers off front and back foot.

The pitch was a good one and the batsmen were in complete command. In the face of that, the bowlers looked fairly impotent to stop the flow of runs, although they did not stop trying. The closure came at tea-time, so we had one session to throw everything at them before our bowlers had a night's rest.

The plan was to be really aggressive, while at the same time looking to correct the errors in length that plagued our bowling on the first day, and I think we managed that pretty well. Sarkar played well, and he got some support from Habibul Bashar, but Stuart MacGill again proved tough for their batsmen to come to terms with, so we were able to capture four wickets before the close of play.

If we can maintain this evening's intensity when play resumes tomorrow, it should not take us too long to wrap things up.

Martin Love

The man with the surname that is a headline-writer's dream has to be about the most relaxed man I know. As I write this I am struggling to think of a single occasion when I have seen Martin Love's heart go above 70 beats per minute. He is the essence of calmness, and that is probably why he took to international cricket so easily when he finally got his chance at the highest level.

Love has certainly had to be patient: he made the most appearances by any Australia player in history in first-class cricket before getting his first Test cap, which came when Darren Lehmann was laid low with a virus during the Ashes series of 2002/03.

After such a long wait he could have been forgiven for being nervous about finally having the chance to play for his country, especially as it came in one of the biggest occasions of all: the Boxing Day Test. But Love took to it like a duck to water, and although he has not been able to nail down a regular spot since that series, having a player of his ability waiting to step into the side is a great position for the team to be in.

I knew of Love's ability long before he popped up on the Test match scene, because I played in age-group cricket against him and his fellow Queenslanders — including Jimmy Maher and Matthew Mott — and it was obvious even then that he was going to be an excellent player.

Along with Damien Martyn, Love is a player who makes batting look so simple when he is flowing — they are both exquisite timers of the ball. His record for Queensland has been an exceptionally consistent one, and in another era he may well have played many more Tests than he has managed so far.

I first played in the same side as Love on the Young Australia tour of the UK in 1995. Back then he was a very quiet bloke who kept himself to himself. He still is quiet; he is not someone who goes around the dressing room shouting or is especially vocal on the field. He leaves that sort of thing to other people.

Having ended the Test series against England in the side, it was Love's misfortune to miss out when we got to the Caribbean and decided to play an extra bowler. He only got a spot in the side for the final match of that series, in Antigua, when I was out with a virus. During that tour he kept his spirits up, despite the disappointment of being a reserve, and came out of his shell more than many of us had seen before — revealing a liking for rum we hadn't known about — but at the same time retaining a great work ethic and his usual calm exterior.

He has tasted county cricket with Durham, and during that spell in the UK broke his right little finger so badly that it no longer straightens. Luckily, that does not seem to have hindered his batting or his slip fielding — his safe hands played a vital role in our victory in that Melbourne Test of 2002.

Maybe it is the fact that Love has a career to fall back on when he finally calls it a day as a cricketer — he is a qualified physiotherapist — that helps keep him so calm. Whatever it is, he is a top-quality player and a great bloke, and the fact that he cannot get a regular game for Australia when most other countries would kill for a player of his ability shows just why we have been so successful in recent years.

Monday 28 July

Australia names a 13-man squad for the VB Series against Bangladesh: Ricky Ponting (captain), Michael Bevan, Andy Bichel, Adam Gilchrist, Jason Gillespie, Ian Harvey, Matthew Hayden, Brad Hogg, Brett Lee, Darren Lehmann, Damien Martyn, Glenn McGrath and Andrew Symonds.

Second Test, day four: Australia 4–556 declared beat Bangladesh 295 and 163 (Sarkar 55, MacGill 5–56) by an innings and 98 runs.

As we hoped, we wrapped up the match before lunch, with Stuart MacGill again our trump card. He picked up his third five-wicket haul in four innings and finished with 17 wickets from two Tests — a worthy man of the series indeed.

The pitch did offer him some spin. The surface reminded me a little of what you might see for a Test at the Gabba: firm, with good pace and some help for the bowler who gets the ball in the right areas. That pitch always impresses me, so the comparison is an indication of how highly I rate the pitch here at Cairns.

The Bangladesh batsmen lacked the discipline to fight it out today, although with four wickets down when play resumed, their cause was already fairly hopeless. That is to take nothing away from our bowlers, and in particular MacGill and Jason Gillespie — they would have been a handful for better players than we saw here.

Their players headed into our dressing room after the match and several of them joined Adam Gilchrist and me for a chat about batting.

They were keen to know how I manage to hook and pull so effectively and I explained that it is all in the way I pick up my bat. As I prepare to face each delivery I have my hands quite high, so that if the ball is banged in short I do not need to make much of an adjustment to play the hook or pull. Other players (Stephen Waugh, for example) tend not to pick the bat up so high. That means they have to make an extra movement to get their hands up to play cross-batted shots; as a result, they do not play them as often as someone like me.

After the match I also chatted with Trevor Hohns about the make-up of the one-day squad for the three-match series to follow, and there was good and bad news. The good news is that Damien Martyn is ready to come back after fracturing his finger during the World Cup. He went through the pain barrier to play in the final just a week after sustaining the injury, and that probably did it no good at all — he has had surgery to try to repair the damage, and missed the whole of the Caribbean tour. Even now, he does not have a full range of movement in the finger, and apparently it is unlikely that it will ever come back. But it is good enough for him to play cricket again and everyone is keen for him to be involved because he is a top-class player — as he showed in the World Cup final.

News on Glenn McGrath is not so positive. He has been having trouble with a loose fragment of bone in his left ankle, and although he, like other fast bowlers, always tapes his ankles to reduce the strain on them, it has been especially uncomfortable towards the end of this Test. We will take advice from Errol Alcott, but I do not think he will be playing in the one-day series to come, and he may well face surgery to clear up the problem.

If McGrath is not fit enough to play then Brad Williams will come into the squad. I feel sorry for Williams in one sense: he has been in this situation, acting as cover or a replacement and not really knowing how long he is going to be with the squad, plenty of times over the past few years. On the other side of the coin, it is a great chance for him to show he deserves to be in the squad full-time and, knowing him, he will be busting a gut to show exactly that if he gets the chance.

Thursday 31 July

Glenn McGrath is ruled out of the one-day series against Bangladesh with an injury to his left ankle. He will undergo surgery on Friday (1 August) and will be assessed in the build-up to the Test series against Zimbabwe in September.

Brad Williams is named as a replacement for McGrath in the one-day squad.

Glenn McGrath

There are two sides to Glenn McGrath, the public and the private, and they are as contrasting as can be. In public he is the man who talks the talk, openly targeting opposition players, and ready and willing to get involved in banter on the field. In private he is quite the opposite: quietly spoken, a devoted family man, and a person of simple tastes.

McGrath is a country boy at heart. He was when I first came across him, at the Commonwealth Bank Cricket Academy in Adelaide, and he remains so even now, despite the deserved trappings of his success at international level. He has a massive property in the outback that he runs with his brother, and I have no doubt that is where he will end up, together with his wife and two children, when his playing days are over. He has even taken helicopter lessons so that running his vast acreage is easier.

Back in the days when we were together at the Academy I do not recall anyone saying McGrath was a bowler who could go on to take well in excess of 400 Test wickets and become one of our all-time great players. He had talent, there was no doubt about that, and he and I enjoyed plenty of battles in the nets as he had the self-confidence to back up that talent. All the same, few could have predicted he would become so successful.

What are the reasons for his success? Discipline and rhythm are key ingredients: he aims to run in and hit a similar spot on the pitch each time — a good length around off-stump. That immediately poses a question for the batsman — whether or not to play at the ball. And when the line of the delivery is allied with a little seam movement, he is likely to have some success.

It is a method of almost boring the batsmen out through sheer accuracy and consistency; one that I have asked Brett Lee to follow (while at the same time maintaining his high pace). Other bowlers, most notably Michael Kasprowicz, have also taken a leaf out of McGrath's book by striving for greater consistency. I think that is part of the reason for Kasprowicz's recent successes.

The idea of discipline and rhythm may seem simple, but simplicity has been McGrath's trademark. After all, he has never really swung the ball, and pace has never really been a weapon of his either. In fact his lack of pace has been a positive benefit. I remember England batsman Michael Atherton commenting on that after the Ashes series in 2001. He said that as a batsman, when he saw a ball seam away, his instinctive reaction was to try to adjust to cover that movement. When he did that against Jason Gillespie he found he almost always missed the ball — it was past him before his adjustment was complete; with McGrath, however, who was just a little slower, the adjustment meant the ball usually took the edge of the bat.

Given McGrath's lack of pace and his desire to maintain such a tight line and length, I have always wondered why more opposition players have not tried to get after him, using their feet and trying to put him off. I can think of just one who has tried: Abdul Razzaq of Pakistan, in Sydney in 2000, who succeeded in hitting McGrath for five fours in a row. The fact that it happens so rarely is a testament to the bowler's skill.

McGrath likes being the aggressor on the field, but I always feel it is a delicate balancing act. There is nothing wrong with a bit of banter — quite often it helps to get him going — but occasionally, as in the Test match in Antigua, it can work against him. John Buchanan was convinced that McGrath's blow-up with Ramnaresh Sarwan affected his bowling. It is something he needs to keep in check.

In the privacy of the team environment McGrath is a bit of a thinker. He is not a great one for leading discussions, but when he talks he usually has something sensible to say about ways to approach opposition batsmen. He understands techniques of bowling — wrist-position, use of the crease, and the strains it puts on the body — as well as anyone I have met, with the possible exception of Dennis Lillee.

One of McGrath's other distinguishing characteristics is his sense of humour — it is, at best, like that of a 5-year-old. He is always the one flicking your ears during an interview, or making faces at you from behind the camera, or hiding your socks in the dressing room, or coming up with a one-line put-down. We all put up with it and give him back whatever we can, just to keep him in his place, but he loves to have the last word in any discussion.

He has always been shrewd, not just in cricketing terms but also in business. He was one of the first players to get his bat sponsored when the ICC relaxed regulations for private advertising on equipment, and that was despite the fact that he has been one of the least successful batsmen in the international game. That in itself was a talking point, which means the sponsorship deal is a success whichever way you look at it.

As for his batting, well, it is better than it used to be. That might not seem to be saying much, but he has been determined to improve right from his early days, when he was a walking wicket for any bowler lucky enough to be in the attack when he came in, and has worked really hard at his game. That improvement with the bat has helped countless players get through to personal landmarks — something McGrath points out to us whenever his batting ability is questioned.

Not many bowlers have gone on playing into their late 30s and remained successful at the highest level. But if any player is capable of bucking that trend it is McGrath, and it will be a massive bonus for Australian cricket if he succeeds.

Saturday 2 August

First one-day international, Cairns: Australia 2–107 beat Bangladesh 105 by 8 wickets.

I had a new experience today — I was booed by an Australian crowd while playing for Australia in Australia.

I remember something similar happened to the Australia side when it played Australia A in the World Series in 1994/95. The crowd decided to barrack for the underdog, the A side that I was a part of, and I remember Australia's captain, Mark Taylor, saying how much he disliked it. But I cannot think of another example of the same thing happening — until today.

The reaction surprised me, but it did not bother me too much. After all, I have played enough international cricket to deal with that sort of thing and still remain focused. In a way I could even understand it. The fans up here do not see much international cricket, so when it does come they want to be entertained. The most likely way for that to happen, given the relative strengths of the two sides, is for us to bat first — that would give the crowd the chance to see at least one of our top-order batsmen play a lengthy innings.

My agenda was slightly different. I wanted to make sure we gave ourselves the best chance to win the game as efficiently as possible; on this occasion that meant bowling first, to exploit conditions at the start of the day. If there was going to be any assistance for the bowlers it would be first thing this morning, and I made my decision with that in mind.

I know there are those who point out that we are in the entertainment business, but we are not in the business of playing social cricket and giving our opposition the best chance of making a game of it. If we are struggling you can be sure no one will be giving us a chance, and nor would we expect them to. That would make a joke of international cricket and I am not about to go down that path just so the public gets a longer game. In any case, it is not so big a jump from giving the opposition a chance to match-fixing, and there is no way I am going to leave myself or my team open to any suggestions in that area.

As it turned out, we crushed them, but even the boo-boys cannot have failed to admire how well Brett Lee bowled. He gave them a fantastic display of fast bowling, which even Dav Whatmore, the Bangladesh coach, appreciated.

What we saw today was Brett at his best. He was genuinely quick, got the ball to swing away late and also bowled that in-between length where the batsman is not sure whether to go forward or back. He must have beaten the bat 15 or 20 times in his opening spell, and the Bangladesh batsmen were simply not good enough to get a touch. In their defence, there would have been plenty of other players struggling in that regard today.

At his worst, Brett will bowl two lengths during a spell — either too full or too short — and with his pace any mistakes are likely to be magnified, because all a batsman has to do is get some wood on the ball and it will usually fly away for four. He can also strive too hard for wickets, and that is when he will start to overstep the crease and bowl no-balls, but today it was one of those magic days when he got everything right.

I have been credited with helping Brett before the second half of last summer's VB Series, when he was struggling with his form in one-day cricket, but what I said to him was simple. I told him to take a leaf out of Glenn McGrath's book and make sure he gets the ball in the right areas. Pace is one of his big assets, but it is nothing without control. As long as he gets the ball in the right areas, around off-stump and on that in-between length, he will succeed at one-day level, because, as he has pace and can swing the ball out when it is new and in when it is older, he will take wickets.

He still has the occasional off day but they are becoming fewer and fewer, and today was definitely one when it all clicked for him. He bowled with great rhythm and even fractured the thumb of Bangladesh wicketkeeper Khaled Mashud, which meant Hannan Sarkar had to keep wicket when we batted.

Our time at the crease was not long: with Matthew Hayden leading the way, we raced to victory with almost 27 overs in hand. I managed to get out looking for the winning runs off the left-arm spin of Mohammad Rafique, but that gave Damien Martyn the chance to complete a leisurely return to international cricket by facing one ball.

All in all it was a successful day, whatever the boo-boys thought.

Sunday 3 August

Second one-day international, Cairns: Australia 1–148 (Martyn 92 not out) beat Bangladesh 147 by 9 wickets.

We juggled the order around ahead of the final match of the series on Wednesday so Damien Martyn, Michael Bevan and Andrew Symonds got the chance to bat. We would not have done that if we had batted first or if we had had a large score to chase, but faced with a modest score against us, we wanted to avoid those three players going into the last game of the series without having batted, because none of them played in the Test series.

Even allowing for Bangladesh's modest attack, we got the chance to witness some awesome batting as Damien Martyn announced his return to the international fold with a blazing innings. All his trademark shots were there, with back-foot cover drives, shots over cover and pulls too — he made batting look ridiculously easy.

He got on a roll when he took 19 runs from an over from Bangladesh captain Khaled Mahmud, and then kept going. He was unstoppable, and would have completed his hundred but for Michael Bevan lifting the tempo at the other end as the target approached.

Symonds was not able to make the most of his chance, but Bevan and Martyn made up for that, and we won with almost 30 overs in hand.

For Bangladesh it will have been a sobering day: once again it clarified just how far they still have to go to reach senior international level.

The boo-boys did not get their chance to have a go at me today because Bangladesh won the toss and batted. I was amazed that they chose that, as it put them under pressure straight away. They have a modest bowling attack that will always struggle to defend scores on good surfaces like this one, and I thought their best hope would have been to bowl first then try to chase down whatever we set them. They obviously thought differently.

We rested Jason Gillespie, but Bangladesh were still unable to get away from us in the early stages of their innings, and then they fell in a heap when faced with the spin of Darren Lehmann and Brad Hogg. Their inability to play spin continues to surprise me; it is something they will have to work on. Lehmann and Hogg took six wickets between them and never looked like being collared. The batsmen did not seem to have a plan against them; or if they did, they did implement it.

After the match we did not sing the team song, even though we had clinched the series. We decided to save that until the end of the series, in Darwin on Wednesday evening.

Wednesday 6 August

Third one-day international, Darwin: Australia 7–254 (Ponting 101, Bevan 57) beat Bangladesh 142 by 112 runs.

At last I managed to get some runs on the board, with a pleasing hundred in conditions that were not ideal for one-day cricket. The pitch was slow — even slower than for the Test we played here — and the outfield was also on the slow side. So, to get my head down and play responsibly, guiding us to a score Bangladesh came nowhere near chasing down, was a source of real satisfaction.

On the face of it, our score of 254 was not a great one given the modest nature of the Bangladesh side. But the pitch played into their hands a little, as it had in the Test, in that the ball did not come onto the bat. Their bowlers do not operate with a great deal of pace, and that made forcing the ball around quite difficult.

It needed a patient approach; that was emphasised by the way we lost cheap wickets either side of my appearance at the crease. Matthew Hayden was caught and bowled chipping a leading edge back to the left-arm spinner Rafique, Damien Martyn chopped on, and Andrew Symonds was run out after I sent him back over a risky single to midwicket.

Hayden tied himself in knots against Rafique, so it was no surprise when he was dismissed. He set himself to sweep the spinner no matter what the bowler delivered, and must have had 10 or 12 goes at the shot without making contact. He then started moving around the crease, trying to put Rafique off, but the spinner held his line and his nerve, and when Hayden went back and tried to work the ball onto the on-side, all he achieved was to pop the ball back to the grateful bowler.

I began my innings determined to be positive, and clubbed Khaled Mahmud, their captain, over long-on for six early on. But the loss of three quick wickets made me rein back, and I concentrated on working the spinners into the gaps.

At the other end, Michael Bevan gave me solid support, and by the time I was out, caught at long-off trying to hit a six in the last but one over of the innings, I was comfortable that we had a more than adequate score to win the match easily — I thought it would have been worth 280 on a ground with a faster pitch and outfield.

I had the impression that some of our batting in this match was carried out with an attitude of near-boredom, given the gulf between the sides, but our bowling did not reflect that. We did a professional job of stifling them. Jason Gillespie was outstanding: he conceded just two runs in his first seven overs, an illustration of his discipline.

At the end of the match the Bangladesh players came into our dressing room for the final time on the tour, and when they left we sang our team song to celebrate a professional job of winning the series 3–0.

So, having played Bangladesh at Test and one-day level, where do they stand in international cricket? Well, although it pains me to write this, I believe there is no way they should be playing Test cricket.

That might sound harsh, but it is merely stating the obvious. I accept that every new side at Test level has taken time to bed in and become competitive, but the scale of Bangladesh's defeats suggests that the problems are more deep-seated than a side trying to adjust to a step up in class.

With one or two exceptions, the players are just not good enough to compete at the top level, and no amount of play against better sides is going to change that. If a player does not have the natural talent to succeed at the highest level, he will not suddenly find it by playing 10, 20 or 30 Tests.

The only way to improve the game in Bangladesh is to get the correct structure in place at home: one that promotes tough cricket on good pitches. At the same time, there needs to be the correct infrastructure around the game, with coaching and support services like physiotherapy and fitness training, as well as coaching programs at the junior levels that ensure that a uniform message is fed down from the very top to the very bottom of the game.

None of this is especially revolutionary. It is just common sense, and something Dav Whatmore, the former Australia Test batsman who is now coaching Bangladesh, will be fully aware of. However, implementing such a plan will take time, and until it starts to come to fruition, I can only see more struggles for Bangladesh at the highest level.

That will not do the game in that country any good, and if the gap between the top sides and those at the bottom of the International Cricket Council's (ICC's) Test ladder continues to be a massive gulf, it will also damage the credibility of Test cricket. I know it is an issue the game's world governing body is aware of, but rather than looking to further expand the game globally, maybe the game would be better served if the ICC threw more weight behind attempts to bring the likes of Bangladesh and Zimbabwe up to speed.

Part 3:
Zimbabwe home series

BEING PART OF HISTORY

Tuesday 16 September

Zimbabwe's senior batsman, Grant Flower, will miss the Test tour of Australia after breaking his right thumb in a Logan Cup match.

Wednesday 17 September

Zimbabwe name a 15-man squad for the two-Test tour: Heath Streak (captain), Tatenda Taibu (wicketkeeper and vice-captain), Andy Blignaut, Gary Brent, Stuart Carlisle, Dion Ebrahim, Sean Ervine, Craig Evans, Gavin Ewing, Trevor Gripper, Douglas Hondo, Stewart Matsikenyeri, Ray Price, Mark Vermeulen and Craig Wishart.

Friday 19 September

Glenn McGrath is confirmed as extremely doubtful for the Zimbabwe Test series as he continues to recover from surgery on his left ankle.

Monday 29 September

Zimbabwe seam bowler Douglas Hondo injures his right thumb in a tour match, making him doubtful for the first Test in Perth.

Wednesday 1 October

Australia names a 13-man squad for the first Test against Zimbabwe in Perth: Stephen Waugh (captain), Ricky Ponting (vice-captain), Andy Bichel, Adam Gilchrist, Jason Gillespie, Matthew Hayden, Justin Langer, Brett Lee, Darren Lehmann, Stuart MacGill, Damien Martyn, Glenn McGrath and Brad Williams.

Martyn returns to the Test squad for the first time since January after recovering from a fractured right index finger, replacing Martin Love from the side that beat Bangladesh in July. Williams is included as cover for Glenn McGrath.

Thursday 2 October

Stephen Waugh hints that retirement may not be too far away. 'There is a good chance this will be the last time I am going to play in Perth,' he said.

Sunday 5 October

Glenn McGrath pulls out of Australia's squad after aggravating his left ankle injury while bowling in the nets in Perth. He faces the prospect of more surgery and more time on the sidelines.

Tuesday 7 October

Western Australia and former Zimbabwe batsman Murray Goodwin alleges that racial discrimination occurs in Zimbabwe cricket. 'You've got guys getting promoted because of performance and other guys getting promoted because of their colour,' he said.

Cricket Australia announces a Spirit of Cricket project designed to ensure that all Australian cricketers from school and park to the elite level understand their obligations to fair play.

The project includes:

- Seeking to educate all captains throughout Australian cricket, from local park cricket up, so that they understand that the Laws of Cricket require them to ensure that they and their teams play the game in the right spirit.
- Introduction of Spirit of Cricket team awards for interstate teams, including Pura Cup, ING Cup, Women's National Cricket League and under-19 and under-17 teams, which play the game in the best spirit, with similar awards for district/premier cricket (to be managed by the six state cricket associations).
- Reviewing and amending the Cricket Australia Code of Behaviour to more closely align it with the International Cricket Council (ICC) code, which covers international cricket.
- Educating state Code of Conduct Commissioners and state and district umpires about the importance of enforcing code of behaviour requirements.
- Promoting Spirit of Cricket messages at all levels of Australian cricket, from children's Have-A-Go clinics upwards.
- Distributing 20,000 copies of the official Laws of Cricket to captains and umpires throughout Australian cricket, with a special message drawing attention to the preamble of the Laws, which requires captains and all players to respect umpires' decisions, their opponents and the traditions of the game.

All Cricket Australia-contracted players put their name to this Spirit of Cricket project; it is something James Sutherland, the Chief Executive, and Chairman Bob Merriman have been discussing with me for the past few months, well ahead of today's announcement.

It is recognition that, as the best cricketing side in the world, we have to set the standard for behaviour as well. Most of us already knew that, but maybe in the past we have felt a little hard done by, believing that Cricket Australia tended to overreact and side with any media criticism of our conduct rather than back us as players fighting it out in tough situations.

I think all of us were shaken from that view by the reaction we saw, not only in Australia but around the world, to the McGrath–Sarwan clash in Antigua. We were seen as out of order, as a team that reacts badly if things go against us.

That is not the image we want. We want to be remembered as a great team, one of the best of all time, rather than as a team that played great cricket but also behaved poorly and lowered the standard of behaviour in the game.

We have retained the right to have some banter on the field with opposition players — that is part of the competitive element of cricket at the highest level — but we have distanced ourselves from sledging and on-field abuse, and this Spirit of Cricket project is an expression of our desire to be seen as appropriate role models on and off the field.

It is something we will police ourselves. We are still playing within the boundaries of the ICC's Code of Conduct, but if any of us feels a team-mate is stepping out of line, it is up to all of us to pull him back. Bad behaviour by one of us will reflect badly on all of us.

Wednesday 8 October

The eve of our first Test of the summer, and for all of us it has been an unusual build-up.

To start with, the Test summer is getting underway at least a month earlier than usual because of our commitment to play in a one-day tournament in India later this month — and, maybe, because of the Rugby World Cup. You do not have to be a marketing expert to know that with that event taking most of November it would be smart for international cricket to take a break then.

The early start has meant that some of us have not played any cricket at all coming into tomorrow's first Test, although the Queensland boys have a club match under their belts thanks to the better weather in that part of the country. We have been practising in the nets at the WACA ground here in Perth, as well as going through a series of fitness checks and tests under the supervision of Errol Alcott, our physiotherapist, and fitness trainer Jock Campbell.

The fact the international summer is kicking off so early means that we will have a very long run of cricket without a break, so it is important that we are in good shape now — which we all should be, following the training programs given to us by Jock — and that any niggling injuries are addressed straight away.

We have lost one player already. Glenn McGrath is now back in Sydney for further treatment on his ankle injury. I always thought it would be tough for him to be fit for this series, as he only had surgery on the problem at the beginning of August. The key now is for him to get the problem fixed, and not think about playing again until he is ready. There is no need for him to rush back — we have the likes of Brad Williams to call on.

The issue of whether we should be playing Zimbabwe has been raised again, as it was during the World Cup, although luckily it has not been something the media or the public appears to have focused on. It may sound naïve, but as a cricketer I would rather not make that decision; I prefer to leave it up to the administrators, as that is what they are there to do — administer the game. That is not to say that as a player I wander around without a thought about the wider world in my head, but if I start getting involved in politics and making moral judgements, where do those judgements stop? I do not know the answer, so I would rather not get involved in the first place.

Zimbabwe is not the side it was when we last played it at Test level, in Harare in October 1999. Then it had Andy Flower, Neil Johnson and Murray Goodwin, all top-class batsmen, as well as another batsman, Grant Flower (who is injured now) and fast bowler Henry Olonga. The touring side, now coached by our former coach Geoff Marsh, has not exactly set the world alight with its form so far on tour, but we will still respect its players.

We have seen most of the squad — we played them in the World Cup earlier this year — so our pre-match meeting did not go into a lot of depth. I think we all believe that if we bowl with discipline we will create chances to take wickets, and, as batsmen, we know that the Zimbabwe bowling attack, while hardworking, is not full of world-beaters.

Our approach is a simple one, basically the same one we adopted against Bangladesh: try to win as quickly and as ruthlessly as possible. That way we can maintain our focus rather than get complacent or allow the game to meander.

Heath Streak is Zimbabwe's main danger. He swings the ball away from the right-handers, but lacks the pace to really test us. That pace is usually supplied by Andy Blignaut, but he is wayward. Sean Ervine will do a steady job bowling medium-pace, and left-arm spinner Ray Price will look to test our patience by operating over the wicket to the right-hander, bowling into the pads.

Thursday 9 October

First Test, day one: Australia 3–368 (Hayden 183 not out, Waugh 61, Martyn 53) v Zimbabwe.

Former Zimbabwe captain Andy Flower, now playing for South Australia, says the issue of promoting players on the basis of colour over ability has been a 'bone of contention' for some time in Zimbabwe cricket. 'Some believe it's the right way forward and some disagree. There are various schools of thought, and there has certainly been an element of it over the years, and probably is now,' he said.

We made about as good a start to the series as we could have hoped for, with Matthew Hayden once again showing us why he has every right to be considered the best batsman in the world.

Hayden was awesome today. After his failures against Bangladesh he looked to me like a man on a mission: he was going to make up for those low scores with a big one here. And as he is not out at the end of today, he could indeed go on and get a really big one.

He took around five hours to get to three figures; this was an indication to me of how much he wanted to reach that mark. Both Justin Langer and I outscored him comfortably when we batted with him, but he was happy to occupy the crease and wait for an over-pitched ball to club through the off-side.

Then, late in the day, when Zimbabwe took the new ball, he suddenly opened his shoulders and took full toll of a tiring attack. He went from 100 to 150 in 32 balls, and when he is in that mood he is impossible to bowl at. When the ball was pitched up he smashed it down the ground for four or six; he was even prepared to use his feet to the medium-pacers to do just that. Then, when the bowlers dragged their length back to compensate, he rocked onto the back foot and pulled or cut the ball away for more runs.

Hayden, and the rest of us, were helped by Zimbabwe's decision to bowl first on a blameless pitch which had little of the pace you normally associate with a surface at the WACA. Maybe that is not so surprising, given the time of year we are playing this Test.

Heath Streak's idea of putting us into bat may have been partly defensive; he may not have wanted to face our seam attack on the first morning of the match. But he may also have thought that if there was going to be any help for him and his fellow bowlers from the pitch, it would be on the first morning. Yesterday Stephen Waugh thought there was enough in the surface to bowl first, but he changed his mind when he saw the pitch this morning, and said he would have batted if he'd had the call.

For me it was a disappointing day. I got a start, but did not go on with it to make a big score. I have not had much preparation because of the early start of the season, but I felt good in nets before the match and felt in great touch out in the middle. A good sign for me is if I hit the ball through the covers with conviction — that means my balance is good and my feet are moving. I was able to put a tick in that box after cover drives off Ray Price and Sean Ervine.

All was going well for me when, out of the blue, I was lbw to Ervine. It was a clever piece of bowling from the medium-pacer, who was the pick of their attack. He generally tried to swing the ball away, but he also angled the odd ball back in, and that was the delivery that got me. I am not sure why I missed it, but looking at replays, maybe I was guilty of trying to hit the ball too square through the on-side and not presenting the full face of the bat. Whatever the reason, it was a frustrating way to get out.

The day began with a minute of silence in memory of the victims of last year's bomb blast in Bali, and we wore black armbands to commemorate the forthcoming anniversary of that tragedy. By the end of play Hayden had put a smile on everyone's faces except the Zimbabwe bowlers.

Friday 10 October

First Test, day two: Zimbabwe 1–79 trail Australia 6–735 declared (Hayden 380, Gilchrist 113 not out, Waugh 78, Martyn 53) by 656 runs.

Fantastic. Awesome. Brilliant. To be Matthew Hayden's team-mate on the day he achieved the world record score is all of those things and more. And those words also go some way to describing the innings of a lifetime by Hayden.

There is no doubt in my mind that the previous record score — the 375 made by Brian Lara against England in Antigua in 1994 — was a better innings, because it came against a better attack, but that takes nothing away from the achievement of Hayden today. You still have to go out and score the runs, no matter who is bowling, and he did exactly that. And not only that: he did it in five sessions of play, which is truly unbelievable.

His innings was so brutal, so awe-inspiring, that Adam Gilchrist's 113 not out at the other end, including a century in 84 balls, seems to have been forgotten. That is bad luck for Gilchrist, but I know he was just pumped to be out on the ground when

Hayden broke the record — just before tea, with a single to mid-off. It reminded me of a story the former Australia opener Arthur Morris told us when he joined us for a team meal during the series against Pakistan in 1999. He said that while everyone remembers Sir Donald Bradman's last Test innings, when he was dismissed for a duck at The Oval in London in 1948, no one seems to recall that he (Morris) was at the other end and went on to score 196. He told the story with a smile on his face; in years to come, Gilchrist may feel that today's events mirror that situation.

It seems strange now, but at the start of play I do not recall anyone talking about the record. The search for individual landmarks like that is not part of our game plan; all we look to do is score quickly, so that we put the opposition under pressure and give ourselves enough time to bowl them out twice.

But by lunchtime, with the big man on 271 and still going strong, the topic did crop up and we began to get quite excited about it. There was some chat in the dressing room, and Stephen Waugh told Hayden to go on and try for the record.

That may have inhibited some players, especially as it is not every day you get the chance to break an individual milestone like that, but if anything Hayden seemed to step up a gear or two. Having Gilchrist playing in exactly the same way will have helped him with that; at one stage it looked like the pair was involved in some sort of batting contest, seeing who could hit the ball hardest and furthest.

Once again it was Hayden's driving, both along the ground and, towards the end of his innings, in the air, that stood out. He did offer one chance, on 335 to deep midwicket, but Trevor Gripper misjudged it completely, prompting a huge shout of joy from quite a few of us in the dressing room viewing area.

By then Hayden had gone past the highest individual score made by an Australian batsman in Tests, the 334 of Mark Taylor and Sir Donald Bradman, and as he ploughed on the only question seemed to be whether he would reach the record by tea. Waugh would not have declared on him at that point if he had not got there, but it would have made for a nervous 20 minutes for all of us if he had still been short of the mark at that point.

As it turned out, we need not have worried. He pushed the ball down the ground and scampered the single in the last over before the break — there was a huge windmill of the bat from Hayden, a hug from Gilchrist, and the whole ground rose to him. The sad part was that only around 8000 fans were there to see it, but I reckon they, and the rest of us, will remember it for a long, long time.

As the players started to come off for tea at the end of the over, Waugh suggested we go down to form a guard of honour for Hayden, so we all raced down the pavilion steps and lined up on either side as he walked off, with a huge grin on his face. A few of us broke ranks to hug him, and the adrenaline was clearly flowing as he made his way up to the dressing room for a sit-down.

A declaration at that point would have been our normal policy, but there was no time pressure, because the team, and Hayden, had scored our runs so quickly. So Waugh said to Hayden that as he was so close to 400, he might as well have a go for that mark after the break — it is not every day you get a chance to scale a height like that.

He failed, sweeping to deep backward square leg three balls after tea, but although that was sad, it would be wrong to be too greedy after such an amazing achievement. At that point Waugh did declare. Now it was time for us to start the search for 20 wickets to win this Test.

In the field there was, almost inevitably, a sense of anti-climax after the excitement of what Hayden had achieved, but we were still able to have a bit of fun at his expense. Damien Martyn and I took some paper towels out onto the ground, and as we lined up at slip alongside him we stuffed them into our ears — to show that we did not want to put up with a session of him talking about his innings non-stop between deliveries. He loved that.

After play the excitement level was up again, as it was anything but a normal close of a day. There was a Channel Nine camera crew and Mark Taylor in the dressing room to interview Hayden, photographers to record the occasion and someone opened a bottle of champagne. There was some banter as he answered Tubby Taylor's questions, and everyone was full of energy, buzzing at what one of us had achieved. Even Tubby came in for some good-natured joking: we told him that the bat with which he'd made the previous highest score by an Australian in Tests was now worth considerably less than it had been at the start of the day.

Matthew Hayden

If you want an example of a player who is mentally tough, it is impossible to go past the imposing figure of Matthew Hayden.

He dominates and intimidates opponents not only through the power and range of his shots, but also through his body language. On top of that, he loves to 'mix it' with opponents; he is like Brian Lara in that a bit of banter with the opposition can often help his focus when he feels the intensity in his game is not there.

It is very rare for him to lose a mental battle like that. I saw him win a classic encounter with Shoaib Ahktar in Sharjah in 2002. Conditions were almost unbearably hot, and Shoaib was steaming in off his long run, trying to bowl as fast as he could.

Hayden's response was to say to the perspiring bowler: 'Is that as quick as you can bowl?', which of course fired Shoaib up even more. It might have seemed like madness to say something like that to one of the quickest bowlers in the world but Hayden knew what he was doing. In that heat Shoaib would burn himself out very quickly. After a couple of overs Hayden added: 'Two overs gone, just one left now, I reckon.' Sure enough, Shoaib ran out of steam and Hayden ended up with a hundred.

I have never run in and bowled at Hayden in a Test match or a one-day international, but it must be an intimidating sight. His size and strength make him an imposing figure, and his power off both front and back foot does not give a bowler much margin for error.

His current success is an amazing contrast to his early days at international level, when he could barely buy a run. For many years, all he had to show for his efforts at the highest level was a scratchy, ugly hundred against the West Indies on a flat pitch at the Adelaide Oval in 1997. When he talked to me about that innings a few years later he said, 'I didn't know how to score runs at this level then.' He certainly has the hang of it now.

What is the difference between his early days and his current, dominating form? Well, at the start of his career I think he was fighting a few things, by trying to become the perfect batsman and looking to develop new shots by spending hours in the nets, hitting ball after ball. Eventually he realised that he had the game to succeed, and that all he had to do to score well at the highest level was master the mental side of the game.

That mental side is all about believing in your ability to play Test and one-day international cricket, backing yourself to play the shots you take for granted at a lower level. I think Stephen Waugh must take some credit for giving Hayden that belief.

Waugh backed him publicly by saying he thought Hayden would finish with a Test average over 50, even though there was no evidence at the time to support such a claim. For Hayden that was a massive vote of confidence, and since then he has gone from strength to strength. In fact, the suggestion that he might end up with an average of 50 is looking a bit conservative at the moment.

Hayden's approach to batting is something a lot of us have learnt from over the past few years. He no longer goes into the nets for hours and hours of practice; instead, he looks for quality over quantity, and makes sure he is fresh and rested for the action out in the middle. I am the same these days. I no longer worry about how many balls I hit in the nets before a Test match; as long as I feel sharp going into a game I am confident that the basics will look after themselves. We play so much cricket these days that net practice on top of regular matches can soon make you stale.

Hayden may not appear to do much more than sit on the pitch in his socked feet the day before a Test, but that is all part of his preparation. He spends time visualising how he will play each bowler, how they will bowl to him and where he will look to hit them — and the method obviously works.

However, that success is not just based on visualisation. It is also based on hard, physical work that he puts in away from the spotlight, at his beach house on the Queensland coast. He spends hours running up and down sand dunes to make sure he is at his best physically at the start of every series. Hayden is a classic example of how physical fitness aids a player's ability to concentrate long and hard in match situations.

That time away on the coast is one reason he is known as 'nature boy'. He loves the outdoor life away from the city, and is never happier than when he is fishing or surfing. It is another way he stays fresh for cricket; he does not let the game consume him. He has a family, hobbies, and even an interest in cooking that is set to involve a book. It all helps him maintain his appetite for cricket.

If you ever spend any time in Hayden's company you will quickly discover that he hates to sit still for any length of time and is very easily bored. I remember in 2000 a few of us went to the cinema in Perth during a Test against the West Indies. He quickly decided that the film on offer it was not very entertaining, but rather than walk out, he stood up and stretched or fidgeted in his seat. At the end of the movie he announced that it was the most boring film he had ever seen. Most of us agreed, but not everyone was as bad at hiding their response as Hayden.

Waugh is definitely a mentor for Hayden; so much so that he has taken on one of Waugh's habits — ranting when he gets out. Every player has his own way of dealing with being dismissed, and the way Hayden does it is by shouting and bawling when he gets back into the privacy of the dressing room. It is in many ways a natural reaction. We are under almost constant scrutiny as players, and it is important to have a release valve for the pressure that builds up as a result of that. The dressing room is the one place where that valve can be opened. All the same, we have had meetings about how we express our disappointment after dismissals, because it is also important to respect the fact that the players who still have to bat need an atmosphere of calm in the dressing room.

Hayden is a fantastic example of what determination and self-belief can achieve. He has gone from being a player who was overlooked for the Commonwealth Bank Cricket Academy to one of the greatest players of all time. He is the ultimate example of 'If at first you don't succeed, try, try, try again.'

Saturday 11 October

First Test, day three: Zimbabwe 239 (Gripper 53) and 2–87 (Vermeulen 50) trail Australia 6–735 declared by 409 runs.

After Hayden's innings of a lifetime we have come back to earth with a bump. True, we bowled Zimbabwe out and have taken two wickets in the follow-on, but we also picked up two injury concerns among the bowlers, with Stuart MacGill and Jason Gillespie both ending the day on the treatment table.

Gillespie left the field after taking both second innings wickets, complaining of a sore side, and with the one-day tour of India to come, as well as the rest of this Test and another in Sydney next week, this is not good news. Side muscle injuries are notoriously slow to heal, so we will not want to rush him back too quickly, especially as, after the one-day tour, there is a Test series against India, the VB Series and a tour of Sri Lanka to follow in quick succession.

MacGill left the field in the middle of an over, complaining of discomfort behind his right knee. Errol Alcott thinks it is a calf injury, but it is too early to tell how bad it is.

It meant we ended the day with Darren Lehmann and Damien Martyn bowling and, as well as putting our designated twelfth man (Brad Williams) on the field, we also had to call on assistant coach Tim Nielsen to do some fielding while we searched around for first-class players to fill the gap, if necessary, for the rest of the Test.

Tim, a former wicketkeeper with South Australia, made one brilliant stop at short midwicket, and I do not think he will let us forget it. For the rest of the session he kept saying, 'Let's see some *real* commitment in the field, eh?'

We bowled steadily through the first part of the day, with each of our four frontline strikers enjoying some success. MacGill produced a couple of classic leg-breaks to get rid of Mark Vermeulen and Stuart Carlisle, while Andy Bichel ran in to get us two breakthroughs in the afternoon: Craig Wishart was caught behind and Craig Evans was bowled.

Brett Lee bowled with some pace as he and Gillespie mopped up the tail, and at the start of Zimbabwe's second innings, when Gillespie took two more wickets — Trevor Gripper caught behind playing a poor defensive shot and Dion Ebrahim bowled off the inside edge — I think we all hoped we could wrap the match up sooner rather than later.

That is still possible, but it will be much harder now if Gillespie and MacGill do not make it back onto the field, and on a pitch which is still a beauty for batting we might just be made to work very hard for the last eight Zimbabwe wickets.

Sunday 12 October

First Test, day four: Zimbabwe 239 and 9–272 (Vermeulen 63, Ervine 53) trail Australia 6–735 declared by 224 runs.

This was an utterly frustrating day which finished with us still one wicket away from wrapping up the Test. A combination of our limited bowling resources, some lower-order toughness from Zimbabwe and two breaks for rain in the last session all combined to ensure that we have to try to finish the job tomorrow.

An idea of how frustrated we were and how depleted our attack was because of the continued absence of Gillespie and MacGill could be seen when Stephen Waugh threw me the ball. I sent down some gentle off-spin, but not even my mother would say I looked very threatening, and I went wicketless.

On a positive note, we should probably be grateful for taking seven wickets during the day given that half our frontline attack spent the day off the field. But the flipside of that was a lot of overs for Darren Lehmann, and that caused his Achilles tendon to flare up. Another injury we could do without.

Lehmann has had problems with his feet and his Achilles tendon for much of the past couple of years, and he took the winter off from county cricket in an attempt to let the problem settle down. It has not done so, and the way he was moving after play tonight suggests that he could be joining the growing list of doubtful starters for next week's Test in Sydney.

We managed to get five wickets relatively quickly before the Zimbabwe lower order dug in. Their resistance was helped by our need to give our two remaining fast bowlers, Andy Bichel and Brett Lee, the chance of a break ahead of taking the new ball. Then the clouds started to roll in, which prompted the umpires to order the floodlights turned on, and finally, in the last session, there were two breaks for rain.

By that stage we needed just one wicket to win the Test — just one ball would have been enough ... Maybe we tried too hard to find it. And Heath Streak and Ray Price, the last pair, were in no mood to surrender without a fight. Zimbabwe will be banking on a day of rain tomorrow. We are still confident, but the weather forecast — showers are predicted — is something that concerns me.

Monday 13 October

First Test, day five: Australia 6–735 declared beat Zimbabwe 239 and 321 (Streak 71 not out, Vermeulen 63, Ervine 53) by an innings and 175 runs.

Australia names a 14-man squad for the second Test against Zimbabwe, in Sydney, starting on 17 October: Stephen Waugh (captain), Ricky Ponting (vice-captain), Andy Bichel, Nathan Bracken, Adam Gilchrist, Matthew Hayden, Brad Hogg, Simon Katich, Justin Langer, Brett Lee, Darren Lehmann, Stuart MacGill, Damien Martyn and Brad Williams.

Western Australia and former Zimbabwe batsman Murray Goodwin is charged with a breach of the Cricket Australia Code of Behaviour following comments attributed to him claiming that racial discrimination exists in Zimbabwe cricket.

It took us 22.2 overs on the last day, but eventually we wrapped up the Test, which brought a massive sense of relief and satisfaction. The win means the innings of Hayden did not go to waste, and we can take heart from a great effort to bowl Zimbabwe out in the second innings with two bowlers out of action.

The expected showers didn't materialise today but we still made things harder than we should have done. Brett Lee bowled Streak with a no-ball, and Andy Bichel took the final wicket, which gave him four for the innings and six for the match. He and Lee shouldered a major burden when Gillespie and MacGill left the field.

There was one small element of discord in the dressing room after play as we celebrated the win. Normally we hang around for a long time after a match, enjoying each other's company, having a drink and maybe even an evening out. But today, with the match finishing before lunch, quite a few of us, including me, left early, after we sang the team song, to fly home for a day before meeting up for the next Test in Sydney. That upset Justin Langer and John Buchanan, who are big believers in making the most of every victory we get, and I could understand their attitude. My attitude was that we will get the chance to do it all again in Sydney after the next Test — win, lose or draw — and with a period away to follow (we are flying to India), I want as much time at home as I can get. We agreed to disagree.

The side for the Sydney Test looks set to have a few changes from the eleven we fielded here. Jason Gillespie is definitely out and, given the nature of his injury, he looks a doubtful starter for the tour of India as well. Stuart MacGill and Darren Lehmann have both been included in the squad, but they are struggling to be fit; with that in mind, Brad Hogg and Simon Katich have also been picked. Nathan Bracken is included in place of Gillespie, but I expect Brad Williams to make his Test debut now, after a couple of years of near misses.

I am pleased for Katich, as I know he has worked hard to get back into the squad after a couple of years in the wilderness. He was part of the squad that toured the UK in 2001, and he played a Test at Headingley when Stephen Waugh was injured, but since then he has slipped down the pecking order. It has taken a move away from Western Australia to New South Wales to reignite his career.

His inclusion is bad luck for Martin Love, who scored a hundred in his last Test innings, against Bangladesh in July, but it may have something to do with Katich's ability as a bowler as well as the runs he has scored. MacGill rates him as one of the best spinners in the country, and the pair formed an effective combination last summer when New South Wales won the Pura Cup.

Tuesday 14 October

New Zealand batsman Nathan Astle is ruled out of the one-day tri-series, the TVS Cup, also involving India and Australia, following the recurrence of a longstanding knee injury. He is to be replaced by Chris Nevin.

Wednesday 15 October

Australia names a 14-man squad for the TVS Cup against India and New Zealand in India: Ricky Ponting (captain), Adam Gilchrist (vice-captain), Michael Bevan, Andy Bichel, Nathan Bracken, Michael Clarke, Jason Gillespie, Ian Harvey, Matthew Hayden, Brad Hogg, Brett Lee, Jimmy Maher, Damien Martyn and Andrew Symonds.

Jason Gillespie is included subject to proving his fitness after suffering a slight tear in his left side muscle during the Perth Test against Zimbabwe.

Darren Lehmann is ruled out of the TVS Cup and the second Test against Zimbabwe after scans of his left foot revealed a torn Achilles tendon. Lehmann is advised to rest for six weeks before he starts rehabilitation, or he will risk rupturing the tendon and ending his career.

Victoria coach David Hookes criticises the Australia selectors' choice of New South Wales' Nathan Bracken in the squad ahead of Victoria's Matthew Inness. 'When they give out the baggy blue cap in New South Wales, they give you a baggy green in a brown paper bag as well, to save making two presentations,' he is quoted as saying.

Today was the climax of a series of meetings and phone calls with chairman of selectors Trevor Hohns as Cricket Australia named the one-day squad I will lead in India.

It has hardly been the easiest few days as we lost Jason Gillespie and Darren Lehmann, on top of Glenn McGrath.

We have gone for Nathan Bracken for a couple of reasons. There is an element of consistency in his selection, because he replaced Gillespie during the World Cup earlier this year, and there is also the fact he has toured India before and has done well in those conditions. Bracken was part of the one-day squad that won a series 3–2 there in 2001, and his experience in those conditions should be invaluable.

I am frustrated to lose Lehmann as he is a really big player for us, not just because of his ability as a batsman, but also because of his experience, which he shares with me. He is a great reader of the game and we will miss his insights on the field, as well as his relaxed attitude off it.

The positive side is that Lehmann's absence gives Michael Clarke another chance to shine at the top level. He filled in for Damien Martyn in the Caribbean and did a solid job; now he will get a chance to show his talents on a different stage.

My concern now is that we seem to be down to bare bones in terms of experience; we cannot afford to lose another player before our departure. Without McGrath, Gillespie and Lehmann it will be tough to win, especially as you can be sure that New Zealand and India, after the beatings we handed them in the World Cup, will be fired up for revenge.

Thursday 16 October

Stuart MacGill is ruled out of the second Test against Zimbabwe after failing to recover from an injury to his right calf sustained during the first Test in Perth.

Second Test, day one: Zimbabwe 8–256 (Carlisle 118) v Australia.

Brad Williams is drafted into Australia's TVS Cup squad after Jason Gillespie is ruled out. Gillespie has not recovered from the side strain he suffered during the first Test against Zimbabwe in Perth.

India name a 14-man squad for the first three matches of the TVS Cup: Sourav Ganguly (captain), Ajit Agarkar, Rahul Dravid, Mohammad Kaif, Murali Kartik, Zaheer Khan, Anil Kumble, VVS Laxman, Parthiv Patel, Aavishkar Salvi, Virender Sehwag, Harbhajan Singh, Yuvraj Singh and Sachin Tendulkar.

Salvi is included despite having missed the second Test against New Zealand after suffering a hand injury, and Ganguly is expected to be fit despite recent minor surgery on a thigh injury. Left-arm seamer Ashish Nehra is left out to allow him more time to recover from ankle surgery.

Although the scoreboard might suggest that we did okay, this was a disappointing day. Conditions were helpful for our attack, but for some reason we just did not click, and they kept us in the field all day.

Stuart Carlisle was one of the beneficiaries of our sloppiness: he scored his maiden Test hundred after we dropped him in the slips on 36. But all credit to him — you still have to take advantage of let-offs like that, and he did.

We were all aware that he had never made a Test hundred before — the giant electronic scoreboard at the Sydney Cricket Ground told us so — and we reminded him of that fact as he got closer and closer to the mark. But he showed a steady nerve and fully deserved to reach three figures.

Brad Williams was one of our line-up, and I was especially interested in seeing how he performed, as he has been called into our squad for the TVS Cup after Jason Gillespie's absence was officially confirmed today. Maybe it was nerves — he is playing his first Test, after all — but although he bowled okay today I was a bit concerned that he did not seem to be charging in as I know he can. I have seen plenty of him over the years and today he did not show the spark I know he possesses. He has some concerns over soreness in one of his knees. I hope that is nothing major; we have lost enough players from the one-day squad already.

Once Zimbabwe won the toss I think they almost felt duty-bound to bat first, no matter what the conditions were, because of what happened in Perth. There they put us into bat and we scored more than 700; Heath Streak was not going to make that mistake again.

Conditions and the atmosphere were not exactly high summer, with the floodlights on in the last session to make sure we got through to the close of play without losing any overs, and there were only around 5000 people in the ground. It all combined to create an unreal atmosphere — we are used to having far more people inside the SCG when we play an international.

We were not as switched on as we could have been and we need to put that right tomorrow. We need two quick wickets to end the Zimbabwe innings, then a positive response.

Saturday 18 October

Second Test, day two: Australia 3–245 (Ponting 137 not out) trail Zimbabwe 308 (Carlisle 118) by 63 runs.

This was a mixed day for me and the team. On the one hand, I had the joy of a Test hundred where I felt I played exceptionally well, and of passing 5000 Test runs. But on the other hand, we lost Brett Lee — not only for the rest of the match, but also for the TVS Cup — because of a torn abdominal muscle.

Lee's loss is the latest in a long line of injury setbacks over the past couple of months. It really does reduce our chances, both in this match and in the one-day series in India. It meant another conversation with Trevor Hohns. We will probably go for Michael Kasprowicz as a replacement in the one-day squad. Kasprowicz has not played international cricket for over two years and is the wrong side of 30, but he is reportedly bowling well and has experience playing in India, having toured there in 1998 and 2001.

The loss of a fifth player to injury has prompted chat in our dressing room about the reasons behind our sudden fitness problems. We have had a great record of players staying fit over the past few years, due in large measure to players' professionalism and the advice and treatment of our medical staff and fitness trainers, so this is a shock to our collective system. Why it is happening now is hard to pinpoint, but any number of suggestions flew around the room. Is it because we have gone straight into Tests without a great deal of cricket beforehand to condition our bodies? Is it a lack of fitness? Is it just bad luck or a coincidence that so many players have broken down?

If you look at each case, I tend to go with the bad luck and coincidence theory. Glenn McGrath's problem with bone spurs in his ankle is nothing to do with how much fitness work he has done over the past few months; it has been an ongoing injury, and is a common one among fast bowlers. Likewise, Darren Lehmann's problem has also been long-term, and has just happened to flare up now. And you could not accuse Stuart MacGill of being underdone, as he has come off the back of a season of county cricket. With Jason Gillespie and Brett Lee — well, muscle injuries are just a hazard of the business of bowling fast, and maybe the fact that both are injured now merely highlights how well we have done in the past to avoid such injuries, especially if you compare us with other Test-playing countries.

Lee's injury left me in a confused state of mind, at least when I was not batting. I was required to do my job, scoring runs to help us win this Test, but I also had my one-day captaincy hat on, thinking about the implications of his loss for the TVS Cup. We are missing another experienced player, and someone who is effective in getting both orthodox and reverse swing with the white ball. We know Kasprowicz can do that too, but he lacks Lee's raw pace. Whether or not the absence of that pace will affect us remains to be seen.

I was able to put all those issues to the back of my mind when I batted, and my reward was a satisfying hundred. Right from the first ball I faced I felt in total control. It was a good length outswinger from Andy Blignaut, and straight away my feet were moving. I pushed the ball into the covers and set off for a single to get off the mark. It was a good feeling, and I built on it.

The best way to describe my innings is to say that I was in what we call 'the zone' all day — that perfect state where your body, your feet, your hands, your head and the bat all move in harmony. You almost seem to anticipate the ball before the bowler delivers it, so you are in position to play it with plenty of time to spare. Every ball you hit seems to strike the middle of the bat, you feel completely confident in your ability to score runs, and there is nothing else on your mind except the next delivery.

As a team we have tried to analyse how a player gets into this mood, but, like most sports psychologists and other sportsmen, we have always failed. The most memorable effort we made was to get Adam Gilchrist to talk us through his innings against India in Mumbai a couple of years ago, when he made a blazing hundred. He then got a pair in the next Test and scored 0 and 1 in the match following that. It just goes to show what an elusive thing 'the zone' is. I guess if it was so simple to get into that state we would be doing it all the time, and cricket would appear a pretty easy game.

Today I used my feet well to the Zimbabwe spinners — Ray

Price, the left-armer, and off-spinner Gavin Ewing — looking to hit them over the in-field. If you do that they are forced to drag their length back a bit, and that allows me to cut and pull, which I was also able to do with comfort.

The fact that I played so well begs the question why I, together with Stephen Waugh, accepted the umpires' offer to go off for bad light in the final session of the day. After all, the floodlights had been turned on. Personally, I do not like batting with a red ball under lights. I cannot put my finger on why; it just feels different and unnatural. The ball seems smaller, its shiny side seems shinier, and there is a different glare off the pitch and the ball. I just do not like it.

And although it is true that I was going well when we went off, and we are in the business of entertaining people, if I had got out it would have created a different situation entirely for a new batsman. In circumstances like that I always remember what Stephen once told me: 'You should never bat in anything other than ideal light if you can help it.' After almost a decade of international cricket it is a conclusion I agree with, and I will not compromise myself or my team in that situation.

We still have three days to play, as well as plenty of batting to come. Providing the weather does not interfere too much, we are still very well placed to force a result out of this match.

Sunday 19 October

Second Test, day three: Zimbabwe 308 and 4–151 lead Australia 403 (Ponting 169, Waugh 61, Katich 52, Price 6–121) by 56 runs.

Queensland fast bowler Michael Kasprowicz is called into Australia's TVS Cup squad in place of the injured Brett Lee.

India captain Sourav Ganguly is ruled out of his side's first two matches in the tournament after surgery to remove an abscess from his left thigh. Rahul Dravid will lead the side in his absence.

We are still extremely confident about winning this match comfortably, as there is little to fear in the pitch, but Zimbabwe fought back well today, reminding us that they have come to play.

I was unable to recapture my form of yesterday and was out in a slightly bizarre way, one of six wickets for the left-arm spin of Ray Price, who fully deserved his haul. I played the ball defensively off the back foot with a loose grip on the bat to try to stun the delivery at my feet rather than allow it to ricochet to a close fielder. But that loose grip was my undoing, because rather than rebound back down the pitch after I hit it, the ball spun back between my legs and onto the stumps before I could react by kicking it away. It was a soft way to get out.

Price bowled 95 per cent of his spell over the wicket, and although that is a negative tactic, it worked. From that line it is almost impossible to get a batsman out lbw because most of his deliveries will pitch outside leg-stump, but it challenges the batsman, because in order to score runs and take the game forward you have to take a risk. With most of his deliveries outside leg-stump, the natural area to score is the leg-side, but to do that you have to hit against his spin, which is taking the ball to the off-side. And at the same time, most of his deliveries are pitching in the footmarks made by bowlers outside that leg-stump.

Price bowled poorly in Perth, but here he gave Zimbabwe a measure of control. He was not scared to flight the ball, got some drift in the air as well as a little spin off the pitch, and produced a useful arm-ball, which swings back into the right-hander.

Our main contributor with the bat was Simon Katich, who made 52 in his first Test innings in more than two years. Katich appears a much more confident player than he did in 2001, and his inclusion here looked fully justified on the basis of this innings. He was well balanced at the crease, and for a player with a short back-lift he hits the ball deceptively hard. Today he punched the ball well off front and back feet, cut and pulled well (as you would expect from someone brought up on the steep-bouncing pitches in Perth), and used his feet well to the spinners, something he has worked on during his time in Sydney.

Katich ensured that we got some sort of lead, though it was not as many as we would have liked, and without Brett Lee in our line-up they made us fight for the four wickets we got before the close of play. Trevor Gripper and Mark Vermeulen both passed 40 and almost took Zimbabwe into a lead before we separated them; by removing that pair by the close of play we have left ourselves with a good chance of wrapping up the match tomorrow.

Monday 20 October

Second Test, fourth day: Australia 403 and 1–172 (Hayden 101 not out, Ponting 53 not out) beat Zimbabwe 308 and 266 (Katich 6–65) by 9 wickets.

We did a professional job of beating Zimbabwe today, with one experienced hand and one newcomer sharing the honours. Simon Katich took six wickets with his left-arm wrist spin to set up the win and Matthew Hayden finished off the match with a brutal hundred, the type he has produced so often in the past three years.

Whether Katich would have bowled so much if Brett Lee had been fit is open to debate, but there is a chance he would have, because the pitch did offer him plenty of turn — I was surprised by how much, actually. It still required him to take advantage of the situation, though, and he did that superbly.

I have seen enough of Katich to know that he has ability with the ball — I'd faced him in the nets on tour. In my first match in charge of Australia at first-class level, against Somerset in 2001, he bowled us to victory with three cheap wickets at the end of the match. But here he showed that his bowling has come on in leaps and bounds in the past couple of seasons, and that he has benefited from his move to New South Wales last summer.

He spun the ball sharply and bowled with good variation, and it was clear that quite a few of the Zimbabwe batsmen had not seen anything quite like him before. For some reason we seem to produce more left-arm wrist spinners than other parts of the world, and the fact that most players from overseas will not have seen many bowlers of this type adds to their value.

I will remember one of Katich's six wickets, as it gave me a nice bruise on my left bicep after I found myself fielding at short leg. Normally I will field close to the wicket on the off-side to the spinner, because I enjoy being around the bat and testing my reflexes. Katich filled the short leg position for much of the Test, but when he was bowling it needed someone else to stand there and I was happy to volunteer.

The first ball of Katich's new spell, to Zimbabwe's wicketkeeper Tatenda Taibu, was a real loosener, short and spinning back into the batsman, the perfect delivery to play the pull shot. In this situation, with the batsman getting into position to hit the ball hard in the vicinity of short leg, the normal response of the fielder is to duck for cover — you usually get your head between your legs, get low to the ground and make sure you are as small a target as possible.

That response did not cross my mind. I had protective equipment on, including an abdominal guard, shin pads and Katich's protective helmet, and was not worried about getting hit by the ball. So although I turned my body slightly in anticipation of the shot, I still kept my eye on the batsman and saw the ball leave the bat.

The ball hit my left bicep and then rolled onto my chest, and as I had my hands up in that area, the next thing I knew I was holding it and starting to celebrate the dismissal — while the batsman looked on in disbelief.

When I saw it later on television replays it looked impressive, but it was a total fluke, and it will not stay with me the way some other catches I have taken in the past will. I think my most satisfying catch at international level is the one I took to get rid of Sachin Tendulkar at Mumbai in 2001. He pulled the ball against Justin Langer at short leg, only for it to loop up towards square leg. I was fielding at midwicket and had to run to my right and then dive full length to hold on. It was a catch that helped turn the Test match our way, and that makes it particularly special.

Of all the catches I have taken in my life, the one that gives me most pleasure to think about is a screamer I held when I was just 13 years old. It was my first A grade match, for Mowbray against Launceston. I was fielding at point and managed to latch onto a square slash from batsman Richard Bennett off the bowling of Troy Cooley (who is now England's bowling coach, after having played first-class cricket for Tasmania and worked with the Commonwealth Bank Cricket Academy). Maybe it is the significance of that match for me that makes the catch so special; today's catch is nowhere near that first one in my mind.

It did help us move closer to bowling Zimbabwe out, though, and once we completed that task, Hayden finished the job with a ruthless innings. I was surprised to find out afterwards that he reached his hundred in just 85 balls; that figure is a measure of just how well he played. A target of 172 could have been a bit awkward if Zimbabwe had managed to get some early wickets, but you could not wish for a better bloke than Hayden at the crease in that situation — he gave them no hope at all.

I had a moment of luck on seven, when I drilled an Andy Blignaut delivery straight to mid-on and was caught. I only survived because it was a no-ball. Apart from that, I felt in control and was happy to play defensively as the winning post got near, just to make sure Hayden got his hundred.

Our win meant a 2–0 series success, but there was not a lot of point in a lap of honour to celebrate, as only just over 1000 fans turned up to watch what turned out to be the final day. It was odd to play a Test in Australia in front of so few fans; we are used to decent crowds at all our matches. The weather did not help — it has been cold and grey for much of the Test — but at times it was difficult to escape the feeling that there would have been more atmosphere if we had played on the moon. With no disrespect to Zimbabwe intended, the gap in quality between the two sides did not increase the pulling power of the series. If we repeat the experiment of early-season Tests, I hope it can be against a more high-profile opposition that might draw more of a crowd.

Unlike the Perth Test, when many of us left early rather than hanging around to celebrate our win, this time we stayed late into the night in the dressing rooms. The Zimbabwe players came in to join us and I had a long chat with Andy Blignaut about the side.

I will accept that the Zimbabwe side is much weaker than it was a few years ago, but then what side would not be if it lost Andy Flower, Neil Johnson, Murray Goodwin and a few other players? Contrary to what the doom merchants are saying, though, I do not believe that Zimbabwe are a hopeless case. Their batting has a pretty solid foundation with the likes of Mark Vermeulen, Trevor Gripper and Stuart Carlisle, and Craig Wishart is a stand-out player for me, as long as he can find some self-belief to go with his obvious ability. If you add lower-order players like Heath Streak, Sean Ervine and Blignaut to that mix, and they all play to their potential, getting runs should not be a problem. Zimbabwe need bowlers: a specialist quick bowler and a specialist wrist-spinner. If they can find them, and both players have some quality about them, then Zimbabwe will be able to compete with any side. Unfortunately, every other Test-playing country is looking for the same two players, and the fact that they are so scarce just highlights Zimbabwe's problem, especially as the country seems to have such a small base of players to pick from.

The public's response to the series, along with the relatively poor crowds for the Bangladesh Top End tour, has confirmed my view that something needs to be done to avoid mismatches at the highest level. These types of games clearly do not appeal to the public, because they are poor spectacles.

Maybe there is mileage in some sort of two-tier system with the top eight countries playing in the highest division, but with the chance for other sides to join them through a promotion and relegation test every four years or so. That way they would have time to build up the proper infrastructure at a domestic level rather than being rushed into Test cricket, as it seems Bangladesh have been, without the infrastructure in place to support international cricket.

The second-tier sides would then spend their time playing against each other in three, four and even five-day matches, to get used to playing that type of cricket. While they do that, there would be nothing to stop them touring first-tier countries to gain experience with the conditions there and get a flavour of the standards they will have to reach to get to the highest level.

A plan like that obviously needs significant investment from the ICC, but to me it is the way to take the game forward. It would be better than seeing less-established countries continually thrashed at Test level and other, even smaller sides taking part in the World Cup and the Champions Trophy when they are patently not ready to play on that stage.

We sang the team song after the Zimbabwe players left, and even had an impromptu game of rugby in the dressing room in honour of the World Cup that is going on at the moment. It was all very relaxed, a good opportunity for us to unwind before returning to play domestic cricket or, in the case of eight of us here, heading off to India in two days' time for the TVS Cup.

Andy Bichel

One player who does not know how to play at anything other than full throttle is Andy Bichel.

He will run in and give you everything with the ball, whatever the score, whatever the conditions, and whether it is the first over of the day or the last. If you are in any doubt about that statement, just speak to Michael Vaughan and Nasser Hussain. He got rid of both of them in successive innings in the final over of a day's play during the Adelaide Test match against England in 2002 — two vital wickets that put us on the road to victory.

His ability, not only with the ball, but also as a brave and underrated batsman and a livewire in the field, means he is always likely to be in the thoughts of the selectors, but with the likes of Glenn McGrath, Brett Lee, Jason Gillespie and latterly Michael Kasprowicz also available, he has not always been able to hold down a regular spot.

He lost his place in the squad for the VB Series finals against India in 2004 and the tour of Sri Lanka that followed, which caused him to express his frustrations publicly. To an extent that was understandable. After all, he had made some crucial contributions to our success in the World Cup, the Caribbean and the home series against Zimbabwe, and felt he deserved some loyalty as a result. The selectors thought differently, and with competition for places so intense, Bichel was the one to miss out. When he was also omitted from the list of contracted players for the 2004/05 season, there were those who believed it spelled the end of his international career. I am not so sure about that, for two reasons.

First, Bichel is a player who thrives on challenges. He overcame the doubters to establish himself in the Test and one-day squad for the two years before his recent omission, and during that he pulled quite a few rabbits out of the hat when the odds were squarely against us. His performances in the 2003 World Cup, and specifically his effort against England at Port Elizabeth, when he took 7–20 and scored an unbeaten 34 to win a match that looked lost, will be remembered long after he packs in the game.

On top of that, Bichel has always been a great team man, and if the selectors are ever casting around for someone the captain can turn to in any situation, they know he is a safe bet. Stephen Waugh once called Bichel Australia's best-ever twelfth man, an indication of how hard he works for his team-mates behind the scenes if he is not in the final eleven, a fate he has endured many times. He always puts aside any disappointment he feels at missing out to ensure that a player has that dry pair of gloves, that drink that was requested at an interval, and whatever else is required to make the job of playing a little easier.

Bichel's ability as a team man extends beyond that: he also takes responsibility when he is in the side. In the Sydney Test of 2003 he dislocated his finger trying to stop a straight drive while he was bowling, but he continued to take part in the match when the easy option would have been to have a sit-down in the dressing room. He even volunteered to act as nightwatchman when we batted, scored useful runs and then played the next few matches in the VB Series with a splint on the finger.

Against Pakistan in Sharjah in 2002, in baking heat, while most bowlers could only manage one-over or two-over spells, he was the man who put his hand up to bowl five and six overs in a row, with every ball hitting the bat as hard as the first. The spell made him dizzy, but it gave his bowling colleagues a break and helped us win the match. That typifies Bichel's attitude.

He is as tough as teak — which is obvious when he takes his shirt off — and is a natural athlete; he also played rugby league as a youngster. There is not a kilo of spare fat on him, and if you ever thought of taking him on in a fight, one look at his upper body would put you off the idea pretty quickly.

Bichel's desire to stay on the park may also have something to do with the fact that he remembers how hard it was for him to break into the side in the first place. Once he is there, you always get the impression that he is going to make sure it will be equally hard for someone else to get him out.

In common with other members of the Queensland 'Mafia', Matthew Hayden and Andrew Symonds, Bichel loves fishing when he is not in the thick of the action on a cricket ground, but when he is playing he is like Glenn McGrath — he needs plenty of work, especially with the ball, to get into a good rhythm. This means he has benefited from his time playing county cricket. He has developed as a player because of the intense program of matches in the UK, while others have been dragged down by the grind of day-in, day-out professional cricket. He is a model professional and a great man to have on your side.

Part 4:
TVS Cup in India (Australia, India and New Zealand)

AS GOOD AS THE WORLD CUP

Thursday 23 October

India seam bowler Lakshimipathy Balaji replaces fellow medium-pacer Aavishkar Salvi for India's first two matches of the TVS Cup. Salvi suffered a hand injury bowling in the nets during the second Test against New Zealand, in Ahmedabad.

TVS Cup, match one, Chennai: India (3 points) 3–141 v New Zealand (3 points) (no result, rain).

Less than 24 hours in the country and already the tournament has begun. And we've had a wake-up call — in more ways than one — to let us know that we will be in action sooner rather than later. India scored quickly, although that is always possible in Chennai, the ground where Matthew Hayden made a double hundred in a Test match almost three years ago, but it was difficult to get too much out of watching the action, because rain cut play to just 26.5 overs.

After last night's media conference, today was a media session for all the players, me included. We do this at the start of every tour we go on now, after starting the practice here in India in 2001. Rather than have our preparations for our opening match interrupted by endless requests for interviews, we set a time and a place — on this occasion the team hotel in Delhi — and any reporter who wants to speak to anyone in the squad can come down and do it today. The session allows the journalists to get as many interviews as they want before the series, and allows us to focus on what we are here for once the session is over. From now on, one player will speak to the media each day.

I did a whole heap of interviews, and if I had a rupee for every time I was asked how we would cope without Glenn McGrath, Jason Gillespie, Brett Lee and Darren Lehmann I would be a rich man. If anyone listened to every interview I did they would have been pretty bored by the end of the hour-long session, because I said the same thing no matter how the question was phrased: the players we have brought in have been around, they are experienced, they deserve their chance and we have full confidence in them.

Saturday 25 October

Today was all about meetings. I met the media, the match referee and umpires and we met as a team to discuss our approach to the series.

The media conference at the ground followed training and was a standard affair, full of questions I have answered already on this trip. My meeting with the match referee and umpires was more interesting. I found out that a complaint against a player can now be lodged by the third umpire on the basis of what he sees on television. Shoaib Akhtar, the Pakistan fast bowler, was found guilty of verbally abusing Paul Adams of South Africa thanks to television pictures, even though the two on-field umpires did not complain. As we have already agreed to try to uphold the Spirit of Cricket, I hope this will not affect us but I mentioned it to the squad when we met as a group later on and it is another reason why we need to be on our best behaviour.

We had a brief chat about how we will bowl to the Indians in this series.

- Sehwag — a great hitter, but has a strange technique, as he tries to stay leg-side of the ball. Likes width and is not as strong through the leg-side. Could be vulnerable to short-pitched bowling.
- Tendulkar — class act. We always have plans for him, but none of them ever really works. Key idea is to try to get him driving, especially outside the off-stump, to see if we can induce an edge; if that fails, try to attack the stumps.
- Dravid — another class act. Very patient and has a good all-round game. Is maybe their best player of short-pitched bowling, as he can either get out of the way or pull with authority. Another player we need to try to get edging the ball, especially early in his innings.
- Ganguly — will murder wide bowling, so the key message is no width. Might be worth going around the wicket to try to take away the angle across him that provides natural width to play his shots. Always potentially vulnerable to short-of-a-length deliveries, especially early on, as he tends to fend them towards the slips, but make sure you do not get too wide or he will cut and carve with real power.
- Laxman — similar to Dravid, although not as good at handling the short-pitched stuff. Maybe we can capitalise on the fact that he does not always use his crease to get right forward or right back early in his innings. Full and fast early on might work.
- Badani — plays spin and medium-pacers pretty well but an unknown quantity against quick stuff. Expected to bat in the middle

order as a finisher, so we can try to build pressure on him with an extra fielder or two inside the circle to test his temperament.

- Patel — handy batsman if he plays to give Dravid a rest from duties behind the stumps. Has plenty to say and is a capable player who likes to go for his shots. Bowl a tight line around off-stump, as he is potentially vulnerable in that area.

We did not dwell too long on the individual players because we had seen most of them in the World Cup. The bowlers had a separate meeting with video to discuss methods of attack anyway. So John Buchanan and I switched the focus to our overall approach to the series.

Sunday 26 October

TVS Cup, match two, Gwalior: India (5 points) 5–283 (Laxman 102, Tendulkar 100) beat Australia (1 point) 9–246 (Gilchrist 83) by 37 runs.

Small periods of poor judgement, first with the ball and then with the bat, cost us in a big way, and we contrived to lose a match we should have won.

Sachin Tendulkar and VVS Laxman scored hundreds, but our bowlers still had a degree of control until we lost the plot towards the end of their innings. Even then we were still in a prime position to win after Adam Gilchrist and Matthew Hayden gave us a great start, but after them we lost our way badly through a needless collapse.

Chasing 284 was never going to be easy, but having reached 0–132 in the 25th over we should have gone on to win the match. It was at that point, when Gilchrist departed, that we lost it. Their bowlers exploited a softening ball and a pitch that lost any pace it had had and we self-destructed.

We knew they would bring the field in with the spinners on, try to build pressure and wait for us to look for the big shots. Our plan should have been to try to get through that period, rotate the strike wherever possible, reduce risks and, if necessary, give up some runs. On Indian grounds it is always possible to make up for a lull in scoring late on if you have wickets in hand, because the outfields are usually lightning fast.

Tonight, unfortunately, we did not follow that strategy. Instead we tried to force the pace, and the result was the loss of four wickets for nine runs. After that it was always going to be tough to win.

India's score suggests that a well-paced innings, but a combination of poor bowling by us in the final five or six overs and the whirling blade of Ajit Agarkar got them out of jail. I thought Laxman, back in the one-day side after missing the World Cup, played for himself, and wanted to make a hundred just to prove a point. It meant he slowed down as he neared three figures, which suited us fine.

As it turned out, though, getting him out was the worst thing we could have done, because Agarkar, together with Yuvraj Singh, took advantage of too many full tosses and half-volleys by our bowlers and lifted the tempo rapidly in the closing overs. They both hit the ball well, and we gave them too many chances to do it.

Tendulkar looked in great touch; he was close to his best today. When he is playing well he presents the full face of the bat to the bowlers, driving the ball down the ground, and he did that today. He looked for the straight and cover boundaries in the first 15 overs, when we had to have the field up inside the circle, and then, once the field restrictions were lifted, he took few risks and gave us no chances.

He showed us how to go about pacing our innings, even though things were made a little harder by the pitch starting to deteriorate, a mass of flying insects attracted by the floodlights, and constant interruptions because of people moving near the sightscreen. Hayden got so upset at one point that he walked all the way to the edge of the boundary to have a go at the stewards for not doing their job. Unfortunately, that is all part of playing in India. We are going to have to get used to things like that and put them to the back of our minds if we are going to make an impact in this tournament.

My dismissal was an example of how we lost the plot. Leg-spinner Anil Kumble bowled me a delivery that was short of a length. Playing back, I went to force it down the ground. However, the ball held up on the pitch and all I succeeded in doing was chipping it back to the bowler. It was a soft way to get out, but I hope that as we become more used to conditions, that type of dismissal will become less common for us.

As if the defeat were not bad enough, we have another injury to contend with, this time to Michael Kasprowicz, who was not even playing in the match. He came to the ground early with Allan Border to get some batting practice, but as he played forward to a delivery he pulled a muscle in his backside. It is a bizarre injury, but it may spell the end of his tour before it has even started. This is a short tour with matches coming thick and fast, and we cannot afford to carry a player who is unable to play for any length of time. Alex Kontouri, our physiotherapist, will treat him. If there is no sign of an improvement we will need to call for a replacement, although who that will be given the injury list we already have is anyone's guess.

Wednesday 29 October

TVS Cup, match three, Faridabad: Australia (6 points) 2–101 beat New Zealand (0 points) 97 by 8 wickets.

I lost the toss but we won the match as our bowlers made the most of Stephen Fleming's decision to bat first.

It was a strange decision. The pitch would have been a beauty if the match had been a day–night game, but with a 9 o'clock start there was still some moisture in the surface and some early morning dampness in the air. Brad Williams and Nathan Bracken made the most of those conditions, which were perfect for bowling.

New Zealand's plight might have been even worse if Williams and Andy Bichel had not struggled to control the white Kookaburra ball as it swung all over the place. We bowled 18 wides, a totally unacceptable number, but luckily for us New Zealand were in no position to make us pay for that generosity.

I do wonder whether it was by accident or design that the pitch for this match looked nothing like the surface on which we played India. That was a dustbowl that turned more and more as the match went on. If it is a policy, I guess you cannot blame India: they will try to play to their strengths and our perceived weakness, and it is up to us to overcome that.

Bracken was the pick of our bowlers, even though Williams was named man of the match — he took one more wicket. I am not sure the Indians have seen anyone swing the ball in this country as much as Bracken does, and both here and in Gwalior he made the openers look very foolish.

In Gwalior he swung the first couple of deliveries back into Virender Sehwag then pushed one across him and got the batsman to edge it to slip. Here he pushed the first ball across Chris Nevin then swung the second back in sharply, having him plumb lbw. Bracken has worked a lot with Bruce Reid, the former Australia left-arm pace bowler, to try to improve his ability to swing the ball back into the right-handers, and on the evidence of this series it has been time well spent.

I feel in terrible form, and it showed as I made a very scratchy 12. It is not as if I have not been practising, but the harder I try, the worse I feel at the crease. The things I am keen to avoid are getting too worked up about the problem and overanalysing it, and practising too much in a bid to get back into some form. It is a case of trying for quality not quantity, and trusting my ability and instincts. Let's hope I find my touch again sooner rather than later.

There was better news on Michael Kasprowicz: he is recovering from his strained backside and so will stay with the tour group.

Brad Williams

If you asked me to define 'wholehearted' and 'committed' I would do it using two words: Brad Williams. I do not think there is a player who puts more into everything he does.

It cannot have been easy for him over the past three years as he hovered around the fringes of the Test side without ever making that final step into the starting eleven, and always reliant on injuries to others to make the one-day line-up.

That frustration boiled over last summer when he was left out of the final eleven again in Brisbane at the start of the India Test series following an excellent TVS Cup. He was critical of the selectors for omitting him, but he quickly realised he had said the wrong thing and apologised. There was no awkwardness when he rejoined the squad for the next Test. Everyone knows that Williams does not have a malicious bone in his body, and Cricket Australia acknowledged that fact by handing him a slap on the wrist for his comments rather than a more severe punishment.

For all his frustration over the past few years, Williams has also had some good times. His successes in the TVS Cup, the VB Series and in finally getting a baggy green cap have been a well-deserved reward for his perseverance.

I first came across Willo in the UK in 1995 when we toured together for Young Australia. Back then he was quick, maybe the quickest bowler in Australia at the time. He was raw, but his pace was enough to concern even the best of players: I remember he terrified the late Hansie Cronje, then playing for Leicestershire, in one match we played on the trip.

On that tour I also got my first look at what a committed cricketer Williams is. He played through horrendous pain in the opening first-class game of the tour after developing blisters all over his feet from bowling in basketball boots with spikes added to them — they offered extra support to his ankles. The blisters were the size of the bottom of a Coke can, but he bowled through the agony they must have caused him and played a part in a win for the side.

His level of commitment was again demonstrated last summer against India, when he hurtled into a boundary board at the Adelaide Oval trying to stop a four. He damaged his left shoulder and was not expected to bowl again in the match, but came out and went through the pain barrier to do just that.

I know the Indian batsmen did not enjoy facing him in the TVS Cup or during our home summer, because he runs in and bangs the ball into the pitch, whatever the conditions. He has been one of the few bowlers who has consistently troubled VVS Laxman, which is a tribute to him considering the number of runs Laxman has taken off us over the years.

Williams is one of the reasons we have been so successful over the past 15 years, because players like him are constantly challenging the senior bowlers — men like McGrath, Lee, Gillespie and Kasprowicz. He is saying: 'If you drop your standards I am there to take your place.' At the same time, when he has linked up with the squad and not made the starting line-up, he has worked tirelessly to ensure that the playing eleven are well looked after. That is the essence of a good team man: a title that sums up Brad Williams perfectly.

Friday 31 October

India captain Sourav Ganguly is ruled out of a return to action for another week as he continues to recover from surgery to remove an abscess from his left thigh.

Western Australia and former Zimbabwe batsman Murray Goodwin is reprimanded by Cricket Australia (CA) Code of Behaviour Commissioner Alan Sullivan QC for remarks he made alleging that racial discrimination occurs in Zimbabwe cricket. Goodwin had pleaded guilty to breaching CA's Code of Behaviour.

Last night I was named Electrolux Wisden International Cricketer of the Year in an award ceremony in Mumbai. Andy Bichel picked up the prize for the best one-day performance of the year for his 7–20 and 34 not out against England in the World Cup match at Port Elizabeth, and Shane Warne's 7–94 against Pakistan in Colombo in late 2002 earned him the award for the best bowling performance in Tests.

It was good to see Warne, who was also at the ceremony, but it was today, away from the public eye, that something just as important took place.

Shane Warne came to see me in my room and we had a 20-minute chat to clear the air ahead of what we both hope will be a comeback by him to international cricket next February, when his year-long suspension for taking a banned diuretic comes to an end.

We have hardly seen each other since the day he left the World Cup squad last February; it seems we have conducted our dialogue through the media in the meantime.

I knew he had been hurt by some of my comments after he returned to Australia. Looking back, it was pretty easy for me to sit in South Africa and sound off about how foolish he had been to do what he did. No one knew that more than him, and given the pressure he and his family were under at the time it was not the most sensitive thing for me to have said. I apologised, and we agreed it was time to move on.

The fact that he came to see me suggests that he has maintained his enthusiasm for the game and wants to come back again. That is great news for us.

Saturday 1 November

TVS Cup, match four, Mumbai: Australia (6 points) 8–286 (Martyn 100) beat India (0 points) 209 (Tendulkar 68, Dravid 59) by 77 runs.

This was a great win for us, just what we needed to stop India gaining any sort of momentum, and almost a carbon copy of the first match we played in the tournament, but this time with the roles reversed.

This time we batted first, made a big score, and then strangled the life out of them on a wearing pitch. It was a hint to India and New Zealand that we are starting to come to terms with conditions: we won thanks to a brilliant innings from Damien Martyn and excellent bowling from Nathan Bracken — and also, perhaps more surprisingly, Michael Clarke.

Martyn played superbly, and put to bed once and for all any suggestion that he cannot play spin. It is a myth that comes from the fact that he plays his cricket in Perth, where very few spinners are found because the rock-hard, fast, bouncy surfaces over there promote fast bowlers. It is a false myth, as he showed in this innings.

Building on the form he showed in the World Cup, where he improved his ability to rotate the strike, Martyn carried on that way today before opening out later on with some lovely drives down the ground and over the in-field. He even attacked Anil Kumble, who had given us so much trouble in our first match in Gwalior, and moved to his second 50 in just 34 balls.

Our healthy total was down not only to Martyn, but also to two excellent partnerships — with Andrew Symonds and Michael Bevan.

Phil Hillyard, © News Limited

Phil Hillyard, © News Limited

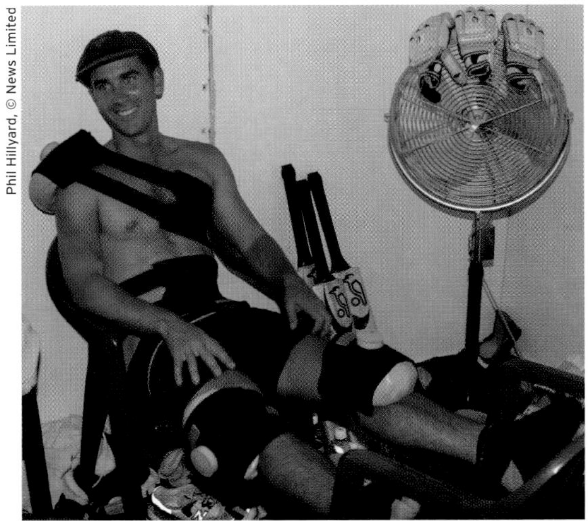

Above A cut above the rest: Justin Langer hits out during his man of the match double — 146 and 78 not out — against the West Indies in the first Test, in Guyana.

Left The aftermath: a sore but satisfied Langer ices down to reduce the aches, strains, blows and bruises resulting from his efforts, which helped us make a winning start to the series.

Right A special moment: Darren Lehmann jumps for joy after reaching his maiden Test hundred during the second Test against the West Indies, in Trinidad — this finally happened more than 13 years after his first call-up for Australia.

Below A job well done: it is no secret how much I admire Darren Lehmann, so it was a pleasure to be with him when he finally cracked the three-figure barrier at Test level.

Phil Hillyard, © News Limited

Phil Hillyard, © News Limited

Left Yes!: I am ecstatic after finally cracking the 200 barrier, during the second Test against the West Indies. Rianna being there made it even better.

Below Every Hogg has his day: celebrations after Brad Hogg bowls Brian Lara around his legs in Trinidad. This was a crucial wicket on our road to victory.

Right Headstrong: I lost my cool after this clash with Mervyn Dillon, after he dismissed me in Trinidad.

Phil Hillyard, © News Limited

Phil Hillyard, © News Limited

Left Waugh hero: In the third Test, in Barbados, Stephen Waugh acknowledges the applause after reaching his 30th Test hundred. This gave him one more three-figure score than Sir Donald Bradman.

Photo courtesy Ricky and Rianna Ponting

Right Cruising: Rianna and me (centre, back) with team-mates and their family members on a catamaran in Barbados before the third Test against the West Indies.

Phil Hillyard, © News Limited

Left Flashpoint: Words between Glenn McGrath and Ramnaresh Sarwan created global attention.

Below The spoils: we celebrate retaining the Frank Worrell Trophy in relaxed fashion in Antigua.

Phil Hillyard, © News Limited

Left The big one: Andy Bichel celebrates removing Brian Lara during the second one-day international, in Jamaica. Bichel dismissed Lara seven times in Test and one-day action, which was a crucial factor in the success of our tour.

Below Take that: Michael Clarke hits out during his 75 not out in St Lucia. The one-day series showcased his exceptional talent — and his need to improve his fitness.

The last Waugh: Stephen Waugh hits out on the way to his 32nd and final Test hundred, against Bangladesh in Cairns.

Above 'This is how you bowl at 150 km/h!': Brett Lee offers advice to Bangladeshi players during the Top End series of 2003.

Below It's good to be back: Damien Martyn shows what we were missing as he returns to international cricket after injury and scores 92 from just 51 balls against Bangladesh in Cairns.

Both of them joined him in rotating the strike in a way we failed to do in Gwalior. India's captain, Rahul Dravid, became more desperate, rotating seven bowlers in his search for wickets. Although we lost four wickets in the last over, we still had a solid total to defend.

Nathan Bracken again bowled beautifully with the new ball; he swung the ball back into Virender Sehwag to trap him lbw with his first delivery. Already he seems to have Sehwag totally at sea, not sure if the ball is going to swing into him or hold its line across him. If Bracken can keep taking such a dangerous strokeplayer out of the equation that would be great news for us.

Despite that early breakthrough, India still made solid progress, and it took a hunch from me to make sure we did not waste our large score. Sachin Tendulkar and Dravid were looking in control, but I wanted to set them a fresh challenge, so I threw the ball to Clarke.

The Indians had used Yuvraj Singh — like Clarke, a part-time left-arm spinner — bowling over the wicket into the bowlers' footmarks outside leg-stump. That forced our batsmen to play against the spin. Yuvraj is not a great bowler, but he walked away with 1–36 in eight overs, and I figured that if Clarke could do much the same job it would put the home side behind the asking rate, which was then almost 6 runs per over. As it turned out, he did even better.

First he bowled Tendulkar as the batsman tried to back away and cut the ball through the wide open spaces on the off-side. Then he had Yuvraj caught off bat and glove as he top-edged a sweep. Then, to complete an impressive trifecta, he removed Dravid, who had also been looking for the wide open spaces on the off-side but only found Andy Bichel at backward point with a clumsy reverse sweep. Clarke picked up a fourth wicket when he bowled Kumble, but by then the writing was on the wall for India. Their defeat was confirmed when Bracken came back to help see off the tail.

Clarke does not have the perfect action for a left-arm spinner — his arm is a bit low and sometimes he tends to fire the ball through too quickly. But he gets plenty of spin on the ball and, as he showed tonight, if you can combine that with getting the ball in the right area you can trouble any player in the world.

To cap a good day, I felt in my best touch of the tournament so far, although given my scratchy play in the previous two matches that does not say a lot. More importantly, we have won two games, each with a full complement of six points. That will go a long way to getting us into the final, and it will put plenty of pressure on the other two sides.

Monday 3 November

India captain Sourav Ganguly has been cleared to play in the match against Australia in Bangalore on 12 November after recovering from surgery to remove an abscess in his left thigh.

TVS Cup, match five, Pune: Australia (5 points) 8–259 (Clarke 70, Bevan 50) beat New Zealand (1 point) 9–258 (Oram 81, McCullum 51, Williams 5–53) by 2 wickets.

The spectators must have loved this match, but it did nothing for my heart rate. The compensation is that we came away with a win that all but assures us of a place in the final.

It is good to know we can come out of a close match with our noses in front, but the reason it was so close was that we did plenty wrong. It took some sensible batting from Michael Clarke and Michael Bevan to get us back into the game after our top order failed, and then some nerveless work from Andrew Symonds at the death to get us over the line.

Even then we had some good fortune — New Zealand dropped two catches in the last over — but we still had to be good enough to take advantage of those errors, and we were. Just.

Once again, the pitch, together with some early morning moisture, weighted conditions far too heavily in favour of the side bowling first. This time I won the toss, and I was happy for our bowlers to take advantage of those conditions.

We reduced New Zealand to 4–21 and then 7–151, but then we lost the plot against an excellent counterattack from Jacob Oram and, towards the end of the innings, Brendon McCullum, and New Zealand finished up scoring far more than they should have.

Even though the ball swung a hell of a lot, there was little excuse for our experienced bowlers delivering 32 wides, but they know that without me having to bang my fist on the table, and I expect it to be worked on ahead of the next match. In defence of our bowlers, they were not helped by having to cope with the swinging ball and also with the need to constantly switch lines because of a left-handed and right-handed combination (Oram and McCullum) in full flow.

The two batsmen deserve some credit for the way they played. With their top order in tatters, it would have been easy to just try to push the ball around and aim to scramble to 200, but they didn't. They took the option of counterattacking, and with our bowlers struggling for control it worked.

Oram drove powerfully and McCullum caused our bowlers

plenty of difficulties; he looked a better player than we saw in the World Cup earlier this year. McCullum drove the ball down the ground, forcing me to keep both mid-on and mid-off back on the boundary; as we needed four men inside the fielding circle, I brought up fine leg. McCullum's answer was to lap-sweep the quick bowlers over the head of that fielder, and his reward was 51 from just 47 balls.

Although the pitch flattened out into a good batting strip, we still managed to get ourselves into early trouble. All our top order got in but did not go on with the job, and I was as guilty as anyone else. I missed a straight half-volley which I tried to play through midwicket. That was bad cricket, and at 4–65 we were in trouble.

Clarke and Bevan pulled us out of the hole, and while Bevan does this sort of thing for a living — as New Zealand will remember, because he scored a hundred to rescue a seemingly hopeless cause against them in Melbourne almost two years ago — Clarke was more of a revelation. He was not fit enough when he was with us in the Caribbean earlier this year, but he has gone away and worked on that aspect of his game during the winter, and now appears to be in excellent shape.

Both Bevan and Clarke got out with work still to do, but we still had Symonds, who has become a reassuring presence in our middle order in the past year. He has obviously grown in confidence after breaking through during the World Cup, and now he is an ideal finisher in this sort of situation. He can knock the ball around into gaps to keep the scoreboard ticking over, as Bevan does so well, but his awesome power also allows him to find the boundary at vital times.

He did that today by hitting Daniel Vettori's last two balls for four and six, placing us in the driving seat with just four required from the last over, but even then there was a sting in the tail. In that last over, bowled by Oram, Brad Williams was dropped behind the wicket by McCullum, the batsmen crossed, then Symonds was dropped by Scott Styris at midwicket, which allowed us to score the winning runs. Sometimes the difference between winning and losing can be as tight as that.

After battling back from losing the toss and being 4–21, New Zealand and Stephen Fleming were pretty upset to let this match slip from their grasp, and I gather it showed in some of Fleming's comments in the post-match media conference. He slammed the conditions at the start of the match and the fact that New Zealand (and Australia) are playing in two sets of conditions in the tournament.

'You can't start this early with wickets like this. There's no point,' he said. 'We've been on the wrong side of it twice, and it makes the next game a lottery too. There are two competitions going on: one for us and Australia, where it seams around and is tough to bat, and another for India, where it gets lower and slower then turns.'

It is easy for me to be relaxed about things — we won — but although I agree with him, I get the impression he is losing his patience after a month in India and that is a dangerous thing to do on tour. If you let foreign conditions get to you it can be a slippery slope, and pretty soon you're wanting to be on the first available plane home rather than focusing on the job at hand, which is winning the next match. New Zealand seem to be in danger of falling into that trap.

Wednesday 5 November

India leg-spinner Anil Kumble will miss his side's match against New Zealand in Cuttack on Thursday following the death of his father. Fellow leg-spinner Sairaj Bahutule, who played a Test against Australia in 2001, takes his place in the squad.

New Zealand all-rounder Chris Cairns will miss the Cuttack match after injuring his hamstring against Australia in Pune.

Thursday 6 November

TVS Cup, match six, Cuttack: New Zealand (5 points) 6–249 (McMillan 82 not out, Styris 68) beat India (1 point) 9–246 (Kaif 64) by 4 wickets.

Friday 7 November

New Zealand all-rounder Scott Styris is fined US$2500 after being found guilty of dissent following his dismissal during the TVS Cup match against India in Cuttack.

Saturday 8 November

I now know what the Beatles must have felt like. When we flew into Guwahati today it was incredible. People were screaming as we got off the plane, and every vantage point was taken in an attempt to catch even a glimpse of us as we made our way through the terminal and onto the team bus.

Once we got to the hotel I had a pre-match media conference about tomorrow's match against New Zealand, and I got another look at the level of enthusiasm for cricket — even for matches which do not involve India. Even though Guwahati is only a country town, about the equivalent in size of Ballarat in Victoria, there must have been 100 local media hanging on my every word. It was quite amazing.

As it turned out, the journalists were not the only people who were hanging on my words — the microphone system sent my voice through the entire hotel. I am not sure what the people trying to have a quiet coffee in the restaurant thought of my views on the TVS Cup!

Sunday 9 November

Sourav Ganguly and Anil Kumble are both confirmed starters for India's next match, against Australia in Bangalore on Wednesday 12 November.

TVS Cup, match seven, Guwahati: Australia (5 points) 7–225 (Bevan 84 not out, Ponting 52) beat New Zealand (1 point) 181 (Styris 54) by 44 runs.

This was an excellent win, because we did it despite resting Adam Gilchrist, Matthew Hayden and Brad Williams, losing the toss and losing early wickets. Somehow, we still managed to compile a winning score.

Like New Zealand in their two previous games against us, we struggled against the moving ball. The fact that we were able to come through and win the match is testament to our strong self-belief and the confidence that has built up in the side over the last few years.

I managed to make a contribution with the bat, at last, and it was just as well — we slipped to 4–61. We experimented with Ian Harvey and Jimmy Maher at the top of the order: they got us off to a quick start but failed to go on with it. With Damien Martyn and Andrew Symonds also failing, we needed all of Michael Bevan's experience in tricky conditions.

My lack of form, plus some extravagant seam movement for Jacob Oram, made the early part of my innings almost laughable. He darted the ball around and might as well have bowled me a guitar, as I would have had more chance of playing that. The one advantage I had was our early scoring rate — 5 runs per over in the first dozen or so overs — which meant we did not need to take too many risks while Bevan and I got established.

We probably took that desire to get established a bit far, because we did lose our way a little in the middle of the innings, maybe placing too high a price on our wickets at the expense of pressing on. Once I realised that I tried to accelerate, but that cost me my wicket.

I went down the pitch to hit spinner Daniel Vettori over cover but got my front foot too close to the ball. That meant I did not have room to swing my bat as freely as I wanted, and I ended up getting a thick inside edge on the ball, sending it to long-off. I was out after doing a lot of the hard work, something several of us in the top order have been far too guilty of in this tournament so far.

My wicket sent us into decline, and we slipped to 7–164 before Andy Bichel joined Bevan. They added 61 from the last eight overs to drag us back to respectability. For New Zealand it must have seemed like a bad dream, as it had been Bevan and Bichel who rescued us against the same opposition in the World Cup match at Port Elizabeth in March.

Our score — 225 — was not great, but the new ball did offer some assistance and our bowlers took full advantage of it. We claimed early wickets, with Nathan Bracken again outstanding. We bowled with more discipline than in Pune, and there was no way back for New Zealand this time.

It is getting towards the end of a long tour for New Zealand — they played two Tests against India before we arrived — and their players seemed to be struggling a bit with tiredness. That impression can also often come from defeat. New Zealand now need to beat India in their last match to have any hope of qualifying for the final; if they do, you can be sure they will be bubbling again.

Monday 10 November

Gilbert Enoka, New Zealand Cricket's sports psychologist, will join the squad in Hyderabad ahead of its match against India. New Zealand must win the game to qualify for the final against Australia.

Tuesday 11 November

We play our last qualifying match before the final tomorrow, against India, and I could not think of many better spots to play it than Bangalore.

Our trip to get here was a long one — a flight from Guwahati to Delhi, then another one from Delhi to here — but one look at our hotel, which is really lovely, made all that travelling worthwhile.

On top of that, the ground is outstanding, with a good pitch, an excellent outfield, and even a clever way of dealing with missiles thrown onto the ground. There is a net suspended from the roof of the popular section of terracing, held in place high above the ground by ropes and sandbags. As soon as the crowd starts to get rowdy and throws anything onto the field, the ropes are cut, and down comes the netting. After that, anything thrown bounces off the net and straight back towards the spectators. It is very simple, but a lot of the best ideas often are.

We trained today, and although we are already through to the final I am keen to keep our feet on the accelerator pedal. Now is not a good time for us to be losing momentum or handing it to India, and we have an added incentive here: a win for us could rub them out of the final. That would be a bonus, as India on their own turf are always a threat. Each side has won one game against the other in this tournament, so if we can win — and win well — tomorrow it will be a huge confidence boost for us for the final, whoever we end up playing.

India have Ashish Nehra, the left-arm fast bowler, back after ankle surgery, and Sourav Ganguly is also due to play after recovering from a thigh injury. Both of them are short of time in the middle, of course, so they are two players we will be looking to put under particular pressure.

Wednesday 12 November

TVS Cup, match eight, Bangalore: Australia (5 points) 2–347 (Gilchrist 111, Ponting 108, Martyn 61 not out) beat India (1 point) 8–286 (Tendulkar 89) by 61 runs.

This was just the sort of performance we were after in the lead-up to next week's final — aggressive, ruthless and intimidating. We crushed India in a game that, looking at the scoreboard, has more than a passing resemblance to the World Cup final in March. I hope India think that way too.

Adam Gilchrist played superbly for his first one-day hundred against India, and I scored a hundred too, ending a horror run. If I had a dollar for every time I have heard someone say, 'It is a different game when you have been at the crease for half an hour', I would have some handy change for my back pocket, but my innings today showed how true a statement that is.

I scratched around early on, unable to time the ball, while my feet felt as if they were set in cement. And when I did get them moving I managed to miss the ball, only for Rahul Dravid to give me a let-off, missing an easy stumping chance. That was my cue to believe it was my day. I decided to be really positive against the spinners and it paid off. The left-armer, Murali Kartik, bowled really well, turning the ball sharply, but without any luck. I came to the conclusion that if I just tried to survive against him he would get me out, so I decided to take the attack to him.

My statistics pretty much tell the story of how I played. My first 50 took 69 balls, but I only needed another 31 deliveries to get to 100, with four sixes in that second half-century. I went for broke, and it was one of those days when that approach paid off.

At the other end I had Gilchrist and then Damien Martyn. Gilchrist took the game away from India right from the start of the day as he laid into Ashish Nehra — the left-arm fast bowler's first five overs cost 44. It was not quite the return to action he was looking for, but it was just what we had wanted, and put him under pressure straight away. Gilchrist hits the ball hard at the best of times, and some of the cover drives he hammered off Nehra were as hard as anything I have seen hit on a cricket ground. Afterwards, even Gilchrist admitted that he had smashed them.

The way he was playing I wondered if he had a chance of a double hundred, but he got out with 16 overs still to bowl. He was replaced by Martyn, who carbon-copied his innings in the World Cup final, scoring at a run a ball but also rotating the strike intelligently so that I could take advantage of my rediscovered form.

My major disappointment of the day was the way we allowed Virender Sehwag to rediscover some form of his own. Nathan Bracken has had him in all sorts of trouble, and again this evening he began as though he had never picked up a bat. But we dropped him three times, and although Sehwag only made 39, it may be enough to convince him he can play against us.

Sachin Tendulkar got 89 and played very well again, and as they passed 150 in the 26th over they were still on course for an assault on our score. But as we discovered on this ground in 2001, when we were chasing more than 300 in a one-day international, a score like that is a tough requirement, and I always felt that as long as we maintained our discipline with the ball it would be difficult for them.

Ian Harvey and Michael Clarke were expensive with the ball but they also picked up vital wickets, and that meant India were never in a position to launch a final assault on our score. In the end they just scraped past 278, which was the score they needed to earn a point — that point puts them level with New Zealand going into the final match of the tournament. That match now becomes a semi-final for the right to play us in Kolkata.

I lost my temper after the match, as I was mobbed by masses of people who somehow got onto the ground for the presentation ceremony. I was incensed by the poor security.

Nathan Bracken

It is Nathan Bracken's misfortune to be playing at a time when we have a solid stock of seam and swing bowlers. Had he been playing in another era, he might have appeared much more regularly at Test and one-day international level.

When he has played he has shown himself to be an ideal foil to the explosive talents of the likes of Jason Gillespie, Brett Lee and Glenn McGrath because of his ability to contain batsmen: when batsmen get to the other end, away from that trio, if they face Bracken they find there are still no easy runs to be scored. The fact that he poses a different challenge to batsmen because he is a left-arm bowler adds to his appeal.

Bracken's bowling may look relatively innocuous from the sidelines, but he gets the ball in the right areas more often than not, and if a bowler does that he will get good players out. Bracken showed this early in his international career, when he toured India with the one-day squad in 2001. We won that series 3–2 and he played a part in all three of our victories, as the Indian batsmen struggled to come to terms with the angle from which he delivered the ball. Bracken's dismissals of Sachin Tendulkar in both Vizag and Margoa were crucial in our achieving the series win.

At that point Bracken looked set for an extended run in the Australian side, especially after he was picked for both the Test and the one-day squad for the Ashes tour later that year. But barely two weeks into the tour he picked up a shoulder injury that meant an early return home and an uncertain future.

Bracken may not always seem the most robust bowler — he is not powerfully built, like, say, Brad Williams — but he has shown over recent times that he has plenty of determination and stamina. He defied a foot injury, that later ruled him out of the one-day series in the West Indies, so that he could be part of the World Cup squad when Jason Gillespie was injured; and during the Test series against India last summer, he kept going in the Sydney Test despite a painful leg strain that kept him out of the VB Series, and he was our most consistent bowler in that Test.

The suggestion that he could not swing the ball back into the right-handers may have counted against him in his early days. Whether that was fair or not, he showed it was no longer true during our TVS Cup triumph in India in late 2003, when he tied the India and New Zealand batsmen in knots with his ability to duck the ball in late or make it hold its line going towards the slips. It was a travesty that he did not win the man of the series award, because he always made early inroads for us with the new ball, and that was enormously important on the easy-paced pitches of the subcontinent, where the ball loses its shine after just a few overs.

In the Tests he played against India during our home summer of 2003/04, Bracken was used in more of a stock bowling role, often going round the wicket, looking for reverse swing away from the right-handers and capable of bowling a good yorker. He did a great job in that role, and his spell on the fourth day of the Melbourne Test, although not many people will remember it, was vital in ensuring that we retained control, built up pressure and ultimately won the match.

I have always found Bracks a pretty shy guy; he's not too talkative in the team environment. He tends to keep himself to himself, at least in my experience, but he is a player I also have plenty of faith in.

Bracken was someone I was very much in favour of when we were hunting around for a replacement for Gillespie in the World Cup. His ability to reverse swing the ball was a key factor in his selection. I knew we were likely to play several games on the dry surface of Port Elizabeth, and those conditions, with the pitch roughing up the ball, are almost guaranteed to foster reverse swing, as Brett Lee proved against New Zealand when he took five late wickets to seal a win in one of our matches there.

The selectors left Bracken off the list of 25 contracted players in 2004, but in fast bowling terms, with the re-emergence of Michael Kasprowicz, the return to fitness of Glenn McGrath and the arrival of Shaun Tait, they were spoiled for choice. Bracken was not the only player who could consider himself unlucky; Andy Bichel also missed out. I hope Bracken takes his omission in the right way and redoubles his efforts to play for Australia again, because I believe he has the potential to be a valuable bowler for us at international level.

Thursday 13 November

India name a list of 20 players from which they will choose their Test squad to tour Australia. The players are: Sourav Ganguly (captain), Ajit Agarkar, Hemang Badani, Lakshimipathy Balaji, Akash Chopra, Deep Dasgupta, Rahul Dravid, Murali Kartik, Zaheer Khan, Anil Kumble, VVS Laxman, Ashish Nehra, Parthiv Patel, Irfan Pathan,

Sadagoppan Ramesh, Aavishkar Salvi, Virender Sehwag, Harbhajan Singh, Yuvraj Singh and Sachin Tendulkar.

India also name their squad for the rest of the TVS Cup, with Aavishkar Salvi replacing Ashish Nehra.

Saturday 15 November

India name a 16-man squad for their Test tour of Australia. It is: Sourav Ganguly (captain), Ajit Agarkar, Akash Chopra, Deep Dasgupta, Rahul Dravid, Zaheer Khan, Anil Kumble, VVS Laxman, Ashish Nehra, Parthiv Patel, Irfan Pathan, Sadagoppan Ramesh, Aavishkar Salvi, Virender Sehwag, Harbhajan Singh and Sachin Tendulkar.

TVS Cup, match nine, Hyderabad: India (6 points) 5–353 (Sehwag 130, Tendulkar 102, Dravid 50 not out) beat New Zealand (0 points) 208 (Styris 54) by 145 runs.

India booked their place in the final against us with a crushing win that showcased the batting talent they have available. Virender Sehwag, well and truly back in form, and Sachin Tendulkar blitzed the ball all over the field in an opening stand of 182, at 6 runs per over, and Rahul Dravid scored his runs at a gallop, from just 22 balls.

Once India scored so many runs there was never a way back for New Zealand; looking at the body language of the players, I think they are glad to be getting on the plane home.

India named their Test squad for the upcoming Australia tour and it does not contain any surprises. They have named a young left-arm fast bowler called Irfan Pathan, and he looks quite an exciting prospect. I've seen a bit of him on television recently when he played in an Asian under-19 tournament in Pakistan. He bowls at a lively pace and can swing the ball, so it will be interesting to see if he can force his way into the side ahead of more experienced players such as Zaheer Khan, Ashish Nehra and Ajit Agarkar.

A few people asked me about the decision to leave out left-arm spinner Murali Kartik. Although he has bowled well against us here, they already have Anil Kumble and Harbhajan Singh in the squad. There may be a time when they will play two spinners, but there will never be a chance for three of them to play in the same match on Australian pitches.

India's batting has picked itself, with the selectors choosing the left-handed Sadagoppan Ramesh as the spare batsman. We have seen plenty of him in the past, both in Australia and in India.

TVS Cup, final, Kolkata: Australia 5–235 (Martyn 61) beat India 198 by 37 runs.

This may seem like an amazing thing to write, and maybe I have been influenced by the odd beer, but I think every member of this playing group rates our success here in India as comparable to the World Cup win in southern Africa earlier this year.

For us to come here with what was called a makeshift side — without Glenn McGrath, Jason Gillespie, Brett Lee and Darren Lehmann — to face an India side on their own turf plus a New Zealand line-up that was acclimatised, and lose just one match, has been a brilliant effort.

We adapted quickly to playing in alien conditions, and that was shown to perfect effect by our display in the final.

We overcame some nerves with the bat to post a defendable but by no means unbeatable score, then bowled and fielded like tigers while India crumpled under the pressure. And after we wrapped up the match, just one glance around the terraces, which emptied in double-quick time, told me all I needed to know about how well we did our job.

As a group we were so euphoric about this win that we sang our team song straight after the last wicket fell, on the middle of the ground. When we got back into the dressing room I told the players just how proud of them I am.

We were fortunate that certain things went our way — the toss, for example — but there is also an element of making your own luck in situations like this, and we did just that.

India did not help themselves by dropping a whole host of catches. The ball seemed to follow VVS Laxman around: he dropped me twice, as well as missing chances from Matthew Hayden and Michael Bevan. Any one of the catches offered by me or Hayden could have given India the opportunity to get into our middle order while the ball was still relatively new.

Although Damien Martyn played with his customary coolness, our total of 235 owed most to Michael Clarke, who played a superb innings. He went in when Martyn was out, with nine overs left. At that point our innings was stagnating. Michael Bevan, who was struggling with a sore groin, could not get the ball away, and I was seriously considering getting a message out to him to retire hurt, but then Clarke suddenly put his foot on the gas.

He scored 44 from just 28 balls — it was just the type of innings

I thought he could play when I got my first decent look at him, in the Caribbean earlier this year. He runs well between the wickets and is now fitter, but more importantly he is able to hit the ball powerfully and has a wide range of shots, which allows him to hit boundaries in lots of areas at the end of an innings. That makes setting a field to him very difficult.

Clarke's innings changed the game: it gave us some momentum and a score we could now defend, as well as taking the wind out of India's sails — their players might have been expecting to chase 210.

The ball was turning and holding up off the surface, and as I said to the players before we went out on the field, no matter how good you are, it would be difficult to chase a score like ours under pressure and with the pitch deteriorating. That was exactly how it turned out.

The atmosphere when we were in the field was just as I had expected. In the middle of a ground like that you cannot hear one voice over another, it is just a constant roar of sound. Rather than being intimidated by it, it gets my adrenaline flowing, and I always play better when that happens.

The noise does not present too many problems for a captain as long as the rest of the players are focused and paying attention, and they were this evening. My work involved lots of hand signals, plenty of chats with Adam Gilchrist between overs — because he is in the best position to see what the bowlers are doing — and good use of the time when wickets fall or we have a drinks break. They are the only times you can get any messages across to all the players at once.

The key wicket for us was Sachin Tendulkar, and Andy Bichel got him. The little master clearly set his stall out to bat through the innings and finish up 100 not out; he felt that if he was there at the end of the innings, India would win. To show his desire to do just that, it took him more than half an hour to find his first boundary, but he had just got into his stride when Bichel got him, with a great ball that nipped back through the gate to beat an attempted push down the ground.

By that stage Brad Williams had already got in on the act, thanks to a fiery confrontation with Laxman that saw him (Williams) get a quiet talking to from the umpires for overstepping the mark.

We wanted to force Laxman onto the back foot, partly because he loves to get forward and drive, and also because with the bounce in the pitch becoming a little uneven, it increased his chances of falling lbw to a delivery that kept low. But to get him back there Williams had to pitch a little short of a length, and that gave Laxman the chance to angle the ball away through the vacant slip area.

To counter that I put myself where third slip would normally be, but as luck would have it, Laxman then edged two fours into the gap between Gilchrist and me. That did not impress Williams, as he explained to Laxman. It left me with a delicate balancing act: I did not want Williams to overdo anything the umpires felt was out of order, but at the same time I did not want to curb his enthusiasm for the job in hand.

I was trying to think of the best way to deal with the issue when Williams ended the debate, bowling Laxman on the back foot with a ball that cut back and kept a little low. He was pretty happy, and so was I.

Our total meant India were never out of the game — the asking rate was never too high — but whenever the home side seemed to have things under control we managed to come up with a wicket. As I said before the innings started, the pressure of chasing a total to win the tournament was a heavy burden, and both Yuvraj Singh, who edged a drive to slip, and Hemang Badani, who top-edged a sweep after playing pretty well, illustrated that point perfectly.

Ian Harvey finished India off with his intelligent mix of seamers, swingers and slower balls, and we won with more than eight overs of the Indian innings unused. All they needed to do was push the ball around for ones and twos and they could have won the match comfortably, but the pressure of the situation told on them as we held our collective nerve.

I do not remember anyone in the squad mentioning our Test loss in Kolkata in 2001, and I do not believe it was of any significance in this match, but I still take great pleasure in this win, especially if it shows India we can beat them at Eden Gardens.

I also hope that with our four-match Test series against the same opposition starting in the next two weeks, and the VB Series to follow, it reinforces any psychological edge we might have over the Indian players. We have beaten them twice: in the last World Cup and now here in their own backyard, and if that sows further seeds of doubt about whether they can beat us, that is good.

We celebrated back in the bar of the hotel, but for me, at least, it was a relatively early night. I can reflect on a great job well done by the players, but the merry-go-round of international cricket means I am already thinking about the flight home and the Test series to follow in two weeks' time.

Part 5: India in Australia

NO FAIRYTALE AT WAUGH'S END

Friday 21 November

India depart for their tour of Australia.

Monday 24 November

Darren Lehmann is ruled out of the Test series with India after an assessment of his Achilles tendon injury. He is unlikely to resume first-class cricket until January, but is given permission to start a rehabilitation program, having had his foot in a protective boot since October.

Glenn McGrath (ankle) and Brett Lee (abdominal muscles and ankle) are continuing their recovery.

Tuesday 25 November

Tour match, day one, Melbourne: The Indians 9–266 (Ramesh 87, Tendulkar 80, Patel 52 not out) v Victoria.

Wednesday 26 November

Tour match, day two, Melbourne: Victoria 5–348 (Hodge 153 not out, Harvey 54 not out) lead the Indians 9–266 declared by 82 runs.

Australia Test captain Stephen Waugh issues the following statement:

'This morning I sent letters to Bob Merriman, James Sutherland and Trevor Hohns of Cricket Australia, advising of my intention to retire from international cricket, as both captain and player, at the completion of the Indian series in Australia.

'The upcoming Sydney Test will be my last for Australia, should I be selected to play. My present form and fitness suggests I could play on, however all good things must come to an end. Sydney is the perfect place to finish.

'The last 12 months have been amongst the most challenging and also the most rewarding of my career. During the last year, the support of the public has been an inspiration for me.

'I have enjoyed playing cricket for my country and wish to thank all my team-mates — both past and present — for their support, friendship and loyalty to me, first as a player and then as a captain. I wish them all, and Cricket Australia, every success in the coming years.

'I also must mention the opposition players, on all levels and from all countries, who have assisted in shaping my cricketing career. I have thoroughly enjoyed the opportunity to play against, and socialise with, each and every one of you. Thank you.

'Perhaps by far the best outcome for me as an individual in retiring is the opportunity to now spend quality time with my family. Lynette, Rosie, Austin and Lily have supported my cricket ambitions in a selfless manner. I look forward now to the opportunity to spend time with them as a more traditional family unit.

'Finally, a thank you to the media, for your support over these years. I look forward to seeing you over the course of the Indian series.'

In some ways Stephen's statement, which he read out at a packed media conference at the Sydney Cricket Ground, was a shock to me, and in other ways it was not.

That might sound mixed up, but I think all of us in the Australia side expected he would be packing in the game sooner rather than later. What did surprise me was his timing — at the start of a massive series. I expected him to make some sort of announcement towards the end of the summer.

I think his idea is to stop a repeat of the merry-go-round of speculation we had during last summer's Ashes series, when the pressure built and built before his hundred in Sydney. That served as a giant release valve and gave him a position of strength from which to carry on. The speculation did not affect us as a team, but Stephen got a bit frustrated at having to answer the same question about his future every time he went in front of the media. This way he will not have to do that.

More than anything else, I think Stephen's decision is an indication that he wants to go out on his own terms. I know he was hurt when he was sacked as one-day captain after our failure to reach the VB Series finals in 2002, and by making his announcement now he has basically ensured that there will be no repeat of that. His form is good, the public loves him, and he has set the stage for his farewell on his home ground, Sydney. Even if he makes a duck in every innings until the end of the year, it would take a brave bunch of selectors to cut him before the final Test.

Given the success I have enjoyed with the one-day side over the past 18 months, I know sections of the media and public will assume I am going to be the next Test captain, but I cannot afford to think too much about that now. After all, the decision is out of my hands. It is something that will be considered by the selectors: Trevor Hohns, David Boon, Allan Border and Andrew Hilditch. They make their recommendation to the board of directors of Cricket Australia and then the 14 directors either agree or disagree with it. I do not know when that decision will be made, but Stephen's announcement means those groups have the luxury of time to consider the options. In the meantime, I have to concentrate on scoring as many runs as I can. If I start to get ahead of myself thinking about what might or might not happen, that will distract me from my primary role — as a batsman — and that will not do anyone any good.

My desire was to let events take their natural course, but there were still plenty of journalists keen for my views on the likelihood that I will take over as captain. I just said that any decisions are out of my hands, and that until they are made it is up to us to focus on getting behind Stephen to give him a winning send-off as captain.

Stephen did not speak to me before his announcement, but I would not have expected him to. The decision was his to make, and has nothing to do with me.

I tried to call him on his mobile after the announcement, but, perhaps not surprisingly, could not get through, so I just left a message congratulating him on his great career. I hope to have more of a chance to chat with him later in the week: as luck would have it, New South Wales are playing Tasmania in an ING Cup game at the weekend, and the two of us will be going head to head as captains. It is strange how things work out like that sometimes.

Stephen Waugh

If you went around all the current and recent members of the Australian squad and mentioned Stephen Waugh's name, I am sure they would all say the same thing: that he has been a tremendous influence on us as a team and as individuals.

That might seem an obvious thing to say given the success we had as a team under his captaincy, but in my case it is not overstating things to say that he played a crucial part in turning my career around.

In my early years I had a reputation — and it was a pretty well-deserved one — for being a bit of a larrikin and a hothead, and it got me into trouble. That trouble included a suspension by the Australian Cricket Board in 1999. I had always tried to be one of the leaders of the player group with tactics and planning, and I thought the suspension meant I could kiss any future captaincy hopes goodbye.

But on the tour of Zimbabwe later that year Waugh came out in the media and said I was the future of Australian cricket. For a player as respected as him, not just in the dressing room but also among the public, to come out and say that gave me a massive boost. It convinced me that maybe I had a future as a leader after all. The rest, as they say, is history.

That summed up one aspect of Stephen's style of leadership. He was never a table-thumping captain who went round the dressing room pumping his fist in the face of each player demanding more and more effort. His belief was that being selected to play for Australia should be motivation enough. Instead he would use the media to build a player up; his comments about me were just one example. He knew I could handle any pressure it might create, as I had coped with it from an early age; far from intimidating me, it made me feel great about myself and changed my mindset.

Stephen's preference was to chat on a one-to-one basis with players, and he did that with me during the Ashes tour of 2001. I started the tour brilliantly, scoring runs for fun in the one-day series. I was promoted to number three in the order for the Test series that followed.

I began that series with a few failures, and Stephen came and chatted to me after the second Test. He didn't say anything earth-shattering, just reinforced the fact that he believed in me in my new role and that I should back myself. The result was another boost to my self-confidence, a hundred in the fourth Test, at Headingley, a strong finish to the series and plenty of runs later from that number three spot.

Stephen loved to 'mix it' with the opposition, but in contrast with his bristling aggression on the field, he was a shy man off the ground and hated confrontation. The best example of that was when he had to go and tell Michael Slater he had been dropped from the Test team, in 2001. What made things doubly awkward for Stephen was that Slats had been a close friend of his for many years. He was so nervous he took team manager Steve Bernard along for support.

Stephen said afterwards that it was one of the toughest things he'd ever had to do. It prompted his recommendation that the captain be removed from the selection process on tour, which was accepted. The change freed him from having to deal with that sort of issue in the future.

The one time he would take his passion off the field was when he was dismissed. He was a great one for yelling when he got out — once he was back in the privacy of the dressing room. Some players (Adam Gilchrist or Damien Martyn, for example) do the opposite: they just sit down in their seat and quietly unwind. Waugh would rarely do that, especially if he was out relatively cheaply, but it was just his way of letting off steam and it was understandable in some ways: the dressing room was about the only place he could do that away from the glare of the media.

Stephen's record shows that he was a great captain, and I believe it stands up to scrutiny, even when we remember that he had so many world-class bowlers to call on. Doubters may point out that he could usually throw the ball to Glenn McGrath, Jason Gillespie, Shane Warne, Brett Lee or a host of other top performers who were the envy of every other Test team, but he was also happy to back his players with attacking field settings that demanded they look for wickets rather than containment. Stephen was, for example, always happy to dispense with a third man in favour of another catcher around the bat — most other sides have now followed suit.

On the field he was never a great talker to the rest of us. He tended to set the field, have some banter with the batsman if he was within earshot — 'mental disintegration' he called it, rather than sledging — but not talk a great deal with the bowler. He usually just expected the bowlers to get on with it. I am more of a regular communicator with the members of the attack; that just reflects different styles of captaincy.

That whole sledging issue used to annoy him when it was brought up by the media, because he felt it was a case of making an issue out of nothing. Most on-field chat does not involve personal abuse of the opposition; abuse is something none of us condone. Generally it is just an attempt to plant some seeds of doubt in the batsman's mind, to get him thinking about the pitch, the field settings, his own inadequacies in coping with a certain type of ball, rather than focusing on the job at hand, which is playing the next delivery. Stephen never saw anything wrong with that and I don't either, and our view is reflected in our Spirit of Cricket document, which allows for that type of banter.

In terms of our approach to batting, Stephen never said we should go out to score at 4 runs per over, but he always wanted us to score quickly to give ourselves as much chance as possible to bowl out the opposition twice. By publicly backing players he gave the batsmen confidence to go out and play in that way without feeling they were playing for their places because he had staked *his* reputation on our success.

Stephen's success as a player and a captain is even more remarkable given his struggles with injury, something that is never really referred to. During his latter years in the side I reckon he spent more time on the massage bench than any other player. He always seemed to be getting treatment for something, but despite the aches and pains brought on by almost 20 years of constant high-pressure cricket, he very rarely failed to make it onto the field. And once he was there he very rarely failed to perform. I remember one occasion when he tore a muscle in his backside yet still led the side in the field. It was Stephen's way of saying, 'I can do it, I can go through pain to succeed, and I expect you to do the same thing.' Usually we did, too: injuries very rarely kept anyone off the field during his time in charge of the side. It was also something we used to motivate us against other teams, especially

England in 2001. We saw their players dropping out of Tests for all sorts of reasons and then taking ages to get fit again, and it helped convince us we were tougher than them.

The demands on an Australian captain are massive, with the media and public always wanting to hear your views on the hot topic of the day. Stephen had the ability — and this is an ability that many others in the team also have — to shut out all distractions once he crossed the boundary rope and walked onto the field. Those demands also ensured that he loved to switch off when he was away from the ground. He was one of a small group of players who would always hunt out the local cinema after play and watch whatever was on offer — it meant that for two hours, no one could reach him and he had nothing else to think about but the film in front of him.

Another way he switched off from cricket was to have his family with him as often as possible; it was under his captaincy that there was a real explosion of family involvement with the team. That trend might have had something to do with the fact the average age of the team has been growing in recent years, which has meant fewer single men and more young children. But Stephen, together with coach John Buchanan, was at the forefront of ensuring that wives, partners and children were looked after, and Cricket Australia has responded by making sure that players have suites rather than basic rooms with a bed and a desk when they travel around Australia.

Stephen's captaincy is a tough act to follow because he was so successful, but it is not something I am complaining about, because it is thanks, in part, to Stephen's faith in me that I have a chance to follow him as Australia's captain.

Thursday 27 November

Tour match, day three, Melbourne: The Indians 9–266 declared and 2–116 (Chopra 55 not out) drew with Victoria 8–518 declared (Hodge 264, Harvey 71).

Australia announce a 12-man squad for the first Test against India starting in Brisbane on 4 December. It is: Stephen Waugh (captain), Andy Bichel, Nathan Bracken, Adam Gilchrist, Jason Gillespie, Matthew Hayden, Simon Katich, Justin Langer, Stuart MacGill, Damien Martyn, Ricky Ponting (vice-captain) and Brad Williams.

Both Gillespie (side) and MacGill (calf) are included after suffering injuries during the series against Zimbabwe.

I am not sure how many players have been told that they will be Australia's next Test captain on the day they are dressed up as a deodorant canister, but that happened to me today.

I was in Woolloomooloo filming a commercial for one of my sponsors, Rexona, when I got a call from Cricket Australia's General Manager, Cricket Operations, Michael Brown. He said the directors had agreed to a recommendation from the selectors that I take over from Stephen for the Test tour of Sri Lanka that starts next February.

It is difficult to explain your emotions when someone tells you something like that. I had been hoping I would get the nod to take over but I had not expected the decision to be made so quickly, so I felt some shock when I heard the news. That was mixed with a massive dose of excitement and pride — something like this is the pinnacle of a cricketer's life.

If the news was a shock, there was more to come. Michael explained that they wanted to make the announcement as soon as possible to prevent the news leaking out and also stop speculation. The result was that I was required in Melbourne for a media conference the next day.

At first, I was not sure about that. I did not want to appear to be undermining Stephen by looming over him before he had even finished the job, but Michael said Stephen was very much in favour of the idea. On top of that, Michael said the idea was to take some of the pressure off me as well: it would mean I would not be asked about whether or not I expected to become the new captain every time I faced the press. Looking at it that way, I was happy to go ahead with the announcement, so Rianna and I flew down to Melbourne in the early evening.

We told our families, but no one else, and had a quiet meal before heading back to the Quay West hotel, where I spent the last part of my day going through the statement I will make tomorrow with Cricket Australia's media manager, Jonathan Rose. As Jonathan said, it is important that I am happy with what goes out into the public domain — it is not every day you are named Australia's next Test captain. I am just hoping there isn't anyone I have forgotten to thank.

Friday 28 November

Reports indicate India have approached former Australia left-arm fast bowler Bruce Reid to act as their bowling coach during their tour of Australia.

Cricket Australia announces that Ricky Ponting will be Australia's 42nd Test captain, following the 3-sponsored Test series against India, subject to form and fitness.

Mr Bob Merriman, Chairman of Cricket Australia, confirms that the Board has accepted the recommendation of the National Selection Panel that Ponting be appointed as Stephen Waugh's successor once Waugh steps down in January.

He also announces that Adam Gilchrist will be appointed Test vice-captain following the forthcoming Test series.

Mr Merriman says that the announcement is being made now so that all players in the team can focus on the important series against India.

'Given the strong public interest in the issue, we thought it would be prudent to avoid any unnecessary speculation and distraction throughout the summer by making this announcement today, so that Stephen, Ricky, Adam and the players can put the question aside and get on with winning the imminent series under Stephen Waugh's leadership,' says Mr Merriman.

Mr Merriman also states that Cricket Australia was concerned that any such speculation would distract from what will be Stephen Waugh's farewell tour.

'Stephen has been Australia's most successful captain in Test cricket, and he has certainly left the game in better shape than when he started his international career 18 seasons ago,' says Mr Merriman. 'We simply cannot thank him enough for his outstanding contribution over this time.

'We are confident that the Australian public will want to farewell him appropriately over the next six weeks as he leads the Australian team in the 3-sponsored series against India.

'The Board has asked Cricket Australia management to plan an appropriate official farewell, and looks forward to a summer celebrating his remarkable career,' said Mr Merriman.

Ponting says that he is delighted by the decision.

'I'm honoured to be named as the Test captain elect,' he says. 'The one-day captaincy has given me a valuable insight into the characteristics required to be a successful leader, and I'm confident I can transfer these skills across to the Test arena.'

Ponting also says that he has learnt a lot playing under Waugh.

'I've learnt a lot about leadership having played under Stephen for many years now, and I feel well equipped to take on what is undoubtedly one of the highest honours in Australian sport,' he said.

'Stephen's record as a player speaks for itself, and he will be remembered as one of Australia's greatest captains. He's a true legend of the game.

'It's important to remember that the approaching summer is about celebrating Stephen Waugh and everything he has contributed to cricket in Australia and around the world, and I look forward to being the best vice-captain I can be throughout the next four Tests.

'I'd like to encourage cricket fans around the country to get out to the Test matches this summer and give Stephen the farewell he deserves.'

Stephen Waugh also voices his support for Ponting's appointment.

'I've always regarded Ricky as an outstanding leader,' he says. 'He's been a very good captain in one-day cricket, and an impressive deputy at Test level. His promotion to Test captain seems the logical move.

'It's good that this announcement has taken place so that we can now all focus on the Test series before us,' says Waugh.

Mr Merriman says that Ponting's appointment signals the dawn of a new era in Australian cricket.

'The Test captaincy is one of Australia's significant leadership roles,' says Mr Merriman. 'Ricky has proven to be an outstanding international captain and leader of men. His record leading up to and through this year's ICC (International Cricket Council) World Cup, in the West Indies, and in recent weeks in India speaks for itself. He has also been a fine Test vice-captain and a strong performer as a member of the Test leadership group.

'We're very excited by the prospect of Ricky's appointment, and look forward to helping him and his team-mates farewell Stephen in the best possible manner, by winning the Test series against India,' says Mr Merriman.

Ricky Ponting's statement upon his appointment as Test captain elect:

'It's a great honour to be named as Test captain elect and I thank the selectors and Cricket Australia's directors for their faith in me.

'Every Australian kid who plays backyard cricket dreams of being Australian Test captain, and I was no different.

'There are many people who have helped me achieve what I have so far. In particular, my beautiful wife Rianna, and my manager Sam. And to my captain Steve, it's an honour and privilege to play with and under you.

'Thank you also to my fellow Australian and Tasmanian team-mates, coaches and support staff, who have helped me succeed as a player and as one-day captain.

'I would also like to congratulate Adam Gilchrist on his appointment as vice-captain elect.

'As I have already stated this week, this time in Australian cricket is not about me, it's about celebrating Steve Waugh. I would have been happy to play out the rest of my career under his inspirational leadership.

'My intention for the next six weeks is to be the best vice-captain I can be and to ensure we play at our best in the imminent series against India.

'Lastly, I would like to take this opportunity to encourage the Australian public to get out and give Steve the farewell he deserves.'

The media conference, at Cricket Australia headquarters, was a very straightforward affair, but that is because this is what they call the honeymoon period. I am under no illusions. I know the questions will get tougher and more searching as time goes on and there are bound to be some prickly issues to deal with, but for now it was smiles all around as I was revealed to the waiting media alongside Cricket Australia Chairman Bob Merriman.

The business of appearing in front of the media is something that goes with the territory of captain, and although I am no expert, I am at least used to sitting or standing in front of a room full of journalists with cameras all around, so apart from the nerves that came from the uniqueness of today's events, it was not too much of an ordeal.

One key question I did have to answer was how my appointment will affect me or the other players in this series against India. I guess it may change how people outside the team see me but I do not think it will be a problem within the dressing room, and as far as I am concerned it is not something I will give much thought to until the time comes for me to take charge. Everyone there knows Stephen is still the captain, and the appointment will not change the way I conduct myself. I have been vice-captain since the West Indies tour and will continue to offer Stephen my advice, but my focus will be on playing as well as I can as a batsman. If I do that, I will be helping to ensure that Stephen gets the send-off he deserves — a series win.

It was a relatively short media conference, because cricket, the thing I am paid to do, appeared on the radar: I had to fly to Hobart for tomorrow's ING Cup game against the NSW Blues. I got a taste of what will be expected of me as I headed out to Melbourne airport to catch my flight. Jonathan Rose came with me, and I did four radio interviews on his mobile during the 30-minute journey.

Saturday 29 November

Tour match, day one, Brisbane: The Indians 3–17 trail Queensland Academy of Sport 6–304 declared (Carseldine 112, Philipson 85) by 287 runs.

I got the chance to wish Stephen all the best for the summer today and he got his chance to congratulate me on my appointment, but there was precious little time for any serious discussion between us.

We were both too caught up in our own and our side's preparations to speak before today's ING Cup match, there was obviously no opportunity for a chat during the game, and as he had to fly off straight after the match there was no chance for a beer then either.

At least the media got the picture they wanted, of Stephen and me tossing up at the start of the match. The events of the past few days certainly ensured a bigger than usual crowd and a correspondingly large media presence, but the match was about Tasmania and New South Wales and the battle for ING Cup points, as I said to my players before the start of the match.

For the record, New South Wales won with ten balls to spare, chasing down our 7–272. I made 12 before Stuart MacGill bowled me round my legs as I missed an attempted sweep. Stephen scored 14. The day was dominated by two left-handers: Michael Di Venuto with 125 for us and Simon Katich, who showed he is in great form ahead of the first Test, with 118.

Sunday 30 November

Tour match, day two, Brisbane: Queensland Academy of Sport 6–304 declared and 2–79 lead the Indians 9–208 declared (Laxman 74) by 175 runs.

Monday 1 December

Tour match, day three, Brisbane: Queensland Academy of Sport 6–304 declared and 6–208 declared (Carseldine 109 not out) drew with the Indians 9–208 declared and 4–121.

Tuesday 2 December

Australia wicketkeeper Adam Gilchrist misses the squad's training session, confined to bed. According to team physiotherapist Errol Alcott, Gilchrist has 'a mild flu and a bit of an infection'. Alcott added that Andy Bichel is also suffering from a similar infection and Matthew Hayden has a foot injury. It is hoped all three players will be fit for the start of the first Test on Thursday.

Wednesday 3 December

Adam Gilchrist is fit to train alongside his team-mates, and Brett Lee takes part in Australia's practice session as he continues his recovery from abdominal and ankle injuries.

This is the ninth year in a row I have been involved in the build-up to the first Test of the summer in Brisbane, and it is still one of my favourite cricketing times of the year.

There is the anticipation of a new series against new opponents, new clothing and equipment to be distributed by Cricket Australia, and a feeling of freshness around the place that is associated with the start of an international summer.

This year is different because we played two Tests in October and have already faced India this season, albeit in a one-day tournament in India, but that does not mean there is any lack of expectation or excitement from me or the rest of the squad.

The key words from our pre-Test meeting were 'discipline' and 'patience'. Everyone expects us to continually bounce the Indian batsmen in an attempt to intimidate them into submission — they are not used to playing on our pitches, and our pitches have much more pace than the surfaces they are used to back home.

But the conclusion of our meeting was that that is not necessarily the right tactic. A plan like that rarely works against good players, and in Tendulkar, Laxman, Dravid and Ganguly (plus a couple of others) they have good players. On top of that, most of us have played in Brisbane often enough to know that getting our faster bowlers to land the ball in the right area often enough, in the corridor around off-stump, is the best way to go about the game. There is always the chance of some movement off the seam or some swing here, and although the short ball will have useful value as a shock tactic against the Indian batsmen, there is no point overdoing it.

On top of that, of course, we are missing our fastest bowler, Brett Lee, as he recovers from injury, and without him any strategy of using short-pitched bowling to unsettle India is limited. He is the one bowler we have at the moment who can act as an enforcer in that regard.

We did not dwell too much on India's batting as most of us have seen them before, especially those who were in India for the TVS Cup last month. We did discuss Aakash Chopra, who is a recent inclusion in the squad. He is a solid opening batsman, a real contrast to the flamboyant strokeplay of Virender Sehwag and several other members of India's top order. He has a sound technique and waits for the bowler to over-pitch, as the drive is his main method of scoring. It might be worth seeing how he handles short-pitched bowling, but for the most part we will look to test him with swing and seam early on, because he has only played Tests in India so far, and the ball tends to do less there than it does here.

We did discuss India's bowling line-up:

- Zaheer Khan — has talent and is able to swing and seam the ball but has been dogged by injuries. Matthew Hayden showed he can be dominated during the World Cup; a positive approach against him here may open up some scars from that tournament.
- Ajit Agarkar — can swing the ball away from the right-hander and is a good competitor. Stephen Waugh rated him

India's best bowler when we thrashed them 3–0 in the series here in 1999/2000. If we show patience against him we can score, because he is liable to bowl the odd loose ball.

- Ashish Nehra — just back from an ankle injury, and we looked to get on top of him straight away during the TVS Cup. He is a good competitor and India may use him as their workhorse, bowling wide of off-stump to defensive fields to try to frustrate us. Does not swing the ball as much as Zaheer.
- Anil Kumble — class act, as his record shows, although he struggled here on the last tour. May be used to keep things quiet while the seam and swing bowlers attack in short bursts at the other end.
- Harbhajan Singh — at his best he is the best off-spinner in the world, with the exception of Muttiah Muralitharan. Not afraid to flight the ball; batsmen need to be aware of the difference between his top-spinner and his off-break — it is hard to tell the difference, especially early in an innings.
- Irfan Pathan — India's wildcard selection. We saw him on television when we were in India. He was playing in an Asian under–19 tournament in Pakistan and was easily the best bowler on display among all the sides that took part. Swings the new ball, can reverse swing the old one, has genuine pace and is a bundle of energy, as you might expect for a teenager. None of us is sure he will play if Nehra, Agarkar and Zaheer are all fit, but he will put pressure on them to perform.

We did not let the meeting drag on — there is no point in talking for the sake of talking. Our way is to impose ourselves on our opponents through discipline and aggression, and that is exactly what we have to do here. Everyone is clear on that; it is now a case of actions, not words.

Thursday 4 December

First Test, day one: Australia 2–262 (Langer 115 not out, Ponting 54) v India.

Thanks to some imposing batting from our top order and some indifferent bowling in helpful conditions, we are in control of this match after a rain-shortened day.

We lost 28 overs from the day's quota but compensated for that by scoring at more than 4 runs per over. That scoring rate meant

India's bowlers were under pressure all day; they will have to show some character to come back tomorrow.

India put us into bat. There were two possible reasons behind the decision. On the one hand, it was humid and overcast, and maybe Sourav Ganguly wanted to see if his bowlers could get any swing and seam movement. On the other hand, maybe there was a defensive element to the thinking — he may not have wanted his batsmen to face our attack in those conditions.

Whatever Ganguly's reasoning, the plan did not work because we scored pretty freely all day. Justin Langer scored a well-constructed hundred. He was the first to admit afterwards that he was not terribly fluent today, but in Test cricket it does not matter how you get runs; it only matters that you get them.

The ball did swing for India's bowlers, but instead of trying to get it in the right area consistently, around off-stump, they fell into the trap of trying to bowl magic balls, the type that pitch on leg and flick the top of off. That meant there was a regular supply of loose deliveries we could score off, and that made it tough for Ganguly to set a field, because we were scoring on both sides of the pitch.

On top of that, we had a couple of breaks for rain, which meant that when the ball was hit into the outfield, it got damp, so it did not swing as much as India was hoping. This was an added complication for their attack.

I made 54 before I top-edged a pull shot at Zaheer Khan. Wicketkeeper Parthiv Patel took the skied catch.

It was a clever piece of bowling from Khan — his bouncer was well outside the off-stump. For me to hit it on the leg-side I had to reach for the ball, reducing the amount of control I had on the shot. On top of that, there was some doubt about whether the ball was short enough for me to play that type of shot in the first place.

I felt it was short enough, and if Khan bowls the same delivery next time I will play the same shot. The way I pick up my bat, with my hands quite high as I prepare to face the ball, allows me to pull quite easily, as I am already halfway into position for that type of delivery. My technique makes it one of my strongest shots, and I would be depriving myself of a strong scoring area if I cut it out of my repertoire. I just have to make sure I execute the shot better next time.

That was a negative from my innings, as was the fact that I got to 54 but did not go on with the job. But at the same time, there were plenty of positive things to come from my time at the crease.

I hammered Ajit Agarkar for plenty of runs, and that is

important because with his ability to swing the ball away from the right-handers, he has the potential to be a real threat if he gets his rhythm and confidence right.

His plan of attack to me was to bowl full and straight, looking for an lbw. My answer was to play as straight as possible. I kept punching him down the ground for boundaries, and he eventually retired from the attack with 5 overs for 40 runs.

My assault on him was not premeditated, but we have the feeling that he is very much a confidence player, so if we can get on top of him he may struggle to bounce back. We saw that with his batting against us in that previous series — he scored a whole heap of first-ball ducks, and by the end of that summer his batting confidence was shattered.

My other major positive was the way I played Harbhajan Singh. India may have been banking on me struggling against him — he dismissed me five times in a row in India in 2001 — but this time I felt I played him very comfortably, and he never looked like getting me out.

Back on that 2001 tour I made the mistake of not trusting my technique against him after he got me out with a freak ball in the first innings of the series. The ball bounced and turned, took my glove, and I was caught at short leg, but rather than accepting that it was a fine piece of bowling on a helpful pitch, I went looking for other ways to try to play him instead of trusting my usual game plan against that type of bowler, which is to use my feet, dominate, and play straight.

I showed I could cope with him in two World Cup matches earlier this year and in the TVS Cup, but I am sure there were still plenty of people wondering how I would cope in Test match conditions with men around the bat. I felt I did just fine, using my feet to smash him straight for six.

That was not a planned shot or part of a plan to be ultra-aggressive either, but I knew that on a first-day Brisbane pitch Harbhajan would not spin the ball a great deal. That gave me a chance to get down the pitch if he flighted the ball. It is a long summer, but I have no concerns about him and felt I won our first battle today.

Langer's hundred was not one of his best, but the rate at which we scored all day still shows how well he played. It was also a vital innings from a team perspective — it showed that we mean business right from the start of the series.

Once Matthew Hayden was out, Langer's continued presence also meant that the Indians had to bowl to left-handers and right-handers all day, and that constant need to switch lines of attack will not have helped their search for consistency.

Friday 5 December

First Test, day two: Australia 9–323 (Langer 121, Ponting 54, Khan 5–95) v India.

Only 16 overs were possible today, but in that time India turned the whole match on its head with some excellent bowling.

The bowlers had clearly learnt from their mistakes of the first day, and they took full advantage of conditions that saw the ball swing around. There was plenty of aggression from them too, and we were unable to cope.

We did not help ourselves either, thanks in part to a bizarre mix-up between Stephen Waugh and Damien Martyn that saw Martyn dismissed; this was the first of three wickets to fall in less than two overs.

Martyn punched the ball through the covers and he and Waugh set off between the wickets as Harbhajan Singh chased the ball. They ran two comfortably, but then Waugh set off for a third, even though Harbhajan was in the process of throwing the ball back.

Martyn hesitated, but Waugh kept running, and with both batsmen virtually at the same end it was clear someone would be run out unless the fielding side made an almighty mess of things. Harbhajan's throw was not brilliant, but the batsmen's problems gave Parthiv Patel plenty of time to gather the ball and get it to Sourav Ganguly at the bowler's end. He whipped off the bails as Martyn made a vain attempt to make his ground.

The rest of the side and I watched the incident unfold on the television inside the dressing room and we were not exactly delighted, especially as Martyn had been playing well at the time. He needs runs, as he has only just come back into the Test side after a long injury lay-off, and there was the added frustration for him of getting out once he had got himself settled at the crease.

The first thing to say is that mix-ups happen in cricket. They are part of the game. But while one batsman had to go, it made no sense that Martyn sacrificed himself for his captain. Martyn was the one who was established; Waugh had just come in and was still to get off the mark.

I asked Martyn what happened out in the middle and he said that although he did not want to take on what eventually became a suicidal third run, he felt he had to because of the cries of the crowd, all of them wanting Stephen Waugh to do well in his last Test at the Gabba.

From a sentimental point of view he did the right thing, but from a cricketing point of view it was wrong, and it was compounded later in the same over when Waugh trod on his stumps as he played a short ball from Khan to fine leg.

It meant we suddenly had two fresh batsmen at the crease. The Indians took full advantage of this by slicing through our lower order.

Waugh had not made a big issue of his impending retirement when we spoke as a team during the build-up to the game, but situations like the one today suggest that the retirement is going to loom large over the series unless we deal with it. We are all desperate to make sure he gets the send-off he deserves — a series win — but we cannot afford to let sentiment take precedence over cricketing sense. That is one lesson we can take from today's events.

Saturday 6 December

Brad Williams apologises to Cricket Australia, Stephen Waugh and chairman of selectors Trevor Hohns after criticising the selectors for picking Nathan Bracken ahead of him for the Brisbane Test.

First Test, day three: India 0–11 trail Australia 323 (Langer 121, Ponting 54, Khan 5–95) by 312 runs.

More rain meant only 6.2 overs today, but instead of wasting our unexpected spare time, we decided to have a clear-the-air meeting about Stephen Waugh's impending retirement and the effect it is having on us.

Damien Martyn has admitted that he felt swept along by the crowd, and the result was his dismissal. Now Waugh has come in for some severe criticism in the media over the mix-up; he has even been criticised for walking out to bat too soon after the previous batsman, Justin Langer, was dismissed. By getting onto the field while Langer was still walking off, Waugh detracted from the applause for Langer's innings of 121, according to some critics.

It is a silly argument, as the International Cricket Council (ICC) is keen on incoming and outgoing batsmen crossing on the field wherever possible — it helps speed up the game. But it is also an indication of the hype that already surrounds Waugh's farewell as Australia's captain.

With three Tests left after this one, that hype is only going to increase, especially with the final match set to take place at his home ground in Sydney.

As was shown yesterday, what is best for Stephen Waugh is not necessarily what is best for the side, and the captain was in full agreement with that sentiment. His message to us was simple: 'Don't let my career and what is happening to me affect what we are trying to achieve,' he said.

We all agreed that the main focus is winning the series and regaining the Border–Gavaskar Trophy. If we can do that, the captain's farewell will look after itself and we will give him the perfect send-off.

In the play that was possible, our last pair — Stuart MacGill and Nathan Bracken — lasted just one ball: MacGill slogged Ajit Agarkar straight up in the air. That left India with 35 overs to face before the scheduled close of play.

In the end, the openers, Virender Sehwag and Aakash Chopra, faced just 6.1 overs from Bracken and Jason Gillespie before the bad weather returned. Although our bowlers ran in hard and beat the bat occasionally, we could not get the breakthrough.

Sunday 7 December

Australia fast bowler Brett Lee comes through his first match action since suffering stomach and ankle injuries during the second Test against Zimbabwe at Sydney in October. He bowls 10 overs for 41 runs in an ING Cup match against Victoria and afterwards declares himself ready to play in the Pura Cup match against the same opponents, starting at the MCG on Friday.

First Test, day four: India 6–362 (Ganguly 144, Laxman 75) lead Australia 323 by 39 runs.

India proved today that Friday's comeback with the ball was no flash in the pan, taking a first innings lead thanks to excellent innings from Sourav Ganguly and VVS Laxman.

Ganguly, in particular, was under pressure as the side's captain and talisman, especially after Sachin Tendulkar was out without scoring and Rahul Dravid made just one, but he decided that attack was the best form of defence, took the battle to our bowlers and got his reward.

Some people may be critical of the way our bowlers played today, but I am not one of them. Although this is the fourth day, we have lost so much time because of weather that the pitch is still in perfect condition. It offered no variable bounce, there was no pace to speak of (this is unusual for the Gabba), and the ball did not swing. Conditions were tailor-made for batting.

There may have been times when we bowled a little too short and wide to Ganguly, but he still had to be good enough to take advantage of that. And once he got past 20 he did so, carving the ball through the off-side.

The lack of pace in the pitch meant that the bowlers were unable to inconvenience the Indian captain with short balls around the ribcage, an area where he has been vulnerable in the past. When we did bang the ball in short he started to hook and pull, a shot he is not always comfortable playing. His ability to play those shots was another indication of the lack of pace in the pitch — and of his growing confidence.

Laxman played a great supporting role, although some of the shots he played meant he was hardly overshadowed. He played one shot through wide mid-on from Simon Katich's left-arm leg-breaks that was brilliant. He waited for the ball to turn into him then whipped it away for four using his bottom hand. I do not think there is a better player of that whip shot in world cricket.

Tendulkar's dismissal was one of three early wickets that gave us hope of gaining a substantial lead, and judging by this evening's television news reports, it seems to have caused a bit of controversy. He played no shot to Jason Gillespie, who got the ball to cut back off the seam. It struck him high on the front pad, and after a long delay umpire Steve Bucknor gave the batsman out.

From my position at second slip I was surprised that the decision went in our favour. I think the same goes for the rest of us. From where I was standing it looked as though the ball was going over the top of the stumps, but the line was pretty good, and that was good enough for umpire Bucknor.

Monday 8 December

Australia name an unchanged 12-man squad for the second Test in Adelaide starting on Friday. It is: Stephen Waugh (captain), Andy Bichel, Nathan Bracken, Adam Gilchrist, Jason Gillespie, Matthew Hayden, Simon Katich, Justin Langer, Stuart MacGill, Damien Martyn, Ricky Ponting (vice-captain) and Brad Williams.

First Test, day five: Australia 323 and 3–284 declared (Hayden 99, Martyn 66 not out, Waugh 56 not out, Ponting 50) drew with India 409 (Ganguly 144, Laxman 75) and 2–73.

The match ended in a draw but we were still able to take some pluses from the final rites, which were played out in bright sunshine, the best weather of the match.

Stuart MacGill mopped up India's tail to finish with four wickets, which will do his confidence a power of good. Then four of us reached 50 and played so well that Stephen Waugh decided to declare and put India's batsmen under pressure when they least expected it.

Our reward was two wickets, but with so much time lost to rain over the first three days there was never any realistic chance of a result. Play was called off with seven overs still to bowl.

Once MacGill had wrapped up India's innings the idea was to go out and bat positively. There was no plan to look for a declaration, but when Matthew Hayden and I were able to score so quickly, especially in the period straight after lunch, it became a possibility.

Hayden was at his best, driving powerfully down the ground and sweeping strongly, although it was the sweep that brought about his downfall when he got a slight top edge to a delivery from Harbhajan Singh. It still required a good catch from Virender Sehwag at deep backward square leg, but Sehwag did hang on, condemning Hayden to his second score of 99 against India: the other was in one-day cricket, at Bangalore in 2001.

Hayden is an unusual cricketer in that he says he never looks at his own score on the scoreboard. I am not sure he always manages to keep to that — he knew he was on 375 when we played Zimbabwe in Perth in October, for example. If he had known he was on 99 today he could have pushed a single, but that is not his way. He will always look to dominate the attack, whether he is on zero or 299, and getting out like this when in sight of another Test hundred will not change him.

Harbhajan was ineffective, failing to spin the ball very much. He was India's chief destroyer the last time the two sides met, in India in 2001, but he did not enjoy conditions at the Gabba. Without spin he has to resort to variations in flight, and that gives batsmen the chance to get down the pitch to him. Both Hayden and I did that whenever we could, looking to unsettle him. Waugh and Damien Martyn also played him fairly comfortably when they came to bat. The fact that he did not pose much of a threat to us today is a real positive to take from the Test.

Waugh declared when he could just as easily have gone on to three figures, a move that would have pushed him closer to Allan Border's record for most Test runs in the process — let's hope this has answered some of those critics who felt he had been a bit selfish in the mix-up with Martyn on Friday. It also added a bit of late spice into the match, which could have died far earlier than it did.

With a maximum of only 23 overs to bowl to India, we had no expectation of winning the Test; the idea was to see if we could get some early wickets and then maybe put a few India players under pressure. We managed the first part of that plan with Nathan Bracken striking twice, but then Rahul Dravid and VVS Laxman played thoroughly well, ensuring that there were no further alarms for India.

One point of interest was the non-appearance of Sachin Tendulkar, who usually comes in at number four. He remained in the pavilion — we took that as a positive for us. Maybe he decided he did not want to risk another failure after his zero in the first innings. Whatever his reason for not batting in his usual position, it robbed him of the chance of time at the crease before the next Test. As far as we are concerned, the more time he spends in the dressing room during this series the better.

We all stayed around after the match, relaxing over a drink in the dressing room. It was the ideal way to unwind after a week of tension, both leading into the Test and during the Test itself. It might seem strange, but matches like this, with large gaps in play, can be more tiring than Tests without any interruptions. That is because in weather-affected matches you have plenty of time to think about the situation you are in, instead of just getting out on the field and batting, bowling or fielding. That can be mentally draining, especially if there is a lot going on around you, as was the case with the focus on Waugh during this match.

Waugh let off some steam in the post-match media conference, accusing sections of the media of 'a lot of finger-pointing [and] a lot of innuendo' concerning his part in the Martyn run-out, and I think all of us are glad to get this Test out of the way. When bad weather intervenes, as it did here, issues like Waugh's retirement and the fuss surrounding it will always grow in size because there is no cricket to write about. A lot of the controversy surrounding Waugh's situation will be reduced if we have a cracker of a Test in Adelaide with plenty of outstanding performances to occupy the minds of the journalists.

What has been made clear by events this week is that India are definitely up for the challenge of playing in Australia. We did not play at our best, and the Gabba pitch was more placid than usual, but India showed just how much talent they have, especially with the bat, and the way the team bounced back with the ball on day two suggests a resilience we did not see in 1999/2000.

Wednesday 10 December

Umpire Steve Bucknor dismisses criticism of his decision to give Sachin Tendulkar out lbw during the first Test in Brisbane. 'I am pretty comfortable with my form,' he said. 'The criticism does not bother me. Mistakes are going to be made. I know that.'

Thursday 11 December

Left-arm spinner Murali Kartik arrives to supplement India's squad as off-spinner Harbhajan Singh struggles to overcome an injury to his spinning finger.

Friday 12 December

Harbhajan Singh's finger injury rules him out of the rest of the series.

Second Test, day one: Australia 5–400 (Ponting 176 not out, Katich 75, Langer 58) v India.

I got massive satisfaction from today's play. I made a big score to put us in charge, and have the chance to ram home that advantage tomorrow, as I am not out overnight.

Not for the first time this year, and I hope not for the last, I felt good right from the start of my innings, and although I offered a chance fairly early on, I was able to take advantage of that let-off and make India pay dearly for it.

The chance came about thanks to the Indian bowlers' tactics. I saw pretty quickly that their plan was to bowl outside my off-stump and wait for me to lose patience and have a go at a wide one. I did, when I was on 17, but Virender Sehwag in the gully could not hold on to it: I sliced a drive at a full-length ball from left-armer Irfan Pathan.

India's bowlers stuck pretty rigidly to that plan, which is well illustrated by the fact that all 17 of the boundaries I hit in reaching my hundred came through the off-side. I look on that as a tick in the box for me: it shows I was able to adapt to those tactics and still score heavily.

My routine before play did not differ from the usual. I had a catch and a stretch and then a light net, by which I mean no more than 5 minutes. As an example of someone at the opposite end of the spectrum, Justin Langer likes to face loads of deliveries in the nets. He feels it gets him into a good rhythm. As long as I feel my feet are moving and I am watching the ball, I am satisfied, although I might have some throw-downs with assistant coach Tim Nielsen to work on a particular shot.

I felt in great form right from the start of my innings, although why that is I am not sure. It is one of those feelings you wish you could bottle so that you could make sure you felt it before every innings. I left my first ball, from Pathan, punched the next delivery, a good length ball, back past the bowler and I was away.

In the next over, from Ajit Agarkar, I hammered him off the back foot through cover for four, and that set the tone for my innings for the rest of the day. I felt assured, and was in that state where my feet were moving, my head was over the ball and I was in total control, without feeling arrogant or overconfident.

I batted for all but the first 20 minutes of the day, coming to the crease when Matthew Hayden was out, but I never felt tired, even at stumps. It was not a very hot day, and that helped, but one of the ways I try to stay fresh out in the middle is by switching off completely in between balls, especially when I am at the non-striker's end. I am completely focused from the moment the bowler turns at the end of his mark, but otherwise I try to let my mind wander, look at the crowd and think of anything other than cricket.

I do not let anything distract me when I am on strike. Sides rarely say anything to me out in the middle. I think they feel it fires me up, but that's not really true: even the odd word that does go on, for example the wicketkeeper geeing up the bowler, passes me by when I'm getting ready to face the ball.

As soon as I get into my stance I focus on the bowler running in, with my eyes trained on his bowling hand. When he is halfway through his run I say, 'Watch the ball' to myself twice, to ensure that my concentration is spot-on, then I respond to whatever delivery is sent down. The method seems to work.

India were not helped by the absence of Zaheer Khan, who picked up a hamstring injury in the Test at Brisbane. It meant a debut for 19-year-old Pathan, the left-arm fast bowler. He never stopped trying today, but with the ball not swinging he was relatively ineffective, as was the rest of India's attack.

Katich played a gem of an innings, showing exactly why the selectors have gone for him to fill the number six slot. He struggled to adapt to the lack of pace in the pitch for his first 20 runs, but once he came to terms with that he timed the ball sweetly. I felt sure he was set for a Test hundred, but he hooked Agarkar to long leg and was caught in the second-last over of the day.

That was a bit of a dampener, but we can still take heart from Adam Gilchrist bringing up our 400 from the final ball of the day. As I stood at the non-striker's end I was hoping he could do it just for the psychological effect it might have on India's bowlers. Sure enough, he pushed the last delivery wide of mid-off for the single that ticked the score over.

There is still plenty of work to do in this Test, despite our solid position. It is an easy-paced pitch and India will not find it too tough to bat on when their turn comes, but we have the advantage of runs on the board, so it will be difficult for us to lose the match from this position. We also have the knowledge that batting last at Adelaide, something India will have to do, can be tough, because the pitch tends to become more uneven as the match goes on.

Saturday 13 December

Second Test, day two: India 4–180 (Laxman 55 not out) trail Australia 556 (Ponting 242, Katich 75, Langer 58, Kumble 5–154) by 376 runs.

Although India took the honours in the last hour of the day, we were well pleased with most of what went before it. First, we pressed on past 550, then we took four good wickets, so although VVS Laxman and Rahul Dravid dug in, we are still in control.

I had the satisfaction of my first Test double hundred in Australia, watched by Rianna. She seems to be my lucky charm — she was there when I made my first Test double hundred, against the West Indies in Trinidad earlier this year. She has brought out the best in me ever since we got together three years ago, and when I reached 200 I blew her a kiss in the members' stand, to the left of the dressing room.

I felt pretty good at the start of the day, not tired or stiff at all, despite having batted for so long yesterday. I did my normal warm-up — a stretch, taking a few catches and 5 minutes in the nets — then went back into the dressing room to get ready to resume my innings.

Like most cricketers, I have the odd superstition. My latest one is to wear the same pair of trousers when I bat. I have had my current pair since the West Indies tour; given the success I have had in them, maybe it is no wonder I want to bat in them all the time. They are instantly recognisable too, at least to me: at the start of the West Indies tour the drawstring around the waist broke and Lucy Frostick, our masseuse, replaced it with a shoelace. After batting in them all day yesterday I took them back to the hotel, rinsed them out in the bathroom and left them to dry overnight.

Before play resumed we had a brief chat in the dressing room. The key message was to capitalise on our position. Stephen Waugh said: 'We may have got 400 yesterday, but let's not take anything for granted.' I went out with that in mind and it, together with the fact that I was batting with the lower order, may have meant I was not quite as positive as I'd been yesterday.

I added 51 with Andy Bichel and another 83 with Jason Gillespie — Gillespie even outscored me as I moved towards 250. Then I threw my wicket away in an annoying way.

All through my innings I had tried to be positive to the leg-spin of Anil Kumble, both in attack and in defence. For example, if I went down the pitch to play him I was fully committed to any shot I played. When I changed that approach it cost me my wicket. I started to go down the pitch to him but stopped, and poked at the ball. All I did was steer it straight to slip. I left the ground to a standing ovation, but I was cursing myself.

My dismissal also cost Gillespie the chance of a maiden Test 50, because Brad Williams and Stuart MacGill both fell in the same over. That wrapped up the innings, and gave Kumble a five-wicket haul. He deserved it for his persistence, but he had to bowl a lot of overs to get it — 43 — and until those three late successes he had 2–154, which suggests our top order played him pretty well.

India started their innings solidly, but after a period where we did not really look like taking a wicket, Bichel changed things around for us either side of the tea break.

He removed both openers, and the prize wicket of Sachin Tendulkar, and when Sourav Ganguly ran himself out we were in total control.

The dismissal of Tendulkar was a great piece of bowling, even though it may not have looked like it. To the average onlooker it may have appeared that all Tendulkar did was edge a wide half-volley, and in a way that was what happened, but bowling a wide, full-length ball to Tendulkar is all part of our plan at the moment.

At his best, Tendulkar presents the full face of the bat to the ball and wants to drive down the ground. But he has made a few low scores recently and, as a result, he is more anxious than normal to get some runs on the board. That seems to be making him play at balls he might not normally look at early in his innings.

Bowling Tendulkar a wide, full-length ball offered him the chance of runs, but there was an element of risk as well. It forced him to play the ball square of the wicket rather than back past the bowler, and so increased the risk of a mistake as he was no longer presenting the full face of the bat to the ball. Our plan worked perfectly here: looking to drive through the covers, the ball took the edge and Adam Gilchrist took the catch.

My double hundred meant that I had to speak to the media again this evening. There was mention of the fact that Dravid and Laxman are together again, as they were in Kolkata almost three years ago. That time they added over 300, batting us out of the Test and turning the series on its head. It was mentioned in the dressing room this evening but only in a light-hearted way — we hope they will not produce anything like that stand again.

We know it is possible: they are two very fine players, and the pitch remains an absolute beauty at this stage. Stuart MacGill managed to get the ball to turn, but it did not do so with any great pace off the surface, so the batsmen were always able to adjust to that turn. There is precious little help for the seam bowlers, no swing to speak of, and no uneven bounce. Although we are very much in control of this Test, it will be hard work if we fail to break this partnership quickly tomorrow.

Sunday 14 December

Second Test, day three: India 7–477 (Dravid 199 not out, Laxman 148) trail Australia 556 by 79 runs.

It was not quite as tough as Kolkata, when we went a whole day without taking a wicket, but it was still a testing day at the office thanks to brilliant batting from VVS Laxman and Rahul Dravid. The pitch remained excellent for batting throughout the day.

It took us until almost tea-time to get a wicket, and although we picked up two more in the final session, Dravid is still at the crease, on the brink of an outstanding double hundred, and India are right in this match.

We could have been in a far better position if I had taken a chance offered by Laxman in the first session of the day.

The chance came from the first ball after the drinks break. I still had a lolly in my mouth and my glasses were perched on top of my cap. I realised I did not have them on as Brad Williams was running into bowl, but thought I could get away with it for that one delivery — then I would put them on and swallow the lolly.

All those thoughts combined to ensure that I was not as switched on as I should have been, and when Williams found the edge of Laxman's bat, I could not hold on to the chance. It was low, fast and to my right at second slip, but I got both hands to the ball. It was the sort of chance I have taken on a regular basis through my Test career. This time I grassed it, and Laxman, on 65, had a reprieve. If ever there was a lesson about being switched on for every ball in the field that was it, and I learnt it the hard way.

Apart from that chance, Laxman played brilliantly, just as he did in that Kolkata Test match. His off-side play is outstanding off front and back foot, but if I had to pick out one shot that stuck in my mind it would be the whip through the on-side from Stuart MacGill's leg-spin. The ball was turning away from him but he went back in his crease, waited until the last possible moment, then used his bottom hand to punch the ball past the right hand of mid-on. He played that shot well in the previous Test too, and reinforced my opinion that no one in world cricket plays the shot better.

As for Dravid, he gave us nothing. Unlike Tendulkar, he was not tempted by anything wide of off-stump; he only looked to play the ball if the bowlers adjusted their line and bowled straighter. If they then got too full in length he would punch the ball either through cover or straight down the ground, all the while also looking for ones and twos to keep the scoreboard ticking over.

Hindsight is a great thing, but maybe we made it a bit too easy for the pair of them by allowing them to score on both sides of the wicket. This is the same mistake we made against Shivnarine Chanderpaul when he took a hundred off us in Guyana in the first Test of the West Indies series.

To test the batsmen's patience, we could have just bowled an off-side line, as India did to me, but there is a chance that tactic would not have worked either. Dravid, in particular, was very selective about what he played at, so there was a chance the game could have ground to a halt. By bowling wide of the stumps we would have reduced the number of ways we could have got him out — bowled and lbw would have been removed from the equation. It is a fine line between limiting the ways in which a batsman can score and going too defensive.

We were also handicapped by an injury to Brad Williams. Chasing after a ball, he slid into a boundary board and damaged his left shoulder. Although it is not his bowling shoulder, the left arm plays an important part in his action, and it may prevent him from bowling again in the match.

Williams' absence could be costly, because the weather warmed up today, and in hot conditions we need as many bowling options as possible. On the other hand, we are still in the lead and India will have to bat last on a surface that traditionally turns more and more and becomes more uneven as the match goes on. We have not seen too much evidence of that so far, but more hot sun will open up any cracks on the pitch, so it could become a factor in the last two days of this match.

Monday 15 December

Zimbabwe name a 14-man squad for the VB Series against Australia and India. It is: Heath Streak (captain), Andy Blignaut, Stuart Carlisle, Sean Ervine, Grant Flower, Travis Friend, Douglas Hondo, Blessing Mahwire, Stuart Matsikenyeri, Ray Price, Vusi Sibanda, Tatenda Taibu, Mark Vermeulen and Craig Wishart.

Second Test, day four: India 523 (Dravid 233, Laxman 148) and 0–37 require another 193 runs to beat Australia 556 and 196 (Agarkar 6–41).

A disastrous batting display has handed India the chance to pinch this Test match, a chance they should never have had after we scored 556 in the first innings.

I am just as guilty as the rest of the side. India kept me pinned down on nought and I ran out of patience, attempted an extravagant back-foot forcing shot off Ajit Agarkar and sliced the ball to gully, where it was caught. Maybe the shot came from overconfidence after my first innings 242. It is a lesson: no matter how many you have scored in your previous effort, you still have to play yourself in the next time you bat. It was a case of riches to rags in one innings.

Every player in the top order will look back at his dismissal and wince. Justin Langer is having trouble with Agarkar swinging the ball back into him, and was trapped lbw as he overbalanced. Matthew Hayden drove loosely at a wide ball from Ashish Nehra and was caught in the covers, and both Damien Martyn and Stephen Waugh were suckered out by Sachin Tendulkar's gentle leg-spinners.

Tendulkar's plan was obvious, at least from the dressing room. He set an off-side based field with a slip, and tossed up his leg-spinners into the rough outside the off-stump. The plan was to challenge the batsman's ego: he would try and clobber Tendulkar through the off-side, even though there was that boundary fielder in place, and perhaps be caught at slip. Both Martyn and Waugh fell into the trap and both were out on the brink of tea. It was dumb batting.

Simon Katich and Adam Gilchrist launched a mini-revival, but then they both threw their wickets away as well. Gilchrist got into a tangle trying to sweep a ball from Anil Kumble that was too full for the shot and managed to get bowled around his legs, and Katich top-edged a pull to be caught at long-leg, in a carbon copy of his first innings dismissal. The only thing to be said in his defence is that by the time he was out he was batting with the tail, so he was looking to play some shots and get as many runs as he could.

Our last five wickets went for just 13 runs, leaving India with 230 to get. Ordinarily I would say we would still be favourites to win, because Adelaide usually becomes difficult to bat on in the final innings of a Test. Three years ago we had to chase 130 against the West Indies, and we slipped to 4–48 before finally getting home by five wickets. But so far at least, the pitch has not shown too many signs of excessive wear, although there was some turn for Tendulkar's leg-spin. On the downside, I know Stuart MacGill is feeling pretty tired after his 43 overs in the first innings; we have to hope he can get himself right for tomorrow's final day.

Although there was some banter between a few of the lads after play, the mood in the dressing room was pretty flat. I know John Buchanan was very frustrated about the way we performed. He explained his feelings in a note he sent around to all our rooms late tonight.

Buchanan likes writing notes. He feels they can sum up his thoughts far better than an unscripted team talk. I know some players prefer a chat, but judging by the length of Buchanan's note, that would have taken quite a while, as he had a fair bit to get off his chest.

He called our batting today 'inept', and that is fair enough, but I am not sure he is right about the possible reasons for the display. He wondered whether outside factors have distracted us, and gave a few examples, such as concern over the new helmet design, sponsor commitments, Waugh's exit from Test cricket and media coverage.

I do not feel any of those factors or any other outside influences have affected me during this Test match. I cannot really comment for any other players, but I am not sure they have been affected much by those factors either.

There are always outside pressures and problems; I should know, having gone through some pretty tough times thanks to my off-field behaviour in past seasons. But one thing most of this squad are very good at is dealing with one issue at a time. When I am on the field, my only thought is the cricket I am playing. When I have a sponsor commitment, that is my prime concern, and when I am with my wife and family they take up all of my time . . . and so on.

What I think we lacked in today's second innings was not so much focus as concentration. I let myself down in that area and maybe, as a batting unit, we were all guilty of that, together with looking too far ahead, thinking of setting up the game by posting a score rather than playing each ball on its merits. Maybe there was complacency too, after scoring 556 and knowing India would have to bat last.

India showed no nerves this evening, setting about the target in very positive fashion. Virender Sehwag was happy to play his shots to any ball off line, and India raced along at 4 runs per over up to the close.

The only positive note was seeing Brad Williams take the field and open the bowling despite his injury the previous day — his left arm had been in a sling then. That is the type of spirit we will need to show tomorrow.

Tuesday 16 December

Second Test, day five: India 523 and 6–233 (Dravid 72 not out) beat Australia 556 and 196 by 4 wickets.

We tried hard, but our best was not good enough, and India have deservedly taken the lead in this series.

There were a number of factors that worked against us. We lost Jason Gillespie with a groin strain midway through the first session, Brad Williams was still struggling for fitness after injuring his shoulder and Stuart MacGill was struggling to come back after his marathon first innings bowling spell, so we were well and truly short of the necessary firepower to test India's line-up, especially on the hottest day of the match. The pitch also failed to misbehave as much as Adelaide pitches normally do on the final day of a Test.

But all those factors are really nothing more than excuses. Rahul Dravid again batted brilliantly, and with the other players in India's top order making useful contributions we were at least 50 runs short of really testing their nerve in the final innings.

Before play began we chatted about John Buchanan's note last night. Most of us disagreed with the suggestion that outside influences are distracting us from the job at hand, but everyone realised that yesterday's batting effort was unacceptable. There was no shouting or finger-pointing. That is not our way. Instead we resolved to refocus our efforts and get the basics right; it is the basics that have got us where we are in world cricket.

Gillespie bowled a miserly opening spell and made the first breakthrough when he removed Aakash Chopra lbw, but when he tried to come back for a second burst it was clear that he was not happy. It is not unusual to see Gillespie doing all sorts of groin, calf and hamstring stretches on his way back to his mark, but he clearly felt that any more bowling would result in serious damage, so off he trooped to be seen by Errol Alcott, our physiotherapist.

MacGill was our main hope, and he got two big wickets when he removed Virender Sehwag and Sachin Tendulkar either side of lunch. Sehwag really is what you might call an ego player — he believes no bowler can tie him down, but that was his undoing. MacGill went around the wicket to him, trying to pitch into the footmarks outside the leg-stump, and rather than wait for a bad ball, Sehwag's response was to try to hit him out of the ground. He missed, and Adam Gilchrist completed the stumping.

Tendulkar is always a big wicket, even though he is struggling for fluency at the moment. MacGill got him with an excellent quicker ball. Tendulkar may have been playing for turn, but the delivery skidded on straight and trapped him plumb in front, half-forward.

When Andy Bichel got rid of Sourav Ganguly, edging low to Simon Katich in the gully, India still needed 60 with six wickets in hand. VVS Laxman then came in and played beautifully, and by the time we got rid of him, pulling a long-hop to midwicket, India wanted only nine more runs.

Dravid was again the key. He played with excellent patience, but we did have a chance to get rid of him. Brad Williams found the edge, but Gilchrist could not hold on to the chance, which was low to his right. Dravid had nine at that point, and he gave us no other opportunities.

Dravid hit the winning runs, cutting a MacGill long-hop to the boundary and sparking wild celebrations among the Indian players. They raced out of the dressing room to embrace Dravid. Ganguly was one of the first onto the field.

Ganguly had a huge grin on his face and was anxious to shake hands with every one of our players. I thought it was a bit rich, because we never saw him doing the same thing when we beat India, and I told him so as we shook hands. His response was: 'Yes, it is very good to win.'

Once we were back in the dressing room the atmosphere was very flat. We knew we had thrown this Test away with one bad display with the bat after a massive first innings score. Against a steady but far from outstanding bowling attack we capitulated, and as a batting group we have not done that for quite some time. It means we are now 1–0 down, and in a four-match series that is already halfway through it will be tough to get back into the series. We know that.

Luckily the flat mood did not last too long. We stayed around for a drink and chat, and a few India players — Dravid, Harbhajan Singh, Tendulkar and Zaheer Khan — came into the dressing room to join us for what turned out to be a very good afternoon and early evening. Harbhajan is set for an operation on his spinning finger next week and is out of the rest of the series, but India will be pretty relaxed, since they managed to beat us even without him and Khan.

Jason Gillespie

Jason Gillespie is a player I have a massive amount of respect for. He has come back from many injury setbacks, some of them career-threatening, to play cricket for Australia, and for that reason alone he deserves all the success he gets. The fact that he is also a lovely bloke only helps. He is a superb team man, and although he is a shy and private person he also gives us plenty to laugh about.

In the past, that shyness has sometimes been misinterpreted. He used to have a reputation for never doing interviews, and that put the noses of a few reporters out of joint. The truth is that he hates talking about himself — and hates talking himself up even more. He prefers to let his actions on the field do the talking.

I will always remember his fury during the Ashes tour of 2001 when a journalist showed him a clipping from a newspaper back home that was advertising his talents for hire, even suggesting film roles as a possibility. The man who placed that advertisement is no longer Gillespie's manager.

He also hates talking about the number of injuries he has had; given his track record in that area, maybe that is no surprise. Some of those injuries were pretty severe — most notably the broken leg and wrist he suffered in a collision with Stephen Waugh in Sri Lanka in 1999.

Gillespie is a very private person. For example, I only found out that he got married after the event. His desire for privacy does not make him any less of a team-mate, though, as anyone who has played alongside him and seen the effort he puts in can vouch for.

He has certainly matured as a cricketer in the time I have known him. When he first broke into the Australian side, as the backup fast bowler in the 1996 World Cup squad, he had a ponytail, barely a season of Sheffield Shield cricket behind him, and was very, very fast.

He debuted the following summer against the West Indies but quickly succumbed to injury, a pattern that was repeated when he toured the UK for the Ashes series of 1997. When he made it onto the field he was lethal, if occasionally wayward — the issue was always making sure he stayed there.

For his improved record in that area he and the Australian team's long-time physiotherapist, Errol Alcott, should share the credit. Gillespie has worked tirelessly to strengthen key areas of his body, and both he and Alcott have looked at modifications to his bowling action to ease the load on those key areas.

Gillespie may not be forever popping up on television, radio or in the newspapers doing interviews, but he has done something that has prompted a fair amount of publicity: he has grown his hair into a mullet.

It started off as a chat with Adam Gilchrist about the hairstyles of 1980s' footballers. Gillespie agreed to try to grow a mullet and, having done it, he decided to keep it, although he does trim it occasionally and also makes the odd comment that he will get it cut off one day. I cannot believe it is any fun to bowl in — or to bat in, for that matter, under a helmet — but he seems to like it and it does not appear to have done his cricket any harm.

Gillespie's hair is usually a talking point in the dressing room, and not just because of his mullet. Although he is not yet 30, he has already gone grey, but he prefers to cover it up. The boys joke about it, calling him 'Jamaican Brown' (the name and shade of hair dye he uses) — I prefer 'Weird Al', as I think his dark mullet makes him look like the pop singer of that name who performed send-ups of hit records in the 1980s.

Gillespie has developed enormously as a cricketer since his days as a tearaway fast bowler in the mid to late 1990s, and I would say he is now one of the best technical bowlers in the game: his wrist position is outstanding, always behind the ball, and that means he lands it on the seam more often than any other bowler in the world today. Add to this his sharp pace and nagging accuracy, and it means he is always asking questions of the best batsmen; I do not think many players like facing him. It also means we can maintain pressure at both ends for long periods, because if Glenn McGrath or Shane Warne is operating with Gillespie, there are very few opportunities for batsmen to score.

Away from cricket Gillespie is a huge fan of World Wrestling Entertainment. He also has a daughter from a relationship when he was still quite young, and when we play a Test in Adelaide he usually gets his daughter along with her friends after play one evening — he loves showing her around the dressing room and introducing her to his team-mates.

Gillespie has grown in stature in the past couple of years, especially since he took up the challenge of leading the attack in the West Indies when Glenn McGrath was absent at the start of that series. With the skill and experience he now has, I believe it is in his power to be remembered as one of Australia's all-time great fast bowlers by the time he retires.

Wednesday 17 December

Glenn McGrath is ruled out of the Test series against India. The NSW fast bowler, out since July with an injury to his left ankle, had hoped to play for his state on Friday but pulled out after complaining of continued pain. A scan showed that the injury has improved, but he is now focusing on a return to action in the new year.

Harbhajan Singh is set to have surgery on his injured right index finger on Friday. He hopes to be fit in time for the tour to Pakistan, set for late February.

Friday 19 December

Jason Gillespie is ruled out of the third Test in Melbourne because of the groin injury he suffered on the last day of the Adelaide Test. Gillespie will spend time with the squad in Melbourne to receive treatment from physiotherapist Errol Alcott in an attempt to be fit for the final match of the series in Sydney, starting on 2 January.

Tour match, day one, Hobart: The Indians 1–37 trail Australia A 5–311 declared (Love 94, Rogers 70, M Hussey 67) by 274 runs.

Saturday 20 December

Tour match, day two, Hobart: Australia A 5–311 declared and 3–57 lead the Indians 245 by 123 runs.

Sunday 21 December

Tour match, day three, Hobart: Australia A 5–311 declared and 7–241 declared (Clarke 131) drew with the Indians 245 and 2–66.

Brad Williams is passed fit for selection for the third Test, in Melbourne, after being put through his paces at the WACA ground in Perth.

Monday 22 December

Australia names a 12-man squad for the third Test, starting on Friday in Melbourne. It is: Stephen Waugh (captain), Andy Bichel, Nathan Bracken, Adam Gilchrist, Matthew Hayden, Simon Katich, Justin Langer, Brett Lee, Stuart MacGill, Damien Martyn, Ricky Ponting (vice-captain) and Brad Williams.

Lee is recalled after ankle and abdominal injuries in place of Jason Gillespie, who is sidelined with a groin strain.

Wednesday 24 December

Australia's captain, Stephen Waugh, says: 'If we hold our catches in Melbourne, we will win.'

Thursday 25 December

Every year on this day Cricket Australia works with Crown Casino to throw a party for players, support staff and families. It involves a Christmas lunch with as much food as you can eat, and toys, arcade games and even a bouncy castle to keep the ever-growing numbers of children entertained.

This year I was joined by Rianna, her parents and her sisters — Natalie, who is 13, and Hayley, who is 11. I think the girls had a great time rubbing shoulders with the squad. It was a thoroughly relaxing day.

Among the players and coaching staff there was the distribution of Secret Santa gifts. When the squad assembled a few days ago, everyone's names were scribbled on pieces of paper and put in a hat. One by one we drew out a name each. Once we had that name, which we were not to reveal to any of the others, we had to go away and get a $10 gift for that person, leaving it under the tree in our function room at Crown when we arrived for lunch.

The idea is to make the gift as daft and amusing as possible — my gift was a pair of socks with an umpire on them, covering up a streaker. The one that stole the show this year was the item given to John Buchanan. His note to us all on the fourth evening of the Adelaide Test somehow got into the hands of the media, who have made a big issue of it over the past few days. The response of one of our squad was perfect: John's gift was an invisible ink pen, something that had his family crying with laughter.

It is not the first time one of Buck's notes has become public knowledge; it has happened at least three times that I can think of since he became coach in late 1999. I know some of the squad are upset that private thoughts get into the public arena, but it does not bother me too much. There is nothing offensive in the note, and the debate in the media about its contents has not affected our build-up to the match.

Friday 26 December

Third Test, day one: India 4–329 (Sehwag 195) v Australia.

Today could, and maybe should, have been a disaster for us. We were sloppy in the field and Virender Sehwag took advantage of a good pitch to hammer an aggressive 195. But we fought back in the final session. Sehwag gave us his wicket, so although India took the honours, we are still in the match.

It could have been even better for us, but Brett Lee, armed with the new ball, dropped a return chance offered by Sourav Ganguly. We have to make sure that is not too costly.

Sehwag will always give you a chance, because he is a naturally flamboyant player, but on a day when there was not much swing and with the outfield fast he rode his luck and cashed in on our mistakes.

We should have dismissed him when we had the chance, inside the first half-hour. He and his partner Aakash Chopra hesitated over a second run, and the return came back to the bowler's end — with the two batsmen virtually at the same end — but Lee's relay to Adam Gilchrist was wild, so Gilchrist could not gather it and Sehwag survived.

Given that reprieve, he took advantage. If we gave him any width he flashed hard at the ball and got it through or over the in-field, and he also punched the ball well down the ground off both front and back foot.

Sehwag does not worry about hitting the ball in the air. Rather than viewing it as a risk, his attitude seems to be that there are no fielders up in the sky to catch it — the same goes for hitting the ball over the fence. He greeted Stuart MacGill with a brilliant extra-cover drive for six that looked as easy as you like yet sent the ball 10 rows back into the southern stand. Even when Sehwag hits the ball at catchable height he generally hits it so hard that taking the catch is a tough assignment.

After lunch he miscued Nathan Bracken to backward point, but Simon Katich dropped what was a regulation catch; at that stage I felt we were looking down the barrel of a large first innings total against us.

I heard a suggestion after play that some reporters thought we looked nervous at times. I certainly did not feel nervous. It is true that we have a few players making their first appearances in a Boxing Day Test, and that can be intimidating: even with a large part of the western side of the ground reduced to a construction site, there was still room for more than 60,000 fans to pack into the ground, and that will have been one of the biggest crowds Bracken, Brad Williams and Katich have played in front of.

On top of that, Lee is making his comeback to Test cricket after injury, and there has been plenty of hype surrounding him in the build-up to this match, especially because he is the first one who will test out the Indian batsmen with some genuine pace in this series. He hit both openers on the helmet and got the wicket of Sachin Tendulkar, so overall it was a satisfactory return for him — though it would have been even better if he had caught Ganguly late on.

I think we are just not used to sides playing the type of bold cricket India has played. Sehwag showed no inhibitions today, and we are not used to players playing that way against us. On top of that we are 1–0 down in the series, and that is also an unusual position for us to be in. We have to come to terms with the pressure that creates, and I thought through the day there were signs that we are doing that.

We showed all our fighting qualities in the last session, after India reached 1–278. At that point, with Stephen Waugh bowling ahead of the second new ball, we had some luck. Rahul Dravid clipped the ball casually straight to midwicket, and then Lee strangled Tendulkar. Lee bowled a half-volley sliding down the leg-side and Tendulkar deflected it fine, only to see Gilchrist get across and take a brilliant one-handed catch. That is the sort of thing that happens to you when you are out of form, as Tendulkar is at the moment.

With Sehwag still in, India were still on top, but with his 200 in sight he got greedy — and paid the price. Katich was bowling, and Sehwag hammered him for six and moved to 195. He tried to repeat the dose next ball but miscued it to long-on, where Nathan Bracken sprawled forward and took a well-judged catch.

I got the impression Sehwag was satisfied with his contribution, but if I was his captain I would have been furious at the way he got out, especially with the new ball less than two overs away: 195 might sound like a lot of runs, but I got 242 in the previous Test and that was still not enough to save us from defeat. Sehwag let us off the hook this evening; now it is up to us to make sure we take the chance he has given us.

To do that we will have to hold our catches, something Lee could not do tonight. He cramped Ganguly with a short delivery aimed at the body. The India captain popped the ball back down the pitch off the leading edge, and although Lee had to change direction from his follow-through in order to reach it, he managed to get both hands to the ball — but could not hold on.

A fifth wicket would have given us a share of the honours today but we were pretty upbeat anyway. One more wicket will take us into India's tail, and if we can wrap up their innings for less than 400 we will have an excellent chance to put the pressure back on Ganguly's side with a decent first innings total, something we are all itching to do after our failure in the second innings in Adelaide.

Saturday 27 December

Third Test, day two: Australia 3–317 (Hayden 136, Ponting 120 not out) trail India 366 (Sehwag 195) by 49 runs.

This was exactly the day we needed: we barged through the opening we created for ourselves in the final hour of play on Friday. We rattled through India's lower order, then two of us made hundreds in reply, and now we can take control of this match if we produce another disciplined day tomorrow.

The mood of the side was just right when we got to the ground. We had a team meeting before we went out for our warm-ups and identified the first session as crucial. As soon as play began, we showed some real intensity. There was no suggestion of nerves today.

Brad Williams typified that intensity. He only picked up one wicket when he bowled, but he gave India's batsmen nothing to hit and showed superb agility, running Ajit Agarkar out from mid-off when the batsmen tried to get off the mark with a suicidal single. Williams raced forward, picked the ball up cleanly then hurled an underarm throw that scored a direct hit on the stumps at the non-striker's end.

After Sourav Ganguly and VVS Laxman made a deceptively calm start, we managed to take the last six Indian wickets for just 16 runs. That included Ganguly, caught in the gully as he fended at a short rising ball from Brett Lee around off-stump. That is an area we feel he is always vulnerable in, and Lee, going around the wicket, found the perfect line and length — and made up for last night's dropped chance off his own bowling.

That performance in the field meant we were back in the match, but there was no point getting ahead of ourselves the way we did in the second innings in Adelaide. This was confirmed when Justin Langer was lbw to Agarkar before lunch. It is the fourth time Agarkar has dismissed him; he is struggling with the way Agarkar is swinging the ball back into him.

That gave me an early chance to get to the crease, and right from the start of my innings I felt in control. The pitch is a good one, and my game plan was exactly the same as it had been in Adelaide, at least in the first innings. I was happy to play with patience against Anil Kumble's leg-spin, and I tried to be positive in everything I did.

At the other end, Matthew Hayden played superbly. He was also in a positive mood, running well between the wickets, keen to sweep Kumble whenever he could, and powerful as ever through the off-side with his drives.

Hayden and I have shared some decent stands over the past few years. The key to a good partnership is good communication. That can mean good, clear calling for running between the wickets or some advice between overs about what a particular bowler is doing.

There are two major advantages of batting with Hayden. One, you are never under pressure to score because he is such a free scorer, and two, his being a left-hander means the bowlers have to constantly change their line of attack if you are rotating the strike well. That was a major factor in our success today.

India were not helped by the fact that Zaheer Khan has clearly not recovered from a hamstring injury he sustained in the first Test. This put added pressure on Kumble to keep things tight at the southern end while Ganguly rotated his remaining seam bowlers at the Members' end.

I rate my innings as one of the best I have played at Test level. Stephen Waugh told me after play finished that I am now level with his brother on 20 Test hundreds, but those things do not matter much to me. What I am interested in is scoring runs when the side needs it most, and today was an example of that: being 1–0 down in the series, we have to win this Test to be in with a chance to regain the Border–Gavaskar Trophy.

It was also satisfying for a personal reason: it means I will make another appearance on the honour board in the dressing room. There are two boards in our room: one for Australia bowlers who have taken five wickets in a Test innings at the MCG, and one for batsmen with Test hundreds on the ground. All my one-day hundreds have been in Melbourne, but before today I only had one Test hundred here, against South Africa in 1997. I looked at the board before my innings and felt it was time I put that right.

I was not entirely happy with our tactics towards the end of the day — Gilchrist came in when Hayden was out. I knew Damien Martyn had been sitting there with his pads on for almost four hours, from when the second wicket fell, and that with less than a hour to play and India's bowlers tiring, Gilchrist may have been able to take advantage of that, but with three days left, I felt we still had plenty of time before we needed to press the accelerator too hard. I thought our first priority should be to establish a first innings lead.

Gilchrist made 14 before he was dismissed, bringing Martyn to the crease. I felt that was a wicket — and an option for later in the innings — that had been thrown away.

Apart from that, we should be happy with the way we progressed today. Now we have to make the most of the position we have worked ourselves into.

Sunday 28 December

Third Test, day three: India 366 and 2–27 trail Australia 558 (Ponting 257, Hayden 136, Kumble 6–176) by 165 runs.

This was another great day for us. With the pitch starting to show signs of wear, we now have a great chance of levelling the series.

It contained a personal highlight for me — my highest Test score. And as I found out from the media afterwards, it makes me the fifth player in Test history to make double hundreds in successive matches. That is a nice honour, especially when the other players include Don Bradman, but as I told the reporters, the key for us is to go on and win the match.

We should be able to do that, but given India's ability to fight back with the bat against us, we will not be taking anything for granted.

My innings has earned me a box of wine from Adam Gilchrist. Before play he asked me what my highest Test score was, and said he would treat me to the wine if I bettered it. That explains my wave to the dressing room when I moved on to 243.

I took very few risks today. My plan was to bat as long as

possible, to build up a substantial lead. That approach needed to be backed up with support at the other end, and I got that through useful stands with Damien Martyn, Simon Katich and Stephen Waugh.

Waugh's effort was especially brave, as he batted with an injured left elbow, courtesy of a stinging blow from the second ball he faced, from Ajit Agarkar. The ball was short and Waugh started to duck, but it did not bounce as much as he thought and instead thudded into the unprotected, bony area right on the joint.

Watching from the non-striker's end, I thought his arm was broken. The blow made a funny, crunching noise and straight away the area began to swell, a lump the size of a golf ball appearing within a minute. Waugh tried to grip the bat but could not, and after he was examined by Errol Alcott, he went off for treatment and an X-ray. That revealed no break and he resumed his innings two hours later, but the injury was clearly paining him. Despite that, he still stuck around to help me add 65, and those runs might prove vital in the final analysis.

When Waugh re-emerged, he was wearing an arm guard to protect the damaged area. I have never worn one, and do not wear an inner thigh guard to protect the inside of my right thigh either. The only protection I wear, apart from pads and gloves, are a thigh pad on my left leg and an abdominal protector. Batting at number three means I am generally facing new or nearly new balls, fast bowlers and the occasional uneven pitch, so it might seem strange not to use that extra padding, but I would rather trust my reflexes. One of the keys to batting is to feel comfortable at the crease, and I would not feel comfortable with so much protection in place. I also remember something Waugh told us about a chat he had with Sir Donald Bradman in 1999. He asked Bradman how many times he had been hit on the hands in his career. The reply was, 'Never.' As Bradman said, the whole point of having a bat was to use it to hit the ball.

When we were bowled out it left India with 11 overs to bat, a perfect spell for us. For our new ball bowlers it meant they could give it everything, knowing they could then rest up after play and be fresh for tomorrow.

In that time we got rid of both openers, Aakash Chopra and Virender Sehwag, confirming our control of the match. Chopra may have been unlucky, as replays suggested the ball that Nathan Bracken got between his bat and body flicked his thigh, not the inside edge. We all heard a noise and appealed, and the umpire gave the decision in our favour. Then Brad Williams, who has been inspirational in the field, dived full length at midwicket to catch Sehwag off Brett Lee.

We were surprised not to see Sachin Tendulkar come out at number four; instead, India's captain, Sourav Ganguly, took the spot. We read that as a positive, because if Tendulkar were in decent form I cannot believe he would be placed further down the batting order. It is another sign that we are on top in this match, but there is still no room for complacency. The pitch has shown signs of uneven bounce, and if India can gain a decent lead they can still make life difficult for us on the final day. We struggled to chase 107 against England last summer in the same situation, so we cannot ease up now.

Monday 29 December

Third Test, day four: Australia 558 require 95 runs to beat India 366 and 286 (Dravid 92, Ganguly 73).

A disciplined bowling performance has left us in sight of a series-levelling win. We need just 95 for that win, and although the pitch has become a little uneven in bounce, we should get those runs pretty comfortably tomorrow.

The bowlers trod a fine line really well. Our plan was to dry up India's run-scoring, as most of their top-order players like to get the scoreboard moving. At the same time, we still wanted to give ourselves a chance of taking wickets. We got the balance right and the results followed.

Brad Williams was the most successful bowler, but I was also impressed with Nathan Bracken, who helped build the pressure on India's batsmen with a great spell around the wicket before lunch. The ball was not swinging for him, but he was able to get the odd ball to seam away from the right-handers, and going around the wicket brought lbws back into the equation for him. He choked the flow of runs, and although he did not get a wicket with that first spell, it set the tone for the rest of the attack.

Williams got one of the key wickets, Sachin Tendulkar, in exactly the same way Andy Bichel had removed him in Adelaide. Williams bowled a tight line around off-stump, offering the batsman nothing to score off, then threw in a wide, full-length ball, inviting the drive. It drew Tendulkar away from his body as he tried to hit the ball too square of the wicket, and presented Adam Gilchrist with a straightforward catch.

The only period of real concern for us was when Rahul Dravid and Sourav Ganguly were in partnership after tea, motoring along at better than a run a minute. With the new ball imminent and the faster bowlers needing a rest, we had to turn to Simon Katich and Stuart MacGill, the latter having bowled impressively in the afternoon session. The two batsmen took advantage of a few loose deliveries, but once the ball was back in the hands of the fast men we regained control pretty quickly. We will always try to get our fastest bowlers on against Ganguly when he comes in, because he plays the short ball poorly, turning his head away from it. Today his innings was split into two — he retired hurt during the morning session, hit on the side of the head by a Brad Williams bouncer, as if to confirm our opinion of his play.

There was no time to start our chase after India lost their final wicket, but that did not concern us. The forecast for tomorrow is good, and although we know India have nothing to lose when they take the field, we will have to bat very poorly not to win this Test now. Rest assured, we are not thinking like that.

Tuesday 30 December

The Australia and India teams combine to raise funds for victims of the earthquake in Bam, Iran. The players of both sides sign Stephen Waugh's Test shirt, which will be framed and placed on the e-Bay website for auction.

Australia names a 13-man squad for the fourth Test in Sydney. It is: Stephen Waugh (captain), Andy Bichel, Nathan Bracken, Adam Gilchrist, Jason Gillespie, Matthew Hayden, Simon Katich, Justin Langer, Brett Lee, Stuart MacGill, Damien Martyn, Ricky Ponting (vice-captain) and Brad Williams.

Third Test, day five: Australia 558 and 1–97 (Hayden 53 not out) beat India 366 and 286 by 9 wickets.

We are level in the series after what was, in the end, a very straightforward win, but one that was tinged with controversy.

A piece of soil about the size of a chocolate bar, located on a good length outside the left-hander's off-stump at the southern end of the ground, cracked and broke in the pitch yesterday, and was replaced overnight by curator Tony Ware.

Replacement of damaged areas around the bowlers' foot holes is covered in the International Cricket Council's regulations and the Laws of Cricket. It is not meant to happen in the 'business' area of the pitch: damage in that area is viewed as natural wear and tear.

I am not sure why Ware acted as he did, but when match referee Mike Procter, together with umpires Billy Bowden and David Shepherd, saw his handiwork they ordered the fresh soil to be removed. It was, before play started.

The piece originally came out of the pitch while India captain Sourav Ganguly was batting yesterday. It was crumbling already, and he flicked it away with his bat. I am not sure why he did that, although all batsmen will tend to brush loose earth away from their line of sight while they are at the crease. I did not feel it was in a crucial area of the pitch, even allowing for the presence of four left-handers in our top seven batsmen.

Ganguly seemed to make a big play of his unhappiness when asked about the matter after the match, but it was all a storm in a teacup and did not affect the final outcome. I do not remember one ball hitting that spot, or anywhere near it, during the 95 minutes it took us to knock off the runs we required.

Our approach today was just to play each ball on its merits and not think too far ahead. We learnt that lesson the hard way in the second innings in Adelaide, and although we lost Justin Langer early on today, lbw again to Ajit Agarkar, Matthew Hayden was in commanding form and he and I snuffed out any hopes of an amazing Indian victory.

Both of us spent a fair while on the pitch during this match, so, as I came off the ground, I was pleased to hear Jock Campbell, our fitness trainer, say that he could not believe how fresh I looked. That is a good sign after all the batting I have done in this series. I have tried to ensure that I get plenty of rest when not playing, and that seems to have been the key to my success. I have also been careful not to practise too much, saving my energy for batting in matches. I am happy with the way my feet have been moving and the way I have been hitting the ball, so my attitude has been to leave well alone. That seems to have worked.

We did a lap of honour with Stephen Waugh after the match, which marked his last Test appearance at Melbourne. But unlike in Adelaide, the Indian players did not come to our dressing room for a get-together after the match. In their absence we relaxed, chatted, listened to music and eventually sang the team song to mark our victory. I am in charge of that, but I wanted Waugh to lead it instead of me. He refused, saying, 'Let me do the last one.' That suggestion means he expects us to win in Sydney. We all want that; let's hope it happens.

Wednesday 31 December – Thursday 1 January

Australia names a 13-man squad for their first four matches in the VB Series, against India and Zimbabwe. It is: Ricky Ponting (captain), Michael Bevan, Andy Bichel, Nathan Bracken, Michael Clarke, Adam Gilchrist (vice-captain), Jason Gillespie, Ian Harvey, Matthew Hayden, Brad Hogg, Brett Lee, Damien Martyn and Andrew Symonds.

Jason Gillespie and Brett Lee return to the one-day squad in place of Brad Williams and Michael Kasprowicz.

Tour match, Perth: The Zimbabweans 240 (Carlisle 100 not out) beat Australia A 232 (S Marsh 57) by 8 runs.

With a Test match less than 36 hours away, New Year's Eve is always a quiet time for us, and this year was no exception. All players and their families gather in team manager Steve Bernard's room at the Quay West hotel, which has a balcony and a view of the Sydney Harbour Bridge. The hotel supplies a chef to cook a barbecue and the balcony gives everyone a great view of the fireworks.

Just for a change this year Rianna and I, along with Damien Martyn, headed off to a restaurant for dinner before rejoining the group to watch the fireworks. It was a really nice evening, socially and weather-wise, in contrast to last year when howling winds forced the cancellation of the display.

Our final practice session before the Test was a hectic one, but only because so many people wanted to see it. The fact that this will be Stephen Waugh's last Test has created a real buzz around the city already, and that is something we are going to have to cope with. Newspapers are producing special souvenir editions, fans are set to turn up with red rags to wave in recognition of the lucky red rag Waugh has had for the past ten years or so, and authorities are expecting large crowds on every day of the Test, which is great — we all like to play in front of a packed house.

Friday 2 January

India batsman Mohammad Kaif will miss the VB Series after damaging his thumb playing for India A.

Fourth Test, day one: India 3–284 (Tendulkar 73 not out, Sehwag 72) v Australia.

After all the hype, today did not turn out quite the way we wanted. India played well, and we were below par, so it was Sourav Ganguly's men that took the first day's honours.

We were not helped by losing the toss on a very good pitch — like every other surface in this series, it played into India's hands through its lack of pace and bounce. But we still did not bowl as well as we could have done and the batsmen were good enough to take advantage of that.

Stephen Waugh is not a man for big speeches, but he did say to us before we started that he wants to keep things as normal as possible. That is easier said than done in his final Test, of course, but he is determined to ensure that we get on with our jobs rather than get deflected by the massive media and public scrutiny of the match.

I do not think there will be a problem, because we are all experienced enough to do that, but we did make one concession to Waugh's farewell before the start of play. At Adam Gilchrist's suggestion we all lined up on the boundary's edge and formed a guard of honour to clap the captain onto the field at the beginning of his last match in charge.

Waugh is not an emotional man, and there were not too many signs of the iceman cracking here either, despite the massive wave of clapping and cheering that greeted his appearance. He patted a few shoulders and shook all our hands as he walked onto the ground, then made a gesture with his right hand to call us onto the field behind him. It was his way of saying it was time to get on with things.

As I said, we were not at our best today. Jason Gillespie, back in the side after his groin injury, in place of Brad Williams, showed signs of rustiness after a couple of weeks out of action, and Brett Lee bowled far too many no-balls — one of them costing us a wicket (when he had Virender Sehwag caught behind). That would have been okay, because he induced an edge from Sehwag again with the next ball, but Simon Katich dropped that chance — it was a carbon copy of his miss of Sehwag in Melbourne.

We were not short of support today and the atmosphere was amazing, with a full house and loads of noise all day. I always enjoy the feeling around the Sydney Cricket Ground when there is a large crowd, because despite the fact that it holds more than 40,000 fans, it still has quite an intimate feel.

Despite our errors we did eventually start taking wickets, but Sachin Tendulkar looked in ominous form during his innings, and that is a bad sign for us. He has made a significant change in his game plan: he has decided to leave all balls that are wide of the off-stump; the type we were tempting him with earlier in the series. That forced us to bowl straighter at him to try to get him out, and when we did that he either punched the ball back down the ground past the bowler using the full face of the bat or, if we drifted onto his pads, clipped the ball away through midwicket.

Tendulkar usually produces at least one hundred against us in a series, and the way he has played so far today means we will have to produce a very good delivery sometime tomorrow to stop him making that kind of score in this match.

Saturday 3 January

Fourth Test, day two: India 5–650 (Tendulkar 220 not out, Laxman 178, Sehwag 72) v Australia.

This is not how it was supposed to be. Instead of today being a fairytale for Stephen Waugh, it has turned into a nightmare for us all as Sachin Tendulkar came good with a high-class double hundred and VVS Laxman again showed us what an outstanding player he is. Together they snuffed out any hopes we had of getting back into the match. It was a boiling hot day, and we were again below par, but I don't want to take anything away from some excellent batting.

The tone for the day was set with a ragged opening spell from Brett Lee. After his no-ball troubles yesterday he tried to compensate, so today his front foot was landing at least half a metre behind the line. But what we gained in a reduced number of extras we also lost in rhythm for Lee. He had none at all, and conceded seven fours in three overs.

Part of the problem seems to be that Lee is physically cooked. He proved his fitness for the Melbourne Test by playing two Pura Cup matches, but that has been counterproductive in the longer term, because those games, together with the Boxing Day Test, have taken a lot out of him. Lee is a great trier and will keep running in, but on the evidence of today there does not appear to be much fuel left in the tank.

Stuart MacGill dropped Tendulkar twice — both were difficult, but possible, chances — but apart from that we never looked like getting him out. Once again he played without taking any undue risk, even late in the day when India might have been expected to press on towards a declaration. There was no sign of that as we walked off; India look set to bat on again tomorrow.

If we were in the same position I do not think we would play it that way, especially on such a good pitch. We would want to give ourselves as much time as possible to bowl the opposition out twice and win the match. However, India only need a draw to retain the Border–Gavaskar Trophy, and with the number of runs they have scored already, it is going to be very tough to prevent that.

Laxman was brilliant again. He really is a difficult player for us. We have tried to come up with plans to get rid of him, but he does not have too many weaknesses in his game, especially on an easy-paced surface like this one. He has a simple method, and is one of the best timers of a cricket ball ever to play the game. We did not get him out until after tea — he was our first success of the day — but Tendulkar, together with Parthiv Patel, ensured more hard labour for us before the close.

The crowd, or at least those who had turned up just to see Stephen Waugh leave international cricket in a blaze of glory, grew more and more frustrated as the day went on, aided no doubt by the hot sun and a few beers, and when MacGill dropped those chances there were a few cat-calls from some spectators. MacGill did not react but it upset Waugh, who pointed to the crest on his battered baggy green as if to say, 'We are all out there trying as hard as we can, playing for our country, and abuse does not help the situation.'

It was a frustrating day, and not a situation many of us have come across too often, especially in this country. All we could do to get through it was to try to enjoy the game: to play with smiles on our faces and stay disciplined. It may seem odd to say that we were trying to smile as India rattled along, but there was nothing to be gained by getting down about it or shouting at each other. We were doing our best, but it was not good enough.

There were some tired players in our dressing room when we got off the ground this evening, and although everyone is still upbeat, it is difficult to see how we can win from here. The key now is to retain our pride — the last thing we want to do is lose. That would hardly be the appropriate send-off for Waugh.

Sunday 4 January

Zimbabwe batsman Craig Wishart injures his left knee during Zimbabwe's build-up to their first VB Series match, against Australia on 11 January.

India name Rohan Gavaskar as the replacement for Mohammad Kaif in India's VB Series squad.

Tour match, Perth: Western Australia 9–286 (Goodwin 77, Meuleman 67, Ervine 5–56) beat the Zimbabweans 216 (Vermeulen 55) by 70 runs.

Fourth Test, day three: Australia 6–342 (Langer 117, Hayden 67, Katich 51 not out) trail India 7–705 declared (Tendulkar 241 not out, Laxman 178, Sehwag 72, Patel 62) by 363 runs.

We had a decent day, but still have a fair bit of batting to do to save this match.

India went past 700 but that did not bother us too much, apart from the obvious fact that it makes any hope we have of avoiding the follow-on — or winning the game — even more remote. We prefer to look on it as a positive: if we are going to save this Test match, India's decision to bat on this morning just means we have less time at bat to get that draw.

Our approach with the bat was not to look too far ahead. It was a case of focusing on each ball bowled, remembering our individual game plans against each bowler and not worrying about the scoreboard. If you look up and see that the opposition has 705 runs it is easy to lose focus and try to hit everything for four or six in an attempt to claw that score back, which leaves you more likely to get out, actually. The best way to deal with the situation is just to play each ball on its merits — you can only get those runs back one delivery at a time.

Justin Langer was our mainstay with the bat and that was pleasing, because he has had some rough moments in this series. He has been troubled by Ajit Agarkar's ability to swing the ball back into him, but today he came to terms with that, helped by a lack of swing on offer for India's bowlers with the new ball.

Langer also stayed more upright in his stance and played the ball a bit later than he has been doing. Part of his problem has been that his head has been following the initial line of the delivery, causing him to be unbalanced when the ball swung back into him from that line. Today he got everything right and his hundred was the reward.

Langer has an excellent record at Sydney — he scored a double hundred here against India in 2000 — so it is hardly surprising that he enjoys playing at this ground. He even treated everyone to an unusual way to get to three figures: with a reverse sweep for four from the left-arm spin of Murali Kartik. I cannot remember seeing him play that shot before, and although he said it was not premeditated, when we met mid-pitch to celebrate his landmark I had to tell him I didn't quite believe that.

I came in after Langer and Matthew Hayden got us off to a great start with a stand of 147 (at almost 5 runs per over). That emphasised how good conditions are for batting. The outfield is fast and the pitch remains excellent, although it is becoming very dry and may well offer India's two spinners, Kartik and Anil Kumble, plenty of assistance on the final day.

Kumble was India's main wicket-taker today, with four wickets, including me. He bowled tidily, as he usually does, but of course that is always easier to do when you have 705 runs behind you.

I never felt threatened by him, but his great skill is in getting the ball in the right area consistently, and he was still good enough to get me out. It was a clever piece of bowling: he bowled me four leg-breaks in a row and then beat me on the back foot with a quicker, flatter delivery that trapped me lbw.

Stephen Waugh made 40 but was undone by an excellent piece of bowling by Irfan Pathan, the young left-arm fast bowler who is only in the side because of Zaheer Khan's hamstring injury. Late in the day he started to get the old ball to reverse swing at a lively pace, and one delivery moved away late enough to catch the edge of Waugh's bat. We all wanted Waugh to go out with a hundred, similar to the brilliant hundred he made against England on this ground last summer, but in keeping with the rest of this Test so far, that particular fairytale turned out to be too much to hope for.

Pathan produced another swinging beauty to account for Adam Gilchrist just before the close of play, and although Simon Katich played really well, we are still miles behind India at this point and will have to fight our backsides off to save this Test.

Monday 5 January

Fourth Test, day four: Australia 474 (Katich 125, Langer 117, Hayden 67, Kumble 8–141) and 0–10 require 423 more runs to beat India 7–705 declared and 2–211 declared (Dravid 91 not out, Tendulkar 60 not out).

Amazingly, we have a chance of pulling off a stunning victory, despite having been outplayed for much of this match.

India gave us that chance. They declared this evening, after having declined to enforce the follow-on when we were bowled out in the mid-afternoon.

We will aim to be positive tomorrow, as we always are, but realistically, scoring more than 400 runs on a final-day pitch that is sure to offer India's spinners some assistance is unlikely. Our best hope is to secure a draw; this would draw the series at 1–1.

Today we saw Simon Katich's maiden Test hundred, which was a superb effort. The fact he played most of his innings in company with the lower order made it an even better display.

India's tactics were strange. Sourav Ganguly, rather than trying to bowl Katich out, dropped the field back for him, allowing singles to be taken. Katich was happy to do that — he had plenty of faith in Jason Gillespie, and the pair added 117 for the eighth wicket.

It meant India did not bowl us out until well after the lunch break, and as they had been in the field for a day and a half, Ganguly decided not to make us bat again, even though we failed by 32 runs to avoid the follow-on mark.

That shut the door on one possible route to victory for us: if we had batted again we may have been able to score quickly enough to set India a teasing last-day target. By batting themselves, India remained in control of the match.

When we took the field for India's second innings, our main hope was to bowl them out for around 100 and then chase the final innings target. We did get an early wicket, and the crowd was right behind us, but beyond that the plan did not work out. India's batsmen produced another dominating performance.

Gillespie had Aakash Chopra caught by Damien Martyn in the gully, but Brett Lee again struggled for rhythm. As in the first innings, he had Virender Sehwag caught behind off a no-ball, and when he did get his feet and the ball in the right place I could not hold onto the edge that came at me from Sehwag's bat. I saw the ball all the way off the bat, but Sehwag played a full-blooded square cut and I was beaten for pace — I was standing very close because of the slowness of the pitch. The ball hit my hands and was gone before I had a chance to react; that just about summed up the way things have gone for Lee in this match.

Rahul Dravid and Sachin Tendulkar played well, and soon it became a matter of trying to keep the batsmen out there for as long as possible so as to delay the declaration — that meant we would have less time to bat and therefore more of a chance to save the Test. The declaration eventually came when Lee hit Dravid on the side of the helmet with a bouncer. It left us with four overs to survive before the close of play.

Matthew Hayden and Justin Langer got through those overs, thank heavens, so if we can score steadily during the first two sessions of the day tomorrow, without losing too many wickets, maybe we will be in a position to have a go at the target after tea. That is still a long way ahead, though; our first priority must be to avoid losing wickets tomorrow morning. One of the criticisms of this side over the last few years has been that we have been poor at playing for draws when the need has arisen — the Kolkata Test against India in 2001 and the Test against England on this ground last summer are two examples. It would be nice to show we can do it if necessary.

Simon Katich

Although he is quietly spoken and seems as gentle as they come, Simon Katich is one of the toughest blokes I know, both mentally and physically. This left-hander loves getting into a contest, and that is perhaps fitting given the battle he has had to get into the Australian side — and to stay there.

He was seen as one of the next big things in Australian cricket when he was picked to tour Sri Lanka and Zimbabwe in 1999, but chickenpox ruined his tour and then cost him the next year of his career, as he suffered from some sort of reaction to the illness that left him with no energy at all. His Western Australia team-mates at that time have told me that when he was not batting or fielding he would usually be flat out in the dressing room, asleep.

He fought his way back to be included in the Australian squad that toured the UK in 2001, and made his Test debut at Headingley when Stephen Waugh was missing through injury. But when Waugh returned for the next match it was back to the sidelines for 'Kato'; another frustrating period followed as he wondered whether or not he would ever add to his single cap.

His chance did come again, but only after he moved across the country — from his home state of Western Australia to New South Wales. I do not know what the politics of that move were, although I heard that part of the reason for his switch was unhappiness at some of the internal goings-on at the WACA. Whatever the reasons, it was a gutsy move for a player everyone in the game always considered a dyed-in-the-wool man of the west.

The move has worked out perfectly for him. Cynics would say the selectors have tended to favour New South Wales players, but the truth of the matter is that the switch gave Katich a chance to develop his game. It allowed him much more of a chance to bowl his left-arm wrist, as pitches in the east are far more conducive to spin than those in Perth, and it also allowed him to develop his play against the turning ball. Those factors combined to put him in the shop window for selection when Darren Lehmann was injured during the series against Zimbabwe in 2003.

Katich did little wrong during Tests against Zimbabwe and India, with his hundred against Anil Kumble on a turning Sydney Cricket Ground pitch one of the innings of the season, but he still lost his spot to Andrew Symonds when we got to Sri Lanka — we opted for a different balance to our side in the first two Tests of that series.

I know that hit him hard, but he kept his head down and did the right thing by scoring runs when he got his next chance, in the final Test of the series, in Colombo. He came in at a crucial stage — when we lost two quick wickets on the fourth morning — and if he had been dismissed quickly we could have lost the match in a hurry. But he dug in, underlining his love of a scrap, and together with Justin Langer saw us to a total that was enough to win the match.

The one thing Katich was unable to do after that match was enjoy too much of a drink to celebrate our victory or his success: the fatigue-related illness he had previously means he can't have more than one or two beers without feeling awful the next day. His tolerance of alcohol is so low these days that his New South Wales team-mate Stuart MacGill calls him Sick Note. Another of his nicknames is Stiffy, as in a stiff neck, because if you are to the side of him he tends to turn his whole body rather than just his head to look at you.

I cannot think of a hairier cricketer in the world than Katich — his arms, especially, are covered in thick dark hair — and he has a reputation for having the biggest appetite in the Australian squad. On the UK tour of 2001 every player was asked to nominate a top five of favourite things for the official Test match magazine, and Katich's top five was all his favourite lunches in county cricket. He nominated Lord's twice on the basis that there is nothing wrong with having second helpings.

I know Katich will not mind me mentioning that because he has a great sense of humour, something he has proved over the years through his support of the Richmond Football Club. Like so many players in our squad, he is as hard as nails, has bags of talent and should be around for several years to come.

Tuesday 6 January– Wednesday 7 January

Nathan Bracken is ruled out of the opening matches of the VB Series because of a hip injury. Brad Williams replaces him in Australia's squad.

Tour match, Adelaide: Australia A 6–327 (North 115, Clarke 93) beat the Zimbabweans 208 (Flower 67, Ervine 51) by 119 runs.

Fourth Test, day five: India 7–705 declared and 2–211 declared drew with Australia 474 and 6–357 (Waugh 80, Katich 77 not out).

We could not pull off a sensational win, but we did manage to emerge from the Test with some honour after spending most of the match staring down the barrel of defeat. It was not quite the ending any of us wanted for Stephen Waugh, but avoiding defeat after chasing the match for so long was still satisfying.

Realistically, it was always going to be tough to win the match from the position we were in at the start of the day, but we all agreed before play that if any team could win from that position it was us, and we felt India knew that too.

The plan was to play each ball on its merits but be positive. If we could keep wickets intact going into the final session, we would have an outside chance of making an assault on the target if we were close enough. However, we lost wickets at awkward times during the day, and we gradually slipped behind the asking rate.

I was trying to be positive, but the spinners, Anil Kumble and Murali Kartik, got the odd ball to turn very sharply and that made it tough to play with any certainty. In the end, though, it was the left-arm fast bowler Irfan Pathan who got rid of me. He ran his fingers down the side of the ball and took the pace off it a little. The delivery held up on the pitch and I popped back a return catch off the outside half of the bat. After a largely satisfying series with the bat it was a low-key way to finish up.

The main focus was on Stephen Waugh and, as ever, he rose to the occasion. He played his favourite shot, the slog-sweep, to the spinners, and when they pulled back their length he responded with another favourite shot of his, the cut. As the match moved into the final hour it was clear that there was no chance of us winning, but there was still a chance Waugh could get a hundred. Everyone, apart from the Indian team, was willing him to get there.

With six overs left he had 20 runs to get. The atmosphere in the dressing room was tense, but in keeping with the rest of this match, there was no fairytale ending. Waugh went for the slog-sweep one more time but miscued it and sent it to Sachin Tendulkar at deep square leg.

Waugh got a fantastic ovation off the ground, not just from the crowd but also from the Indian players, and most of the spectators seemed to be waving red rags as he left. There was not much sentiment from Waugh as he left the field, which is typical of the man: just a wave of the bat and a jog up the steps, back into the dressing room.

The sentiment came afterwards, when a few of us carried him shoulder-high on a lap of the ground. It was a strange feeling. It was great to walk around the ground with Waugh and see and hear and feel this amazing reception for him, but it was also odd to think that he would never be part of the playing group again. I have played my whole Test career with Waugh either around the side or as captain, and not seeing the name Waugh on the scoreboard — both Stephen and Mark have left the international scene — will take some getting used to.

Our time as a squad in the dressing room was pretty chaotic. First Waugh had to go and speak to the media, and when he got back, there were dozens of well-wishers around. Once everyone had shaken his hand, poet Rupert McCall read us his tribute to the captain, which was excellent, and we enjoyed Waugh's company in the dressing room as captain one last time.

We also broke with tradition in two ways. First, after clearing all those people not involved with the team from the dressing room, we sang the team song even though we did not win the Test. I cannot recall us doing that at any other time during my career but it was a unique occasion; everyone felt it was the right thing to do, and it left Waugh pretty emotional.

The other thing we did was leave the dressing room relatively early. Usually at the end of a home series we hang around for hours talking and relaxing, because it is the last time we will see some of the players for a while — not every member of the squad plays in both forms of the game. This time we left to head off to a party thrown by Waugh's manager, Robert Joske.

It was a pretty select evening, topped off by Jimmy Barnes belting out 'Khe Sanh', one of the team's traditional favourites after we win a Test, and everyone joined in.

Unfortunately, by the time we got to the party I was feeling pretty unwell. It started after I was dismissed. I developed a headache and my body started to feel achy, but I put it down to the pressure of the situation and the fact that I had batted a long time in the series. I kept going until we got to Joske's house, but I was sick after just one drink, and although I was desperate to stay and be a part of this special evening, I spent most of the party going back and forth to the bathroom. I had to leave before the rest of the squad.

I got back to the hotel and felt so bad I did not have the energy to get into bed, so I slept fully clothed on top of the sheets. Just as in the West Indies last year, I spent the night going from boiling hot to freezing cold, and most of the time I was awake I was in the bathroom being sick.

It was not the ideal build-up to the first VB Series match. In the morning I did not feel well enough to fly to Melbourne with the rest of the one-day squad. I rang Steve Bernard, and he arranged for me to stay in Sydney for an extra day. Errol Alcott called a doctor to take a look at me.

I gradually felt a little better as the day went on — the doctor gave me some medication — but although I am going to fly to Melbourne to meet up with the rest of the squad tomorrow, I will need to be feeling much better to play in Friday's match.

Part 6: VB Series

WORK, REST AND WINNING

Thursday 8 January

Zimbabwe batsman Craig Wishart is ruled out of the VB Series with a knee injury. Dion Ebrahim is called up as replacement.

I was well enough to travel to Melbourne for tomorrow's opening match against India, but I still do not feel all that great. I have stopped being sick, but I am not sure I will be well enough to play; I still feel sore, and far from my best.

I did not practise today, but that did not worry me. I am happy with the way I have been playing and have spent plenty of time at the crease during the Test series.

What I did do was take part in the squad meeting we had to address how we will play.

I did not want it to be a long meeting, and not just because I wanted to go for a lie-down. Apart from Brett Lee and Jason Gillepsie, the rest of the squad played against India less than two months ago, so there was no point going over old ground just for the sake of it.

However, we did discuss how to bowl to a few of their batsmen, particularly as the pitches here in Australia will have some more bounce than the pitches we played on in India. This is what we said:

All India's batsmen – Do not be shy in using the short ball.

Sehwag – Likes width, so cramp him up, leaving no room to free his arms outside off-stump. Do not bowl too full to him.

Tendulkar – Early on try to get him bowled or lbw; he has a high percentage of dismissals like that in one-day cricket.

Ganguly – Like Sehwag, cramp him, give him no width; he will carve the ball through the off-side. Likes to use his feet to hit over the in-field in the first 15 overs, so do not worry about letting him have the odd short ball to pin him back.

Dravid – Look to bowl a fuller length to him compared with the other India batsmen. He plays the pull shot better than anyone else in the Indian top order.

Laxman – Be patient with him around the off-stump. Do not worry too much if he gets a hundred in 130 balls; that will put pressure on the players at the other end.

India are a very fine side, but in one-day cricket our record against them is excellent, especially here in Australia. We have nothing to fear tomorrow.

Friday 9 January

VB Series, match one, Melbourne: Australia (5 points) 288 (Symonds 88, Clarke 63, Agarkar 6–42) beat India (1 point) 270 (Ganguly 82, Tendulkar 63) by 18 runs.

This was not a perfect performance, but it was a great win. India were full of confidence after the Test series, but this result will have taken some wind out of their sails by reminding them that we have a great one-day record against them.

The result also means we have got off to a good start, which is not something we have always managed to do in one-day series. The first match of a home summer always follows on from the Test series, and it has often taken us until match two or three to start playing winning one-day cricket. We even lost the first match of the TVS Cup last year. It is more a mental thing, a question of getting the right tempo of play for one-day cricket, and today we did it well enough to win. I hope this says we mean business.

There were plenty of positives, not least the batting of Andrew Symonds and Michael Clarke. They came together when we were in some trouble, at 4–89, and played superbly. Although we lost those four early wickets, our scoring rate was still almost 6 runs per over when they joined forces, and rather than play conservatively to try to rebuild the innings, they kept that momentum going.

There were some big shots played with Symonds clobbering the ball down the ground and pulling savagely. Clarke got back in his crease and cut and pulled Anil Kumble, even when the ball appeared too full for the shot. But on top of those crowd-pleasing shots, there was also sensible rotation of the strike. It kept the scoreboard moving — and upset Kumble, who loves to work on one batsman for a few balls in a row, either to set him up for a particular type of dismissal, as he did with me in the Sydney Test, or just to build up pressure.

Symonds and Clarke also had the benefit of knowing that they were not the last two frontline batsmen — we had Michael Bevan to come in behind them. It may look as if we are playing one batsman too many but I like the balance of this side; it allows us to bat deep but still have four specialist bowlers, plus Symonds and Clarke as a fifth and sixth option.

The other major plus in our performance was our fielding. It is something we have spoken about a lot over the past year or so, with Mike Young, one of our coaching staff, stressing that it is no good going out and buzzing around for 10 or 15 overs and then letting that level of intensity drop off as the innings progresses. I see our ability to maintain that intensity in the field through a full 50 overs as a gauge of how well we are going overall, and tonight we were excellent in that way, with Michael Clarke and Ian Harvey pulling off a couple of pieces of brilliance when it really mattered, and sealing the win.

India wanted 32 in a little more than four overs, with six wickets in hand and the two batsmen at the crease, Sourav Ganguly and Yuvraj Singh, both going well. The batting side should win those types of finishes more often than not, but that is the time when great fielding can really turn things around, as happened tonight.

First, Clarke held onto a scorching drive from Yuvraj at midwicket. Then, next ball, Ganguly was run out by a brilliant pick and throw from the bowler, Harvey, after a mix-up with Sanjay Bangar, the new batsman. Suddenly India had two new batsmen on nought; we were able to ram home that advantage.

I also managed to make a contribution in the field, which pleased me after I'd had a soft dismissal when I batted, checking a drive to give a return catch to the medium-pacer Lakshimipathy Balaji. Sachin Tendulkar was going well and India were scoring at around the required rate of 6 runs per over when the little master tried to clip Symonds over my head at midwicket.

There is an element of luck to a catch above your head, especially if it is high enough to make you jump: you have to time your jump perfectly, hope you get your hand in the right place and then hope the ball sticks. I managed to combine all three elements, and pulled down a satisfying grab. I even managed to shock myself — after I felt the ball go into my hand and I landed safely I did not know what to do to celebrate. I ended up more or less standing there and being engulfed by my team-mates.

It was not all plain sailing for us. Our top order, including me, did not fire, and that is a concern. We cannot expect Symonds, Clarke and Bevan to bail us out all the time. We also failed to bat out our full 50 overs, which in a tight match like this could have been crucial. When we were seven wickets down and had more than six overs to go I kept sending out messages between overs to push the ball around rather than go for big shots, but those messages fell on deaf ears.

We rested Brett Lee from this match because he is very tired after a heavy program of cricket over the past four weeks. The Sydney Test showed that he needed a break. It is now up to him to recharge his batteries — and work on his run-up and his line and length in the nets. He has already proved what an effective one-day bowler he is when he gets everything right.

Saturday 10 January

Medium-pacer Amit Bhandari is added to India's squad for the VB Series.

Sunday 11 January

VB Series, match two, Sydney: Australia (6 points) 8–225 beat Zimbabwe (0 points) 126 (Williams 5–22) by 99 runs.

This ended up being a straightforward win for us but it was a poor game of cricket, thanks to a shocking pitch — it was about as different from the one we used here for last week's Test as it would be possible to get.

The ideal one-day surface is firm but with some pace, so the ball does not deviate very much and allows batsmen to play their strokes. This pitch offered seam movement and a degree of uneven bounce with the new ball, and when the spinners came on the ball turned quite a bit, but, more importantly, it also held up on the surface, making strokeplay very difficult.

In the curator's defence, I am not sure how much time he had to produce the pitch. After all, the Test match ended just five days ago. Also, no matter how poor the pitch, five of our top seven batsmen got past 20, and with a start like that, at least one of us should have gone on to reach a half-century.

At the same time, Brad Williams showed how unsuitable the pitch was for one-day cricket as he ripped through the Zimbabwe top order bowling fast off-cutters. He dismissed Mark Vermeulen and Grant Flower with balls that came back a long way. When Zimbabwe were 5–17 it was just a question of Heath Streak's side trying to achieve respectability.

Tatenda Taibu, Streak and Sean Ervine helped it do that, but there was no way Zimbabwe could win after making a start like that, even allowing for our modest total. This meant an early night for us and a chance for me to head home to Wollongong for a couple of nights before the trip to my home state of Tasmania for our next match, in Hobart.

Wednesday 14 January

VB Series, match three, Hobart: India (6 points) 3–211 (Sehwag 90) beat Zimbabwe (0 points) 6–208 (Streak 59 not out) by 7 wickets.

Thursday 15 January

Australia announce that Brett Lee will return to action for Australia's VB Series match against Zimbabwe on 16 January. Lee replaces Jason Gillespie, who is rested, while left-arm wrist-spinner Brad Hogg is also named in the starting 11, in place of Ian Harvey, also rested for the match.

Friday 16 January

VB Series, match four, Hobart: Australia (6 points) 7–344 (Gilchrist 172, Hayden 63) beat Zimbabwe (0 points) 6–196 (Streak 64 not out) by 148 runs.

It is early days in this VB Series, but it is already clear which two teams are going to be playing in the final. Zimbabwe are a poor side and we showed that today with a crushing win.

They have some solid performers, but not enough class with bat or ball to test us or India, and that was shown clearly by the gulf between the two sides at the Bellerive Oval.

The major focus for the first half of the match was on whether or not Adam Gilchrist would become the first player to score 200 in a one-day international. Stephen Waugh tipped him to do it four years ago, and he will not have too many better chances to reach that landmark than he had today.

The pitch was superb, the outfield fast and Zimbabwe's attack limited, but in the end he fell 28 runs short when he was dismissed with more than five overs left.

I felt certain Gilchrist would get 200, and said so when I came off the field after adding 106 with him for the second wicket. My share of that stand was just 37, which indicates how well he played.

Apart from his dismissal, of course, the main factor working against him was the unusually low percentage of fours and sixes he hit. Gilchrist struck 13 fours and three sixes, and 96 of his runs came in singles. Many of those were hammered straight to fielders on the boundary, at long-on, long-off, deep cover or deep square leg, and all it would have needed was to convert six or seven of those to fours for him to reach the landmark comfortably.

In the end he did not even have the satisfaction of reaching the highest score made by an Australian batsman in one-day cricket: he fell one run short of equalling Mark Waugh's innings of 173 against the West Indies at Melbourne in 2001. Everyone in the players' viewing area knew about that record but I do not think he was aware of it. Records never play much of a part in Gilchrist's thinking.

The problem of making such a big score in the first innings of a match like this against a side that is not really equipped to chase it down is that the second half of the match can drag; it was hard to avoid just going through the motions, especially after we took early wickets to remove even the slightest chance of Zimbabwe launching a genuine challenge. There is also the issue of professional pride, and we were all forced to call on that to stop switching off.

However, there was also the chance to see Brett Lee and Brad Hogg in action for the first time in the series, and both of them took the chance to get some match practice under their belts ahead of more serious challenges to come. Both bowled well but it is difficult to gauge how well they are going until they come up against the likes of Sachin Tendulkar and VVS Laxman, later in the tournament.

Sunday 18 January

VB Series, match five, Brisbane: India (5 points) 4–303 (Laxman 103 not out, Tendulkar 86, Dravid 74) beat Australia (1 point) 284 (Hayden 109) by 19 runs.

If there was any suggestion we might slip into complacency in this VB Series, that thought was well and truly knocked out of the picture tonight with a sobering loss.

On a roasting hot afternoon India thumped us around for the highest score ever made in a one-day international at the Gabba, and despite a top-quality hundred by Matthew Hayden, we could not overhaul the target.

There is plenty for us to reflect on. Once again, too many of our top order got starts but did not go on with the job. That, in the end, was probably the main reason we lost the match. We reached a point when we needed 100 at a run a ball and Hayden and Michael Clarke were going well, but by then we had lost four wickets, which meant we had little margin for error. When both players were out in quick succession, it was asking too much for Michael Bevan and the lower order to win from that position.

Hayden did play a loose drive and got out two balls after being dropped at long-on, but there is no way we can blame him for our defeat. It was his innings that kept us in the hunt; what it needed was someone to stay with him and make a similarly big contribution.

My failure was typical of our disappointing top-order display.

Adam Gilchrist and Hayden got us off to a rapid start, which is always useful when chasing a large score — it means batsmen coming in later are not under so much pressure to score quickly right from the start of their innings. But rather than consolidate, I tried to keep the momentum going, looking to take full advantage of the fact that the fielding restrictions were still in place.

Balaji banged the ball in short of a length and I tried to swing it over the leg-side, but all I succeeded in doing was getting a massive top-edge straight up in the air. It was a poor shot.

And batting was not our only concern. Brett Lee was wayward and the Indian batsmen picked him off for 83 runs from his 10 overs. It was a complete contrast to the tidy way he bowled in Hobart, although he was bowling to better players here. He struggled for rhythm and was generally either too full or too short in length. If he gets his length wrong he can go for runs even if he is swinging the ball, because a batsman only needs to get half a bat on the ball to send it flying away to the boundary. We need to work with him before the next match to try to get things right.

Although VVS Laxman scored most runs for India, reaching his hundred and bringing up the 300 off the last ball of the innings when he clobbered an Ian Harvey full toss over midwicket for four, it was Sachin Tendulkar who played India's stand-out innings. He injured an ankle early on but refused a runner, even when Sourav Ganguly came out fully padded up; he probably felt it would only cause confusion in the middle.

The way Tendulkar played showed that he did not really need a runner. He batted with plenty of patience, waiting for us to bowl too full at him — and when we did, he punched the ball straight down the ground. He also clipped Lee through midwicket when he bowled straight. Rahul Dravid also played expertly, working the ball around to rotate the strike so that he kept the scoreboard ticking over even though he did not hit many boundaries.

This win will be a real boost for India as it will convince them that they can now beat us in this form of the game. Our task is to ensure that this was a one-off.

Monday 19 January

Matthew Hayden is to be rested from Australia's match against India in Sydney on 22 January. Hayden is replaced by NSW left-hander Simon Katich, and will rejoin the squad before the match against Zimbabwe in Adelaide, scheduled for 26 January.

We are all in a state of shock today. Former Australia batsman David Hookes has died after an incident outside a pub in Melbourne on Sunday night.

I found out this morning that he was badly injured when I got a call from media manager Jonathan Rose. I turned on the television and was shocked to hear the accounts of what happened. We headed to the airport after breakfast for the flight to Sydney. None of the squad, most of whom knew him, could take in the situation. There was near silence on the bus.

Then, this evening, news came through that his life support machine had been turned off. A life gone after a needless incident at the end of what should have been a happy day following Victoria's ING Cup win over South Australia.

He and I were not close friends, but I met Hookesy regularly, especially on overseas tours, where he often worked as a television commentator, and it was always good to share a drink. We had a common interest in the AFL and our chats usually involved the relative merits of the Adelaide Crows and my team, the Kangaroos. We also enjoyed a game of golf and often chatted about that too. He hosted an excellent sports show on Victorian radio station 3AW every weekday evening, and whenever I was able to, I was happy to do an interview for him.

Hookes' death has hit some members of the squad harder than others, but we have all been affected by it — he was an Australia cricketer and someone all of us knew or knew of. For me, it is a sobering lesson about how much I take life, and everything I have from that life, for granted. As Hookes' death has shown, things can change in an instant when you least expect them to. It is a reminder that we should all make the most of everything we do.

Tuesday 20 January

Zimbabwe batsman Mark Vermeulen suffers a skull fracture after being hit over the right eye by a short ball from India's Irfan Pathan.

India vice-captain Rahul Dravid is fined 50 per cent of his match fee for a Level 2 breach of the International Cricket Council's Code of Conduct. Match referee Clive Lloyd imposed the fine after finding Dravid guilty of changing the condition of the ball.

Television pictures appeared to show Dravid rubbing a lolly into the ball during India's match against Zimbabwe in Brisbane.

VB Series, match six, Brisbane: India (5 points) 6–255 (Dravid 84, Yuvraj 69) beat Zimbabwe (1 point) 231 by 24 runs.

Wednesday 21 January

Wicketkeeper Adam Gilchrist is to be rested from Australia's VB Series matches against Zimbabwe in Adelaide (26 January) and Melbourne (29 January). He is replaced by NSW wicketkeeper Brad Haddin, and will rejoin the squad before the match against India in Perth on 1 February.

We practised today in preparation for the match with India and I spent a long time working with Brett Lee, trying to get him bowling the right length.

Before the session we took a moment, as a squad, to reflect on David Hookes' death. We all joined arms on the field and Adam Gilchrist said the incident highlighted how much we should value life. Hookesy's passing shows that life and health are more important than anything we may achieve on the field.

Thursday 22 January

Zimbabwe batsman Mark Vermeulen undergoes surgery in Brisbane to repair the skull fracture he suffered against India on Tuesday.

Sri Lanka retain Hashan Tillakaratne as its Test captain for the upcoming three-match series against Australia that starts in March. Marvan Atapattu retains his role as one-day captain for the five-match series that precedes the Tests.

VB Series, match seven, Sydney: Australia (5 points) 8–225 (Gilchrist 95) beat India (1 point) 4–296 (Yuvraj 139, Laxman 106 not out) by 2 wickets (Duckworth–Lewis method).

India will feel that this is a match they should have won. Sourav Ganguly's side produced another dominating display with the bat and then had the best of the bowling conditions after a delay for rain.

But we kept fighting — as well as doing our best to throw the match away, it has to be said — and in the end it was Brett Lee who sealed the victory, with the help of a dramatic six over extra-cover in the final over.

We were definitely helped by that rain break, as it reduced our target score, and it's always easier to maintain a relatively high run rate over a shorter period of time. But at the same time, the break also seemed to freshen up the pitch, and that assisted India's bowlers.

Lee's six capped a pretty good day for him. He bowled well, which suggests that the work we did in the nets on Wednesday has paid dividends. He maintained a reasonable line and length despite

India having a left-handed and right-handed batting combination for much of their innings — something that gave Andy Bichel and Ian Harvey a real problem.

We did not bowl especially well, but VVS Laxman and Yuvraj Singh deserve some credit for the way they played. Laxman did not score very freely, but he did rotate the strike well, giving plenty of it to Yuvraj as the innings went along; and Yuvraj once again showed us what a fine striker of the ball he is.

We first saw him in the ICC Knock-out tournament in Kenya in 2000, where he hammered a rapid half-century that helped India beat us. He has very quick swing of the bat that despatches the ball away at a rapid rate. Like many subcontinent players, he also uses his wrists very well, manoeuvring the ball into unusual areas. One of his strengths is his ability to whip straight balls backward of square on the leg-side, and he did that today.

We were chasing almost a run a ball from the start of our innings. Adam Gilchrist's response was to go on the attack right from the time he reached the crease. He went off at such an amazing rate, playing a shot a ball, that the Indians started to try to slow the game down: they had lengthy consultations between bowlers and fielders as they realised rain was coming.

When that break did come, it lasted more than 90 minutes, and when we got back onto the field we needed 152 runs from 24.2 overs, a rate not much above our original requirement. The Indians seemed to know it left us with a good chance of winning and again they tried to slow the match down, maybe in the hope of making us lose our patience — or perhaps in the hope that more rain would come.

The tactics frustrated me, and maybe contributed to my dismissal, which was basically caused by a lack of concentration. I tried to guide a slower ball from Irfan Pathan to third man but succeeded only in getting a thin edge through to the wicketkeeper, just as I was starting to find my touch.

India's negative mindset cost them the match. Sourav Ganguly's gentle medium-paced bowling was tough to hit after the rain break, because he nipped the ball around off the seam, but rather than try to bowl us out they tried to restrict us. With a relatively small target after the interruption we were always within striking distance of winning, and in the end we just managed to sneak home.

Andrew Symonds, Michael Bevan and Michael Clarke all got starts, but none of them was able to go on and see us through to victory — it was left to Lee and Bichel to do that in the end.

I would not claim to be a fortune-teller, but as the situation got tense in the final over I predicted to Duncan Kerr, our dressing room attendant, that Lee would strike the decisive blow with a six over extra-cover. But I was still amazed when Lee came up with the shot.

He has always been strong in that area, and he has been experimenting in practice with a new grip on the bat to try to improve his leg-side play. Afterwards he told me that he abandoned that new grip and went back to what he knew best out in the middle, and that six was his reward.

This is a big win, because it came after India made another big total against us. I am sure the India players thought they had the match won, especially when we lost wickets midway through our chase. Instead, we got up in the final over. I hope it sows some seeds of doubt in their minds and makes them wonder if they can win games against us when the situation gets really tight.

Brett Lee

Brett has been one of the biggest breaths of fresh air in Australian cricket since I became involved at international level, but the one thing that has become crystal clear over the past 12 months is that we must manage him better if we are to get the very best out of him.

That management process works in two ways. First of all, we must get him on the field and make sure he stays there. He has the ability to bowl fast, and he can swing the new ball away from the right-handers and the old ball back into them through reverse-swing. That is a lethal combination, but we have to make the most of it, and to do that we have to use him more wisely.

We cannot have a repeat of the situation either side of Christmas 2003, when he played back-to-back Pura Cup matches to prove his fitness after injury, then played back-to-back Test matches straight afterwards. He was on his knees by the time we got to Sydney for the last of those four matches, which meant we did not get the best out of him in that Sydney Test match or in the first half of the VB Series that followed.

We have to accept that Lee cannot bowl at top pace for 40 overs an innings; we have to use him in shorter bursts in order to maximise his effectiveness. I have been impressed with the way England has handled Simon Jones after his serious knee injury. They use him as a shock bowler rather than giving him an enormous amount of work. That is the way we have to look at Lee — he has the priceless gift of being able to bowl at 150 kilometres per hour, and not too many can do that.

One of the difficulties with a plan like this is that when you have a real diamond like Lee, the temptation is always to try to get a bit more out of him, especially as he is a willing workhorse — if you throw him the ball he will continue to try to bowl fast even when it is not in his or the side's best interests. We have to be a bit smarter in the way we handle him, because Glenn McGrath is not going to be around forever, and we need Lee to step up and be one of our spearheads in the future.

Looking after Lee's workload is one way we can manage him better; the other way is by communicating with him on a regular basis.

After I took over as one-day captain in 2002, John Buchanan and I sat down with him and laid things out. 'We cannot afford you to be conceding 60 runs per innings and bowling no-balls,' we told him. He went away and worked on his control and his problem with overstepping, and the result was his terrific performance in southern Africa.

He bowled superbly in that tournament, but still needed guidance, even during matches. I would signal from second slip, telling him what length to bowl at each batsman, and he responded — and played a major role in winning the World Cup for us.

I heard about Brett's ability to bowl fast long before I saw him for the first time. Rodney Marsh, the then boss of the Commonwealth Bank Cricket Academy, made some pretty big statements about him, and Rodney is not prone to giving someone a big rap just for the sake of it, so I knew Lee must be something special.

Then, during the Carlton & United Series of 1999, I spoke to a few of the England players who had faced him that summer and they were also raving about 'Shane's brother'. At that stage, Brett's older brother Shane was the Lee in the Australian squad. It did not take long for the situation to be reversed, with Brett taking all the headlines. Shane has been forced to retire because of a knee injury.

The issue over whether or not Brett throws the ball blew up in 2000 and there have been whispers about it occasionally since then. I have never had any doubts about the purity of his action. We all got behind him at the time, but we never discussed the matter as a team and it is not something we have ever regarded as a problem.

One of the joys of having Brett in the side, apart from his tremendous natural ability, is that he always seems to have a smile on his face, and he clearly loves playing the game. He is someone who is incredibly gifted at whatever he turns his hand to, whether it is selling suits — which he did before he became a successful player — or playing guitar in a band alongside his brother Shane and other mates from the New South Wales team.

He is also an expert at sleeping — I have never known anyone to sleep as much as he does. He will often train in the morning and then go back to bed for a few hours before getting up again after lunch. And when he goes to bed it is next to impossible to wake him, as he is a very deep sleeper. I remember when he was recalled to the side for the Perth Test against England in 2002, the media manager was hammering on his hotel door trying to get him up to speak to reporters but Brett slept on, emerging bleary-eyed after about 40 minutes, wondering what all the fuss was about.

That situation also showed why he is regarded as king of the one-liners in the dressing room. He popped his head out of the door with his hair sticking up, and when someone pointed it out he said it was not a problem, adding, 'I've been brushing my hair with a balloon.'

Add to Lee's talent with the ball his underrated talent with the bat and his electric ability in the field and you have someone who is a fairly complete package. It is now up to us to ensure that we get the most out of that package.

Friday 23 January

The India team is fined for its slow over rate during Thursday's VB Series match against Australia in Sydney. Each player is fined 15 per cent of his match fee, with Sourav Ganguly, as captain, suffering a 30 per cent fine, plus an additional 50 per cent fine for a Level 2 breach of the part of the ICC's Code of Conduct that refers to 'conduct contrary to the spirit of the game'.

Saturday 24 January

VB Series, match eight, Adelaide: India (5 points) 7–280 (Laxman 131, Dravid 56, Gavaskar 54) beat Zimbabwe (1 point) 6–277 (Carlisle 109, Ervine 100) by 3 runs.

Monday 26 January

VB Series, match nine, Adelaide: Australia (5 points) 7–279 (Bevan 75, Ponting 63) beat Zimbabwe (1 point) 8–266 (Flower 94) by 13 runs.

Although the margin of this win was only 13 runs, we were in fact never likely to lose the match. Our total was solid without being out of sight, but once Jason Gillespie, Brett Lee and Brad Williams restricted the Zimbabwe top order, they were always behind the asking rate.

It is in situations like this, where the result is never really in doubt as long as we retain our professional approach, that the media look to find another angle, and in this case they have settled on the form of Damien Martyn.

While most of our top order has made at least one significant contribution in this series, Martyn is the odd man out — so far, at least. That has not always been his fault. He has not always had the chance to build a decent innings, which was why we gave him the opportunity today to open the innings. He has done the job before, even scoring a hundred against Zimbabwe as opener in Perth in 2001, and on a warm day and with a decent pitch to bat on this was his chance to return to his best.

It did not quite work out that way. He played one superb cover drive but then flashed a drive square of the pitch to be brilliantly caught by Dion Ebrahim. Even players in great form can fall in that way, but more often than not it seems to happen when a player is short of runs.

Not that long ago Martyn scored a brilliant hundred to help us win a match in the TVS Cup in Mumbai, and in that same tournament he partnered me in a substantial stand in Bangalore. But he has also gone almost two years without a Test match hundred, and although that is a different form of the game, it is a statistic that is being used to beat him at the moment.

Martyn is probably my closest friend in the current Australia squad, but that does not mean I am blind to the calls for his head. That is not a decision I have to make — the captain is not a selector — but I am sure Trevor Hohns and his colleagues will stick with Martyn for the time being.

Martyn is down on form and confidence, there is no doubt about that, but it makes no sense to dump a player of his ability just for that. He has a great deal of experience, and it is far better to back him — as we did today by promoting him — than to just toss him aside and call in a replacement who may take time to bed in.

I played pretty well and felt set for a hundred, but was undone by a brilliant piece of fielding by Andy Blignaut. I skipped down the pitch to Ray Price's left-arm spin, clipped the ball to Blignaut's right at midwicket and called 'Wait' to my partner, Michael Bevan, because I expected the ball to beat the fielder and go for runs. In a flash Blignaut stopped the ball and threw it back to the wicketkeeper while still on his knees. I saw what was happening too late and tried to regain my ground, but was out by a fraction. It was frustrating, but it was also a piece of fielding I would have been proud of.

Damien Martyn

There are a few players — like Shane Warne or Glenn McGrath — who revel in the limelight, but Damien Martyn is not one of them. One journalist I know refers to Martyn as Australian cricket's best-kept secret, and that just about sums him up: he's happy to be in the background while others take the headlines.

I think that desire stems from a tough period he went through in the early to mid-1990s, when he slid from golden boy to forgotten man in very quick time.

He had been marked down as a rising star of Australian cricket from an early age, and captained the under-19 side — which also included Adam Gilchrist and Michael Kasprowicz — before going on his first Ashes tour at the age of 21.

Maybe that level of success came too quickly for him and he thought he was a world-beater, but when he failed at the highest level, most notably against South Africa in a closely fought Test in early 1994, he immediately found himself on the other side of the fence, in the glare of bad publicity, and it affected him quite badly.

Even now he hates being interviewed, although he accepts that it is part and parcel of his life as an Australian cricketer. The unhappy memories of 1994 and the couple of years that followed may have been behind his gesture to a television cameraman as he struggled for runs during the recent VB Series.

When he was dropped by the selectors in 1994 he went back to Western Australia, but for several years he could not score anywhere near the number of runs he should have or needed to in order to get back into the Test side. But thanks in large part to his state captain, Tom Moody, and his coach, Wayne Clark, he got himself back together and started the journey back up the ladder to the Australian side.

One of the things Martyn put in place at that time was a dietary and training regime that has left him in good shape ever since. He trained as hard as anyone to drop weight and increase strength and stamina, and the great thing is that once he got back into the Test side he maintained and even intensified that regime. I use him as an example to anyone who thinks they have made it once they break into the Australian team. As Martyn showed second time around, making the team is where the hard work begins.

He has had to be patient. After breaking back into the one-day side in the summer of 1997/98, it took him another two years to win back his Test place — when I missed the tour of New Zealand through injury. Even then, though he performed solidly, he did not become a regular again until the Ashes tour of 2001. On that trip, when he scored Test hundreds at Edgbaston and Headingley, he showed everyone how good a player he is.

In contrast with Hayden and Gilchrist, who frequently bludgeon the ball with raw power, Martyn's play is typified by timing, especially through the off-side. He is one of the best players in the world at hitting through or over cover, and I hope he can continue to display that talent for a few years to come.

Tuesday 27 January

We delayed our departure for Melbourne and our next match in the VB Series in order to attend David Hookes' funeral at the Adelaide Oval this morning.

It was a touching ceremony, and was attended by everyone from the general public right up to movie actor Russell Crowe. I sat next to Darren Lehmann, Hookes' great friend and someone who was next to him during the incident that led to his death, just over a week ago. Lehmann managed to keep himself together pretty well through the ceremony.

There was one particularly moving moment when the Robbie Williams song *Angels* was played. The giant video screen at the ground cut to a shot of two people in the crowd, a young lad on the grass bank in front of the scoreboard, cricket bat in hand, running to and hugging his father. The timing of the shot, with the music playing, could not have been better — it brought a lump to my throat.

Wednesday 28 January

Tour match, Canberra: The Indians 8–254 (Badani 100) beat the Prime Minister's XI 6–253 (Brown 80, North 74) by 1 run.

Thursday 29 January

Ricky Ponting is to be rested for the VB Series match against India in Perth on 1 February. Adam Gilchrist will lead the side, with Simon Katich replacing Ponting in the squad for the match.

VB Series, match ten, Melbourne: Australia (3 points) 9–263 (Bevan 56) v Zimbabwe (3 points). Match abandoned because of rain.

This was a frustrating day. We posted a decent score in cool, overcast conditions, and on an MCG pitch that offered Zimbabwe's seam bowlers some assistance. Then, as we prepared to go out for their innings, it began to rain — and it didn't stop for the rest of the evening.

There was plenty to keep me occupied, though. Michael Bevan had injured a rib in a previous match and it began to give him real discomfort as he batted. When he came off the field he went and had an X-ray, and it confirmed there is a crack. That meant we needed a replacement for the match in Perth; it also brought into question Bevan's place in the one-day squad for the tour of Sri Lanka that starts in a couple of weeks.

Andrew Hilditch was the selector on duty at the match, so he and I discussed who might step in. We spoke of the possibility of Darren Lehmann coming back into the squad, but the selectors are against that idea at the moment. He has just returned to action for South Australia after a long period out of the game with an Achilles tendon injury and they want to see how he copes with the next couple of matches: he has an ING Cup match on Friday and a four-day Pura Cup match that starts two days later. My view is we would get a better idea of his fitness by playing him in Sunday's VB Series match, because there is less opportunity for a player to coast at international level than at state level, but I did not win the debate.

The player who will step in is Michael Hussey, a left-hander who has built a reputation as a fine one-day player over the past few years. He started off as an opening batsman and still does that job in first-class cricket, but he slid down the order in the one-day game and now plays a similar role to Bevan for his state, Western Australia. The selectors are keen to have a look at him at international level, and as Sunday's match is at his home ground it is, in many ways, the ideal time to introduce him. It shows that we have more than one option, and that is a very good thing.

Bevan is naturally desperate to tour Sri Lanka, and is keen for us to give him as much time as possible to be fit. Team doctor Trefor James confirmed that it would be possible for him to be right for the first one-day international in three weeks' time. We will monitor his progress over the next week or so — Bevan remains in the mix for the trip at this stage.

Before the rain ruined the match Damien Martyn got some time in the middle, and although he did not make a big score, his 42 from 40 balls was evidence that he is finding his form again. He played very well, again opening the innings, but his dismissal suggested that luck is still not really going his way. It was raining — one of several showers we had through the day — and the umpires were about to take the players off, but they opted to complete the over in progress first. Of course that was the over in which Martyn was trapped lbw. It left him pretty frustrated.

Michael Bevan

When the history of one-day cricket is written, you can be sure that Michael Bevan will get a pretty big mention. He has been an amazing player in the short form of the game, and his average — more than 50 runs per innings over a sustained period of time — is unlikely ever to be matched or bettered.

It is possible to argue that the average is inflated by a large number of not outs, and that is true. But it also reflects the fact that more often than not Bevan has been undefeated because he has either seen his side to victory or helped it post a defendable score when batting first.

To watch Bevan at the crease in a one-day game is an amazing sight. He has so much experience that he instinctively knows how to handle each situation, and he has got us home on many occasions when all seemed to be lost: Sydney 1997 against the West Indies, Melbourne 2002 against New Zealand, two World Cup games at Port Elizabeth against England and New Zealand in 2003, and plenty of other matches.

Bevan is especially skilful at batting with the lower order. If tailenders are kept scoreless for any length of time in a one-day game they will usually look for a big shot. Bevan is a huge calming influence in those situations, virtually telling the batsmen how to play each over. The chase against England during the World Cup was a case in point. As each lower order player came in, Bevan would spend half a minute or so telling him how they could win the game, and then kept reinforcing the message after every over.

For Bevan not to have made more of his talents at Test level is one of the great mysteries of the game, especially given his run-scoring feats in the first-class game, where he is New South Wales' leading all-time batsman.

There has been a question mark over the way he handled short-pitched bowling when he last played at Test level. That has been something he has tried to address, and as recently as a couple of years ago he worked with a baseball coach in an attempt to master the hook and pull shots.

Perhaps another factor in his failure to play more Tests has been his apparent reluctance to bowl more often. Bevan was a good enough wrist-spinner to take 10 wickets in a Test match against the West Indies in 1997, and if he had persisted with his bowling he surely would have earned further caps.

I know everyone in authority I spoke to always wanted him to bowl more often, but for some reason he never seemed to do so for New South Wales and in the absence of match practice it meant that when he came into the one-day international side it was not something any captain was prepared to gamble on.

Maybe that reluctance to bowl has something to do with longstanding groin problems that have bothered him more and more over recent years. He has been increasingly prone to niggling injuries, and the groin problem he suffered before the 2003 World Cup almost ruled him out of the tournament.

Bevan is a private man and likes doing things his own way, and when he was younger he had a reputation as a bit of a hothead. In the days when players had to share rooms on tour he was not the most popular room-mate, as he insisted on quiet and total darkness in the room as soon as he was ready for sleep, which even extended to covering up the power light on the television that indicated it was connected to the electricity. That is not to say he is unpopular; far from it. It is just that he is an individual and it is always a case of recognising that fact and giving him some space.

The selectors' decision not to name Bevan in the 2004 list of Cricket Australia contracted players suggests that his international career is over. But knowing him, and knowing that he has made a career out of turning around seemingly hopeless situations, I am sure he will be out to prove them wrong.

Friday 30 January–Saturday 31 January

Michael Hussey is named as Michael Bevan's replacement for the VB Series match against India in Perth.

Sachin Tendulkar and Virender Sehwag are both confirmed starters for the Perth match on Sunday. Tendulkar has recovered from the ankle injury he suffered in Brisbane, and Sehwag has recovered from a shoulder strain.

Damien Martyn is reprimanded by Cricket Australia after he is seen on film making a raised-finger gesture to a cameraman recording the squad's departure from its Melbourne hotel.

I headed back to Wollongong for a break but my phone has still been busy. Cricket Australia let me know about the incident involving Damien Martyn and I spoke to him before a media release was issued confirming his reprimand.

He feels under the media spotlight at the moment, but I reminded him that that was no excuse, especially as it went against our commitment at the start of the season to uphold the Spirit of Cricket.

I also took the chance to see how he is feeling. He is a little bit low. He likes to know that he is contributing to the success of the side, and at the moment does not feel that he is doing that. I told him how highly everyone in the team rates him, and also reminded him of the vital part he played in our success only a couple of months ago in

India. I hope it made him feel better; I also hope that a few days at home in Perth during this match will lift his spirits. It can be tough for players from the west during a domestic summer, because most of the season is played out in the east — trips home are far more time-consuming and harder for them to slot in.

Sunday 1 February

VB Series, match eleven, Perth: Australia (6 points) 5–204 (Gilchrist 75, Symonds 73) beat India (0 points) 203 by 5 wickets.

I did not see much of this match, but what I did see was very encouraging, especially with the finals series coming up at the end of the week.

We took advantage of a fast, bouncy pitch at the WACA ground to unnerve a few of India's top order through some aggressive fast bowling, then Adam Gilchrist and Andrew Symonds blitzed their attack by adding 122 in 16 overs. We won with a massive 18 overs in hand. It was great entertainment and something for India to think about.

The way their top order struggled against our fast bowlers in what were typical Perth conditions shows what a different Test series it might have been if we had played a Test, especially the first one, in the west. It could have knocked the stuffing out of a few of India's players right at the start of the summer and we could have gone on to dominate the series. Unfortunately that did not happen, and the India batsmen were more than a match for us on the pitches that were produced.

Tuesday 3 February

Australia names a 13-man squad for the VB Series finals. It is: Ricky Ponting (captain), Michael Clarke, Adam Gilchrist, Jason Gillespie, Ian Harvey, Matthew Hayden, Brad Hogg, Michael Kasprowicz, Simon Katich, Brett Lee, Damien Martyn, Andrew Symonds and Brad Williams.

Sri Lanka's selectors name a 25-man training squad for the upcoming one-day series against Australia. It is: Marvan Atapattu (captain), Russel Arnold, Upul Chandana, Kumar Dharmasena, Tillakaratne Dilshan, Buddhika Fernando, Dinusha Fernando, Chamila Gamage, Darshana Gamage, Avishka Gunawardena, Rangana Herath, Dinuka Hettiarachchi, Saman Jayantha, Sanath Jayasuriya, Mahela Jayawardene, Romesh Kaluwitharana, Thilina Kandamby, Nuwan Kulasekara, Kaushal Lokuarachchi, Muttiah

Muralitharan, Ruchira Perera, Kumar Sangakkara, Chamara Silva, Chaminda Vaas and Nuwan Zoysa.

Fast bowler Dilhara Fernando is left out of the squad; he is suffering the latest in the series of back injuries that have dogged his career.

VB Series, match twelve, Perth: India (6 points) 6–136 beat Zimbabwe (0 points) 135 by 4 wickets.

I did not watch much of the final qualifying match on TV, but from what I did see, India once again struggled to come to terms with the extra bounce in the Perth pitch, even against a Zimbabwe attack that lacks a genuinely fast bowler of high quality. Zimbabwe could even have won the match if they had taken all their catches.

With the 12 qualifying matches now over, everyone can focus on the finals series, although it has been pretty obvious almost from the start of the tournament that we would be meeting India in the final.

Zimbabwe have not won a match in eight attempts, and although they came close to beating India in three of their four meetings, the results have made the tournament far too predictable. Many of the matches cannot have been much fun to watch, and some of them were not great fun to play in either. I realise there will always be some sides that are stronger than others in international cricket, but I hope the ICC can do something to help lift the standards of the teams at the lower end of the ladder, because putting an inferior product on show does nobody any good.

MIKE HUSSEY

If other countries are looking for reasons why Australian cricket is currently so strong then they do not need to look much further than a player like Mike Hussey.

That might seem a strange thing to write, given he has played a single one-day international, but it is the pressure he and players like him continue to apply to the guys in the Australian squad that helps keep those of us on the inside so hungry for success. If there was no competition for places from outside, players might be tempted to cruise without pushing themselves all the time.

I have not yet played with Mike as his solitary appearance came in Perth when I was resting ahead of the VB Series finals of 2004, but the way he has developed his game has certainly impressed me. He started off as a solid opener but in recent years he has reinvented himself in the one-day game as an explosive finisher for the Western Warriors in the ING Cup, batting at high tempo towards the end of an innings. On top of that, he is an electric fielder and also bowls useful medium pace, another aspect of his game he has developed in recent seasons. It is that complete package — a phrase used a lot in one-day terms these days — which makes him such an attractive proposition for the selectors.

Mike is another player who has benefited from playing county cricket in the UK, like Michael Kasprowicz. It is not something that will suit everyone but Huss used the opportunity county cricket provides to play lots of innings in different conditions and varying situations to develop his game, and the results have been obvious. He is certainly a more complete player than he was before he went away. While he was in the UK he also got the chance to captain county side Northamptonshire and that will have aided his development still further.

Having quality players like Mike around is exciting for me, because I know we have the potential to remain strong even if injuries hit us; which is reassuring given the heavy international program we have over the next year or so.

Thursday 5 February

Glenn McGrath's return to competitive action has been postponed again. The fast bowler, who has been recovering from ankle surgery, was hoping to prove his fitness for the forthcoming tour of Sri Lanka by playing in a second XI match for New South Wales against Tasmania in Hobart, starting on 9 February, but he is still not quite ready for the outing.

India spinner Anil Kumble is rated a 50–50 chance to be ready for the first VB Series final as he battles to recover from a shoulder injury.

Friday 6 February

VB Series, first final, Melbourne: Australia 3–224 (Ponting 88, Hayden 50) beat India 222 (Badani 60 not out, Agarkar 53) by 7 wickets.

This match was the perfect start to our finals campaign. We intimidated India's batting with some aggressive fast bowling and then, after they gained some respectability through useful innings by Hemang Badani and Ajit Agarkar, our top order hammered India's bowling into submission. It meant the match was not a fantastic spectacle, but I was more than pleased with our performance — parts of our cricket were excellent. India now have it all to do to force this series into a third final.

That is something we are desperate to avoid. This year it is due to take place in Adelaide next Tuesday: this would mean another flight and then just one day at home before the Allan Border Medal day in Melbourne on Thursday 12 February, with the departure to Sri Lanka the day after that. I know we should look forward to every international match, but three days at home and away from the spotlight is priceless — it would give everyone the chance to recharge their batteries before the trip to Sri Lanka.

If we play on Sunday (in Sydney) the way we did here, India will struggle to take the series to a decider. We bowled and fielded with real purpose today, especially in the first part of their innings, and that was where the match was won and lost.

Jason Gillespie found some bounce bowling short of a length from the southern end of the ground, and made life miserable for Virender Sehwag, who flapped a short ball to Adam Gilchrist. Then Brett Lee knocked over the big wicket of Sachin Tendulkar with some seriously quick bowling.

Lee pinned Tendulkar back in his crease then beat him through the gate with a rapid ball that was pitched up slightly further than the others. Tendulkar's crouching down on his haunches after he played the shot suggested that the ball had kept low, but in reality he was just beaten for pace.

Ian Harvey and Brad Williams kept up the pressure, with Harvey grabbing the wicket of Sourav Ganguly, helped by excellent work from Gilchrist. Ganguly loves to waltz down the pitch to the seam bowlers, so that he can free his arms and hit them down the ground, but he was penned in his crease when Gilchrist decided to stand up to the stumps — that brought into play the threat of being stumped. Restricted by Gilchrist's move, Ganguly tried to cut a ball that was too close for the shot; he could only edge it, and Gilchrist took a fine catch.

By the time Badani and Agarkar joined forces India were 6–75, but both of them batted very well. We have seen Badani play well in the past — he got a hundred against us in Pune in a one-day international in 2001 — but Agarkar was a revelation, especially as he has made countless noughts against us. He is obviously a very nervous starter, but once he gets settled he can strike the ball cleanly, as he did today, especially over mid-off and wide mid-on. It was a relief when we eventually dismissed him, with almost ten overs left.

If Agarkar had stayed with Badani until the end of the innings we could have been chasing 250, but the way we batted, even that would not have been a tough task. Gilchrist got us off to a rapid start with 38 from 20 balls, then I maintained the tempo with Matthew Hayden.

Hayden kept the scoreboard ticking over by feeding me the strike — I felt in great form right from the start of the innings. Melbourne is my lucky one-day ground in Australia. It is the only place in Australia where I have reached three figures in this form of the game, and I felt as though I would do it again tonight.

The rest has obviously done me no harm. My feet moved well and I picked up the ball very early, swivelling on a few pull shots when the bowlers dropped short, as well as punching the ball through extra-cover if the ball was over-pitched. My balance was also good, and I was able to clip the ball through midwicket without falling over to the off-side, something I do when I am out of form.

By the time I feathered a catch to the wicketkeeper we wanted less than 30 to win. Damien Martyn and Andrew Symonds finished off the job. There were plenty of smiles and shouts in the dressing room when it was all over, but no one is making the mistake of thinking the job is done yet.

Sunday 8 February

Michael Bevan is passed fit to tour Sri Lanka.

VB Series, second final, Sydney: Australia 5–359 (Hayden 126, Martyn 67, Symonds 66) beat India 151 by 208 runs.

This win shows why we are the best side in the world. After a long home season when we have not always been at our best, we played out of our skins in all departments of the game and completely overwhelmed India.

The scale of India's defeat suggests that they ran out of steam at the vital stage of the one-day campaign, but to put it in those simple terms would be to imply that they lost the match. That was not the case here. We won it, with some aggressive cricket that India just could not cope with.

Our batting was built around three major contributions, with Matthew Hayden scoring a brilliant hundred, Damien Martyn offering sensible support for 67 and Andrew Symonds adding the icing on the cake with a blazing 66 from just 39 balls. Any fight the Indians had after Hayden's pummelling was knocked out of them by Symonds and Michael Clarke, who made 33 from just 20 balls to see us to the same massive score we reached in the World Cup final 11 months ago.

Until Hayden tired, he'd had a chance of a double hundred. He raced to 50 from just 37 balls, bullying the bowlers by clubbing them back over their heads and then pulling and cutting them for further boundaries when they pulled their lengths back. Hayden made spinner Murali Kartik's life a misery when he came on to bowl, sweeping him mercilessly. We were racing along at 6 runs an over even after the fielding restrictions were lifted at the end of 15 overs.

Martyn showed why he is such a valuable member of the one-day side, doing the same job he has done with me at the other end so often in the past, rotating the strike to get the form player back to face the bowling, and making sure the runs do not dry up at one end by scoring at almost a run a ball.

When he and Hayden were out in quick succession there was a chance that India could peg us back to around 300, which would have been an achievable target on an excellent pitch and with a fast outfield. But Symonds and Clarke put paid to that idea with some awesome hitting. Symonds, in particular, took us from a point where 290 was a likely score to that 350 total. And that was way beyond India.

Apart from my dismissal, out to a stupid shot where I had a brain explosion and tried to hit Irfan Pathan out of the ground, it was one of those days where everything went right. It showed when it came our turn to field as well: we had both openers caught at short fine leg by Brett Lee.

I would like to say it was planning, but the truth is, it was a total fluke. We had to have two fielders outside the 30-yard circle in the first 15 overs, and normally they are fine leg and third man. But we knew India had to attack right from the start of the innings if they were going to get anywhere near our total, and we felt their batsmen would find it easier to hit the ball to deep square leg than to fine leg, especially if our new ball bowlers were going to try to maintain an off-stump line. So we opted for that square leg fielder on the boundary, which meant fine leg had to be up inside the circle.

It was not a catching position; we were just lucky that Lee has such great reflexes. He took two blinding catches there off Jason Gillespie, getting rid of first Virender Sehwag, then Sachin Tendulkar.

Sehwag hit the ball straight at Lee, but Lee still had to react quickly, because the batsman was clipping away a delivery that had been bowled at around 145 km/h. That made his grab of Tendulkar even better: on that occasion the ball was wide of him, but he dived and plucked the ball out of the air quite brilliantly.

That gave us a massive boost — and knocked the wind out of India's sails. Our mood was pretty well illustrated by Martyn's run out of Dravid: it was a direct hit from cover with only one stump to aim at. I always say that our fielding is a barometer of how well we are going as a side, and Lee's two catches and that piece of work told the story today.

It was as emphatic a win in a finals series as you could wish to see, and a great boost to our morale ahead of the series in Sri Lanka. We played as if we wanted the extra couple of days at home — and after a performance like that, everyone deserves that time.

After the match and the presentations, we were joined in the dressing room by a few of the Indian players, to reflect on the end of a long and tough battle in both forms of the game: Tests and one-day internationals.

I spent the evening chatting with Rahul Dravid, and he showed me what a decent and generous man he is. He said he had followed my career from the time I first broke into the Australian side and was delighted for me at how far I have come both within the team and as a player. It just goes to show that although we play it tough on the field, there is still room for sentiment and friendships in a competitive environment.

We sang the team song, led by Adam Gilchrist, for one last time in this home summer, and it reminded me of something. As I have become Test captain, I should now pass over the honour of leading the team song in that form of the game to another player. I have just over a month to come up with the name of a team-mate to fill that role.

Monday 9 February

Irfan Pathan is reprimanded for a breach of the ICC's Code of Conduct after mocking Damien Martyn when he dismissed him in Sunday's second final of the VB Series, in Sydney.

Australia announce a 15-man squad for the one-day series in Sri Lanka starting on 20 February. It is: Ricky Ponting (captain), Michael Bevan, Michael Clarke, Adam Gilchrist, Jason Gillespie, Brad Haddin, Ian Harvey, Matthew Hayden, Brad Hogg,

Michael Kasprowicz, Simon Katich, Brett Lee, Damien Martyn, Andrew Symonds and Brad Williams.

Tuesday 10 February

Shane Warne made his long-awaited comeback to cricket today, playing for Victoria's second XI against the Queensland Academy of Sport at the Junction Oval in Melbourne.

Judging by the amount of coverage in the media, anyone would have thought it was the start of World War III, but that is the pulling power of Warne. Although rain meant he did not bowl, it is still good to know he is back playing cricket again.

I have spoken to him at various times through the summer — he has been working for Channel Nine in its commentary team — and he has retained the enthusiasm he showed me when we met in my hotel room in India during the TVS Cup last November.

He has the chance to play some cricket between now and when the Test squad for the tour of Sri Lanka is named, in about ten days' time, and as long as he can convince everyone that he is fit and can still land the ball where he wants with plenty of spin on it, I cannot see why we would not pick him for the trip.

He has been rushed back into the side before after long breaks, though, and it has not always worked. I can remember his return after shoulder surgery in 1999 and after a broken finger in 2001 as two examples of Warne returning to the side before he was ready, and his form and figures showed that it did not work. However, this time he is not returning from injury, and the 12 month rest may have done him some good. It has been 12 months without a high workload on his shoulder, spinning fingers and left knee; if that means we get an extra year or two out of him, that is a bonus out of a sad episode for him and Australian cricket.

Thursday 12 February

Ricky Ponting is named the Allan Border Medallist for 2004 at an awards dinner at Crown Casino, Melbourne.

Ponting polled 139 votes (cast by players, umpires and the media) and is the fifth winner of the award, which honours Australia's outstanding international cricketer over the previous 12 months.

He was 48 votes clear of second-placed Matthew Hayden and 69 votes clear of Adam Gilchrist, who finished third.

Ponting follows previous winners Glenn McGrath (2000), Stephen Waugh (2001), Matthew Hayden (2002) and Adam Gilchrist (2003).

Gilchrist was named one-day international player of the year, Simon Katich was named state player of the year and South Australia fast bowler Shaun Tait was named the Bradman young cricketer of the year.

Part 7:
Australia in Sri Lanka

MISSIONS ACCOMPLISHED

Friday 13 February

I might have scooped the most prestigious individual award in Australian cricket last night, but that didn't qualify me for special privileges this morning — like a sleep-in. I had to be up at 7 o'clock to get ready for a round of breakfast media interviews about my success at the AB Medal.

Not that I needed too much incentive to get up: after all, it was the day I travelled to Sri Lanka for my first tour as not only one-day but also Test captain. Going there on the back of a fantastic season for me personally is the perfect platform. It's now up to me to maintain the standards I've set myself.

Very quickly I began to spot a pattern emerging at the media interviews, with quite a few interviewers focusing on my dress at the dinner rather than my efforts as a cricketer. I had opted for a pin-striped suit, no tie and a wide-lapelled shirt, and it was my fashion sense that seemed to attract the most questions. I treated it in a fairly light-hearted way but was still a bit taken aback by the number of comments my clothes seemed to provoke.

At 9.30 it was time for my pre-departure media conference about the Sri Lanka tour. Even there some reporters seemed keen to quiz me on my choice of clothes the previous evening — Channel Seven sent a reporter specifically for that purpose. It must have been a slow news day.

The key message I wanted to get across at the press conference was about the type of cricket I want us to play on the tour. I am looking for us to play the same attacking brand of cricket overseas as we do at home. Having said that, I am also mindful of the conditions we're likely to find in Sri Lanka. It will be hot, the pitches will offer turn, and patience may well be the key. I want us to marry a patient approach with our natural desire to dominate — that combination will make us extremely tough to beat.

There were also questions, inevitably, about Shane Warne and whether or not he will be picked for the Test series. That squad is to be named next Friday (20 February). I am not a selector, so it is not my place to go around making public pronouncements on who should or should not be in that squad, but I tried to talk Warne up as much as I could and I think most people expect he will be on that list when it comes out. He has so much experience and, hopefully, his year-long enforced rest will have allowed him to recharge his batteries. Of course he has not bowled very much lately, but with a player of his class and ability — and who, these days, keeps himself very fit — I don't think that should be an issue.

There was no media to do out at the airport, just some photographers and cameramen there to record us checking in and heading to the departure gate. I said goodbye to Rianna with the promise that I would see her in a few weeks' time — she's coming to Galle for the first Test — and then we were off. It was the type of departure most of us have done countless times, but for me there was an added thrill: I am captain of the whole trip. I can't wait for the cricket to start.

Saturday 14 February

We arrived in Sri Lanka in the early hours after a stop in Singapore that saw us collect our coach, John Buchanan. He'd opted out of the AB Medal night to spend some more time with his family, and then Cricket Australia allowed him to fly straight to Singapore from Brisbane.

As usual, Buchanan had a huge grin on his face — as well as his video camera in his hand — when we ran into him, but by the time we got to Colombo most of us were well past grinning. Even though we get to fly business class, a long-haul flight can take it out of you, and this one was no exception. By the time we cleared customs it was 2 o'clock in the morning, local time, and everyone wanted just one thing: a bed to sleep in. I felt really shattered, not just because of the late hour, but also, I think, because of all the events of the past 24 hours or so. When I was awarded the AB Medal and then doing all the media around that and this tour, I think the adrenaline was flowing, but on the plane that buzz soon stopped and tiredness kicked in.

We were met by Chitral Mendis, our liaison officer for the tour, and he whisked us onto the team bus for the drive into Colombo, a trip of about 45 minutes. Even coming through the airport at night you could feel the humidity in the air. That is something we will have to get used to for the next six weeks or so. Our ability to cope with conditions will be a key to our success on this trip. Once at the hotel, we were presented with garlands of flowers around our necks and the all-important keys to our rooms. It was off to bed, and nothing but sleep to think about.

The first commitment for most of the players was at 4 o'clock: a meet the media session. I was excused, as I had spoken to the media before departure and I am slated to appear at a pre-series launch along with the Sri Lankans in a day or so.

Once that was over it was time for our first team meeting of the tour. Rather than focusing on tactics, this one was all about logistics — and there was a bit of fun thrown in by Adam Gilchrist at the end. Reg Dickason, our security manager, gave us a list of dos and don'ts; the don'ts included travelling by tri-shaw. These are the three-wheel taxis that dodge in and out of traffic. Some are more reliable than others, as Zimbabwe captain Heath Streak found out 18 months ago during the Champions Trophy. His taxi flipped over and he dislocated his shoulder — it put him out of cricket for a few months. As Reg pointed out, we can do without that sort of accident.

Alex Kontouri, our physiotherapist, then chatted to us. Alex is with us because our long-time physio, Errol Alcott, is taking some well-deserved time away to work with Russell Crowe on a movie project. Errol will be missed, as he has been in the job for almost 20 years, but having Alex, who was also with us for the TVS Cup, is a real bonus. Not only is he a great operator, but he is also an expert in all things Sri Lankan — he was physiotherapist to their squad for most of the past decade. Alex gave us a list of approved restaurants, handed out malaria tablets and reminded us that with the heat and humidity we should try to drink water whenever possible, including decent amounts at breakfast. Ideally, we should get a couple of litres into us before play every day, as well as making sure we top up throughout the day with more water and Gatorade. Most of us are aware of the need to stay hydrated, but it is one of those things you can never remind players of too much.

For my part, I wanted to put a flag down straight away. The one thing I do not want on the trip is whingeing. The pitches, the practice facilities, the temperature and humidity, the umpiring — or anything else, for that matter — are all facts of life in this part of the world and we just have to get used to them. Moaning and looking for excuses will only bring us down and, after all, all those conditions will be the same for the other side. Everyone agreed with my approach, which is pleasing but also not surprising. We have adopted the same type of attitude on all our recent tours, especially to the subcontinent. All the same, I thought it was worth repeating.

Business over, it was time for Gilchrist, ever the king of the social scene on tour, to take over. He wanted everyone to reassemble in the hotel bar later and to come prepared with a special fact about themselves, something no one else knew.

It was a great idea, and although some of the resulting information is not fit for a family diary, other snippets gave us a whole new view on members of the touring party. Simon Katich, for example, said he has little or no sense of smell — just about the only thing he can smell is embrocation. Jason Gillespie tried to learn to play the saxophone as a youngster because he liked the theme from *The Pink Panther*. He gave it up when he kept leaving his instrument on the bus and had to make regular trips to the bus station to see if someone had handed it in. Michael Kasprowicz had us in fits of laughter when he revealed that he took dancing lessons as a 12-year-old in an attempt to impress a girl.

My fact was about the way I spent my last night in Australia before my first Ashes tour, in 1997. Rather than sit at home nervous about the trip or go out and have a few drinks, I went to Hobart in the back of a van with one of my greyhounds, Josie's Joy. She was racing that night, but was considered a real roughie, priced around $26 and given no chance. I spent the whole of the trip south patting her to try to keep her calm in the van, but once we arrived at the track she started to bark. She had never done that before, but right up until the start of the race she did not stop barking. It turned out to be a good sign — she won the race and gave me a memorable moment before the Ashes tour.

As for Gilchrist, his fact was a really odd one. He said that at school he used to sign autographs and give them out to people, saying they should keep them, because he would be famous one day. One day at a Sydney Test a couple of years ago, Gilchrist was on the players' balcony waiting to bat when someone shouted up to him. He thought he recognised the bloke, and it turned out to be someone he had been to school with. The bloke asked him if he remembered signing those autographs all those years ago — and then handed him one, saying he had kept it all that time. A bizarre story, but part of a great night that got us all together and laughing at the start of the trip.

Sunday 15 February

Today was our first workout of the tour, a light skills session at the R Premadasa Stadium, about 20 minutes' drive from the hotel. The Premadasa is one of three Test grounds I've played on in Colombo;

the others are the P Saravanamuttu Stadium and the Singhalese Sports Club. The Premadasa is a bit of a concrete bowl, with stands all the way around the ground. That means there is rarely any sort of a breeze on the field. Sri Lanka tend to play a lot of one-day cricket there, because it is the only venue in Colombo that has floodlights. The last time we were here was for the semi-final of the Champions Trophy in September 2002 and we were completely outplayed by the home side; they packed the side with spinners. I am banking on us not batting as badly during this series, because we have two matches at the ground during the one-day series.

The trip to the Premadasa was also the first chance we had to see our baggage master for the trip, Siripala. He is only about 170 centimetres tall and is as skinny as a rake, but he is also as strong as an ox, as he showed us almost straight away, carrying Alex's medical coffin cases around as if they were empty cardboard boxes. It really is amazing, as he seems to have no fat on him at all.

The workout session went pretty well, I thought, with a good level of intensity. After that I had a brief chat to the Australian media, doing a one-day series preview for Monday's papers, and then caught up separately with Malcolm Conn, the cricket writer for *The Australian*. I have signed a deal with them to write a column during the tour, which Malcolm will write with me, so we chatted about the type of thing the paper will want.

This evening we had a function at the Australian High Commission. These types of functions occur whenever we travel overseas. This one was pretty low key, which is what we prefer. As players, we tend to dislike formal sit-down meals that take hours and hours. This was just a relaxed barbecue, with music from a group of ex-pat Australians and no speeches. It all added up to an enjoyable evening.

Monday 16 February

Another day and another practice session at the Premadasa Stadium, this one a bit more intense than yesterday's. That might have something to do with the way we are starting to adapt to the heat and humidity — and the fact that we are getting over our jetlag. After all, it is still less than 72 hours since we arrived in the country.

The trip to and from the Premadasa Stadium is an amazing experience, especially if you are a petrol head. Just along from the ground is a very long road lined with shop after shop selling nothing but automotive parts. A lot of the traders seem to major in spares for tri-shaws, but I would hazard a guess that there has not been a car or bike part ever made that you would not find in one of those shops.

Back at the hotel this evening it was my turn to face the local media, as I took part in Sri Lanka Cricket's official launch of the tour. It was an amazing experience — there must have been at least 10 people on the top table, including me, Marvan Atapattu, Sri Lanka's one-day captain, and their Test captain, Hashan Tillakaratne.

The launch began with speeches galore, from dignitaries and sponsors; they must have taken at least 40 minutes. Then, finally, it was down to questions for me and the two Sri Lankans, but that did not go like clockwork. Atapattu and I were at different ends of the table, which meant that every time one of us was asked a question, all the reporters and television crews had to stand up, go to the top table and move their microphones to one of us. It was painful.

There was also an awkward moment for Tillakaratne, courtesy of one of the local reporters, who asked him about the 'Spirit of Cricket' code. The idea of playing the game in the right way, hard but fair, is now included at the start of the Laws of the game; on top of that, Australia have adopted their own set of standards. When Tillakartne was asked about his thoughts on the Spirit of Cricket he replied that what happens on the field stays on the field, suggesting that if any ill feeling occurs it is up to those on the ground to deal with it there and then.

The local reporter — obviously not Tillakaratne's biggest fan — loved that reply. He immediately fired back, saying that was not the way Tillakaratne had responded when Nasser Hussain was alleged to have sledged Muttiah Muralitharan during the Kandy Test match against England before Christmas — the Sri Lankans complained to the match referee about that incident. Tillakaratne is under pressure anyhow: sections of the media here want him sacked as captain and replaced by Atapattu.

Tuesday 17 February

Practice match, Moratuwa: Sri Lanka Cricket President's XI 8–283 (Mubarak 56, Jayantha 50) lost to the Australians 5–284 (Ponting 57) by 5 wickets.

This was a useful workout at a ground about 40 minutes' drive south of Colombo, and it also gave us an early lesson in the conditions in this part of the world. We made an early start — 10 o'clock — which meant there was some humidity around. That caused the ball to swing, but instead of being able to exploit those conditions, the bowlers found it difficult to control the ball. We conceded 25 wides, which is totally unacceptable; if we do that in the two day games we have in the one-day series, the chances are we will lose. It is something for the bowlers to work on.

In one sense we were lucky to discover the problem so early. Originally we were going to bat first; we were going to have an agreed toss, because it was just a practice match. In the end, however, that did not happen, because the home side's captain, Russel Arnold, refused to go along with the idea. So we got to bowl first instead.

One thing that we did agree on was that it was a 13-a-side match, although only 11 players could bat or were allowed in the field at any one time. That ensured we could give everyone — except Michael Bevan, who was still resting the rib injury he suffered during the VB Series — a chance of some action. I used nine bowlers. The spinners, Brad Hogg, Simon Katich and Michael Clarke, performed best, but overall it was a performance in the field that suggested we needed the run.

There were fewer problems with the bat. The President's XI took just two wickets, and three of us retired out to make sure all the top order got some time in the middle. Andrew Symonds, who has a big chance of making the Test squad because of his ability to bowl spin and seam and his skills with the bat and in the field, caused most fuss, hitting a straight six into the press box and sending the reporters scurrying for cover.

I was surprised there were not many people there to watch the match; I had been expecting quite a crowd. There were a few stray dogs wandering about the place, though, and they kept our boundary riders company during our time in the field.

Wednesday 18 February

Sri Lanka name a 15-man squad for the first two one-day internationals against Australia, calling up batting all-rounder Saman Jayantha for the first time and recalling leg-spinning all-rounder Kaushal Lokuarachchi.

Former Sri Lanka captain Arjuna Ranatunga, who led his country to World Cup success against Australia in 1996, labels Ricky Ponting's side 'unimpressive' in the Australian media.

The bus trip from Colombo to Dambulla is a tough one. It takes over 4 hours, and even though we had a police escort it is impossible to get up a decent speed because the roads in Sri Lanka are not the best. They are fairly narrow, tend to wind around rather than go in a straight line, and have lots of pot holes. On top of that they have all sorts of vehicles on them, ranging from tri-shaws, cars and even carts pulled by donkeys or oxen to massive trucks complete with blaring horns.

The main rule of the road in Sri Lanka seems to be that you must overtake whenever you can. The fact that sometimes other vehicles are coming in the other direction appears to be only a minor concern. Our police escort meant we were kings of the road for our trip and overtook everything in sight, but we still got a chance to see the other vehicles in action. It is a wonder there are not masses of accidents every day. I guess the state of the roads helps reduce the number of accidents in a funny sort of way — it is just not possible to drive fast.

All the way along the route north we passed through towns and villages with shops on either side of the road selling anything from biscuits to cricket bats. And every so often we passed the local equivalent of a roadhouse, complete with petrol pumps and a café attached.

We stopped at one of those roadhouses about halfway to Dambulla, and it was there that Brad Hogg gave us all a laugh, even though he did not intend to. As we got off the bus he looked at his watch and asked team manager Steve Bernard how far we had to go. 'Probably another 2 hours,' came the reply. 'So when will we get there?' asked Hogg. Classic.

Those 2 hours passed quietly, with most of the boys watching DVDs on their laptops. Eventually we pulled into the long dirt road that leads to the Kandalama Hotel. The fact that the road has not been concreted is the first indication you get that the hotel is doing all it can to be as eco-friendly as possible. It is built in an area of great natural beauty — there is a massive lake nearby, as well as all sorts of plants and animals — and the owners have undertaken to disturb the local environment as little as possible. That even extends to ensuring that all vehicles turn their engines off once they get to the front of the hotel, even if they are waiting for guests to come out.

We were escorted up the steep driveway by two guards on horseback. There was also an elephant around as we got off the bus. Needless to say, John Buchanan was in his element with his video camera. The way we were made to feel so welcome was great.

To get the cobwebs out of the system after our long bus trip we headed to the ground in the late afternoon, about 30 minutes' drive away, to check out the facilities and the pitch. It is a relatively new venue, only staging its first one-day international three years ago, and it was only built six months before that. The idea behind the venue was to capitalise on the fact that it rarely rains in this part of Sri Lanka; this makes it pretty different from Colombo. Last year it staged a one-day tournament involving Pakistan, Sri Lanka and New Zealand when all the grounds in Colombo were waterlogged.

The history of matches at the ground makes interesting reading: the scores are mainly very low, some less than 150, and there is no real pattern to the results: sides batting first and second have both enjoyed their share of success, and spinners and seamers have all exploited the conditions. Alex Kontouri has already told us that the Sri Lankan players do not really enjoy playing here, because unlike other grounds in this country, they do not really understand the conditions. That is a positive for us even before we walk onto the ground.

Two pitches have been prepared for the two matches we have here, with a further two pitches for net practice at either end of the square. The match pitches look very dry, and one of them even has a series of white marks all over it, thanks to a practice game the Sri Lankans played on it last night. The pitches look as if they should offer plenty of turn.

The one thing we do not know is how the pitch or the atmosphere will behave at night; that is something that would be useful to understand, because the first of our two matches here is under lights. Unfortunately, only one day–night international has ever been played here, and that was last November. England managed to lose it by 10 wickets before the sun set and the lights kicked in. The light towers seem to be a bit lower than the ones we are used to in Australia, but all the squad have played plenty of night cricket, so we hope there will not be any surprises we cannot handle.

The hotel is not only a fair distance away from the ground but it is also a fair trek from the town of Dambulla, and none of us really fancied making that trip to get some food when we got back from the ground. Luckily, the hotel's buffet was fantastic, so most of us tucked into a great meal to end the day.

Thursday 19 February

A busy day began at breakfast with a chat to the Australian media. An early media briefing for them is likely to be the order of the day throughout the trip, because Sri Lanka is 5 hours back from eastern summer time — leaving our chat until lunchtime would really push them up against their deadlines.

The chat this morning had two purposes: they wanted me not only to preview the one-day series starting tomorrow but also to look ahead to the announcement of the Test squad, which will be made in Melbourne tomorrow morning.

The keys for us, as I said later at the team meeting, are aggression and energy in the field, especially while the ball is hard and the bowlers are fresh, as well as patience with the bat, making sure we keep wickets in hand for the final overs. That was the way we beat Sri Lanka twice in the World Cup, even managing to get the better of them on a slow, low pitch in Port Elizabeth in the semi-final, and I do not see any reason to change that game plan now.

I had already spoken with Trevor Hohns about the Test squad, but of course I was not in a position to give too much away; it will be interesting to see how many of the choices the media guess correctly. Shane Warne has been recalled, and Stuart MacGill is also included, which means no place for Brad Hogg. There is no place for Michael Clarke either, with Andrew Symonds included. Clarke is unlucky; it is Symonds' ability to bowl medium-pace as well as off-spin that has won him the spot. We are expecting the pitches to offer plenty of turn, which means MacGill and Warne are both likely to play, and if that is the case we need someone who can bowl medium-pace to support the two frontline pace bowlers we would also include. Symonds fits that bill, and his ability to bowl some spin as well means he offers extra options. And with his batting coming on in leaps and bounds and his fielding an obvious asset, he is, as Hohns put it to me, 'the complete package'. Michael Kasprowicz has also been included. This is his first call-up to the Test squad since 2001: he has forced his way back in through sheer consistency. Justin Langer told me Kasprowicz was the best bowler he faced this season in state cricket, and the selectors have been getting the same story from everyone else they ask. Also back is Darren Lehmann, who is fit again after a horror season with injuries. It is no secret how much I value his cricket brain — he is a go-to man for me when I want advice on the game. On top of that he is a top-class player of spin. He will be a massive asset to our squad.

We had a light final practice at the ground and I was also involved in the customary match referee's meeting, as were Marvan Atapattu and the umpires. The meeting is a chance for the referee, in this case former South Africa all-rounder Mike Procter, to make both sides aware of any changes to the playing conditions and how he wants the series conducted. It is also an opportunity for either captain to ask him or the umpires how certain issues will be interpreted. I was keen to stress to the umpires and the referee that I wanted to see consistency when it came to changing balls during an innings. The problem arises because the white ball gets discoloured during play. If the umpires feel the ball being used has got too dirty and is therefore too tough to see, they will order it changed. That can be a huge advantage to the batting side, because the replacement ball usually swings less and is harder, and therefore easier to hit. All I asked was that the umpires are consistent in their decisions over whether or not they change the ball. It is no good opting not to change it during the first innings of a match but then doing so in the second innings with, say, five overs left, when the batting side is struggling and the bowlers are getting good reverse swing. My view is that it should be changed at the same point in both innings or not at all.

Atapattu and I also agreed that if a fielder claims a low catch the batsman will take the fielder's word that the ball had carried and walk off rather than wait for the third umpire to rule on the matter. This is an issue that has been festering for quite some time, as some batsmen have tended to stay put rather than walk off, knowing they will get the benefit of the doubt if the matter is referred to the third umpire: TV replays tend to be inconclusive. That, in turn, has led to some needle between teams. Both Atapattu and I hope our agreement will take the heat out of this potential flashpoint.

Back at the hotel it was time for our final team meeting before the match. We have an experienced bunch of players and everyone is pretty familiar with our game plan, so there was no need to go into any great depth apart from stressing the basics: aggression with the ball, especially when it is hard and new, bowlers not to give any width, energy in the field, rotation of the strike when batting and keeping wickets in hand for a final assault at the end of our innings. It was all pretty straightforward, but worth reminding everyone about.

One thing I did stress was that everyone should be clear on how they are going to play when their turn comes to bat. I am not a believer in having a team plan to combat certain bowlers. After all, each player is different, so having the same approach would make no sense. All I ask is that whatever a player's plan, he is clear about it and feels confident enough to execute it. Matthew Hayden, for example, will look to sweep whenever he can against the spinners. My plan will be to get down the pitch in an attempt to push the field back and also break up their rhythm. Rotating the strike with a partner, especially if he happens to be left-handed, is also a useful weapon, as it stops bowlers settling into one line of attack.

With the formal business over, we then had to decide who should get the Dhaktari uniform for the first time on the tour. The Dhaktari is a longstanding tradition within the Australian team on tour. It is a collection of shocking clothes awarded to a member of the touring party who makes a fool of himself or herself. The recipient then has to wear the outfit all evening — ideally, out for a meal.

The outfit on this trip has been donated by Adam Gilchrist: it is a retro tracksuit modelled on the Australian team's outfit at the 1968 Olympics. It is red and green, has a massive collar and comes complete with a headband and a fake Olympic medal. After his question to Steve Bernard on the way to Dambulla, there was only one possible winner — Brad Hogg.

Friday 20 February

Australia announce a 15-man Test squad to take part in the three-match series with Sri Lanka. It is: Ricky Ponting (captain), Adam Gilchrist (vice-captain), Jason Gillespie, Matthew Hayden, Michael Kasprowicz, Simon Katich, Justin Langer, Brett Lee, Darren Lehmann, Stuart MacGill, Damien Martyn, Wade Seccombe, Andrew Symonds, Shane Warne and Brad Williams.

First one-day international, Dambulla: Australia 6–262 (Gilchrist 66, Ponting 58) beat Sri Lanka 178 (Jayawardene 61, Sangakkara 58, Hogg 5–41) by 84 runs.

We made the perfect start to the one-day series, doing exactly what I'd hoped we would do — playing aggressively and stamping our authority on the opposition. It was an emphatic performance, and I reckon we have given them plenty to think about already.

We got just about everything right, starting with my winning the toss, which gave us the chance to bat with the pitch at its best. Then we managed to nullify the threat of Muttiah Muralitharan and keep wickets in hand for a late onslaught, which was led by Andrew Symonds, fresh from the news of his inclusion in the Test squad. When we bowled we showed plenty of aggression, our fielding and catching were excellent, and Brad Hogg ran through them at the end as the pitch turned more and more, claiming his first five-wicket haul in one-dayers.

The pitch played a lot better than any of the previous scores on it suggested it would. It was slow, but we expected that, and by and large it did not do anything outrageous. Matthew Hayden was dropped from the first ball he faced, from Chaminda Vaas — he had pushed hard at the ball — but gradually he and Adam Gilchrist got used to the pace of the surface and carved out a vital stand, the first-ever three-figure partnership at the ground.

I was delighted with the way I played. I had to start against spin, with Muralitharan and Upul Chandana, the leg-spinner, in operation, but I took my time and, apart from a four through midwicket off Chandana, I was content early on to push the ball around for ones and twos and get used to the pace of the surface and the conditions. There was not a lot of scope for risk-taking early on in any case, as Hayden got out within three overs of me arriving at the crease. That meant Sri Lanka had two relatively new batsmen to attack, so it was up to Damien Martyn and me to ensure that they did not get any further encouragement — for a while at least.

Thanks to the start Hayden and Gilchrist gave us, there was no huge rush, so sensible knocking of the ball into gaps was the order of the day. And even though Martyn departed with 12 overs to go, we still brought up the 200 in the 42nd over.

At that point I decided, with seven wickets in hand, that it was time for me to get on with it. I had Michael Bevan at the other end and I knew he would look to knock it around and rotate the strike; that gave me a licence to play some big shots, especially with the likes of Andrew Symonds and Michael Clarke still in the pavilion.

I clobbered Sanath Jayasuriya through extra-cover and was feeling very positive, but my next shot was my undoing. I tried to go down the ground, but the ball held up on the pitch a little and I got it on the inside half of the bat. Instead of clearing the ropes I ended up finding the fielder at long-on, and that was that.

At least it let Symonds in with a few overs in hand. Straight away he played with real confidence, working the ball into the gaps and clobbering Jayasuriya through midwicket for four. We lost momentum at the other end as Muralitharan finally got some success, but overall I was happy with the way we dealt with him. He may have gone for only 30 runs in his 10 overs, but he did not run through us — and, more importantly, we got a look at his new delivery, the doosra, the ball that spins away from the bat like a leg-break.

He bowled it far too much, but I am not complaining. It meant we got more of a chance to have a close look at the wrist action he uses to deliver the ball. I was actually surprised that he used it as much as he did. I believe his biggest weapon is the big-spinning off-break, and I think he should concentrate on that and just use the other ball as a surprise tactic; by bowling the doosra so much today he has given us an advantage for the rest of the tour.

Sri Lanka chose to finish our innings with the spin of Jayasuriya and it cost them, as Symonds clobbered him for 20. He was left not knowing where to bowl, as he was hit for fours through extra-cover, long-on and midwicket and finally a six way back over long-off. That effort from Symonds summed up how he has matured at this level over the past year and how he is really thinking about his cricket. When he went in, with eight overs to go, he assessed the situation and played himself in, knocking the ball around and waiting for the right ball to hit before launching his assault at the end. Maybe before last year's World Cup he would have gone out and just slogged the ball up in the air straight away; he is better than that now. He has shown that consistently enough over the past year to earn his call-up to the Test squad. I have no doubt that he fully deserves it.

Symonds' onslaught turned our total from a very useful one into something that was formidable, and meant that the pressure was on Sri Lanka from ball one of their innings. It showed in their approach. Their running between the wickets was panic-stricken and we exploited that to get rid of both openers.

First Jayasuriya went, in an ugly mix-up over a second run to fine leg. There was no decent communication between him and his partner, Romesh Kaluwitharana, and in the end, Gilchrist had time to gather Brett Lee's slightly wayward return, turn and underarm it onto the stumps with Jayasuriya still short of his ground after being sent back. Then Kaluwitharana was short of his ground in the next over, when I scored a direct hit at the striker's end after Marvan Atapattu pushed the ball into the off-side and set off. Kaluwitharana, maybe still thinking about the run-out in the previous over, was late to respond and finished up centimetres short.

Our only real concern during Sri Lanka's innings was the partnership between Kumar Sangakkara and Mahela Jayawardene. They added 121, and got Sri Lanka to the stage where they needed a gettable 7 runs an over from the last 17 overs, with wickets in hand. But I was always confident, even when those two were together, because no matter how well a pair is playing, it is tough to maintain that sort of run rate over that length of time. And in this case, the pitch was showing some signs of wear and they had a lengthy tail, with Chandana coming in at number seven.

Sure enough, once Lee had removed Sangakkara, edging a cut shot through to Gilchrist, the end came fairly swiftly. Lee, incidentally, bowled beautifully, swinging the new ball and then firing up for that breakthrough in mid-innings, just when we needed it. Jason Gillespie was impressive too. It seems that no matter what the conditions and the surface are like, we can still trouble Sri Lanka with pace if our quick bowlers get it right.

Hogg rattled through the lower order like a hot knife through butter, in a spell that showed everything that is good about his bowling. His first six-over spell was pretty ordinary, but when I brought him back he got some momentum in his approach to the crease and got some real action on the ball — and the results followed. He is at his best when he bustles in, and that is exactly what he did in his final spell.

He spun the ball sharply, and the Sri Lanka lower order batsmen had all sorts of problems picking him. I guess that may be because left-arm wrist-spinners are not all that common around the world, although Australia have had their share and we have two in this squad — Simon Katich is the other. Hogg was named man of the match, and the massive novelty cheque he was given went straight into the bottom of his coffin when he got back into the dressing room after the presentation ceremony. His performance was just the sort of response you want from a player after he's been left out of the Test squad. It sums up his attitude to the game, but I do not think it will alter the selectors' thinking about the make-up of that squad. They have picked what they believe are our best two wrist-spinners — Shane Warne and Stuart MacGill — and I cannot ever see a time when we would play three in a match, especially after the way our quicks bowled here. That is for the future, though; for now, Hogg and the rest of us can enjoy this win.

Brad Hogg

If you asked me to name the player in the Australian squad with the most energy, there could only be one choice: Brad Hogg. I do not think I have ever seen him stay still for any prolonged length of time — it is no wonder there is not a kilo of spare fat on him.

The selectors must take a lot of credit for backing my hunch to bring him back into the squad after several years in the wilderness. He responded by being a key member of our World Cup-winning side as well as an effective bowler in one-day cricket after that tournament.

Before the World Cup there seemed no way in for Hogg, as Shane Warne was apparently nailed on as our number one spinner, and backup was likely to come from Nathan Hauritz, who had experience of the conditions, having toured South Africa in 2002 and done well there.

Despite that fact, and without any disrespect to Hauritz, I had a feeling for Hogg. I'd had my eye on him for some time, having been impressed by him when we played against each other, and I felt he offered something different. Left-arm wrist-spinners are not common in domestic cricket, let alone at international level, and the fact that he was also a useful lower order batsman and stunning in the field meant he was someone who was more than just a one-trick pony.

Even so, he was not expected to play a major role in the tournament, despite useful displays when Shane Warne was injured during that summer's VB Series; but when Warne was sent home for a drugs offence the picture suddenly changed: Hogg was our frontline spinner.

He responded brilliantly, with only Sri Lanka's Muttiah Muralitharan (among the spinners) taking more wickets, and he even forced his way into the Test side later in the year, against the West Indies and Zimbabwe.

Hogg — or George as he is sometimes affectionately known (that is his first name, although he is always called by his second name, Brad) — is, more than most players, someone who requires self-confidence. There are some players — Matthew Hayden for example — who can scrap their way to an 'ugly' hundred without being in their best form, but Hogg needs to be buoyant about his own game in order to perform well.

Hogg gets much of his confidence through practice, and he would practise or play every hour of every day if he could. He is constantly trying to improve and feel good about his bowling and his cricket — sometimes we have to rein him back in and tell him to relax for a while rather than have a training session just for the sake of it.

He also gets a fair deal of confidence from rhythm, something he got spot on in Sri Lanka in early 2004. Before the tour he was racing in to bowl and was not properly balanced at the crease, but in Sri Lanka he approached the crease more slowly, more deliberately, and the reward was his first five-wicket haul at one-day level, in Dambulla.

That was doubly pleasing because it came on the same day as it was announced that Hogg had been left out of the squad for the Test series that followed the one-day matches. Knowing how hard he can be on himself and his own performances, I was delighted to see that he responded in the right way — with a great display — rather than getting down about missing out on the second half of the tour.

Hogg is someone who has experienced life away from cricket. He has worked as a postman, and I think this extra life experience makes him even more determined to make the most of his opportunity now that it has come along — especially as this is something of a second coming for him: he played a Test match way back in 1996 in India, plus a handful of one-day games, before going missing at international level for several years.

Hogg is also someone who can give everyone a laugh. He often inadvertently puts his foot in his mouth. There are a few examples of 'Hogg-isms' in this diary, but one I have not mentioned elsewhere springs to mind. During the one-day series in Sri Lanka, he became increasingly irritated by fans hanging around in the lobby of our hotel and pestering players for autographs when they were trying to relax away from the hurly-burly of playing and practice. The problem did not crop up in Dambulla, but in our hotel in Colombo, Sri Lanka's capital city, it was a constant issue. One day a few of us were trying to enjoy a quiet drink in the hotel's coffee shop when some autograph hunters appeared, and although we all signed, the intrusion upset Hogg. 'Don't these Colombians ever give it a rest?' he said.

Hogg's energy is infectious around the team, which means he is a pleasure to have in the squad. And although he is past 30, his excellent fitness levels, combined with the fact that spin bowlers tend to be like fine wine and mature with age, suggest that he has plenty to offer in the next few years.

Saturday 21 February

A few of the players — those not involved in yesterday's win — went to the ground for a light practice session, but for most of us, today was all about relaxing. We have five matches in nine days in this series, so it is important to rest as much as possible between games. Everyone will be feeling the workload by the end of the series, especially when we get back to Colombo where it will be much hotter. Here there is a slight cooling breeze to provide a little respite from the humidity.

There was a pool session to allow us to stretch out the muscles we used last night, and Lucy Frostick, the team's masseuse, had a full day of work with the bowlers, who were all getting treatment from her after their first international match in ten days or so, but players were mostly left to their own devices.

I opted for some time on the internet, which might not have been such a good idea: I was gutted to see that Melbourne had beaten the Kangaroos in the Wizard Cup, the AFL's pre-season tournament. I was especially sick because I thought the game was on Sunday and was going to send the players a good luck text message.

At least Jock Campbell gave us all a laugh. He set out for a jog around the lake that our hotel overlooks, but halfway round he discovered it was impassable. He ended up having to wade around up to his waist in water — he looked pretty shabby by the time he got back. Adam Gilchrist also confirmed the hotel's reputation for being close to nature, as a monkey joined him at his window for breakfast this morning.

Sunday 22 February

Second one-day international, Dambulla: Sri Lanka 245 (Jayasuriya 55, Clarke 5–35) beat Australia 5–244 (Hayden 93, Ponting 69) by 1 run.

I am not quite sure how to describe my feelings at the moment. It is enough to say that this was a shocking loss and a bitter disappointment. We really should have won the match comfortably.

When I was batting with Matthew Hayden we were cruising, wanting less than 100 with nine wickets and 19 overs in hand. The ball was turning, but the pitch held up far better than we thought it would. After getting ourselves into that position, there is no excuse for losing the game and letting Sri Lanka back into the series — even though Chaminda Vaas bowled exceptionally well at the death.

And to make matters worse, when we got to Colombo late this evening I found out that Adam Gilchrist and Andrew Symonds have to face a hearing for dissent after Symonds was given out then reinstated following an lbw appeal. All in all, today was not one of our — or my — better days.

Things did not start impressively, because when we arrived at the ground we found out that we were playing on the pitch that had been used on Friday. Logic suggested that we would use the fresh second pitch that had been prepared, but Sri Lanka obviously felt they would have a better chance of winning if they played on Friday's worn strip, which would obviously favour their spinners far more. It created a hurdle for us before a ball was even bowled.

We made one change, with Ian Harvey coming in for Brad Williams. Conditions did not suit Williams on Friday and we felt that Harvey, with his mix of slower balls and cutters, as well as his ability with the bat, would give us extra options.

I lost the toss and Sri Lanka decided to bat, presumably hoping that the pitch would deteriorate as the match went on. I was not too worried about bowling first. I hoped Jason Gillespie and Brett Lee would be able to spook the Sri Lanka top order again, just as they had done on Friday.

Unfortunately, that did not happen. Both men were off their game; Lee, in particular, was struggling. He bowled four no-balls and a wide in his opening three overs and had no rhythm at all. He conceded 19 runs and allowed Marvan Atapattu and Sanath Jayasuriya to get off to a flying start.

I tried to shut things down with Harvey, but Jayasuriya, after spending a couple of overs getting used to him, helped himself to three fours in one over, with a slashing cut, a delicate glance and a meaty pick-up over midwicket. They scored 89 from the first 15 overs, and on a pitch where batting was expected to get harder as the day went on, that was far too many.

Gradually, however, we managed to rein things back. Symonds, who started off bowling his seamers, switched to off-spin and had two appeals against Jayasuriya turned down in quick succession. First there was an appeal for a stumping, rejected after a referral to the third umpire, then we went up for a catch to Gilchrist as Jayasuriya missed a clumsy attempt at a sweep. There was definitely a noise, but the benefit of the doubt, in the flurry of arms, glove and bat, went to the batsman.

It was encouraging stuff in one way, especially as Brad Hogg was settling into his work at the other end, but the fact that our spinners were making them work hard for runs also had a downside: it suggested that batting against their slow bowlers might also be tough later in the day. And in any case, we still needed a wicket.

That was where I came in, with what I have to admit was one of the best pieces of fielding I can remember producing. The funny thing about it was that it felt as if it happened in the blink of an eye, so quickly in fact that I couldn't remember how I had done it when I tried to re-run it in my mind after the event.

Atapattu clipped the ball to my left at midwicket and I dived full length and managed to get it in my left hand. Atapattu, whose call for the run it was, thought the ball was past me and set off — he was now committed beyond the point of no return and that convinced me that I could run him out easily by running in 10 metres and removing the bails. But he made good ground and, as I saw him out of the corner of my eye, I realised I had to throw the ball. Otherwise, by the time I got there, he might have made it. That added an element of difficulty, because I was side on and had just one stump to aim at.

Luckily I scored a direct hit. I knew he was gone straight away, though it was referred to the third umpire for confirmation. It was just the break we needed, and with Symonds following it up soon afterwards, trapping Jayasuriya on the back foot, suddenly we had two new batsmen to bowl at.

All credit to Kumar Sangakkara and Mahela Jayawardene, who rebuilt the innings pretty well. Without taking any undue risks against our spinners, they nudged the ball around, keeping wickets in hand and the scoreboard ticking over, and when I called Lee back, in the hope that he might find some better rhythm, they took him for 20 from three overs.

The way Lee was bowling meant it would be tough for me to give him his full ration of 10 overs, so I threw the ball to Michael Clarke, not only to get through a few of Lee's overs but also to see if he could work a trick for us. He was something of a golden arm for me during the TVS Cup in India, and once again he did not let me down — although even in my wildest dreams I never thought he would end up with 5–35.

Clarke got the ball in the right area, spun it a little, and they panicked. At least that was how it seemed to me. At the same time we switched up a gear in the field, found some sharpness that may have been missing in the first 10 or 15 overs, and managed to bowl the home side out with a ball unused.

Sri Lanka's collapse left me a bit shocked — it is not something you expect from a side full of experienced players, and I am not sure what to put it down to apart from steady bowling from Clarke, backed up by Harvey, solid fielding and a lack of clear thinking by the batting side. They were well placed to get at least 270 but fell well short of that, which gave us a huge lift going into the interval. We knew it was still going to be a tough chase, though.

At this point I had a think about our tactics for the chase. Looking at Sri Lanka's line-up and their choice of just one seam bowler, Vaas, I figured our openers were likely to face an off-spinner. If that bowler did his job and got some turn against our two left-handers at the top of the order, he could take one side of the field right out of play at a time when we really needed to press on — while the ball was hard and coming onto the bat.

I chatted it over with Hayden and Gilchrist and both of them agreed that we should try to keep a left-hand and right-hand combination in the innings wherever possible, to break up the bowlers' lines. That meant opening with a right-hander. The choices to slot in with Hayden were Symonds, Damien Martyn or Clarke, and although the first two had done the job before, I preferred to keep them in the middle order, so I decided on using Clarke. I think I also hoped that his bowling would have given him some extra confidence.

Things did not go quite according to plan. Clarke took first strike and managed to slice a drive from Vaas straight to backward point before an off-spinner had even bowled a ball. I guess that is why captaincy can sometimes be such a thankless task.

Gilchrist had his pads on, but as it was the right-hander who had been was dismissed I went in. After taking my time to have a look at conditions I got the scoreboard moving with a pull shot for six off Vaas followed by a slashing four through backward point, both of them coming right off the middle of the bat.

Gradually we assumed control, and Sri Lanka started to become bothered. Wicketkeeper Romesh Kaluwitharana was spoken to by umpire Billy Bowden for an over-enthusiastic lbw appeal against me when Muttiah Muralitharan turned one sharply, and then, to cap his misery, he missed a stumping chance after Hayden charged down the pitch to Kumara Dharmasena and missed a big drive. I found out afterwards that I had ticked past 7000 one-day runs. It all seemed to be going very well — until I started the slide by getting out needlessly.

The sweep is not my strongest shot, but this time I managed to middle it perfectly. The only problem was that I hit it too well, and rather than getting us a single, or maybe more, the ball ended up carrying all the way to the boundary, where Vaas took a straightforward catch.

I was furious with myself because I knew how difficult it would be for a new batsman starting out now. The pitch was getting slower and slower and Sri Lanka's spinners would not be easy to face first up. On top of that, Vaas is a master at taking the pace off the ball by running his fingers down the side of it as he bowls. That is exactly how he got Martyn, deceiving him with a slower ball. Martyn picked it late and checked his shot, but ended up chipping it to short extra-cover where Atapattu took a low, tumbling catch.

There was now a lot of pressure on Hayden to bat through the innings, but for once he was not able to see us through: like me, he was guilty of a poor choice of shot. We still wanted less than a run a ball, so there was no need to take undue risks, but his desire to be positive got the better of him and he lofted the ball to long-off. Jayawardene did not pick it up at first. He came running in, only to realise that the ball was away to his right and going pretty quickly. He managed to adjust at the last second and in the end held on to a cracking catch at chest height.

The match was just starting to get away from us when suddenly there was added drama involving Symonds and Gilchrist. The batsmen crossed when Hayden was out, so Symonds was on strike, and on the next ball he attempted to pull Dharmasena through the leg-side. The ball turned and kept low, but he got a pretty solid bottom edge onto it before it thudded into his pads.

There was an instinctive appeal for lbw, and almost straight away Peter Manuel, the umpire at the bowler's end, upheld it. Symonds was clearly disappointed with the decision, but had just started to make his way off the ground when, from my seat on the boundary's edge, I could see the two umpires consult. After a brief chat they went to the huddle of Sri Lanka players with Atapattu in the middle of it and then, with Symonds by now about halfway back to the dressing room, they called him back — Manuel made the signal of both arms across his chest to indicate that he had changed his decision. It was a brave call by the umpire, but I have to say that having heard the nick from the boundary edge, it was the right one; his first call was obviously wrong.

At this point I decided to head back into the dressing room to have a look at the incident on the TV. It has to be said that TV pictures often make incidents look far worse than they are in reality, especially when they are replayed time and again from every angle, but the replays this time did show Symonds' disappointment with the decision and I suspected he would face a charge of dissent. At that point I had not picked up Gilchrist's response to the decision.

Our good fortune over that decision did not last long. Gilchrist chipped a catch straight back to Vaas in the next over, leaving us in real trouble. At that point, 5–192 in the 42nd over, I thought we were out of the game, and I guess in a sense we did well to get so close to pulling off the win. But if Hayden and I had seen it through as we should have done, it would never have come to that.

When Gilchrist got back to the dressing room he told us he had heard Symonds' inside edge at the non-striker's end and expressed his disappointment at the decision. It made me wonder if he might also be facing a visit to the match referee after the game. But that was for the future. For now it was up to Symonds and Michael Bevan to see us home.

We really threw the match away, but the Sri Lankans still deserve credit for the way they held their nerve, and Atapattu handled his bowlers pretty skilfully at the death. He saved Muralitharan and Vaas to bowl the last two overs, but that would not have been significant if leg-spinner Upul Chandana and Dharmasena had not been able to bottle things up themselves, conceding four and five runs respectively in the 46th and 47th overs, varying their pace and getting some sharp spin.

We needed 17 from the final two overs, the first of which was bowled by Muralitharan. After Symonds got a single from the first ball, Murali looked as though he would keep Bevan scoreless. He opted to go around the wicket, spinning the ball sharply, and it was difficult to see how Bevan could lay a bat on the ball. Then, out of desperation, Bevan resorted to the slog-sweep and got enough bat on ball to clear the boundary at wide midwicket. We got nine off the over, and with Symonds on strike we had a real chance of taking the match at the last gasp, with eight still needed.

We reckoned without Vaas. He bowled a beautiful last over, right up in the blockhole, giving neither Symonds nor Bevan any room to swing their arms or get under the ball to belt a boundary that would have eased the tension. He conceded just three singles from the first five balls, which meant Bevan needed a second six to win the match — a four would have given us a tie, which would have been some sort of consolation.

Again the ball was full, but although Bevan did manage to get under the ball, it sliced high off a thick top edge to extra-cover. Sangakkara, running back from inside the circle, tried to take the catch — ironically that almost gave us the tie, because he could not hold on as he dived, instead deflecting the ball away from the stumps. Luckily for him it ricocheted to a team-mate, and the ball was returned before either Symonds or Bevan could even think about a fourth run.

The post-match media activity was almost all concerned with the events surrounding the changed lbw decision, but there was not a lot I could say, as I had not been on the field at the time. On top of that, even though I had not heard anything at that point, I knew there was every chance there would be a hearing, so I was reluctant to get too deeply involved in passing comment on the incident for fear of getting into trouble myself.

The mood on the bus going back to Colombo could easily have been downbeat after a frustrating loss like that, but I think we rebounded pretty quickly. Gilchrist pulled out his video camera and went up and down the bus, with everyone given the task of contributing one sentence. The result was a bizarre story that gave us a laugh, as did a viewing of some *All Aussie Adventures* — thanks to Brad Williams' portable DVD player, which he rigged up to the television on the bus.

We got to Colombo at about 11 o'clock to discover that a hearing had been called for tomorrow morning.

Monday 23 February

With Adam Gilchrist and Andrew Symonds charged with dissent, I was up at 10 o'clock to get ready to attend the hearing — only to find out it had been postponed, first until late afternoon and then until the next day. This is, apparently, to give both sides a chance to prepare their cases.

The charge has been laid by Peter Manuel and it is no real surprise to me that it has happened. We will find out tomorrow whether the powers that be think Gilchrist and Symonds have overstepped the mark. One thing is for sure, though: the incident has not got our plan to accept all close decisions without question off to the best of starts.

Without the hearing to occupy my time I had a quiet day, surfing the internet and also having a recovery session with Jock Campbell. This usually involves some stretches or walking and maybe some laps of the pool. The idea is to get rid of any stiffness from the game and the bus trip that followed it. We are all used to following that routine now and it seems to keep us in pretty good shape.

Tuesday 24 February

Sri Lanka name an unchanged 15-man squad for the third and fourth matches of the one-day series.

It could have been worse, but it is still not the ideal build-up to a crucial match tomorrow. Adam Gilchrist has been fined 50 per cent of his match fee for a show of dissent, but Andrew Symonds has been found not guilty of the same offence, with match referee Mike Procter saying 'there is a very fine line between disappointment and dissent'.

I did not need to attend the hearing after all, but I know Gilchrist was extremely disappointed at copping the fine. I think he feels he might be getting a reputation, because he was charged with a similar offence during the Sydney Test against England last year. I know Symonds is also feeling pretty bad for Gilchrist — not only was

Ian Munro, © News Limited

Jackson Flindell, © News Limited

Above The record: Matthew Hayden, looking as fresh as a daisy, celebrates his world record 376th run, against Zimbabwe in Perth.

Right The taste of success: Hayden toasts his achievement in the dressing room.

Above So lonely: we may be the best side in the world, but not many Sydneysiders wanted to watch us beat Zimbabwe.

Right 'You beauty!': I celebrate with Matthew Hayden as he reaches his hundred and takes us to victory over Zimbabwe in Sydney.

Left Bracks attack: Nathan Bracken, who led our attack brilliantly during the TVS Cup in India.

Below 'How about that then?': (left to right) Jimmy Maher, Adam Gilchrist and Michael Kasprowicz celebrate our TVS Cup final win over India in Kolkata.

Patrick Hamilton, © News Limited

Left Leap of faith: India captain Sourav Ganguly celebrates his hundred in Brisbane. It was an innings that set the tone for India's defiance throughout the Test series.

Ray Titus, © News Limited

Below Brilliant: Rahul Dravid drives during his outstanding double of 233 and 72 not out in Adelaide. These were the innings that won the second Test for India.

Left Pulling out all the stops: Virender Sehwag clobbers a four during his 195 in the third Test, at the Melbourne Cricket Ground. The careless shot that caused his dismissal helped turn the match our way.

Below Getting stuck in: Brad Williams's wholehearted commitment and determination typified our approach in Melbourne as we levelled the series.

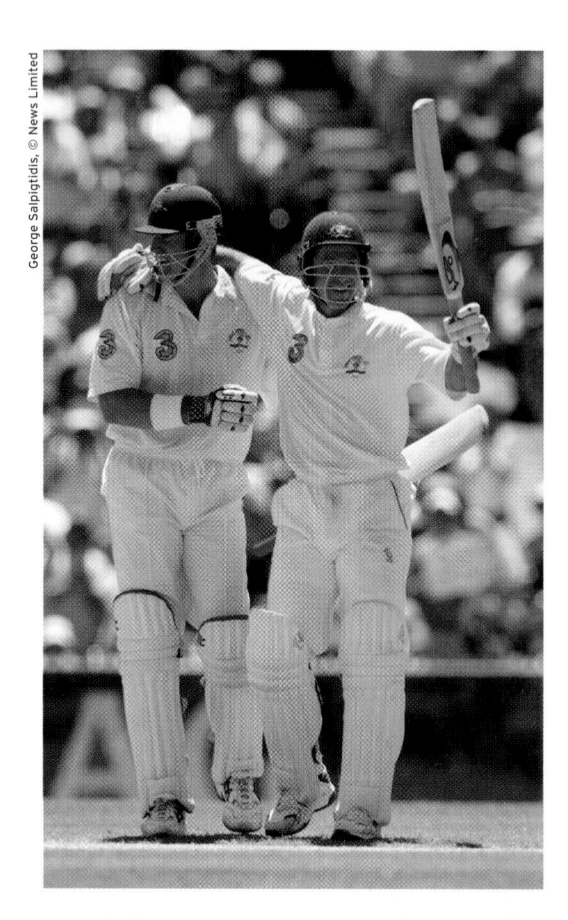
George Salpigtidis, © News Limited

Left Victory: Matthew Hayden and I celebrate winning the third Test against India, a success we both played key roles in achieving.

Below Guard of honour: we welcome Stephen Waugh onto his beloved Sydney Cricket Ground at the start of his final Test match, against India.

Phil Hillyard, © News Limited

Above No wonder we couldn't get him out: Sachin Tendulkar displays the textbook style that brought him an unbeaten 241 during the Sydney Test.

Below Waugh's end: Stephen Waugh waves to the adoring Sydney crowd after his final, unforgettable Test.

Above left Power play: Adam Gilchrist helped maintain our one-day edge over India with a blazing 95 from 72 balls during the VB Series group game in Sydney.

Above right Hammer blow: Matthew Hayden snuffed out India's hopes of taking the VB Series to a third final with a ruthless 126 in Sydney.

Right Bingo time: 'Bing' Lee celebrates after his dramatic six in the final over of the VB Series match against India gave us a narrow win.

it his mistake that caused the incident, but also he managed to get off without any punishment at all.

The incident has sparked plenty of debate, especially in the media, about whether or not an umpire should ever change his decision and whether or not there is a need to use technology instead of an on-field official. I am quite happy with the way things are at the moment, with technology impacting on but not dominating the decision-making process in a Test or one-day international through the use of the third umpire for line decisions. I cannot see any need to go further than that at this stage, given the ICC's commitment to get the best officials in place; if they do that, a better quality of decision-making should follow. All we really ask for, as players, is consistency from umpires. If we get that, I think most players will not be able to find much to complain about. As for the umpire ever changing his decision — well, we have committed to accept their decisions whether we think they are right or wrong, because that is the foundation on which the game of cricket is built. I hope we can do that for the rest of the tour; it will reflect badly on us if we do not.

We had a team practice session at the Premadasa Stadium this afternoon and it gave us a chance to have a look at conditions there. The last time we played here — in the semi-final of the Champions Trophy in September 2002 — we were thumped, thanks in large part to some pretty poor batting against a Sri Lanka team that was packed with spin bowlers. I like to think our approach over the first two matches in this series, where we managed more than 500 runs in two innings on a slow pitch offering sharp turn, suggests that we have come to terms with the problems the spinners pose. However, the only way to prove that is to win this series. That task will start again tomorrow, on a pitch that today looks much as we expected: very dry, and sure to offer plenty of help to the spinners at some stage.

Simon Katich was feeling in a generous mood and gave Chitral Mendis, our liaison man, a pair of his sunglasses. Chitral did not take them off for the entire session, or during the trip back to the hotel, and while he was in the dressing room he kept walking past the metallic fridge there, checking his reflection. Chitral is an excellent man, and that was a nice touch from Katich.

Wednesday 25 February

Third one-day international, R Premadasa Stadium, Colombo: Sri Lanka 8–226 (Jayawardene 80) lost to Australia 5–227 (Ponting 63) by 5 wickets.

This was a great win, especially as I thought we were set for another loss when we were five wickets down and running out of overs. At that point Sri Lanka's spinners were strangling the life out of our innings, and it looked as if it would be a re-run of the second game in Dambulla, with us failing to make the most of a promising position.

I need not have worried. Andrew Symonds was still there, and he showed again how much his game has developed over the past year: 12 months ago I am not sure he could have played the type of innings he produced tonight, but now he has so much belief in himself that he backed himself to win the game — and did just that.

At the other end was Michael Clarke, who played a fantastic innings that gave us some momentum just when we needed it. In the end we got home with more than an over to spare, which was amazing considering that we needed almost a run a ball when the pair came together.

Those two made sure we got over the line, but credit should also go to Jason Gillespie and Michael Kasprowicz, who gave us a dream start at the other end of the match and helped ensure that although Sri Lanka got away from us at the end of their innings, they were never going to post a score that was beyond us.

Kasprowicz came in for Brett Lee: we figured he deserved his chance, and also felt that with his ability to bowl off-cutters and get the ball to reverse swing late on, he might find conditions to his liking. As it turned out, it was his opening burst, in partnership with his great mate Gillespie, that helped decide the match. The pair of them love World Wrestling Entertainment and early on they had the Sri Lankan batting in a headlock: Kasprowicz gave nothing away at one end and Gillespie opened up the top order at the other.

We soon discovered that the pitch gave plenty of help to the new ball bowler. There was a little swing and seam but, more importantly, there was bounce and carry for both Gillespie and Kasprowicz and they exploited it perfectly, starting in the first over.

Our plan with Sanath Jayasuriya is to try to make sure we never give him any width to free his arms and swing hard, because he can really hurt us if he gets on a roll. Instead we try to cramp him for room by bowling just short of a length at his body. He grips the bat very low and is not a natural hooker, so he does not like that line of attack.

Gillespie found a short ball for Jayasuriya that bounced more than the batsman expected. He tried to run it down to third man but we had positioned Clarke around where third slip would normally be and the ball went straight to him. That was not the only success we had with that 'floating' slip: Kumar Sangakkara fell in similar fashion a little later on, with Matthew Hayden taking the catch that time.

The idea behind using a fielder in that position rather than a man at first slip is pretty straightforward. It allows the bowlers to operate just short of a driving length; if the batsman then tries to run the ball down the third man to get off strike, he runs the risk of being caught by that fielder if the ball bounces a bit more than he expects — which is exactly what happened today. Things do not always work out so well, but today was one of those times when the plan worked perfectly.

Those two wickets for Gillespie book-ended his dismissal of Marvan Atapattu, with a ball that cut back sharply off the seam and cannoned into the top of his stumps off the inside edge. It was another beautiful piece of bowling, as the ball came back at pace. By removing Sri Lanka's three leading batsmen, Gillespie did more than enough to claim the man of the match award he was later given.

With Kasprowicz and Gillespie bowling so well, I wanted to keep them going for as long as possible — the chance of getting more wickets would increase our stranglehold on the match. At the same time I was aware that they were my only two frontline quick bowlers and I needed something from them for later on. On top of that, I had to be careful not to bowl them into the ground — it was really hot in the middle. I gave them a breather after Gillespie bowled eight overs and Kasprowicz seven, and initially I was still able to retain control, thanks to Brad Hogg and Ian Harvey. Hogg, in particular, caused Arnold all sorts of problems. He could not seem to pick which way Hogg was spinning the ball, so it came as no surprise when he was dismissed, slogging the ball high to deep midwicket.

But that was our last success for some time. Mahela Jayawardene and Tillakaratne Dilshan played with increasing freedom, and even when Dilshan edged a drive at Symonds' arm-ball, the total continued to mount.

Jayawardene skilfully pushed the ball into gaps while Upul Chandana nudged the ball around in support, even though he appeared to be struggling with illness. He was not helped by the high humidity out in the centre, and towards the end of his innings he called for a runner. Dilshan came out, but managed to get run out looking for second run to Hogg at long-on.

A return from the deep by Hogg also saw off Jayawardene, just as he was starting to lift the tempo with off-side fours off first Ian Harvey and then Kasprowicz. With four overs to go, I was pretty content. But that was before Chaminda Vaas and Kumara Dharmasena spoiled the party a little with a late flourish.

Because I'd bowled Kasprowicz and Gillespie for so many overs at the start of the innings, I had to rely on Symonds towards the end of the innings. Vaas managed to get under a delivery from him and sent it over midwicket for six. The opening bowlers also struggled to contain the hitting, as Dharmasena moved around his stumps effectively, scoring runs on both sides of the pitch. He sliced Gillespie backward of square for four and then glanced Kasprowicz fine for another boundary with long leg up in the circle.

Sri Lanka scored 41 from their final four overs, which was too many with seven wickets down, but I felt their 226 was a target we could achieve fairly comfortably — even after we made a rotten start.

Matthew Hayden injured his knee sliding over the boundary rope stopping a cover drive from Chandana when we were in the field, and he was in a fair amount of pain when he went out to open the innings. That may have accounted for his loose drive at Vaas — Muralitharan took the catch comfortably at cover.

I came in and got off the mark with a single to midwicket. Then, still in the same over, Adam Gilchrist edged a drive into the hands of Jayawardene at first slip. Suddenly we were 2–4 after three overs. We had plenty of rebuilding to do.

The plan for me and Damien Martyn was simple: nothing too flashy, just rotate the strike, build a partnership and be prepared to put away the bad ball. We managed to do that, even though batting was not easy. The new ball proved tough to score off, as it had in Sri Lanka's innings, but not for the same reason. Then it was the extra bounce that Gillespie and Kasprowicz got, as well as the seam movement, that proved tough for their batsmen to deal with; now it was a hint of swing from Vaas and Nuwan Zoysa. The slower balls from those two bowlers were also gripping the pitch when they hit the seam, and that made it very difficult to time the ball.

One ball from Zoysa cut back so sharply it hit me in the abdominal protector before rushing past Sangakkara behind the stumps for four. The speed of the outfield was one factor in our favour: it was rock hard and the grass was cut short, so almost anything that beat the field was a boundary. The hardness of the ground made it very tough to field on — it felt like diving on concrete when you went down to stop a ball — but on surfaces like that it is a case of putting your body on the line. I lost some skin from my knees during the match and I was not the only one.

As in the second match at Dambulla, we gradually recovered from a poor start and got ourselves into a position of strength. Martyn and I just knocked their spinners around, looking for gaps and rotating the strike. We scored at 4 and 5 runs per over in relative comfort. With 20 overs left we needed less than 100 to win.

At that point things started to go wrong. Again, I was the player who started the slide, with another poorly executed shot. I am not sure why, but after playing pretty well with the full face of the bat I opted to try to run a ball from Vaas down to third man — but I chose the wrong delivery to do it. It was a slower ball, and I was through my shot a little too quickly. As a result, I got an inside edge back onto my stumps — a soft way to get out at a crucial stage of the match.

We always stress the need to avoid two established batsmen getting out in quick succession: that allows the bowling side to build pressure by having two new players to bowl out. Unfortunately, soon after I was out Martyn followed, run out at the non-striker's end backing up too far after Jayasuriya, who was bowling, quickly gathered a straight drive from Symonds and threw down the stumps. The heat may have contributed to Martyn's dismissal — he was pretty drained by then — but it still presented us with a real problem. And things only got worse: Michael Bevan was also run out soon afterwards.

Symonds clipped the ball out to deep midwicket and looked for two, but Bevan was a little slower than usual to get into his stride. Jayawardene, the fielder, picked that up and threw to the bowler's end. Bevan was well short of his ground; there was no need to refer the decision to the third umpire.

We had gone from 2–133 to 5–159, and with 12.3 overs left we appeared to be heading for a pretty likely defeat. But that was clearly not what either Symonds or Clarke was thinking.

What was most impressive was the way neither man panicked. Rather than looking for big shots they began their partnership by looking for the gaps and keeping the strike rotating; Clarke, in particular, was quick to turn ones into twos as he started to throw the pressure back onto the Sri Lanka fielders.

We still needed 52 from the final eight overs when the two players decided it was time to pick up the tempo. Symonds clobbered a sweep off Muralitharan through square leg for four, then hit Chandana through midwicket for another boundary when the leg-spinner dropped short, then took a single to get Clarke back on strike.

Chandana had not been well when he batted, and now he seemed to be showing some signs of fatigue, which was hardly surprising — it was still very humid out there. His next ball was a big full toss on leg-stump, and Clarke's first instinct was to try to clobber it for six.

He gave it a full swing of the bat out towards deep square leg — my first thought was that he had hit it straight down the throat of the fielder on the boundary and I shouted 'No!' as soon as he struck it. Luckily, I was wrong: he'd got more than enough bat on ball to clear the ropes. All of a sudden we were in the middle of a match-turning over.

If that six was not enough, Clarke played perhaps the shot of the night in the next over, this time off Muralitharan. The master spinner has trapped plenty of players with deliveries that turn so quickly that the batsman cannot adjust once he has opted to play back, but Clarke has such quick reflexes, and such a quick swing of the bat, that he can almost defy physics. Muralitharan's off-spinners were pitching at least 30 centimetres outside off-stump, and turning and bouncing enough to comfortably miss leg-stump, but Clarke was up to the challenge: giving himself room, he cut the ball through backward point like a bullet for four, bringing up the 200. Our confidence surged, and the body language of the fielding side began to look flat.

We still wanted 26 from five overs. Symonds put the matter almost beyond doubt with another remarkable shot, this time off Vaas: he clobbered him over extra-cover for six. It was an amazing shot, especially when he confirmed what we saw on the TV replay — it came off somewhere near the bottom of his bat.

We cruised home with nine balls in hand, an amazing margin of victory given our earlier struggles, and exactly the shot in the arm we needed after the loss in Dambulla. It was a happy dressing room, made even happier by another one of Hogg's classics as we debated the arrangements for practice tomorrow.

John Buchanan and Jock Campbell told Hogg to take it easy and not bother having a net session. Hogg disagreed. 'I just want to bowl 12 balls tomorrow, that's all,' he said.

'Why 12?' asked Jock.

'Four leg-breaks, four wrong 'uns and a flipper,' came the reply.

Jock was confused. 'That's only nine, what about the other three?' he asked.

'They are spares, in case I get any of the other nine wrong,' said Hoggy. He is a gem.

Michael Clarke

In an era when the average age of the Australian side has been rising, there is always going to be an extra weight of expectation on a young player when he comes into the squad, but I am confident Michael Clarke can handle it.

To me he comes across as someone who is pretty level-headed, despite the success he has had relatively early in his career. And the good news is that he seems hungry for more success, rather than believing he has made it now that he is on the list of contracted players.

I saw that hunger first-hand in Sri Lanka when, as part of the one-day side, he was left out of the squad for the Test series that followed. Rather than sulk or get upset, he responded in the best way possible: by taking five wickets with the ball in the next game and then playing a match-winning innings with the bat in the game after that.

During that Sri Lanka tour I took the opportunity to have a word with him about handling all the expectations placed on him by himself and others; I feel there are similarities between us, not only in the instinctive way we play but also in the way we were hyped as youngsters.

I tried not to give him advice, because he is more advanced in his thinking and maturity than I was at his age, but I did say I was around if he wanted someone to chat with about the way he is going about his life and his game. I have been in the situation he is in now, and have made mistakes — if I can help him avoid making similar errors, that has to be a good thing.

Clarke impressed me with his attitude in the wake of the West Indies tour. It was his first overseas trip after breaking into the one-day side during the VB Series in 2003, and it was clear during the tour that he was not fit enough. Playing the role he was — batting in the latter stages of a one-day innings — he needed to be able to scamper between the wickets as though his life depended on it and then immediately regain his breath and composure so that he could think clearly and hit good shots. He coped, but not as well as he should have, and it was something he clearly needed to work on.

To his credit, he did just that through the winter, and when he went to India for the TVS Cup he was in much better shape, which helped him play a crucial innings for us in the final.

My one concern with Clarke is that by spending so much time away with the one-day side, his first-class opportunities — and, as a result, his form — may suffer. There have been plenty of examples of players on the fringes of the squad who have been overlooked for Test selection because others from outside the group have been scoring runs or taking wickets in Pura Cup and

ING Cup matches and have had the chance to press their claims to the selectors.

I do not want to see that happen to Clarke; I would like to see him slotted into the Test side at the earliest possible opportunity, as I believe we have to make the most of his talent. However, at the same time I realise he may have to bide his time; there is no slot available at the moment and there are plenty of other fine players pressing their case for inclusion. I am pleased he has decided to go and play some county cricket in the UK during the winter of 2004 — that will give him the chance to improve his game by playing plenty of first-class cricket in conditions different from those he may be used to.

His potential as a Test and one-day player is increased because he can bowl some useful left-arm spin. At a time when we have generally played just four frontline bowlers, having someone else who is able to send down 10 overs a day is a priceless asset. That, together with his electric skills in the field, will always help his case for selection.

Clarke is a confident person, very sure of himself, and he showed that right from the time he made his international debut, against England in Adelaide in 2003. Not many players could have arrived for the match at the eleventh hour as he did, replacing the suspended Darren Lehmann, and still perform well, but he bowled tidily, fielded brilliantly and then played a nerveless innings to seal the win.

I am sure some of Clarke's confidence results from the fact that he is a New South Wales player — that is a state where a youngster has to prove himself in pretty impressive company. At the same time, however, he is not arrogant. In fact, I have always found him quite the opposite, but if he has something to say on the field he will say it, and he is constructive in team meetings.

A performance like Clarke's debut, allied with his efforts since then, convinces me that he has what it takes to succeed at international level. I hope the selectors give him every opportunity to establish himself — he has a great deal to offer Australian cricket.

Thursday 26 February

Five of the players — Jason Gillespie, Brad Williams, Simon Katich, Michael Bevan and Brad Hogg — practised at the ground, but for the rest of us it was a day of rest. I started with a lie-in, followed by some recovery work with Jock Campbell, then surfed the internet. It was very hot, and with the prospect of it being pretty similar tomorrow, I could not see the point in doing anything that might cost me some energy before then.

I did make the effort to join Damien Martyn and Matthew Hayden for a very sociable drink in the Galle Face Hotel at the end of the day and I am glad I did — not only because of the company, but because of the setting. It is a beautiful old building across the road from our hotel, and it overlooks the sea, so it is the perfect place to watch the sun go down.

Hayden spent most of the day having treatment for the leg injury he picked up diving in the field yesterday. I know Alex Kontouri was not too hopeful about Hayden playing tomorrow when he first saw him, but now both of them seem quite confident about the big man making it, which is encouraging.

Friday 27 February

Fourth one-day international, R Premadasa Stadium, Colombo: Australia 233 (Ponting 67, Symonds 53) beat Sri Lanka 193 (Sangakkara 101, Kasprowicz 5–45) by 40 runs.

It may be because this performance is fresh in my mind, but I am convinced that our win tonight, which sealed the one-day series with one match in hand, was one of our best of recent years.

We had setbacks with the bat and in the field, but rather than crumble, we hung in there. That tenacity was rewarded with a great spell from Michael Kasprowicz which got us home — with, in the end, quite a bit to spare.

We could have won more easily than we did, though. We should have got more than 233, especially after we reached 5–201 with ten overs to go. But Sri Lanka fought back hard at that point and we had to be grateful for an intelligent innings from Michael Clarke, along with support from Jason Gillespie, to get us to that 233.

Kumar Sangakkara's innings — one of the best I have seen at this level for as long as I can remember — threatened to take the series to a final match decider, until a combination of his fatigue and Kasprowicz's persistence saw him off. Once we got that opening we bolted through to the finish line, silencing 40,000 noisy fans.

It was another roasting hot day, and I was again disappointed — but not surprised — to see that the locals had opted to follow the lead of the matches at Dambulla and use a pitch for the second time rather than produce a new strip. It meant we could expect some really sharp turn late on in the match, so chasing would be tough. Clearly, it would be better to bat first; I managed to secure us that right by winning the toss again.

Adam Gilchrist fell early, walking for a thin edge down the leg-side off Nuwan Zoysa, and that brought me to the crease. I have felt in great form throughout the tour and today was no exception. I passed 50 — for the fifth time in five innings — but once again was not able to go on with the job and get the big score we needed. That is frustrating, and it's something I hope I can put right once the Test series gets underway.

Straight away today I was into my stride. I clipped my first ball through midwicket for four, but my confidence almost proved my undoing. After I ducked under the bouncer that followed, Zoysa gave me a well-disguised slower ball that was full and outside the off-stump. My eyes lit up and I went for a big drive, only to check my shot when I saw that the ball had been held back on me. The result was that I chipped the ball towards mid-off, but although Sanath Jayasuriya timed his jump pretty well, he just could not get high enough off the ground to haul it in — instead, with the outfield once again rock hard and running fast, I picked up a second boundary.

I whipped Zoysa for a second four through midwicket two overs later, and when Chaminda Vaas dropped short I was back and in position quickly to pull him high and handsome over square leg for successive sixes. It was one of those innings when I saw the ball early, my feet moved quickly and everything hit the middle of my bat.

At the other end I lost two partners. First Matthew Hayden was the victim of some good thinking by the Sri Lankans. He likes to bat out of his crease and drive the new ball bowlers, but Sangakkara spotted this and decided to stand up to the stumps. It meant Hayden was penned back and, instead of being able to move down the pitch, he had to look for other areas to score in because with Sangakkara standing up it increased the risk of the batsman being stumped. He decided that with fine leg up in the circle he would try to paddle Vaas away in that area. Unfortunately, his execution was not quite right — he managed to find the fielder rather than the gap, with Zoysa taking a sharp catch.

Damien Martyn came in, but departed pretty quickly, the victim of another good catch by Zoysa, this time at short cover after Martyn produced a loose drive off the leg-spin of Kaushal Lokuarachchi. Suddenly we were 3–62. That brought Andrew Symonds to the crease. Straight away he looked as though he was taking up where he left off on Wednesday night, cutting Lokuarachchi for four to get underway then settling in nicely and rotating the strike, mainly by punching the spinners down the ground for singles.

We took the total to 3–136 with 22 overs in hand, and looked set for a score well in excess of 250 when Muttiah Muralitharan got me with one of his trademark balls, a big spinning off-break. I played back, looking to work it on the leg-side, but was beaten by the speed and amount of turn he got on the ball and was trapped plumb in front. What's more, I knew that ball was probably the last of Murali's spell: this was his sixth over in succession. The Sri Lankans like to use him in the middle overs to try to get a breakthrough, but if it does not come they take him off — which puts the pressure for a breakthrough back on the other bowlers, of course — because the captain is keen to keep a few overs for him at the end of the innings. I was right: as soon as I was out they whipped Muralitharan out of the attack, but now there was less pressure on the bowlers who followed, because they had a new batsman to bowl at.

Sri Lanka were also a little lucky that the new batsman was Michael Bevan. He has been struggling for form on this trip and was handicapped today by a groin strain, so we did lose some momentum during that period. In fact, that loss of momentum may have contributed to Symonds' dismissal. Having played beautifully and without too many risks, he suddenly tried to lift the tempo and slog-swept Muralitharan right off the middle of the bat — straight to Saman Jayantha at deep midwicket. Now we were five down.

There was still no need to panic. Bevan had taken time to play himself in, and with Clarke joining him we still had every reason to believe we could comfortably top 250. But that was before a disastrous 12 ball spell when we lost four wickets for five runs. Suddenly we were faced with the prospect of being bowled out well ahead of our 50 overs.

A collapse like that just goes to show that you can never take things for granted, no matter how experienced you are. As the wickets fell, we all recognised the need for someone to dig in, especially as we had a top-order batsman, Clarke, still there, but the players who went in just found silly ways of getting out and suddenly our last pair were together with eight overs to go.

Bevan had never really looked comfortable, so it was no surprise when, looking to turn the ball on the leg-side, he got a leading edge back to the bowler, Muralitharan. That brought in Ian Harvey, and he got underway with a cracking square cut for four, but he was then guilty of ball-watching rather than looking for a single when he played the ball to backward point. Clarke set off but Harvey was slow to respond, and in the end he was miles short of his ground when the throw came in to the bowler's end.

That meant Brad Hogg was on strike for the first ball of the next over, which was leg-spin from Chandana, and straight away he was plumb lbw, playing half-forward to a ball that turned enough to beat the bat — he'd been trying to work it on the leg-side. Michael Kasprowicz then managed to play the rest of the over looking as though he had never picked up a bat, finally thin-edging a cut shot through to the keeper.

We had gone from 5–201 to 9–206: there could be no better illustration of the difficulties of batting in the second half of the innings on a Sri Lankan pitch. The ball turns sharply and it can be tough to get established, but if you manage it, you really have to make the most of your opportunity rather than leaving it for someone else. That has been my mistake throughout this one-day series.

Clarke responded to the situation sensibly, pushing the ball around while Gillespie gave him good support at the other end. At the same time, Clarke did not ignore the chance to put away the bad ball, as he did when Vaas gave him some width outside the off-stump.

He played really well — 36 from 32 balls — but in the end he decided to look for big shots an over or two earlier than he might have done with number 11 for company. Trying to drive Upal Chandana over long-on for six, he miscued and hit it straight to the fielder on the boundary. We were gone, and we had failed to use 14 balls of our innings. It might not sound a lot, but if you think of it in terms of a possible 14 singles, you realise it could add a fair chunk to your total.

I was not unhappy with 233; it was a reasonable score. As I said to the players before we went out to field, it was a second-day pitch, and with the ball likely to grip and die off the surface, as well as turn sharply for our spinners, it was not going to be an easy chase for Sri Lanka.

My view seemed to be confirmed almost straight away. Kasprowicz removed Sanath Jayasuriya with his second ball. It was a great delivery that bounced and moved away from the batsman. Unfortunately, all that did was bring in Sangakkara, who played a gem of an innings, which for a long time looked destined to take the match away from us.

Right from the start he looked in great touch, with two boundaries in that opening Kasprowicz over: one through backward point and the other a lovely cover drive. He flew to 50 from just 45 balls, including 11 fours. The match was racing away from us at breakneck speed.

Sangakkara's skill made it look as if Kasprowicz was bowling very badly to him — Sangakkara kept hammering him through point, at one stage scoring three fours in a row through that area. In reality, Kasprowicz was bowling perfectly well; it's just that Sangakkara plays the ball with the face of the bat open, so even when the bowler gets the ball reasonably tight into his body he can still get it away square of the wicket on the off-side. It means a bowler's margin for error is very small, especially as Sangakkara is also skilled at working the ball through the leg-side if the bowler strays onto the line of middle stump.

Our one piece of good fortune was that Marvan Atapattu, at the other end, was struggling to find his timing, especially as Sangakkara was dominating the strike. We could tell he was getting frustrated, and sure enough, rather than opt to play second fiddle to the man on form, he threw his wicket away, running down the pitch to Hogg and lofting him straight to Bevan at long-on.

It was the breakthrough we needed, but at first there was no sign that it would be decisive. Mahela Jayawardene came in and pushed the ball around nicely while Sangakkara continued to play his strokes. Our main hope was that Sangakkara would tire — the humidity was still high and he had already kept wicket throughout our innings. When Symonds and Hogg could not get us another wicket I brought back Gillespie. By this stage Sri Lanka needed less than 100 to win and had more than 20 overs in hand, so while Gillespie was not the last throw of the dice, it was vitally important that we broke up the batting pair. Luckily, Gillespie succeeded: Jayawardene played a wild attempted cut shot, completely out of character with the rest of his innings.

That wicket gave me renewed belief that we could win. I sprinted off to go to the bathroom while the new batsman came out, and as I reached our viewing area I shouted to John Buchanan and anyone else who cared to listen: 'If we can get Sangakkara we will win.'

It was Kasprowicz who got that breakthrough. I brought him on to replace Gillespie — I wanted to save Gillespie for a couple of overs at the end in case the match got tight and he had already bowled eight overs. Kasprowicz was the natural replacement. He started the over by conceding the two runs that saw Sangakkara to his hundred, then produced a ball that went across the left-hander. He edged a tired wave at the ball and Gilchrist accepted the chance. Now we had two new batsmen to bowl at, and the pressure was on them rather than us.

Harvey intensified that pressure by removing Jayantha via a great catch from Gilchrist, standing up to the stumps, and Sri Lanka lost their last recognised batsman in Tillakaratne Dilshan when he was short of his ground attempting a quick single at midwicket, which was where I was. I was moving to my right to get the ball, away from where I needed to throw it, but still managed to flick it back across my body to the bowler's end, where Symonds, over the stumps, having taken over the bowling from Kasprowicz, produced a great bit of work to whip the bails off.

Sri Lanka still had dangerous lower order hitters, as we had seen in Wednesday night's game, when they added 41 from the last four overs, but I was determined we were not going to give them even a sniff of a chance, so I recalled Kasprowicz.

With his first ball he found some extra bounce that forced Chandana into giving Gilchrist his fifth catch. That put us firmly in the box seat, but there was still time for me to lose my cool with the umpires. That wicket prompted them to get together and decide to change the ball, a decision which made me furious. Right at the start of the series I asked for consistency in the decision to change the ball, because it is something that usually works in favour of the batting side. The replacement ball is usually harder and therefore easier to hit, and it also tends to offer less reverse swing. I reminded Billy Bowden, the senior umpire on the ground, that I had pleaded for consistency and that the ball had not been changed either during our innings or during our run chase when we batted second under lights two days ago. I got quite heated. He pointed out that there had been no complaint about the ball by our batsmen in either of our last two innings. He had a fair point, but I just felt that everything I had said before the series had been ignored; that is why I got a bit hot under the collar.

It did not matter. Kasprowicz found some swing with the replacement ball and picked up Vaas — giving Gilchrist a record-equalling sixth catch — and Lokuarachchi in the same over, and when Hogg trapped Zoysa in the next over with a perfectly pitched flipper we were home, with plenty to spare.

We were ecstatic, as anyone watching could tell from our reaction out on the ground. Winning the one-day series is the first part of our target on this tour, and we have achieved that first goal with a match to spare. The success has once again confirmed our place as the best one-day side in the world.

We sang our team song, led by Gilchrist, in the rooms after the match, but did not hang around there too late. As we packed up to leave the ground our baggage man, Siripala, managed to fall over under the weight of bags he was picking up — luckily, he was fine. He is amazingly strong for someone built so slightly.

We headed back to the hotel to celebrate in the bar and wait for the members of the Test squad — Justin Langer, Darren Lehmann, Stuart MacGill, Wade Seccombe and Shane Warne — to arrive from Australia, something they didn't do till well after midnight. It was great to see the Test squad boys but they were pretty tired, so after a short while with us they just wanted to get some sleep. It turned out a couple of them had some company, because the hotel was overbooked. Warne had to share with Harvey and Darren Lehmann had to share with Clarke. No one seemed too concerned, though. After all, we were all on a high, celebrating a great series win.

Michael Kasprowicz

If you had to name one player who does not have an enemy in the game, the chances are it would be Michael Kasprowicz. He is the gentle giant of Australian cricket, and over the past year he has come back into contention for Test and one-day honours at a time when the careers of many fast bowlers are starting to wind down.

It has been a long journey back to this point for Kasper, and he must have wondered if his time had come and gone as the selectors looked at a host of bowling options before he was finally recalled during the VB Series in 2004.

He had last played in 2001, when he and the rest of the Australian attack had the misfortune to run into the broad bats of VVS Laxman and Rahul Dravid. Since then, however, he has almost reinvented himself, and he is now producing the most effective bowling of his international career.

Kasprowicz has sacrificed much of his ability to find orthodox swing in the search for extra pace, and although he is no Brett Lee, he is still capable of hurrying up even the best players. His height means he can find disconcerting bounce from most surfaces, and he is one of the best exponents of reverse-swing in world cricket.

He bowled so well in Sri Lanka that the selectors are likely to have a major problem on their hands in the near future when Brett Lee regains full fitness. Then they will have four fast bowlers — Lee, Kasprowicz, Jason Gillespie and Glenn McGrath — jostling for three places ... unless they decide to repeat the tactic of the West Indies tour and choose five bowlers. I think that is unlikely, because it would make our tail too long. So one of the quartet is set to miss out, and given the way Kasprowicz has performed, it would be tough if he were the man to go.

Whether or not he plays, Kasprowicz is a great man to have around. He has a great sense of humour, something he showed when quizzed about the fact that he always seems to be chosen for tours to the subcontinent — he has two tours of India and one to Sri Lanka under his belt — instead of tours to more fashionable places, such as the West Indies, England or South Africa. 'I like cocktails with little umbrellas in them too,' he said, suggesting he would not mind a trip to the Caribbean if there was one on offer.

That sense of humour was also on show on the India tour of 2001, when he — along with Damien Fleming and Jason Gillespie — kept us entertained. That trio are huge fans of World Wrestling Entertainment and they used a camcorder to make a spoof documentary paying homage to their wrestling heroes. They even dressed up in ridiculous masks and outfits — it was brilliant.

Kasprowicz is a natural sportsman, and could have found success in rugby union. He played at age-group level and was sounded out even in recent years about playing part-time in his home state; he knocked it back when there were complications over insurance cover because of his cricket commitments.

At that stage he doubted whether he would ever play for Australia again, but his continuing excellence has earned him another chance and he has taken it with both hands. With his economical approach to the crease, his bowling know-how and his growing level of success at international level, Kasprowicz could be around for a while yet.

Saturday 28 February

It really is amazing — Shane Warne seems to be news wherever he goes. He has not been on tour for 24 hours yet, but already the trip seems to have taken on a higher profile than it had before.

Everyone is clambering over each other to hear what he says about his hopes for this trip. The demand for words from our champion leg-spinner was so great that he held a media conference at 3 o'clock this afternoon, just before we had a team walk along the sea front opposite our hotel. I do not know what he said at the media conference, but whatever it was, it certainly prompted the television cameramen and photographers to come out in force for what we all thought was a fairly low-key recovery session after yesterday's one-day international. We were mobbed by journalists looking for pictures of our walk, with Warne the centre of attention.

Then we had selection issues to discuss. The selectors want me to rest from either tomorrow's one-day international or the three-day lead-up game before the first Test. We decided it would be the one-dayer. As it is my first Test tour as captain I am keen to play in the lead-up match, particularly as that match will include players like

Michael Kasprowicz and Warne, both of whom have been out of the Test scene for a while. It will be a useful exercise for all of us — and for me to get into captaincy mode in the longer form of the game. So I will sit out tomorrow's match.

That means Adam Gilchrist will have to play; after a fair amount of thought, it was decided that he will also keep wicket. Originally the idea was for Brad Haddin — our back-up keeper in the one-day series and someone who has stood in for Adam Gilchrist in the past at home and abroad — to keep while Gilchrist had a run around in the field. But after Gilly thought about it, he decided that if he was going to play he might as well keep wicket — so now Haddin will get the chance to stretch his legs and test out his throwing arm.

Haddin has been unlucky, as has Simon Katich, because of the way the series has gone. Originally we wanted to rest a few players for the fourth match (if we had sealed the series by then), but things did not work out that way and those two have been left to kick their heels. Both will play tomorrow, although the exact make-up of the side will have to wait until just before the toss — we are waiting on a report on Michael Bevan's fitness. He came to me at the start of our time in the field yesterday complaining of a groin strain, and although he made it back onto the field later, after treatment from Alex Kontouri, we want to make sure he is right to play before throwing him into a one-day international, especially as we have fit players in reserve.

Sunday 29 February

Fifth one-day international, Singhalese Sports Club, Colombo: Australia 7–198 lost to Sri Lanka 7–202 by 3 wickets.

After the excitement of winning the series on Friday, this match ended up as a let-down for us. Sri Lanka managed to gain a consolation victory that will lift their self-belief for the Test series.

We will be accused of a lack of intensity and focus and the old saying about dead rubbers will resurface after a defeat like this; it is something we always get when we lose a match like this. But as I watched from the sidelines, I thought we did okay.

It needs to be remembered that we went into this match with quite a few players who have not played a lot of cricket on the trip — and we left out Jason Gillespie, Ian Harvey, Matthew Hayden and me. Despite that, when we took the home side's seventh wicket, with

63 still required, I think most people around the ground would have had us favourites to win the match.

Sri Lanka were able to get home quite comfortably, as it turned out: they still had a recognised batsman at the crease — Russel Arnold, who played pretty well — and at the other end, the big left-arm seam bowler Nuwan Zoysa played a remarkable innings, full of clean hitting. It was one of those days when everything he touched turned to gold: he bowled well too, leading the attack in the absence of the injured Chaminda Vaas.

Gilchrist bit the bullet and batted first even though it was a day game and all our information about the ground suggested that the ball would swing and seam early on. It did just that, and batting against their attack of Zoysa and Nuwan Kulasekera, a skiddy little medium-pacer, was far from easy, especially for Haddin, who was playing his first one-day international of the tour.

Sri Lanka bowled well, and that, combined with a few questionable pieces of judgement from our batsmen, cost us wickets and the chance to build early momentum. Haddin tried to drive a ball over the in-field but instead skied it to mid-off, Michael Clarke top-edged an ambitious pull to Muralitharan, Simon Katich ran himself out looking for a dicey second run to third man, and Damien Martyn, having played himself in, was bowled trying to steer Muralitharan to third man for a single.

In the end it took a sensible stand from Andrew Symonds and Brad Hogg to get us up to a total that was defendable. They came together at 6–120 in the 35th over and decided that with 15 overs left they could not afford to accelerate too early, in case either of them got out — with only four wickets in hand, there was not a lot of batting to come.

They pushed the ball around for ones and twos for almost ten overs before trying to press on a little harder in the final six overs. That approach was shown to be correct, as we managed to add 58 runs in that time.

Symonds hit straight and hard, with four off Upul Chandana and six off Muralitharan, and Hogg was nudging and deflecting, placing the ball well to pick up ones and twos and offering Symonds good support. The fact that we had a left-hand and right-hand combination at the crease also helped, as it always does, by forcing the bowlers to keep changing their line.

As Hogg and Symonds pushed the ball around before their late assault, the crowd near our dressing room area became distracted — and not just because the match had hit a bit of a flat spot. The newly arrived Test squad members turned up at the ground for a practice session and, as usual, it seemed everyone wanted to say hello to Shane Warne.

The practice nets are behind our dressing room, but after the session Warne had to come around the front of the stand to do an interview for the television channel broadcasting the match. To get there he had to get quite close to the public area, because the gate around the back of the dressing rooms was shut. That upset our security manager, Reg Dickason: he is particularly concerned about Warney's safety. Warne and Arjuna Ranatunga, the former Sri Lanka captain, do not see eye to eye and have been having a war of words in the media, and while no one is expecting Ranatunga to come along to the ground and belt Warne, all it would take is for one of his supporters to take offence at something that has appeared in the media and Warne could be in real danger. However, none of this actually happened.

I thought we bowled pretty well to get so close to defending a relatively low score, and was especially impressed with Symonds; he gave us real cause for optimism for the Test series ahead. He bowled his off-spinners really well to an attacking line just outside off-stump, and spun them sharply, bowling Tillakaratne Dilshan with an absolute beauty through the gate and having Chandana caught at short leg off bat and pad. Kasprowicz and Brad Williams also bowled well on a pitch that did not offer them a great deal, and Hogg, although he was expensive, got Kumar Sangakkara with a great piece of thinking, bowling him around the legs first ball after switching to around the wicket. He spotted Sangakkara taking a big stride back and across to play him on the leg-side, and that made him think he could clip the leg-stump, something he did superbly well when Sangakkara missed his attempted leg-glance.

Even though I was not captain today, I spoke to the media after the match about the series as a whole. The lack of media conference facilities at the ground means that any chats I have with the press have to take place out on the field after the presentation ceremony, which is not ideal. Everyone is standing up, so the chats are usually quite short and to the point, which is a plus for everyone, but the downside is that you tend to get crowded by people not related to the media — and it can also be pretty hot out there.

I said I was disappointed to lose the match and felt that if luck had gone our way we could have won the series 5–0 rather than 3–2. We lost the second match by just one run, after having the worst of conditions, and would have won today's match as well but for that late stand between Zoysa and Arnold. On that basis I was pretty pleased with the way things have gone for us on the tour so far.

Trevor Hohns was heading home after the match, so we picked the side for the three-day match that starts on Tuesday during the day. We opted to rest Gilchrist, Hayden, Martyn and Gillespie, so the match is certain to be billed as a bat-off between Symonds, Katich and Lehmann for two spots in the middle order.

This will be tough on Katich, who made a brilliant hundred in our last Test, against India in Sydney, but if the pitch in Galle is as we expect, with not much grass and likely to favour spin, he will be the one who will miss out. A pitch like that means we will play both leg-spinners, Warne and Stuart MacGill, so we will need someone who can act as a third seamer, and Symonds fits that bill. Lehmann was one of our best players before he got injured, and with his ability against spin he should come straight back in.

Despite having lost, we hung around in the dressing room after the match — it was a chance for everyone to reflect on the one-day series over a beer. The one-day players departed last, with our liaison officer and team manager Steve Bernard taking them, along with Trevor Hohns and his wife, who had been with us throughout the one-day series, out to the airport for the flight home. Bernard, meanwhile, is flying to Zimbabwe, to link up with Cricket Australia's General Manager, Cricket Operations Michael Brown. They will be going through security and logistical arrangements for our tour there, due to start in May; we will not see him until we get to Galle at the end of the week. It is amazing that one tour is not even halfway through and we are planning for the next one. I guess that is what international cricket is all about these days.

Wade Seccombe and Brad Haddin

There are plenty of players in Australian cricket who must sometimes wish they'd been born in another era, and it would be no surprise if Brad Haddin and Wade Seccombe were two of them. At another time — in the mid-1980s, for example, when Australia tried any number of wicketkeepers before finally discovering Ian Healy — either man may well have become a regular at international level. Instead, both have found themselves jostling for position behind Adam Gilchrist, which is something of a thankless task given his brilliance on either side of the stumps.

Seccombe is used to waiting, having been Ian Healy's understudy at Queensland, but that role also meant he got plenty of chances to impress at state level when Healy was away on international duty, and he built a reputation as one of the best keepers in the country.

I had already seen his skills first-hand by that time, as he attended the Commonwealth Bank Cricket Academy during my second year in Adelaide. He was an excellent keeper, even at that age, but his batting was well and truly his weaker suit, and it drove the head coach, Rod Marsh, to distraction.

I remember on one occasion, after a net session where Seccombe had barely laid bat on ball, a frustrated Marsh said, only half-joking: 'Don't even try any more. Just concentrate on your keeping.' Luckily, Chuck disregarded that advice, and through sheer determination and perseverance has turned himself into a more than capable middle-order player.

The fact that he was able to do that does not surprise me: Seccombe is one of the hardest trainers in the game. At home in Brisbane he rides a bike wherever he can — he used to ride BMX bikes competitively when he was a teenager, and his playing number for Queensland is the same as the one he had when he was a racer — and he will often jog back to the hotel from the ground after a day's play.

He is also an intelligent man, and worked in Queensland Cricket's marketing department before quitting that job to tour with the Australia side to the UK when he was chosen as backup to Gilchrist in 2001. That sort of assignment is never easy, because if the first-choice player stays fit there is not much cricket for the backup to play. Seccombe made the best of it, relishing the chance to stay in shape by training as hard as any player on the trip and also proving a superb support to the one-day and Test playing elevens. When Brett Lee was injured on the last day of the tour, during The Oval Test match, Chuck went on as substitute for the last rites of the match — the chance for him to field in a Test was a well-deserved reward for his efforts.

On that trip Seccombe and another player who did not figure in the Test side, Damien Fleming, invented a new game, foccer, which even earned some space in the local media. Rather than just kick a soccer ball around or hand-pass and punt a football about as a way to warm up before or warm down after a day's play, the pair of them decided to combine the two games and play soccer using an Australian rules football.

The sight of blokes running around trying to control, pass and kick an oval-shaped ball as though it was round was an amazing laugh, although it was no fun trying to head it — and I am not sure what any fans who watched us must have thought.

Brad Haddin is easily more talented with the bat than Seccombe, and though it is a tough label to have, he has the potential to be the new Gilchrist, at least in one-day cricket. He played a brutal innings for New South Wales against Tasmania at Bankstown a couple of seasons ago, and while the boundaries were relatively short, he still struck the ball with immense power and timing.

Haddin's keeping has benefited from spending plenty of time up at the stumps to Stuart MacGill and Simon Katich on turning pitches in Sydney, and if he can continue to take his game forward, it will be a tough choice for the selectors when the time comes to find a replacement for Gilchrist.

In common with most keepers around the world, Haddin is a real chatter on the field, but off the ground he is a different bloke entirely. He is respectful, and calls you by your name — when we met he called me Ricky, which was unusual: most people just call me Punter, my nickname — but I liked that. I told him he could call me Punter now, just like everyone else.

Monday 1 March

The main focus of today was rest after the one-day series, and so although the new arrivals and those of the original squad who have not figured much so far on the trip did some extended work in the nets, for most of us it was a fairly light session. We played some touch football as a loosening-up exercise, and there was catching and throwing practice plus batting and bowling for those who felt they needed it.

I spoke to the media in the morning. The numbers of Australian journalists have now swelled: Jim Wilson from Channel Seven and ABC Radio's Jim Maxwell have both arrived. It turns out that the ABC is not covering the series live: Maxwell is just sending back updates of each day's play. That seems a real shame. Apparently it is all about the budget — this year also has the Olympic Games and our tour of India.

The media merry-go-round continued in the afternoon, with Adam Gilchrist heading out to the local television studio to take part in a live link-up to Australia for a sports panel show with Tony Squires. It turned out Mark Waugh was in the studio in Australia and Gilchrist reported a bit of good-natured banter between the two during the program. They know each other pretty well, as they opened the batting together for years in one-day cricket, and Junior Waugh was part of this squad till about 18 months ago.

We had a team meeting in the evening to make sure our focus is now on the longer form of the game. The tour match is only three days long, rather than the four-day matches we play at first-class level in Australia. I said the idea is to make sure that everyone playing gets at least one decent bat and all the bowlers get a good workout. I am especially keen for Warne to get a long bowl, because he has not had much cricket since returning to action last month.

We also used the meeting to outline our no-whingeing policy to the recently arrived players and to find out if any of the Test squad had a funny fact to give us that no one else knew. Stuart MacGill came up with a cracker: he said that while he was at the Commonwealth Bank Cricket Academy he worked on the ghost train at the Royal Adelaide Show, and his job was to scare people. I wonder what members of the public thought as they hurtled around the ride and MacGill jumped out at them.

Tuesday 2 March

Tour match, Colombo Cricket Club, Colombo, day one: The Australians 6–484 (Lehmann 134, Ponting 116, Katich 116) v Sri Lanka Cricket President's XI.

Today went just about as well as it could have. All our top order players batted for long periods and three of us scored hundreds.

I was one of them, at last managing to convert a start into a three-figure score, and I did it from the unaccustomed position of opening the innings. With Matthew Hayden resting, we needed someone to bat alongside Justin Langer at the top of the order; I opted to take on the challenge because it would give the other players a chance of some time at the crease against spin bowling.

I decided that it would be pointless promoting Simon Katich, Darren Lehmann or Andrew Symonds to do the job because they would then be batting against the new ball and seam bowlers, and if they bat in a Test match they will be coming in at number five or six, which means the chances are they will be facing slow bowling.

I felt in good form throughout my innings and that helped us maintain momentum at the start of the day, because Langer took some time to find his feet. The conditions were just about as far removed from those at the WACA ground in Perth as you could wish to find. He was still not in great touch by the time he was out, making 35 in 100 balls, but the time he spent at the crease will be invaluable for him for the Tests.

Lehmann and Katich were the other two players to score hundreds, and both played well. Katich has really developed his play against spin over the past couple of years, since his move to New

South Wales, as he showed when he scored 125 and 77 not out against India in January, and once again today he was happy to use his feet and skip down the pitch or wait if the ball was short. Lehmann, by contrast, was full of nudges, deflections, clubbing bottom-handed drives and cuts — by the end of the innings he was even standing outside leg-stump to the spinners. He does this to open up the off-side for his strokes, as well as to give the bowlers a different problem to think about. He is supremely confident about his ability to manoeuvre the ball wherever he wants, and used his time at the crease well today.

After play we had a warm-down in the hotel pool before I went to the airport with Chitral Mendis to meet Rianna. His contacts at the airport even managed to get me past customs so I was able to meet her in the baggage hall, which was a nice surprise for her after her long journey.

Wednesday 3 March

Tour match, Colombo Cricket Club, Colombo, day two: The Australians 6–484 declared and 4–250 (Symonds 119 not out, Langer 63) lead Sri Lanka Cricket President's XI 166 (Gunawardene 70, Lee 4–29) by 568 runs.

This was another brilliant day for us ahead of the first Test. All the bowlers had a workout as we knocked the home side over — more quickly than I could have hoped for — and then Andrew Symonds spent some quality time in the middle, as did Justin Langer, who showed signs of coming to terms with conditions after his lengthy spell at the crease in the first innings.

What pleased me most of all was the way Brett Lee bowled. He showed us his full box of tricks. With the new ball he bowled with good pace, swinging the ball in to the left-handers and away from the right-handers. His length was also excellent: not so full that he could be driven or sliced away for cheap runs and not so short that he could be cut or pulled. His effort left me really excited about the Test. He has troubled the Sri Lanka top order in the past, and on this form he will do that again, whatever the type of pitch we play on.

I might even take some credit for Lee's electric start to the day — he took two wickets in the first over. At our warm-down in the pool after the first day's play I said to anyone who wanted to listen: 'Bing [Lee] will take two wickets in the first over tomorrow: Russel Arnold and Gunawardene, both lbw.' He did take two wickets in that first over too, and one of them was Arnold, lbw first ball. Lee's ability to swing the new ball back into left-handers means he always has a chance of picking up an lbw against them early on, while batsmen are still trying to get used to conditions. Lee did not get a chance to remove Gunawardene in that first over — he was leaning on his bat at the non-striker's end — but he did make sure my prediction came at least partly true, by taking a second wicket four balls later, removing Saman Jayantha, a right-hander who played in the one-day series, with a top-class yorker. I wish I had that kind of foresight when it comes to predicting winners at the dog track.

The only downside with bowling the home side out so quickly — we finished their innings by mid-afternoon — was that Shane Warne only got 6.2 overs of bowling. I am sure he will get a much longer bowl in the second innings. His fellow leg-spinner, Stuart MacGill, bowled impressively, taking three wickets. It seems all the jigsaw pieces are falling into place for the Test series.

That appeared to be confirmed when Symonds helped himself to an unbeaten hundred when we batted again (I opted not to enforce the follow-on). He has carried the confidence gained from his performances in one-day cricket into the longer form of the game and is absolutely at the top of his form at the moment. On that basis alone I think now is the right time to pick him for the Test side; however, the final decision will have to wait until we get the chance to look at the surface in Galle and the selectors make their decision.

I have been really pleased with the way we have approached this match so far. It would be easy enough — but not acceptable — for us to just go through the motions. It is hot, some of the players have just come off the back of a tough one-day series, and the first Test is at the back of everyone's minds, whether they will admit it or not. But we have played with a real hunger and purpose so far, and if we can finish things off tomorrow, it will be the perfect lead-in to that first Test. It will also show Sri Lanka that we really do mean business — so far in this match, we have dominated a side that is full of players hoping to get into the Test squad.

Thursday 4 March

Sri Lanka name a 15-man squad for the first Test, in Galle: Hashan Tillakaratne (captain), Marvan Atapattu (vice-captain), Upul Chandana, Kumar Dharmasena, Tillakaratne Dilshan, Avishka Gunawardene, Sanath Jayasuriya, Mahela Jayawardene, Nuwan Kulasekera, Kaushal Lokuarachchi, Muttiah Muralitharan, Thilan Samaraweera, Kumar Sangakkara, Chaminda Vaas and Nuwan Zoysa.

Tour match, Colombo Cricket Club, Colombo, day three: The Australians 6–484 declared and 4–250 declared beat Sri Lanka Cricket President's XI 166 and 323 (de Silva 92, Ramyakumara 67, Samaraweera 50) by 245 runs.

Just when things were going so well, we have suffered a setback: Brett Lee has picked up an ankle injury, which has taken the gloss off our win against the side of Sri Lanka Test hopefuls. A scan has shown that there is no structural damage, but I am already more or less resigned to being without Lee in the Galle Test match.

Lee has a high pain threshold and will run through a brick wall if you ask him to, so when he came to me in his fourth over today and said he had to go off, I feared the worst straight away.

It turns out he has had a problem with his left ankle for a while, at least going back to the Sydney Test against India. On the second morning of that match his front foot was landing well behind the front line; at the time we all assumed it was because he was trying to get over the no-ball problem he'd had the previous day. In fact he was doing it to avoid landing around the hole dug by the bowlers' front feet on the first day — if you have a sore ankle and land awkwardly around a hole like that, it will hurt.

Lee told me he'd had some pain in the ankle during the one-day series. That surprised me — it was the first I'd heard of it. The bowlers all strap their ankles up for extra support before they take the field but obviously that is not enough for Lee now, and if he is struggling at this point it is difficult to see how we can take him into a Test match, even with four days' rest. Conditions are roasting hot here, with high humidity, and even if we expect a lot of the bowling to be done by spinners, we cannot afford to lose a member of our attack during the match. The scan was a positive, though. Alex Kontouri will now treat and monitor Lee over the next few days.

We won the match very comfortably after I declared on our overnight score. All our frontline bowlers had a decent workout, with Shane Warne making up for his lack of overs in the first innings with a long bowl this time around. The President's XI captain, Thilan Samaraweera, batted for a long time against him but Warne did not show him too many variations — Samaraweera has been named in Sri Lanka's squad for the Test match, so there's no need to give away everything just yet.

John Buchanan and assistant coach Tim Nielsen left early to head down to Galle and have a look at the pitch. They were joined by Matt Hayden, his wife, Kellie, and Jock Campbell; Hayden and Campbell are making the trip to give themselves the chance of a surf tomorrow morning. Our hotel in Galle is right on the beach, and apart from the high humidity the place is very similar to Barbados.

Friday 5 March

Today was all about trying to figure out whether or not Brett Lee has a chance of playing in the Test, which starts on Monday. Once we arrived in Galle, in the early afternoon, we had a meeting involving me, Brett, Alex Kontouri, John Buchanan, Tim Nielsen and Allan Border, who will be the selector on duty during the Test series.

We all wanted to know where Lee thought he was in terms of fitness for a five-day match, and he was honest enough to say that although he was confident he could bowl through one day, he was not sure how he would cope if he had to back it up with another day of bowling straight afterwards. Alex agreed with that assessment, and added that we would be taking a risk to pick Lee, especially if the plan is to go in with just two quick bowlers — and that is our plan.

I also chatted with Buchanan about his first impressions of the pitch, and he thinks it will offer a fair amount of turn. He is also not sure whether it will last five days. Like the rest of us, he wants to have another look at the surface as the match gets closer.

Saturday 6 March

The United Cricket Board of South Africa announces that it has agreed to stage the inaugural ICC Super Series in September 2005. It will involve the reigning Test and one-day international champions, Australia, playing three one-day matches and a Test against a Rest of the World side.

Today was our main training session at the venue before the Test, and after a chat during that session with Allan Border, I think we have settled on our side. We will play two fast bowlers and the two leg-spinners, which means Symonds will make his Test debut and Darren Lehmann will come back into the side after injury. This means no place for Simon Katich.

Before chatting to Border I had a look at the pitch, and my first impression is that we may be in for a three-day Test. The surface is dry and cracked and there appears to be crumbling and dusting around the cracks already. I think it may break up quite badly. Of course, trying to figure out how a pitch will play 48 hours before a match is hardly an exact science, but one way or the other I think we will get a result in this Test match.

Border and I wondered whether or not we could go into the match with three fast bowlers and try to unsettle Sri Lanka's batsmen that way. We saw in Dambulla that even when the surface is slow they are not happy if our quick bowlers get it in the right areas, and if the pitch does break up and become uneven it might be an advantage to have bowlers who will hit the surface harder, because that could make the ball misbehave far more.

On balance, however, we decided that we would be fighting the conditions if we went down that path. Sri Lanka obviously expect the pitch to offer some turn: they have four frontline spinners and two more part-timers in their squad. If we do go in with three quick bowlers it would mean leaving out one of Australia's two best spinners — either Shane Warne or Stuart MacGill. Together with Glenn McGrath, Warne has been our best bowler for a decade, and MacGill averages almost five wickets per Test through his career.

I know there is a view that they do not bowl well in tandem, but I do not agree with that. When they are both fully fit and on form they can be formidable, as they showed against South Africa at Sydney two years ago, when they bowled us to a four-day victory. The one remaining question we need to answer is who our two quick bowlers will be. One of them is obviously going to be Jason Gillespie, and the other will be either Michael Kasprowicz or Brad Williams. Brett Lee did not train today, and I think we have all but publicly put a line through his name for this Test. He had some more treatment from Alex Kontouri, but with conditions really hot again, there is no way we can take a risk with a bowler we are not sure will last the course.

Williams has never let us down in the past, but neither has Kasprowicz, and after the way he bowled in the one-day series I think we are likely to go with him to play what will be his first Test since the India tour three years ago. I think he believed his international days were over, so it just goes to show that if you keep bowling well and taking wickets the selectors cannot ignore you forever.

This evening we had a great team dinner that brought home to me, if I did not realise it already, that I am about to captain Australia in a Test match for the first time. The dinner was on the lawn of the hotel overlooking the sea and was attended by not only the touring party but also Michael Brown of Cricket Australia, directors Jack Clarke, Bob Horsell and Allan Border, and partners of the players, including Rianna. It was hardly a formal function, but Michael

Brown spoke on behalf of Cricket Australia and then Adam Gilchrist got up and said a few words, wishing me luck on behalf of all the lads. He also added a couple of great touches of his own to top off proceedings. First he played a video in which all the lads had recorded a good luck message for me, and then he presented me with a Test match shirt signed with messages from the whole squad. The evening left me feeling very humble, and also very proud to be captain of this group of players.

Sunday 7 March

We had our final team meeting ahead of the Test today and we used it to let all the players and support staff know that we have settled on a side. After my discussions with Allan Border yesterday, the only issue we had to resolve was which quick bowler we would pick to support Jason Gillespie. We settled on Michael Kasprowicz. There were congratulations all round for Andrew Symonds, who will make his debut, and for Darren Lehmann, Shane Warne and Michael Kasprowicz, all of them back after lengthy absences. Typically, Simon Katich, Brad Williams and Brett Lee were there to shake the hands of the players who were picked ahead of them. The way players all pull together, even when they are not in the final eleven, is one of the major strengths of our unit, and has been ever since I can remember.

Despite the fact that we have chosen our eleven, I told everyone I did not want to read about it in tomorrow morning's newspaper. I am keen to keep the Sri Lankans guessing about the make-up of our side — I do not want to give them too much time to plan how they will deal with our new-look attack.

Having said that, I reckon they will have already guessed that Lee is not going to play. He did not train again, and as he has not bowled since he pulled up injured on Thursday they will know we are unlikely to take a risk with him.

We discussed tactics. Our general policy with the ball is to be pretty aggressive to their batsmen without overdoing the short stuff; with individual players we will try to bowl certain lines:

- Jayasuriya — short of a length in at his body, giving him no width. That will take away his big shots through the off-side.
- Atapattu — maintain a line tight to the off-stump but do not get too straight, as he can get the ball through the on-side. Try to bring him forward to drive, because he does not

always get his front foot right to the pitch of the ball and can be vulnerable to the ball that cuts back.

- Sangakkara — like Jayasuriya, do not give him width. Good player of quick bowling but not all that strong down the ground, driving back past the bowler.
- Jayawardene — be disciplined with a line around off-stump, as he is a candidate to nick a catch behind the stumps. He is a compulsive hooker, so do not be afraid to use the short ball.
- Dilshan — something of an unknown quantity, but seems to like to play his shots. Try to frustrate him by stopping boundaries.
- Tillakaratne — a blocker, so having him at the crease may not hurt us too much. He is under pressure for his place as captain so we should keep it tight to increase that pressure. Angle the ball across him with pace and try to avoid feeding him his favourite stroke, the on-drive.
- Samaraweera — has a good technique but is not always convincing against the short ball. Test him out in this area.

We also assessed the Sri Lanka bowling:

- Vaas — swings the ball back into the right-handers. Watch out for his change of pace.
- Zoysa — like Vaas, can swing the ball back in and also has a good slower ball. Will get extra bounce with the new ball thanks to his height.
- Muralitharan — as with all Sri Lanka's bowlers, have a game plan against him and stick to it. Try to be positive and not let him get on top.
- Chandana — can spin the odd ball very sharply but is inconsistent. Sit on him and wait for the bad ball.
- Dharmasena — likes to bowl maidens, so be positive against him.

After we finished with the Test match business we got a briefing from Michael Brown and Steve Bernard about their trip to Zimbabwe. Bernard makes pre-series trips every time we are due to tour a country, and this time he reported that after checking out the venues we are set to play at, as well as holding meetings with local officials and also the Australian High Commissioner, he feels there is no reason why our tour there, starting in May, should not go ahead. That was about the end of the chat on that subject; the minds of most people are on tomorrow's match first and foremost and, as players, we are pretty relaxed about letting Cricket Australia make decisions on whether or not tours should go ahead. They have pulled us out of trips in the past if they have felt we would be in danger, and if there is any hint of that this time I know they will do the right thing again.

We already had the standard pre-series meeting involving the match referee, the two captains, the team managers and the umpires by this stage. We have a new match referee for this series: Chris Broad, the former England opening batsman, is taking over from Mike Procter. The main point of business for me was that Hashan Tillakaratne agreed to go along with what we agreed with one-day captain Marvan Atapattu: batsmen should walk off if a fielder claims a low catch, without waiting for referral to the third umpire.

Before the team meeting, a few of us, as well as some of Cricket Australia's directors, attended the unveiling of a plaque commemorating the co-operation between Sri Lanka and Australia during World War II. Catalina flying boat services used to travel on missions between our two countries during the war, something that is already commemorated with a plaque in Perth, next to the Swan River. With the unveiling of the plaque here in Galle, the missions are now recognised here in Sri Lanka as well.

My manager, Sam Halvorsen, has arrived, and he brought with him something that confirms what I am about to do over the next five days: the captain's blazer. I will be wearing it tomorrow for the first time when the coin is tossed at 10 o'clock. I can hardly wait.

Monday 8 March

First Test, day one: Sri Lanka 1–81 trail Australia 220 (Lehmann 63, Muralitharan 6–59) by 139 runs.

As first days go this was not one of our best. It was a bit of an anticlimax for me personally after all the build-up to my first Test as captain. Put simply, we played poorly and paid for it; however, the match is not out of our reach yet.

Despite what the scoreboard said, I did not think we batted really badly. It was just that all the frontline batsmen made tiny errors of judgement that cost us wickets when we had been looking pretty comfortable. One look at that scoreboard shows each one of our top five batsmen got his eye in; it was just that no one went on with it.

Our score — 220 — is below par but not disastrous. Mind you, Sri Lanka's batsmen put conditions into perspective in the final session, when they moved pretty comfortably along. It means we need a big day tomorrow if we are to get back into the match.

The day started well. I got a good night's sleep, certainly better than Rianna, who always seems to get more nervous than me, and felt calm, rested and ready for action when we arrived at the ground. Once there I had a chat with John Buchanan and Allan Border and that confirmed we would go with the side we had decided on.

That meant a Test debut for Andrew Symonds. Allan Border presented him with his cap in front of the rest of the squad before our warm-ups. We always ask a former Australia player to present a debutant with his baggy green because it stresses our cricketing history to a newcomer; the interesting thing about today's ceremony was that Border appeared more nervous than Symonds. Border is one our greatest players and captains, but he was really tongue-tied as he tried to find the right words with which to hand Symonds his cap. Maybe it has something to do with the fact that he has known Symonds since the start of Symonds' career with Queensland, a decade ago, and has also played alongside him, so he knows how much this moment means.

The only slight hitch in proceedings before play was that Hashan Tillakaratne was late for the toss, at least according to the clock on the ground. I was out there at 10 o'clock, complete with the captain's blazer, and there was no sign of him for a couple of minutes. It was hot out in the middle, even at that time, especially with a blazer on, but I had the last laugh — I called correctly when he spun the coin and was happy to bat first. I always call heads, for no reason I can think of except it is what Stephen Waugh used to call, and today it proved a good omen. The pitch looked better than it did a few days ago, and the cracks I saw then certainly did not appear to be any wider, but the surface was still very dry, and I have no doubt it will offer turn and play some tricks towards the end of the match, so the chance to avoid batting last was one I was happy to take.

Sri Lanka obviously expect the pitch to help the spinners: they picked just one seam bowler, Chaminda Vaas, which meant we had the unusual sight of Kumara Dharmasena, the off-spinner, opening the bowling in a Test match. I am not sure how many times that has happened in the past. We were all interested to see how much turn he would get from the surface.

The first few overs were pretty uneventful, with Matthew Hayden and Justin Langer trying to play themselves in. Hayden thumped Vaas down the ground for four and also pulled him powerfully away backward of square leg when he dropped short, while Langer was happy to push the ball around. Langer's game plan against spin clearly involved playing the sweep shot whenever possible, as he showed when he top-edged a paddle around the corner from the very first ball he faced from Dharmasena. Luckily there was no one there to accept the chance, so he picked up two runs.

Hayden survived a sharp chance back to Vaas as he tried for a drive. This was a good indication of the lack of pace in the surface, and a replay of the life the same bowler gave him at the start of the one-day series, in Dambulla. For a while our two openers seemed to be going along nicely — until Langer was undone by some sharp turn and a lack of bounce from Dharmasena.

He tried to cut a short ball but it spun and kept low. Langer may have been unbalanced, falling away to the leg-side as he played the shot, but all he managed to do was get a fine under-edge to the ball. Kumar Sangakkara, behind the stumps, took a good low catch at the second attempt.

That was my cue for action. When I am waiting to go into bat I usually sit just outside the dressing room, to help me get used to the light. I also tend to have a bottle of water by my side, which I sip from time to time, as well as a pack of chewing gum. As soon as I put my gear on I slip a gum into my mouth. How much I go through depends on how long I am waiting to bat — I have been known to go through the whole pack.

When the wicket falls I have a swig of water, dispose of the gum and then get on my way. I usually try to get out onto the ground as quickly as possible. As I walk out I go through some light stretches, just to try to get any tension I may be feeling out of the system.

Even though this was my first time as Test captain, I did not feel any extra nerves. In fact I felt pretty relaxed as I got ready to face up. Hayden was at the other end, and I have batted with him many times before. It is not as if I have not been captain before — I've done the job more than 60 times at one-day level. The Test captaincy is a massive honour, of course, but I am not, by nature, someone who gets very nervous or makes a big deal out of things. I just focus on what I have to do at the time — and right now my job was batting.

There was some chat around the bat from the Sri Lankans as I took my guard from the umpire: suggestions that it was spinning a long way already, that kind of stuff. Nothing I have not come across many, many times before. I am pretty good at blocking chat like that out. Right from the start of my innings I felt in good touch: I have passed 50 in each of my previous innings on tour. I always take middle stump as my guard; something I picked up as a junior and have always stuck with. I might change it to, say, off-stump, if I am looking to combat an off-spinner who is turning the ball a long way, or a left-arm bowler angling the ball across me. That helps me know where my off-stump is, which means I am in a better position to leave the ball if it is wide.

I got underway on the fourth ball, leaning on a drive through the covers from Dharmasena; I was happy to use my feet if any of the Sri Lanka spinners were giving the ball any flight. When the leg-spinner Upul Chandana replaced Dharmasena I paddled him away fine for four. I felt I was playing myself in nicely, with no real alarms.

Hayden and I were going well. He seemed to be getting into his stride, clubbing three fours in one over off Chaminda Vaas, two through midwicket when he dropped short and another one down the ground when he adjusted his length and bowled too full. He is usually immaculate with his length, so he may have been tiring. That would not be surprising — it was his eighth over in really hot conditions.

In the next over, from the opposite end, Muttiah Muralitharan came into the attack. Hayden and I knew the importance of this passage of play. When we were here in 1999 a few of our batsmen struggled to come to terms with him, and that was a major factor in our loss of that series. Hayden was on that tour but was the reserve batsman and did not play in a Test. He has a deserved reputation for playing spin well, but his desire to dominate proved his undoing here.

Muralitharan knew Hayden would look to sweep him whenever he could — that is one of Hayden's strongest shots. Hayden also feels it is a relatively safe shot, even though he is sweeping against the spin, because he gets a big stride in. If he misses the ball it will almost always miss off-stump or hit him on the pad outside off-stump, which removes the danger of being out lbw.

Muralitharan tried to counter the sweep shot by having two men out on the boundary, one square of the wicket and another at an orthodox backward square position, but Hayden backed his ability and decided to play the shot anyway. He hit it well, but maybe there was a hint of top-edge involved. Anyhow, it carried a long way, but near Chandana, the squarer of those two fielders on the boundary. Chandana almost misjudged it — it was travelling a bit faster than he expected — but he leapt to his left and pulled in an excellent catch. Now we were two wickets down.

Even though I was joined by a new batsman, Damien Martyn, I

saw no need to rein myself in if the ball was there to hit, and when Muralitharan tossed the ball up I was happy to go after him. I clipped him through midwicket then skipped down the pitch and lofted him over mid-on for successive fours. Round one to me. He now knew I was not afraid to loft him over the in-field. He hates conceding runs, so he dropped his mid-on back three-quarters of the way to the boundary.

I thought that was short-sighted. He could have chosen to back himself by keeping the fielder up, saving one and daring me to try to hit over the top again. Instead he gave me ground, which was good as far as I was concerned.

By now I felt I was hitting the ball really well. I was playing positively and felt on top of Sri Lanka's attack. Maybe that attitude, together with a fine piece of bowling, was my undoing, because in the next over I was on my way back to the pavilion.

I had already shown my desire to get down the pitch whenever the spinners gave the ball any air, and facing up to Chandana, I made my way down the pitch again. This time, though, the bowler must have seen me coming: he dragged his length back a touch and that, together with a poor choice of shot, removed me.

Rather than just hitting straight, with the full face of the bat, I tried to whip the ball through the on-side. This was not the wisest shot against a bowler spinning the ball away from me and, sure enough, he beat my outside edge; Sangakkara completed a good bit of stumping — the ball also bounced a fair bit. It was a frustrating end to a promising innings, especially as I had played myself in. Suddenly we were 3–76 and in a little trouble.

Luckily, Darren Lehmann and Martyn put things into perspective in the half-hour that remained before lunch: they accumulated another 33 runs with clips backward of square and deflections into the gaps, although neither man was afraid to play a bigger shot if the chance came along. Martyn drove Chandana through the covers beautifully and followed that with a well-timed clip through midwicket off Muralitharan, and Lehmann was down the pitch as soon as Muralitharan gave the ball some air, lofting him straight for an effortless six. At lunch the score was 3–109, and although Sri Lanka would have been the happier of the two sides, we were still pretty well placed, despite losing at least one wicket more than we would have wanted.

By tea the picture had changed considerably, and the balance of power was well and truly in Sri Lanka's favour. We lost three more wickets — three of our frontline batsmen — and were barely past

200. It was not a great position given that we are expecting batting to get harder as the match goes on.

The three wickets we lost in the session were down to a mixture of bad luck and poor execution; a similar story to the first session. Martyn, having shaped up well against the spinners, suddenly had a rush of blood and paddled the ball straight to a leg-slip that had only been posted there the ball before. Symonds, wearing his baggy green cap for the first time, was undone by a ball from Muralitharan that turned sharply: he was given out caught off bat and pad at slip. He did not think he got a touch on the ball, and the replays were pretty inconclusive as the ball turned through the gate and lobbed up, but umpire Rudi Koertzen's finger went up and he had to go. Then Gilchrist, never the best starter against spin, decided, after being beaten and almost bowled by what looked like a top-spinner from Muralitharan, that attack was the best form of defence. He played a slog-sweep, only to find Dharmasena at deep midwicket — the fielder had been placed there specifically for the shot.

Lehmann, together with Shane Warne, shored up our position either side of tea, showing that batting was far from impossible. Warne did not look very comfortable against Muralitharan, but against the other bowlers he looked perfectly at ease, thumping Chandana for successive fours over the in-field. At the other end, Lehmann mixed patient accumulation of singles with the odd aggressive shot, striking Dharmasena straight down the ground and, when he was replaced by Chandana, greeting the new bowler with a powerful shot through extra-cover.

We hoped those two could keep going in much the same way after the tea break, but things very quickly fell to pieces after the interval and Sri Lanka wrapped up our innings with little fuss. Lehmann was always going to be the key wicket, and he fell in an unusual way, bowled round his legs by Muralitharan's doosra as he got too far across his stumps trying to push the ball on the on-side. Lehmann will often move around his crease to try to put the bowler off — he did this in the game before the Test — but on this occasion Muralitharan, coming around the wicket, managed to outsmart him.

With our last remaining frontline batsman gone, the rest of our resistance crumbled pretty quickly. Warne was out in the next over, from Vaas, the victim of a fine piece of bowling. The left-armer will swing the odd ball back into a right-hand batsman, and that will make you look to play at balls wide of off-stump that you would usually leave alone because you are worried about the ball coming back into you. That was exactly what Vaas did to Warne here, swinging one back in then tempting him with wider balls that did not swing. Warne had already played and missed at one delivery; then he got a touch to a second one and was gone.

Muralitharan made short work of our tail, bowling Kasprowicz through the gate as he looked for an ambitious drive and then trapping Stuart MacGill lbw, playing half-forward with his bat well behind his pad. It was a sorry end to our innings, with Muralitharan picking up six wickets on a pitch supposedly at its best for batting.

Our low score was more due to our own failings than to any major drama with the surface. We all knew that, and it was put into perspective by the way Sri Lanka began their reply.

There was no lack of effort from Jason Gillespie and Kasprowicz, but Marvan Atapattu and Sanath Jaysuriya looked comfortable, without threatening to take the game away from us. Jayasuriya popped back a low catch off the leading edge to Gillespie, but he could not hold onto it. Apart from that, there were no chances to speak of in the first few overs.

Kasprowicz could not find a great deal of swing, so he went around the wicket to Jayasuriya to try to give him something different to think about, but Jayasuriya's reply was emphatic: he glanced fine and then slashed square, producing boundaries from two successive balls.

The time had come for a change, and I opted to give Warne the opportunity ahead of Symonds or MacGill. I did not see any sign of nerves from him but I knew he was bound to be a little jittery. It was only natural after 12 months out of the game. The other players have helped him slot back in as if he has never been away, but I figured it would be best to get him into the action straight away rather than give him a chance to get even more nervous standing at slip.

Warne will usually start with a quick, flat delivery, just to get his radar going. He did that, and after he had got that one out of his system, Jayasuriya responded with successive shots through the covers that brought him two and four, and followed them with a glance off his hip for a single. Atapattu followed that by working the ball through square leg for another run, making it eight off Warne's first over.

It was not the perfect start for him but I knew he would settle into his work. He became more and more relaxed and, sure enough, in his third over he got us the breakthrough we needed. Jayasuriya looked to sweep, but was deceived by a ball that held back on him and was through the shot a little early. The ball thumped him on the pad — there was little doubt from what Gilchrist said that it was plumb lbw.

That wicket, with five overs to go, gave us some heart, but Sangakkara did his best to knock the wind out of our sails in the last passage of play. He looked Sri Lanka's best player in the one-day series and he continued to look good here, clipping Warne through midwicket for four and, in the final over of the day, skipping down the pitch to MacGill and picking him up effortlessly over wide mid-on for six. He finished the day on 16 from just 16 balls, giving us plenty to ponder as we left the field.

When we got back to the dressing room, and later as we warmed down in the hotel pool, the mood was still upbeat. We knew we'd had a bad day but at the same time we knew there was no point in moping about it. If there is one positive thing we can take out of today's events it is that we had this collapse on the first day of the series, in the first innings. It will remind everyone that patience is required on these pitches, against these bowlers, in these conditions. We forgot that today and got burnt. Let's hope the lesson has been learnt.

Andrew Symonds

I have been given a fair amount of credit for getting the best out of Andrew Symonds, a serial underachiever for so many years who finally clicked under my captaincy at the World Cup and has not looked back since. However, the truth is that John Buchanan should take the majority of the credit for Symonds' emergence on the international stage.

When other people may have been inclined to give up on the player who often looked so good before giving away his wicket in frustrating fashion, Buchanan continued to back him — and we have seen the fruits of that support over the past year or so.

I could always see that here was a special talent: a player who could hit the ball miles, could bowl either seam or spin (depending on conditions) and would be ranked as one of the best fielders in the world in any position. So how did we go about getting the best out of him?

Symonds' natural talent made me believe he was worth a punt for a place in the World Cup squad — he gave our side some added balance, increasing our batting and bowling depth. I said as much to the selectors, and Buchanan, who had coached him for many years with Queensland, agreed.

Then, when Symonds was named in the squad, I took a leaf out of Stephen Waugh's book of man management and publicly said how highly I rated him as a player. I hoped that would be a boost to his self-confidence.

Once he was on board, I asked Buchanan what we needed to do to unlock Symonds' talent once and for all. Buchanan's answer was simple: 'He needs direction but keep things simple, don't try to blind him with too many theories. Just give him a job and he will go away and do it to the best of his ability.'

His job in that first match of the World Cup was to try to bat through the innings after we lost early wickets, and he certainly managed that. In fact he made 143 not out — it was the start of his emergence as a player of genuine international class.

Symonds himself must take a lot of the credit for the way he has developed since the start of the World Cup, of course. I know he spent some time talking to Matthew Hayden, who is a close friend and who struggled to come to terms with international cricket before making an impact; whatever Hayden told his mate seems to have worked.

People's impression of the old Symonds was that he often went out and tried to slog the ball around from ball one, with regular failures the result. But from the World Cup onwards he has appeared to have much more of a plan. He now aims to build an innings, work the ball around and then finally explode in the closing overs. His ability — he has a wide range of shots and can hit boundaries anywhere on the field, and can do it at important times — allows us to think of him as a finisher, someone to close out a one-day game when we bat second.

His bowling is already effective in one-day cricket but I would like to see him develop it more, especially his off-spin. I want him to make a nuisance of himself and bowl more during his spells in county cricket and also work with a leading spin coach whenever he can, because I think he has real potential as a spinner. He has the height to generate bounce, and he tries to spin the ball rather than just rolling it out of the fingers, which is a useful start.

Symonds bowled his spinners effectively in the one-day series in Sri Lanka, dismissing good players through the gate between bat and pad, but he was a lot less effective during the Test series that followed, as the home side's players targeted him as inexperienced and a weak link in our attack. If he can improve his off-spin he not only increases his chances of being selected for future Test tours, but he will also give us extra options with the ball, especially in spin-friendly countries like India and Sri Lanka.

The good news for us is that Symonds did not look out of his depth at Test level, even though he did not rip up the record books. And with his brilliance in the field in any position, he made sure he has a good chance of remaining in the selectors' thoughts for the longer form of the game for some time to come.

That is fortunate for him, because it means he can find another excuse to wear his baggy green cap — it never seemed to be off his head during the Test series in Sri Lanka. In fact it is difficult to think of a player who has been more outwardly proud to wear his cap.

Symonds has a great cricket brain, and his improved form at international level has seen him more and more willing to make suggestions for tactics both in the dressing room and on the field. His emergence as a player has benefited us in many ways.

He is now a married man, tying the knot with his long-term partner, Brooke, after we got back from Sri Lanka. He loves hunting and shooting in the outback, getting away from the hustle and bustle of city life whenever he can, and when we are travelling around as a group it is not unusual to see Symonds with a copy of a hunting, shooting or fishing magazine while most of the rest of the squad have copies of *Inside Edge*, *Inside Sport*, *FHM* or *Sports Illustrated*.

Fishing is a passion he shares with Hayden; they owned a boat together, which was famously overturned by a freak wave — with them in it — a few years ago. They had to swim back to shore despite the threat of sharks, but as far as I know they still go fishing together whenever they get the chance.

Symonds' emergence has been a real plus during my time as Australian captain, and I hope the best is still to come from this talented all-rounder.

Tuesday 9 March

First Test, day two: Sri Lanka 6–352 (Dilshan 104, Jayawardene 68) lead Australia 220 by 132 runs.

This was a tough day at the office, but we never let our heads drop, and with the pitch showing no sign of deteriorating too much yet, we are not totally out of the match at this stage. All the same, we do need a good session tomorrow morning.

It was another hot and humid morning, and I chose to open the bowling with Shane Warne and Michael Kasprowicz. With only two quick bowlers in the side, our plan is to use them as attacking defensive bowlers once the hardness goes out of the ball, if that makes any sense: they will run in hard and try to hit the pitch, but at the same time they will be operating to defensive fields, with maybe just one slip and men in front of the bat looking to cut down scoring opportunities. That way they can shut up one end while we attack with the spinners.

That is the theory. Kasprowicz managed to get a breakthrough in the first hour, when he bent low in his follow-through to pick up a great return catch as the dangerous Kumar Sangakkara checked an attempted drive. Kasprowicz produced an excellent five-over spell for just 13 runs. He was bowling well, but I was keen not to over-bowl him. The heat and humidity are amazing, and if you overwork a bowler early in the day, the chances are he will have nothing in the tank when you ask him to come back later.

I replaced him with Jason Gillespie, and he did an equally impressive job, bowling six overs for just 12 runs and taking the vital wicket of Marvan Atapattu. We regard him as the glue that sticks the Sri Lanka top order together; he is a really patient player with a great range of shots, but he is usually happy just to accumulate while the strokemakers like Sanath Jayasuriya and Sangakkara look to get after the bowling at the other end. Strangely, he seemed to get a bit frustrated at the way first Kasprowicz then Gillespie tied him down today, and his response was a really loose back-foot forcing shot that he dragged back onto his stumps.

That wicket left Sri Lanka at 3–123, and I felt we were still very much in control of proceedings. However, from that point we just could not force another breakthrough. Mahela Jayawardene and Tillakaratne Dilshan played thoroughly well. Neither of them appeared troubled by Warne, even though I bowled him long enough to find some rhythm, and when Stuart MacGill replaced him they were content to wait for the bad ball that came along every so often and put it away for four.

Dilshan is light on his feet and likes to drive through the off-side; Jayawardene likes to use the pace of the ball, and gets a fair percentage of his runs through square cover and backward point. They complemented each other well, and when I threw the ball to Symonds for an over before lunch, Jayawardene hit him for successive fours through extra-cover and then midwicket.

I kept Symonds going after the interval to see if he could find any turn, or any of the magic he had during the one-day series, but both batsmen seemed determined to hit him out of the attack. I am not sure whether that was because they saw him as a threat (he'd got both of them out in the one-day series) or whether they wanted to make sure the Test new boy did not get a chance to settle, but they both tried to attack him at every opportunity and his first four overs of the day cost 29. When you add that to the three I gave him last night — which cost 20 — his figures were looking sorry, but I saw no sense in taking him off: it would only dent his confidence, and I was sure he would settle.

Looking back, maybe we should have had a different plan about how he should bowl to start with. He began trying to bowl a very attacking line outside off-stump, trying to take wickets, but he really is not the finished article as an off-spinner yet and maybe that sort of approach was asking too much of him first up. Perhaps we should have looked to get him bowling straighter to start with and then, once he had some rhythm and confidence, alter the line.

I felt justified in keeping him on, because he did settle into a better rhythm, and he did pick up a wicket in a dismissal that was similar to many of ours yesterday. Jayawardene was clearly planning to press on, but he tried to drive through the off-side and executed the shot poorly. Playing with an open face of the bat, he sliced his drive straight to Matthew Hayden at backward point, who made a low catch look easy. That was four wickets down and Sri Lanka still 22 behind.

That brought Tillakaratne in, and he ensured that our pursuit of wickets stalled. He can be a hugely annoying player to bowl to because he attempts very little: he leaves the ball that is well outside off-stump and forces you to bowl at him. Once you do get straighter, he works you through the on-side. He also has terrifically strong wrists and is capable of whipping the over-pitched ball past the left hand of mid-on.

The one plus about having him at the crease is that the scoreboard never races along, but today he knew there was no hurry, and with conditions so hot and humid every extra minute in the field was hard work for our bowlers.

At the other end, Dilshan played beautifully. He was happy to skip down the pitch to the spinners when they flighted the ball: two successive shots off Warne really stick in my memory — for all the wrong reasons. Warne was bowling around the wicket into the footmarks outside the batsman's leg-stump, and Dilshan came down the pitch, staying to the leg-side of the ball and lifted him first for four over long-off then straight for six. They were great shots that required precise footwork and execution — and they were not unlike the way VVS Laxman tormented Warne in India three years ago.

Warne was clearly not at his best, and neither he nor MacGill got the same amount of turn out of the surface as the Sri Lanka spinners did on day one. But Warne stuck to his task and was never afraid to try things, like having two fielders on the drive in the hope of inducing a false stroke out of the rough. And in the end he got his reward, when Tillakaratne, maybe put off from lunging too far forward because of those fielders, played back and was trapped lbw by a delivery that turned back into him and kept low.

Thilan Samaraweera replaced him, and that, at least, ensured that Sri Lanka did not get away from us too much — he was content to block almost everything bowled to him. He has a sound technique, Test figures that suggest he can play and the odd delightful attacking shot. But he was not helped by a groin injury that meant he required a runner, and he managed just six scoring strokes in the hour and a half up to the close. That suited us just fine, because our bowlers were tiring.

While Tillakaratne was in we were not being hurt too much by the speed of their batting. That meant I was reluctant to take the new ball — the old one was quite soft. A newer, harder ball would come off the bat faster and we had two well-set batsmen in; we could not really afford to let them get away any further. However, when Warne broke through I knew we had to think about taking the new ball, and we did after 97 overs. This gave us an added advantage: Gillespie and Kasprowicz had a longer rest than they might otherwise have enjoyed.

The harder ball, combined with the extra pace onto the bat, can often bring a change in tempo in the match, especially after a period of intense cricket involving the spinners, and today was no exception. Dilshan was in the 90s when our new ball pairing came back into the attack. He was keen to get to three figures and crashed Kasprowicz through the covers to climb to 96. He should have been dismissed next ball, but Warne dropped what was a tough catch, high to his left at first slip. It was a difficult chance, and it could be argued that Adam Gilchrist should have gone for it, but it flew high and quick. It was exactly the sort of chance we needed to take to keep a toe-hold in the match. Reprieved, Dilshan picked up three more runs before scampering the single to point off Gillespie that left him celebrating a well-deserved hundred.

Luckily for us, he did not add too many more. Kasprowicz bowled him a rapid bouncer, which he was keen to hook, but the ball was onto him far more quickly than he expected. Dilshan caught the ball somewhere near the splice of his bat but still followed through with the shot. It carried a fair way back over mid-on, where Justin Langer was fielding. Langer took a moment to sight it, then began back-pedalling furiously, before grasping it above his head and rolling backwards, still clinging to the ball. It was a great catch, and a great wicket for Kasprowicz; it also meant we were now into Sri Lanka's tail, which was an added bonus.

It was our last success of the day. The pace bowlers were spent after bowling six-over spells, and the new batsman, Upul Chandana, and Samaraweera, both played the leg-spin of MacGill and Warne without too many alarms. That was frustrating, and so was the sight of Kasprowicz trotting off after injuring his shoulder diving to save a boundary late in the day. With only two frontline fast bowlers in the side that was the last thing we needed, and the news from Alex Kontouri when I got back to the dressing room at close of play was not great. Kasprowicz has a sprain in his right (bowling) shoulder joint, and although it is not connected to the shoulder reconstruction he had four years ago, it means his chances of bowling again in the match must be small.

It is not the first time one of our players has been injured in that way. Brad Williams injured his shoulder on an advertising board in Adelaide last December, and I managed to break my ankle attempting a sliding save on the boundary in Sydney four years ago — that injury that cost me a Test and one-day tour of New Zealand and a one-day series in South Africa.

Officials have responded to our committed fielding by bringing boundary ropes in from perimeter advertising boards to lessen the danger of us crashing into them. Kasprowicz's problem tonight was just a case of landing awkwardly on the rock-hard ground as he rolled over trying to flick the ball back. I know some critics argue that we should not be diving around like that — especially the fast bowlers, and especially at the end of a long day in the field — but I am not going to tell players not to follow their gut instinct, which is to try to save runs. In Kasprowicz's defence, he has probably done the same thing thousands of times before with no ill effects; I think it says a lot about what it means to this team to save every run. I do not see too many other sides doing the same thing; maybe that commitment is part of what makes this team so successful.

On a positive note, Brett Lee had a bowl before play and looked in very good order. He got the ball through well and did not seem too troubled by his ankle, but as Alex Kontouri said, we will see how he pulls up tomorrow, and if he is struggling we will have to send him home.

We are not out of this match yet, especially as the pitch seems to be playing okay so far, but experience tells me that with three days left we will have to fight very hard if we are to get even a draw. That fight starts again tomorrow morning.

Wednesday 10 March

First Test, day three: Australia 220 and 2–193 (Hayden 106 not out) lead Sri Lanka 381 (Dilshan 104, Jayawardene 68, Warne 5–116) by 32 runs.

We are right back in the Test match. Despite not having Michael Kasprowicz to bowl for us this morning, we managed to take Sri Lanka's last four wickets with barely a whimper, and then a more patient approach from us second time around paid dividends.

Shane Warne bowled much more like his old self this morning — and picked up a well-deserved five-wicket haul that gave us a chink of a chance in the match. That chink was exploited by Matthew Hayden, who made a battling hundred. It was not one of his most flamboyant knocks, but it was full of discipline and good shot selection, and that was exactly the type of approach we needed after our effort in the first innings.

Not everything is perfect. Brett Lee was struggling to put weight on his ankle when he woke up today, so we decided to send him home. And then I was run out in foolish fashion in an attempt to get Hayden to his hundred; it was a total waste of a wicket.

The announcement about Lee was made at lunchtime and Allan Border came down to the dressing room after play to talk through possible replacements. In the end we decided that rather than go for someone like Glenn McGrath, now apparently fit again after his long-term ankle injury, or another lively fast–medium seamer, we should get a like-for-like replacement for Lee: a crackerjack fast bowler who could give us raw pace if we needed it. On that basis, the only choice was Shaun Tait, a youngster from South Australia who has been impressing good judges this season and who played against the Indians for Australia A earlier in the summer. I faced him in the nets at Adelaide on Test and one-day duty there and can vouch for the fact that he is quick. Chances are he will not play here, but it will be good to get him involved at a higher level than he is used to, away from the pressures of the exposure he might get being in the squad in a home series, and it will let him see what he has to do to get to the next step on the ladder. Border said he would go back to the other selectors, but he did not see a problem. All being well, we will make an announcement tomorrow.

The first session of the day was obviously a crucial one for us, especially as Kasprowicz's sore shoulder prevented him from bowling. It meant that if Sri Lanka got on top of us early on we did not have a lot of options — we could be facing a long haul to even draw the game.

As it turned out, Warne, together with Jason Gillespie and Stuart MacGill, stuck their hands up and produced the goods. Warne's success may have been partly due to a chat we had after play last night.

We agreed that he had struggled for rhythm on the second day. He said part of the reason may have been a stiff breeze across the ground that left him feeling unbalanced as he got into his delivery stride. On top of that, we agreed he may have been guilty of bowling the ball a little too slowly. The Sri Lanka batsmen are masters in their own conditions, and that lack of pace on the ball, together with the slow nature of the pitch, meant they were able to wait for the turn before deciding where to play him. By pushing it through a bit quicker, we agreed, he would be removing the option of playing him off the pitch — and he may get some more drift on the ball. Quite often when Warne pushes the ball through a bit faster, the pace on the ball, combined with the revolutions he puts on it, causes it to dip, making the batsman unsure of the length of each delivery. That was the theory and, being the genius he is, Warne was able to put it into practice in a beautiful spell of bowling.

He, Gillespie and MacGill bowled exceptionally well, but we were also helped by some pretty timid batting from the Sri Lankans. They added just 29 runs in 21.4 overs for the last four wickets, and I got the impression that they did not know what to do or how to do it. If they had come at us with attacking intent, especially as we had limited bowling options, they could have taken the game away from us in that first session; instead, they seemed to freeze, and we were able to take advantage of that fact.

Although Warne got the glory, with three of the four wickets that fell, a lot of the credit should go to Gillespie, whose opening spell of seven overs cost just nine runs. It was exactly the type of bowling we want from our fast men in these conditions with an old ball: it was the attacking defence I have previously referred to, staying aggressive but tight while the spinners weave their magic at the other end.

That spell helped ensure that Sri Lanka scored just 17 runs in the first hour. However, they did not lose a wicket either. That was a concern, but then all of a sudden they fell in a heap.

First, Warne found the perfect leg-break for Upul Chandana, who edged a forward push to Gilchrist. Then Chaminda Vaas played back to a ball angled across him from MacGill and the resulting edge was pouched by Hayden at slip. Kumara Dharmasena edged another Warne leg-break to Hayden, then Muttiah Muralitharan offered next to no resistance, chipping a simple caught and bowled back to Warne to give him his fifth wicket.

At the other end was Thilan Samaraweera, left stranded on 36 after almost three hours at the crease — he did little for his side except stall any momentum they had. He looked solid enough but he did not really hurt us, and that was the key issue from my perspective.

It took us just over 90 minutes to bowl them out this morning. That had the disadvantage of leaving us with an awkward little period for the openers to negotiate before lunch. But openers are used to doing that and Justin Langer and Matthew Hayden coped pretty well. Muralitharan bowled the last over before the interval, and we were all interested to see how much spin he would get off the surface. He did turn the ball, but Langer coped, even paddling him fine for four.

I think we were all conscious of how we got things wrong in the first innings, so we were keen to put things right this time. The key for us was — and still is — trying to bat for a long time. It is not that runs are unimportant, but we know we are all aggressive players, so if we look to occupy the crease the runs will come.

That was exactly how the two openers played it after lunch. Langer, with only one match in these conditions before the Test, looked less fluent than Hayden, but they kept the scoreboard ticking over at 3 runs an over, and after a five-over burst from Vaas straight after the interval, the match settled into a battle between Sri Lanka's spinners and our batsmen.

The heat and humidity were still pretty unpleasant, and both men swapped their batting helmets for caps once Vaas was out of the attack. Langer was content just to work the ball through the on-side for ones, in order to rotate the strike; Hayden played most of the big shots. He struggled to make contact with his favourite sweep shot against the part-time off-spin of Tillakaratne Dilshan, but when Dharmasena tossed the ball up he was down the pitch and lofted him straight for six.

We were not dominating proceedings but we were not looking in too much trouble either, and faced with that, Hashan Tillakaratne kept shuffling his bowling pack, looking for a breakthrough. The sixth change he made, bringing on Sanath Jayasuriya, brought him the wicket he wanted.

The left-arm spinner operating into the rough outside the left-hander's off-stump is always going to be a handful, especially bowling at the pace Jayasuriya does. He tries to push the ball through, and pitching on crumbling foot holes it can make the ball keep low. That was exactly what happened to Langer as he played back. The ball turned, kept low and he was trapped plumb in front.

When I came in we were still 70 behind. As in the first innings, I felt pretty relaxed. After all the time I spent in the middle during the one-day series, I felt confident enough in the way I was playing Muralitharan to cut him away for four when he dropped short and then, when he tossed the ball up, I was down the pitch and whipping him through wide mid-on for another boundary. He and Jayasuriya experimented with bowling over and round the wicket in an attempt to break up the rhythm Hayden and I established, but the only real problem we had before tea was a near run-out.

We were keen to keep rotating the strike but it almost cost us a wicket. Hayden dropped Jayasuriya out on the off-side, looking for a quick single. I set off but was sent back — it was pretty obvious there was not a run there, thanks to quick work by Kumar Sangakkara. He was out from behind the stumps in a flash, had his right glove off and sent a low return to the bowler's end. I was still short of my ground when Jayasuriya dropped the ball. It was a lucky let-off.

Unfortunately we did not learn from it, and in the last session I was run out in stupid fashion. Sri Lanka's players were flat and adopted some curious defensive fields with mid-off and mid-on pushed back halfway to the boundary, giving us singles which we were happy to take. The pressure was off us and we had moved into the lead by the time Hayden reached 99.

All of sudden there was more energy about Sri Lanka in the field, but that should not have been a concern. They were obviously keen to stop Hayden getting to three figures, and Jayasuriya, who was bowling, was also keen to keep him fretting, one short of the milestone, for as long as possible.

We had both seen tactics like it a hundred times before. Jayasuriya would halt play to move a fielder maybe a metre this way or a metre that way. All of us captains have done it. Then, as he ran in to bowl the first ball of his over to Hayden, he pretended that he lost his grip on the ball and had to go back to his mark to prepare again.

I could see what was happening, so I went down the pitch to Hayden and told him to stay calm and maintain his focus. But just for a split second the red mist descended: he clipped one off his toes and called me for a single to get to his hundred.

As non-striker, you want to be quickly out of the blocks when your partner calls you through on 99. I did not look where Hayden had hit the ball; I just trusted his call and set off. But as I saw on the replay when I got back to the dressing room, he hit it almost straight to the right hand of Chandana, Sri Lanka's best fielder, and that meant I was struggling. Chandana sent in a bullet-like return right next to the stumps and I was short of my ground, a fact which was confirmed by the third umpire a minute or so later.

I was really angry when I got back to the dressing room. Not only was it a wicket thrown away, but also, once again, I had failed to make the most of a good start.

Luckily we did not lose any more wickets up to close of play. Damien Martyn played sensibly, and also took some of the weight of responsibility off Hayden in the run-up to stumps. It was another hot day and Hayden had given an awful lot in terms of concentration, so Martyn took most of the strike in the last ten overs of the day.

Hayden was subdued when he reached his hundred, no doubt thinking about the run-out, but was fine, if pretty tired, when he came back into the dressing room after play. There was no point him having a guilt trip over the matter or me getting carried away. I got my frustrations out of my system when I got back to the dressing room — these things happen in cricket. You just wish that they never happen to you.

Warne spoke to the media after play tonight and said that 100 might be tough for Sri Lanka to get in the last innings. I think that is a little bit of wishful thinking — and I would like a few more than 100 as a lead in the final innings. The positive is that we are right back in the Test, and if we bat with the same discipline tomorrow that we showed today, we have a great chance of getting a win out of the match.

Shane Warne

If you have ever wondered who gave me the nickname Punter, the answer is Shane Warne.

It came about when he visited Adelaide to train at the Commonwealth Bank Cricket Academy before his first overseas tour with the Australian side, to Sri Lanka in 1992. I was at the Academy at the time and would regularly go to evening greyhound racing at the local track. Warne noticed it and the nickname was born.

At that time we all knew Warne had talent. I remember the size of his fingers — they were like Cuban cigars — the way they gripped the ball, and the sound the ball made fizzing through the air as it revolved on its way down to you as a batsman, a sign the bowler is putting some serious spin on it. But despite that, I do not think any of us expected him to become as successful as he has. At the time spinners were not very fashionable in world cricket, and for him to go on and almost single-handedly reinvent the art of leg-spin worldwide is a testament to his talent.

Throughout my time playing for Australia Warne has been the superstar of the team, and that has helped the rest of us in more ways than one. In addition to the way we have benefited from his skill as a cricketer, we have also seen what it is like for a person to live his life under constant scrutiny. We have seen first-hand the mistakes he has made and how he has dealt with the fall-out from those mistakes. That, in turn, has given us a lesson in how we should conduct ourselves in the glare of the public eye.

When Warne returned to the side in Sri Lanka after his year-long ban it really did feel as though he had never been away. That is a credit not only to him for the way he slotted back into the squad, but also to the rest of the players for the way they made him feel welcome straight away. It helps that everyone knows we will always benefit from having a world-class performer around, but most of all it also shows that everyone recognises him as a good bloke.

However, despite Warne's success, it may surprise people to know that he, like many players at the top level, is not always the confident person he comes across as in public, and that although he has achieved more than almost anyone else in the history of the game, he is still nagged by self-doubt. He was nervous coming back to the Test side, and those nerves were magnified by the fact that he was just short of 500 wickets — it showed in his first full day of bowling, in Galle during the first Test.

After play he and I chatted, and we agreed that he needed to bowl the ball quicker and with more over-spin, because the way he had been bowling was giving the Sri Lanka batsmen, all very experienced at playing spin bowling, time to either come down the pitch and play him or wait in their crease and play for spin off the pitch. Warne made the adjustment next day, took a five-wicket haul and ended the series with 26 wickets.

One major disappointment for me is that it is highly unlikely we will see Shane again in one-day cricket. I was surprised at his decision to pack it in at one-day international level, because I still believed he had something to offer in that form of the game.

Given the unsatisfactory way he left the one-day arena, with a ban for a drugs offence rather than with a World Cup medal around his neck, I believe there is a large part of him that would still like to play one-day internationals. However, it would take one of the selectors to ask him to play for that to happen, because I do not think he will risk coming out of retirement and then not being picked. It is not a combination of events I can see happening, and in some ways that is a shame.

On the other hand, Warne's decision to play just one form of the game may well benefit us in the long run in Tests. He believes that by playing just Tests he can extend his career by a year or two, and that has to be good news for us considering the way he has bowled since returning from suspension.

It may also be the start of a trend that runs through our side because of the amount of cricket we are playing. This year, for example, after the tour of Zimbabwe, we were due to play a home series against Sri Lanka, a one-day series against India and Pakistan in Holland, the ICC Champions Trophy in England, then another Test series in India before a full home summer of Tests and a VB Series, then a tour of New Zealand in the autumn and an Ashes trip to follow. With a schedule like that, it may well be inevitable that some players, especially bowlers, will start to pick and choose what cricket they play just to try to stay fit and keep themselves in the game for longer.

Not that Warne needs to worry too much about his fitness at the moment, in my opinion. Although he has got plenty of kilometres on the clock on his right shoulder and his spinning fingers, overall he is now probably the fittest he has been since he started playing for Australia. He has always had powerful fingers and a well-developed shoulder, despite surgery to both areas, but over the last couple of years he has lost a lot of his body fat and trimmed down so that he now looks like a genuine elite athlete.

After his ban there will always be whispers about how he got into his current shape. All I can say is that I saw plenty of examples of the work he did in the gym, both on his own and with fitness trainer Jock Campbell. He admitted to us in the dressing room that he has become a gym junkie.

Maybe John Buchanan can claim partial credit for this transformation after his comments about Warne during our tour of India in 2001 — he publicly criticised Warne's fitness levels during that trip. That made Warne furious, but it obviously struck a chord somewhere in his brain, because he has worked hard to improve the situation and Australian cricket has benefited.

Warne's switch to such a punishing fitness regime relatively late in his career has been combined with a rigorous diet that has all but ruled out his favourite pizzas; that just shows me that the hunger is still there, at least in cricketing terms. That is reassuring, because it would be very easy for him to step aside. He is well set-up for life after cricket, with everyone expecting him to join the Channel Nine commentary team. He even has his own brand of wine to promote.

He obviously feels he still has plenty to achieve in the game, and one of those things is a Test hundred. It is quite amazing that a player with his natural ability with the bat has not reached three figures, not even at first-class level for Victoria or English county Hampshire.

I remember the closest he ever came to the mark, against New Zealand in Perth in 2001. It would be great if he could go one better than he did on that occasion, when nerves got the better of him and he played a wild shot and was caught on the boundary for 99. He came off and spent the next 20 minutes sitting on a plastic chair in the shower room, still with his batting gear on, distraught at his failure, while the selector on duty for the match, his first captain for Australia, Allan Border, tried to console him.

I think we would all love to see Warne put the record straight with a hundred before he finally calls time on his brilliant career. That would top things off nicely.

Thursday 11 March

First Test, day four: Sri Lanka 381 and 0–3 require another 349 runs to beat Australia 220 and 8–512 declared (Hayden 130, Lehmann 129, Martyn 110, Muralitharan 5–153).

At the risk of being over-optimistic after a brilliant performance with the bat, I think there is only one side that can win this match now, and it is not Sri Lanka. Damien Martyn and Darren Lehmann batted with fantastic discipline to score hundreds, and they have given us a platform from which we can go on and take the lead in the series if we can bowl well tomorrow.

At the start of the day we were all keen to avoid getting too far ahead of things — we only led by 32 at that point. The plan when we began was nothing more specific than to bat and bat and bat, and then bat some more, making sure our position was rock solid. After working so hard to get back into the match, none of us wanted to throw that work away by pushing on too soon.

The idea was to see where we were at the close, but Lehmann and Martyn were playing with such assurance that we started to get it into our heads that we could bowl tonight. The intention was to give them at least five overs to face. But then clouds started rolling in and it looked as if it might rain, so we changed the plan again: it would make no sense to close the innings only for Sri Lanka to be reprieved with the offer of bad light. Then the weather changed again — the clouds cleared — so we did declare. This gave us three overs at their openers, two of them by Shane Warne, and although we did not break through, I think we are all confident that we can put the home side under a fair deal of pressure tomorrow.

That situation had looked a million miles away in the first hour of the day, when Hayden, maybe struggling to back up his great effort of yesterday, found the going really tough. He is as mentally tough and fit a player as you could meet, but the shots he played in that first hour suggested to me that the heat and humidity on Wednesday had taken a lot out of him.

Rather than continuing where he left off last night, he played some pretty extravagant shots, and had a fair amount of luck even before he was dismissed. In Muttiah Muralitharan's second over of the day, Hayden appeared to edge a chance behind the wicket, but Kumar Sangakkara could not hold on. In the next over, he got a leading edge that just looped over Marvan Atapattu at extra-cover. In the fourth over, from Upul Chandana, he charged down the pitch and was only saved from being bowled or stumped by an inside edge; and when he got back on strike against Muttiah Muralitharan, he started to back away and give himself room to hit through the off-side, something I could not remember him doing the previous day.

He called for fresh batting gloves after half an hour, and the message that went out with them was to keep battling away, but playing the way he was it was only a matter of time before he was dismissed. He was eventually removed when he got a thin top edge to an attempted sweep at Muralitharan, with the ball going in a gentle arc to Mahela Jayawardene at slip. Despite his odd choice of shots this morning, it was an excellent innings. Now we needed another partnership.

Lehmann joined Martyn and the two of them, having looked our most assured players on day one, played superbly. It was not that they dominated the attack; what they did was give Sri Lanka's bowlers absolutely no hope at all. They played each ball on its merits and the Sri Lanka spinners struggled to break through. We started to take control.

Lehmann was the more aggressive of the two batsmen. He was happy to use his feet whenever he got the chance, and happy to hit down the ground if the opportunity presented itself, which it did with successive balls from Chandana before lunch. Martyn, in contrast, scored most of his boundaries through the off-side, in the area between extra-cover and backward point, but if the bowlers strayed onto his pads, as Kumara Dharmasena did in the morning session, he was quick to clip it through midwicket.

Both players showed amazing concentration in trying conditions; they were determined not to give their wickets away. For both, of course, getting a three-figure score meant a great deal, though for different reasons. For Martyn it gets a monkey off his back, silencing the talk about the fact that it has been two years since his last Test hundred. It also ends any suggestion that he cannot play spin. That is a charge most West Australian players have to put up with, and it comes because they do not see a lot of it. He put that myth to bed today. Scoring a hundred in these conditions — on a turning pitch, and against the most effective spinner in the world: Muralitharan — says a lot about his character.

Lehmann, on the other hand, is widely regarded as a top player of spin and today he showed why he has that reputation. I know he was determined to repay the faith we showed by picking him after his six months away through injury, and I think he was also hoping that getting some runs would help him put the death of David Hookes behind him. He took Hookes' death pretty hard — they were great mates, and he was present at the incident that led to it. When he got to 100 he looked up to the heavens; I know he dedicated his innings to his former mentor.

The pitch has held up a lot better than we thought it would. At the start of the match I was certain it would be over in three days; it just goes to show how hard it is to read pitches correctly. I had a look at the pitch when we were out there tonight: the footmarks are quite deep and the cracks have opened up a little, as you would expect in the type of heat we have had over the past few days. But the recent history of the ground suggests that it is possible to survive for long periods in the final innings of a match — England batted for more than 100 overs here to save a Test in December.

Lehmann has not played a lot of cricket in the last few months, which meant he became pretty fatigued as the day went on. We did all we could to try to keep him going, sending out ice-vests, an umbrella for shade and even a chair for him to sit on during drinks breaks. He enjoyed the chair and the ice-vests, but the umbrella did not work quite as we planned — the breeze across the ground blew it inside out. That was the end of that experiment!

By the time Martyn was out we had a lead of 290 and were well into the final session. Andrew Symonds, the next man in, was given the go-ahead to lift the tempo. It was the perfect situation for him and he obliged with a rapid-fire 24, sweeping Muralitharan fine on the leg-side, clubbing Chandana through midwicket for two successive crunching fours and also getting Muralitharan backward of point for another boundary. Unfortunately, he then failed to read the doosra and was stumped.

Lehmann eventually slogged one up in the air and was caught, and Adam Gilchrist and Shane Warne also fell in the pursuit of quick runs. With the clouds hovering, Jason Gillespie and Michael

Kasprowicz pushed the ball around for a while — until we got past the 350 lead, the light improved and we felt in a position to close the innings.

Kasprowicz was still not fit enough to bowl this evening, but Alex Kontouri reckons that with another evening of treatment he could have a go tomorrow morning. With him off the field tonight I opened up with Warne. Some spinners hate operating with the new ball because the sharp new seam can cut their fingers as they look to get some action on the ball; others feel they cannot get a decent grip on it because of the lacquer coating on the leather. Warne has strong, tough fingers and those sorts of things have never seemed to bother him. Plus, his confidence is sky-high after his five-wicket haul in the first innings. Using Warne at the start also gave me a chance to see how much spin he would get — and whether or not he could find some extra bounce with the new ball — and how their openers would cope with men around the bat and nothing to play for except the close of play.

Sri Lanka opened with Kumar Sangakkara instead of Sanath Jayasuriya — who was off the field for much of the day after suffering a cut to the webbing near his right thumb — and he and Marvan Atapattu coped pretty well, as the ball did turn for Warne but did not do anything unexpected. All the same, we were pretty confident in our dressing room tonight. Sri Lanka have a long way to go to save the match, let alone win it.

Friday 12 March

First Test, day five: Australia 220 and 8–512 declared beat Sri Lanka 381 and 154 (Warne 5–43) by 197 runs.

At the start of the day I would not have believed that we could win this Test match by just after 2 o'clock. The pitch had held up much better than we expected, there was a question mark over the fitness of one of our bowlers, and I thought Sri Lanka's batsmen would be tough nuts to crack in their own conditions.

I reckoned without some fantastic work by our bowlers, with Shane Warne and Stuart MacGill outstanding. And to cap off a memorable first Test as captain, we saw Warne take his 500th Test wicket, an amazing achievement by an amazing bowler.

Right from the start things fell into place for us. First, there was the news that Michael Kasprowicz was fit to bowl. That was a great effort by him and a great effort by Alex Kontouri: I know Kasprowicz was worried about the whole tour when he suffered the injury. But he made it onto the ground and bowled an important opening spell that got us our first breakthrough — and earned him his 50th Test wicket.

Although I think we always knew it was going to be a day dominated by spin, our plan first up was to try to hit Sri Lanka hard with our fast bowlers and do some damage while they were still fresh and the ball was still hard. Kasprowicz and Jason Gillespie both ran in hard, and Kasprowicz was rewarded with a wicket in the third over of the day.

His ability to swing the ball back into left-handers with the new ball makes him a danger in much the same way as Brett Lee is a danger, although Kasprowicz is not quite as quick. Today he found the perfect delivery for Kumar Sangakkara: full, swinging, and catching the batsman on the back foot.

But that was our only wicket in the first hour. Gillespie, in particular, was keen to bowl as straight as possible, on the off-chance that a ball might misbehave, and in getting close to the stumps at the bowler's end — trying to bowl wicket to wicket — he twice kicked them over in his delivery stride. Marvan Atapattu and Mahela Jayawardene survived that opening burst, but Jayawardene did play and miss on more than one occasion. However, he also edged Gillespie for four through third man. I thought Jayawardene looked uncomfortable when the ball was banged in short at him, and we experimented with a leg-gully at one point, to see how he would cope, but he managed to either play down or avoid any balls angled in at his body after that.

After 45 minutes I got my two trump cards, Warne and MacGill, into action in tandem, and after spending an over or two finding their range and the pace to bowl at on this pitch, they started to wreck the Sri Lanka batting.

Both men found extravagant turn, and Atapattu was the first to fall victim to it. Warne served up a leg-break that pitched short of a length and Atapattu, after first playing back, then appeared drawn to it — and guided it straight to Matthew Hayden's hands at slip.

Tillakaratne Dilshan, the new batsman, responded in emphatic fashion, skipping down the pitch to club Warne through mid-on for four. The battle was on, but it was Warne who won it, trapping the batsman lbw with a perfectly pitched slider. Dilshan, playing half-forward, was looking for turn but there was none — the ball cannoned into his front pad and he was gone. It was like quite a few of Warne's dismissals of Pakistan batsmen in Sharjah on our tour there 18 months ago, when batsmen who were unsure what was being bowled played for turn that never appeared.

Now wickets started falling in a hurry: two more tumbled in successive overs. First Jayawardene was the victim of a perfectly pitched leg-break from Warne that found the edge as he pushed forward; Hayden was again the man with safe hands at slip. Then MacGill got in on the act with a beautifully pitched googly that spun across Sanath Jayasuriya, again taking the edge — and for the third time Hayden was there to gobble up the chance. That was 5–56 and Sri Lanka were in disarray.

It meant we now had the last two recognised batsmen at the crease: Hashan Tillakaratne and Thilan Samaraweera. Although they are both players who could block for a living, they were not going to hurt us, so I could crowd them a little more. With the spinners bowling so well I could have four or even five close catchers plus Adam Gilchrist around the bat, and in the last over before lunch it almost paid dividends.

All those fielders hovering makes a batsman reluctant to push forward to every ball, because on a fifth-day pitch the odd delivery can jump unexpectedly and take the glove or inside edge, giving all the catchers a chance. That may have been in Tillakaratne's mind when he played back to MacGill.

A fifth-day pitch can also cause the odd ball to keep low, and that was exactly what happened here. The batsman was right back on his stumps, and only the possibility that he may have got an inside edge on the ball saved him from certain dismissal.

The day had started hot and sunny, but by the time we left the field at the interval the clouds were starting to roll over the ground. There was no immediate threat of rain, but the weather was definitely another reason for us to maintain our intensity after the break.

I need not have worried, as the lads came out full of energy, and MacGill struck with a brilliant piece of bowling in his first over of the afternoon session. The delivery he sent down must have looked to Samaraweera as if it was angling way down the leg-side, so he made a move to pad it away. But MacGill had tried to spin the ball hard and that caused the ball to dip in flight at the last minute, which meant that the batsman's pad was suddenly in the wrong place. Instead of hitting the pad, the ball turned sharply after pitching and ripped between his legs, plucking out the off-stump and earning MacGill his 150th Test wicket. It was superb stuff.

At the other end I put Gillespie on after lunch, to see if he could find any reverse swing or uneven bounce in the surface. He was tidy, but after three overs from him I decided to go back to the partnership that had served us so well before the interval, and with his second ball back Warne gave us the vital breakthrough that broke the back of Sri Lanka's resistance — and earned him his 500th wicket.

With just the tail for company Tillakaratne decided to be positive: he thumped Warne's first ball through mid-on for four. But to the next delivery, a full ball from around the wicket into the rough outside the left-hander's off-stump, he suffered through being too positive.

Any cross-bat stroke with the ball coming out of the bowlers' footmarks is fraught with danger, and this ball bounced just a little bit more than Tillakaratne expected, took a big top edge and headed almost straight up in the air. At least half the side could have got under the ball and caught it, but in the end it was Symonds, running in from midwicket, who accepted the chance.

We all knew the significance of the moment and everyone wanted to hug Warne as he celebrated. He was quite emotional, which is pretty understandable after all he has been through over the past year, and I know that no matter what he has said in the media to play down the achievement of reaching 500 wickets, it is something he is unbelievably excited about. I still had to convince him to hold the ball up and show the crowd the same way our bowlers do when they take five wickets. And there was time for some humour from a few of the lads as we huddled around him. Everyone was slapping Symonds on the back — the word was he would now be a rich man because he would be a part of all the 500 wicket memorabilia pieces that would flood the market.

Joking and landmarks aside, there was still a match to be won. We finished things off pretty quickly after that, even though Upul Chandana hit a few defiant blows. Because so many of us were so close to the bat he tried to go over the in-field. He succeeded a couple of times, but I knew that if he continued to play that way it would only be a matter of time before we got him, and indeed he miscued one to deep mid-off, where Justin Langer took the catch.

There was time for Kumara Dharmasena to give Warne his tenth wicket of the match, and another catch to Hayden, which turned out to be a record-equalling seventh in the match for him. Muralitharan, who had no hope of batting for 3½ hours to save the game, ran down the pitch and surrendered meekly, giving us the win — and another wicket to MacGill (his fourth).

We were ecstatic, and rightly so, because this was a great team performance. Any number of our players could have been man of the match, but in the end the television commentators who made the decision gave it to Hayden for his hundred and his record number of catches, although I think he would have been disappointed if he had dropped any of them. Personally, I may have given it to Darren Lehmann for his effort in both innings, but Damien Martyn and Warne also had strong claims. In the end it did not matter — we won, and that is the main thing.

For a captain, the period straight after the end of a match is a busy time, with not only the presentation ceremony but also the post-match media conference to deal with. That was on the ground, as usual, and with quite a few of the players wanted by media outlets it was some time before we all got back to the dressing room as a team and started to celebrate properly with a few drinks, the odd cigar for a couple of the players and, on this occasion, a massive number of well-wishers calling or dropping in. With a few family members and friends in the dressing room as well, it was quite a crowded place for a while. Stephen Waugh, Trevor Hohns and James Sutherland all rang to pass on their congratulations to me, Warne and the rest of the touring party.

Eventually the well-wishers slipped away and I had a chance to deal with an issue that has caused me a few anxious moments since I was confirmed as captain — who should lead the singing of the team song.

Traditionally the captain does not fill this slot, so when I became one-day captain I passed the job in that side on to Adam Gilchrist. Now, for the Test squad, I narrowed my list of candidates down to Gilchrist and Langer. I came up with Langer's name because although we all value playing for Australia so much, he really epitomises the spirit we aim to show every time we walk onto the field and is always quick to remind us how much we should value the chance to pull on the baggy green cap. On top of that, as someone who is only part of the Test squad, he does not get to sing the song as much as the players who play both forms of the game.

However, I did not want to offend Gilchrist, so I chatted it through with him before I made my decision: Gilchrist thought Langer was a good idea. All I had to do now was pick the right time to tell him. I knew everyone in the team was waiting for me to make the announcement — I wanted to be a bit subtle about the whole thing. I texted out the message 'Mate, I want you to sing the team song' on my phone, pretended I had received a message and handed it to Langer so he could see what the message said.

His reaction told me I had made a good choice. He put his head in his hands twice, seemed close to tears, and went to the showers. I followed him in there and he said, 'Thanks. This is the greatest moment of my career.'

His plan for his first song in charge was quite novel. He got everyone onto the team bus and we headed to the top of the fort that overlooks the ground. Right at the top we all took our shirts off, including Cricket Australia director Allan Border, and off we went into the song, just as the sun was setting. Langer led us with plenty of passion, as you might expect.

It was a fitting finale to a great day. We had come to terms with the conditions and managed to beat Sri Lanka after conceding a healthy deficit; now it is up to us to ram home the advantage we have fought so hard to achieve.

Saturday 13 March

There were a few sore heads today but there was no chance for a long lie-in because we headed off to Kandy straight after breakfast.

If we travelled by road it would have taken more than 6 hours, even though it is only a little more than 200 kilometres. Faced with that trip, which would not have been too pleasant, even on a large bus, we split into two groups. Most of the squad went by helicopter, which took off from just outside the ground, and a few of us — me, Rianna, Steve Bernard and his partner Judy, Allan Border, media manager Jonathan Rose, Andrew Symonds' fiancée Brooke and liaison officer Chitral Mendis — travelled by sea plane.

It was a 40-minute flight and we put down in a dam about 25 minutes' drive from the Earl's Regency Hotel, our base in Kandy. The journey itself was very straightforward and comfortable but the arrival was a bit tougher because the water level of the dam is pretty low. That meant we had a fair climb to get to our transport to the hotel, but we all made it in the end.

We arrived before the rest of the squad, which threw the hotel's plans to welcome us into confusion. As soon as we walked through the front doors Queen's 'We Are The Champions' was played at very high volume and rose petals started falling from above us. It was a lovely gesture, but as I was the only player in the group it felt as if they had overdone things a little. Anyhow, the rest of the lads told me that when they arrived exactly the same thing happened, so all was well in the end.

The hotel has a decent-sized pool, so Jock Campbell led us in a recovery session in there in the afternoon. Shane Warne was even happier than normal after he got the news that St Kilda had won the Wizard Cup, the AFL's pre-season competition. We also got the chance to meet and greet the newest member of our tour party: Shaun Tait. He quickly picked up the nickname Sloon — which is what the receptionists at the hotel call him; they cannot seem to master Shaun. Jason Gillespie also calls him Larry, after a character called Larry Tait from the 1960s' television show 'Bewitched'.

We seem to have timed our arrival at the hotel well: it is holding an Australian food festival and Steve Bernard and I were asked to officially open it this evening. A barbecue followed, but I am not sure they've got the hang of it yet — they decided to cook it indoors, which meant the restaurant finished up being very hot and very smoky, even though the food was fine.

Sunday 14 March

Sri Lanka name a 16-man squad for the second Test, in Kandy, recalling left-arm spinner Rangana Herath in place of Kumara Dharmasena. Uncapped batting all-rounder Saman Jayantha has been placed on standby in case batsmen Sanath Jayasuriya (split webbing on right hand) and Thilan Samaraweera (groin injury) fail to recover.

This is normally our major training day, two days before a Test, but today things did not work out as we hoped. The practice pitches were damp and green, and rather than put up with that, most of the batsmen decided against having a hit.

I was one of those who chose not to bat, so after a game of touch rugby to warm up and some catching practice, I sat out the rest of the session. I am happy with the way I have been hitting the ball so far on the trip and 10 minutes in a net with the ball flying around would only dent my confidence. Justin Langer did have a bat, facing Brad Williams, and said afterwards that Williams was bowling well.

This is the ground where Jason Gillespie and Stephen Waugh collided almost five years ago — Gillespie broke his wrist and leg and Stephen had his nose splattered across his face. Gillespie later told us that as practice catches were being knocked into the air today he'd had a flashback of the incident. He asked Darren Lehmann to hit him some catches away from everyone else, because he was nervous about colliding with the rest of the group. It was a shocking injury, which he has done well to recover from, and while I do not expect it to affect him in the game, it is worth keeping an eye on him.

While we were at the ground the ground staff went through their paces with massive plastic sheets that will be used to cover the ground. Last year the first day and a half of Sri Lanka's Test with New Zealand was washed out due to a wet outfield but that does not look as though it will happen this time — the sheets look as if they cover every metre of the field. They were needed this afternoon, as the rain absolutely hammered down. So much for a drought in this area. Let's hope it will clear up in time for the match on Tuesday.

Monday 15 March

I spoke to the media first thing this morning and the main topic of conversation was the weather. It was raining heavily again, and even though the number of covers they have at the ground means we should be able to play if we get a break in the clouds, there has to be a question mark over the way the pitch will behave. With all this rain, the surface may not be as well prepared as the curator would like; there may also be some moisture around, which could lead us to play three fast bowlers rather than the two we opted for in Galle.

That is a decision for tomorrow — because of the rain, we could not get a final look at the pitch this afternoon; our final training session was cancelled.

We still had our team meeting. In the absence of a final eleven, I told everyone to prepare themselves to play. There was not a lot else to add. We all know where we need to be bowling to the Sri Lanka players, and the two innings in Galle have taught us a lot about the best way to go about batting over here. It is now just a case of us executing those plans and tactics correctly when we get out into the middle — whenever that might be.

There was something special during the meeting. Ben Romalis, our video analyst for this trip, and Tim Nielsen put together a photo montage of action from the first Test using favourite bits of music from each player. It was really well done and included, for example, a shot of Darren Lehmann looking up to the heavens when he reached his hundred, to the tune of 'Angels' by Robbie Williams, the song that also featured at David Hookes' funeral. A few shots of Damien Martyn featured at the same time as a song by the rapper 50 Cent, which everyone thought was very funny — Martyn is the only member of the squad that seems to like his music.

After the meeting, John Buchanan, Allan Border, Steve Bernard and I had a separate chat with Shaun Tait. It was partly to let him know about our commitment to the Spirit of Cricket, which we agreed on as a squad at the start of the season, and partly to let him know why he is here. It is easy for a young player in this situation to feel a bit unsure of himself, especially if he has not played a lot of cricket: he is suddenly surrounded by players with vast experience at the highest level and is left wondering whether or not he really deserves to be around. As Border said, he does deserve this call-up, because he has had an excellent domestic season. He has been identified as a youngster with talent and now it is up to him to watch, learn and show a willingness to work hard — he needs to show he is ready to take the next step. My first impressions of him are very good. He seems a nice lad, and I hope he will get plenty out of the opportunity he has been given.

Tuesday 16 March

Second Test, day one: Sri Lanka 7–92 trail Australia 120 (Hayden 54) by 28 runs.

It is difficult to know where to start describing today. Usually, if 17 wickets fall on the opening day of a match it means the pitch is a minefield. In this case, that would be unfair. The pitch did offer plenty of assistance to fast and slow bowlers, but I do not think it was as bad as the scores suggest.

When we batted there was plenty of movement in the air and off the pitch for Sri Lanka's seam bowlers and Muttiah Muralitharan spun the ball sharply, reaching 500 Test wickets in the process. But quite a few of our batsmen managed to contribute to their own downfall.

By the time we came to bowl, just before tea, there was still something there for the bowlers, and Michael Kasprowicz, Jason Gillespie and even Andrew Symonds were darting the ball around, while Shane Warne got some very sharp spin. Despite all that, Sri Lanka should not have lost seven wickets by stumps.

When I woke up and saw the weather was fine I headed down to the ground pretty early, before 8 o'clock, to get a look at the pitch. There was some moisture in the surface, which meant there was a case for including a third fast bowler at the expense of Stuart MacGill, but I was happy to go with the same side we fielded in Galle, and Allan Border agreed. I knew Gillespie and Kasprowicz could do an effective job, and having two leg-spinners meant we had a chance of exploiting the pitch later on, as it began to wear.

For Warne and MacGill to bowl last, we needed to bat first, which was always going to be a risk in bowler-friendly conditions. But I was happy to bite the bullet if I won the toss, safe in the belief that we had players capable of knuckling down, as we'd showed in the second innings in Galle.

As it turned out, the coin again came down 'heads', but that part of my theory was proved wrong, as we contributed to our own downfall with some poor batting. But given my time again I would make the same decision.

Given our low score, it is amazing to look back now and see that Matthew Hayden and Justin Langer managed to survive the first hour without being parted. In the dressing room we thought that was a great effort. Sri Lanka had opted to play Nuwan Zoysa as seam bowling support for Chaminda Vaas, and Langer, in particular, played and missed plenty of times as the ball swung and seamed around. Hayden looked more assured at the other end but still needed a life — which he got when Hashan Tillakaratne dropped him at first slip off Zoysa.

For once our scoring rate was slow, although both batsmen did their best to try to rotate the strike. One effort to do that almost cost Hayden his wicket: he pushed the ball to extra-cover and set off. If Sanath Jayasuriya's throw had hit the stumps he would have been out, but it missed, narrowly.

We thought we had won the first battle when Vaas was rested after a six-over spell, but he was replaced by Muralitharan. We knew he would be just as dangerous, because he would be able to get turn off the damp surface. Zoysa, meanwhile, kept going, and it was he who got the first breakthrough.

Zoysa is a curious character. He has all the ingredients necessary to make him a top-class fast-medium bowler: he is tall, gets bounce, and is able to swing and seam the ball around thanks to a great wrist position behind the ball that means he gets the seam upright on its way down to the batsman almost every time. But he sometimes gives the impression that he would rather be elsewhere, and if you get on top of him he can go to pieces.

Unfortunately, today he was right on his game, and he trapped Langer with a great late in-swinger. After swinging a couple away, he got a ball to come back sharply, and Langer, fooled by the previous deliveries, was trapped in front playing no shot.

That brought me to the crease. Despite the tough conditions, I felt in great form straight away, as I had for the whole tour so far. With the ball swinging I was keen to get forward and present the full face of the bat. I got underway with successive drives for four from Zoysa, the first straight back past the stumps and the second through mid-off.

Hayden was trying to dominate Muralitharan and had some success, edging him to third man for four and getting two more runs to long-leg off an inside edge, then playing a more authentic shot through mid-off for another boundary. Between us we took 19 off two successive overs, which hinted that we were starting to get away from Sri Lanka.

Tillakaratne responded by whisking Zoysa out of the attack and bringing back Vaas, and with the fifth ball of his new spell he dismissed me, although I cannot say I was happy with the decision.

After working the ball through square leg for two runs, I realised he was swinging the ball in quite sharply. I made a big play of taking up my stance well outside the crease, even asking for fresh guard from umpire Dave Orchard. I was still batting on middle stump, as I always do, but opting to take the guard down the pitch — I reckon I was about a metre out of my crease as I prepared to face Vaas.

Batting so far down the pitch is not always a good idea, especially against very fast bowling, because it reduces the time you have to react before the ball gets to you. But Vaas is around medium pace, so I believed I still had enough time to respond to whatever he bowled me.

My plan was to get as far forward as I could in order to reduce the time the ball had to swing before it reached me — and also to make it tough for the umpire to give me out lbw. Given the distance between me and the stumps, the umpire would be guessing about whether or not the ball would go on to hit those stumps if I was hit on the pad, and I felt it protected me against an lbw decision. It turned out I was wrong.

Vaas bowled me a full length in-swinger. I got a big stride in before the ball rapped me on the front pad, and so was more than a little surprised to see Orchard's finger go up in response to the appeal. Television replays when I got back to the dressing room suggested that the ball may have gone on to hit the stumps, but I felt I was so far down the pitch and the ball still had so far to travel that the umpire was guessing I was out rather than being absolutely certain about the decision.

Whatever I felt about it, I still had to go, and so did two others before the lunch break, which we took at an uncomfortable 4–61. Damien Martyn, who replaced me, was trapped on the back foot by a ball from Muralitharan that turned sharply and beat his defensive stroke, and Darren Lehmann, for the second time in the series, got too far across and was bowled around his legs, this time by Zoysa.

Hayden was still there, but conditions were tough: the ball continued to swing, seam and spin, and our slide continued. Two more careless dismissals after lunch added to our problems.

We needed someone to hang around with Hayden but Symonds decided he was going to attack, and threw the kitchen sink at a wide half-volley from Zoysa, only to edge it to first slip. The ball was travelling fast and it took at least three grabs before a relieved Tillakaratne hung on. Then, two balls later, Adam Gilchrist, also trying to be positive, edged a drive through to Kumar Sangakkara. Now we were 6–84.

Hayden was the only man to stand firm while the carnage at the other end continued, but he fell in the next over, playing back to Muralitharan's doosra and being trapped plumb lbw as he looked to work it square on the leg-side.

With all our leading batsmen out, it was now just a matter of time. Could we even scramble to three figures? We did that, thanks to Warne and Gillespie, but the end was not long delayed. Gillespie edged another doosra low to slip, then Kasprowicz entered the record books as Muralitharan's 500th wicket when he was bowled through the gate looking to drive.

For a bloke who has a reasonable batting record in first-class cricket Kasprowicz really has struggled on this tour, and his dismissal here was a carbon copy of the way he was out in the first innings at Galle. He is one of only two players I can recall who think they can cover drive Muralitharan; the other one is Glenn McGrath. Kasprowicz is clearly not picking Muralitharan, so maybe John Buchanan or I need to have a chat with him about his game plan against the spinners.

MacGill hung around with Warne to add 14 for the last wicket, until Warne lofted Vaas to deep mid-off, where Muralitharan, who I reckon would have wanted to keep the match ball in any case, pouched the catch and put it in his pocket. We were all out for 120. Even allowing for helpful bowling conditions, it was a pretty sorry display.

Not that there was any need for me to say that. Everyone in the dressing room knew we had performed badly. Now we had to hit back while there was still some moisture left in the pitch. Luckily, we ended up doing this very well.

We had a brief spell bowling at Sri Lanka before tea and managed to get one wicket — Kasprowicz swung the ball back into

Sanath Jayasuriya and trapped him lbw — but then there was a 20-minute break either side of the interval as a squall of wind and rain blew through. The wind was quite strong for a while, strong enough to rip a banner that had been unfurled on some scaffolding next to the sightscreen at the far end of the ground to celebrate Muralitharan's 500th wicket.

Kasprowicz bowled pretty quickly either side of the rain break, and as well as getting some swing, he also got steep bounce; this really disconcerted Avishka Gunawardene, who was in the side in place of the injured Thilan Samaraweera. One short ball even managed to clear Gilchrist for four byes — it was the result of a technique Kasprowicz had picked up from watching Vaas.

Vaas is barely above medium pace, but he has developed a way of getting his bouncers to climb quite sharply. He cuts his fingers down the side of the ball to make sure the seam is rotating, but also tries to land it with the seam horizontal to the pitch. That way, when the ball then bounces up, it starts to rise a bit like a flying saucer in one of those old science fiction films. If he gets it right, the ball can lift far more quickly than you might expect — this ball is quite a useful weapon. A few of our quick bowlers have noticed Vaas do it and have tried to copy him, and Kasprowicz seems to have got the technique sorted out.

Once we returned after the tea break, our bowlers quickly got to work. We bowled with plenty of aggression, and with conditions still offering a lot of help, we really got into them. Kasprowicz, having forced Gunawardene onto the back foot before the break, bowled a slightly fuller length to him straight after the interval and got his reward when he trapped him lbw. Then he made it three wickets out of three when he had Marvan Atapattu, another player he disconcerted with the short ball, gloving to Gilchrist down the leg-side.

Even though the pitch was still offering seam movement, the short ball was pretty effective. Mahela Jayawardene, as in the first Test, did not seem to know whether to hook or duck, and Sangakkara chose the wrong ball to try to pull, succeeding only in getting a short one from Gillespie high on the bat and lobbing it straight to Symonds at square leg. He may have been surprised by that delivery — we did not have two men out for the lofted hook shot, after all — so perhaps we won a war of bluff and double bluff there.

Just as we had, Sri Lanka desperately needed someone to get his head down and play a long innings. Jayawardene turned out not to be the man for that job: he fell to a horrible shot. Warne, who replaced Kasprowicz, started with two full tosses, one of which Jayawardene clubbed through midwicket for four. That seemed to make him keen to dominate. But rather than play a low-risk shot next, he went for another boundary, backing away and trying to hit over extra-cover — this is a difficult shot even when the ball is not turning. Warne got the ball to spin away, so it caught a thick outside edge and lobbed gently to Symonds at backward point. A wicket thrown away.

The folly of that shot was shown next ball, when Sri Lanka lost another wicket. Tillakaratne Dilshan followed Jayawardene back to the pavilion, having fallen victim to exactly the same ball that had dismissed him the second innings in Galle: he pushed half-forward looking for turn, but Warne fooled him again with a slider that skidded straight on and hit him plumb in front of the stumps.

By this stage the light was closing in but we were keen to press on as far as we could, because the way things were going, there was a chance we could get a first innings lead. Warne was getting significant turn, beating Vaas through the gate with a ball that spun sharply and only missed the stumps because of some extra bounce. He was troubling both Vaas and Tillakaratne, especially when he went around the wicket; they weren't sure what to play and what to leave, because some balls were turning so much. It was that uncertainty that brought about our last success. Tillakaratne pushed forward to Warne without any real conviction. His bat was half-hidden behind the pad, but it was exposed enough to catch the finest of outside edges ... Gilchrist did the rest.

There was time for just one more over but we left the field more than happy with the way we had fought back. When we got back to the dressing room I said to Martyn that there was no way the wicket played poorly enough for 17 wickets to fall; he agreed. It was just poor batting. As at Galle, it is something we will have to put right once we get Sri Lanka's last three wickets.

Wednesday 17 March

Second Test, day two: Australia 120 and 2–221 (Gilchrist 140 not out, Martyn 64 not out) lead Sri Lanka 211 (Vaas 68, Warne 5–65) by 130 runs.

After a pretty disastrous first half of the day, both personally and from a team point of view, I am more than happy with our position.

We let Sri Lanka get away from us in the first session: they played aggressively and earned a lead of 91. That soon looked like a big deficit after we lost both openers cheaply and I was lying on the treatment table thanks to a freak injury I suffered while fielding.

But Adam Gilchrist, well supported by Damien Martyn, came to our rescue with the type of innings that only he can play, and we finished the day on top. If we bat well tomorrow we should be in a position to dictate terms in the rest of the match.

I sprained my upper back, so I hope these two can bat for a little longer yet to give me the best chance of being fit to bat myself.

It happened when Sri Lanka were nine wickets down and their last-wicket partnership, between Chaminda Vaas and Muttiah Muralitharan — which ended up being worth 79 runs — was just starting to get annoying.

Vaas was on strike to Warne towards the end of an over and I was hustling in from cover to try to save one so that we had Muralitharan on strike for the next over. The ball was played to my right, and as I twisted to try to move towards it I felt something grab in my back. It was painful, but I was able to continue — until a few balls later, when I went down for the count.

That ball was played down towards the bottom end of the ground, not far from the sponsor's mat that is laid out on the field, and after bending down to pick it up, I found I could not stand up. My back had seized up completely.

I lay down, feeling a bit embarrassed at picking up an injury this way, and Alex Kontouri ran out to treat me. Even in these types of situations humour is never far from the surface in our team, and someone pointed out that I had gone down in Kandy's equivalent of the Bermuda Triangle: I was lying in the same area where Jason Gillespie and Stephen Waugh had collided back in 1999. Funny though that remark is now, I cannot say I was laughing my head off when it was made, as I was lying on the ground in pain.

Alex manipulated me enough to get me back on my feet and I hobbled to the dressing room. I then spent most of the rest of the day on the treatment table as he tried to free up the affected area. Between spells of treatment I stood up and picked up a bat to see if I could swing it — I could still feel the problem area, somewhere between my shoulder blades, grabbing a little. Alex told me he would treat me again later tonight and again tomorrow morning, and seemed quite hopeful that I would be able to bat at some stage, depending how long our innings lasts.

Either side of my departure from the field we lost control of the match, thanks to some aggressive hitting from Vaas, well supported by an unorthodox innings from Muralitharan.

Right from the start of the day it was clear that Sri Lanka had decided to be positive rather than just get out pushing and prodding. Nuwan Zoysa was caught behind in Kasprowicz's second over of the day, edging a firm-footed drive at a ball angled across him — but only after he got off the mark with a sweetly timed extra-cover drive.

Vaas, at the other end, made his intentions clear by hitting Kasprowicz through midwicket before lofting Warne over mid-off for another boundary. Warne's response was to go around the wicket, but Vaas responded to that by slog-sweeping him from outside off-stump over midwicket for four more.

Kaushal Lokuarachchi was also keen to play his strokes, and after a slightly lucky four to fine leg off Kasprowicz to get off the mark, he drove the same bowler through backward point for four to take Sri Lanka into the lead.

I opened up with Kasprowicz and Warne because they were our most dangerous bowlers last night. I hoped Kasprowicz would be able to get some swing, either orthodox or reverse, and I also know that Warne has a happy knack of knocking over lower-order players.

Sure enough, after a bright and breezy contribution Lokuarachchi fell, top-edging a sweep off Warne straight to short fine leg. At that point, even though we had lost the lead, Sri Lanka's advantage was only 12, and the last man, Muralitharan, was striding to the crease.

He had given us no trouble in Galle, and clearly Vaas had little faith in him, at least at first, because he started to try to farm the strike, looking for big shots at the start of the over and then trying to give Muralitharan no more than one, or at most two, balls at the end of an over.

Hindsight is a wonderful thing, so Kasprowicz will know now that he did not bowl very well to Muralitharan. The little spinner is not the bravest batsman in the world, and is not keen to get into line, so a yorker can always be an effective ball. But while his technique might not be the best, he does have a very good eye and his hand–eye coordination is excellent, and today he played some brilliant shots.

When Kasprowicz dropped short and tried to target the batsman's body, Muralitharan pulled him for four. The next ball was pitched up, and he played it over extra-cover for another boundary. He then swung Kasprowicz over mid-on for two more, and followed that with a six into the old pavilion at midwicket off another short ball.

By this stage I was lying on the treatment bench, but I could hear the increasingly excited cheers of the crowd and I realised the last-wicket pair were starting to pile on the runs.

Gilchrist, who had taken over from me when I left the field, whipped Kasprowicz out of the attack and brought on MacGill, but he was treated just as harshly, being swiped for two fours and a six over the leg-side. Perhaps Muralitharan's best shot was a sweetly timed on-drive off Warne that sailed over the ropes at wide midwicket, after seemingly no bat-swing at all.

By now Vaas had given up all idea of protecting Muralitharan — but he was also enjoying himself, passing 50 and launching Warne for six over long-on and fours through cover and straight down the ground. The pair had secured Sri Lanka's highest-ever tenth-wicket partnership in Test history by the time Muralitharan went for one big shot too many and lofted Warne to Symonds at long-on. He had made 43 from just 28 balls.

The lads returned to the dressing room disappointed at what had happened. Our openers now had four overs to bat before lunch and, more importantly, we had to decide who was going to bat at number three, because I was in no condition to take my place.

I would love to claim the idea to move Gilchrist up the order was mine, but I have to admit that it was John Buchanan's. He asked me if I had any thoughts on the batting order, and after I suggested that everyone should just move up a place and I would slot in whenever I was fit enough to bat, Buchanan suggested Gilchrist should bat at first wicket down. At first I thought Martyn would be the better bet, as he has been in good form, but I chatted with Martyn and he thought promoting Gilchrist was a good idea, because Gilchrist has been struggling for form, especially against Muralitharan, and the chance to bat against the new ball and get his eye in before the slow bowlers come on might be just what he needs. Most importantly of all, Gilchrist was happy with the plan — he headed off to get his batting gear on.

Our plan may have been to get him in earlier than normal, but I do not think any of us wanted him on his way to the middle just one ball into the afternoon session. Straight after the interval Matthew Hayden pushed forward to Vaas and lobbed back a simple chance to the bowler off bat and pad. And soon after, Zoysa deceived Justin Langer for the second time in the match. We were 2–26, and in real trouble.

After being dismissed playing no shot to an inswinger in the first innings, Langer had been keen to play as much as he could against

Zoysa, to avoid falling the same way again. The flip-side of that idea was that he ended up playing at balls he might normally leave alone. That was how he was dismissed this time: following a ball that bounced and left him edging a straightforward catch to Kumar Sangakkara.

Gilchrist started scratchily, as you might expect for a player who'd scored just four runs in his previous three innings. But the beauty of Gilchrist is that he does not let that sort of information clutter his mind. All he does is play each ball on its merits, no matter what form he is in, and that means he is only ever a couple of cleanly struck shots away from being in form again. That was exactly how it worked out here.

He got going with a crisply struck four through extra-cover off Vaas, and clubbed two more fours through the off-side off the same bowler as soon as Langer was out. At that point, however, we had one of our big breaks.

Martyn had not scored when Zoysa got a ball to bounce and leave him off the pitch. With his feet not yet moving well, Martyn edged it low to second slip, but Mahela Jayawardene could not hang on. It was a tough chance, but one that should have been taken. Reprieved, Martyn got underway with two fours off Muralitharan, although one of them was off a thick outside edge, before unfurling a lovely cover-drive off Vaas for another boundary.

As the hardness left the new ball, batting suddenly began to look much more straightforward than it had in the first innings. It was by no means plain sailing — Vaas was still troubling Martyn with his in-swing — but Gilchrist was keeping the scoreboard moving, with shots that included a beautifully struck six over long-off when Hashan Tillakaratne introduced Lokuarachchi.

Gilchrist took on the bowlers and played some really bold shots. When Zoysa dropped short outside off-stump he upper-cut him over backward point for four. And he was happy to sweep Muralitharan as he grew in confidence against him, clubbing him through midwicket for four. Martyn caught the mood when he played the shot of the innings, a back-foot punch through cover off the same bowler.

As the partnership grew and we moved past Sri Lanka's score, Tillakaratne turned to Sanath Jayasuriya's skiddy left-arm spinners in an attempt to halt the flow of runs, and it was off his bowling that Gilchrist had his one major stroke of luck. Moving down the pitch to loft Jayasuriya over long-on, he hit it well but almost not well enough — Avishka Gunawardene made good ground to his left to get under the chance. He caught the ball as he leapt backwards, but as he did so he carried the ball over the boundary rope for six. This moved Gilchrist into the nineties.

There was no hanging about for Gilchrist, and he reached three figures with an emphatic four through the covers off Vaas. It is amazing to think that with this hundred he has now reached three figures against every Test team apart from Bangladesh. This is a remarkable record when you realise that he has only been playing Test cricket since late 1999.

Gilchrist's effort, and his partnership with Martyn, clearly left Sri Lanka frustrated; they probably thought they had us on toast after Hayden and Langer were out. Muralitharan was still spinning the odd ball sharply, but both batsmen were now in total control, and the home side was left hoping for some reverse swing with the old ball, something they tried to encourage by bouncing their throws in from the outfield. It was all to no avail, though, and by the time our batsmen accepted an offer of bad light, with four overs still to bowl, you could tell from their body language that Sri Lanka's players were pleased to get off the field. They would be hoping to regroup tomorrow.

It is never easy to continue momentum into a fresh day, but I hope we can do it and set them a stiff target.

Adam Gilchrist

If you hear someone in the Australian team refer to Churchy, they are talking about Adam Gilchrist.

Adam is one of my oldest friends in the squad and the source of his nickname is the 1997 Ashes tour — a trip he had to leave early after damaging knee ligaments playing soccer during a warm-up.

On that tour he was the reserve wicketkeeper to Ian Healy and so was not very well known; at that stage he had played just a handful of one-day internationals. He was yet to move to the opening position he has made his own over the past six years.

During a county match against Derbyshire a few of the players, including Adam, went for a walk around the ground to buy ice-creams, and as they did so a young lad came up to the group and asked for autographs. When it came to Adam he said: 'I know who you are. You're Eric Gilchurch.' The name Gilchurch stuck within the squad — it has now evolved to Churchy.

I do not know when Adam will retire from cricket — we have never discussed that — but when he does he will do so as someone who has changed the game forever, and not many players can claim to have done that.

His powerful hitting at the top of the order in one-day cricket has helped revolutionise the type of totals sides try to achieve in the shorter form of the game, as players from other countries have mirrored his style. And in Test cricket his performances have altered the way other Test sides have selected their squads.

Before Gilchrist's emergence on the Test scene, other teams were always content if their wicketkeeper averaged 25 runs per innings with the bat. If the player averaged 30, they felt they had an exceptional performer. Gilchrist's average, which is more than 50, has illustrated how important it is for a wicketkeeper to score big runs, and now England, New Zealand and Sri Lanka have all opted for wicketkeepers who can provide runs as well as safe glovework.

The strange thing is, I do not think anyone was really aware of his true potential as a batsman through his early years. When I first toured with him, with the Commonwealth Bank Cricket Academy to South Africa when I was 16, he was regarded as a really talented wicketkeeper–batsman, but no one would have predicted the impact he would have on international cricket.

Gilchrist's success as a batsman is based on the fact that he hits the ball very hard and very often. His grip of the bat helps: he holds it high on the handle, which gives him plenty of leverage. Add to that his strong wrists and forearms and a very rapid swing of the bat and you have a player who is a nightmare to bowl to.

Plenty of sides have tried to find a way to reduce Gilchrist's effectiveness, but as his averages show, most have drawn a blank. During the recent Test series against India, Sourav Ganguly's side decided to bowl straight and full at him, trying to make him play down the ground. That method was allied with an attempt to swing the ball back into him, something Heath Streak, the former Zimbabwe captain, had success with a few times.

Gilchrist's figures during that India series were modest by his own high standards, suggesting that the plan worked, but plans against him are never foolproof. Why? Well, he plays very aggressively, so he puts a bowling side under a lot of pressure — plans can, and often do, go out the window under his barrage of attacking shots.

As a bowler running in to Gilchrist, you know that if you over-pitch you will get hit; if you bowl short you will get hit; and if you give him any width you will get hit. His approach gives a bowler so little margin for error that even the best-laid plans can collapse.

One of the strengths of many members of this Australian side is their ability to focus totally on the job at hand when they cross the boundary rope, and Gilchrist is no exception. He has his fingers in plenty of pies off the field, with media and commercial deals, including one that has him linking up with our overseas tour sponsors Travelex, but once he gets on the field he shuts everything else out, and his play reflects that.

His style as a batsman also means he can never be classed as out of form the way most of the rest of us can. He plays in an uncomplicated fashion whether he is on nought or 150, and he plays exactly the same way whether his past three innings have been hundreds or noughts. His method is simple: if the ball is there to hit he hits it, regardless of the match situation.

My first impression of Gilly on the Academy tour all those years ago was that he was a good bloke, and that has only been reinforced in the 14 years since. He is an ambitious man, and I am sure he would love to be Australia's Test captain, but he was still happy to step aside for me to take over as vice-captain to Stephen Waugh when the selectors suggested it in early 2003.

That is just one example of his desire to put others and the team ahead of himself. The idea of team is something he is very strong on, a fact best illustrated by the way he always volunteers to be on any social committees we put together when we are on tour. He is always the man at the forefront of arranging team outings and meals to maintain the spirit we have within the group.

All of the above obviously paints a rosy picture of relations between captain and vice-captain, but we do not agree on everything. We disagree fundamentally on the idea of a player 'walking' if he knows he is out. I believe the umpire, not the batsman, should be the one making that decision. I know he had become frustrated at the way he felt sportsmanship had faded from the game, and that was his response: to 'walk' whenever he knew he was out. I accept his right to play the game in the way he sees fit, but you will not see me following suit or advising any other players to follow his lead, although they are free to do so if they want.

All these words on Gilchrist and I have not even mentioned his wicketkeeping. History shows that he is one of the taller players to succeed in that role, but the fact that a gasp goes around the ground whenever he drops a ball — which is not very often — shows what a high standard he has set in the role.

He came into the Test side in 1999 with the hardest possible task ahead of him — to fill the gloves of Ian Healy, a player who had been Test keeper for more than a decade and had made his reputation with brilliant work up at the stumps to Shane Warne. On top of that, Gilchrist's debut came at Healy's home ground, the Gabba in Brisbane, amid whispers in the media that the local hero had been pushed out to accommodate him. The cry was, 'How will we ever replace Ian Healy?'

That would have been more than enough for most players to cope with on debut. Gilchrist handled it, together with the attendant media pressures, brilliantly. He started off with six dismissals, including a superb leg-side stumping, as well as

81 from just 88 balls, and he has not missed a Test since. The cry now is, 'How will we ever replace Adam Gilchrist?', and with all due respect to Healy, Gilchrist's achievements with bat and gloves will make that one of the toughest tasks the selectors have ever had.

That time may come sooner rather than later. Although we have never discussed retirement dates, I feel certain Gilchrist's business and media interests will ensure that he does not play as long as he might, and that he will go out of the game while he is still at the top. He has a full life outside cricket and a young family. But whenever he does retire, he will do so in the knowledge that he has done a massive amount for Australian cricket.

Thursday 18 March

Second Test, day three: Australia 120 and 5–320 (Gilchrist 144, Martyn 104 not out) lead Sri Lanka 211 by 229 runs.

Rain robbed us of half a day today but I am not unduly worried about that. What it has done is take some time out of the match, and if we can bat well tomorrow it means Sri Lanka will have fewer overs available to get whatever target we can set them. That in turn means they could be batting for a draw rather than a win, allowing us to set more attacking fields and build more pressure on them. That is the ideal scenario, but it is still a long way away.

We managed to make good progress today, maybe losing one more wicket than was ideal, but with Damien Martyn reaching another richly deserved hundred and Andrew Symonds still there, we have some firepower left at our disposal.

Martyn's innings is another feather in his cap, especially as he started the tour with a question mark over his head in the eyes of many in the media. He has shown incredible patience here and has given the perfect demonstration of how we should play in these conditions.

Before the series started, when I chatted to any of our batsmen, we all agreed that the important thing is to try to bat for a long time and not worry about the scoreboard. We have not talked about run rates, target scores during a day's play or even stopping Muralitharan getting wickets. The aim is simply to play it as you see it, while at the same time removing as many risks as you can.

Martyn has done that perfectly — I can think of barely a single ball he hit in the air during this innings. He has had a small amount of luck, but every batsman needs that to make a big score.

Yesterday he was missed low down by Mahela Jayawardene at slip, before he had even scored, and today the same fielder put him down in the same position when he had added just a single to his overnight score. There was no doubt that the ball had carried and Nuwan Zoysa, the unlucky bowler, was distraught.

In Jayawardene's defence, I have found fielding at slip in Sri Lanka one of the hardest jobs in my career. First, you have to try to maintain your concentration for every ball despite the heat and humidity. However, the main difficulty comes from having to stand so close because of the lack of pace and bounce in the pitches. It means that most edges come at you hard and low; it is very rare that you get a chance at a comfortable height.

Martyn went on to make the most of that let-off, but his partner at the other end, Adam Gilchrist, was unable to build on yesterday's effort. Hashan Tillakaratne opened up with Muttiah Muralitharan, and in his second over of the day he beat Gilchrist, who pushed half-forward to the doosra. It turned back, hit him in front of middle stump and that was it.

I was feeling a lot better when I woke up this morning. My back was not too sore and I had a reasonable range of movement, made better by a trip to Alex Kontouri before we left for the ground and more treatment after we arrived. I was feeling so confident that I decided to have a few throw-downs on the outfield before play, just to see how I would go hitting the ball. That felt okay, so I settled on batting at number six.

Darren Lehmann replaced Gilchrist, and he started off looking in great touch, easing Muralitharan through extra-cover to get off the mark and clipping the same bowler through midwicket when he tightened up his line into the batsman's pads.

Chaminda Vaas replaced Zoysa and Lehmann greeted him with a square drive for four. But the bowler then got his revenge, bringing one back into the left-hander. After some thought, umpire Steve Bucknor raised the finger. There was some suggestion that Lehmann may have got an inside edge onto the ball, but when I spoke to him afterwards he said he was not sure he hit it and that the decision was fair enough.

That brought me to the crease. I had no concerns about straight bat shots, having practised them without any trouble before play; my main concern was trying to hit with a cross bat, either cutting, pulling or sweeping, shots that involve some twisting of the trunk area. It is all very well to tell yourself not to play shots like that, but when you have been playing them all your career, instinct can take over when you see a ball pitched in a certain place. That worry was in the back of my mind.

I laid the issue to rest pretty quickly, as Muralitharan bowled me a ball I tried to paddle away on the leg-side. I did not make contact, but it did not cause me any discomfort either — that gave me a licence to play with a lot more freedom.

With Muralitharan in the attack, our battle was renewed. I tried to hit him over mid-on as soon as he flighted the ball enough to let me get down the pitch at him. Sure enough, he tossed the ball up with mid-on up close to save the single and I took up the challenge, managing to middle the ball well enough for it to bounce out of the ground off a tin roof covering one of the stands to the left of the old pavilion.

At the other end Martyn was in no rush at all; he added just 26 runs in the 2-hour morning session. That might seem slow going, but I was not concerned. Our challenge was to bat out the day, because the pitch seemed to be getting better and better. Even now, at close of play, the idea remains simply to bat for as long as we can: the longer we bat, the more chance we have of the pitch wearing, and that will give our leg-spinners the chance to be effective.

I felt good in that morning session, ending it with an emphatic off-drive through Muralitharan at mid-off for four. However, my happiness at the way I was batting did not last long into the afternoon — umpire Dave Orchard gave me another decision to be unhappy with. As in the first innings, Vaas was the bowler.

Given the way Vaas dismissed me in the first innings, swinging the ball back into me, I made an even bigger play of looking to get forward this time around. Vaas's response was to drag his length back a bit, and he got the ball past my inside edge. It flicked my back thigh, went through to Kumar Sangakkara, the Sri Lankans appealed and I was given out.

I admit there was a noise, and the umpire may also have been able to see a deflection, but there was no way he could be certain the ball had hit the bat. I stood there for a second or so after his finger went up, a bit stunned and also a little angry — once again on this tour I have failed to go on and make a big score after getting myself settled in. But because of my responsibilities as captain, and because we have all signed up to uphold the Spirit of Cricket, I had to drag myself off the ground as cheerfully I could, and as there was no knock on the door from the match referee after play, I guess I managed it okay. The dismissal left us with our last two recognised batsmen at the crease and a lead only just over 200, so it was a vital time in the match.

Martyn was in no mood to give things away. He ploughed on, reaching his hundred just after I was dismissed, with a slightly streaky edge through third man for four. While the shot that brought him to three figures may not have been a thing of beauty, his innings has been unbelievably valuable, and as he is still there — now with Symonds — we are hoping he can press on to get us a few more yet.

I talked to him when he came off the field as first bad light and then a torrential rain storm forced play to be abandoned in mid-afternoon, and though he is pretty tired now, after so long without a big score he has the taste for them again and is determined to get as many runs as he can. I stressed to him that all we want is more of the same, just sensible accumulation. If we can get another 100 or even 150 it will make life very tough for Sri Lanka in the fourth innings.

Friday 19 March

Second Test, day four: Sri Lanka 211 and 7–301 (Jayasuriya 131) require another 51 runs to beat Australia 120 and 442 (Martyn 161, Gilchrist 144, Muralitharan 5–173).

We are on the brink of history tonight after a day of mounting tension, and while I am confident we can finish the job, Sri Lanka have given us a real run for our money, with former captain Sanath Jayasuriya leading the way.

We know how dangerous a player he is and we have managed to keep him quiet so far in the series, but he decided to go for broke this afternoon. He had some luck early on, and then played quite beautifully until Jason Gillespie, during an excellent spell, managed to get rid of him and get us back in control of proceedings.

Even then Sri Lanka were still playing positively, and although we have removed all their recognised batsmen, they still have Chaminda Vaas at the crease. He seems to have taken up where he left off in the first innings: he has played spin and pace with equal ease, and while he is there we know Sri Lanka have a fighting chance.

We got our lead up to 351 thanks to Damien Martyn's determination and, for once in the series so far, some resistance from the tail. Even Stuart MacGill, whose batting has gone downhill badly in the last couple of years, managed to hang around while 34 were added for the last wicket, and those runs are looking priceless at the moment.

Amazingly, Martyn was dropped by Mahela Jayawardene again off Nuwan Zoysa, this time when he had added just eight to his overnight score. The ball was angled across the batsman and he pushed at it, but the ball was dropping as it got to the fielder at second slip. Jayawardene did appear to get his hands under the ball, but he could not hold on. If we win this Test those misses by him are going to be ones Sri Lanka will really regret.

The plan was to bat as long as we could, and early in the day we made pretty good progress. Martyn got underway with a delightful back-foot punch through cover off Vaas before he was dropped, and Andrew Symonds clubbed fours through extra-cover in successive overs from Muttiah Muralitharan and Zoysa.

Muralitharan began around the wicket to Symonds, a sure sign he was getting the ball to spin, and it was from that angle that he managed to get his man. Symonds tried to sweep a delivery pitched around middle stump, but it straightened, and although he got a good stride in, umpire Dave Orchard said the ball would have gone on to hit the stumps and raised his finger.

Now Martyn was left with the tail, but they all gave him pretty good support. He never tried to protect them and they responded by playing sensibly — with the odd big shot thrown in for good measure — as we took our lead past 300.

Both Shane Warne and Jason Gillespie were disappointed with the shots they played to get out: they simply picked the wrong balls to be aggressive with. Warne miscued Muralitharan to deep mid-off without getting to the pitch of the ball and Gillespie drilled an on-drive low and hard to mid-on.

That brought in Michael Kasprowicz, and with him came a hint of controversy. He edged Zoysa low towards first slip. Avishka Gunawardene claimed the catch but Kasprowicz hung around. That was completely contrary to what Hashan Tillakaratne and I had agreed before the series: I had instructed all our batsmen to walk off the ground if a fielder said he was happy he had taken a low chance cleanly.

I stood up on the balcony and started waving Kasprowicz to get off the ground but he stayed in the middle; the umpires signalled for a television replay, which showed the ball had reached the fielder on the half-volley.

Even though Kasprowicz was given not out, the incident left me feeling pretty embarrassed after everything I'd said before the series, and it was not until Kasprowicz was out — later in the same over — that I found out what had happened.

Kasprowicz told me that in keeping with what was agreed, he'd been happy to walk off, but umpire Orchard, who had seen the incident from square leg, came forward and said he was not convinced the catch had been taken cleanly. He told Kasprowicz to stay put, and it was at his insistence that the replay was called for.

When we were eventually bowled out we had one over to bowl before the lunch break and after that over I talked with Orchard out in the middle; I wanted to get his version of events before we went off the field. Some onlookers thought I was complaining, saying that there was time for another over before the interval, but I was just trying to clarify what had happened when Kasprowicz was batting. Orchard confirmed what Kasprowicz told me, that it was his idea for the third umpire to be called. I was happy that as a team, we had not gone back on the pre-series agreement with Sri Lanka.

After Kasprowicz's dismissal, Martyn and Stuart MacGill took our lead past 350. Martyn was able to pass 150 for the first time in Tests, thanks to a beautifully timed on-drive for six off Muralitharan, and MacGill got in on the act with a few unorthodox shots of his own, pulling Zoysa through mid-on for four and following that with another boundary through extra-cover when the bowler pitched up.

Martyn was last out, stumped off Muralitharan after batting for just under nine hours. He played a fantastic innings in trying conditions, with heat and humidity a constant problem. Even though the pitch was now in excellent shape, I felt we were in a strong position to win the match unless they played exceptionally well.

Nothing that happened early in Sri Lanka's innings changed my view. Marvan Atapattu was given out lbw, hit as he made a belated attempt to get forward to Gillespie, and Kasprowicz did exactly what he did to Avishka Gunawardene in the first innings all over again. He forced the batsman back with a succession of short balls before bowling a fuller length and trapping Gunawardene lbw on his crease.

Gillespie and Kasprowicz attempted the same thing to Jayasuriya, peppering him with short balls to try to pin him on the back foot. Our usual tactic against him is to cramp him for room and tie him up with short stuff; our problem today was that with only two quick bowlers we did not have unlimited resources to keep doing that.

Faced with these aggressive tactics, Jayasuriya clearly decided to attack or die trying. When Gillespie pitched the ball up he twice hit him through cover for four. This aggressive approach earned him a life when he drove hard at Kasprowicz.

The ball flew off the edge to Martyn's left at third slip, and although he got a hand on the ball, all he could do was parry it for two runs. Just as important as the drop, however, was the sight of Martyn's right index finger afterwards: it looked just the way it did when he fractured it so badly in Durban during last year's World Cup, and the end tip went black very quickly. Fearing the worst, I sent him off straight away to get it seen to by Alex Kontouri. Alex's initial view is positive, and he does not think it is fractured again, but Martyn spent the rest of the day off the field getting it iced, trying to reduce any pain and swelling.

Jayasuriya is a real danger if he is aggressive and has his eye in when the spinners come on, and that was exactly what happened today. I gave Gillespie seven overs after the lunch break and Kasprowicz six, but I could not keep them going forever in the conditions we had today, especially if I wanted anything out of them in the last session.

I threw the ball to Warne and Symonds first up: Warne because of the control and confidence he brings to proceedings, and Symonds because he spins the ball away from the left-handers, and we had two at the crease now — Jayasuriya and Kumar Sangakkara.

At first the pair looked in little trouble, with both batsmen thumping Warne through cover for four. Then I replaced Symonds with MacGill, and Jayasuriya greeted him with a lofted shot over mid-off for another boundary.

The pair were playing very comfortably and brought up a 50 partnership in less than 12 overs. Then Warne got us the breakthrough we desperately needed, removing Sangakkara with a lovely piece of bowling. The batsman skipped down the pitch to drive, found the ball dipping on him and checked his shot at the last minute, but only managed to chip a catch back to Warne.

That left Sri Lanka 3–98, but rather than lie down and submit, Jayasuriya decided to lift the tempo, which was already high — they had been motoring along at more than 4 runs per over. He drove MacGill through mid-off for another four, and then, when I replaced Warne with Kasprowicz, to see if there was any hint of reverse swing, crashed Kasprowicz's first ball over cover for six. It was an amazing shot.

Jayasuriya's battle with MacGill looks pretty one-sided on paper, and there is no question the batsman won it hands down. But all the time MacGill was convinced he would get him out, and there was the odd close shave for Jayasuriya as he continued to play his shots — even though MacGill landed the ball pretty consistently in the rough outside the left-hander's off-stump. By now, Jayasuriya was in a mood to punish any error in line or length, and in successive overs from

MacGill he thumped him through midwicket twice and swept him fine for three fours, bringing up a brilliant individual hundred inside 38 overs.

At the other end Jayawardene was something of an onlooker, but playing steadily enough, and suddenly Sri Lanka were almost halfway to the target and the pitch was playing easily ... we needed something to happen. I talked to Adam Gilchrist and Darren Lehmann, and we decided to try to take the momentum out of Sri Lanka's innings by posting a third man and a deep point for Jayasuriya facing Gillespie. It meant that shots that had been going for four were now going for just a single. That bought us some time and gave the batsmen something to think about.

It was Gillespie who got us our next breakthrough. He drew Jayawardene into a push away from his body, which Gilchrist took behind the stumps. Our relief was massive, as it gave us a new batsman to attack, but Jayasuriya kept on attacking at the other end, even though he required treatment for cramps in his hands.

He clobbered MacGill twice through extra-cover for four, then danced down the pitch to loft him for a straight six, and in the same over we were no-balled for having three fielders behind square leg. An over later, umpire Dave Orchard gave Gillespie a warning for running down the pitch.

It was up to us to pull ourselves together, and thanks to great spells by Gillespie and Warne, we got our composure back. Warne locked things down, conceding just nine runs in his first four overs back in the attack and having two massive appeals for lbw — against Tillakaratne Dilshan, to another slider, and against Jayasuriya, sweeping — both turned down.

Gillespie, meanwhile, ran in aggressively, hit the pitch hard and tried to rattle both batsmen. He got his reward with the big wicket of Jayasuriya, out to a tired shot slashing away from his body and giving Gilchrist a straightforward edge away to his left. One look at our reactions when he held onto that catch will have told everyone watching how important we thought that wicket was.

It brought in Tillakaratne, with half the side out and 134 still required. His appearance caused another whiff of controversy, in an incident that also involved me. Tillakaratne had already driven Warne through mid-on for four — one of his signature shots — when he tried to repeat the dose and got a thick inside edge that sent the ball onto his pad. The ball then popped up in front of him on the off-side and I threw myself forward at silly point to cling on one-handed.

But as I did so I also saw his bat coming across my line of vision. I managed to hang on to the ball, and was ecstatic to do so, but when I said to the other lads, 'Did you see that? He tried to hit me with the bat!', they all thought I was joking — none of them had picked up on it. It was only when we got back into the dressing room afterwards and I pointed it out when the dismissals were shown on television that they saw what I meant.

I gather the match referee asked for an informal chat with Tillakaratne about what he thought he was doing, and I believe he said he was not sure where the ball was. Luckily, it did not matter because I took the catch, but maybe we could have been talking about the Sri Lanka captain out obstructed the field tonight rather than simply caught Ponting bowled Warne.

Even though six wickets were now down, the Sri Lankans still kept playing their shots and putting us under pressure. Vaas came in and got off the mark with a classy clip through midwicket off Warne, and Dilshan showed Gillespie the full face of the bat when he drove him straight as an arrow for four.

One of Gillespie's strengths is his ability to hit the seam regularly, and he managed it again as a response to that shot, cutting one back at Dilshan and catching him a blow in the midriff that had him down for treatment for five minutes. We all smile about that sort of blow, but if it happens to you there is nothing worse. At Gillespie's pace it can make you feel sick; no one really questioned the time Dilshan took to get back on his feet.

I used that time to chat with Lehmann at mid-on about how he thought things were going. He knows Gillespie pretty well and I wanted to get a feel for how much longer he thought I could bowl him — it was already the ninth over of his spell. Lehmann thought he could give us one more, which he did, and after that I threw the ball to Kasprowicz, but it was Warne who got us our last wicket of the day.

He had already dismissed Dilshan twice in the series as he pushed half-forward to the slider, and maybe as a result of that the batsman hung back more than he might have done. But playing back turned out to be a fatal mistake: Warne ripped a leg-spinner past his outside edge and into the middle and off-stumps and we had got rid of Sri Lanka's last recognised batsman with 78 still required. It was a big wicket.

By now it was getting gloomy — it was the latest we had played on any of the four days — but Vaas and the new batsman, Kaushal Lokuarachchi, seemed to be seeing the ball okay as they continued to attack us. Lokuarachchi hit one slog-sweep shot right out of the middle of the bat for four off Warne, but I was not too unhappy seeing him play that way because he was out doing the same thing in both the first innings here and the warm-up match before the first Test. Vaas, meanwhile, took two fours off Warne's last over of the day, one through third man off a thick outside edge and one a high-class extra-cover drive.

Both men looked in great touch, and I was not disappointed when we went off for the evening just after Sri Lanka brought up their 300. We now have a chance to rest and freshen up, which is especially important for our faster bowlers, and Sri Lanka have an opportunity to think about how close they are to a famous win. The question now is whether they will rise to the challenge or crack under the pressure.

Saturday 20 March

Second Test, day five: Australia 120 and 442 beat Sri Lanka 211 and 324 (Jayasuriya 131, Warne 5–90) by 27 runs.

We have done it! We have achieved what we set out to do at the start of this tour: win both the one-day series and the Test series. And we sealed the Test prize by holding our nerve in a tense finale, with Shane Warne, someone who has always thrived in situations like that, getting us over the line.

It is impossible to downplay the significance of our achievement. We came here off the back of a tough domestic season, into hot, humid conditions on pitches where we have not always been at our best, and we have come through it successfully. The only thing left to do now is complete the job next week in Colombo with a series whitewash — but for now all I want to do is savour today's victory.

I slept pretty well last night, but as soon as I was awake my mind was racing. I chatted to John Buchanan over breakfast about his thoughts on our plan of attack. We both agreed that what has become our motto on this trip, the idea of attacking with the ball to defensive fields, was the correct approach.

The drive to the ground takes about 25 minutes, and I sat with Allan Border, who did his best to ease the tension with a bit of a joke. 'It takes a good side to win here,' he said, a reference to the last Australian team to win a series in Sri Lanka, which was back in 1992 — a side he captained. Equalling that side was our challenge.

When we arrived at the ground we gathered as a squad in the dressing room and attempted to flesh out the plan. The idea we came up with was trying to cut off the big shots. I was convinced Sri Lanka would be feeling the pressure every bit as much as we were, and the best way for their batsmen to ease that pressure was by scoring runs quickly. So the longer we could keep them out there without too many boundaries leaking away, the more the pressure would build on them. They only had three wickets in hand, so we hoped the pressure would bring wickets.

We settled on the idea of opening up with Jason Gillespie and Warne. Gillespie had been excellent on the fourth evening, finding a touch of reverse swing, and I knew we could rely on him to keep it fairly tight at one end while we used Warne as more of an attacking weapon.

We knew Sri Lanka would be tense, but there was tension in our side too, and I think it showed in the first couple of overs. We all knew we were close to the series win, and the prospect of failing here and having to do it all again in Colombo next week was almost too much to bear at the end of a long summer. It is at times like this that you need someone to stand up and take responsibility, and that is exactly what Warne and Gillespie did today.

Warne bowled the first over of the day and conceded three singles, two of them to long-off (the field was set back), and although every run was cheered by the biggest crowd of the match, let in free for the occasion by Sri Lanka Cricket, it was a quiet start in cricketing terms.

That all changed in the next over, bowled by Gillespie. To the first ball, Chaminda Vaas, trying for a big drive through the off-side but not moving his feet, inside-edged the ball perilously close to his stumps and past Adam Gilchrist's right hand for four. He followed that with a single to square leg but could not get back for two because Andrew Symonds was quickly onto the ball. After Kaushal Lokuarachchi squeezed another run backward of square on the off-side, Vaas ended the over with another drive — this time he nailed it right out of the middle of the bat, back past Gillespie for four more.

Ten came from that over, but looking back, that may have worked in our favour in a funny sort of way. It got the adrenaline flowing for Vaas and made him want to continue to play his shots, and when he did, he played straight into our hands.

We dismissed him in Warne's next over, the third of the day, but not before more drama. A leg-bye got Vaas on strike and he continued his policy of attacking by going down the pitch and lofting the bowler out towards deep midwicket. We had a deep midwicket and a long-on but he managed to find the gap between the two and pick up another boundary. They needed 33 to win.

Warne tossed the next ball up outside the off-stump and Vaas went for another big drive, but this time he did not pick the gap. Instead he drilled it straight to Symonds at extra-cover — who dropped it. You would hardly credit that, on two counts. First, it was amazing that Vaas managed to find the fielder at all, as we had a deep point and long-off, but no one apart from Symonds in front of the wicket on the off-side. And if you had wanted anyone to be in front of that ball it would surely have been Symonds, one of the best fielders in the world in any position.

I was watching the action from midwicket and saw the ball all the way to Symonds. I could not believe it had gone down; he slumped to his knees after grassing it.

But we all had to pick our heads up and try to create another chance, and that was exactly what happened two balls later. Vaas obviously thought it was going to be his day, and he tried to hit Warne over wide midwicket again, but this time the ball turned, and although he went through with the shot, he got it off a thick inside edge that sent the ball squarer than the shot he hit for four earlier in the over.

Langer was out on the midwicket boundary and he cradled the ball into his midriff, prompting a massive outpouring of relief from all 11 Australians on the field. Among the first to get to him to offer congratulations was Symonds, and no wonder!

Vaas dragged himself off the ground, obviously devastated. I was not surprised he played that shot — we had planned for him to do just that — but he will sit back and wonder why he did it, as he had 90 overs today to get the runs required. It goes to show what tension can do to even the most experienced players, and there are few more experienced than Vaas — he has been playing international cricket for almost ten years.

We still had to maintain our focus. Nuwan Zoysa hurt us in the one-day international in Colombo when we thought we had the game won, so we had to keep the pressure on. Gillespie did that in his next over, conceding just one single — for Lokuarachchi, to third man. That meant Lokuarachchi would still be the striker when Warne came on.

It also meant Zoysa was at the non-striker's end in that over, and his actions were bizarre, to say the least. He did not try to sledge Warne; instead he moved his bat as close as he could to the place where Warne's front foot landed in his delivery stride. Warne was clearly upset and said to Zoysa, 'If you keep doing that, make sure you back it up with the way you are playing', as well as raising the matter with umpire Steve Bucknor. Bucknor was having none of that type of behaviour from Zoysa and made sure he knew it. Zoysa apologised to us later, and said it was part of a plan to put Warne off. I am all for doing it with the odd word here and there, and even some aggressive batting, but I think that was taking things a bit too far.

Warne managed to complete a maiden, which left Zoysa on strike to Gillespie. Our big fast bowler made short work of him, banging in a short ball which Zoysa gloved through to Gilchrist as he attempted an ambitious hook shot. It brought Muralitharan in with 32 still required, and after what happened in the first innings, there was no way we were taking him lightly.

Gillespie tried to pitch the ball up, but even though Muralitharan backed away to square leg, he still got enough bat on the ball to send it through extra-cover for four. With the match so tight, a few shots like that could cost us the win, so after a chat with Lehmann I decided to push all the fielders — apart from me at midwicket — out to the boundary. I figured Muralitharan was not a number 11 for no reason, and that if he was starved of boundaries he would lose patience and slog the ball up in the air sooner or later.

Muralitharan survived the last ball of the over, which meant Lokuarachchi was now on strike to Warne, and once again I opted for an in–out field, with men at midwicket, backward point, extra-cover and short fine leg and the rest protecting the fence. I need not have worried, because Warne produced a high-class top-spinner next ball to wrap up the match, pinning Lokuarachchi plumb in front of all three stumps.

When umpire Bucknor gives an lbw he nods his head a split second before he raises his finger, and when he did that this time it was the start of a wild celebration in the middle of the pitch as we all rushed in to hug Warne and celebrate the win. It was a massive outpouring of the tension we had all been feeling as the match ran towards its conclusion.

The support staff and reserve players were just as excited as the players on the field, and as we raced off the ground and up the dressing room steps everyone was shaking hands, hugging each other and shouting, and Buchanan had his video camera at the ready, as ever. We had a few minutes to ourselves in the dressing room to take in what we had achieved, then it was time to go back out onto the field for the presentation ceremony, with Warne claiming the man of the match award from the television commentators for his 10 wickets in the match and, no doubt, his decisive contribution on the final morning.

As you might expect with a series win, there was plenty of media interest, and it was as I was coming back from one of my media commitments that I saw Lehmann, sitting outside the dressing room on his own, with his feet dangling over the railing, crying his eyes out.

He was obviously really upset and I asked him what the problem was. He said it was nothing and he would be back in the dressing room to join everyone else in a minute or two, but he was so distressed I asked him again what was wrong and whether there was anything I could do to help.

He would not tell me what the problem was and said he would be okay in a while, so I reluctantly left him alone. It was only later I found out that Kandy was the scene of David Hookes' only Test hundred. His death has hit Lehmann harder than anyone else in the team.

It was almost two hours before we finished all the media commitments and could sit down as a team in the dressing room and savour our win together. But there was no team song at the ground: Langer had decided it should take place on the way back to Colombo instead.

With our police escort, we set off on the 3-hour drive. After stopping at a roadhouse on the way for some snacks, Langer eventually got the bus and our escort to stop on a bridge about halfway between Kandy and Colombo. The police officer in charge of our escort agreed to shut the bridge, but said he could only do it for 5 minutes — otherwise he would lose his job. Langer was more than happy with that amount of time, and he got us all together to sing our team song there and then. There were a few locals around and some traffic backed up in either direction — we were on the main north–south road — but no one seemed to mind too much. I wonder if the Sri Lanka cricket team would get the same reaction if they closed a section of the Tullamarine freeway out of Melbourne so they could celebrate a win over us!

The song itself prompted a couple of funny moments. Shaun Tait did not know the words, which is hardly surprising as he has been with us less than a week. Also, as we were in a huddle, he dropped his bottle of beer and it smashed. A splinter of glass went into Warne's sandal between two of his toes, and when he went to pick it out after the team song he actually managed to cut his spinning finger. There was some blood, but it is not serious, thank heavens, and he will be fine for the third Test, on Wednesday.

We eventually arrived in Colombo in the late afternoon, and a few of the touring party met up with wives, partners and families. We all got washed and changed — most of us were still in our playing gear — and then everyone went across to the Galle Face Hotel for a few sundowners. I saw Jim Maxwell of the ABC there, and he reckoned it was the first time he could remember Australia had won a close Test match. I was sure he was wrong, but I could not think of an example to prove it . . . and I still cannot.

We ended the evening with a celebratory meal in the Japanese restaurant at the Hilton before a few of the more adventurous lads kicked on to see what Colombo's nightlife had to offer. A chance to let some hair down was exactly what everyone deserved.

Sunday 21 March

I was not at my best this morning. The few drinks I'd had last night left me pretty groggy, and I was still asleep at 11 o'clock when Jonathan Rose rang me to make sure I had seen a copy of my latest column for *The Australian* newspaper which will be published tomorrow. It is part of his job to check on that sort of thing, but if he had not rung I think I could have slept all day.

Judging by how quiet our hotel corridor has been today, I think that is exactly what some of the boys did, although most of them had to get up this evening and go to the nearby Colombo Plaza hotel for an official function with the Sri Lanka team. There were presentations to Shane Warne and Muttiah Muralitharan for taking 500 Test wickets, and speeches by Bob Merriman, the chairman of Cricket Australia, and Duleep Mendis of Sri Lanka Cricket.

It was a function I missed, because I am due to attend another event tomorrow night. I used my free time to take my wife out for dinner. We had a very pleasant evening at an Italian restaurant close to the Hilton. It was a relaxing day, but starting tomorrow we have to get back into playing mode and focus on the last week of the trip.

Monday 22 March

Shaun Tait is quick. I speak from experience — he thumped me on the helmet with a very rapid short ball during net practice today. It shook me up briefly and, worst of all, broke my helmet, but apart from a small cut I am fine.

The blow came about from a short ball that hurried onto me quicker than I expected. It thumped me on the left side of the helmet above my left ear and I went down. At first I thought nothing more of it. My head was ringing, but otherwise I felt fine, and I got up pretty quickly. I was getting ready to face the next ball when I thought it would be a good idea just to check and see if my helmet was damaged, and when I took it off I could see blood inside it.

Blood started to run down my face but I did not want the photographers or cameramen to see it — I did not want a scare story about my fitness appearing before the Test. I put my hand up to wipe the blood away and marched out of the net to see Alex Kontouri. He was not sure if I needed a stitch in the wound and asked me to see Trefor James, Cricket Australia's doctor, who just happens to be out here on holiday. Trefor thought the wound was fine to leave as it was, so all I am left with is a small cut and a broken helmet.

That is frustrating, because I am not comfortable in the new type of helmet that has been produced. I am wondering what I can do with the Test match just a couple of days away — Albion, the company that supply Cricket Australia with caps and helmets, no longer makes the type I like. The new-style helmet is comfortable to wear and I am happy to use it for fielding, but I struggle to use it for batting.

It has more padding in it than the older type, so it is wider, but for me that means that when I get into my stance and turn to look at the bowler over my left shoulder, the grille hits that shoulder. Also, I find it is less effective for me in absorbing sweat, so sweat runs down the front of my face. Some of the boys love the new helmet, but it is just not for me. I will have to come up with some sort of plan, because I cannot wear my broken one against Chaminda Vaas and Nuwan Zoysa in this Test.

Tait was impressive today, and not just because of the pace he bowled against me. He maintained his focus after sending me out of the net, almost cleaning up Langer next ball with a delivery that whistled over his helmet, and later rapping Katich on the gloves. He is still young, and there is plenty of potential there.

Before I was hit I had a chat with Allan Border about our side for this Test as we looked at the pitch. This ground has a history of helping seam bowlers more than others, and we saw that when we played a one-day international here late last month.

At the same time, the pitch looks dry, so there is the temptation to play two spinners again. If we do opt for a third seamer it will be Brad Williams ahead of Tait; that would also mean picking Katich ahead of Andrew Symonds. The idea with Symonds was always to play him only if we picked both Shane Warne and Stuart MacGill, so he could act as a third seamer. If we play the third quick bowler here, Symonds' role as a third seamer no longer exists, and Katich is ahead of him as a batsman at this stage. Border and I agreed to have a think about things and discuss it again tomorrow.

My evening was taken up with a function for our sponsors, Travelex, with Rianna alongside me. Adam Gilchrist was there as well and he was very excited. He holds a position with the company and during a media session he held today he was asked a question on financial trends by a business writer. He was pretty happy with the way he answered it — it looks as if he has his career after cricket sorted out already.

Shaun Tait

The fact that Cricket Australia blocked UK county Glamorgan's attempt to sign Shaun Tait as a short-term replacement for Michael Kasprowicz when the latter was picked for the tour of Zimbabwe shows how much the selectors think of him.

Tait has the priceless asset of pace — I can vouch for it after my experience against him in the nets in Colombo.

With the schedule we have over the next 12 to 18 months it is vital that we have quality cover for our established fast bowlers — Jason Gillespie, Glenn McGrath, Brett Lee and Michael Kasprowicz — and Tait fits that bill.

My hope is that if we expose him to the international set-up as we did in Sri Lanka, he can see how our senior bowlers go about preparing for big matches and also speak to them about how he should go about bowling in various situations.

On top of that, I hope that being involved in the international scene will mean that if the time comes for him to make his debut it will not be so much of a shock to his system as if he came into the dressing room without knowing many of the players.

My first impressions of him — including the pace at which he bowls — have been very good. He is a polite young bloke, a good listener and someone who could have a very bright future.

Tuesday 23 March

We had our final pre-Test meeting of the tour today, and one of the main topics of conversation was what has become known as dead rubber syndrome. Rightly or wrongly, we have a reputation for not playing well at the end of series we have won. It was something that always bothered Stephen Waugh, and despite his efforts as captain it is still a topic of conversation in the media; after losing the last Test and the final three one-day internationals in the West Indies last year it seems to be back on the agenda now.

What I had to say to the players on the subject was simple: 'I know everyone is looking forward to the flight home, to getting back to Australia, seeing family and friends and having some time off, but as far as I am concerned that can all look after itself.

'All I want now is one more week of the best cricket we can play. That is all. If we do that, we can all go home happy.'

The one thing I was not able to do at the meeting was shed any light on what our team will be — we are still wrestling with the selection possibilities. My gut feeling is that we will go with three fast bowlers, including Brad Williams in place of Stuart MacGill; that would also mean Simon Katich coming back into the side in place of Andrew Symonds, but I would like a final look at the pitch tomorrow morning before I confirm those thoughts with Allan Border, who will then liaise with the other selectors by phone.

It would be great if we could get Katich back into the side. I know he has been down lately after missing out on the first two Tests, though he has never shown it around the rest of the team. Leaving him out of these first two matches was one of the toughest choices I have been involved with since I became captain; the only thing I can compare it with is leaving Ian Harvey out of the World Cup final in Johannesburg. Symonds has fitted in well, but if we do go in with three seamers, Katich will get his place back and I know he will not let us down.

One thing that was not raised at the team meeting was the likelihood of Shane Warne breaking Courtney Walsh's Test wickets record. After 20 wickets in the first two matches, he needs eight to equal Walsh's mark of 519 and nine to go past it. I know Warne will put enough pressure on himself to perform well without us adding to any of the hype that surrounds him, so I left the subject well alone, and no one else mentioned it.

I may have found an answer to my helmet problem. Matthew Hayden also favours the older design, and he has a spare which he has been carrying around with him. He says I can borrow it, so I will bat in it against the quicker bowlers and then swap it for my own cracked version when the spinners come on. That might seem odd, but I am comfortable in my own gear — and not even a top-edge from a sweep shot should damage my helmet any more as it would not have that much pace on it.

I am also on my own for the last week of the tour: Rianna flew home today. I will miss her like crazy, but I have plenty to occupy my mind over the next week.

Wednesday 24 March

Third Test, day one: Australia 6–314 (Lehmann 104 not out, Ponting 92) v Sri Lanka.

We got a solid start to the Test today, thanks to a patient innings from Darren Lehmann. I passed 50 as well, but in keeping with the story of my tour so far, I managed to get out when I really should have gone on to make a big score.

The same could be said for a few in our top order, even allowing for unpleasantly hot conditions. There was barely any sun all day but the heat and humidity were amazing. I thought it even got to the Sri Lanka players in the field, which is quite something.

Before play we bit the bullet and decided to go in with three seamers, including Brad Williams instead of Stuart MacGill. That opened the way for Simon Katich to come back into the side to replace Andrew Symonds. Despite our seam-based plan of attack, I did not feel we had to bowl first when I won the toss — for the third time in the series. The pitch is bone dry, and although it should turn later, maybe it will also break up a little, and our fast bowlers should be able to exploit any uneven bounce that follows from that.

Watching the first few overs, I had the impression Sri Lanka were not very focused. The heat was intense, even at the start of play at 10.30, the series had been decided, and Justin Langer and Matthew Hayden started in comfortable fashion against Chaminda Vaas and Nuwan Zoysa. A couple of sloppy returns to Kumar Sangakkara — one of which (from Zoysa) jarred the wicketkeeper's right thumb so painfully he required treatment — as well as two sets of overthrows, seemed to confirm my view.

Hayden clearly wanted to dominate: the way he walked down the pitch to Zoysa and smashed him back down the ground sent a clear signal to the Sri Lankans that it could be a long day in the field for them. And it looked even longer when Zoysa pulled up in his next over with what appeared to be a calf or knee injury. He headed off the ground and away to the local hospital for a scan; after just 35 minutes the home side was a bowler down.

To make matters worse for them, there did not appear to be much swing with the new ball for Vaas. However, he is a clever bowler, so he adapted to the conditions — and got his reward. Because of the lack of swing, he took second slip out and placed him at midwicket, and then surprised Langer with a well-directed bouncer. It looked to me like the type he has bowled throughout the series, the one that climbs higher than you expect, thanks to the horizontal seam position. Langer, who is a pretty good hooker, got into a real mess and just lobbed the ball up to midwicket for a simple catch. It looked like a careless shot, but it was really the result of an excellent piece of bowling.

That brought me to the crease to face Vaas and Thilan Samaraweera, back in the side after injury and bowling in place of the injured Zoysa. Muttiah Muralitharan may be Sri Lanka's leading bowler, but he dislikes bowling with a relatively new ball because he struggles to grip it. Once the lacquer that coats the ball wears off he is quickly into action.

I got going with an on-drive for four from Samaraweera, skipping down the pitch as he gave the ball a little more flight, and then hit Vaas through midwicket for a second boundary. I hit that one uppishly, but managed to get it wide enough of the fielder, Tillakaratne Dilshan, not to be too concerned.

Hayden's determination to dominate proved his downfall. Sri Lanka's spinners, especially against players like Hayden, Lehmann and me, have tended to bowl to a strange field, with some men, like mid-on, mid-off and midwicket, neither in positions to save one nor back on the boundary. They are in a no-man's land, daring us to try to hit it over them, but if we are patient, as Lehmann and I were later in the day, it is a field that works well for the batsmen — rather than just looking for the big shots, we could take single after single without any risk, simply by pushing the ball back past the bowler.

Hayden, however, fell into the trap and looked for the big shot. He tried to hit Samaraweera down the ground without getting to the pitch of the ball, and all he succeeded in doing was lobbing a catch to Upul Chandana, the substitute fielder, at deep mid-off. It was a wicket thrown away and Hayden knew it.

That brought in Damien Martyn, and also heralded the introduction of Muttiah Muralitharan, but only after I had taken Vaas for four through extra-cover and then driven him straight for three more runs. He was exhausted by this stage, having bowled for the first 90 minutes of the day — I thought it was a strange decision by Hashan Tillakaratne to keep him going that long: he bowled well, but it was an amazingly hot day, they were down to just one seam bowler (because Zoysa was off the field), and they would be sure to need Vaas to come back later in the day.

Muralitharan started with a maiden over to Martyn, but when I got on strike to him I wasted no time in skipping a pace down the pitch to clip him through wide midwicket for four when he gave the ball a little extra flight. We almost have a routine now: when I play a shot like that he immediately puts the mid-on fielder back towards the fence because he hates conceding runs. I wonder why he does not back himself against me, keep the fielder up and dare me to try to play the shot again. If it costs him even 20 extra runs, surely it would be well worth it.

Martyn looked in excellent touch, as you might expect after his innings in Kandy, easing Samaraweera through point with a cut shot and then following that with a clip through midwicket for four more. He had an alarm when he edged Muralitharan just short of Mahela Jayawardene at slip just before lunch, but that was about the only moment of concern for either of us before the interval. I was feeling so confident I even brought out a slog-sweep against Muralitharan in the last over before the break, middling it for four. My attitude is that a bad ball is a bad ball, whether it is the first over of the day or the last over before a break.

We were a comfortable 2–96 at the break, but the picture changed in the second over after the interval, when Martyn was dismissed by Vaas. He bowled a lovely leg-cutter that gripped on the pitch then moved away, and Martyn was in good enough form to get a touch through to Sangakkara.

That break gave Sri Lanka renewed heart at the start of the session. Luckily, for the first part of the afternoon we had some good fortune. The left-arm spinner Rangana Herath, recalled after almost four years out of the side, settled in to a long spell. Lehmann and I both miscued drives to him as we tried to hit down the ground. I also managed to get a leading edge to a ball I tried to work on the leg-side, but it fell safely on the off-side, and Lehmann (on 16) edged a cut at Muralitharan only for Jayawardene to drop yet another chance. He was little unlucky, because he was going one way and the ball then got a slight deflection off the wicketkeeper's gloves, which took some pace off it. He got to it with a dive to his left, but couldn't hold onto it.

I had one brain explosion just after that: I tried to slog Herath out of the ground and missed completely. The ball was not straight, thank heavens, and I was safe. With that out of my system Lehmann and I produced a fluent hour of batting up to the brink of the tea break.

The field was set back and Sri Lanka seemed intent on playing a patience game, but it was still not easy — the heat was a major factor

Hamish Blair, © Getty Images

Phil Hillyard, © News Limited

Above left Fashion plate: Rianna and I arrive at Crown Casino in Melbourne for the Allan Border Medal Awards Dinner, February 2004.

Above right Trunk call: Brad Williams and I take it easy in Dambulla during the one-day series against Sri Lanka.

Below Return of the king: Shane Warne arrives in Colombo for the Test series against Sri Lanka, marking the end of his 12-month absence from international cricket. Behind Shane is Reg Dickason, our security manager; coach John Buchanan is there to record the event.

Phil Hillyard, © News Limited

Above The first supper: our meal before the first Test in Sri Lanka turned into a good luck dinner for me as I prepared to lead Australia for the first time in Test cricket.

Below 'All the best, mate!': Adam Gilchrist offers a few words of support and encouragement on behalf of the squad during the meal at the Lighthouse hotel in Galle.

Above 'Here goes, then!': me looking pensive just before I became Australia's 42nd Test captain.

Right 'Heads!': my call as Sri Lanka captain Hashan Tillakaratne tosses the coin on my first day as Test captain, Galle, 8 March 2004.

Right Swept away: Matthew Hayden shows why he is regarded as one of the best sweepers in the modern game, scoring a match-turning 130 in Galle.

Below Back to his best: Damien Martyn silences his critics with a sublime 110 in Galle; it was his first Test hundred in two years.

Phil Hillyard, © News Limited

Above History man: Shane Warne celebrates after his dismissal of Hashan Tillakaratne takes him to 500 Test wickets.

Below Spin twin: Stuart MacGill played a key role in our win in Galle and reached 150 Test wickets during the match.

Phil Hillyard, © News Limited

Right If the cap fits, wear it: Andrew Symonds, complete with his treasured baggy green cap, savours our success in Galle. The cap was rarely off his head for the rest of the tour.

Above Yes!: we celebrate a great team effort in Galle. We snatched a victory from the jaws of defeat, and it felt like a very special achievement for my first Test as captain.

Right Put your shirt on: Jason Gillespie and Michael Kasprowicz just before we sang our victory song on top of the Dutch fort in Galle which provides a spectacular backdrop to the cricket ground.

Above History man II: Muttiah Muralitharan celebrates joining the 500 Test wicket club after bowling Michael Kasprowicz in Kandy.

Below left Back to reality: physiotherapist Alex Kontouri escorts me off the ground in Kandy after I injured my back during the second Test against Sri Lanka.

Below right Driving force: Adam Gilchrist responded to his promotion in the order in Kandy with a blazing 144 that turned the Test our way.

Phil Hillyard, © News Limited

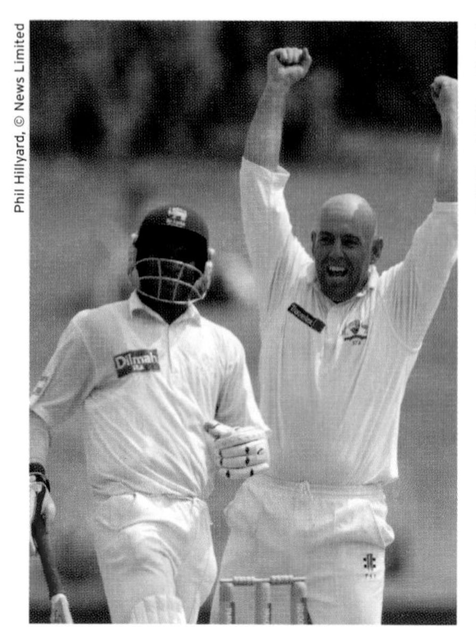

Phil Hillyard, © News Limited

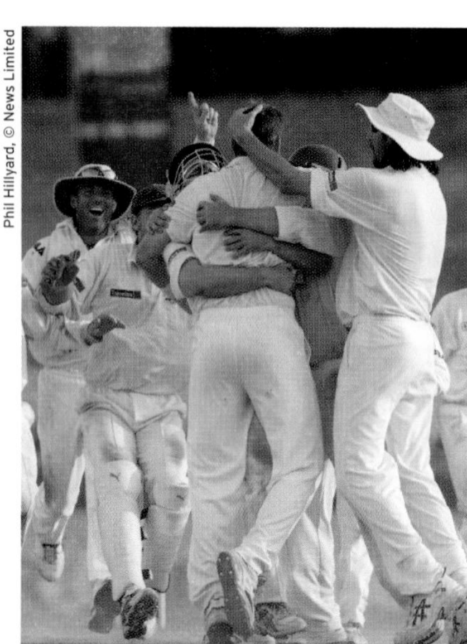

Above left 'Well bowled, Shrek!': Darren Lehmann celebrates one of his six wickets in the Colombo Test.

Above right Moment of victory: Michael Kasprowicz is engulfed after taking the final wicket in Colombo; that win sealed our Test series against Sri Lanka 3-0.

© Getty Images

© Getty Images

Above left Tough talk: me during the difficult media conference following our arrival in Zimbabwe.

Above right Driving force: Michael Clarke on his way to a maiden international hundred during the one-day series in Zimbabwe – a rare highlight of an awkward tour.

for us. When I scored a hundred on this ground in 1999 I did not need to change my gloves once, and changing them is not something I like doing; once I am wearing the gear I am batting in, I like to stick with it through an innings. It is just a comfort thing. But during this innings, batting for just over 3 hours, I had to change my gloves three or four times, because the pair I was using kept being soaked through with sweat.

Sri Lanka's over rate was painfully slow even given that there was no way you could rush around in the field in those conditions, but as Lehmann and I became more confident, there were signs they were flagging — Chandana, normally one of their livewires and still on as a replacement for Zoysa, produced a tired dive over the ball at backward point. We took advantage of the deep-set field as well, and I chipped Muralitharan over the man at midwicket for four as he was just over halfway to the fence. Muralitharan seemed out of sorts for much of today, and was not likely to feel any better after Lehmann drove him for four through mid-off and followed that with a thumping straight six (the ball had been tossed up a little higher as a response to the four).

Tillakaratne, desperate for a breakthrough, recalled Vaas 20 minutes before tea but that only lifted our scoring rate. He came nicely onto the bat and Lehmann twice cut him backward of square on the off-side. We were playing with more and more confidence, but that confidence eventually proved my undoing.

I was feeling like a million dollars, and probably believing that I was finally going to make a big score. Vaas over-pitched and I on-drove him for four, then he threw the ball out wider and I hit him through extra-cover for four more; these were my best shots of the innings. The adrenaline was flowing — and then Vaas suckered me. He bowled me another wide, full-length ball, but this time he took the pace off it. I do not know what came over me. Having hit two fours already in the over I was looking for a third, even though there was every chance it was the last over before tea and we had Sri Lanka on toast. Anyhow, having picked up relatively late that it was a slower ball I checked my shot, but all I succeeded in doing was bunting it to Muralitharan's left at mid-off, where he took a smart catch at waist height.

It was a carbon copy of the way Vaas got me in the semi-final of last year's World Cup in South Africa, except that this time I'd had a Test century within my grasp. I was livid with myself as I walked off the ground with the rest of the players — the umpires had called 'tea' — not only for throwing that personal milestone away, but also for breaking one of our rules on the tour: trying to bat a long time and not worrying about run rate. It was a careless shot.

Lehmann tired in the last session but, unlike me, he avoided the temptation to give his wicket away carelessly. He did have some good fortune, miscuing a slog-sweep at Muralitharan only for it to fall safe between two fielders at deep mid-on and then surviving a run-out chance when Sangakkara dislodged the bails before gathering the ball after Katich called him for a single. Those errors aside, he just ploughed on, gathering singles — thanks to the deep-set field — and putting away the bad ball whenever it came along.

When he reached his hundred, thanks to a cover-drive for four off Herath, he looked towards the dressing room with a big grin on his face, lifted his bat and then made a gesture as if to uncork a bottle of wine. That comes from an agreement he has with Jock Campbell, our fitness trainer. Every time Lehmann gets a hundred, one of them has to shout the other an expensive bottle of red wine, which they then share over a meal. Lehmann's gesture was saying it is Jock's turn to buy the wine.

We lost two wickets in that last session, both to Muralitharan: first Katich, caught and bowled as he looked to work a ball away on the leg-side, and then Adam Gilchrist, well taken at slip by Sanath Jayasuriya as he played back to a ball that turned across him. Jayasuriya is still wearing a hefty bandage on his right hand after splitting the webbing next to his thumb in Galle, but despite that problem Sri Lanka have obviously decided that he is a better bet in that position than Jayawardene, whose confidence as a catcher appears to be shot at the moment. This one was a sharp chance, but Jayasuriya made it look easy.

Lehmann walked off at 104 not out after playing a fantastic innings. I knew he was capable of playing that way — it is why I have so much faith in him as a player. He kept his patience, even during a spell when Muralitharan came over the wicket and pitched the ball outside his leg-stump. As Lehmann said later, that was a really boring period of play for him, because he likes to get on with it, but he knew that was exactly what Muralitharan wanted: for him to take a risk. Lehmann is wise enough to know that with the ball pitching there, the only way he could get out was by playing a stupid shot, so he just cut out any element of risk and waited for a ball he felt comfortable hitting — and in the end, the scoreboard shows who won the day.

All the same, I would be a bit more comfortable if we had lost one or maybe two wickets less today. We are in a strong but by no means imposing position now, and the chances of us getting to that place of strength rest pretty squarely with Lehmann when he resumes tomorrow.

Thursday 25 March

Third Test, day two: Sri Lanka 2–239 (Atapattu 109 not out, Jayasuriya 71) trail Australia 401 (Lehmann 153, Ponting 92, Muralitharan 5–123) by 162 runs.

Today was not one of our best of this tour. After Darren Lehmann carried us past 400, I was optimistic about our chances of making inroads into Sri Lanka's batting, but we were poor with the ball and the home side rattled along at almost four runs per over in the last two sessions.

We could have been in an even weaker position had it not been for Lehmann managing to strangle two wickets when I threw the ball to him. While Sri Lanka are still more than 150 runs behind, we have a lot of work to do to keep them in our sights, because the pitch is playing pretty well at the moment.

It is easy to be critical about the way we bowled — we conceded a lot of fours, especially with the new ball — and a couple of the journalists I spoke to afterwards brought up the subject of the dead rubber syndrome. That seems to be something we just cannot get away from. Our performance with the ball today did not help our efforts to do so, but I thought the way we batted on the first day, scoring more than 300 runs, showed that we are here to play, not just make up the numbers. Also, it is not just about us: there are two sides out there, and Sri Lanka are allowed to play well too.

The day did not start well, because I found out during warm-ups that I had been dismissed yesterday one short of 6000 Test runs. I am not one for facts and figures, and unless people tell me these sorts of things I usually have no idea how many runs I have, but hearing that news made me even more annoyed with the way I had thrown my innings away when I was well set. At least I have that landmark to look forward to in the second innings.

The first session of play went pretty well for us. Lehmann ploughed on, had a good partnership with Shane Warne, and we kept Sri Lanka in the field for the whole of the first session. Our plan at the start of the day was to get as many runs as we could — we had no set figure in mind — and for the remaining tail-enders to play around Lehmann. After Warne, none of them lasted very long, and Muralitharan picked up another five-wicket haul.

Lehmann played exactly as he did yesterday, accumulating runs sensibly. Apart from a big six over midwicket off Muralitharan, he did not really try to open his shoulders until Brad Williams came in at number 11. Then he started refusing singles and looking for big shots, clubbing Muralitharan for fours through square leg and extra-cover and reaching his 150. Then he tried to hit Muralitharan over extra-cover again, but succeeded only in lofting the ball to Sanath Jayasuriya, who ran in off the boundary to take the catch.

The plan with the new ball was to try to bowl with some aggression, as we have throughout the tour, but today the pitch was flat, the weather was roasting hot again, and Jason Gillespie and Michael Kasprowicz were both just a little off their game. We started leaking runs at an alarming rate. The 50 came up in just eight overs as we gave both Marvan Atapattu and Sanath Jayasuriya too much width, and once they got a taste for the action they continued to play their shots, even when I tried to ring a few changes.

Williams replaced Gillespie, who had conceded seven fours in five overs, and was greeted with a cover-drive for four from Marvan Atapattu, and Warne was clipped through wide mid-on by the same player when he came into the attack.

Kasprowicz tried to use the bouncer against Jayasuriya, but the batsman was happy to hook and twice got the ball away for four. When I switched Gillespie to Kasprowicz's end to see if he would have more joy there, he conceded four more boundaries to Atapattu in his first three overs.

Sri Lanka's scoring rate was topping 5 an over, and not even Warne could stop the flow of runs — Jayasuriya waltzed down the pitch and clubbed him over wide midwicket for six and then drove him for four more through the covers. It was an act of desperation as much as anything else that saw me throw the ball to Lehmann.

His bowling is not a thing of beauty: he has a scuttling approach to the crease and a low, slinging arm action, but he knows exactly what he wants to do with the ball, and usually achieves it. In one-day cricket he is a bowler I generally look to use in most matches.

His start today was not the best — Jayasuriya clubbed a full toss over square leg for four — but just as I was wondering when we were ever going to get a wicket, Lehmann came up with the goods, although it was more luck than judgement. He tossed the ball up and Jayasuriya, moving down the pitch, tried to hit him over long-on for six but instead miscued it towards long-on. Gillespie, who was back on the fence, ran in and took the catch, sprawling on his backside. In terms of a needless wicket it was just like the dismissal of Hayden or me yesterday, but it got us a breakthrough and that was all that mattered to us.

That wicket came just ten minutes before tea. We were hoping for a change in fortune in the last session but it did not come along, although Lehmann did get us another wicket. Kumar Sangakkara looked in good touch, as he has been for the whole tour. He is never worried about using his feet to slow bowlers, and skipped down the pitch to Warne to ease him past mid-on for four, swept him for another boundary and also pulled Lehmann through square leg for four. But when he pushed at a ball from Lehmann that skidded on rather than turned, there was a noise, we all went up and umpire Steve Bucknor sent Sangakkara on his way. Later, when we got back to the dressing room, replays on the TV suggested that the ball may have flicked the pad rather than the outside edge, but it was good enough for Bucknor, and I was happy to take anything on offer.

Atapattu never really looked in any difficulty, although Kasprowicz did trouble him with one short ball, which he miscued just short of me at midwicket. I had taken up a spot there less for the catch and more to allow the faster bowlers to bowl a bit straighter than in their first spells. With the new ball we will often have just two fielders on the leg-side, a long-leg and a mid-on, but that can stop the bowlers aiming at the stumps — they are worried about being hit through the vacant midwicket area. However, if they are not spot-on with their line they can end up bowling too wide of off-stump and giving the batsmen too much width; that may have been what happened today.

Atapattu reached his hundred with one of his signature shots — a flowing cover-drive for four off Williams — and with Mahela Jayawardene frustrating us at the other end by running the ball to the vacant third man area for successive boundaries, also off Williams, I was pretty glad to get off the field at close of play with a chance to regroup. Allan Border spoke to me after play about the issue of posting that midwicket to allow the bowlers to bowl straighter; it is something we will address when we have a chat as a team before play tomorrow morning. One way or another, we have to slow Sri Lanka's scoring rate. We cannot let them continue as they did today.

Friday 26 March

Third Test, day three: Australia 401 and 3–80 lead Sri Lanka 407 (Atapattu 118, Tillakaratne 73 not out, Jayasuriya 71) by 74 runs.

A great effort by the bowlers got us back into the Test. There was a hint of controversy too, with Justin Langer having to front up to a hearing this evening charged with bringing the game into disrepute.

I will deal with that incident first. It took place just over an hour into the day's play. We made a great start, picking up three wickets in the first half-hour, but were then held up by Hashan Tillakaratne and Thilan Samaraweera. The left-handed Tillakaratne glanced Brad Williams to long-leg for a single and the field changed over for Samaraweera, a right-hander.

As everyone got ready for that next ball, Shane Warne at slip saw a bail on the ground and asked Dave Orchard, the umpire at square leg, what had happened. Orchard said, 'Is that an appeal?' and I responded with a 'Howzat?' Orchard conferred with Steve Bucknor, called for the third umpire, Peter Manuel, to have a look at the incident, and after what seemed like an age, the word came back to the officials out in the centre via their two-way radios that one of our players had knocked the bail off.

We thought nothing more of it, but then Steve Bernard called Langer aside when we came off for lunch and asked him if he could explain what happened with the bail falling to the ground. Langer said he did not know what Bernard was talking about, but Bernard said he had seen the footage from one of the run-out cameras that is fixed in place to look at the stumps, and either Langer or me — he could not tell which of us it was — had knocked the bail off as we ran to our fielding positions. I knew it was not me but Langer said it was not him either: he was shocked when Ben Romalis called up the action on his laptop and showed Langer what the fuss was about.

Langer was mortified at how bad it looked, but swore he did not have any recollection of the incident. He went out of his way as we went back on the field after lunch to explain that and also to apologise to the on-field umpires. But after tea Bernard was informed that a charge had been lodged against Langer by third umpire Manuel and we would have to attend a hearing after play.

Unlike earlier in the tour, after the one-day match in Dambulla, I did attend this hearing. I was a bit fired up, as I thought it was all a waste of time. I said to match referee Chris Broad that there was no way Langer would have deliberately knocked a bail off to try to cheat a batsman out — with all the cameras around the ground these days, not to mention the two run-out cameras focused solely on the stumps, it would be impossible to get away with it even if he had wanted to do it deliberately and I did not believe Langer would do that. An issue like that would be bound to be referred to the third umpire and it would show all too clearly that the batsman was not to blame. Langer said he would probably have touched the bails like that thousands of times through his career as he swapped sides of the pitch, and he could never recall one falling off before. Dave Orchard, one of the on-field umpires, noted that the grooves on top of the stumps used for this match are very shallow and said he had noticed the bails blow off a few times during the match already. I found that a bit of a shock — I had not noticed any breeze — but he said it had happened.

All that appeared to back up Langer's defence that it was an accident and not a deliberate attempt to cheat, and with that the charge was thrown out. It was a daft thing to happen: there was no need for a hearing to get to the bottom of it. Luckily, common sense prevailed.

Even more luckily, Langer's concentration was not affected in the final session of the day when he was called on to bat, with the match in the balance. He has not been in the best of form on the trip so far but he stuck it out doggedly, and without him we might have been in an even trickier situation than we are at the moment. With the loss of two late wickets, Sri Lanka are marginally ahead in the match; we will need another disciplined innings of the type Darren Lehmann played on the first day to ensure that we set the home side a challenging total.

We began the day with a team meeting in the dressing room to discuss what went wrong yesterday and what we could do right today. We normally have a chat before play; this one turned into quite a detailed planning session, and I am glad I listened to what most of the players suggested rather than go my own way — if I had done that the day might have had a totally different outcome.

I opened the chat by suggesting that we should try to get really negative and bore them out. I said we should bowl wide outside off-stump, set an off-side field and put the pressure on them to try to push the scoring rate along.

Matthew Hayden disagreed quite strongly with that, and he persuaded the other players to his way of thinking. He wanted us to attack rather than defend, to try to hit the stumps and therefore have a stronger on-side field, like the one we finished with last night. He wanted us to try to get the Sri Lanka batsmen out rather than wait for them to make a mistake. Everyone else agreed.

So that was our plan. We started with just one slip, a gully, a cover fielder and also a midwicket. And in the first 30 minutes of the day Jason Gillespie and Michael Kasprowicz executed the plan perfectly. With just his third ball Gillespie found a perfect line around the off-stump and Mahela Jayawardene edged a catch to Adam Gilchrist. Then with his next delivery, a top-class leg-cutter, he bowled Tillakaratne Dilshan, who has shown signs throughout the series of being a poor starter.

He could not get the hat-trick against Hashan Tillakaratne, but we looked far more purposeful today, and after Gillespie almost picked up a third wicket when he forced Marvan Atapattu to edge low past Gilchrist, Kasprowicz finished the job when he found a perfect off-cutter than burst between the batsman's bat and pad to pluck out Atapattu's off-stump.

It was a dream start for us, but if ever Sri Lanka wanted two batsmen to rebuild an innings from that sort of position, they had the right men for the job in Tillakaratne and Samaraweera, both of them happy to block the living daylights out of everything we could send down at them.

In all fairness to them, they played a few shots too. When Williams, who came on in place of Kasprowicz, over-pitched, Samaraweera drove him straight for four, and both batsmen took boundaries off Shane Warne, Tillakaratne twice clipping him through midwicket before lunch and Samaraweera producing a perfect cover drive.

I delayed taking the new ball in order to give Warne a decent spell — and to see if Williams could make the old one reverse swing — but when the breakthrough did not come I claimed it seven overs late, after 87 overs, about 15 minutes before lunch. Williams shared it with Gillespie, not just because he was bowling with a good rhythm, but also because Kasprowicz needed some recovery time after his morning spell. He got that at lunch, with all the bowlers having ice-baths to get their temperatures down — we have used these, together with ice-vests and ice-collars, throughout the trip. All have become standard items for the tours to this part of the world. The bath is usually a giant wheelie bin, filled to the brim with ice-cold water. It may not sound pleasant, but you are only in there for a short period of time and it does its job.

When we returned to the field, it took just over half an hour of all-out effort from Kasprowicz and Gillespie to get us the breakthrough we so desperately needed. It eventually came after I missed a chance to heap the pressure on Tillakaratne. There has been talk in the local media that he is playing for his spot in the side: he has struggled for runs lately, and Atapattu, the one-day captain and Test vice-captain, making 118 here can only have added to the need for him to get runs. But when Kasprowicz swung one across him and found the outside edge I could not hang onto the chance diving away to my left at second slip. It was the kind of catch I have taken plenty of times before: it came quite quickly and was at ankle height, and I saw it all the way, but it just did not hit in the middle of my hand. Down it went. And as if that was not bad enough, he edged the next ball all the way along the ground past me for four. I stood there with my hands on my knees at that, feeling more frustration than you can imagine. The bowlers had worked so hard in the heat to create the chance and I had put it down. It is never good to dwell on those sorts of things in the field — you just have to concentrate on the next ball and be ready to catch the next chance that comes your way — but just for a moment I forgot that golden rule, and if I could have screamed I would have.

In the next over we did get the breakthrough, thank heavens, but it was Samaraweera and not Tillakaratne who departed. Gillespie thinks he has found a weakness to the ball angled in at Samaraweera's ribs: he generally looks to defend rather than hook balls in that area. Gillespie got the ball to bounce a bit more than the batsman expected. It took the glove, and Gilchrist flew down the leg-side to take a superb one-handed grab.

That was a relief, and as Sri Lanka were still 74 runs behind at that point, we even had hopes of pinching a small first innings lead. However, Chaminda Vaas showed all the confidence he had gained from his two innings in Kandy and struck some lovely shots, gradually bringing the home side closer to our score.

Gillespie tested him out with a couple of short balls: he was happy to hook, hitting Gillespie twice through square leg for four. When Warne came on Vaas drove him twice through the covers and pulled him through square leg for another boundary.

Tillakaratne was still nowhere near his best, but as he reached 50 with an extra-cover drive for four off Warne he was clearly growing in confidence. He took the seventh-wicket stand past 50 with four more, clipped through wide mid-on off Darren Lehmann — I had sent him on in the hope that he could get us another wicket out of nowhere, as he did yesterday.

Vaas was playing with real assurance, but then, out of nowhere, he suddenly ran down the pitch, aiming a massive slog at Warne, and was bowled. It was a bizarre shot, especially as he and Tillakaratne had been playing so well, but it opened up an end for us and Lehmann followed it up in the next over: he had Nuwan Zoysa, now apparently fit again, stumped as he was pushing lazily forward.

Rangana Herath survived until tea but fell soon afterwards to his first attacking shot, driving Warne straight to Damien Martyn at short extra-cover. Muralitharan slogged a couple to take Sri Lanka into the lead, but the innings was wrapped up when Kasprowicz took some revenge for the hammering he had copped off the spinner in Kandy. It was a case of bluff and double bluff again, as instead of trying for the yorker that he did not use in Kandy, Kasprowicz banged the ball in short, where Muralitharan, already backing away to square leg, could only swat it off the splice of the bat to Warne at midwicket.

Sri Lanka were all out for 407. After the start they made yesterday I was happy to settle for that, especially if we could bat well in the second innings, set them a target and put their batsmen under pressure on the final day, as we did in Galle.

At the close of play today that plan still looks possible, but losing three wickets (even though one of those wickets was the nightwatchman, Gillespie) has made the task a bit harder.

Matthew Hayden looked in pretty good touch again, skipping down the pitch to Vaas to pick him up over midwicket for four and driving Zoysa, now fit enough to bowl again, through mid-off and down the ground. But after trying to get forward, as he usually does, he found himself trapped on the crease by one from Vaas that kept low; there was not much doubt he was out lbw.

I was left with my heart in my mouth after the second ball I received — I padded up to one from Vaas and survived a massive lbw shout. I was happy to push the pad at the ball because, once again, I had taken my guard a long way down the pitch to try to counter Vaas's swing, make him bowl a slightly shorter length and give me more of a chance if I was hit on the pad. Vaas did get the ball to swing back in, but I was so far down the pitch umpire Bucknor would have really been guessing about whether or not the ball would have gone on to hit the stumps, so I got the benefit of the doubt.

I went past 6000 Test runs two balls later, pushing the ball through mid-off for two runs to get off the mark, but found I had to be pretty wary: the surface was showing signs of wear, which is hardly surprising after a few days in these temperatures. One off-cutter from Vaas went through the top of the pitch and forced me to adjust in a hurry as it cut away and bounced awkwardly, and in my desire to get forward and smother the spin of the left-armer Herath I almost overbalanced and survived an appeal for a stumping — this time a confident one by Kumar Sangakkara that was referred to the third umpire.

Langer looked scratchy at the start of his innings and got off the mark by edging Vaas through the vacant third slip area, but the longer he spent in the middle the more settled he looked. I really felt the two of us were going to get through to the close of play, but in the last but one over of the day I was out to a nice piece of bowling by Herath.

It was a classic left-arm spinner's dismissal. He drew me forward with some nice flight, then spun the ball away from me: it took the outside edge and slip took the catch. Samaraweera, the man in that position, juggled it once at ankle height, but he clung on. Gillespie came in for the last nine balls of the day.

The sight of a nightwatchman will have surprised a few people, because we have not used one for several years. During the West Indies Test series in the summer of 2000/01 we had a team meeting and decided not to use them in future. That decision was based on the idea that a batsman should not need to be protected, and to an extent that is true. But my view is that it is up to the batsman who is next in to decide whether or not he wants a nightwatchman, and I happen to believe that in this part of the world they can be very useful. It can be very difficult to go in on turning pitches, with a couple of overs to go and in fading light, and try to start an innings with the ball turning sharply, especially if the batsman has been in the field for most of the day. It is better to have that batsman fresh and ready to bat the next day; if the nightwatchman can tire the bowlers a little by hanging around the following morning, that is even better.

Gillespie will not get the chance to do that this time because he was out in the last over of the day, caught at leg-slip by Jayawardene as he managed to play the ball off the inside edge through his legs. It gives the scoreboard a better look as far as Sri Lanka are concerned, but Gillespie did his job saving Martyn from having to bat tonight, and that is the most important consideration.

Saturday 27 March

Third Test, day four: Sri Lanka 407 and 0–18 require another 352 runs to beat Australia 401 and 375 (Langer 166, Katich 86).

After a first half-hour when we looked like falling into a tail-spin, brilliant innings from Justin Langer and Simon Katich have put us in with a great chance of winning this match tomorrow — and with it achieving a clean sweep of the series.

The pair played with real patience — that seems to have been a key word when I flick back through this diary of the tour — and in Langer's case a fair amount of courage. He suffered severe leg cramps during lunch and collapsed when he went out after the break, so he needed a runner for the second part of his innings.

The pitch settled down after a frantic start. It will offer Shane Warne some turn and maybe provide our faster bowlers with some uneven bounce tomorrow, but it will be hard work to dig out 10 Sri Lanka players. We should have the chance to build some pressure against them by maintaining attacking fields, though, and that can do funny things to batsmen. I know Sri Lanka will be desperate to avoid the prospect of losing all three Tests in the series — there is no way I would swap their position for ours.

The start of the day was more or less a repeat of yesterday, except that this time we were batting. Damien Martyn, who came in after Jason Gillespie, was trapped on the back foot by Rangana Herath in the fourth over, having already edged a delivery from the same bowler past slip, and Darren Lehmann was caught behind cutting at Muttiah Muralitharan with the ball bouncing and turning alarmingly. Kumar Sangakkara took that edge somewhere around shoulder height. Katich came in next.

Langer watched all this from the non-striker's end. His answer was to be as positive as possible. Twice he swept Herath powerfully along the ground for four, the first time through Sanath Jayasuriya's hands on the boundary, and then through mid-on. And when Herath gave the ball a little more flight, Langer went down the pitch and drove him over long-on for six to reach his fifty.

It was Langer who did most of the scoring as the partnership with Katich took shape. Katich took his time to find his feet; hardly surprising as this is his first match since before the first Test. Muralitharan went round the wicket to try to pitch into the footmarks outside the left-handers' off-stump. Langer's answer was to clout him for successive fours through the off-side; this forced a change in line from the bowler.

Langer tried to sweep whenever he could, even though it is not his best shot, and it almost brought about his downfall when he was on 98, when he top-edged Herath in the direction of short fine-leg. Luckily for him, Muralitharan slipped as he tried to push off towards the ball. Another sweep, two overs later, brought Langer to 100, and by the time lunch arrived we were back on an even footing, at 5–182.

When Langer got back to the dressing room we were all delighted for him, because he has had a lean tour, but any pleasure we felt was short-lived — his leg muscles cramped up when he had an ice bath to try to cool down. First it was his calf muscle, then his hips; it was all Alex Kontouri and Jock Campbell could do to get him ready to go out again after the interval. He made it to the middle, but after playing out a maiden to Thilan Samaraweera he cramped up again when Katich called him through for a single to mid-on. He managed to make that, but then went down like a stone at the striker's end and needed more treatment, more drinks and even a switch from his helmet to his baggy green cap to get him going again. Typically, his first scoring shot after the hold-up was a straight six; he was clearly still in pain, though, and Hayden went out to run for him two overs later.

Through the afternoon session it was Katich who had whatever luck was necessary for them to stay together. He forced a ball off his hip through the hands of short leg after he'd added just a single to his lunchtime score of 19, edged Muralitharan past slip on 29, and, on 47, survived a low but relatively straightforward chance to Sangakkara off the inside edge as he pushed forward at Chaminda Vaas. I would normally expect Sangakkara to catch that, and I think fatigue may have been a factor in it going down: it was roasting hot out there all day again. The fact that we were able to keep Sri Lanka out in the field for as long as we did was an added bonus from the way Langer and Katich played.

Langer gave Sri Lanka nothing, especially in that afternoon session. He and Katich weathered an awkward spell from Nuwan Zoysa when he was getting the ball to reverse swing back into them at lively pace, and it was only after tea that he began to look like getting out. Vaas took the new ball just before the break, and after the break he started to nip the ball back off the seam and into Langer, who was trying to drive. He inside-edged at least half a dozen attempted cover drives into his front pad before finally dragging one back onto his stumps, but by then we were past 300. It was a courageous innings spanning almost 7 hours, and he and Katich have put us in the box seat in this match.

After his innings he said to me that he'd never had any intention of retiring hurt despite his cramps; I wouldn't have expected him to, because he is as tough as teak. He said all he could think about was what Allan Border said to Dean Jones during the tied Test in Madras in 1986 as Jones was being sick by the side of the pitch in temperatures that must have been a bit like this. Border urged more out of Jones and he produced it. Langer said that by the end he was also cramping in his hamstrings and thighs, but he just wanted to stick it out there as long as he could.

Katich was something of a silent partner in the stand, even though his contribution was vital to the cause, but after the tea break he began to play some shots, clipping Vaas through midwicket and hooking Zoysa for another four when the ball was banged in at him. When the spinners came back into the attack he drove Thilan Samaraweera straight for four and then danced down the pitch to loft Muralitharan for six. He was closing in on 100 when he played back to Muralitharan's doosra, tried to work it on the leg-side, missed and was trapped in front. I wondered if the ball pitched outside leg-stump, but when I asked Katich he said he thought he was plumb.

We hadn't planned to declare tonight, but as our position got stronger it entered our heads and we had the ideal man to press on in Adam Gilchrist. He played himself in very carefully before exploding, hitting Herath for two of the biggest sixes I have seen, over wide midwicket. In the end he was left stranded as the tail folded, but that was no bad thing: it gave us what turned out to be five overs at Sri Lanka's openers this evening.

Kasprowicz tried to test out Jayasuriya with a couple of bouncers, but when he pitched up he was slashed three times in succession through cover for four. That is a warning to us to be on top of our game tomorrow — if he plays an innings like the one he played in Kandy, life could still get awkward for us.

Sunday 28 March

Second Test, day five: Australia 401 and 375 beat Sri Lanka 407 and 248 (Samaraweera 53, Jayasuriya 51) by 121 runs.

Reflecting on today's events, it feels like a dream come true. Not only have we beaten Sri Lanka in Sri Lanka, we have swept the board, becoming the first country to come here and do that in a three-match Test series. For that to happen in my first series as captain is almost too good to be true — but after the way we played, it is nothing we do not deserve.

I admit I was nervous at the start of the day, because I wanted the win here so much. I wanted to start as captain by setting a high standard in this sort of game, with the series already decided, and having done that makes me feel fantastic.

What pleased me even more than the win was the reaction of the players to the result. You just had to see the way we celebrated on the ground straight after Michael Kasprowicz took the final wicket to know what it means to everyone. This has been a great team effort.

Even though the day had a perfect ending, I would be lying if I said there were not times when I thought we would have to settle for a draw. I never seriously thought Sri Lanka would get the runs and beat us on a last-day pitch, but the surface was very placid, and their top order did not appear to have too many troubles against our quick bowlers once the ball got soft. However, we persevered, and kept nipping out wickets at vital times until it was a case of whether or not the Sri Lanka lower order could handle the pressure. The answer was an emphatic no.

The plan at the start of the day was to hit Sri Lanka with our quick bowlers while the ball was still hard and both Kasprowicz and Jason Gillespie were still fresh. We began with a deep backward point about two-thirds of the way to the boundary for Sanath Jayasuriya, knowing that he might struggle to resist having a cut at a short wide one, and if he did make decent contact it could well fly in the air in that region.

Gillespie struggled with his line to Jayasuriya to start with, sliding three balls down the leg-side in his first over, but once he got his radar working he came perilously close to trapping Jayasuriya lbw — only an inside edge saved the batsman.

Even with that deep fielder in place Jayasuriya was happy to have a go at anything outside off-stump, and twice he hit Gillespie through the off-side for four, so it was round one to the batsman.

For Marvan Atapattu we put two men in front of the wicket, one on either side, at short extra-cover and short midwicket. There were a couple of ideas in play here. It could make him reluctant to get forward for fear of offering a bat–pad chance as he attempted to drive, or it could challenge his ego and make him more likely to look for the big drive to get rid of the fielders in his eye-line. Either way it would work in Kasprowicz's favour as he tried to trap Atapattu with an off-cutter — as he did in the first innings. Sure enough, that was exactly what happened. Atapattu went for the big drive, was not quite far enough forward, and the ball went between bat and pad and plucked out his off-stump. It was great bowling by Kasprowicz.

That wicket was a major relief, because by that stage we had already missed an opportunity to take Jayasuriya out. Kasprowicz again tested him with a short ball, which he played at and missed, trying to upper-cut it over the slips. Then, next ball, he angled one across the left-hander, drew a tentative push from Jayasuriya, and Adam Gilchrist put down the chance, moving to his left in front of

Shane Warne. The ball was travelling quickly, but it was the sort of catch Gilchrist usually hangs on to.

After 50 minutes I made a double change, bringing on Brad Williams and Warne. Warne began with a short cover fielder to Thilan Samaraweera, in to replace Atapattu, and was happy to toss the ball up outside the off-stump, trying to encourage the drive. It cost him four runs from his first ball, and Samaraweera showed he was not going to be intimidated, skipping down the pitch and driving well through wide mid-off for four more.

At the other end Williams twice induced thick edges to third man from the same batsman, but although he ran in as hard as he could, he did not look very effective; the two Sri Lanka batsmen started to look comfortable. Jayasuriya on-drove Williams for four, then they took 11 off a Warne over, with Samaraweera driving the leg-spinner through extra-cover and then clipping him to midwicket for boundaries.

With 15 minutes to lunch I threw the ball to Lehmann, as I had done in the first innings, to see if he could get us a wicket — and, amazingly, he did with his first ball. And again as in the first innings, it was the vital one of Jayasuriya, who had just reached his fifty.

Lehmann's opening delivery, from over the wicket, bounced and turned a little into the left-hander, and that seemed to surprise Jayasuriya — all he could do was jab at it. The ball took a thick inside edge and ballooned up to Simon Katich at short leg. It was a great wicket.

That was our last success before the interval, and though I would have liked another wicket in the session, I was happy enough to see the back of both openers. It was now a case of building on that after lunch.

I felt Warne was our most likely match-winner, so the plan after lunch was to open up with him while using the seamers in short, sharp bursts as attacking defensive bowlers. The role of the seamer in this situation is to hit the pitch hard, bowl with plenty of aggression and also be disciplined with lines and lengths, in order to allow the leg-spinner at the other end to attack without worrying that we are conceding runs at both ends.

Kasprowicz and Warne opened up, but after a couple of overs they swapped ends. Warne had barely bowled from the dressing room end in the match and I wanted to see if there was anything there for him. On top of that, the breeze had swung around and Kasprowicz fancied a go at the other end to see if it would help his reverse swing.

We were creating half-chances at this stage, but nothing was quite coming off for us. Samaraweera clipped Kasprowicz to midwicket with the ball just reaching me on the half-volley, and Mahela Jayawardene was almost run out at the bowler's end when Katich made a brilliant stop and throw from point as the batsmen hesitated over a single.

Both Jayawardene and Samaraweera showed a willingness to use their feet to Warne in attack and defence, and Jayawardene gave a sign of his confidence by driving Warne high and handsome over long-on for six. While that battle was taking place at one end, I brought on Gillespie in place of Kasprowicz and he tried to unsettle Samaraweera with similar tactics to those he used with success in the first innings. He tried to dig the ball into Samaraweera's ribs, even going around the wicket at one point, posted a leg gully and also had two men out for the hook shot. On one occasion he came mighty close to inducing a glove down the leg-side, but Samaraweera's response was impressive: he picked up a short ball with a straight bat and deposited it out towards square leg to reach his fifty.

Not a lot seemed to be happening for us, but with just half an hour to go before tea we suddenly got the break we needed, and again it was Lehmann who did it. Samaraweera had used his feet impressively to the spinners throughout his innings, but this time he showed his hand a little too early. Lehmann saw him coming down the pitch and pitched the ball a bit shorter. It meant Samaraweera was not to the pitch of the delivery and it turned past his outside edge as he looked to adjust by playing defensively, giving Gilchrist the simplest of stumping chances. It was a soft end to a good innings.

Lehmann managed to get another wicket before tea, sending us off at the final break with a real spring in our steps. Again he found a little turn, this time to Jayawardene, and as the batsman pushed forward there was a noise as the ball got through to Gilchrist. We all appealed and Steve Bucknor agreed it had touched the outside edge; Jayawardene was not so sure.

Lehmann did a superb job with the ball in this match. He took six wickets, including Jayasuriya twice when he was threatening to take control of the situation; just as importantly, Lehmann offered me control, particularly in the first innings. Why he was so successful here I am not sure. Maybe it is because after facing Warne, Gillespie, Kasprowicz and Williams, the batsmen relaxed. After all, batsmen in this part of the world are brought up playing spin and, with all due respect to Lehmann, he cannot be the most fearsome prospect they have encountered. Whatever the reason for his effectiveness, we were grateful.

The loss of those two wickets before the break meant all Sri Lanka had to play for in the last session was a draw. If they'd had eight wickets in hand and 170 to get after tea they would still have had a chance of a win, however slight, and we would have had to consider that, but with only six wickets left, a late charge was out of the question. That added to the pressure the remaining batsmen were under — we could really start to crowd them. That pressure may have helped cause the downfall of Kumar Sangakkara.

Usually he is quite positive in attack and defence, but today, with men hemming him in and Warne bowling into the rough outside his off-stump, he tried to play with the lightest of grips on the bat as the ball bounced and turned. He was conscious of the need to not allow the ball to fly off to one of the close-in fielders, but with such a light grip the ball spun back off the face of the bat, through his legs and onto the stumps. It was a little unlucky — you might struggle to get out like that even if you tried. Today it happened because of the pressure we created. It meant half their side was now out, with 30 overs still to go.

Hashan Tillakaratne came in and straight away we got ready to cut off his favourite stroke through wide mid-on with a short mid-on and a short midwicket. He is a cool customer and loves nothing better than this type of situation — and is never too fazed if he is not scoring. We hoped those fielders would at least give him something to think about.

Tillakaratne's response was to block, and it took him almost 25 minutes to get off the mark, with two runs steered backward of point off Lehmann. Tillakaratne Dilshan, at the other end, had his own plan to save the match. He clearly decided that if he tried to block he would get a ball that would get him out sooner or later, especially with men around the bat; his plan was to play his shots.

He hit Lehmann through cover and midwicket for fours, then used his feet to Warne to clobber a powerful drive through mid-off, then eased another delivery through point — and followed that in Warne's next over with another four through the covers. It was exciting stuff, but we were happy to see him playing that way, because while he kept attacking it gave us a chance to get him out — we only needed one error of judgement on his part. Sure enough, Warne held his nerve, tossed the ball up high and Dilshan, looking to drive again, was not quite to the pitch. The ball sliced off a thick outside edge to Damien Martyn at mid-off and it was another precious wicket in our quest for the win.

Chaminda Vaas came in and looked secure, playing Warne as

well as any of Sri Lanka's frontline batsmen. His method was to play him off the back foot wherever possible, waiting for the ball to turn into him and working it off his hip. If Warne over-pitched, Vaas was happy to drive him through the covers; this forced Warne to alter his approach, and he tried a spell over the wicket.

The final hour of the match started with Sri Lanka still six wickets down. An over later I decided to take the new ball. There were 14 overs left, and I figured that even if Kasprowicz and Gillespie could not get a breakthrough I still had a chance to go back to Warne with a harder ball for a few overs, as a last throw of the dice.

I need not have worried: in his second over, Gillespie produced a beauty that cut back at Tillakaratne and trapped him plumb on the crease. The batsman seemed to indicate that he'd got an edge on the ball — he lifted his bat in exaggerated fashion in front of his face — but we did not think so, and neither did umpire Bucknor.

Ten and a half overs to go, and we still required three wickets. Nuwan Zoysa and Vaas hung around for three and a half of those, and with every over they stayed together I considered tinkering with the attack. Eventually I opted to get Warne back on, not only because I thought he was our main weapon even against two left-handers, but also because I thought Zoysa would not enjoy facing him in this pressure situation — especially after the antagonism between them towards the end of the Kandy Test.

Sure enough, Zoysa tried to play a wild drive to the first ball he faced from Warne — without getting anywhere near the pitch of the ball — and was bowled. It was a poor shot at the best of times, but when your side is trying to save a Test, it was a shocker. I guess you could put it down to pressure.

By now it was 5.20 in the afternoon and the sun was getting low. Umpire Bucknor came to have a chat with the close fielders to remind them to keep still as the ball was being bowled, because there were shadows across the pitch.

Rangana Herath survived the rest of Warne's over and Vaas then played out a maiden from Gillespie. Twice Gillespie tested him with the short ball but he was having nothing to do with an attacking shot now and both times just ducked underneath it. Another maiden from Warne to Herath left us with four overs to get the two wickets and at that point I switched things around again, giving Lehmann another go. I wondered whether he might be able to get us another wicket from somewhere, as he had six times already, but although he switched from over to round the wicket during his over Herath played him safely.

Although Warne was now bowling over the wicket, Vaas was still trying to play him off the back foot, and that proved to be his downfall. He went back to a ball that, although short, skidded onto him, and umpire Bucknor judged that the ball would have gone on to hit leg stump. We were now just one wicket away from victory and had 15 balls to go.

Although the situation was tense, Muttiah Muralitharan seemed as cool as you could imagine, and played the last three balls of Warne's over with relative comfort. That left me with a decision to make: did I stick with Lehmann or pick another option for the last but one over of the day?

After a bit of thought I threw the ball to Kasprowicz. We had not seen Herath against a quick bowler, and Kasprowicz's natural swing into the left-hander would bring the lbw into play. On top of that, if he got a single to get off strike, Muralitharan would face Kasprowicz, and Muralitharan would be far happier against a spinner than against a quick bowler.

That was my thinking, and it took Kasprowicz just four balls to prove me right. He arrowed an in-swinger into Herath's pads and brought the finger of fate from Dave Orchard — and the start of wild scenes of joy from the Australians on the pitch, plus our reserve players and support staff, plus the dozens of Australia supporters in the stands.

The reserves greeted us on the boundary edge and we then raced up to the dressing room to share the pleasure with John Buchanan, Tim Nielsen and the rest of team management.

The presentation ceremony is a bit of a blur. Luckily, Jonathan Rose produced a quick list of people I had to thank as I took the microphone after an interview for TV with former Australian spinner Bruce Yardley. Those I wanted to thank included the players, team management and sponsors — and also the supporters who have followed us, although in all the excitement I almost forgot them, and it took some frantic arm waving from Rose to remind me.

There was some added drama to come: we found out Muralitharan had been reported to the ICC for a suspect bowling action. We were briefed about it by Bob Merriman, the Cricket Australia Chairman, and Steve Bernard in the dressing room after the presentation. It meant the media were keen to get my reaction, but I was not going to get involved in the rights and wrongs of Muralitharan's action — there have been plenty of people who have suffered by going down that path in the past. He is an amazing talent, there is no doubt about that, but it is up to the ICC, not me, to decide whether or not he has a legal action.

We sang the team song in the dressing room this time, with shirts off again (except for Lucy Frostick, our masseuse!). Justin Langer got Wade Seccombe up to join him in leading it — Langer wanted to show that our success here has been thanks to the people off the field as much as those on it. Those players who have not played have been tireless, sometimes covering 10–15 kilometres a day, believe it or not, running drinks and gloves out to us during the action. On top of that, they get our meals ready for us in the dressing room and put our needs at practice ahead of their own, even though they are all busting a gut to get into the side themselves. That was a perfect gesture by Langer.

During our time in the dressing room, Stuart MacGill pulled me aside and said he had decided not to make himself available for the Zimbabwe tour. He stressed that he still wants to play for Australia, but the problems in that country at the moment make him feel he would rather not play cricket there. I get on pretty well with MacGill and I think he likes my captaincy style — I talk to him a fair bit out on the field rather than leaving him to his own devices — but I was not about to try to talk him out of his decision. I figured he would not have come to me in the first place unless he had thought long and hard about it already. It is his choice and he has made it.

After such a great day and a great win, the evening wound up relatively early. That was because most of the players flew out tonight, either off to the UK for county cricket or home to Australia. I was the odd man out, staying in Colombo overnight before flying to India on Monday evening for a week of servicing some sponsors of mine, Cricketnext.com.

We had a farewell in a small function room on the sixth floor of the hotel with some drinks and snacks, but after that I was left to my own devices — I ended up having a drink with Muralitharan. He was pretty philosophical about being called before the ICC again; he has been through it plenty of times in the past. Apparently the ball that has been questioned in the report is his doosra, the ball that spins away from the right-hander like a leg-break. He is a bit confused, because he told me he has been bowling it for five years and this is the first time it has been questioned in this way. He may even have to travel to the University of Western Australia to have it assessed. They have a special biomechanical facility there and he has been put through his paces there in the past.

Apart from chatting about his current problem, Muralitharan was very complimentary about the way we played him during this tour. He said that although he has taken, I think, 28 wickets in the series, he could not recall any side, even India in India, playing him any better than we did, and he thought Darren Lehmann played him better than anyone he has ever bowled to. That is quite a feather in our caps.

So there was no big celebration for me — just a few drinks with Muralitharan and the satisfaction of a great job well done.

Monday 29 March

I had a lie-in until around 11 o'clock this morning. I figured I deserved one. I did not have to check out of the hotel until the evening, so I spent most of the day making sure my diary of the tour was up to date and watching the Pakistan–India Test match from Multan on the TV. It looked at one stage as though Virender Sehwag was going to break Matthew Hayden's world record score, but he finally fell just after reaching 300. However, with India topping 700 by the time I turned the coverage off, there was still not much for the home side to cheer.

I also took a call from Trevor Hohns, who told me that the selectors had picked the 25 contracted players for the next 12 months and the list would be released in the next few days. Among the big names to miss out are Michael Bevan, Andy Bichel and Nathan Bracken. That is tough on all three of them, as each has a case for inclusion. The job of the selectors is really difficult at the moment, because we have so many high-class players around. Now it is up to those three to prove the decision wrong.

Packing took a lot longer than I thought — I seem to have more luggage than when I arrived six weeks ago. It cost me an excess baggage charge when I checked in for my flight, but that was a small price to pay for an amazing six weeks in my life, six weeks that I could not have bettered if I had tried.

Part 8: Australia in Zimbabwe

WHEN CRICKET TAKES A BACK SEAT

Friday 2 April

Heath Streak, Zimbabwe's captain, reportedly resigns as captain after apparently making a series of demands of the Zimbabwe Cricket Union's (ZCU's) board of directors during its quarterly meeting. The demands are believed to include a review of the national side's selection process with the new panel to be made up of players with first-class or Test experience. The ZCU issues a statement that Streak has been sacked as captain, adding that he has retired 'from all forms of cricket', something he denies. The ZCU announces that Tatenda Taibu will take over as captain.

Tuesday 6 April

Streak issues a statement through his father, Denis, in which he denies resigning as national captain. 'Heath at no time tendered or threatened to tender his resignation as captain or as a national player, as alleged by the ZCU,' says Denis Streak, adding, 'All he said was that if his concerns were not addressed he would consider possible retirement from international cricket.'

The statement also claims that the ZCU has acted unlawfully in terminating Heath Streak's position as captain and a member of the national squad.

Thursday 8 April

A group of senior Zimbabwe players, represented by Heath Streak, Grant Flower and Andy Blignaut, ask the ZCU to reverse the decisions to sack Streak and elevate Tatenda Taibu to the captaincy.

Saturday 10 April

An official of the ZCU claims to have sacked up to a dozen players for not turning up to play in a round of domestic matches. The group reportedly believed they had been excused from playing in the matches so they could continue to try to find a solution to the growing crisis surrounding Zimbabwe cricket.

Thursday 15 April

Thirteen of Zimbabwe's leading players refuse to make themselves available for the five-match one-day series against Sri Lanka as the dispute with the ZCU continues.

The ZCU names a 14-man squad, without any of the so-called rebel players, for the series but expects those rebel players to turn up for practice on 16 April. If not, 'action will be taken against them in terms of their contract', according to a ZCU statement.

Friday 16 April

The Times newspaper reports that the players in dispute with the ZCU are to have their contracts terminated.

Tuesday 20 April

First one-day international, Bulawayo: Sri Lanka 4–144 (Sangakkara 73 not out) beat Zimbabwe 6–211 (Taibu 96 not out) by 12 runs (Duckworth–Lewis method).

Wednesday 21 April

Australia names their Test and one-day international squads for the forthcoming tour of Zimbabwe.

Test squad: Ricky Ponting (captain), Adam Gilchrist, Jason Gillespie, Matthew Hayden, Michael Kasprowicz, Simon Katich, Justin Langer, Darren Lehmann, Damien Martyn, Glenn McGrath, Shane Warne, Cameron White and Brad Williams.

One-day squad: Ricky Ponting (captain), Michael Clarke, Adam Gilchrist, Jason Gillespie, Ian Harvey, Matthew Hayden, Brad Hogg, Michael Kasprowicz, Darren Lehmann, Glenn McGrath, Damien Martyn, Andrew Symonds, Shane Watson and Brad Williams.

Stuart MacGill makes himself unavailable for the tour, citing moral reasons. 'I do not believe the situation in Zimbabwe is such that I can tour at this stage,' he says in a statement.

Cricket Australia Chief Executive Officer James Sutherland says he accepts MacGill's decision and that it will not have a bearing on whether or not he is considered for future tours. He adds: 'We go there [to Zimbabwe] to play cricket with other cricketers, to fulfil our obligations to world cricket through the ICC's future tours program, and for no other reason.'

The tour sees recalls for Glenn McGrath and Shane Watson after long-term injury lay-offs. Victoria's Pura Cup-winning captain, leg-spinning all-rounder Cameron White, gets a first call-up at senior international level. Of the Test squad that toured Sri Lanka, Andrew Symonds is omitted.

The tour is set to involve two Test matches and three one-day internationals.

Thursday 22 April

Second one-day international, Bulawayo: Sri Lanka 1–139 (Jayantha 74 not out) beat Zimbabwe 136 by 9 wickets.

Friday 23 April

Cricket Australia Chief Executive Officer James Sutherland is quoted in the *Sydney Morning Herald* newspaper as saying he is confident no other players will join Stuart MacGill in pulling out of Australia's tour of Zimbabwe.

'I'd be very surprised if anyone did, based on the conversations we've had with the players along the way,' he says.

Reports suggest that the ZCU has sent a proposal to the rebel players to try to end the ongoing dispute.

Saturday 24 April

Reports suggest that the ZCU's offer of conciliation is rejected by the rebel players.

Sunday 25 April

Third one-day international, Harare: Sri Lanka 1–40 beat Zimbabwe 35 by 9 wickets.

Tuesday 27 April

Fourth one-day international, Harare: Sri Lanka 9–223 (Sangakkara 63, Chandana 51) beat Zimbabwe 151 (Ebrahim 50 not out) by 72 runs.

Wednesday 28 April

The ZCU announces that the rebel players are set to resume training in two days' time [Friday 30 April] and are back in consideration for selection. The announcement follows suggestions of a possible compromise between the two sides.

Thursday 29 April

Fifth one-day international, Harare: Sri Lanka 7–246 (Arnold 51 not out) beat Zimbabwe 9–221 (Taylor 74, Muralitharan 5–23) by 25 runs.

Zimbabwe's rebel players issue a deadline of Tuesday [4 May] for the ZCU to agree to arbitration or they will resume their refusal to play.

Saturday 1 May

Heath Streak, Sean Ervine, Trevor Gripper and Ray Price, all of them part of the group of players in dispute with the ZCU, are included in a Zimbabwe A side to play against the touring Sri Lankan side. Ervine top-scores with 75 as Zimbabwe A score 294 on the first day of the three-day game.

Monday 3 May

Trevor Gripper top-scores for Zimbabwe A with 97; the match with the Sri Lankans ends in a draw.

Tuesday 4 May

Heath Streak, Sean Ervine, Trevor Gripper and Ray Price are named in a 17-man squad for Zimbabwe's first Test against Sri Lanka starting on Thursday, but all four of them pull out after the rebels reject the ZCU's offer of non-binding arbitration.

The ZCU has given the players until Friday 7 May to end their boycott or face the prospect of being sacked.

Twenty South Africa-based reporters release a letter they have written to ICC Chief Executive Malcolm Speed complaining about the expulsion from Zimbabwe of two cricket writers due to cover the Zimbabwe–Sri Lanka series. The letter also calls on the ICC to put pressure on the ZCU to end its imposition of a US$600 fee for reporters to be accredited.

Thursday 6 May

First Test, day one, Harare: Sri Lanka 0–67 trail Zimbabwe 199 (Muralitharan 6–45) by 132 runs.

Friday 7 May

First Test, day two, Harare: Sri Lanka 7–456 (Atapattu 170, Jayasuriya 157) lead Zimbabwe by 257 runs.

Reports suggest there is still hope that the ZCU–player dispute will be resolved despite the passing of the ZCU's earlier deadline of 7 May for the players to agree to end their boycott.

ICC President Ehsan Mani is reported to be critical of the stance the players have taken. He is quoted as saying: 'By walking out on their team-mates on the eve of a Test match, the rebels have placed Tatenda Taibu and his team in an invidious position.'

He adds: 'If the rebels believe that walking out will result in other countries interfering in Zimbabwe cricket, I think that they have been very badly advised. Many of our members have faced similar issues and are very strongly of the view that the only way to find a solution is at the local level.'

Saturday 8 May

First Test, day three, Harare: Sri Lanka 541 beat Zimbabwe 199 and 102 (Zoysa 5–20) by an innings and 240 runs.

Muttiah Muralitharan takes 2–37, with the wicket of Mluleki Nkala taking him past Courtney Walsh's world record of 519 Test wickets.

Monday 10 May

The ZCU announces that it has sacked the 15 rebel players in dispute with it. One of the players, Grant Flower, says: 'It means that this is the end. I don't know what happens now. All I know is that we are fired.'

Today was the start of what could be a very testing few weeks for the whole squad. We met up in Brisbane ahead of the tour of Zimbabwe.

The testing part of the tour is unlikely to be the cricket: the home side is in turmoil because of a dispute between the players and the Zimbabwe Cricket Union (ZCU) that began when Heath Streak was sacked as captain. Most of the white players in the squad stood down in protest and a shadow side has already been thrashed by Sri Lanka in five one-day internationals and a Test match.

The morality of going on a tour to a country where President Robert Mugabe is reportedly ignoring the basic human rights of many members of the population has already caused some debate among the public, the media and politicians, and now there is the added complication of the prospect of playing against a shadow side which is clearly not up to competing at international level. We want to play a full-strength Zimbabwe side — without wanting to sound big-headed, playing against a weakened line-up is of no use to anyone. If we play the lesser side, we should win without stretching ourselves, and of course being thrashed will do the shadow players no good. Zimbabwe's performances against Sri Lanka — they were bowled out for 35 in a one-day international and lost the first Test in three days — do not bode well for our series if the dispute is not resolved.

My own view is that if our safety and security — Cricket Australia's main criteria for considering any overseas trip for us — are guaranteed, as they appear to be, the tour should go ahead. I want to leave the politics and morals of the situation to the administrators and just get on with my job: playing cricket and leading the Australia cricket team to success. My only reservation about the trip concerns whether or not the dispute is resolved and therefore whether or not we end up playing a sub-standard side. We will set off, and hope that the issues will be sorted out.

Whether that will happen or not is pure guesswork at the moment; from this distance, at least, the situation is confused and pretty fluid. Since the dispute started I have seen stories saying that the groups are making the right noises about coming together — but nothing has been sorted out yet, which is a bit of a worry.

I have not spoken to any Zimbabwe players, either the so-called rebel ones or members of the current side, and I am not sure any other Australian players have either. I am happy to stay at arm's length at this stage. I don't want to be seen as interfering, and we are being kept informed of developments on a regular basis by Cricket Australia (through Michael Brown, the General Manager of Cricket Operations) and through the news stories that appear in the newspapers, on television and on the internet every day.

Brown has also been in touch with senior players Adam Gilchrist and Damien Martyn to gauge their views on the tour and bring them up to speed on the subject. I have also been speaking to them fairly regularly, as they are two of my closest friends among the squad. I think their views are similar to mine — if the safety and security aspects of the tour are okay we should go — but I think all three of us have the odd question mark in our minds over the rights and wrongs of the trip.

However, despite those question marks, I do not believe anyone will follow Stuart MacGill's lead and pull out of the trip. Cricket Australia has pulled us out of tours in the past — Sri Lanka in 1996 and Pakistan in 2002 — if it feels our safety could be compromised, and if it believes we should go on this trip I think the players will have enough faith to toe the line and go with that decision.

I know it has been argued that we are only going so that we stay on the right side of the International Cricket Council (ICC), which is keen to see its 10-year program of Tests and one-day internationals between member countries observed, but I am certain our administrators are not thinking that way.

From a purely personal point of view, I do not feel I know enough about the situation in Zimbabwe to be able to make a judgement on the rights and wrongs of touring there. That is not to say I am blind to the news reports, but as a sportsman I do not believe it is right for me to be making political decisions. But if you pushed me I'd have to say I think it is right we are going because we are going as cricketers to play against cricketers. Our actions have nothing to do with anything political as far as I am concerned; this is about sport. Although I am not naïve enough to think sport and politics are never mixed, at the same time I think we have a duty to try to ensure they do not mix wherever possible.

As for whether or not others will follow MacGill's lead and pull out of the trip, if they are going to do it they have left it very late. I am as sure as I can be that it will not happen, because most are reluctant to give others the chance to take their spots. I read an interview with Michael Kasprowicz in which he said as much, and you can understand his point of view. He has taken three years to get back into the squad and now he is back he wants to stay there. By not touring he would hand his place to another player, and if that player did well that could be the end of Kasprowicz's career.

When the dispute between the ZCU and the players started last month, one of my first thoughts was that we should use the situation — playing a weakened opposition — to rest several players and send a weakened squad ourselves. We have a huge amount of cricket coming up over the next 12 months, including a home Test series with Sri Lanka in July, the Champions Trophy in England in September and a Test series in India before our own summer domestic program, so it makes sense to keep players like Jason Gillespie, Matthew Hayden and Adam Gilchrist as fresh as possible.

However, after thinking about it I changed my mind. To start with, we would probably be accused of cheapening the value of playing for Australia if we picked a squad that was not the strongest available. It might also be seen as a comment on the dispute in Zimbabwe: 'If you don't pick your best side, neither will we.' That is something I am keen to avoid getting caught up in.

The selectors have picked our best available side, and for several players it is a big tour, despite the slightly unreal atmosphere around it at the moment. Chief among those players is Glenn McGrath, who is back with the squad for the first time since continued ankle trouble forced him to pull out of the Test series against the same opponents last September.

McGrath is attempting a comeback to the top level at an age when most players are considering throwing away their bowling boots for good. There is the odd precedent for bowlers continuing to excel at international level into their 30s — Curtly Ambrose, Courtney Walsh and Sir Richard Hadlee, for example — but it is still a major test for McGrath, perhaps the biggest of his career. He has arrived back with the squad fitter than ever thanks to work he has done with the Olympic rowing team, but he is a bowler who needs lots of bowling to get into his rhythm, so he will have plenty of work to do to get back to his best.

Cameron White and Shane Watson are two young players who are also desperate for the tour to go ahead. White, who captained Victoria to the Pura Cup despite his relative inexperience, is a replacement for MacGill, as he bowls leg-spin, but he also brings some useful batting skills and brilliance in the field into the mix. No one is pretending he is as good a bowler as MacGill, but with MacGill and our other Test leg-spinner, Shane Warne, both the wrong side of 30, we need to have one eye on the future. This trip will be a great opportunity for us to have a long look at White, and it will give him the chance to work with Warne and see how the senior spinner prepares for a Test.

Watson is on the comeback trail, more than 12 months after breaking down with a stress fracture of the back. That fracture cost him a place in the World Cup squad, which he had won on the basis of showing signs of coming to terms with international cricket. He has had a fantastic domestic season with the bat for Tasmania, and impressed when he resumed his bowling career with a remodelled action in the second half of the summer. A genuine all-rounder has been the one missing ingredient in the Australian side during my time at international level, especially since Stephen and Mark Waugh concentrated more and more on their batting, and we hope Watson will be the one to fill that slot.

The past month has been a mix of the madcap and the relaxed. At one end of the scale was my trip to India for Cricketnext.com. This took place at the end of the Sri Lanka Test series. I made several appearances in shopping malls, and the level of excitement and interest in me was frightening. I was able to get into the malls without too many problems, but once people realised I was there it was pandemonium. On one occasion in Mumbai I was mobbed by so many people the security guards had to link arms around me to stop me being buried by people — it took a massive effort to get me back to a waiting car.

Once I was in the car I could not go anywhere, because people surrounded that too, and in their excitement they started rocking it. Eventually a way was cleared and we managed to get moving, but 50 metres down the road we had to stop at traffic lights, which meant the fans were able to catch up — they did, and then started clambering around the car again. It was all good-natured, but slightly unnerving; it also gave me an early insight into the type of reception we can expect when we play our Test series in India at the end of this year.

Once I got home from India I spent the Easter break with Rianna and my family in Tasmania, including a few rounds of golf with Dad. It was great to see everyone again, especially as it was the first time we'd all caught up since the success of the Sri Lanka tour. From there it was back home to Wollongong and a chance to relax — and to make sure this diary was up to date.

Our time here in Brisbane has been billed as a pre-tour camp, but although we have had medical tests under the supervision of Dr Trefor James, and been briefed today by Michael Brown and Peter Young of Cricket Australia and Tim May, the Chief Executive of the Australian Cricketers' Association, our stay basically boils down to practice sessions.

Not all members of the Test and one-day squads are here: Kasprowicz, Darren Lehmann, Ian Harvey, Warne, Michael Clarke, Brad Hogg and Andrew Symonds are in the UK playing county cricket and will fly direct to Zimbabwe. For the rest of us it is a chance to get bats and balls back into our hands after a month-long break, something that is quite unusual in this era of back-to-back tours and Tests. The break means we are all raring to go. There is a real enthusiasm about the group; the whole issue of the rights and wrongs of the trip seems to have been put to one side by everyone as they focus on cricket skills.

Cricket Australia's Commonwealth Bank Centre of Excellence is now based in Brisbane, and our stay here gives us the chance to use the facilities at a time when most states are restricted to indoor practice. State coaches have been invited to see how we go about our preparations, and contracted players not in the touring squad, such as Mike Hussey of Western Australia and South Australia's Shaun Tait, are also here so they can get another taste of being around the international squad. Xavier Doherty, the promising wrist-spinner from Tasmania, is also here.

John Buchanan spoke to the media today during a break and confirmed that we are very much focused on the tour happening, and concentrating on our cricket. It would be nice to think that will remain the focus for us and for the media during the next month but I am not certain it will turn out that way.

Shane Watson

If there is any justice in the world, Shane Watson will have a long and fruitful international career. He has had so many setbacks in his career already — and has come back more determined after each one of them — that he deserves his tilt at the big time.

It took him a while to come to terms with international cricket when he was first picked in 2002, but by the time we got to the eve of the 2003 World Cup he was showing signs of developing into a genuine all-rounder. Unfortunately, he was then ruled out of the tournament with a stress fracture of the back.

It was his fourth such injury — he'd had three previous ones when he was a teenager — but rather than complain about it or get down, he went through the hours of rehabilitation required and finally came back into the one-day squad for the tour of Zimbabwe.

Watson is no stranger to doing things the hard way: he also made the tough decision to leave his native Queensland when he felt his way to first-class cricket was blocked, and headed to Tasmania. For someone from the sunshine state, life in Hobart can be just about as different as it gets, but he bit the bullet and has proved a fantastic and popular signing for my home state, producing outstanding displays with bat and ball.

The opportunities he got with Tasmania may, in a funny way, have hindered his progress at international level, but that has been no one's fault. He got the chance to bat in the top order in Tasmania, but then when he played at international level he was expected to bat at number seven or eight and improvise for quick runs or finish a match off. It was not something he had done much and it has taken him some time to get used to it.

The bonus of his year away from the international scene is that it has allowed him to develop his batting. As he recovered from his back injury he played for Tasmania initially as a specialist batsman; with this came the pressure of not having his bowling to fall back on if he failed, as he may have done in the past. Watson's response was to have a stellar season in 2003/04. By the time he started bowling again he was justifying his spot in the state side through batting alone.

There is no doubt that he is a better cricketer now than when he made his international debut, but that is no surprise, because he was initially picked after barely a season of first-class cricket, and more on potential than on sustained performance. However, a player with Watson's work ethic was always likely to develop; he trains as hard as any young cricketer I know.

We saw that potential first-hand when he scored an unbeaten hundred for the Australian side against South Africa A in a tour match in Port Elizabeth in 2002. He also showed his flair for the big occasion by reaching three figures with a six.

Watson is a solid unit of a man, but there is barely a kilo of spare flesh on him — his powerful upper body could have been cloned from Andy Bichel. Like Bichel, he is also a genuinely nice bloke, without a mean bone in his body.

I did have one criticism of him as a youngster when he first broke into the Australian team: he would have a go at himself if he bowled a bad ball. I think that is a sign of weakness; it is exactly what I want to see from a bowler if I am batting, especially if I have just clobbered the ball to the boundary. I want Watson to set himself high standards, and I know that he does, but I do not want him to get too down on himself if he does not reach them. Instead, he needs to keep asking himself how he can improve and then working on what he decides he needs.

As a Tasmanian, I am a little sorry Watson has decided to move back to his home state to be close to his family and friends, but if he continues his development as a player he may not be playing state cricket very much in the next few years anyway — having him in the national side would have to be good news for Australian cricket.

Tuesday 11 May

John Buchanan's media briefing yesterday did not go down very favourably. His statement that we are just focusing on the cricket has been portrayed by some reporters as narrow-minded, and it looks as if we are deliberately ignoring the continuing dispute between the ZCU and the so-called rebel players.

I can understand how reporters may have arrived at that view. Buchanan was keen to avoid passing any judgement on the ZCU situation or on the political situation in Zimbabwe, so he stuck to what he knows best: our cricket. But the truth is that cricket *is* what we are all focusing on, so we are in a no-win situation. If we say that cricket is all we are interested in we are accused of putting our heads in the sand and ignoring the political and moral problems in Zimbabwe and the ongoing dispute. But if we start to comment on those issues we could be accused of interfering. I realise MacGill has taken a stand for what he believes in, but as I said earlier I just want to focus on the cricket and leave the politics to others.

One thing everyone seems to agree on is that the game would be best served by us playing a Zimbabwe side made up of its best available players, but no one knows whether or not that will happen. In the meantime, all we can do is get ready for the trip and leave the politics to other people.

Today we had former Australia wicketkeeper Ian Healy in to talk to us about his old job and how he feels it relates to everyone on the field. Shane Warne used to call him the drummer in the band, someone who dictates the pace and rhythm of the rest of the group, and that is a fair way of describing what Healy did and what every keeper should do. To start with, he is likely to touch the ball more than anyone else during the course of a day, as deliveries that beat the bat and throws from the outfield all come his way; because of that, he is in a unique position to dictate the tempo at which the fielding side plays the game. Also, his position directly behind the stumps gives him a unique view of what each bowler is doing with the ball and how each batsman is coping with the bowling. It all combines to make him the focal point of the fielding effort, and that, plus the encouragement he can offer the bowlers and fielders, helps drive a side on.

We also practised today, which gave me a chance to study Shane Watson and Cameron White at close quarters. I saw Watson's remodelled action for the first time, and it looked good. He has adjusted his delivery to try to take the pressure off his lower back — the recent injury was, I think, the fourth set of stress fractures he has had in that area. The most obvious change I could see was the way he winds up before bowling the ball. His bowling arm now goes back almost like a javelin thrower's, and on today's evidence it seems to be a pretty effective method. He bowled with good pace, probably quicker than I have seen him bowl before, and he also swung the ball away from the right-handers. Previously he tended to angle the ball in, and the only movement away from right-handed batsmen was off the seam. Now he has added away-swing to his armoury; that will make him doubly effective if he can maintain it.

White is a different type of leg-spinner from Shane Warne. He bowls the ball a bit quicker and with a flatter trajectory, but he has plenty of variety. In addition to his leg-spinner he has a top-spinner, a googly and a delivery that slides onto the batsman quickly from the front of the hand. I was also impressed by his control — he did not bowl too many bad balls. On this evidence he could be a real asset for us in the subcontinent, because he bowls the ball at a good pace, which stops the batsman getting down the pitch to hit him. He is also a useful batsman and a great athlete.

I finished the day with an interview for Fox Sports, discussing the tour of India we are due to go on later this year. Matthew Hayden, Glenn McGrath and Adam Gilchrist also did interviews, and the theme of each one was the same: we were asked about our memories of the last time we toured there, in 2001. Those three players all had good memories — McGrath bowled brilliantly, Gilchrist made a superb hundred in Mumbai and Hayden made a hundred in Mumbai and a double century in Chennai. My memories are not quite as happy, because although I made a century in a one-day international in Vizag, I managed just 17 runs in three Tests. I hope to put the record straight when we go back in October.

Wednesday 12 May

Today saw me involved in the first of what I expect will be a whole host of media conferences over the next few weeks. This one, also including James Sutherland and vice-captain Adam Gilchrist, was our pre-departure briefing for the reporters — we fly to Zimbabwe tomorrow.

Sutherland's presence ensured that Gilchrist and I avoided any really tricky political questions on Zimbabwe; that subject was addressed by him. Sutherland stressed that safety and security — the only two reasons we would cancel the tour — are not a problem, so the trip is going ahead.

I said the issue of playing a weakened Zimbabwe side was not something the players have addressed as a group at this stage, because we hope it will not come to that. Our hope is that the Test and one-day series will see Zimbabwe put out their best players; there is no point speculating about anything that may or may not happen before we get ready for that first match.

All we want to do is play for our country — something I am sure we have in common with a group of young players I met at lunchtime today, when I presented caps to the latest intake of Centre of Excellence scholars. Cricket Australia's Commonwealth Bank Centre of Excellence is the new name for the Cricket Academy. Greeting all the players was a special occasion for me, because I was in their position over a decade ago. The Academy has a great record of producing players for international cricket — I could not help wondering if I would still be around when any of this group break into the Test or one-day line-up.

After the day's formalities, and on top of a practice session first thing this morning, we flew to Sydney for tomorrow morning's departure. We checked into the airport hotel and Rianna was there to meet me and take me to see a house we are thinking of buying.

Now that Rianna has finished her law degree at Wollongong University we are planning to move to Sydney, but I am finding the whole process of buying a house quite tough.

We saw one place we both liked, but when the owners found out I was the interested party they decided to try to bump up the asking price. We pulled out of the deal, and now Rianna does all the house-hunting on her own; I only get to look at a property once she is completely satisfied with it. Even then we have to make sure the owners are not around when we have a look. We both like the house we saw tonight, so we will put in an offer.

Thursday 13 May

The tour has not started on a very good note. We had not even arrived in Zimbabwe when we found out one of their best players will not be facing us.

Four of us — Matthew Hayden, Adam Gilchrist, Damien Martyn and me — were having a coffee in Johannesburg airport while we waited for our connecting flight to Harare when Hayden spotted Zimbabwe all-rounder Sean Ervine.

We had a chat with him and discovered that he is moving to Perth to be with his girlfriend, Melissa Marsh, the daughter of our former coach Geoff, now in charge of the Zimbabwe team.

Ervine scored a century in this year's VB Series match against India in Adelaide, and also bowled well against us in the Perth Test last year. If he tries to qualify for Australia it could benefit us in the long term, but Zimbabwe can ill afford to lose a young player of his talent on top of the other high-quality players they have lost in recent years. The fact that he has decided to go seems to suggest that the dispute between the ZCU and the players is not anywhere near being settled.

The impression I got from our chat with Ervine was that he did not know what was happening in the dispute; he only knew that it was still going on. The one crumb of comfort for us is that I think he still expects a few of the so-called rebel players to feature against us. He was one of the group who played for Zimbabwe A against Sri Lanka before the first Test between the two countries at the start of this month, the time when the dispute seemed to be moving closer to a resolution. Since then, positions on both sides seem to have hardened, and Ervine has finally had enough.

Our meeting with Ervine took the wind out of our sails after a very positive journey to South Africa and an equally positive arrival. The journey saw us all — with the exception of our fitness trainer, Jock Campbell — upgraded from our usual business class seats to first class. Jock was desperate to get a seat in the 'bubble' of the plane, the business class seats directly behind the pilot's cockpit, because that is usually a very quiet area, with no children. He was so keen he swapped his seat with team manager Steve Bernard, but once we got on board it turned out his original seat had been in first class. He ended up in business class and the rest of us all finished up in first class and really enjoyed that extra bit of luxury on a journey that takes more than 12 hours.

One of the advantages of first class travel is that it guarantees you a seat that becomes completely flat, so you can get a decent sleep. But as our trip was east to west, and started in the morning, I found it tricky to get to sleep; I had only woken up a few hours earlier. Wide awake, I watched the film *Seabiscuit*, an enjoyable story about a racehorse that thrilled America in the 1930s, and read some golf magazines I'd bought before we boarded the flight.

When we arrived in Johannesburg quite a few of the squad felt at home right away, because we were shown into a lounge that had pictures of last year's World Cup triumph on the walls. It is hard to believe it is more than 12 months since we won that tournament. So much has happened since then, but the memories are still fresh in my mind and it was nice to have them jogged today.

Our connecting flight got us into Harare at about 10 o'clock at night, which was about 6 o'clock on Friday morning in Sydney — we had been travelling about 20 hours by that stage. We were all pretty tired, so it was good to see a friendly face waiting for us: we were greeted by our security officer for the trip, Darren Maughan, wearing his red Australian World Cup tie. Maughan was with us during the World Cup last year and was a very popular addition to our tour group then. He was nicknamed Pirate by Darren Lehmann because he has only one eye; the empty socket is filled by a glass eye. I don't know how he lost his eye, but rest assured, he is as tough as teak. He did a great job in keeping us safe during the World Cup and I am sure his presence will help ease any concerns members of the squad may have about our security.

My initial feeling about Zimbabwe — just from the airport and the trip to our hotel — was the same as when we were here for the

World Cup match last year. Then, as now, we arrived with suggestions that there might be trouble and demonstrations, but in reality the place was very quiet. The time of night has something to do with that, but Harare is a capital city. As we travelled to the team hotel from the airport there were very few people around on the streets and it was very dark, with few street lights to light the way.

We were given confirmation that Darren Lehmann, Shane Warne and Michael Kasprowicz had arrived during the day, so we all headed straight to bed as soon as we reached the hotel.

Friday 14 May

Second Test, day one, Bulawayo: Sri Lanka 0–18 trail Zimbabwe 228 (Ebrahim 70) by 210 runs.

The ZCU issues a statement saying it is giving the rebel players a further 21 days to make themselves available for selection.

If today is an example of what is ahead of me over the next few weeks I am not going to enjoy this tour very much.

We had our first media conference of the tour at 11 o'clock, and most of the questions did not involve cricket; instead they focused on the moral and political problems that surround the tour. By the end of the session I was thoroughly fed up.

I was not surprised that questions about whether or not we should be undertaking the tour came up. What I was surprised about was how persistent and ferocious the questioning was. There were some tough questions about the morality of dealing with President Mugabe's country and even whether or not we would shake hands with him if he turns up at any matches. That was a potential issue before our trip to Bulawayo for the World Cup last year, because Mugabe is Patron of the Zimbabwe Cricket Union. It disappeared as an issue when the World Cup organisers said Mugabe would not be attending any matches, so we were able to play without it being a distraction.

Team manager Steve Bernard was on hand to deal with the political issues and he handled himself brilliantly, staying cool despite the barrage of questions. We both repeated that we are here as cricketers, not politicians, and that although we are not turning a blind eye to any of the problems in Zimbabwe we are only here to play the matches scheduled under the ICC's 10-year program.

We were hoping for an enjoyable tour, but Sean Ervine's departure and the continuing dispute between the ZCU and the players, together with the political overtones of today's conference, suggest that is unlikely to be what we'll get.

With jetlag still very much an issue we did not have a training session; instead we just walked around the gardens that back onto the team hotel in the centre of Harare. In contrast to the scenes I encountered in India last month, there were no cheering crowds or mobs rushing up to us for autographs. In fact there were very few people around, despite the fact that it was the middle of the day and a weekday. That struck me as odd; a few of the other players commented on it as well.

Our arrival has coincided with the start of the second Test of the Zimbabwe–Sri Lanka series in Bulawayo, and we watched some of that match on the TV during the afternoon. It was a useful exercise because there are many players in the Zimbabwe side we have not seen before. This is partly because the dispute with the rebel players still has not been settled — with only eight days until our first Test begins, that is a bad sign. Zimbabwe did not disgrace themselves today, scoring 228, but Sri Lanka scored 541 against them in the first Test, so the home side's effort is unlikely to be enough to keep it in the match for long.

We ended the day with a team meeting to set the agenda for the tour. Obviously, facing a second-string Zimbabwe side is far from ideal — on today's evidence, they will be unlikely to test us very much. However, I do not expect anyone to coast through the trip; that would be disrespectful to the game and to our opponents. In any case, every member of our squad has professional pride. And there are also players in the squad who have plenty to play for: Cameron White and Glenn McGrath, for example.

My message was a simple one, and similar to what I said before the Bangladesh series at home last winter: 'No matter which players they put out against us, we are here to play the best cricket we can, and if that means winning Tests in two or three days, then that is what we will do. I want us to be tough and aggressive, and if they are a second-rate side I want us to embarrass them. We have made our reputation by winning and winning well, and it is up to us to maintain that form here.'

Saturday 15 May

Second Test, day two, Bulawayo: Sri Lanka 1–443 (Atapattu 202 not out, Sangakkara 186 not out) lead Zimbabwe 228 by 215 runs.

Zimbabwe all-rounder Sean Ervine announces his retirement from international cricket. Ervine has moved to Australia to be with his girlfriend, the daughter of Zimbabwe coach Geoff Marsh.

If any of us wondered how good the Zimbabwe attack is without its frontline players, we got our answer today: it is very poor.

We watched on a TV in the dressing room after our morning practice session as Sri Lanka moved towards a close of play score of 1–443. We saw Sanath Jayasuriya get out, the only wicket of the day for the home side, and also saw Kumar Sangakkara dropped second ball. Apart from that it was very one-sided: Sangakkara and Sri Lanka captain Marvan Atapattu did much as they pleased against Zimbabwe's inexperienced attack.

The one reassuring thing for me was that none of the players watching with me resorted to rubbishing the Zimbabwe bowlers or questioning why we are here to play a side that is clearly nowhere near the required standard for international cricket. In line with what I said last night, everyone is concentrating on preparing to play and ensuring that we set our own standards, no matter what the standards of the sides we will face.

The practice session was our first of the tour and went well. But the pitches we practised on were not great; there was some uneven bounce, which meant conditions were not ideal.

Sunday 16 May

Second Test, day three, Bulawayo: Zimbabwe 228 and 2–44 trail Sri Lanka 3–713 declared (Sangakkara 270, Atapattu 249, Jayawardene 100 not out) by 441 runs.

Zimbabwe batsman Dion Ebrahim is banned for one Test match by International Cricket Council (ICC) match referee Mike Procter for comments he made about the bowling action of Sri Lanka spinner Muttiah Muralitharan.

Ebrahim was asked in a radio interview about a leg-break that Muralitharan bowled to him during the second Test in Bulawayo and he reportedly responded by saying it was 'the first legal delivery he bowled'.

Sri Lanka inflicted further humiliation on Zimbabwe today, scoring 3–713 before showing some mercy by declaring. Given that we beat Sri Lanka 3–0 less than two months ago, this suggests that our matches against Zimbabwe could be even more one-sided.

In one sense it would give us little or no satisfaction to win matches like that: it would not be a challenge. On top of that, it would degrade international cricket, which is meant to be the highest form of the game. But what can we do? We are here to play the matches whether we like it or not. I hope the results today just reinforce our resolve to win the Tests and one-day matches as quickly as possible. That is the best way to stop us coasting through the tour.

One reporter has suggested to me that we should try to win a Test in one day, just to highlight what he sees as the farcical nature of the tour. It was something the late David Hookes said we could do against Bangladesh last year. We did not manage it then, but we will never have a better chance to do it than in this Test series. It might be a way to approach a match that will stop us going through the motions, although as I have said before, I do not believe that will happen. I just think we are all too professional for that.

We had our final training session before tomorrow's first match of the tour, against Zimbabwe A, and afterwards a few of us headed to a gym at the Zimbabwe Cricket Academy, a 15-minute bus ride away. During the trip we saw very few people around and no queues for food or petrol — the sorts of sights that were reported and shown on television and in the media during the World Cup last year. I am not sure where those queues have gone, or where the people have gone either; we have not seen many people around anywhere in the first few days of our stay. It adds an air of unreality to the whole situation.

The gym we visited was an excellent facility. It just goes to show that if Zimbabwe cricket get their act together the resources are here to ensure that they have a chance to succeed at international level. Unfortunately, the dispute is still unresolved, and a further nail was hammered into the coffin today with a report that Geoff Marsh will be quitting as coach when his term ends in September.

I feel sorry for Marsh. He was our coach when we won the 1999 World Cup and loved the job, but he quit soon afterwards to spend more time with his family. A close friend of his died while we were on tour in Sri Lanka and that death made him reassess his priorities, but cricket coaching is in his blood and when the chance to work again at international level came up with Zimbabwe he grabbed it.

Gradually, however, he has been ground down by the loss of players like Andy Flower and Henry Olonga for reasons that do not appear to have a great deal to do with cricket. It has meant that the team has not been as competitive as he would have liked it to be. Marsh is a good coach, but not even the best coach in history can turn a team of largely inexperienced players, some of them not of the required standard, into world-beaters.

The current dispute has been the last straw for Marsh. He has been careful to avoid taking sides, but he has been in a no-win situation: if he sided with the so-called rebel players he would have been sacked by the ZCU, but staying on to coach the new team members means he has been criticised by the rebels for having no principles. He has had enough, and it is not difficult to appreciate his feelings.

It will be interesting to see who we face tomorrow, because most of Zimbabwe's young players are now in the Test side. Tomorrow's match will give us a pretty good indication of the depth of talent available in this country.

Because the match is not first-class, we have asked for all 13 players in our squad to be allowed to take part, although only 11 will be able to field at any one time and only 11 players can bat in any innings. This will ensure that everyone gets some sort of workout before the Test, which is still scheduled to start this weekend.

Monday 17 May

Second Test, day four, Bulawayo: Sri Lanka 3–713 declared beat Zimbabwe 228 and 231 (Taylor 61) by an innings and 254 runs.

Tour match, day one of two, Harare: The Australians 1–151 (Langer 79 not out) are level with Zimbabwe A 151.

Even though today was the first playing day of our tour, most of the action seemed to be taking place off the field.

While we were playing our match at the home of the Zimbabwe Cricket Academy, our team manager, Steve Bernard, was joined by Vince Hogg, the Managing Director of the ZCU; there was also news that Malcolm Speed, the ICC's Chief Executive Officer, has flown to Harare to try to understand and resolve the players' dispute.

I am not sure what Hogg said to Bernard, but Speed's arrival is acknowledgement from the ICC that the current situation in Zimbabwe is unacceptable. The ICC has previously maintained that it will not get involved in the internal workings of a member country's cricket administration, and I can understand that, but the integrity of international cricket has suffered: without their best players, Zimbabwe were bowled out for 35 in a one-day international, and today they lost the second Test in Bulawayo by an innings and 254 runs inside three days.

The runs being scored and the wickets being taken against this Zimbabwe side are counting towards players' international records, but everyone knows they are cheap successes because the players Zimbabwe are putting on the field are not their best. I hope the issue is resolved by this weekend, when we are due to play against the home side in the first Test.

If it is not, what do we do? Unless we are told otherwise, we will have to play the Tests and the one-day internationals. Doing that will give us no pleasure, because we know the matches will not be a true test of our abilities, but if the ICC says the show must go on, that is what must happen. The simple fact is they run the game and we play it.

Today we got a look at the depth of Zimbabwe talent below the Test side and it was a shock. The players we came up against on the first day of our warm-up match were, by and large, not very good; if this is Zimbabwe's second-best side, the situation is worse than we realised. It reinforced our hope that the current dispute will be resolved before Saturday — sub-standard international cricket will do the credibility of the game no good at all.

There was some value in today's play, because Glenn McGrath got his first bowl in a match for Australia since the series against Bangladesh almost 10 months ago. He got a wicket in his first over, but overall he lacked rhythm. This was no surprise: he is a bowler who thrives on hard work, something he has missed being out of action for so long. McGrath is his own toughest critic, and straight after Zimbabwe A were dismissed he headed to the practice nets, where he worked for two hours trying to rediscover that rhythm.

There was one curious side to the day: we heard that Australia's Prime Minister, John Howard, has become involved in the latest controversy concerning Sri Lanka's spinner, Muttiah Muralitharan. The dispute over Muralitharan's doosra has been rumbling on ever since we left Sri Lanka at the beginning of April, and now the Prime Minister has been quoted on the subject.

The reports are that Howard was asked about Muralitharan's bowling action at a function last week, and he said his understanding was that the spinner did throw the ball. On radio today he was asked about the issue again, and he referred to the biomechanical tests Muralitharan has undergone in Perth that apparently indicate an illegal degree of bend in the bowler's arm. I am not sure how this story developed, but know it will be widely reported in Sri Lanka and hope it does not affect our series against them in Darwin and Cairns. After the controversy here in Zimbabwe, that is all we need.

Tuesday 18 May

Tour match, day two of two, Harare: The Australians 448 (Ponting 87, Langer 84, Hayden 61) drew with Zimbabwe A 151.

This was another day when events off the field overshadowed events on it.

That was no surprise really. To start with, we had what amounted to a glorified public net session before the match was called off as a draw with the final session left unused.

On top of that we got a sense that the future of this tour will be decided very soon. Peter Chingoka, the ZCU Chairman, and Vince Hogg, the Managing Director, both appeared at the ground to chat with our team manager, Steve Bernard, as did Malcolm Speed of the ICC — it all took attention away from what was happening on the field.

It turns out the ZCU cancelled a meeting with Speed, who flew from London especially to see its representatives. That prompted the ICC to set up a teleconference of all its Test-playing members this Friday to discuss the situation. I am not sure what that means for us at this stage.

There was plenty of chat and speculation among the squad, especially as most of us were in the dressing room for most of the day — we were batting. I think we all expect the tour to go on, but Friday's teleconference might change that, especially if the ICC decides to suspend Zimbabwe, as some reporters suggested to me it might. In truth, no one is really sure what is going on, so every time Bernard's phone rang today everyone's head shot around, half expecting it to be news that we are on the next flight out of here.

It is not the ideal environment in which to prepare for a Test but that is exactly what we must do. John Buchanan spoke to the media after today's play, emphasising that we are all trying to keep our minds on what we are here to do: to play cricket. Unless we are told otherwise, we have to assume we will be starting a Test match on Saturday.

The final day of the match was something of a non-event. Most of the batsmen, including me, spent some valuable time at the crease. My original plan was to declare and let the bowlers have another run-out in the final session, but for one reason or another, none of them wanted to do that. Jason Gillespie and Cameron White were happy with the work they had done in the first innings, Glenn McGrath had done plenty of work in the nets on top of his first innings bowling, Shane Warne and Michael Kasprowicz had no need to bowl again because they have been playing county cricket for the whole of the past month, and Brad Williams was stiff and sore after his first bowl for a month so did not feel able to bowl again, even if he'd wanted to.

One other consideration would have been the crowd, but there were next to no spectators. Armed with all that information, and with little chance of a result, I approached the opposition captain and the umpires and they agreed to end proceedings early. Part of me is wondering whether that was the end of the only match we will play on this trip.

Wednesday 19 May

Today was another example of the confusion in which we are operating. Every day since we have been here there have been stories suggesting that there has been a complete breakdown in relations between the rebel players and the ZCU and stories that say a resolution between the two groups is imminent. Today was no exception.

One story on the internet suggests that the so-called rebel players are willing to play against us in the one-day series that follows the Tests. In the same story there is also a suggestion that the Test series will be cancelled and one-day matches will be played instead.

No one knows whether or not the story is true, and we have seen so many of these stories now that we have learnt to ignore them. All we are focusing on is Saturday's first Test: we are still preparing to play in that match.

Those preparations did go on hold for a while, though, as we took a day off. For me and a few others in the squad that involved a game of golf. I headed off to a course about 20 minutes' drive away from our hotel in the centre of Harare and had a relaxing afternoon with Shane Warne, Damien Martyn, Darren Lehmann, Justin Langer, Adam Gilchrist and assistant coach Tim Nielsen.

The course was dry but in pretty good condition, and it was an opportunity to forget about the issues surrounding the tour for a few hours. Warne has his own clubs with him but the rest of us used borrowed sets, which were very good quality.

Most of the squad plays golf, but some — like Warne, Nielsen, Martyn and me — are keener on the sport than others. If the cricket coming up is as poor as I fear it might be, and if it does not last the distance, the chance to lower our golf handicaps might be the best thing to come out of this trip. I hope that is not the case.

Thursday 20 May

After a day of meetings and discussions it looks as if we will not be playing the Test series against Zimbabwe.

I had a meeting with Cricket Australia's Michael Brown this evening and he briefed me on the developments. Although there is likely to be further discussion between Peter Chingoka of the ZCU and Cricket Australia (CA) Chairman Bob Merriman, who flew into Harare today along with fellow CA director Tony Harrison and selector David Boon, the basic idea seems to be that we will play only the one-day internationals that were originally set for the end of the trip. If that is the case, they will be brought forward, we will fly in our one-day players, and the whole tour could be done and dusted within the next 10 days.

My reading of the situation is that by postponing the Test series, the ZCU might be trying to buy itself more time to get its house in order. The stories I have seen on the internet suggest that tomorrow's ICC teleconference is set to suspend the ZCU from playing Tests in any case, so by opting out of this series of its own accord it might be trying to show that it is aware of its responsibilities to the international game and is willing to do something to repair the situation. However, all that is just a guess on my part.

Brown told me the ZCU's original proposal was for us to play five one-day internationals, but Cricket Australia rejected that idea. That seems fair enough to me. We are only due to play three matches at the end of the tour, and if, at a later date, the Test series is played, it would mean Zimbabwe getting an additional two matches which were not part of the original agreement. If we are not going to be facing Zimbabwe's best players I cannot see any point in playing those two extra matches anyway, as they would not test us a great deal. And it is not as if we need the practice at that form of the game — we play enough of it already.

None of this has been agreed to yet, and until it is there will be no announcements, but it is expected to be confirmed tomorrow morning. At that point the rest of the squad will be told, then the media.

It all seems a shocking waste of time, especially for those of us who are playing only the Tests: Shane Warne, Simon Katich, Justin Langer and Cameron White. They have been here for a week, played very little cricket, and will fly home — or in Warne's case, back to the UK — without a great deal to show for their time apart from some extra frequent flyer points. Even worse, it is likely to mean more hanging around for those of us who play both forms of the game, while we wait for the one-day players to fly in and then build up to the one-day series.

It should mean more time to work on the golf handicap, but even that might not be possible. This afternoon we were told to stay in the hotel because of the possibility of a political demonstration taking place on the streets. From our hotel rooms we could not see any sign of trouble, but a warning like that is another indication of the problems in this country. Darren Maughan, our security officer, went out to see what was happening, but said he did not see a great deal.

Safety and security have always been the only reasons we would call off a tour, and despite today's warning there is no suggestion that we will go home without fulfilling whatever fixtures we are asked to play. Maughan said today's demonstration was all part of the conflict between government and opposition groups, and that we are not a target.

Friday 21 May

Zimbabwe name a 14-man squad for their three-match one-day series against Australia, brought forward to 25, 27 and 29 May following the cancellation of the two-match Test series between the two countries. The squad is: Tatenda Taibu (captain), Elton Chigumbura, Dion Ebrahim, Douglas Hondo, Alester Maregwede, Stuart Matsikenyeri, Tawanda Mupariwa, Waddington Mwayenga, Mluleki Nkala, Tinashe Panyangara, Edward Rainsford, Vusumuzi Sibanda, Brendan Taylor and Mark Vermeulen.

Today the speculation and predictions finally ended with the news that the Test series has been called off. The official wording is that the two matches have been deferred, but there is no date available in the foreseeable future when they might be played.

The news was confirmed to me at 9 o'clock this morning when I met with Michael Brown, Bob Merriman, Tony Harrison, Steve Bernard, John Buchanan and Jonathan Rose, Cricket Australia's media manager. Once Merriman and Brown had explained the situation, which was much as Brown had relayed it to me last night, the rest of the squad were invited in and briefed.

So the Test tour is over before it has begun, which is a bizarre feeling. I am especially sad for Cameron White, who must have been so full of expectation and excitement on his first senior tour. He has been denied the chance to work with Shane Warne before and during a Test match, something that could have been very useful in his development.

One thing that happened today will ensure that he at least has some sort of record of this tour — we had the official Test squad photograph taken. Given that we have played just one two-day warm-up match it might seem an odd thing to do, but a tour is a tour, and in 50 years' time it will be good to have a team photograph as a record of a very curious week.

The first of the three one-day matches is not until next Tuesday, so rather than practise for the sake of practising, John Buchanan and I told the players staying on that today and tomorrow are days off; we will resume training on Sunday. We hope that by then the players picked for just the one-day squad will have arrived and we can start to get our heads around the idea of the one-day matches.

At 11.15 Merriman and I had a media conference. He dealt with most of the questions, because they related to logistics and the politics of the situation. I answered questions about how the situation affects the players; the reality is that it does not affect us very much. We are professionals, and although we are disappointed not to be playing Test cricket, we are also relieved not to be playing what would have been very one-sided matches.

From a personal point of view, I am disappointed at the distinction that has been drawn between Tests and one-day internationals. If the situation here dictates that the Tests are called off, why not the one-day matches as well? I realise that some countries have international status at one-day level only, but Zimbabwe is not one of them, so if the crisis surrounding cricket in this country means we cannot or should not be playing Tests, I do not believe we should be playing one-day cricket either.

One of the reasons the Tests have been 'deferred' is to avoid cheapening that form of the game: Zimbabwe are clearly not competitive at Test level without their so-called rebel players. But playing one-day matches seems to me to be cheapening that form of the game as well. Zimbabwe are not competitive in that form of the game either, as was shown when they lost a recent series against Sri Lanka 5–0. Cheapening the one-day game is sad, because for many players it is the only form of international cricket they play. We all accept that Test cricket is the pinnacle of the game, but one-day cricket also involves representing your country, is watched by many more people than Test cricket and is the only form of the game that involves a World Cup. There are league ladders for Test and one-day international cricket now but the World Cup is the tournament that, I believe, is still associated with the tag of World Champions. That all means the integrity of one-day cricket should be protected just as much as that of Test cricket.

Shane Warne wasted no time flying out, managing to get on a flight to the UK today, but for White, Simon Katich and Justin Langer there was an extra night's wait to get home to Australia. The silver lining in all this for them is getting to spend an extra couple of weeks at home with their families, something that is very precious to players in this era of almost non-stop cricket.

Saturday 22 May

Today's day off meant golf, and with little else to do we even managed to get John Buchanan playing. Buchanan usually prefers to go out and have a look around when we go on tour, but the political climate in this country means that wandering around the streets alone is something our security officer, Darren Maughan, has discouraged us from doing. Fuel shortages mean that driving around the countryside is not much of an option either, so golf has suddenly become very appealing, even to someone like Buchanan. On today's evidence it is a shame he plays so infrequently — he is a useful player.

Matthew Hayden, Jason Gillespie, Jock Campbell and our masseuse, Lucy Frostick, went fishing, while Maughan and Glenn McGrath went hunting at a game reserve. I did not hear how McGrath got on, but Lucy Frostick caught a large bass — which impressed Hayden, who is an expert fisherman.

On a previous trip to Zimbabwe most of the squad went to Victoria Falls by train. It is a long trip, maybe 12 hours, and the spare time in the itinerary now means it would be possible, but no one has mentioned it. It is not something that appeals to me — I am happy playing golf.

Of course I cannot play golf all the time, so I still have plenty of free time on my hands. I am cursing my decision not to bring some DVDs with me. I have a decent-sized collection of around 100 DVDs at home, and when we were on tour in Sri Lanka I often relaxed in my room watching one on my laptop. But I did not pack any for this trip and am now regretting it — the local television stations are not great.

We eat almost all our meals in the hotel too, so the whole place can occasionally feel very claustrophobic, especially when we are not practising. Luckily, four new players arrived today, which lightened the mood. Michael Clarke, Shane Watson, Ian Harvey and Andrew Symonds joined us for the one-day series and, after a meeting in the team room to welcome them, the whole squad had a meal together. The arrival of new players should help give the rest of us a fresh injection of enthusiasm — something we need after more than a week of hanging about without much cricket, and with only the prospect of playing three matches that could be of low quality to look forward to.

Sunday 23 May

There was some relief today from the boredom a few of us are starting to feel: we had a practice session before the first one-day international, which is to be played in two days' time. After all the waiting around, I think most of us, certainly those who have been here since the start of the tour, are looking forward to the first match just for something to do, never mind what the standard of play is.

The new players brought some added buzz, but I felt a bit flat during the session and I don't think I was alone in that. It was not a case of players not trying — bowlers bowled and batsmen batted — but I am not sure how much enthusiasm there is for this one-day series. We all travelled here hoping to play Zimbabwe's best side but that is not going to happen and, without being arrogant, we know we should be able to beat the reserve side without too many problems unless something disastrous happens. That flat feeling is something we will have to address before the match. We are the best side in the world and I want us to play like that, no matter who we are up against.

As for this Zimbabwe side, we do not know a great deal about it. We have played against some of them during the recent VB Series — players like Mark Vermeulen, Dion Ebrahim, Stuart Matsikinyeri, Douglas Hondo and the captain, Tatenda Taibu — and the all-rounder Mluleki Nkala toured Australia for the Carlton & United Series in 2001. But most of them are new names to us; it will be interesting to see how they cope with playing against us.

The plus for Zimbabwe's side is that weaknesses can more easily be hidden in one-day cricket than in Tests, where there is plenty of time and scope (through attacking fields) to exploit technical and mental failings. Even a poor side can scramble to 150 or 180 in a one-day game, because the pitch in that form of the game is usually batsman-friendly and the opposition's best bowlers can only operate for 10 overs.

A poor side's bowling is more likely to be exposed in a one-day game, though, precisely because its best bowlers can only operate for 10 overs each — that exposes any lack of depth in that department. On top of that, its fielding will be put under intense pressure.

Zimbabwe's players have nothing to lose, because everyone is expecting us to thrash them, but I am hoping that will bring out the best in them. If they do play above themselves that in turn should lift our level of performance. The prospect of three dull matches with us just going through the motions to beat Zimbabwe is not something that appeals to any of us.

The final member of the one-day squad, Brad Hogg, arrived today and, just as we did with the other players yesterday, we all got together for a meal this evening. Hogg is one of the most enthusiastic cricketers I have ever met, and his hyperactivity around the place could be another valuable tool in ensuring that we all stay positive.

Monday 24 May

We have not even played a match yet and already we have injury problems. Ian Harvey has hurt his groin and is in doubt for tomorrow's match. Harvey injured himself attempting a slog-sweep at the bowling of Brad Hogg during a net session, and although he went off for treatment straight away, there is a major question mark over his place in the side.

It is never good to have a player injured, especially someone as talented as Harvey, but in some ways it helps us: if he is not fit, it makes the job of selecting the side a little easier. Everyone is keen to play, especially those of us who have been hanging around for 10 days, but we can only play 11 of the squad in any one match.

We did have one piece of good news on the fitness front: it seems Brad Williams will be fit. He was very stiff and sore after his bowl in the match against Zimbabwe A, with aches and pains in his thigh and back. But after a long spell today he said he felt great, so unless he deteriorates overnight he should be available for this match.

Williams is desperate to play because his tour of Sri Lanka did not go as well as he'd hoped. He lost his place in the one-day side and then only figured in the final Test of the series, failing to take a wicket. He has been on the fringes of the squad for the past three or four years, is determined to claim a permanent place and so is keen to impress at every opportunity.

Although Zimbabwe are unlikely to provide very tough opposition, in some ways that is ideal, especially for Shane Watson and Glenn McGrath, both of whom are coming back from long-term injuries. These matches against Zimbabwe will give them the chance to return to international action without too much pressure. At the same time, they will allow the selectors to assess their progress. It will be interesting to see how McGrath and Watson respond. However, if Williams is fit, Watson will have to wait his turn until later in the series.

The media conference today was odd — there appears to be very little local interest in the match. Unlike the conference we held when we arrived in the country, there were very few journalists at this event, and most of them were Australian reporters covering the tour for newspapers back home. There were no questions like those at that first conference of the tour either, which was good; most dealt with the match and what it will be like to be playing after such a long build-up.

I said it was a relief to be finally contemplating some cricket, and that feeling was echoed by the other players at this evening's team meeting. I used the meeting to reinforce what I said to the Test squad at the start of the trip: no matter how good or bad the Zimbabwe side is, I want our aim to be a simple one — to crush them as quickly as possible. International cricket is no place for sympathy, and I do not want us to show the opposition any tomorrow.

Tuesday 25 May

First one-day international, Harare: Australia 3–207 (Ponting 91, Martyn 74 not out) beat Zimbabwe 9–205 (Taylor 59, Taibu 57) by 7 wickets.

What a difference seven months makes. In October, after playing two Tests at home against Zimbabwe, I felt they were not too far away from having a side that could at least compete at Test and one-day level. True, they had lost some very good players, but there was still some decent talent there, and if they had been able to find a quality fast bowler and a wrist-spinner there were signs the team could hold its own in the world game.

Since then things have changed a fair bit, and today we got a first-hand view of what that change means. Without most of the squad that toured Australia last year, and without a great depth of talent to call on as replacements, Zimbabwe look in a mess, and we beat them today without raising a sweat, even though we were pretty poor.

I cannot put my finger on too many specific incidents that show we were poor — we were just generally sloppy in the field and did not bowl very well. Despite that, we won the match with more than 10 overs to spare.

It may seem I am being unfairly harsh on Zimbabwe: the scorecard suggests that it was a competitive match. But while the home side had the odd player who stood out, the overall standard of its play was low. I lost count of the number of times top order batsmen played and missed, and as I said in the build-up to the match, even a poor side can always scramble to 150 or 180. They got more than that today, but it was mostly because we were rusty and the pitch was easy-paced and offered little help to our bowlers.

One of the reasons for our rustiness was that this was our first serious outing since the end of March. Even the best players need time to get back into the swing of things after a lay-off, and we showed signs of that today. I do not believe it was a lack of intensity on our part. We obviously knew Zimbabwe would not be the best side we had ever faced, but each person in our side has pride in his own performance.

On top of that rustiness, Glenn McGrath may have been suffering a few nerves. Attempting a comeback after almost a year out of the side, and at an age when most fast bowlers are retiring, adds up to a fair amount of pressure. The result was that McGrath had a serious lack of rhythm in his bowling today, especially in his first spell, which was one of the more bizarre pieces of cricket I have seen in the last decade.

I had Michael Kasprowicz and Brad Williams in the side, but I gave McGrath the new ball alongside Jason Gillespie. I wanted to get him involved in the action as quickly as possible when Zimbabwe opted to bat first. But after setting the field and taking my place at second slip alongside Matthew Hayden (first slip) and Adam Gilchrist, I was shocked to see him coming into bowl off six paces.

McGrath has bowled off a short run-up before, most notably in the Champions Trophy in Sri Lanka in 2002, but that run-up was 15 or 20 paces — and he bowled well using it. It turns out this new, much shorter run-up was something he had worked on in the nets, and Gillespie and John Buchanan, maybe trying to make him feel a bit more relaxed after his long lay-off, told him he had good pace and momentum using it. The reality today was that he had neither and it looked awful. Hayden, Gilchrist and I thought the run-up was some sort of joke at first — we really were as amazed as that — and could not understand what was going on as the ball arrived at the other end very gently. That feeling was shared throughout the side. After his first spell I urged him to go back to his old-fashioned longer run, and he did. With that run-up there was at least more pace on the ball as it reached the batsman, but he was still struggling for rhythm.

Maybe the shorter run-up is McGrath's way of trying to ease the strain on his ankle, the problem that has sidelined him for so long. But his approach to the crease clearly still needs plenty of work; that is something I hope we can give him in this series.

Although he was disappointing — and disappointed — there is little chance of McGrath sitting out the last two matches. He needs the match practice and, on top of that, there is no chance of Williams playing again. His thigh-muscle injury was fine today but his back gave him real problems and I had to send him off the field. He has a high pain threshold but was clearly in discomfort, and was fighting for breath at the end of his mark. He wanted to keep bowling, because he has not had many chances to establish himself at the top level, and he probably feels that if he lets someone else take his spot he might not get back in. All the same, there was no way he could continue — if he did, there was every chance he would do further damage to his back. I sent him off for an assessment by Alex Kontouri. We do not have a definitive diagnosis yet, but he will obviously not be fit enough to play again on this trip. There is no point in him sitting around for a week, so we will send him home, where he can get a verdict on the injury and begin his recovery.

Ian Harvey was not fit for today's match but should be fine for Friday; we are also hoping Matthew Hayden will be okay for that match, despite injuring his back in the field today. He was severely handicapped when he went out to bat, and failed to score, but he is a fast healer, as he showed during the one-day series in Sri Lanka. He will do some work with Alex Kontouri, and I expect he will be able to play on Friday.

I managed to score a few runs when we chased down the target, and may have got a hundred if I hadn't lost the strike to Damien Martyn and then fallen to one of the best catches I have ever seen. I reckon I was on about 88, and we needed 40 to win, when Martyn started to play expansively. The strike went in his favour, and suddenly I wanted nine runs to reach three figures with only nine runs left for victory.

I went for broke and smashed a low full toss wide of long-on. The fielder, Vusi Sibanda, ran 10 to 12 metres to his right, threw himself full length and clung on one-handed. For those who remember, it was reminiscent of Adam Dale's famous catch for Queensland in a domestic one-day game in Australia a few years ago, only this one was better, because the ball was travelling harder and flat.

I was disappointed to get out, of course — you always want to get to a landmark, no matter what the game — but my failure to get a hundred today is not something that is going to eat away at me. We won, which is the important thing. However, we must play much better than we did today in the remaining matches in the series.

One point of interest was the numbers of people watching, or rather not watching, the match: the crowd was very small. Before we came to Zimbabwe Darren Lehmann spoke to Andy Flower, the former Zimbabwe captain, and Flower said that one of the reasons we should tour was to give Zimbabweans a chance to watch us. I can only assume that those Zimbabweans who wanted to see us watched the match on TV or listened on the radio, because there were not many at the ground. On the other hand, given the problems this country is having, maybe it is not surprising the crowd was so small — I am sure locals have more important things to think about than cricket.

Wednesday 26 May

Brad Williams returns home for an assessment of the back injury he suffered in yesterday's one-day international in Harare.

Today was a chance for everyone to think about how we played in the first match of the series, and to relax before tomorrow's second meeting with Zimbabwe. I chose to spend it playing golf and it turned out to be a good choice: Damien Martyn and I beat assistant coach Tim Nielsen and selector David Boon in a competitive four-ball.

Martyn cannot grip the golf club quite as well as he used to, thanks to the finger injury he suffered during last year's World Cup: the fracture to his right index finger means it will not bend all the way around the club. However, he showed no sign of any difficulty today and played a solid round. I managed to shoot 70, 2 under par for the course, and our joint effort was too good for Nielsen and Boon.

Most of the rest of the squad stayed in their rooms and read books or watched DVDs; Glenn McGrath and Jason Gillespie went hunting. The results of that trip gave us all a laugh when we met up this evening, as McGrath revealed that all Gillespie had managed to shoot was a dove. Somehow the ideas of going hunting and killing the international sign of peace do not go all that well together — Gillespie was mortified at what he had done.

We had a brief team meeting this evening but it was more of a social gathering than an assessment of what we did on Tuesday and what we need to do tomorrow. Everyone is aware of the need for us to improve, and I will be looking for a sign of that when we take the field. Rather than name an eleven I told everyone to be ready to play, because we will choose the side after we get to the ground and assess the fitness of Ian Harvey and Matthew Hayden.

Thursday 27 May

Second one-day international, Harare: Australia 8–323 (Hayden 87, Lehmann 67) beat Zimbabwe 184 (Taylor 65) by 139 runs.

Today was my 200th one-day international, but apart from reaching that landmark, it is not a match that will linger for a long time in my memory.

It was a poor — and at times extremely boring — game of cricket as we racked up a large score on a very easy-paced pitch and then faced a Zimbabwe batting line-up whose sole aim was to reach a score that was respectable. They did achieve that, thanks to some dogged batting in the top order, but once again the home side's lack of depth was evident: they lost their last seven wickets for just 21 runs.

We used the match to shuffle our batting order around, but that was not a deliberate attempt to criticise the status of the match as a full international or to belittle the opposition. Instead, it was an acknowledgement that on a short tour like this we have to be fair to everyone in the squad and give players the opportunity to perform. It was not as if we sent in bowlers like Glenn McGrath or Jason Gillespie to open the batting; it was more just a shuffling of the available batting resources.

Before our warm-ups for the match I was presented with a

signed shirt to mark my 200th match. It was not an official presentation — that will come if I reach the 300-game mark, something Stephen Waugh did a couple of years ago. On that occasion he received a framed and mounted one-day cap. My presentation today was run by assistant coach Tim Nielsen, who wrote on the shirt: 'Congratulations Ricky Ponting on 200 one-day games from vinonline.co.zx'.

The website address is made up — Vinny is Nielsen's nickname — and reflects one of his activities on this trip: he and Darren Lehmann have been acting as bookmakers for the rest of the squad. We have not been betting on cricket; we speculate on Australian rugby league, rugby union and AFL matches. Nielsen and Lehmann get details of the weekly matches and post them on a whiteboard in our team room at the hotel, together with odds for each match. We then bet on the outcome of those matches and the results are later posted on the board. It is not a contest between us; it is just one way of using our allowances. These are paid in Zimbabwe dollars and we will not be able to change the money when we leave this country — no one wants it, and the money would not buy very much, because the exchange rate is something like 4000 Zimbabwe dollars to one US dollar at the moment.

Matthew Hayden and Ian Harvey were both passed fit to play, and Hayden made a typically well-constructed 87 with the rest of the line-up playing around him. Glenn McGrath got through another eight overs but is still searching for some sort of rhythm, and Darren Lehmann capitalised on some low-quality batting by Zimbabwe's middle and lower order to pick up four very cheap wickets.

The quality of the cricket was a reminder of the problems Zimbabwe are having at the moment, but after the match we got a taste of another side of life here. We all attended a barbecue put on by Kelvin Maughan, the brother of our security officer Darren.

Kelvin Maughan has a large house on an estate that backs onto a golf course; the house also boasts a big backyard and a swimming pool. It was a lovely evening, and as we were joined by Darren's family, who had travelled for several hours from his home in Bulawayo to be with us all, it would have been easy to believe we were enjoying ourselves somewhere in Australia rather than away from home.

Darren's family are obviously deeply concerned about what is happening in this country, but at the moment things are still working out for them. They are good people, so I hope it stays that way.

Friday 28 May

The cricket might not be very good on this tour but I am getting a chance to improve my golf. I had another game today, this time with Damien Martyn against Tim Nielsen and Darren Lehmann, and managed to better my effort of Wednesday, this time shooting a 3 under par round of 69.

I was happy with that but it was not enough to avoid defeat at the hands of Nielsen and Lehmann. They played excellent golf, especially when you bear in mind that we were all using borrowed clubs, so even though we lost I had the consolation of knowing we had been involved in a decent sporting competition. I wish I could say the cricket on this trip has been similarly competitive.

Training today for tomorrow's final match was optional, and one player — Shane Watson — took part. So far he has not been involved in the series but he will definitely get his chance tomorrow; this will be the next step back on the road to a regular place in the side after his long-term injury. He has a great attitude, and if he can introduce consistency to his game and stay fit he could be an important player for Australia for the next decade.

Saturday 29 May

Third one-day international, Harare: Australia 2–199 (Clarke 105 not out) beat Zimbabwe 196 (Chigumbura 77, Gillespie 5–32) by 8 wickets.

Another day, another one-sided game, and mercifully the series is over. There was a personal landmark for us to be pleased about today, though: Michael Clarke made his maiden one-day hundred.

There will be plenty of detractors who will say it has come against a sub-standard side, and that is correct. But the runs still have to be made, and a three-figure score at any level of the game is not to be rubbished. I hope that even though Zimbabwe are not a very good side, today's innings will play an important part in Clarke's development: it should help convince him that he has the ability to make big scores at the highest level. He has never been short of self-belief, but it is one thing to have that and another to put it into action and produce a big score, and that is what he did here.

In some ways Clarke can thank Elton Chigumbura for the chance to score a hundred. We had Zimbabwe over a barrel thanks to some excellent bowling by Jason Gillespie, but then Chigumbura came in and hit the ball very hard, giving the home side a decent total.

There were no wickets for Glenn McGrath, who continues to struggle. It is too early to say he has 'gone' as an international cricketer, because you can never write off a player who has achieved as much as he has. What I can say is that he has been nowhere near his best form on this trip; and that is no surprise considering the amount of time he has been out of the game. He has always needed hard work to achieve his rhythm, and he clearly lacked that rhythm here. On the positive side of the coin, he has returned to his longer run-up and as a result has bowled better than that opening spell in the first match ... though that would not be hard to do.

The match finished early, as we won with almost 20 overs to spare. That gave us the chance to watch some English soccer on the dressing room TV. Most of us have at least a passing interest in the game, because there are quite a few Australians playing over in the UK and there are plenty of matches covered on Fox Sports and SBS back home. Today's match was the play-off for a place in the Premier League, with the winning club expected to get a windfall of around $60 million. That meant there was plenty of passion on show, and we stayed glued to the action as Crystal Palace beat their London rivals, West Ham, 1–0.

We also sang the team song, as we do at the end of every series, but it would be fair to say that it lacked a little bit of passion, reflecting the flat nature of this series. There was, however, a pleasing task to perform while we were in the dressing room: we presented John Buchanan with a World Cup ring. The idea of the ring came from Stephen Waugh, and is based on the way sportsmen in the US receive a ring when they win a major championship. Waugh suggested that Cricket Australia replicate that, and when we won the World Cup in 1999 it gave rings to all the players in the squad.

The coaching staff did not receive them, but when two members of that staff, coach Geoff Marsh and fitness trainer David Mission, left their jobs, the players chipped in to buy them rings to commemorate their role in the success.

After our win in 2003 the players again received the rings — but John Buchanan did not, so again we clubbed together to get him one, and today, after the match, we presented it to him, something he was clearly touched by. There is a school of thought that believes Buchanan has little to do because he is in charge of such a talented group of players, but he has been a crucial part of our success since he joined up in October 1999. His skill is in drawing our attention to small details, what you might call the 'one-percenters' that make the difference between winning and losing, and that is why, in one-day cricket especially, we have won so many close games over the past few years. Buchanan was also responsible for bringing in a specialist fielding coach, Mike Young, before our World Cup win last year, and that was an inspired move. Young, who comes from baseball, played a vital part in our success. That is one example of Buchanan's willingness to go outside cricket to see if we can improve.

Once we finished in the dressing room we headed to the bar of the Harare Sports Club for a function held by the ZCU to thank us for taking part in the tour. It was a low-key event that involved the presentation of a tie to each member of the touring party and a few beers and a chat to the Zimbabwe players and officials.

It is a tough time for Zimbabwe, and not just in a cricketing sense, and I got the impression that they are extremely grateful we made the effort to tour. However, when we will next tour this country is anyone's guess.

Sunday 30 May–Monday 31 May

It would be wrong to say my biggest achievement in the last two weeks has been improving my golf — in that time I also played three times for my country. But if you take away the time I spent on the golf course, I have to admit I travelled home feeling that I had not achieved a great deal during my time in Zimbabwe.

We have fulfilled our cricketing obligations to the ICC by playing the one-day series, but I think we are all delighted the trip is over. The quality of the cricket was poor, and in that sense we felt we would have been better off resting at home before the series against Sri Lanka. That is not to suggest that any of us felt anything other than immense pride in playing for our country; it is just that we did not get any satisfaction from playing such a poor-quality opposition.

Hindsight is a wonderful thing: if we had known the dispute between the players and the ZCU would not be resolved, I think there would have been far more reluctance among the players to tour. And I think Cricket Australia would have pushed the ICC to get the whole tour called off.

We travelled in the hope of playing the best available Zimbabwe side, but the team we faced was nowhere near international standard, and that is not good for cricket at the highest level. If Zimbabwe continues to play international cricket it will cheapen the game: batsmen and bowlers will be scoring runs and taking wickets against players who are not good enough to be playing at that level.

That presents a problem for the future of the game in Zimbabwe. As I said when we came up against Bangladesh last year, players without the required talent will not become good enough by playing 30, 40 or 50 one-day matches or Tests, even if those matches are against the best opposition. Instead they will get beaten time and again, and that is hardly likely to inspire a new generation of Zimbabwe players to take up the game — they will have no role models to look up to. Also, the credibility of the international game will suffer, because one-sided spectacles will turn people off supporting the game.

It really is difficult to see a way forward for Zimbabwe cricket at the moment. The problems here, as in Bangladesh, need to be addressed from the grass roots up, with coaching and development programs, a proper domestic structure and decent facilities. Some of those facilities are in place already, as is some sort of first-class structure. However, the dispute between the ZCU and the leading players is sucking out what little talent remains in the country. And I am sure many in Zimbabwe feel there are more important things to worry about than cricket, especially the economic problems we experienced first-hand.

In the worst-case scenario, given the already crowded schedules, opposition players may opt out of tours to Zimbabwe to rest in preparation for matches against better sides. The alternative is players rewriting the record books via cheap wickets and runs — this is what happened to Sri Lanka on the tour of Zimbabwe that was on when we arrived.

We flew home via Johannesburg and arrived in Sydney on Monday. I had one last task to perform: a media conference at the airport. Luckily, this was nowhere near as testing as the one I faced on my arrival in Harare. I was asked about the state of Zimbabwe cricket.

'It is clear that the ZCU needs to get its affairs in order,' I said. 'Ideally, it first needs to resolve the players' dispute; until that happens, I would favour a total ban on Tests and one-day international cricket.'

My personal view is that Zimbabwe should be dropped into a second tier of teams which would play each other over a prolonged period for the right to have a crack at the bigger cricketing countries.

That way the integrity of the game at the highest level would be protected and there would be an incentive to develop the game in other countries.

I realise that supporting a second tier is a costly business, but the ICC must have money to spare after the success of events like last year's World Cup. It has shown a willingness to explore the idea, with regional competitions involving Namibia, Scotland, Holland, Ireland, Canada and the US starting this year. However, until Bangladesh and Zimbabwe are dropped into that tier, the integrity of elite level cricket will continue to suffer.

But that is for others to resolve. My primary concern has to be Australian cricket and after the events of the past 14 months I think it is safe to say we are definitely still travelling in the right direction. For me it has been an amazing journey. I have assumed the captaincy of the Test side to go with the one-day leadership, we have kept on winning and my own game has gone from strength to strength. Can it get any better? It is tough to see how it can, but that will be my aim and the aim of the rest of the players and support staff. That is the way we will stay on top of the cricketing world.

2003–2004 Statistics

COMPILED BY ROSS DUNDAS

2002–03 WEST INDIES v AUSTRALIA

AUSTRALIAN TEST SQUAD

Stephen Waugh (captain) NSW; Ricky Ponting (vice-captain) Tas; Andrew Bichel Qld; Adam Gilchrist WA; Jason Gillespie SA; Matthew Hayden Qld; Brad Hogg WA; Justin Langer WA; Brett Lee NSW; Martin Love Qld; Darren Lehmann SA; Stuart MacGill NSW; Damien Martyn WA; Glenn McGrath NSW; Ashley Noffke Qld. Damien Martyn withdrew from the tour due to injury and was replaced by Michael Clarke NSW. Jimmy Maher Qld was called to join the tour as a reserve wicket keeper. Brad Williams joined the tour as a cover for Glenn McGrath.

INTERNATIONAL LIMITED OVERS SQUAD

Ricky Ponting (captain) Tas; Adam Gilchrist (vice-captain) WA; Michael Bevan NSW; Andrew Bichel Qld; Jason Gillespie SA; Nathan Hauritz Qld; Ian Harvey Vic; Matthew Hayden Qld; Brad Hogg WA; Brett Lee NSW; Darren Lehmann SA; Jimmy Maher Qld; Damien Martyn WA; Glenn McGrath NSW; Andrew Symonds Qld. Damien Martyn withdrew from the tour due to injury and was replaced by Michael Clarke NSW.

Team Management: John Buchanan (Coach), Steve Bernard (Team Manager), Tim Nielsen (Assistant Coach/Performance Analyst), Errol Alcott (Physiotherapist), Jock Campbell (Physical Performance Manager), Jonathan Rose (Media Manager).

AUSTRALIAN TOUR RESULTS

Test matches – Played 4: Won 3, Lost 1.
First-class matches – Played 6, Won 4, Lost 1, Drew 1.
Wins – West Indies (3), University of West Indies Chancellor's XI.
Losses – West Indies.
Draws – Guyana Board President's XI.
International limited overs – Played 7: Won 4, Lost 3.

CARIB BEER XI v AUSTRALIANS at Everest Cricket Club Ground, Georgetown, April 5, 6, 7, 2003. Match drawn. Australian XI 3 dec 377 (JL Langer 60, ML Hayden 102, ML Love 56, SR Waugh 106*, DS Lehmann 43*; D Mohammad 2/107). Carib Beer XI 132 (IH Jan 42*, CS Baugh 32; JN Gillespie 2/13, AJ Bichel 2/10, SCG MacGill 2/49, GB Hogg 4/23). Australian XI 196 (DS Lehmann 42, ML Love 59; A Sanford 3/28, OAC Banks 3/65, D Mohammad 2/45). Carib Beer XI 6 for 402 (IH Jan 44, DS Smith 37, N Deonarine 141*, CS Baugh 115*; GB Hogg 5/112).

FIRST TEST

WEST INDIES v AUSTRALIA
Bourda, Georgetown. April 10,11,12,13, 2003.
Toss: West Indies. Australia won by nine wickets.

WEST INDIES				
WW Hinds c Langer b Hogg	10		lbw b MacGill	7
DS Smith lbw b Lee	3		c Gilchrist b Gillespie	62
D Ganga b Gillespie	0		c Lee b Lehmann	113
BC Lara (c) lbw b Bichel	26		hit wicket b Hogg	110
MN Samuels c Hayden b Hogg	0		c Ponting b MacGill	7
S Chanderpaul lbw b Bichel	100		c Gilchrist b Gillespie	31
RD Jacobs (+) not out	54	(9)	c Lehmann b MacGill	11
VC Drakes c Gilchrist b Bichel	0	(7)	lbw b Gillespie	14
M Dillon lbw b MacGill	20	(8)	lbw b Gillespie	0
PT Collins st Gilchrist b MacGill	3		not out	1
JJC Lawson b Lee	0		lbw b Gillespie	0
EXTRAS (B 10, LB 2, W 3, NB 6)	21		(B 6, LB 13, W 1, NB 22)	42
TOTAL	237			398

FOW 1st Inns: 9 10 47 47 53 184 184 222 236 237
FOW 2nd Inns: 52 110 295 303 354 382 384 391 397 398

Bowling: First Innings: Lee 10.3–1–41–2, Gillespie 12–3–40–1, Bichel 8–1–55–3, Hogg 8–1–40–2, MacGill 12–2–49–2. Second Innings: MacGill 31–5–140–3, Hogg 15–1–68–1, Lee 14–4–57–0, Gillespie 20.2–5–39–5, Bichel 13–4–40–0, Waugh 8–1–29–0, Lehmann 4–0–6–1.

AUSTRALIA			
JL Langer c Hinds b Drakes	146	not out	78
ML Hayden run out (Drakes)	10	c (sub) Deonarine b Lawson	19
RT Ponting c Samuels b Drakes	117	not out	42
DS Lehmann c (sub) Bernard b Drakes	6		
SR Waugh (c) lbw b Dillon	25		
AC Gilchrist (+) c and b Lawson	77		
GB Hogg lbw b Collins	3		
AJ Bichel c Hinds b Drakes	39		
B Lee c Dillon b Drakes	20		
JN Gillespie b Lawson	7		

AUSTRALIA *continued*			
SCG MacGill not out	4		
EXTRAS (B 18, LB 5, W 2, NB 10)	35	(B 1, LB 2, W 2, NB 3)	8
TOTAL	489		1 for 147

FOW 1st Inns: 37 285 300 319 349 362 447 473 485 489
FOW 2nd Inns: 77

Bowling: First Innings: Dillon 23–1–116–1, Collins 23–1–96–1, Lawson 21–0–111–2, Drakes 26.1–5–93–5, Samuels 21–6–49–0, Ganga 1–0–1–0. Second Innings: Dillon 6–0–21–0, Drakes 8–0–28–0, Collins 6–2–14–0, Lawson 9–2–31–1, Samuels 9.1–1–41–0, Ganga 4–0–9–0.

Umpires: EAR De Silva & RE Koertzen (TV Umpire – EA Nicholls)

SECOND TEST

WEST INDIES v AUSTRALIA
Queen's Park Oval, Port of Spain. April 19, 20, 21, 22, 23, 2003.
Toss: Australia. Australia won by 118 runs.

AUSTRALIA			
JL Langer lbw b Dillon	25	lbw b Drakes	3
ML Hayden lbw b Dillon	30	not out	100
RT Ponting st Baugh b Samuels	206	c Baugh b Dillon	45
DS Lehmann c Baugh b Drakes	160	b Dillon	66
AC Gilchrist (+) not out	101		
GB Hogg not out	17		
SR Waugh (c)			
AJ Bichel			
B Lee			
JN Gillespie			
SCG MacGill			
EXTRAS (B 11, LB 7, W 7, NB 12)	37	(B 12, LB 6, W 1, NB 5)	24
TOTAL	4 dec 576		3 dec 238

FOW 1st Inns: 49 56 371 542
FOW 2nd Inns: 12 118 238

Bowling: First Innings: Dillon 28.5–1–124–2, Collins 25–2–123–0, Drakes 33–3–112–1, Samuels 26–2–111–1, Bernard 11–1–61–0, Sarwan 2–0–7–0, Hinds 7–0–20–0. Second Innings: Dillon 18.2–0–64–2, Drakes 20–4–61–1, Samuels 21–1–65–0, Collins 7–1–30–0.

WEST INDIES			
WW Hinds c Hayden b Lee	20	b MacGill	35
DS Smith c Gilchrist b Gillespie	0	lbw b Gillespie	0
D Ganga c Hayden b Lee	117	c Hayden b Gillespie	2
BC Lara (c) b Hogg	91	c Hayden b MacGill	122
RR Sarwan b Lee	26	c Lehmann b Bichel	34
MN Samuels c Bichel b MacGill	68	lbw b Bichel	1
DE Bernard b Gillespie	7	c Hayden b Bichel	4
CS Baugh (+) hit wicket b MacGill	19	c Langer b Hogg	1
VC Drakes lbw b Lee	24	not out	26
M Dillon lbw b Gillespie	0	c Bichel b Lee	13
PT Collins not out	7	lbw b Gillespie	5
EXTRAS (B 4, LB 15, W 2, NB 8)	29	(B 25, LB 7, W 3, NB 10)	45
TOTAL	408		288

FOW 1st Inns: 4 25 183 258 279 300 367 376 384 408
FOW 2nd Inns: 2 12 107 213 222 228 238 238 270 288

Bowling: First Innings: Lee 23–4–69–4, Gillespie 28–9–50–3, Bichel 12–1–58–0, MacGill 27–4–98–2, Hogg 22–3–98–1, Waugh 7–2–16–0. Second Innings: Lee 19–4–68–1, Gillespie 17.2–3–36–3, Bichel 13–3–21–3, Lehmann 7–0–20–0, MacGill 20–6–53–2, Hogg 13–1–58–1.

Umpires: EAR De Silva & RE Koertzen (TV Umpire – B Doctrove)

UNIVERSITY OF WEST INDIES VICE CHANCELLOR'S XI v AUSTRALIANS at Three Ws Oval, Bridgetown, April 26, 27, 28, 2003. Australians won by six wickets. University of West Indies Vice Chancellor's XI 290 (CH Gayle 129, JAM Haynes 58; GD McGrath 2/41, GB Hogg 3/94, SCG MacGill 5/40). Australian XI 6 dec 358 (JL Langer 96, JP Maher 142, SR Waugh 46; CD Collymore 2/54, CO Obuya 2/77, RL Powell 2/66). University of West Indies Vice Chancellor's XI 162 (PA Wallace 53; SCG MacGill 5/45, GB Hogg 2/34). Australian XI 4 for 95 (MJ Clarke 47).

THIRD TEST

WEST INDIES v AUSTRALIA

Kensington Oval, Bridgetown. May 1, 2, 3, 4, 5, 2003.
Toss: West Indies. Australia won by nine wickets.

AUSTRALIA				
JL Langer c Chanderpaul b Banks	78		lbw b Lawson	0
ML Hayden c Gayle b Drakes	27		not out	2
RT Ponting run out (Best/Baugh)	113			
DS Lehmann lbw b Drakes	96	(3)	not out	4
SR Waugh (c) b Lawson	115			
AC Gilchrist (+) c Smith b Banks	65			
AJ Bichel c Lara b Banks	71			
B Lee b Lawson	11			
JN Gillespie not out	18			
SCG MacGill b Lawson	0			
GD McGrath				
EXTRAS (B 3, LB 3, W 3, NB 2)	11		(B 2)	2
TOTAL	9 dec 605			1 for 8

FOW 1st Inns: 43 151 292 331 444 568 580 605 605
FOW 2nd Inns: 0

Bowling: First Innings: Lawson 32.3–2–131–3, Best 20–1–99–0, Drakes 30–2–85–2, Banks 40–2–204–3, Gayle 31–5–79–0, Sarwan 1–0–1–0. Second Innings: Lawson 1–0–2–1, Banks 1–0–2–0, Gayle 0.3–0–2–0.

WEST INDIES				
CH Gayle b Gillespie	71		st Gilchrist b MacGill	56
DS Smith c Gilchrist b Gillespie	59		lbw b Lee	5
D Ganga c Bichel b Lehmann	26		lbw b Lee	6
RR Sarwan c Gilchrist b Lee	40		lbw b MacGill	58
S Chanderpaul c Lee b MacGill	0	(6)	c Gilchrist b Gillespie	21
OAC Banks c Ponting b Gillespie	24	(7)	c Hayden b MacGill	32
CS Baugh (+) c Ponting b MacGill	24	(8)	run out (Gillespie/Gilchrist)	18
BC Lara (c) lbw b Bichel	14	(5)	lbw b Bichel	42
VC Drakes c Lee b MacGill	11		b MacGill	0
TL Best not out	20		c Bichel b MacGill	0

WEST INDIES *continued*				
JJC Lawson st Gilchrist b MacGill	1		not out	5
EXTRAS (B 11, LB 16, NB 11)	38		(B 13, LB 25, W 1, NB 2)	41
TOTAL	328			284

FOW 1st Inns: 139 142 205 206 245 245 281 291 324 328
FOW 2nd Inns: 14 31 94 187 195 256 256 261 265 284

Bowling: First Innings: McGrath 18–7–25–0, Gillespie 21–9–31–3, Lee 25–8–77–1, MacGill 39.5–8–107–4, Lehmann 9–2–26–1, Bichel 16–3–35–1. Second Innings: McGrath 18–4–39–0, Gillespie 28–11–37–1, MacGill 36–11–75–5, Lee 15–6–44–2, Bichel 12–2–35–1, Ponting 2–0–6–0, Waugh 4–1–6–0, Lehmann 1–0–4–0.

Umpires: DR Shepherd & S Venkataraghavan (TV Umpire – EA Nicholls)

FOURTH TEST

WEST INDIES v AUSTRALIA
Recreation Ground, St John's. May 9,10,11,12,13, 2003.
Toss: Australia. West Indies won by three wickets

AUSTRALIA				
JL Langer c Banks b Lawson	42		c Lara b Gayle	111
ML Hayden c Drakes b Lawson	14		run out (sub) CS Baugh	177
ML Love b Banks	36	(4)	c (sub) MN Samuels b Banks	2
DS Lehmann c Jacobs b Lawson	7	(5)	b Dillon	14
SR Waugh (c) c Jacobs b Dillon	41	(6)	not out	45
AC Gilchrist (+) c Chanderpaul b Dillon	33	(3)	c (sub) MN Samuels b Banks	6
AJ Bichel c (sub) MN Samuels b Lawson	34		c Smith b Dillon	0
B Lee c Jacobs b Lawson	9		c (sub) SC Joseph b Dillon	18
JN Gillespie c Jacobs b Lawson	6		c Lara b Drakes	5
SCG MacGill c Sarwan b Lawson	2		c Lara b Dillon	0
GD McGrath not out	5		c Ganga b Drakes	14
EXTRAS (B 2, LB 3, W 2, NB 4)	11		(B 4, LB 9, NB 12)	25
TOTAL	240			417

FOW 1st Inns: 27 80 93 128 181 194 224 231 233 240
FOW 2nd Inns: 242 273 285 330 338 343 373 385 388 417

Bowling: First Innings: Dillon 18–2–53–2, Lawson 19.1–3–78–7, Drakes 15–2–42–0, Banks 20–2–62–1. Second Innings: Lawson 6–1–17–0, Dillon 29–3–112–4, Banks 37–5–153–2, Drakes 19–1–92–2, Gayle 13–1–30–1.

WEST INDIES				
CH Gayle b McGrath	0		c Waugh b Lee	19
DS Smith c Gilchrist b Lee	37		c Gilchrist b Gillespie	23
D Ganga c Gilchrist b Bichel	6		lbw b McGrath	8
VC Drakes lbw b Lee	21	(9)	not out	27
BC Lara (c) c Langer b Bichel	68	(4)	b MacGill	60
RR Sarwan c and b Bichel	24	(5)	c and b Lee	105
S Chanderpaul b McGrath	1	(6)	c Gilchrist b Lee	104
RD Jacobs (+) run out (Lee)	26	(7)	c Gilchrist b Lee	0
OAC Banks not out	13	(8)	not out	47
M Dillon b Lee	12			
JJC Lawson c Love b MacGill	14			
EXTRAS (LB 8, W 3, NB 7)	18		(B 9, LB 9, W 1, NB 6)	25
TOTAL	240			7 for 418

FOW 1st Inns: 1 30 73 80 137 140 185 197 224 240
FOW 2nd Inns: 48 50 74 165 288 288 372

Bowling: First Innings: McGrath 17–6–44–2, Gillespie 17–3–56–0, Bichel 14–4–53–3, Lee 15–2–72–3, MacGill 2.3–0–7–1. Second Innings: McGrath 25–10–50–1, Gillespie 25–10–64–1, Lee 23–4–63–4, Bichel 15–3–49–0, MacGill 35.5–8–149–1, Waugh 5–0–25–0.

Umpires: DR Shepherd & S Venkataraghavan (TV Umpire – B Doctrove)

INTERNATIONAL LIMITED OVERS GAME 1

WEST INDIES v AUSTRALIA
Sabina Park, Kingston. May 17, 2003.
Toss: West Indies. Australia won by 2 runs (D/L method).

AUSTRALIA	
AC Gilchrist (+) c Samuels b Dillon	21
ML Hayden c Gayle b Dillon	7
RT Ponting (c) c Collymore b Gayle	59
DS Lehmann c Powell b Banks	55
A Symonds c Dillon b Banks	18
MG Bevan not out	43
IJ Harvey not out	48
AJ Bichel	
B Lee	
GD McGrath	
GB Hogg	
EXTRAS (LB 6, W 9, NB 4)	19
TOTAL	5 for 270

FOW: 35 47 133 169 183

Bowling: Dillon 9–1–53–2, Drakes 8–0–50–0, Collymore 10–0–49–0, Samuels 6–0–26–0, Gayle 9–0–42–1, Banks 8–0–44–2.

WEST INDIES	
CH Gayle c Hogg b Lee	37
RL Powell c Gilchrist b Lee	37
DS Smith c Gilchrist b Harvey	26
BC Lara (c) c Gilchrist b Harvey	23
RR Sarwan not out	47
MN Samuels c Symonds b Harvey	2
OAC Banks run out (Hayden)	12
CS Baugh (+) b McGrath	7
VC Drakes b Symonds	1
M Dillon not out	8
CD Collymore	
EXTRAS (LB 2, W 1, NB 2)	5
TOTAL	8 for 205

FOW: 75 75 124 133 137 161 176 185

Bowling: McGrath 8–1–34–1, Lee 8–2–52–2, Bichel 7–1–38–0, Harvey 7–0–37–3, Symonds 7–0–42–1.

Umpires: B Doctrove & DR Shepherd (TV Umpire – EA Nicholls)

INTERNATIONAL LIMITED OVERS GAME 2

WEST INDIES v AUSTRALIA
Sabina Park, Kingston. May 18, 2003.
Toss: West Indies. Australia won by eight wickets.

WEST INDIES	
CH Gayle c Gilchrist b Bichel	28
DS Smith c and b Lee	1
MN Samuels c Gilchrist b McGrath	6
BC Lara (c) c Gilchrist b Bichel	5
RR Sarwan c Hayden b Gillespie	14
RL Powell c McGrath b Hogg	32
OAC Banks c Gilchrist b Lee	29
CS Baugh (+) b McGrath	29
VC Drakes b McGrath	1
M Dillon not out	3
CD Collymore lbw b McGrath	0
EXTRAS (B 2, LB 4, W 9)	15
TOTAL	163

FOW: 4 21 43 50 75 103 157 160 163 163

Bowling: McGrath 10–2–31–4, Lee 7–0–22–2, Gillespie 9–0–28–1, Bichel 5–0–27–2, Hogg 10–3–27–1, Symonds 8–0–22–0.

AUSTRALIA	
AC Gilchrist (+) c Samuels b Collymore	27
ML Hayden c Collymore b Banks	51
RT Ponting (c) not out	57
A Symonds not out	17
MG Bevan	
GB Hogg	
AJ Bichel	
B Lee	
JP Maher	
JN Gillespie	
GD McGrath	
EXTRAS (LB 10, W 3, NB 1)	14
TOTAL	2 for 166

FOW: 50 120

Bowling: Dillon 10–1–45–0, Collymore 8.1–1–35–1, Banks 10–0–42–1, Drakes 1–0–6–0, Gayle 6–0–28–0.

Umpires: EA Nicholls & DR Shepherd (TV Umpire – B Doctrove)

INTERNATIONAL LIMITED OVERS GAME 3

WEST INDIES v AUSTRALIA
Beausejour Stadium, Gros Islet. May 21, 2003.
Toss: West Indies. Australia won by 25 runs.

AUSTRALIA	
JP Maher (+) c Smith b Banks	17
ML Hayden c Baugh b Dillon	20
RT Ponting (c) run out (Collymore)	32
A Symonds b Gayle	75
MJ Clarke not out	75
MG Bevan not out	32
GB Hogg	
AJ Bichel	
NM Hauritz	
JN Gillespie	
GD McGrath	
EXTRAS (LB 2, W 2, NB 3)	7
TOTAL	4 for 258

FOW: 25 48 79 178

Bowling: Dillon 10–1–36–1, Collymore 10–0–52–0, Banks 7–0–38–1, Hinds 7–0–42–0, Gayle 10–0–50–1, Samuels 6–0–38–0.

WEST INDIES	
CH Gayle c Clarke b Hauritz	43
DS Smith c Maher b McGrath	9
RR Sarwan c Gillespie b Hauritz	15
BC Lara (c) b Bichel	4
WW Hinds run out (Bevan/Maher)	42
MN Samuels c Clarke b Gillespie	37
RL Powell c Clarke b Gillespie	26
OAC Banks run out (Hogg)	3
CS Baugh (+) not out	24
M Dillon run out (Symonds)	4
CD Collymore not out	8
EXTRAS (LB 3, W 14, NB 1)	18
TOTAL	9 for 233

FOW: 20 67 70 85 150 181 181 186 197

Bowling: McGrath 10–1–35–1, Gillespie 10–1–48–2, Bichel 10–1–44–1, Hauritz 10–1–50–2, Hogg 10–0–53–0.

Umpires: B Doctrove & DR Shepherd (TV Umpire – EA Nicholls)

INTERNATIONAL LIMITED OVERS GAME 4

WEST INDIES v AUSTRALIA
Queen's Park Oval, Port of Spain. May 24, 2003.
Toss: Australia. Australia won by 67 runs.

AUSTRALIA	
AC Gilchrist (+) b Hurley	84
ML Hayden c Hurley b Drakes	44
RT Ponting (c) c Hurley b Powell	38
A Symonds b Collymore	24
MJ Clarke not out	55
MG Bevan c Lara b Drakes	21
GB Hogg	
IJ Harvey	
B Lee	
JN Gillespie	
GD McGrath	
EXTRAS (LB 9, W 9, NB 2)	20
TOTAL	5 for 286

FOW: 78 148 200 223 286

Bowling: Dillon 10–0–46–0, Collymore 9–1–58–1, Gayle 10–0–52–0, Hurley 10–0–57–1, Drakes 10–0–62–2, Powell 1–0–2–1.

WEST INDIES	
CH Gayle lbw b Harvey	84
RL Powell c Ponting b Gillespie	8
WW Hinds lbw b Lee	3
RR Sarwan lbw b McGrath	16
BC Lara (c) c Hayden b Symonds	40
MN Samuels c Hogg b Harvey	27
RD Jacobs (+) run out (Lee)	13
RO Hurley run out (Symonds/Gilchrist)	0
VC Drakes lbw b Gillespie	9
M Dillon not out	0
CD Collymore run out (Ponting/Harvey)	2
EXTRAS (B 4, LB 4, W 8, NB 1)	17
TOTAL	219

FOW: 20 33 77 146 174 197 201 217 217 219

Bowling: Lee 8–1–30–1, Gillespie 8–0–30–2, McGrath 7–0–21–1, Hogg 9–1–41–0, Harvey 9.3–0–58–2, Symonds 4–0–31–1.

Umpires: RE Koertzen & EA Nicholls (TV Umpire – B Doctrove)

INTERNATIONAL LIMITED OVERS GAME 5

WEST INDIES v AUSTRALIA
Queen's Park Oval, Port of Spain. May 25, 2003.
Toss: West Indies. West Indies won by 39 runs.

WEST INDIES	
CH Gayle lbw b Lee	5
WW Hinds c Gilchrist b Bichel	79
BC Lara (c) c Gilchrist b Bichel	80
RR Sarwan c Gilchrist b Lee	32
MN Samuels lbw b Lee	42
RL Powell not out	20
RD Jacobs (+) not out	7
RO Hurley	
DE Bernard	
M Dillon	
CD Collymore	
EXTRAS (B 1, LB 11, W 11, NB 2)	25
TOTAL	5 for 290

FOW: 5 183 192 263 264

Bowling: McGrath 10–0–46–0, Lee 10–2–56–3, Harvey 10–1–46–0, Bichel 10–0–67–2, Hauritz 6–0–38–0, Clarke 4–0–25–0.

AUSTRALIA	
AC Gilchrist (+) c Hinds b Collymore	11
JP Maher c Hurley b Collymore	21
RT Ponting (c) c Hinds b Dillon	10
A Symonds b Samuels	77
MJ Clarke c Lara b Dillon	39
MG Bevan c Samuels b Dillon	31
IJ Harvey b Gayle	2
AJ Bichel b Samuels	7
B Lee c Gayle b Sarwan	6
NM Hauritz not out	20
GD McGrath not out	3
EXTRAS (LB 15, W 8, NB 1)	24
TOTAL	9 for 251

FOW: 18 43 57 149 182 189 202 219 229

Bowling: Collymore 8–0–25–2, Dillon 9–0–40–3, Hinds 1–0–3–0, Powell 1–0–8–0, Gayle 10–0–44–1, Sarwan 10–0–53–1, Samuels 10–0–48–2, Lara 1–0–15–0.

Umpires: B Doctrove & RE Koertzen (TV Umpire – EA Nicholls)

INTERNATIONAL LIMITED OVERS GAME 6

WEST INDIES v AUSTRALIA
Queen's Park, St George's. May 30, 2003.
Toss: Australia. West Indies won by three wickets.

AUSTRALIA	
AC Gilchrist (+) c Lara b Samuels	64
ML Hayden c Hinds b Collymore	29
RT Ponting (c) run out (Lara/Samuels)	2
A Symonds c Lara b Sarwan	16
DS Lehmann c and b Gayle	43
JP Maher c and b Gayle	19
GB Hogg c Gayle b Samuels	0
AJ Bichel c Lara b Gayle	41
B Lee c Powell b Collymore	14
NM Hauritz run out (Bernard)	2
JN Gillespie not out	1
EXTRAS (LB 8, W 10, NB 3)	21
TOTAL	252

FOW: 90 105 105 149 177 178 193 243 250 252

Bowling: Collymore 10–1–46–2, Dillon 8–0–52–0, Samuels 10–1–39–2, Drakes 6–0–21–0, Bernard 2–0–17–0, Sarwan 4–0–32–1, Gayle 10–1–37–3.

WEST INDIES	
CH Gayle c Gilchrist b Lee	18
WW Hinds not out	125
BC Lara (c) c and b Symonds	15
RR Sarwan c Symonds b Lee	50
MN Samuels b Lee	0
RL Powell c and b Lehmann	1
RD Jacobs (+) c Maher b Bichel	8
DE Bernard lbw b Gillespie	7
VC Drakes not out	0
M Dillon	
CD Collymore	
EXTRAS (B 4, LB 15, W 8, NB 3)	30
TOTAL	7 for 254

FOW: 23 67 181 181 193 213 244

Bowling: Lee 9.4–2–50–3, Gillespie 9–2–33–1, Bichel 10–0–52–1, Symonds 4–0–19–1, Hogg 10–1–35–0, Hauritz 5–0–35–0, Lehmann 1–0–11–1.

Umpires: RE Koertzen & EA Nicholls (TV Umpire – BEW Morgan)

INTERNATIONAL LIMITED OVERS GAME 7

WEST INDIES v AUSTRALIA
Queen's Park, St George's. June 1, 2003.
Toss: Australia. West Indies won by nine wickets.

AUSTRALIA	
AC Gilchrist (+) b Samuels	5
ML Hayden c Bernard b Dillon	8
RT Ponting (c) not out	2
DS Lehmann c Samuels b Gayle	107
A Symonds c Hinds b Gayle	48
MJ Clarke st Jacobs b Gayle	1
IJ Harvey run out (Lara)	4
GB Hogg b Gayle	53
B Lee c Samuels b Gayle	4
JN Gillespie not out	0
GD McGrath	
EXTRAS (LB 3, W 10, NB 2)	15
TOTAL	8 for 247

FOW: 17 18 125 127 133 228 246 246

Bowling: Samuels 7–0–39–1, Dillon 10–0–46–1, Collymore 9–0–39–0, Sarwan 4–1–22–0, Drakes 10–0–52–0, Gayle 10–0–46–5.

WEST INDIES	
CH Gayle b Symonds	60
WW Hinds not out	103
BC Lara (c) not out	75
RR Sarwan	
MN Samuels	
RL Powell	
RD Jacobs (+)	
DE Bernard	
VC Drakes	
M Dillon	
CD Collymore	
EXTRAS (LB 2, W 7, NB 2)	11
TOTAL	1 for 249

FOW: 116

Bowling: Lee 6–0–36–0, Gillespie 10–1–41–0, McGrath 6–0–29–0, Symonds 5–0–36–1, Hogg 10–0–47–0, Harvey 5–0–31–0, Lehmann 1.3–0–27–0.

Umpires: B Doctrove & RE Koertzen (TV Umpire – EA Nicholls)

2002–03 WEST INDIES–AUSTRALIA TEST AVERAGES

Batting	Team	M	Inn	NO	Runs	HS	50	100	Avrge	Ct/St
RT Ponting	Aus	3	5	1	523	206	–	3	130.75	3
SR Waugh	Aus	4	4	1	226	115	–	1	75.33	1
AC Gilchrist	Aus	4	5	1	282	101*	2	1	70.50	12/3
JL Langer	Aus	4	8	1	483	146	2	2	69.00	3
BC Lara	WI	4	8	–	533	122	3	2	66.63	4
ML Hayden	Aus	4	8	2	379	177	–	2	63.17	7
DS Lehmann	Aus	4	7	1	353	160	2	1	58.83	2
OAC Banks	WI	2	4	2	116	47*	–	–	58.00	1
RR Sarwan	WI	3	6	–	287	105	1	1	47.83	1
S Chanderpaul	WI	3	6	–	257	104	–	2	42.83	2
CH Gayle	WI	2	4	–	146	71	2	–	36.50	1
AJ Bichel	Aus	4	4	–	144	71	1	–	36.00	5
D Ganga	WI	4	8	–	278	117	–	2	34.75	1
RD Jacobs	WI	2	4	1	91	54*	1	–	30.33	4
DS Smith	WI	4	8	–	189	62	2	–	23.63	2
VC Drakes	WI	4	8	2	123	27*	–	–	20.50	1
GB Hogg	Aus	2	2	1	20	17*	–	–	20.00	–
TL Best	WI	1	2	1	20	20*	–	–	20.00	–
MN Samuels	WI	2	4	–	76	68	1	–	19.00	1
GD McGrath	Aus	2	2	1	19	14	–	–	19.00	–
ML Love	Aus	1	2	–	38	36	–	–	19.00	1
WW Hinds	WI	2	4	–	72	35	–	–	18.00	2
CS Baugh	WI	2	4	–	62	24	–	–	15.50	2/1
B Lee	Aus	4	4	–	58	20	–	–	14.50	4
JN Gillespie	Aus	4	4	1	36	18*	–	–	12.00	–
M Dillon	WI	3	5	–	45	20	–	–	9.00	1
PT Collins	WI	2	4	2	16	7*	–	–	8.00	–
DE Bernard	WI	1	2	–	11	7	–	–	5.50	–
JJC Lawson	WI	3	5	1	20	14	–	–	5.00	1
SCG MacGill	Aus	4	4	1	6	4*	–	–	2.00	–

Bowling	Team	Overs	Mds	Runs	Wkts	Avrge	5wi	10wm	Best
JN Gillespie	Aus	168.4	53	353	17	20.76	1	–	5/39
JJC Lawson	WI	88.4	8	370	14	26.43	1	–	7/78
DS Lehmann	Aus	21.0	2	56	2	28.00	–	–	1/6
B Lee	Aus	144.3	33	491	17	28.88	–	–	4/63
AJ Bichel	Aus	103.0	21	346	11	31.45	–	–	3/21
SCG MacGill	Aus	204.1	44	678	20	33.90	1	–	5/75
M Dillon	WI	123.1	7	490	11	44.55	–	–	4/112
VC Drakes	WI	151.1	17	513	11	46.64	1	–	5/93
GD McGrath	Aus	78.0	27	158	3	52.67	–	–	2/44
GB Hogg	Aus	58.0	6	264	5	52.80	–	–	2/40
OAC Banks	WI	98.0	9	421	6	70.17	–	–	3/204
CH Gayle	WI	44.3	6	111	1	111.00	–	–	1/30
PT Collins	WI	61.0	6	263	1	263.00	–	–	1/96
MN Samuels	WI	77.1	10	266	1	266.00	–	–	1/111
DE Bernard	WI	11.0	1	61	0	–	–	–	–
TL Best	WI	20.0	1	99	0	–	–	–	–
D Ganga	WI	5.0	–	10	0	–	–	–	–
WW Hinds	WI	7.0	–	20	0	–	–	–	–
RT Ponting	Aus	2.0	–	6	0	–	–	–	–
RR Sarwan	WI	3.0	–	8	0	–	–	–	–
SR Waugh	Aus	24.0	4	76	0	–	–	–	–

2002–03 WEST INDIES–AUSTRALIA INTERNATIONAL LIMITED OVERS

Batting	Team	M	Inn	NO	Runs	HS	50	100	Avrge	Ct/St	Stk–Rt
WW Hinds	WI	5	5	2	352	125*	1	2	117.33	4	79.10
CH Gayle	WI	7	7	–	275	84	2	–	39.29	5	77.03
A Symonds	Aus	7	7	1	275	77	2	–	45.83	3	77.90
BC Lara	WI	7	7	1	242	80	2	–	40.33	5	82.31
AC Gilchrist	Aus	6	6	–	212	84	2	–	35.33	11	80.92
DS Lehmann	Aus	3	3	–	205	107	1	1	68.33	1	82.66
RT Ponting	Aus	7	7	2	200	59	2	–	40.00	1	79.37
RR Sarwan	WI	7	6	1	174	50	1	–	34.80	–	78.38
MJ Clarke	Aus	4	4	2	170	75*	2	–	85.00	3	86.29
ML Hayden	Aus	6	6	–	159	51	1	–	26.50	2	69.13
MG Bevan	Aus	5	4	2	127	43*	–	–	63.50	–	87.59
RL Powell	WI	7	6	1	124	37	–	–	24.80	2	99.20
MN Samuels	WI	7	6	–	114	42	–	–	19.00	5	72.61
CS Baugh	WI	3	3	1	60	29	–	–	30.00	1	58.25
JP Maher	Aus	4	3	–	57	21	–	–	19.00	2	50.44
IJ Harvey	Aus	4	3	1	54	48*	–	–	27.00	–	114.89
GB Hogg	Aus	6	2	–	53	53	1	–	26.50	2	88.33
AJ Bichel	Aus	5	2	–	48	41	–	–	24.00	–	97.96
OAC Banks	WI	3	3	–	44	29	–	–	14.67	–	45.83
DS Smith	WI	3	3	–	36	26	–	–	12.00	1	65.45
RD Jacobs	WI	4	3	1	28	13	–	–	14.00	–/1	80.00
B Lee	Aus	6	3	–	24	14	–	–	8.00	1	53.33
NM Hauritz	Aus	3	2	1	22	20*	–	–	22.00	–	122.22
M Dillon	WI	7	4	3	15	8*	–	–	15.00	1	125.00
VC Drakes	WI	5	4	1	11	9	–	–	3.67	–	64.71
CD Collymore	WI	7	3	1	10	8*	–	–	5.00	2	43.48
DE Bernard	WI	3	1	–	7	7	–	–	7.00	1	63.64
GD McGrath	Aus	6	1	1	3	3*	–	–	–	1	60.00
JN Gillespie	Aus	5	2	2	1	1*	–	–	–	1	90.91
RO Hurley	WI	2	1	–	0	0	–	–	0.00	3	0.00

Bowling	Team	Overs	Mds	Runs	Wkts	Avrge	5wi	Best	RPO
CH Gayle	WI	65.0	1	299	11	27.18	1	5/46	4.60
B Lee	Aus	48.4	7	246	11	22.36	0	3/50	5.05
M Dillon	WI	66.0	3	318	7	45.43	0	3/40	4.82
GD McGrath	Aus	51.0	4	196	7	28.00	0	4/31	3.84
AJ Bichel	Aus	42.0	2	228	6	38.00	0	2/27	5.43
CD Collymore	WI	64.1	3	304	6	50.67	0	2/25	4.74
JN Gillespie	Aus	46.0	4	180	6	30.00	0	2/30	3.91
IJ Harvey	Aus	31.3	1	172	5	34.40	0	3/37	5.46
MN Samuels	WI	39.0	1	190	5	38.00	0	2/39	4.87
OAC Banks	WI	25.0	0	124	4	31.00	0	2/44	4.96
A Symonds	Aus	28.0	0	150	4	37.50	0	1/19	5.36
VC Drakes	WI	35.0	0	191	2	95.50	0	2/62	5.46
NM Hauritz	Aus	21.0	1	123	2	61.50	0	2/50	5.86
RR Sarwan	WI	18.0	1	107	2	53.50	0	1/32	5.94
GB Hogg	Aus	49.0	5	203	1	203.00	0	1/27	4.14
RO Hurley	WI	10.0	0	57	1	57.00	0	1/57	5.70
DS Lehmann	Aus	2.3	0	38	1	38.00	0	1/11	15.20
RL Powell	WI	2.0	0	10	1	10.00	0	1/2	5.00
DE Bernard	WI	2.0	0	17	0	–	0	–	8.50
MJ Clarke	Aus	4.0	0	25	0	–	0	–	6.25
WW Hinds	WI	8.0	0	45	0	–	0	–	5.63
BC Lara	WI	1.0	0	15	0	–	0	–	15.00

2003–04 AUSTRALIA v BANGLADESH

TOURING PARTY

Khaled Mahmud (captain), Al Sahariar Rokon, Alok Kapali, Anwar Hossain, Habib-ul-Bashar, Hasib-ul-Hassan, Hannan Sarkar, Javed Omar, Khaled Mashud, Manjural Islam, Mashrafe Bin Mortaza, Mohammad Ashraful, Mohammad Rafiq, Sanwar Hossain, Tapash Baisya, Tareq Aziz, Tushar Imran. Coach: DF Whatmore.

QUEENSLAND ACADEMY OF SPORT INVITATION v BANGLADESHIS at Allan Border Field, Albion, June 27, 28, 29, 2003. Queensland Academy of Sport Invitation won by 29 runs. Queensland Academy of Sport Invitation 201 (LA Carseldine 92, JR Hopes 53; Tapash Baisya 3/33, Khaled Mahmud 2/34). Bangladeshis 9 dec 203 (Mohammad Ashraful 39, Alok Kapali 55, Khaled Mashud 38; DR MacKenzie 2/37, JR Hopes 4/35). Queensland Academy of Sport Invitation 176 (DM Payne 52, LA Carseldine 31*; Manjural Islam 2/37, Alok Kapali 4/27, Anwar Hossain 3/37). Bangladeshis 145 (Hannan Sarkar 33, Habib-ul-Bashar 33; JR Hopes 2/25, DR MacKenzie 3/28, CP Simpson 2/15).

AUSTRALIAN CRICKET ACADEMY v BANGLADESHIS at Allan Border Field, Albion, July 3, 4, 5, 2003. Bangladeshis won by two wickets. Australian Cricket Academy 3 dec 258 (ML Innes 128*, RJG Lockyear 90). Bangladeshis 7 dec 232 (Javed Omar 59, Habib-ul-Bashar 99; AJ Nye 2/40, CJ Ferguson 2/5). Australian Cricket Academy 4 dec 203 (AJ Nye 89*, CJ Ferguson 48*; Mashrafe Bin Mortaza 2/31). Bangladeshis 8 for 232 (Mohammad Ashraful 61, Alok Kapali 44; MF Cleary 2/45, PC Worthington 3/31).

NORTHERN TERRITORY CHIEF MINISTER'S XI v BANGLADESHIS at Marrara Cricket Ground, Darwin, July 10, 11, 12, 13, 2003. Bangladeshis won by two wickets. Northern Territory Chief Minister's XI 189 (MJ Clarke 79; Manjural Islam 2/23, Khaled Mahmud 3/43, Mashrafe Bin Mortaza 3/28). Bangladeshis 139 (Hannan Sarkar 34; BJ Hatton 2/20, NM Hauritz 2/37). Northern Territory Chief Minister's XI 136 (KE Vowles 34; Manjural Islam 2/23, Tapash Baisya 3/19, Mohammad Ashraful 2/21). Bangladeshis 8 for 187 (Javed Omar 44, Al Sahariar Rokon 41; A McAdam 2/30, NM Hauritz 2/48).

FIRST TEST

AUSTRALIA v BANGLADESH
Marrara Cricket Ground, Darwin. July 18, 19, 20, 2003.
Toss: Australia. Australia won by an innings and 132 runs.

BANGLADESH				
Hannan Sarkar lbw b McGrath	0		c Gilchrist b Gillespie	35
Javed Omar c Gilchrist b Gillespie	5		lbw b McGrath	5
Habib-ul-Bashar b Lee	16		b MacGill	54
Mohammad Ashraful c Gillespie b McGrath	23		c Gilchrist b Lee	7
Al Sahariar Rokon b Lee	0		c and b MacGill	36
Alok Kapali lbw b MacGill	0		lbw b MacGill	0
Khaled Mashud (+) lbw b McGrath	11		c Gilchrist b MacGill	6
Khaled Mahmud (c) c Gilchrist b MacGill	21		b Gillespie	5
Mashrafe Bin Mortaza c Gilchrist b Gillespie	3	(10)	run out (Lehmann)	15
Tapash Baisya not out	2	(9)	lbw b MacGill	4
Manjural Islam c Langer b Lee	1		not out	0
EXTRAS (B 1, LB 5, W 6, NB 3)	15		(LB 6, W 2, NB 3)	11
TOTAL	97			178

FOW 1st Inns: 4 26 36 39 40 60 87 91 94 97
FOW 2nd Inns: 8 89 112 112 112 122 143 152 171 178

Bowling: First Innings: McGrath 13–6–20–3, Gillespie 8–1–27–2, Lee 8.2–2–23–3, MacGill 13–4–21–2. Second Innings: McGrath 10–0–25–1, Gillespie 16–3–48–2, Lee 12–5–34–1, MacGill 13.1–1–65–5.

AUSTRALIA	
JL Langer lbw b Alok Kapali	71
ML Hayden b Mashrafe Bin Mortaza	11
RT Ponting c Javed Omar b Tapash Baisya	10
DS Lehmann c Javed Omar b Mashrafe Bin Mortaza	110
SR Waugh (c) not out	100
ML Love b Mashrafe Bin Mortaza	0
AC Gilchrist (+) b Manjural Islam	43

AUSTRALIA *continued*	
B Lee run out (Tapash Baisya)	23
JN Gillespie not out	16
SCG MacGill	
GD McGrath	
EXTRAS (B 5, LB 8, W 7, NB 3)	23
TOTAL	7 dec 407

FOW 1st Inns: 13 43 184 243 244 313 377

Bowling: First Innings: Manjural Islam 24–4–78–1, Mashrafe Bin Mortaza 23–7–74–3, Tapash Baisya 21.5–4–69–1, Khaled Mahmud 28–2–98–0, Alok Kapali 18–2–65–1, Mohammad Ashraful 2–0–9–0, Habib-ul-Bashar 1–0–1–0.

Umpires: RE Koertzen & DR Shepherd (TV Umpire – SJA Taufel)

SECOND TEST

AUSTRALIA v BANGLADESH

Bundaberg Rum Stadium, Cairns. July 25, 26, 27, 28, 2003.
Toss: Australia. Australia won by an innings and 98 runs.

BANGLADESH			
Hannan Sarkar lbw b MacGill	76	c Hayden b MacGill	55
Javed Omar c Gilchrist b Lee	26	lbw b Gillespie	8
Habib-ul-Bashar c and b MacGill	46	c Langer b Lee	25
Mohammad Ashraful c Gilchrist b Gillespie	0	c Ponting b MacGill	0
Sanwar Hossain b MacGill	46	c Ponting b MacGill	16
Alok Kapali c Love b MacGill	5	c Langer b MacGill	17
Khaled Mashud (+) c Love b Gillespie	44	lbw b Gillespie	14
Khaled Mahmud (c) lbw b MacGill	0	c Lee b MacGill	17
Tapash Baisya c Gilchrist b McGrath	25	lbw b Gillespie	0
Mashrafe Bin Mortaza c Lee b Gillespie	8	not out	3
Anwar Hossain Monir not out	0	b Gillespie	4
EXTRAS (LB 8, NB 11)	19	(LB 2, NB 2)	4
TOTAL	295		163

FOW 1st Inns: 47 155 156 156 170 230 230 281 295 295
FOW 2nd Inns: 12 87 90 90 123 136 156 156 156 163

Bowling: First Innings: McGrath 17.1–2–57–1, Gillespie 25–7–57–3, Lee 18–1–88–1, MacGill 24–9–77–5, Waugh 5–3–4–0, Lehmann 3–1–4–0. Second Innings: McGrath 15–9–22–0, Gillespie 12.4–3–38–4, MacGill 20–3–56–5, Lee 11–2–45–1.

AUSTRALIA	
JL Langer c Javed Omar b Mashrafe Bin Mortaza	1
ML Hayden b Sanwar Hossain	50
RT Ponting c Mohammad Ashraful b Sanwar Hossain	59
DS Lehmann c Mohammad Ashraful b Tapash Baisya	177
SR Waugh (c) not out	156
ML Love not out	100
AC Gilchrist (+)	
B Lee	
JN Gillespie	
SCG MacGill	
GD McGrath	
EXTRAS (LB 11, W 1, NB 1)	13
TOTAL	4 dec 556

FOW 1st Inns: 14 105 132 382

Bowling: First Innings: Mashrafe Bin Mortaza 25–7–60–1, Tapash Baisya 26–5–96–1, Anwar Hossain Monir 21–4–95–0, Khaled Mahmud 19–3–75–0, Sanwar Hossain 30–2–128–2, Alok Kapali 14.2–0–69–0, Mohammad Ashraful 4–0–22–0.

Umpires: RE Koertzen & DR Shepherd (TV Umpire – SJ Davis)

QUEENSLAND ACADEMY OF SPORT v BANGLADESHIS at Technical and Further Education Ground, Innisfail, July 31, 2003. Bangladeshis won by four wickets. Queensland Academy of Sport 7 for 175 (CA Philipson 67, CD Hartley 41*; Hasib-ul-Hassan 3/39, Khaled Mahmud 2/33). Bangladeshis 6 for 176 (Hannan Sarkar 35, Alok Kapali 36, Khaled Mashud 37*; CP Simpson 2/28).

INTERNATIONAL LIMITED OVERS GAME 1

AUSTRALIA v BANGLADESH
Bundaberg Rum Stadium, Cairns. August 2, 2003.
Toss: Australia. Australia won by eight wickets.

BANGLADESH	
Hannan Sarkar run out (Martyn/Hogg)	1
Al Sahariar Rokon c Hayden b Lee	8
Habib-ul-Bashar c Gilchrist b Lee	0
Alok Kapali b Lee	0
Sanwar Hossain c Gilchrist b Lee	7
Tushar Imran c Ponting b Gillespie	28
Khaled Mashud (+) lbw b Gillespie	18
Khaled Mahmud (c) not out	25
Mohammad Rafiq c Symonds b Gillespie	3
Hasib-ul-Hassan c Gilchrist b Bichel	6
Mashrafe Bin Mortaza c Gilchrist b Bichel	0
EXTRAS (LB 1, W 5, NB 3)	9
TOTAL	105

FOW: 2 9 14 19 33 66 76 80 105 105

Bowling: Gillespie 10–3–23–3, Lee 8–1–25–4, Bichel 5–0–24–2, Hogg 10–0–27–0, Symonds 1–0–5–0.

AUSTRALIA	
AC Gilchrist (+) c Hannan Sarkar b Mashrafe Bin Mortaza	18
ML Hayden not out	46
RT Ponting (c) b Mohammad Rafiq	29
DR Martyn not out	0
DS Lehmann	
MG Bevan	
A Symonds	
GB Hogg	
B Lee	
JN Gillespie	
AJ Bichel	
EXTRAS (W 6, NB 8)	14
TOTAL	2 for 107

FOW: 29 107

Bowling: Mashrafe Bin Mortaza 7–0–40–1, Hasib-ul-Hassan 5–0–31–0, Khaled Mahmud 5.3–0–29–0, Mohammad Rafiq 5–2–7–1.

Umpires: DR Shepherd & SJA Taufel (TV Umpire – PD Parker)

INTERNATIONAL LIMITED OVERS GAME 2

AUSTRALIA v BANGLADESH
Bundaberg Rum Stadium, Cairns. August 3, 2003.
Toss: Bangladesh. Australia won by nine wickets.

BANGLADESH	
Hannan Sarkar (+) c Gilchrist b Harvey	19
Javed Omar c Gilchrist b Bichel	11
Habib-ul-Bashar c and b Symonds	31
Sanwar Hossain c Ponting b Hogg	3
Al Sahariar Rokon c Martyn b Hogg	8
Tushar Imran c Bichel b Hogg	2
Alok Kapali c Martyn b Lehmann	34
Khaled Mahmud (c) run out (Lehmann)	11
Tapash Baisya c Bevan b Lehmann	2
Mohammad Rafiq c Bevan b Lehmann	6
Hasib-ul-Hassan not out	0
EXTRAS (LB 2, W 16, NB 2)	20
TOTAL	147

FOW: 37 46 52 84 86 101 121 133 144 147

Bowling: Lee 9–2–24–0, Bichel 10–0–29–1, Harvey 7–1–21–1, Hogg 10–0–31–3, Symonds 5–0–24–1, Lehmann 4.1–0–16–3.

AUSTRALIA	
A Symonds c Sanwar Hossain b Hasib-ul-Hassan	7
MG Bevan not out	40
DR Martyn not out	92
RT Ponting (c)	
DS Lehmann	
ML Hayden	
AC Gilchrist (+)	
GB Hogg	
IJ Harvey	
B Lee	
AJ Bichel	
EXTRAS (W 4, NB 5)	9
TOTAL	1 for 148

FOW: 17

Bowling: Tapash Baisya 5–0–31–0, Hasib-ul–Hassan 6–0–37–1, Khaled Mahmud 3–0–34–0, Mohammad Rafiq 4–0–29–0, Sanwar Hossain 2.2–0–17–0.

Umpires: SJ Davis & DR Shepherd (TV Umpire – PD Parker)

INTERNATIONAL LIMITED OVERS GAME 3

AUSTRALIA v BANGLADESH
Marrara Cricket Ground, Darwin. August 6, 2003.
Toss: Australia. Australia won by 112 runs.

AUSTRALIA	
AC Gilchrist (+) c Hannan Sarkar b Mohammad Rafiq	31
ML Hayden c and b Mohammad Rafiq	42
RT Ponting (c) c Tushar Imran b Tapash Baisya	101
DR Martyn b Alok Kapali	1
A Symonds run out (Sanwar/Sarkar)	0
MG Bevan b Mashrafe Bin Mortaza	57
IJ Harvey c Mohammad Rafiq b Mashrafe Bin Mortaza	5
GB Hogg not out	4
AJ Bichel	
JN Gillespie	
BA Williams	
EXTRAS (LB 7, W 5, NB 1)	13
TOTAL	7 for 254

FOW: 54 112 113 114 241 247 254

Bowling: Mashrafe Bin Mortaza 10–2–41–2, Tapash Baisya 10–0–63–1, Khaled Mahmud 8–0–57–0, Mohammad Rafiq 10–0–31–2, Alok Kapali 10–1–43–1, Sanwar Hossain 2–0–12–0.

BANGLADESH	
Hannan Sarkar (+) lbw b Gillespie	1
Javed Omar lbw b Harvey	16
Habib-ul-Bashar c Ponting b Bichel	2
Sanwar Hossain c and b Hogg	27
Tushar Imran run out (Hogg/Gilchrist)	1
Mohammad Ashraful b Harvey	4
Alok Kapali c and b Hogg	49
Khaled Mahmud run out (Williams/Hogg)	5
Tapash Baisya c Ponting b Harvey	11
Mohammad Rafiq not out	8
Mashrafe Bin Mortaza b Harvey	2
EXTRAS (LB 11, W 5)	16
TOTAL	142

FOW: 4 24 27 30 36 102 119 119 136 142

Bowling: Gillespie 10–6–16–1, Williams 10–2–32–0, Bichel 10–1–35–1, Harvey 6.3–0–16–4, Hogg 10–0–32–2, Symonds 1–1–0–0.

Umpires: DR Shepherd & SJA Taufel (TV Umpire – SJ Davis)

2003–04 AUSTRALIA–BANGLADESH TEST AVERAGES

Batting	Team	M	Inn	NO	Runs	HS	50	100	Avrge	Ct
DS Lehmann	Aus	2	2	–	287	177	–	2	143.50	–
ML Love	Aus	2	2	1	100	100*	–	1	100.00	2
AC Gilchrist	Aus	2	1	–	43	43	–	–	43.00	9
Hannan Sarkar	Ban	2	4	–	166	76	2	–	41.50	–
JL Langer	Ban	2	2	–	72	71	1	–	36.00	3
Habib-ul-Bashar	Ban	2	4	–	141	54	1	–	35.25	–
RT Ponting	Aus	2	2	–	69	59	1	–	34.50	2
Sanwar Hossain	Ban	1	2	–	62	46	–	–	31.00	–
ML Hayden	Aus	2	2	–	61	50	1	–	30.50	1
B Lee	Aus	2	1	–	23	23	–	–	23.00	2
Khaled Mashud	Ban	2	4	–	75	44	–	–	18.75	–
Al Sahariar Rokon	Ban	1	2	–	36	36	–	–	18.00	–
Javed Omar	Ban	2	4	–	44	26	–	–	11.00	3
Khaled Mahmud	Ban	2	4	–	43	21	–	–	10.75	–
Tapash Baisya	Ban	2	4	1	31	25	–	–	10.33	–
Mashrafe Bin Mortaza	Ban	2	4	1	29	15	–	–	9.67	–
Mohammad Ashraful	Ban	2	4	–	30	23	–	–	7.50	2
Alok Kapali	Ban	2	4	–	22	17	–	–	5.50	–
Anwar Hossain Monir	Ban	1	2	1	4	4	–	–	4.00	–
Manjural Islam	Ban	1	2	1	1	1	–	–	1.00	–
SR Waugh	Aus	2	2	2	256	156*	–	2	–	–
JN Gillespie	Aus	2	1	1	16	16*	–	–	–	1
SCG MacGill	Aus	2	–	–	–	–	–	–	–	2
GD McGrath	Aus	2	–	–	–	–	–	–	–	–

Bowling	Team	Overs	Mds	Runs	Wkts	Avrge	5wi	10wm	Best
SCG MacGill	Aus	70.1	17	219	17	12.88	3	1	5/56
JN Gillespie	Aus	61.4	14	170	11	15.45	–	–	4/38
GD McGrath	Aus	55.1	17	124	5	24.80	–	–	3/20

continued

Bowling	Team	Overs	Mds	Runs	Wkts	Avrge	5wi	10wm	Best
B Lee	Aus	49.2	10	190	6	31.67	–	–	3/23
Mashrafe Bin Mortaza	Ban	48.0	14	134	4	33.50	–	–	3/74
Sanwar Hossain	Ban	30.0	2	128	2	64.00	–	–	2/128
Manjural Islam	Ban	24.0	4	78	1	78.00	–	–	1/78
Tapash Baisya	Ban	47.5	9	165	2	82.50	–	–	1/69
Alok Kapali	Ban	32.2	2	134	1	134.00	–	–	1/65
Anwar Hossain Monir	Ban	21.0	4	95	0	–	–	–	–
Habib-ul-Bashar	Ban	1.0	–	1	0	–	–	–	–
Khaled Mahmud	Ban	47.0	5	173	0	–	–	–	–
DS Lehmann	Aus	3.0	1	4	0	–	–	–	–
Mohammad Ashraful	Ban	6.0	–	31	0	–	–	–	–
SR Waugh	Aus	5.0	3	4	0	–	–	–	–

2003–04 AUSTRALIA–BANGLADESH INTERNATIONAL LIMITED OVERS

Batting	Team	M	Inn	NO	Runs	HS	50	100	Avrge	Ct	Stk–Rt
RT Ponting	Aus	3	2	–	130	101	–	1	65.00	4	71.04
MG Bevan	Aus	3	2	1	97	57	1	–	97.00	2	81.51
DR Martyn	Aus	3	3	2	93	92*	1	–	93.00	2	163.16
ML Hayden	Aus	3	2	1	88	46*	–	–	88.00	1	67.69
Alok Kapali	Ban	3	3	–	83	49	–	–	27.67	–	70.94
AC Gilchrist	Aus	3	2	–	49	31	–	–	24.50	6	90.74
Khaled Mahmud	Ban	3	3	1	41	25*	–	–	20.50	–	51.90
Sanwar Hossain	Ban	3	3	–	37	27	–	–	12.33	1	48.05
Habib-ul-Bashar	Ban	3	3	–	33	31	–	–	11.00	–	42.31
Tushar Imran	Ban	3	3	–	31	28	–	–	10.33	1	68.89
Javed Omar	Ban	2	2	–	27	16	–	–	13.50	–	25.23
Hannan Sarkar	Ban	3	3	–	21	19	–	–	7.00	2	31.82
Khaled Mashud	Ban	1	1	–	18	18	–	–	18.00	–	42.86
Mohammad Rafiq	Ban	3	3	1	17	8*	–	–	8.50	2	39.53
Al Sahariar Rokon	Ban	2	2	–	16	8	–	–	8.00	–	38.10

continued

Batting	Team	M	Inn	NO	Runs	HS	50	100	Avrge	Ct	Stk-Rt
Tapash Baisya	Ban	2	2	–	13	11	–	–	6.50	–	41.94
A Symonds	Aus	3	2	–	7	7	–	–	3.50	2	36.84
Hasib-ul-Hassan	Ban	2	2	1	6	6	–	–	6.00	–	28.57
IJ Harvey	Aus	2	1	–	5	5	–	–	5.00	–	71.43
GB Hogg	Aus	3	1	1	4	4*	–	–	–	2	133.33
Mohammad Ashraful	Ban	1	1	–	4	4	–	–	4.00	–	50.00
Mashrafe Bin Mortaza	Ban	2	2	–	2	2	–	–	1.00	–	22.22
B Lee	Aus	2	–	–	–	–	–	–	–	–	–
AJ Bichel	Aus	3	–	–	–	–	–	–	–	1	–
JN Gillespie	Aus	2	–	–	–	–	–	–	–	–	–
DS Lehmann	Aus	2	–	–	–	–	–	–	–	–	–
BA Williams	Aus	1	–	–	–	–	–	–	–	–	–

Bowling	Team	Overs	Mds	Runs	Wkts	Avrge	5wi	Best	RPO
IJ Harvey	Aus	13.3	1	37	5	7.40	–	4/16	2.74
GB Hogg	Aus	30.0	–	90	5	18.00	–	3/31	3.00
AJ Bichel	Aus	25.0	1	88	4	22.00	–	2/24	3.52
JN Gillespie	Aus	20.0	9	39	4	9.75	–	3/23	1.95
B Lee	Aus	17.0	3	49	4	12.25	–	4/25	2.88
DS Lehmann	Aus	4.1	–	16	3	5.33	–	3/16	3.84
Mashrafe Bin Mortaza	Ban	17.0	2	81	3	27.00	–	2/41	4.76
Mohammad Rafiq	Ban	19.0	2	67	3	22.33	–	2/31	3.53
Alok Kapali	Ban	10.0	1	43	1	43.00	–	1/43	4.30
Hasib-ul-Hassan	Ban	11.0	–	68	1	68.00	–	1/37	6.18
A Symonds	Aus	7.0	1	29	1	29.00	–	1/24	4.14
Tapash Baisya	Ban	15.0	–	94	1	94.00	–	1/63	6.27
Sanwar Hossain	Ban	4.2	–	29	0	–	–	–	6.69
BA Williams	Aus	10.0	2	32	0	–	–	–	3.20
Khaled Mahmud	Ban	16.3	–	120	0	–	–	–	7.27

2003–04 AUSTRALIA v ZIMBABWE

TOURING PARTY

Heath Streak (captain), Tatenda Taibu (vice-captain), Andy Blignaut, Gary Brent, Stuart Carlisle, Dion Ebrahim, Sean Ervine, Craig Evans, Gavin Ewing, Trevor Gripper, Douglas Hondo, Stewart Matsikenyeri, Ray Price, Mark Vermeulen, Craig Wishart. Coach: Geoff Marsh. Bowling Coach: Bruce Reid. Blessing Mawhire will travel with the squad to Australia to further his development.

ROCKINGHAMMANDURAH INVITATIONAL XI v ZIMBABWEANS at Setters Hill, Baldivis, September 28, 29, 30 2003. Match drawn. Zimbabweans 149 (SM Ervine 41; DJ Wates 4/22, T Gilbert 3/35, AC Voges 2/15). RockinghamMandurah Invitational XI 123 (L Ronchi 44; SM Ervine 5/37, RW Price 2/20). Zimbabweans 9 dec 255 (CB Wishart 116, SM Ervine 51; JJ Taylor 3/34, AK Heal 3/53, AC Voges 2/42). RockinghamMandurah Invitational XI 6 for 135 (CJ Simmons 35, L Ronchi 47; SM Ervine 2/21, RW Price 4/55).

CRICKET AUSTRALIA CHAIRMAN'S XI v ZIMBABWEANS at Lilac Hill Park, Caversham, October 1, 2003. Zimbabweans won by seven wickets. Cricket Australia Chairman's XI 240 (DR Martyn 31, RJ Campbell 65, GB Hogg 38; HH Streak 4/32, AM Blignaut 3/47). Zimbabweans 3 for 241 (MA Vermeulen 61, SV Carlisle 89*, CB Wishart 63*).

WESTERN AUSTRALIA v ZIMBABWEANS at WACA Ground, Perth, October 3, 4, 5, 2003. Match drawn. Zimbabweans 330 (MA Vermeulen 38, CB Wishart 100, HH Streak 45, AM Blignaut 57; P Wilson 4/41, DJ Wates 2/97, J Angel 2/74). Western Australia 6 dec 207 (MJ North 59, SW Meuleman 47, PC Worthington 30*; HH Streak 3/35, AM Blignaut 2/63). Zimbabweans 6 dec 146 (TR Gripper 54, MA Vermeulen 30; P Wilson 3/26, DJ Wates 2/53). Western Australia 4 for 266 (MEK Hussey 79, RJ Campbell 59, PC Worthington 45, MJ North 31*; TR Gripper 2/57).

FIRST TEST

AUSTRALIA v ZIMBABWE
WACA Ground, Perth. October 9, 10, 11, 12, 13, 2003.
Toss: Zimbabwe. Australia won by an innings and 175 runs.

AUSTRALIA	
JL Langer b Ervine	26
ML Hayden c Carlisle b Gripper	380
RT Ponting lbw b Ervine	37
DR Martyn c Wishart b Gripper	53
SR Waugh (c) c and b Ervine	78
DS Lehmann c and b Ervine	30
AC Gilchrist (+) not out	113
AJ Bichel	
B Lee	
JN Gillespie	
SCG MacGill	
EXTRAS (B 4, LB 10, W 1, NB 3)	18
TOTAL	6 dec 735

FOW 1st Inns: 43 102 199 406 502 735

Bowling: First Innings: Streak 26–6–131–0, Blignaut 28–4–115–0, Ervine 31–4–146–4, Price 36–5–187–0, Gripper 25.3–0–142–2.

ZIMBABWE				
DD Ebrahim b Gillespie	29		b Gillespie	4
TR Gripper c Lehmann b Lee	53		c Gilchrist b Gillespie	0
MA Vermeulen c Hayden b MacGill	38		c Gilchrist b Lee	63
SV Carlisle c Hayden b MacGill	2		c Hayden b Lehmann	35
CB Wishart c Gilchrist b Bichel	46		lbw b Bichel	8
CN Evans b Bichel	22		b Lehmann	5
T Taibu (+) lbw b Gillespie	15		c Gilchrist b Bichel	3
HH Streak (c) b Lee	9	(9)	not out	71
SM Ervine c Waugh b Gillespie	6	(8)	b Bichel	53
AM Blignaut lbw b Lee	0		st Gilchrist b Lehmann	22

ZIMBABWE *continued*			
RW Price not out	2	c Waugh b Bichel	36
EXTRAS (LB 10, W 2, NB 5)	17	(B 4, LB 6, W 5, NB 6)	21
TOTAL	239		321

FOW 1st Inns: 61 105 120 131 199 200 231 231 231 239
FOW 2nd Inns: 2 11 110 112 118 126 126 209 247 321

Bowling: First Innings: Lee 15–4–48–3, Gillespie 25.3–9–52–3, Bichel 21–2–62–2, MacGill 21–4–54–2, Lehmann 2–1–3–0, Waugh 5–1–10–0. Second Innings: Lee 35–8–96–1, Gillespie 3–0–6–2, MacGill 3.4–1–10–0, Bichel 28.2–15–63–4, Lehmann 31.2–15–61–3, Martyn 13–5–34–0, Waugh 8–2–26–0, Ponting 5–1–15–0.

Umpires: S Venkataraghavan & P Willey (TV Umpire – SJ Davis)

SECOND TEST

AUSTRALIA v ZIMBABWE
Sydney Cricket Ground, Sydney. October 17, 18, 19, 20, 2003.
Toss: Zimbabwe. Australia won by nine wickets.

ZIMBABWE			
DD Ebrahim b Lee	9	c Katich b Williams	0
TR Gripper c Gilchrist b Bichel	15	c Hayden b Katich	47
MA Vermeulen lbw b Williams	17	c Waugh b Williams	48
SV Carlisle c Ponting b Bichel	118	c Williams b Katich	5
CB Wishart c Gilchrist b Williams	14	st Gilchrist b Katich	45
T Taibu (+) c Gilchrist b Hogg	27	c Ponting b Katich	35
HH Streak (c) lbw b Hogg	14	run out (Katich/Gilchrist)	25
GM Ewing c Martyn b Lee	2	c Gilchrist b Hogg	0
AM Blignaut not out	38	c Williams b Katich	44
RW Price c Williams b Bichel	20	lbw b Katich	0
NB Mahwire c Gilchrist b Bichel	6	not out	1
EXTRAS (B 4, LB 12, W 3, NB 9)	28	(B 6, LB 5, W 1, NB 4)	16
TOTAL	308		266

FOW 1st Inns: 15 45 47 95 151 218 222 243 296 308
FOW 2nd Inns: 0 93 103 114 176 212 216 230 244 266

Bowling: First Innings: Lee 23–5–78–2, Williams 23–6–58–2, Bichel 24.2–7–66–4, Hogg 23–8–49–2, Waugh 4–0–7–0, Katich 7–0–25–0, Martyn 3–1–9–0. Second Innings: Williams 16–8–56–2, Bichel 19–5–64–0, Hogg 31–9–70–1, Katich 25.5–3–65–6.

AUSTRALIA			
JL Langer c Streak b Blignaut	2	c Taibu b Streak	8
ML Hayden c Carlisle b Blignaut	20	not out	101
RT Ponting b Price	169	not out	53
DR Martyn lbw b Price	32		
SR Waugh (c) c Carlisle b Price	61		
SM Katich b Price	52		
AC Gilchrist (+) b Streak	20		
GB Hogg c Ebrahim b Price	13		
AJ Bichel c Wishart b Blignaut	5		
B Lee not out	6		
BA Williams c and b Price	7		
EXTRAS (LB 2, W 1, NB 13)	16	(B 3, LB 3, NB 4)	10
TOTAL	403		1 for 172

FOW 1st Inns: 7 51 148 283 306 347 375 384 394 403
FOW 2nd Inns: 21

Bowling: First Innings: Streak 21–3–83–1, Blignaut 20–2–83–3, Mahwire 10–1–61–0, Price 41.3–6–121–6, Ewing 11–1–53–0. Second Innings: Streak 9–1–46–1, Blignaut 4–0–35–0, Price 12.1–0–63–0, Gripper 1–0–2–0, Ewing 3–0–20–0.

Umpires: BF Bowden & S Venkataraghavan (TV Umpire – PD Parker)

2003–04 AUSTRALIA–ZIMBABWE TEST AVERAGES

Batting	Team	M	Inn	NO	Runs	HS	50	100	Avrge	Ct/St
ML Hayden	Aus	2	3	1	501	380	–	2	250.50	4
AC Gilchrist	Aus	2	2	1	133	113*	–	1	133.00	9/2
RT Ponting	Aus	2	3	1	259	169	1	1	129.50	2
SR Waugh	Aus	2	2	–	139	78	2	–	69.50	3
SM Katich	Aus	1	1	–	52	52	1	–	52.00	1
DR Martyn	Aus	2	2	–	85	53	1	–	42.50	1
MA Vermeulen	Zim	2	4	–	166	63	1	–	41.50	–
SV Carlisle	Zim	2	4	–	160	118	–	1	40.00	3
HH Streak	Zim	2	4	1	119	71*	1	–	39.67	1
AM Blignaut	Zim	2	4	1	104	44	–	–	34.67	–

continued

Batting	Team	M	Inn	NO	Runs	HS	50	100	Avrge	Ct/St
DS Lehmann	Aus	1	1	–	30	30	–	–	30.00	1
SM Ervine	Zim	1	2	–	59	53	1	–	29.50	2
TR Gripper	Zim	2	4	–	115	53	1	–	28.75	–
CB Wishart	Zim	2	4	–	113	46	–	–	28.25	2
T Taibu	Zim	2	4	–	80	35	–	–	20.00	1
RW Price	Zim	2	4	1	58	36	–	–	19.33	1
CN Evans	Zim	1	2	–	27	22	–	–	13.50	–
GB Hogg	Aus	1	1	–	13	13	–	–	13.00	–
JL Langer	Aus	2	3	–	36	26	–	–	12.00	–
DD Ebrahim	Zim	2	4	–	42	29	–	–	10.50	1
BA Williams	Aus	1	1	–	7	7	–	–	7.00	3
NB Mahwire	Zim	1	2	1	7	6	–	–	7.00	–
AJ Bichel	Aus	2	1	–	5	5	–	–	5.00	–
GM Ewing	Zim	1	2	–	2	2	–	–	1.00	–
B Lee	Aus	2	1	1	6	6*	–	–	–	–
JN Gillespie	Aus	1	–	–	–	–	–	–	–	–
SCG MacGill	Aus	1	–	–	–	–	–	–	–	–

Bowling	Team	Overs	Mds	Runs	Wkts	Avrge	5wi	10wm	Best
JN Gillespie	Aus	28.3	9	58	5	11.60	–	–	3/52
SM Katich	Aus	32.5	3	90	6	15.00	1	–	6/65
DS Lehmann	Aus	33.2	16	64	3	21.33	–	–	3/61
AJ Bichel	Aus	92.4	29	255	10	25.50	–	–	4/63
BA Williams	Aus	39.0	14	114	4	28.50	–	–	2/56
SCG MacGill	Aus	24.4	5	64	2	32.00	–	–	2/54
SM Ervine	Zim	31.0	4	146	4	36.50	–	–	4/146
B Lee	Aus	73.0	17	222	6	37.00	–	–	3/48
GB Hogg	Aus	54.0	17	119	3	39.67	–	–	2/49
RW Price	Zim	89.4	11	371	6	61.83	1	–	6/121
TR Gripper	Zim	26.3	0	144	2	72.00	–	–	2/142
AM Blignaut	Zim	52.0	6	233	3	77.67	–	–	3/83
HH Streak	Zim	56.0	10	260	2	130.00	–	–	1/46
GM Ewing	Zim	14.0	1	73	0	–	–	–	–
NB Mahwire	Zim	10.0	1	61	0	–	–	–	–

continued

Bowling	Team	Overs	Mds	Runs	Wkts	Avrge	5wi	10wm	Best
DR Martyn	Aus	16.0	6	43	0	–	–	–	–
RT Ponting	Aus	5.0	1	15	0	–	–	–	–
SR Waugh	Aus	17.0	3	43	0	–	–	–	–

2003–04 TRI-NATION INTERNATIONAL LIMITED OVERS

TOURING PARTY

Ricky Ponting (captain) Tas, Adam Gilchrist (vice-captain) WA, Andy Bichel Qld, Michael Bevan NSW, Nathan Bracken NSW, Michael Clarke NSW, Ian Harvey Vic, Matthew Hayden Qld, Brad Hogg WA, Jimmy Maher (Qld), Damien Martyn WA, Andrew Symonds Qld.

Brett Lee NSW and Jason Gillespie SA withdrew before the start of the tour and were replaced by Michael Kasprowicz Qld and Brad Williams WA.

Team Management: John Buchanan (Coach), Steve Bernard (Team Manager), Tim Nielsen (Assistant Coach/Performance Analyst), Errol Alcott (Physiotherapist), Jock Campbell (Physical Performance Manager).

INTERNATIONAL LIMITED OVERS GAME 1

INDIA v NEW ZEALAND at MA Chidambaram Stadium (Chepauk), Chennai, October 23, 2003. No result. India 3 for 141 (V Sehwag 31, SR Tendulkar 48*). No award.

INTERNATIONAL LIMITED OVERS GAME 2

INDIA v AUSTRALIA
Captain Roop Singh Stadium, Gwalior. October 26, 2003.
Toss: India. India won by 37 runs.

INDIA	
V Sehwag c Hayden b Bracken	0
SR Tendulkar c Gilchrist b Bracken	100
VVS Laxman run out (Symonds)	102
Yuvraj Singh c Symonds b Williams	44
AB Agarkar c Symonds b Bracken	22
M Kaif not out	1
PA Patel (+)	
RS Dravid (c)	
Harbhajan Singh	
AR Kumble	
Zaheer Khan	
EXTRAS (LB 7, W 6, NB 1)	14
TOTAL	5 for 283

FOW: 1 192 256 264 283

Bowling: Bracken 10–0–53–3, Williams 10–0–67–1, Bichel 7–0–39–0, Harvey 8–0–46–0, Hogg 10–0–47–0, Symonds 5–0–24–0.

AUSTRALIA	
AC Gilchrist (+) b Zaheer Khan	83
ML Hayden st Patel b Kumble	47
RT Ponting (c) c and b Kumble	2
DR Martyn b Sehwag	16
A Symonds lbw b Zaheer Khan	1
MG Bevan b Sehwag	18
IJ Harvey b Tendulkar	4
GB Hogg st Patel b Harbhajan Singh	29
AJ Bichel c Kaif b Zaheer Khan	14
BA Williams not out	11
NW Bracken not out	7
EXTRAS (LB 4, W 4, NB 6)	14
TOTAL	9 for 246

FOW: 132 135 140 141 176 177 185 225 229

Bowling: Zaheer Khan 10–0–49–3, Agarkar 6–0–42–0, Kumble 10–2–28–2, Harbhajan Singh 10–0–43–1, Tendulkar 6–0–39–1, Sehwag 7–0–36–2, Yuvraj Singh 1–0–5–0.

Umpires: K Hariharan & NA Mallender (TV Umpire – AV Jayaprakash)

INTERNATIONAL LIMITED OVERS GAME 3

AUSTRALIA v NEW ZEALAND
Nahar Singh Stadium, Faridabad. October 29, 2003.
Toss: New Zealand. Australia won by eight wickets.

NEW ZEALAND	
CJ Nevin lbw b Bracken	0
SP Fleming (c) c Gilchrist b Bracken	2
L Vincent c Bichel b Williams	0
SB Styris c Ponting b Williams	7
CD McMillan lbw b Bichel	24
JDP Oram c Gilchrist b Bracken	0
CZ Harris lbw b Harvey	14
BB McCullum (+) c Martyn b Williams	5
DL Vettori lbw b Harvey	0
PA Hitchcock c Hayden b Williams	10
DR Tuffey not out	3
EXTRAS (LB 12, W 18, NB 2)	32
TOTAL	97

FOW: 0 11 11 20 21 73 77 80 80 97

Bowling: Bracken 9–2–25–3, Williams 9.4–1–22–4, Bichel 7–0–29–1, Harvey 8–2–9–2.

AUSTRALIA	
AC Gilchrist (+) c and b Oram	29
ML Hayden not out	51
RT Ponting (c) c McCullum b Tuffey	12
DR Martyn not out	2
A Symonds	
MG Bevan	
IJ Harvey	
GB Hogg	
AJ Bichel	
NW Bracken	
BA Williams	
EXTRAS (LB 5, NB 2)	7
TOTAL	2 for 101

FOW: 47 90

Bowling: Tuffey 6.4–0–51–1, Oram 7–1–31–1, Hitchcock 2–0–8–0, Vettori 1–0–6–0.

Umpires: DR Shepherd & S Venkataraghavan (TV Umpire – I Sivaram)

INTERNATIONAL LIMITED OVERS GAME 4

INDIA v AUSTRALIA
Wankhede Stadium, Mumbai. November 1, 2003.
Toss: Australia. Australia won by 77 runs.

AUSTRALIA	
AC Gilchrist (+) c Kaif b Harbhajan Singh	41
ML Hayden c Yuvraj Singh b Zaheer Khan	0
RT Ponting (c) lbw b Agarkar	31
DR Martyn b Agarkar	100
A Symonds c Harbhajan Singh b Yuvraj Singh	48
MG Bevan c Kaif b Agarkar	42
MJ Clarke run out (Tendular/Agarkar)	2
AJ Bichel b Agarkar	1
GB Hogg not out	0
NW Bracken	
BA Williams	
EXTRAS (B 4, LB 2, W 8, NB 7)	21
TOTAL	8 for 286

FOW: 9 55 93 171 282 283 286 286

Bowling: Zaheer Khan 7–0–64–1, Sehwag 4–0–28–0, Harbhajan Singh 10–0–44–1, Kumble 8–0–50–0, Agarkar 9–0–37–4, Tendulkar 4–0–21–0, Yuvraj Singh 8–1–36–1.

INDIA	
V Sehwag lbw b Bracken	0
SR Tendulkar b Clarke	68
VVS Laxman c Gilchrist b Bichel	21
RS Dravid (c) c Bichel b Clarke	59
Yuvraj Singh c Gilchrist b Clarke	9
M Kaif c Gilchrist b Bracken	10
AB Agarkar c Symonds b Bracken	2
PA Patel (+) c Clarke b Hogg	16
Harbhajan Singh c and b Bracken	6
AR Kumble b Clarke	6
Zaheer Khan not out	5
EXTRAS (LB 2, W 4, NB 1)	7
TOTAL	209

FOW: 0 38 137 153 172 175 178 185 200 209

Bowling: Bracken 10–2–29–4, Williams 5–0–20–0, Bichel 6–0–31–1, Symonds 10–0–57–0, Hogg 5.2–0–28–1, Clarke 10–0–42–4.

Umpires: AV Jayaprakash & NA Mallender (TV Umpire – K Hariharan)

INTERNATIONAL LIMITED OVERS GAME 5

AUSTRALIA v NEW ZEALAND
Nehru Stadium, Pune. November 3, 2003.
Toss: Australia. Australia won by 2 wickets.

NEW ZEALAND	
CJ Nevin lbw b Williams	0
SP Fleming (c) c Harvey b Symonds	40
L Vincent c Ponting b Williams	1
SB Styris lbw b Williams	0
CD McMillan b Williams	0
CL Cairns lbw b Bichel	27
JDP Oram b Symonds	81
CZ Harris c Harvey b Williams	1
BB McCullum (+) not out	51
DL Vettori b Harvey	18
DR Tuffey not out	1
EXTRAS (LB 4, W 32, NB 2)	38
TOTAL	9 for 258

FOW: 3 10 11 21 68 130 151 219 246

Bowling: Bracken 10–3–39–0, Williams 10–1–53–5, Bichel 9–0–59–1, Harvey 9–1–33–1, Symonds 10–2–56–2, Clarke 2–0–14–0.

AUSTRALIA	
AC Gilchrist (+) c Vettori b Tuffey	25
ML Hayden c Styris b Tuffey	9
RT Ponting (c) b Styris	16
DR Martyn b Tuffey	10
MJ Clarke b Tuffey	70
MG Bevan c Harris b Cairns	50
A Symonds not out	37
IJ Harvey c Styris b Vettori	19
AJ Bichel c McCullum b Vettori	9
BA Williams not out	3
NW Bracken	
EXTRAS (LB 2, W 8, NB 1)	11
TOTAL	8 for 259

FOW: 34 40 54 65 173 204 231 244

Bowling: Tuffey 10–2–30–4, Oram 9.5–0–65–0, Cairns 10–0–48–1, Styris 7–1–31–1, Vettori 8–0–59–2, Harris 5–0–24–0.

Umpires: K Hariharan & DR Shepherd (TV Umpire – AV Jayaprakash)

INTERNATIONAL LIMITED OVERS GAME 6

INDIA v NEW ZEALAND at Barabati Stadium, Cuttack, November 6, 2003. New Zealand won by four wickets. India 9 for 246 (VVS Laxman 31, M Kaif 64, RS Dravid 31, HK Badani 41, Zaheer Khan 33*; DR Tuffey 3/31, SB Styris 3/38, DL Vettori 2/39). **New Zealand** 6 for 249 (SB Styris 68, CD McMillan 82*; Zaheer Khan 2/49). Man of the Match: SB Styris.

INTERNATIONAL LIMITED OVERS GAME 7

AUSTRALIA v NEW ZEALAND
Nehru Stadium, Guwahati. November 9, 2003.
Toss: New Zealand. Australia won by 44 runs.

AUSTRALIA	
IJ Harvey c Nevin b Tuffey	25
JP Maher (+) lbw b Tuffey	3
RT Ponting (c) c McMillan b Vettori	52
DR Martyn c McCullum b Mills	0
A Symonds c McCullum b Mills	18
MG Bevan not out	84
MJ Clarke c McMillan b Vettori	2
GB Hogg c Styris b Harris	9
AJ Bichel not out	15
MS Kasprowicz	
NW Bracken	
EXTRAS (LB 9, W 7, NB 1)	17
TOTAL	7 for 225

FOW: 33 33 34 61 139 141 164

Bowling: Tuffey 10–1–60–2, Mills 8–0–36–2, Oram 10–0–47–0, Vettori 10–0–20–2, Styris 9–1–38–0, Harris 3–0–15–1.

NEW ZEALAND	
CJ Nevin c Ponting b Bracken	2
SP Fleming (c) c and b Harvey	29
L Vincent c Hogg b Bracken	12
SB Styris c Ponting b Hogg	54
CD McMillan c Maher b Bichel	0
JDP Oram lbw b Hogg	14
CZ Harris run out (Ponting)	38
BB McCullum (+) c Maher b Kasprowicz	7
DL Vettori run out (Bichel/Kasprowicz)	0
KD Mills c Maher b Bracken	4
DR Tuffey not out	0
EXTRAS (B 4, LB 6, W 9, NB 2)	21
TOTAL	181

FOW: 7 38 66 68 88 143 169 170 181 181

Bowling: Bracken 7.3–0–34–3, Kasprowicz 8–0–28–1, Bichel 7–0–21–1, Harvey 4–0–14–1, Hogg 10–0–39–2, Symonds 4–0–14–0, Clarke 5–0–21–0.

Umpires: K Hariharan & DR Shepherd (TV Umpire – I Sivaram)

INTERNATIONAL LIMITED OVERS GAME 8

INDIA v AUSTRALIA
M Chinnaswamy Stadium, Bangalore. November 12, 2003.
Toss: Australia. Australia won by 61 runs.

AUSTRALIA	
AC Gilchrist (+) c Zaheer Khan b Kumble	111
ML Hayden run out (Ganguly/Dravid)	44
RT Ponting (c) not out	108
DR Martyn not out	61
MJ Clarke	
MG Bevan	
A Symonds	
IJ Harvey	
MS Kasprowicz	
AJ Bichel	
BA Williams	
EXTRAS (B 1, LB 9, W 12, NB 1)	23
TOTAL	2 for 347

FOW: 119 198

Bowling: Nehra 10–0–80–0, Zaheer Khan 10–0–67–0, Kumble 9–0–60–1, Sehwag 5–0–36–0, Kartik 10–2–51–0, Ganguly 2–0–10–0, Yuvraj Singh 4–0–33–0.

INDIA	
V Sehwag b Harvey	39
SR Tendulkar b Harvey	89
VVS Laxman c Symonds b Clarke	18
SC Ganguly (c) c Bichel b Symonds	37
RS Dravid (+) c and b Kasprowicz	34
Yuvraj Singh lbw b Symonds	20
M Kaif b Symonds	8
Zaheer Khan run out (Bichel/Gilchrist)	2
AR Kumble not out	12
M Kartik not out	4
A Nehra	
EXTRAS (B 4, LB 7, W 11, NB 1)	23
TOTAL	8 for 286

FOW: 103 148 172 217 254 254 258 277

Bowling: Williams 8–0–43–0, Kasprowicz 10–0–37–1, Bichel 9–0–46–0, Symonds 9–0–42–3, Harvey 10–0–71–2, Clarke 4–0–36–1.

Umpires: AV Jayaprakash & DR Shepherd (TV Umpire – K Hariharan)

INTERNATIONAL LIMITED OVERS GAME 9

INDIA v NEW ZEALAND at Lal Bahadur (Fateh Maidan) Stadium, Hyderabad, November 15, 2003. India won by 145 runs. India 5 for 353 (V Sehwag 130, SR Tendulkar 102, SC Ganguly 33, RS Dravid 50*; SB Styris 2/46). **New Zealand** 208 (SB Styris 54, BB McCullum 31; Zaheer Khan 3/30, AB Agarkar 2/28, AR Kumble 2/36, M Kartik 2/38). Man of the Match: V Sehwag.

FINAL

INDIA v AUSTRALIA
Eden Gardens, Kolkata. November 18, 2003.
Toss: Australia. Australia won by 37 runs.

AUSTRALIA	
AC Gilchrist (+) b Agarkar	7
ML Hayden c Laxman b Zaheer Khan	19
RT Ponting (c) c Laxman b Kartik	36
DR Martyn c Yuvraj Singh b Sehwag	61
A Symonds c Badani b Harbhajan Singh	10
MG Bevan not out	40
MJ Clarke not out	44
IJ Harvey	
AJ Bichel	
NW Bracken	
BA Williams	
EXTRAS (B 4, LB 7, W 7)	18
TOTAL	5 for 235

FOW: 16 32 112 129 170

Bowling: Agarkar 8–2–50–1, Zaheer Khan 6–0–29–1, Salvi 3–0–23–0, Kartik 10–1–30–1, Harbhajan Singh 10–1–34–1, Sehwag 8–0–35–1, Badani 5–0–23–0.

INDIA	
SR Tendulkar b Bichel	45
V Sehwag c and b Bracken	5
VVS Laxman b Williams	22
RS Dravid (c+) b Clarke	49
Yuvraj Singh c Hayden b Symonds	4
HK Badani c Symonds b Clarke	30
AB Agarkar not out	26
M Kartik b Harvey	1
Zaheer Khan b Harvey	0
Harbhajan Singh c Symonds b Harvey	2
AM Salvi b Harvey	0
EXTRAS (B 4, LB 5, W 5)	14
TOTAL	198

FOW: 8 36 99 110 159 168 186 186 198 198

Bowling: Bracken 8–1–15–1, Williams 7–1–30–1, Bichel 8–0–51–1, Harvey 4.5–0–21–4, Symonds 7–0–36–1, Clarke 7–1–36–2.

Umpires: AV Jayaprakash & DR Shepherd (TV Umpire – K Hariharan)

2003–04 TRI-NATIONS INTERNATIONAL LIMITED OVERS

Batting	Team	M	Inn	NO	Runs	HS	50	100	Avrge	Ct/St	Stk-Rt
SR Tendulkar	Ind	7	7	1	466	102	2	2	77.67	–	89.27
AC Gilchrist	Aus	6	6	–	296	111	1	1	49.33	6	107.64
RT Ponting	Aus	7	7	1	257	108*	1	1	42.83	4	79.32
DR Martyn	Aus	7	7	2	250	100	2	1	50.00	1	80.91
MG Bevan	Aus	7	5	2	234	84*	2	–	78.00	–	72.22
RS Dravid	Ind	7	6	1	227	59	2	–	45.40	1/1	94.19
VVS Laxman	Ind	7	7	–	222	102	–	1	31.71	2	76.29
V Sehwag	Ind	6	6	–	205	130	–	1	34.17	–	88.36
SB Styris	NZ	6	5	–	183	68	3	–	36.60	6	78.21
ML Hayden	Aus	6	6	1	170	51*	1	–	34.00	3	79.44
CD McMillan	NZ	6	5	1	126	82*	1	–	31.50	3	64.62
MJ Clarke	Aus	5	4	1	118	70	1	–	39.33	1	94.40
A Symonds	Aus	7	5	1	114	48	–	–	28.50	6	76.51
BB McCullum	NZ	6	5	2	113	51*	1	–	37.67	5	71.52
Yuvraj Singh	Ind	7	7	1	113	44	–	–	18.83	3	93.39
JDP Oram	NZ	6	5	–	112	81	1	–	22.40	2	78.32
M Kaif	Ind	6	5	2	98	64	1	–	32.67	3	66.22
SP Fleming	NZ	5	4	–	95	40	–	–	23.75	–	54.60
HK Badani	Ind	2	2	–	71	41	–	–	35.50	1	87.65
SC Ganguly	Ind	2	2	–	70	37	–	–	35.00	–	112.90
AB Agarkar	Ind	6	4	1	57	26*	–	–	19.00	1	111.76
CZ Harris	NZ	6	5	–	54	38	–	–	10.80	2	41.54
CL Cairns	NZ	3	2	–	50	27	–	–	25.00	–	76.92
IJ Harvey	Aus	6	3	–	48	25	–	–	16.00	3	100.00
Zaheer Khan	Ind	7	4	2	40	33*	–	–	20.00	2	160.00
AJ Bichel	Aus	7	4	1	39	15*	–	–	13.00	3	79.59
GB Hogg	Aus	4	3	1	38	29	–	–	19.00	1	63.23
DL Vettori	NZ	6	4	–	37	19	–	–	9.25	1	82.04
L Vincent	NZ	6	5	–	36	22	–	–	7.20	1	42.35
CJ Nevin	NZ	5	5	–	32	29	–	–	6.40	1	49.23
AR Kumble	Ind	5	2	1	18	12*	–	–	18.00	1	45.00
PA Patel	Ind	3	1	–	16	16	–	–	16.00	–/2	51.61

continued

Batting	Team	M	Inn	NO	Runs	HS	50	100	Avrge	Ct/St	Stk-Rt
BA Williams	Aus	6	2	2	14	11*	–	–	–	–	70.00
Harbhajan Singh	Ind	5	3	–	13	6	–	–	4.33	1	72.22
SV Bahutule	Ind	1	1	–	11	11	–	–	11.00	–	84.62
KD Mills	NZ	3	2	1	11	7*	–	–	11.00	1	57.89
PA Hitchcock	NZ	2	1	–	10	10	–	–	10.00	–	52.63
NW Bracken	Aus	6	1	1	7	7*	–	–	–	2	70.00
M Kartik	Ind	4	3	2	6	4*	–	–	6.00	–	42.86
DR Tuffey	NZ	6	4	3	4	3*	–	–	4.00	1	21.05
JP Maher	Aus	1	1	–	3	3	–	–	3.00	3	30.00
AM Salvi	Ind	1	1	–	0	0	–	–	0.00	–	0.00
A Nehra	Ind	1	–	–	–	–	–	–	–	–	–
MS Kasprowicz	Aus	2	–	–	–	–	–	–	–	1	–

Bowling	Team	Overs	Mds	Runs	Wkts	Avrge	5wi	Best	RPO
NW Bracken	Aus	54.3	8	195	14	13.93	–	4/29	3.58
DR Tuffey	NZ	49.4	5	267	11	24.27	–	4/30	5.38
BA Williams	Aus	49.4	3	235	11	21.36	1	5/53	4.73
IJ Harvey	Aus	43.5	3	194	10	19.40	–	4/21	4.43
Zaheer Khan	Ind	50.0	2	288	10	28.80	–	3/30	5.76
AB Agarkar	Ind	37.0	2	198	8	24.75	–	4/37	5.35
MJ Clarke	Aus	28.0	1	149	7	21.29	–	4/42	5.32
SB Styris	NZ	36.0	2	172	7	24.57	–	3/38	4.78
DL Vettori	NZ	39.0	–	180	7	25.71	–	2/20	4.62
A Symonds	Aus	45.0	2	229	6	38.17	–	3/42	5.09
AJ Bichel	Aus	53.0	–	276	5	55.20	–	1/21	5.21
AR Kumble	Ind	37.0	3	174	5	34.80	–	2/28	4.70
Harbhajan Singh	Ind	40.0	1	162	4	40.50	–	1/34	4.05
M Kartik	Ind	40.0	4	153	4	38.25	–	2/38	3.83
KD Mills	NZ	26.0	–	141	4	35.25	–	2/36	5.42
GB Hogg	Aus	25.2	–	114	3	38.00	–	2/39	4.50
V Sehwag	Ind	24.0	–	135	3	45.00	–	2/36	5.63
CL Cairns	NZ	20.0	–	111	2	55.50	–	1/16	5.55
CZ Harris	NZ	17.5	–	92	2	46.00	–	1/15	5.16

continued

Bowling	Team	Overs	Mds	Runs	Wkts	Avrge	5wi	Best	RPO
MS Kasprowicz	Aus	18.0	–	65	2	32.50	–	1/28	3.61
JDP Oram	NZ	49.5	1	309	1	309.00	–	1/31	6.20
SR Tendulkar	Ind	21.0	–	125	1	125.00	–	1/39	5.95
Yuvraj Singh	Ind	19.0	1	106	1	106.00	–	1/36	5.58
HK Badani	Ind	8.3	–	44	0	–	–	–	5.18
SV Bahutule	Ind	3.0	–	24	0	–	–	–	8.00
SC Ganguly	Ind	2.0	–	10	0	–	–	–	5.00
PA Hitchcock	NZ	5.0	–	25	0	–	–	–	5.00
A Nehra	Ind	10.0	–	80	0	–	–	–	8.00
AM Salvi	Ind	3.0	–	23	0	–	–	–	7.67

2003–04 AUSTRALIA v INDIA

TOURING SQUAD

Sourav Ganguly (captain), Rahul Dravid (vice-captain), Ajit Agarkar, Akash Chopra, Anil Kumble, Ashish Nehra, Deep Dasgupta, Harbhajan Singh, Irfan Pathan, Parthiv Patel, Sachin Tendulkar, Sadagoppan Ramesh, Virender Sehwag, VVS Laxman, Zaheer Khan. Coach: John Wright.

Aavishkar Salvi was injured prior to the start of the tour and was replaced by Lakshmipathy Balaji. Murali Kartik added to the squad mid December.

VICTORIA v INDIANS at Melbourne Cricket Ground, Melbourne, November 25, 26, 27, 2003. Match drawn. Indians 9 dec 266 (S Ramesh 87, SR Tendulkar 80, PA Patel 52*; MWH Inness 4/64, CL White 4/59). Victoria 8 dec 518 (MTG Elliott 48, BJ Hodge 264, J Moss 42, IJ Harvey 71, CL White 39; A Nehra 2/91, Harbhajan Singh 2/159). Indians 2 for 116 (A Chopra 55*, S Ramesh 36).

FIRST TEST

AUSTRALIA v INDIA

Brisbane Cricket Ground, Brisbane. December 4, 5, 6, 7, 8, 2003.
Toss: India. Match drawn.

AUSTRALIA				
JL Langer lbw b Agarkar	121	(2)	c Patel b Agarkar	0
ML Hayden c Laxman b Zaheer Khan	37	(1)	c Sehwag b Harbhajan Singh	99
RT Ponting c Patel b Zaheer Khan	54		c Sehwag b Nehra	50
DR Martyn run out (Harbhjan/Patel/Ganguly)	42		not out	66
SR Waugh (c) hit wicket b Zaheer Khan	0		not out	56
SM Katich c Patel b Zaheer Khan	16			
AC Gilchrist (+) c Laxman b Zaheer Khan	0			
AJ Bichel c Laxman b Agarkar	11			
JN Gillespie run out (Harbhajan/Agarkar)	8			
NW Bracken not out	6			
SCG MacGill c Chopra b Agarkar	1			
EXTRAS (B 4, LB 7, W 2, NB 14)	27		(B 4, NB 9)	13
TOTAL	323			3 dec 284

FOW 1st Inns: 73 162 268 275 275 276 302 310 317 323
FOW 2nd Inns: 6 146 156

Bowling: First Innings: Zaheer Khan 23–2–95–5, Nehra 15–4–51–0, Agarkar 25.1–5–90–3, Harbhajan Singh 14–1–68–0, Ganguly 1–0–8–0. Second Innings: Zaheer Khan 3–0–15–0, Agarkar 12–3–45–1, Nehra 19–1–89–1, Harbhajan Singh 21–1–101–1, Tendulkar 2–0–9–0, Sehwag 5–1–21–0.

INDIA				
A Chopra c Hayden b Gillespie	36		c Langer b Bracken	4
V Sehwag c Hayden b Bracken	45		c Martyn b Bracken	0
RS Dravid c Hayden b Gillespie	1		not out	43
SR Tendulkar lbw b Gillespie	0			
SC Ganguly (c) c Gillespie b MacGill	144			
VVS Laxman c Katich b MacGill	75	(4)	not out	24
PA Patel (+) c Bichel b Gillespie	37			
AB Agarkar c Hayden b Bichel	12			

INDIA *continued*			
Harbhajan Singh not out	19		
Zaheer Khan b MacGill	27		
A Nehra lbw b MacGill	0		
EXTRAS (LB 6, W 1, NB 6)	13	(NB 2)	2
TOTAL	409		2 for 73

FOW 1st Inns: 61 62 62 127 273 329 362 362 403 409
FOW 2nd Inns: 4 4

Bowling: First Innings: Gillespie 31–12–65–4, Bracken 26–5–90–1, Bichel 28–6–130–1, MacGill 26.1–4–86–4, Waugh 7–3–16–0, Katich 2–0–16–0. Second Innings: Gillespie 5–1–17–0, Bracken 4–1–12–2, MacGill 4–0–32–0, Bichel 3–0–12–0.

Umpires: SA Bucknor & RE Koertzen (TV Umpire – PD Parker)

SECOND TEST

AUSTRALIA v INDIA
Adelaide Oval, Adelaide. December 12,13,14,15,16, 2003.
Toss: Australia. India won by four wickets.

AUSTRALIA			
JL Langer c Sehwag b Kumble	58	lbw b Agarkar	10
ML Hayden c Patel b Pathan	12	c Sehwag b Nehra	17
RT Ponting c Dravid b Kumble	242	c Chopra b Agarkar	0
DR Martyn c Laxman b Nehra	30	c Dravid b Tendulkar	38
SR Waugh (c) b Nehra	30	c Dravid b Tendulkar	42
SM Katich c Sehwag b Agarkar	75	c Nehra b Agarkar	31
AC Gilchrist (+) c Sehwag b Agarkar	29	b Kumble	43
AJ Bichel c Chopra b Kumble	19	b Agarkar	1
JN Gillespie not out	48	c Patel b Agarkar	3
BA Williams b Kumble	0	not out	4
SCG MacGill lbw b Kumble	0	b Agarkar	1
EXTRAS (LB 8, W 1, NB 4)	13	(B 2, LB 2, W 1, NB 1)	6
TOTAL	556	196	

FOW 1st Inns: 22 135 200 252 390 426 473 556 556 556
FOW 2nd Inns: 10 18 44 109 112 183 184 188 192 196

Bowling: First Innings: Agarkar 26–1–119–2, Pathan 27–3–136–1, Nehra 25–3–115–2, Kumble 43–3–154–5, Sehwag 5–0–21–0, Tendulkar 1–0–3–0. Second Innings: Agarkar 16.2–2–41–6, Pathan 7–0–24–0, Nehra 7–2–21–1, Kumble 17–2–58–1, Tendulkar 6–0–36–2, Sehwag 3–0–12–0.

INDIA			
A Chopra c and b Bichel	27	lbw b Gillespie	20
V Sehwag c Hayden b Bichel	47	st Gilchrist b MacGill	47
RS Dravid c Bichel b Gillespie	233	not out	72
SR Tendulkar c Gilchrist b Bichel	1	lbw b MacGill	37
SC Ganguly (c) run out (Williams/MacGill)	2	c Katich b Bichel	12
VVS Laxman c Gilchrist b Bichel	148	c Bichel b Katich	32
PA Patel (+) c Ponting b Katich	31	b Katich	3
AB Agarkar c MacGill b Katich	11	not out	0
AR Kumble lbw b MacGill	12		
IK Pathan c and b MacGill	1		
A Nehra not out	0		
EXTRAS (B 4, LB 2, W 2, NB 2)	10	(B 3, LB 6, W 1)	10
TOTAL	523	6 for 233	

FOW 1st Inns: 66 81 83 85 388 447 469 510 518 523
FOW 2nd Inns: 48 79 149 170 221 229

Bowling: First Innings: Gillespie 40.5–13–106–1, Williams 23–7–72–0, Bichel 28–3–118–4, MacGill 44–8–143–2, Katich 16–3–59–2, Waugh 9–2–15–0, Ponting 1–0–4–0. Second Innings: Gillespie 10.2–2–22–1, Williams 14–6–34–0, MacGill 24.4–3–101–2, Bichel 11.4–2–35–1, Katich 8–1–22–2, Waugh 4–0–10–0.

Umpires: RE Koertzen & DR Shepherd (TV Umpire – SJ Davis)

AUSTRALIA A v INDIANS at Bellerive Oval, Hobart, December 19, 20, 21, 2003. Match drawn. Australia A 5 dec 311 (MEK Hussey 67, CJL Rogers 70, ML Love 94, MJ Clarke 38*; A Nehra 2/33). Indians 245 (A Chopra 46, SR Tendulkar 36, V Sehwag 30, PA Patel 49; MJ Nicholson 4/25, SW Tait 3/85). Australia A 7 dec 241 (BJ Hodge 33, MJ Clarke 131*; IK Pathan 2/40, L Balaji 3/87). Indians 2 for 66.

THIRD TEST

AUSTRALIA v INDIA
Melbourne Cricket Ground, Melbourne. December 26, 27, 28, 29, 30, 2003.
Toss: India. Australia won by nine wickets.

INDIA				
A Chopra c Katich b MacGill	48		c Gilchrist b Bracken	4
V Sehwag c Bracken b Katich	195		c Williams b Lee	11
RS Dravid c Martyn b Waugh	49		c Gilchrist b Lee	92
SR Tendulkar c Gilchrist b Lee	0	(5)	c Gilchrist b Williams	44
SC Ganguly (c) c Langer b Lee	37	(4)	b Bracken	73
VVS Laxman c Hayden b MacGill	19		c Hayden b MacGill	18
PA Patel (+) c Gilchrist b Bracken	0		not out	27
AB Agarkar run out (Williams)	0		b Williams	1
AR Kumble c Langer b Williams	3		lbw b Williams	0
Zaheer Khan not out	0		c Hayden b Williams	1
A Nehra c Gilchrist b MacGill	0		c Hayden b MacGill	0
EXTRAS (LB 3, W 1, NB 11)	15		(B 4, LB 3, W 1, NB 7)	15
TOTAL	366			286

FOW 1st Inns: 141 278 286 311 350 353 353 366 366 366
FOW 2nd Inns: 5 19 126 160 253 258 271 271 277 286

Bowling: First Innings: Lee 27–7–103–2, Bracken 28–6–71–1, Williams 20–6–66–1, MacGill 15–3–70–3, Katich 4–0–18–1, Waugh 9–0–35–1. Second Innings: Lee 22–3–97–2, Bracken 25–13–45–2, Williams 22–5–53–4, MacGill 26.5–5–68–2, Katich 4–0–16–0.

AUSTRALIA			
JL Langer c Tendulkar b Agarkar	14	lbw b Agarkar	2
ML Hayden lbw b Kumble	136	not out	53
RT Ponting st Patel b Kumble	257	not out	31
AC Gilchrist (+) c Nehra b Kumble	14		
DR Martyn c Patel b Agarkar	31		
SR Waugh (c) lbw b Kumble	19		
SM Katich c Chopra b Kumble	29		
B Lee c Laxman b Kumble	8		
NW Bracken c and b Tendulkar	1		
BA Williams not out	10		

AUSTRALIA *continued*			
SCG MacGill lbw b Agarkar	0		
EXTRAS (B 4, LB 8, W 5, NB 17)	39	(B 4, LB 2, W 1, NB 4)	11
TOTAL	558		1 for 97

FOW 1st Inns: 30 264 295 373 437 502 535 542 555 558
FOW 2nd Inns: 9

Bowling: First Innings: Agarkar 33.2–5–115–3, Zaheer Khan 25–4–103–0, Nehra 29–3–90–0, Kumble 51–8–176–6, Tendulkar 13–0–57–1. Second Innings: Sehwag 3–0–7–0, Agarkar 7–2–25–1, Nehra 6–3–16–0, Kumble 6.2–0–43–0.

Umpires: BF Bowden & DR Shepherd (TV Umpire – RL Parry)

FOURTH TEST

AUSTRALIA v INDIA
Sydney Cricket Ground, Sydney. January 2, 3, 4, 5, 6, 2004.
Toss: India. Match drawn.

INDIA			
A Chopra b Lee	45	c Martyn b Gillespie	2
V Sehwag c Gilchrist b Gillespie	72	c Gillespie b MacGill	47
RS Dravid lbw b Gillespie	38	not out	91
SR Tendulkar not out	241	not out	60
VVS Laxman b Gillespie	178		
SC Ganguly (c) b Lee	16		
PA Patel (+) c Gilchrist b Lee	62		
AB Agarkar b Lee	2		
IK Pathan not out	13		
AR Kumble			
M Kartik			
EXTRAS (B 4, LB 5, W 4, NB 25)	38	(LB 3, W 1, NB 7)	11
TOTAL	7 dec 705		2 dec 211

FOW 1st Inns: 123 128 194 547 570 671 678
FOW 2nd Inns: 11 73

Bowling: First Innings: Lee 39.3–5–201–4, Gillespie 45–11–135–3, Bracken 37–13–97–0, MacGill 38–5–146–0, Waugh 2–0–6–0, Katich 17–1–84–0, Martyn 9–1–27–0. Second Innings: Lee 12.2–2–75–0, Gillespie 7–2–32–1, MacGill 16–1–65–1, Bracken 8–0–36–0.

AUSTRALIA				
JL Langer c Patel b Kumble	117		c Sehwag b Kartik	47
ML Hayden c Ganguly b Kumble	67		c Dravid b Kumble	30
RT Ponting lbw b Kumble	25		c and b Pathan	47
DR Martyn c and b Kumble	7		c (sub) Yuvraj Singh b Kumble	40
SR Waugh (c) c Patel b Pathan	40		c Tendulkar b Kumble	80
SM Katich c Sehwag b Kumble	125		not out	77
AC Gilchrist (+) b Pathan	6		st Patel b Kumble	4
B Lee c Chopra b Kumble	0			
JN Gillespie st Patel b Kumble	47	(8)	not out	4
NW Bracken c Agarkar b Kumble	2			
SCG MacGill not out	0			
EXTRAS (B 6, LB 9, W 3, NB 20)	38		(B 6, LB 7, W 2, NB 13)	28
TOTAL	474			6 for 357

FOW 1st Inns: 147 214 229 261 311 341 350 467 473 474
FOW 2nd Inns: 75 92 170 196 338 342

Bowling: First Innings: Agarkar 25–3–116–0, Pathan 26–3–80–2, Kumble 46.5–7–141–8, Kartik 19–1–122–0, Ganguly 1–1–0–0. Second Innings: Agarkar 10–2–45–0, Kumble 42–8–138–4, Pathan 8–1–26–1, Kartik 26–5–89–1, Tendulkar 6–0–36–0, Sehwag 2–0–10–0.

Umpires: BF Bowden & SA Bucknor (TV Umpire – PD Parker)

2003–04 AUSTRALIA–INDIA TEST AVERAGES

Batting	Team	M	Inn	NO	Runs	HS	50	100	Avrge	Ct/St
RS Dravid	Ind	4	8	3	619	233	3	1	123.80	4
RT Ponting	Aus	4	8	1	706	257	2	2	100.86	1
VVS Laxman	Ind	4	7	1	494	178	1	2	82.33	5
SR Tendulkar	Ind	4	7	2	383	241*	1	1	76.60	3
SM Katich	Aus	4	6	1	353	125	2	1	70.60	3
ML Hayden	Aus	4	8	1	451	136	3	1	64.43	9
V Sehwag	Ind	4	8	–	464	195	1	1	58.00	8
SC Ganguly	Ind	4	6	–	284	144	1	1	47.33	1
JL Langer	Aus	4	8	–	369	121	1	2	46.13	3

continued

Batting	Team	M	Inn	NO	Runs	HS	50	100	Avrge	Ct/St
SR Waugh	Aus	4	7	1	267	80	2	–	44.50	–
DR Martyn	Aus	4	7	1	254	66*	1	–	42.33	3
JN Gillespie	Aus	3	5	2	110	48*	–	–	36.67	2
PA Patel	Ind	4	6	1	160	62	1	–	32.00	8/3
A Chopra	Ind	4	8	–	186	48	–	–	23.25	5
AC Gilchrist	Aus	4	6	–	96	43	–	–	16.00	10/1
Zaheer Khan	Ind	2	3	1	28	27	–	–	14.00	–
BA Williams	Aus	2	3	2	14	10*	–	–	14.00	1
IK Pathan	Ind	2	2	1	14	13*	–	–	14.00	1
AJ Bichel	Aus	2	3	–	31	19	–	–	10.33	4
AB Agarkar	Ind	4	6	1	26	12	–	–	5.20	1
AR Kumble	Ind	3	3	–	15	12	–	–	5.00	1
NW Bracken	Aus	3	3	1	9	6*	–	–	4.50	1
B Lee	Aus	2	2	–	8	8	–	–	4.00	–
SCG MacGill	Aus	4	5	1	2	1	–	–	0.50	2
A Nehra	Ind	3	4	1	0	0*	–	–	0.00	2
Harbhajan Singh	Ind	1	1	1	19	19*	–	–	–	–
M Kartik	Ind	1	–	–	–		–	–	–	–

Bowling	Team	Overs	Mds	Runs	Wkts	Avrge	5wi	10wm	Best
AR Kumble	Ind	206.1	28	710	24	29.58	3	1	8/141
AB Agarkar	Ind	154.5	23	596	16	37.25	1	–	6/41
JN Gillespie	Aus	139.1	41	377	10	37.70	–	–	4/65
Zaheer Khan	Ind	51.0	6	213	5	42.60	1	–	5/95
SM Katich	Aus	51.0	5	215	5	43.00	–	–	2/22
BA Williams	Aus	79.0	24	225	5	45.00	–	–	4/53
SR Tendulkar	Ind	28.0	–	141	3	47.00	–	–	2/36
AJ Bichel	Aus	70.4	11	295	6	49.17	–	–	4/118
SCG MacGill	Aus	194.4	29	711	14	50.79	–	–	4/86
NW Bracken	Aus	128.0	38	351	6	58.50	–	–	2/12
B Lee	Aus	100.5	17	476	8	59.50	–	–	4/201
IK Pathan	Ind	68.0	7	266	4	66.50	–	–	2/80
SR Waugh	Aus	31.0	5	82	1	82.00	–	–	1/35
A Nehra	Ind	101.0	16	382	4	95.50	–	–	2/115

continued

Bowling	Team	Overs	Mds	Runs	Wkts	Avrge	5wi	10wm	Best
Harbhajan Singh	Ind	35.0	2	169	1	169.00	–	–	1/101
M Kartik	Ind	45.0	6	211	1	211.00	–	–	1/89
SC Ganguly	Ind	2.0	1	8	0	–	–	–	–
DR Martyn	Aus	9.0	1	27	0	–	–	–	–
RT Ponting	Aus	1.0	–	4	0	–	–	–	–
V Sehwag	Ind	18.0	1	71	0	–	–	–	–

2003–04 VB SERIES

AUSTRALIAN SQUAD: Ricky Ponting (captain) Tas, Adam Gilchrist (vice-captain) WA, Michael Bevan NSW, Andrew Bichel Qld, Nathan Bracken NSW, Michael Clarke NSW, Jason Gillespie SA, Ian Harvey Vic, Matthew Hayden Qld, Brad Hogg WA, Brett Lee NSW, Damien Martyn WA, Andrew Symonds Qld, Brad Williams WA. Brad Haddin NSW, Simon Kasprowicz Qld, Simon Katich NSW and Mike Hussey WA included to the squad to cover injuries.

INDIAN SQUAD: Sourav Ganguly (captain), Rahul Dravid (vice-captain), Ajit Agarkar, Hemang Badani, L Balaji, Sanjay Bangar, Murali Kartik, Anil Kumble, VVS Laxman, Ashish Nehra, Parthiv Patel, Irfan Pathan, Yuvraj Singh, Virender Sehwag, Sachin Tendulkar. Mohammad Kaif withdrawn due to injury early in the series and replaced by Rohan Gavaskar. Amit Bhandari added to the squad on January 10.

ZIMBABWE SQUAD: Heath Streak (captain), Tatenda Taibu (vice-captain), Andy Blignaut, Stuart Carlisle, Sean Ervine, Grant Flower, Travis Friend, Douglas Hondo, Blessing Mahwire, Stuart Matsikenyeri, Ray Price, Vusi Sibanda, Mark Vermeulen. Craig Wishart withdrawn during the series and replaced by Dion Ebrahim.

Date	Venue	Batting First	Batting Second	Result	Man of Match	Attendance
Jan 9	Melbourne	Australia 288	India 270	Aus by 18 runs	A Symonds (A)	63271
Jan 11	Sydney	Australia 8/225	Zimbabwe 126	Aus by 99 runs	BA Williams (A)	19494
Jan 14	Hobart	Zimbabwe 6/208	India 3/211	Ind by 7 wkts	V Sehwag (I)	3109
Jan 16	Hobart	Australia 7/344	Zimbabwe 6/196	Aus by 149 runs	AC Gilchrist (A)	12715
Jan 18	Brisbane	India 4/305	Australia 284	Ind by 19 runs	VVS Laxman (I)	35052
Jan 20	Brisbane	India 6/255	Zimbabwe 9/231	Ind by 24 runs	Yuvraj Singh (I)	9638
Jan 22	Sydney	India 4/296	Australia 8/225	Aus by 2 wkts (D/L)	Yuvraj Singh (I)	39088
Jan 24	Adelaide	India 4/296	Zimbabwe 8/225	Ind by 3 runs	VVS Laxman (I)	8680
Jan 26	Adelaide	Australia 7/279	Zimbabwe 8/266	Aus by 13 runs	GW Flower (Z)	27612
Jan 29	Melbourne	Australia 9/263	Zimbabwe	No result	No award	15218
Feb 1	Perth	India 203	Australia 5/204	Aus by 5 wkts	AC Gilchrist (A)	18858
Feb 3	Perth	Zimbabwe 135	India 6/136	Ind by 4 wkts	IK Pathan (I)	4053

Finals

Date	Venue	Batting First	Batting Second	Result	Man of Match	Attendance
Feb 6	Melbourne	India 222	Australia 3/224	Aus by 7 wkts	RT Ponting (A)	44835
Feb 8	Sydney	Australia 5/359	India 151	Aus by 208 runs	ML Hayden (A)	39760

(Player of the Series: AC Gilchrist)

INTERNATIONAL LIMITED OVERS GAME 1

AUSTRALIA v INDIA
Melbourne Cricket Ground, Melbourne. January 9, 2004.
Toss: Australia. Australia won by 18 runs.

AUSTRALIA	
AC Gilchrist (+) c Pathan b Agarkar	34
ML Hayden c Yuvraj Singh b Agarkar	20
RT Ponting (c) c and b Balaji	18
DR Martyn c Balaji b Agarkar	0
A Symonds c Kumble b Agarkar	88
MJ Clarke c Laxman b Kumble	63
MG Bevan c Ganguly b Sehwag	1
IJ Harvey c Tendulkar b Agarkar	28
AJ Bichel run out (Balaji)	1
JN Gillespie not out	8
BA Williams c Yuvraj Singh b Agarkar	0
EXTRAS (LB 10, W 14, NB 3)	27
TOTAL	288

FOW: 59 70 70 89 232 233 258 272 287 288

Bowling: Agarkar 9.3–1–42–6, Pathan 10–0–61–0, Balaji 9–0–52–1, Kumble 10–0–56–1, Bangar 3–0–19–0, Ganguly 5–0–40–0, Sehwag 2–1–8–1.

INDIA	
V Sehwag b Harvey	35
SR Tendulkar c Ponting b Symonds	63
SC Ganguly (c) run out (Harvey)	82
VVS Laxman c Clarke b Symonds	16
RS Dravid (+) c Harvey b Clarke	16
Yuvraj Singh c Clarke b Harvey	25
SB Bangar c Ponting b Harvey	3
AB Agarkar c Clarke b Gillespie	1
IK Pathan c Hayden b Williams	3
AR Kumble c Clarke b Williams	5
L Balaji not out	0
EXTRAS (B 1, LB 8, W 11, NB 1)	21
TOTAL	270

FOW: 103 134 168 195 257 257 260 263 266 270

Bowling: Gillespie 10–1–50–1, Williams 9–0–52–2, Bichel 6–0–38–0, Harvey 10–1–52–3, Symonds 10–0–47–2, Clarke 4–0–22–1.

Umpires: SA Bucknor & SJA Taufel (TV Umpire – RL Parry)

INTERNATIONAL LIMITED OVERS GAME 2

AUSTRALIA v ZIMBABWE
Sydney Cricket Ground, Sydney. January 11, 2004.
Toss: Australia. Australia won by 99 runs.

AUSTRALIA	
AC Gilchrist (+) c Taibu b Blignaut	34
ML Hayden b Streak	14
RT Ponting (c) c Carlisle b Blignaut	21
DR Martyn c and b Flower	21
A Symonds c Hondo b Ervine	42
MG Bevan c Flower b Flower	3
MJ Clarke c Sibanda b Ervine	40
IJ Harvey c Ervine b Ervine	22
AJ Bichel not out	11
JN Gillespie not out	1
BA Williams	
EXTRAS (LB 4, W 6, NB 6)	16
TOTAL	8 for 225

FOW: 42 73 77 112 118 184 192 222

Bowling: Streak 10–2–36–1, Hondo 5–1–35–0, Ervine 10–0–53–3, Blignaut 5–0–21–2, Price 10–0–34–0, Flower 10–0–42–2.

ZIMBABWE	
V Sibanda c Williams b Gillespie	7
SV Carlisle c Hayden b Williams	1
MA Vermeulen b Williams	5
GW Flower lbw b Williams	0
S Matsikenyeri c Gilchrist b Williams	0
T Taibu (+) c Gilchrist b Symonds	29
HH Streak (c) st Gilchrist b Clarke	46
SM Ervine c Ponting b Symonds	14
AM Blignaut c Ponting b Williams	4
RW Price b Gillespie	0
DT Hondo not out	1
EXTRAS (B 1, LB 6, W 12)	19
TOTAL	126

FOW: 2 13 13 14 17 90 119 122 124 126

Bowling: Gillespie 8–0–21–2, Williams 8.3–2–22–5, Bichel 6–2–24–0, Harvey 4–0–14–0, Symonds 6–1–24–2, Clarke 5–0–14–1.

Umpires: RE Koertzen & SJA Taufel (TV Umpire – RL Parry)

INTERNATIONAL LIMITED OVERS GAME 3

INDIA v ZIMBABWE at Bellerive Oval, Hobart, January 14, 2003. India won by seven wickets. Zimbabwe 6 for 208 (SV Carlisle 36, HH Streak 59*, SM Ervine 48*; V Sehwag 2/40). India 3 for 211 (V Sehwag 90, SR Tendulkar 44, SC Ganguly 32*). Man of the Match: V Sehwag.

INTERNATIONAL LIMITED OVERS GAME 4

AUSTRALIA v ZIMBABWE
Bellerive Oval, Hobart. January 16, 2004.
Toss: Australia. Australia won by 148 runs.

AUSTRALIA	
AC Gilchrist (+) b Ervine	172
ML Hayden c Sibanda b Streak	63
RT Ponting (c) c Matsikenyeri b Flower	37
DR Martyn not out	47
A Symonds run out (Matsikenyeri/Ervine)	0
MG Bevan c Streak b Ervine	7
MJ Clarke c Vermeulen b Streak	0
AJ Bichel b Streak	0
GB Hogg not out	6
B Lee	
BA Williams	
EXTRAS (B 1, LB 5, W 4, NB 2)	12
TOTAL	7 for 344

FOW: 140 246 310 310 326 332 333

Bowling: Streak 10–1–50–3, Hondo 6–0–41–0, Blignaut 8–0–66–0, Ervine 9–0–65–2, Price 10–0–59–0, Flower 6–0–40–1, Matsikenyeri 1–0–17–0.

ZIMBABWE	
DD Ebrahim c Gilchrist b Symonds	21
V Sibanda c Gilchrist b Lee	1
MA Vermeulen c Gilchrist b Williams	1
GW Flower run out (Hogg/Symonds)	40
SM Ervine c Bichel b Hogg	8
HH Streak (c) not out	64
T Taibu (+) c Hayden b Bichel	44
S Matsikenyeri not out	1
AM Blignaut	
RW Price	
DT Hondo	
EXTRAS (LB 11, W 5)	16
TOTAL	6 for 196

FOW: 15 19 36 52 93 195

Bowling: Lee 10–1–29–1, Williams 8–0–25–1, Bichel 9–0–31–1, Symonds 10–0–48–1, Hogg 10–0–36–1, Clarke 3–0–16–0.

Umpires: SJ Davis & RE Koertzen (TV Umpire – PD Parker)

INTERNATIONAL LIMITED OVERS GAME 5

AUSTRALIA v INDIA
Brisbane Cricket Ground, Brisbane. January 18, 2004.
Toss: India. India won by 19 runs.

INDIA	
SC Ganguly (c) c and b Williams	18
SR Tendulkar c and b Symonds	86
VVS Laxman not out	103
RS Dravid (+) c Williams b Harvey	74
Yuvraj Singh b Lee	5
RS Gavaskar not out	2
HK Badani	
IK Pathan	
AR Kumble	
L Balaji	
A Nehra	
EXTRAS (B 4, LB 2, W 6, NB 3)	15
TOTAL	4 for 303

FOW: 37 147 280 295

Bowling: Gillespie 10–0–40–0, Williams 8–0–40–1, Lee 10–0–83–1, Harvey 10–0–61–1, Symonds 8–0–47–1, Clarke 4–0–26–0.

AUSTRALIA	
AC Gilchrist (+) c Balaji b Pathan	21
ML Hayden c Dravid b Pathan	109
RT Ponting (c) c Laxman b Balaji	7
DR Martyn c Yuvraj Singh b Balaji	1
A Symonds c and b Gavaskar	20
MJ Clarke c Dravid b Pathan	42
MG Bevan not out	41
IJ Harvey c Gavaskar b Nehra	13
B Lee c Kumble b Balaji	6
JN Gillespie c Pathan b Balaji	6
BA Williams run out (Dravid)	0
EXTRAS (B 1, LB 3, W 12, NB 2)	18
TOTAL	284

FOW: 46 86 94 141 204 224 249 266 282 284

Bowling: Nehra 10–0–53–1, Pathan 9.4–0–64–3, Balaji 10–0–48–4, Kumble 10–0–53–0, Gavaskar 9–0–56–1, Ganguly 1–0–6–0.

Umpires: SA Bucknor & PD Parker (TV Umpire – SJ Davis)

INTERNATIONAL LIMITED OVERS GAME 6

INDIA v ZIMBABWE at Brisbane Cricket Ground, Brisbane, January 20, 2004. India won by 24 runs. India 6 for 255 (SC Ganguly 33, RS Dravid 84, Yuvraj Singh 69; HH Streak 2/48, SM Ervine 3/47). Zimbabwe 9 for 231 (GW Flower 36, SV Carlisle 34, SM Ervine 39, DD Ebrahim 39; L Balaji 2/37, SC Ganguly 3/55). Man of the Match: Yuvraj Singh.

INTERNATIONAL LIMITED OVERS GAME 7

AUSTRALIA v INDIA
Sydney Cricket Ground, Sydney. January 22, 2004.
Toss: India. Australia won by two wkts (D/L Method).

INDIA	
SC Ganguly (c) c Gilchrist b Lee	1
PA Patel (+) c Gilchrist b Gillespie	28
VVS Laxman not out	106
RS Dravid c Gilchrist b Bichel	12
Yuvraj Singh lbw b Lee	139
RS Gavaskar not out	2
HK Badani	
AB Agarkar	
M Kartik	
IK Pathan	
L Balaji	
EXTRAS (LB 1, W 5, NB 2)	8
TOTAL	4 for 296

FOW: 1 63 80 293

Bowling: Gillespie 10–0–50–1, Lee 9–0–46–2, Bichel 9–0–60–1, Harvey 10–0–68–0, Symonds 7–0–42–0, Clarke 5–0–29–0.

AUSTRALIA	
AC Gilchrist (+) c and b Kartik	95
SM Katich c Ganguly b Pathan	2
RT Ponting (c) c Patel b Pathan	42
DR Martyn c Patel b Pathan	0
A Symonds c Agarkar b Ganguly	16
MG Bevan b Ganguly	12
MJ Clarke c Badani b Ganguly	21
IJ Harvey run out (Agarkar/Ganguly)	1
AJ Bichel not out	2
B Lee not out	12
JN Gillespie	
EXTRAS (B 7, W 15)	22
TOTAL	8 for 225

FOW: 24 150 150 154 176 195 202 210

Bowling: Agarkar 7–1–47–0, Pathan 7–1–51–3, Balaji 5.5–0–40–0, Ganguly 7–0–41–3, Kartik 7–0–39–1.

Umpires: SA Bucknor & DJ Harper (TV Umpire – SJA Taufel)

INTERNATIONAL LIMITED OVERS GAME 8

INDIA v ZIMBABWE at Adelaide Oval, Adelaide, January 24, 2004. India won by three runs. India 7 for 280 (VVS Laxman 131, RS Dravid 56, RS Gavaskar 54; HH Streak 3/53, DT Hondo 2/59). Zimbabwe 6 for 277 (SV Carlisle 109, SM Ervine 100; AB Agarkar 3/39). Man of the Match: VVS Laxman.

INTERNATIONAL LIMITED OVERS GAME 9

AUSTRALIA v ZIMBABWE
Adelaide Oval, Adelaide. January 26, 2004.
Toss: Australia. Australia won by 13 runs.

AUSTRALIA	
ML Hayden c Ebrahim b Blignaut	20
DR Martyn c Ebrahim b Streak	9
RT Ponting (c) run out (Blignaut/Taibu)	63
MG Bevan c Ervine b Hondo	75
MJ Clarke run out (Flower/Taibu)	36
A Symonds c Hondo b Streak	34
BJ Haddin (+) lbw b Streak	14
GB Hogg not out	1
B Lee not out	6
JN Gillespie	
BA Williams	
EXTRAS (B 1, LB 9, W 9, NB 2)	21
TOTAL	7 for 279

FOW: 25 84 128 205 230 271 272

Bowling: Streak 10–0–45–3, Blignaut 9–0–53–1, Ervine 5–0–41–0, Hondo 6–0–45–1, Price 10–0–40–0, Flower 10–0–45–0.

ZIMBABWE	
GW Flower c Haddin b Gillespie	94
T Taibu (+) b Williams	9
TJ Friend b Lee	8
SV Carlisle c (sub) Harvey b Williams	15
SM Ervine c Lee b Hogg	33
HH Streak (c) c and b Symonds	28
DD Ebrahim st Haddin b Symonds	11
S Matsikenyeri b Clarke	5
AM Blignaut not out	31
RW Price not out	13
DT Hondo	
EXTRAS (B 11, LB 1, W 5, NB 2)	19
TOTAL	8 for 266

FOW: 29 55 90 159 169 191 206 229

Bowling: Gillespie 10–2–40–1, Lee 8–0–32–1, Williams 8–1–38–2, Hogg 10–0–40–1, Clarke 7–0–57–1, Symonds 7–0–47–2.

Umpires: SA Bucknor & SJ Davis (TV Umpire – DJ Harper)

INTERNATIONAL LIMITED OVERS GAME 10

AUSTRALIA v ZIMBABWE
Melbourne Cricket Ground, Melbourne. January 29, 2004.
Toss: Zimbabwe. No result.

AUSTRALIA	
ML Hayden b Hondo	23
DR Martyn lbw b Streak	42
RT Ponting (c) c Mahwire b Price	35
MJ Clarke b Mahwire	11
IJ Harvey run out (Blignaut/Taibu)	23
MG Bevan run out (Blignaut/Taibu)	56
BJ Haddin (+) b Streak	32
GB Hogg run out (Streak)	0
AJ Bichel not out	23
B Lee c Blignaut b Ervine	3
BA Williams not out	0
EXTRAS (LB 7, W 4, NB 4)	15
TOTAL	9 for 263

FOW: 59 69 97 139 155 213 214 252 257

Bowling: Streak 10–0–47–2, Blignaut 4–1–23–0, Hondo 4–0–35–1, Mahwire 6–1–35–1, Ervine 7–0–36–1, Flower 9–0–42–0, Price 10–0–38–1.

ZIMBABWE
GW Flower
V Sibanda
SV Carlisle
SM Ervine
T Taibu (+)
HH Streak (c)
DD Ebrahim
AM Blignaut
RW Price
DT Hondo
NB Mahwire

Umpires: RE Koertzen & PD Parker
(TV Umpire – RL Parry)

INTERNATIONAL LIMITED OVERS GAME 11

AUSTRALIA v INDIA
WACA Ground, Perth. February 1, 2004.
Toss: India. Australia won by five wickets.

INDIA	
V Sehwag c Lee b Gillespie	32
SR Tendulkar c Hayden b Lee	5
VVS Laxman c Gilchrist b Lee	1
RS Dravid (+) c Hussey b Williams	13
SC Ganguly (c) c Gilchrist b Bichel	1
Yuvraj Singh c Gilchrist b Symonds	47
RS Gavaskar b Lee	6
AB Agarkar run out (Katich/Hussey)	9
IK Pathan c Bichel b Symonds	20
M Kartik not out	32
L Balaji run out (Martyn/Gilchrist)	11
EXTRAS (LB 7, W 16, NB 3)	26
TOTAL	203

FOW: 20 32 50 57 79 101 129 142 172 203

Bowling: Gillespie 10–0–51–1, Lee 10–2–22–3, Williams 7–2–23–1, Bichel 7–0–44–1, Symonds 10–0–37–2, Hussey 3–0–15–0, Clarke 2–0–4–0.

AUSTRALIA	
AC Gilchrist (c+) c Balaji b Pathan	75
ML Hayden c Gavaskar b Agarkar	0
DR Martyn c Laxman b Agarkar	2
MJ Clarke c Sehwag b Balaji	2
A Symonds c Laxman b Pathan	73
SM Katich not out	18
MEK Hussey not out	17
B Lee	
JN Gillespie	
BA Williams	
AJ Bichel	
EXTRAS (B 1, LB 2, W 14)	17
TOTAL	5 for 204

FOW: 14 16 37 159 165

Bowling: Agarkar 9–0–56–2, Pathan 8–0–69–2, Balaji 10–1–37–1, Kartik 5–0–39–0.

Umpires: SA Bucknor & DJ Harper (TV Umpire – SJA Taufel)

INTERNATIONAL LIMITED OVERS GAME 12

INDIA v ZIMBABWE at WACA. Ground, Perth, February 3, 2004. India won by four wickets. Zimbabwe 135 (S Matsikenyeri 36; IK Pathan 4/24, A Bhandari 3/31). India 6 for 136 (VVS Laxman 32, HK Badani 34*; AM Blignaut 2/41, SM Ervine 2/29). Man of the Match: IK Pathan.

POINTS TABLE

	Played	Won	Lost	No Result	Bonus Points	Points	Net run rate
Australia	8	6	1	1	4	37	1.0999
India	8	5	3	–	4	29	0.2816
Zimbabwe	8	–	7	1	3	6	1.3260

FIRST FINAL

AUSTRALIA v INDIA
Melbourne Cricket Ground, Melbourne. February 6, 2004.
Toss: India. Australia won by seven wickets.

INDIA	
V Sehwag c Gilchrist b Gillespie	3
SR Tendulkar b Lee	8
VVS Laxman c Symonds b Williams	24
RS Dravid (+) c Hayden b Harvey	12
SC Ganguly (c) c Gilchrist b Harvey	6
Yuvraj Singh c Gilchrist b Lee	21
HK Badani not out	60
AB Agarkar c Lee b Clarke	53
IK Pathan run out (Clarke/Gilchrist)	19
AR Kumble run out (Clarke/Gilchrist)	2
L Balaji b Gillespie	2
EXTRAS (LB 6, W 2, NB 4)	12
TOTAL	222

FOW: 6 14 48 48 75 75 177 209 217 222

Bowling: Gillespie 10–0–39–2, Lee 9–0–34–2, Williams 10–1–38–1, Harvey 10–0–40–2, Symonds 7–0–47–0, Clarke 3–0–18–1.

AUSTRALIA	
AC Gilchrist (+) c Tendulkar b Balaji	38
ML Hayden c and b Balaji	50
RT Ponting (c) c Dravid b Balaji	88
DR Martyn not out	20
A Symonds not out	10
MJ Clarke	
SM Katich	
B Lee	
JN Gillespie	
BA Williams	
IJ Harvey	
EXTRAS (B 6, LB 2, W 8, NB 2)	18
TOTAL	3 for 224

FOW: 48 187 193

Bowling: Agarkar 9.1–0–58–0, Balaji 10–1–52–3, Pathan 8–0–36–0, Kumble 7–0–36–0, Sehwag 5–0–29–0, Ganguly 1–0–5–0.

Umpires: SA Bucknor & SJA Taufel (TV Umpire – DJ Harper)

SECOND FINAL

AUSTRALIA v INDIA
Sydney Cricket Ground, Sydney. February 8, 2004.
Toss: India. Australia won by 208 runs.

AUSTRALIA	
AC Gilchrist (+) c Ganguly b Nehra	29
ML Hayden b Tendulkar	126
RT Ponting (c) c Dravid b Pathan	4
DR Martyn c Badani b Pathan	67
A Symonds b Nehra	66
MJ Clarke not out	33
SM Katich not out	11
IJ Harvey	
B Lee	
JN Gillespie	
BA Williams	
EXTRAS (LB 6, W 15, NB 2)	23
TOTAL	5 for 359

FOW: 62 73 230 248 347

Bowling: Pathan 10–0–75–2, Balaji 9–0–65–0, Nehra 10–0–63–2, Kartik 7–0–51–0, Sehwag 5–0–30–0, Ganguly 1–0–9–0, Tendulkar 8–0–60–1.

INDIA	
V Sehwag c Lee b Gillespie	12
SR Tendulkar c Lee b Gillespie	27
VVS Laxman c and b Lee	5
SC Ganguly (c) c Symonds b Harvey	3
RS Dravid (+) run out (Martyn)	0
Yuvraj Singh c Gilchrist b Harvey	4
HK Badani run out (Gilchrist/Symonds)	18
IK Pathan b Lee	30
M Kartik c Gilchrist b Williams	23
L Balaji b Williams	2
A Nehra not out	14
EXTRAS (LB 7, W 4, NB 2)	13
TOTAL	151

FOW: 22 49 49 52 56 59 99 123 136 151

Bowling: Gillespie 9–1–52–2, Lee 10–1–39–2, Williams 6.2–1–12–2, Harvey 5–2–30–2, Symonds 3–1–11–0.

Umpires: DJ Harper & RE Koertzen (TV Umpire – SJA Taufel)

2003–04 VB SERIES INTERNATIONAL LIMITED OVERS

Batting	Team	M	Inn	NO	Runs	HS	50	100	Avrge	Ct/St	Stk-Rt
AC Gilchrist	Aus	8	8	–	498	172	2	1	62.25	16/1	121.46
VVS Laxman	Ind	10	10	3	443	131	–	3	63.29	12	82.34
ML Hayden	Aus	9	9	–	425	126	2	2	47.22	5	81.89
A Symonds	Aus	9	9	1	349	88	3	–	43.63	4	93.82
RT Ponting	Aus	9	9	–	315	88	2	–	35.00	4	82.68
Yuvraj Singh	Ind	9	8	–	314	139	1	1	39.25	4	92.63
RS Dravid	Ind	10	9	–	277	84	3	–	30.78	5	74.86
SM Ervine	Zim	8	7	1	265	100	–	1	44.17	2	100.00
MJ Clarke	Aus	10	9	1	248	63	1	–	31.00	4	89.86
SR Tendulkar	Ind	7	7	–	236	86	2	–	33.71	2	78.15
SV Carlisle	Zim	7	6	–	223	109	–	1	37.17	2	65.78
HH Streak	Zim	8	7	3	211	64*	2	–	52.75	2	68.73
DR Martyn	Aus	10	10	2	209	67	1	–	26.13	–	89.70
MG Bevan	Aus	7	7	1	195	75	2	–	32.50	–	83.33
GW Flower	Zim	7	6	–	195	94	1	–	32.50	3	67.01
V Sehwag	Ind	6	6	–	195	90	1	–	32.50	3	83.33
SC Ganguly	Ind	9	9	1	177	82	1	–	22.13	5	75.32
HK Badani	Ind	8	6	3	133	60*	1	–	44.33	3	68.21
T Taibu	Zim	8	6	–	113	44	–	–	18.83	5	47.88
RS Gavaskar	Ind	6	6	2	90	54	1	–	22.50	4	83.33
IJ Harvey	Aus	7	5	–	87	28	–	–	17.40	1	89.69
IK Pathan	Ind	10	7	3	85	30	–	–	21.25	2	80.19
DD Ebrahim	Zim	6	5	1	80	39	–	–	20.00	3	72.73
AB Agarkar	Ind	6	4	1	75	53	1	–	25.00	1	65.22
M Kartik	Ind	4	2	1	55	32*	–	–	55.00	2	82.09
S Matsikenyeri	Zim	5	5	1	51	36	–	–	12.75	2	68.92
AM Blignaut	Zim	8	5	1	50	31*	–	–	12.50	3	94.34
PA Patel	Ind	3	3	–	47	28	–	–	15.67	4	67.14
BJ Haddin	Aus	2	2	–	46	32	–	–	23.00	1/1	73.02
AJ Bichel	Aus	6	5	3	37	23*	–	–	18.50	2	88.10
V Sibanda	Zim	6	5	–	32	12	–	–	6.40	2	37.65
SM Katich	Aus	4	3	2	31	18*	–	–	31.00	–	68.89

continued

Batting	Team	M	Inn	NO	Runs	HS	50	100	Avrge	Ct/St	Stk-Rt
RW Price	Zim	8	4	2	31	18*	–	–	15.50	–	88.57
B Lee	Aus	8	4	2	27	12*	–	–	13.50	6	93.10
MA Vermeulen	Zim	4	4	1	22	14+	–	–	7.33	1	36.07
MEK Hussey	Aus	1	1	1	17	17*	–	–	–	1	73.91
TJ Friend	Zim	4	4	–	16	8	–	–	4.00	2	34.78
L Balaji	Ind	10	4	1	15	11	–	–	5.00	6	34.01
JN Gillespie	Aus	8	3	2	15	8*	–	–	15.00	–	71.43
A Nehra	Ind	4	1	1	14	14*	–	–	–	–	350.00
NB Mahwire	Zim	2	1	1	8	8*	–	–	–	1	29.63
AR Kumble	Ind	5	2	–	7	5	–	–	3.50	2	100.00
GB Hogg	Aus	3	3	2	7	6*	–	–	7.00	–	100.00
SB Bangar	Ind	2	2	–	3	3	–	–	1.50	–	33.33
DT Hondo	Zim	7	2	1	1	1*	–	–	1.00	3	33.33
BA Williams	Aus	9	3	1	0	0*	–	–	0.00	3	0.00
A Bhandari	Ind	1	–	–	–	–	–	–	–	–	–

Bowling	Team	Overs	Mds	Runs	Wkts	Avrge	5wi	Best	RPO
IK Pathan	Ind	89.4	4	497	16	31.06	–	4/24	5.54
HH Streak	Zim	72.0	7	338	15	22.53	–	3/45	4.69
BA Williams	Aus	64.5	7	250	15	16.67	1	5/22	3.86
L Balaji	Ind	90.0	6	441	13	33.92	–	4/48	4.90
SM Ervine	Zim	63.3	2	361	12	30.08	–	3/47	5.69
B Lee	Aus	66.0	4	285	12	23.75	–	3/22	4.32
AB Agarkar	Ind	52.4	4	281	11	25.55	1	6/42	5.34
JN Gillespie	Aus	77.0	4	343	10	34.30	–	2/21	4.45
A Symonds	Aus	68.0	2	350	10	35.00	–	2/24	5.15
IJ Harvey	Aus	49.0	3	265	8	33.13	–	3/52	5.41
AM Blignaut	Zim	53.0	2	301	6	50.17	–	2/21	5.68
SC Ganguly	Ind	30.0	–	189	6	31.50	–	3/41	6.30
DT Hondo	Zim	45.0	1	293	5	58.60	–	2/59	6.51
A Nehra	Ind	36.0	2	199	5	39.80	–	2/63	5.53
MJ Clarke	Aus	33.0	–	186	4	46.50	–	1/14	5.64
RW Price	Zim	70.0	–	324	4	81.00	–	1/38	4.63
A Bhandari	Ind	7.4	–	31	3	10.33	–	3/31	4.04

continued

Bowling	Team	Overs	Mds	Runs	Wkts	Avrge	5wi	Best	RPO
AJ Bichel	Aus	37.0	2	197	3	65.67	–	1/31	5.32
GW Flower	Zim	52.4	–	256	3	85.33	–	2/42	4.86
V Sehwag	Ind	22.0	1	107	3	35.67	–	2/40	4.86
GB Hogg	Aus	20.0	–	76	2	38.00	–	1/36	3.80
AR Kumble	Ind	47.0	2	227	2	113.50	–	1/38	4.83
HK Badani	Ind	7.0	–	31	1	31.00	–	1/31	4.43
SB Bangar	Ind	11.0	–	61	1	61.00	–	1/42	5.55
RS Gavaskar	Ind	9.0	–	56	1	56.00	–	1/56	6.22
M Kartik	Ind	26.0	–	178	1	178.00	–	1/39	6.85
NB Mahwire	Zim	6.0	1	35	1	35.00	–	1/35	5.83
SR Tendulkar	Ind	8.0	–	60	1	60.00	–	1/60	7.50
TJ Friend	Zim	5.0	–	24	0	–	–	–	4.80
MEK Hussey	Aus	3.0	–	15	0	–	–	–	5.00
S Matsikenyeri	Zim	1.0	–	17	0	–	–	–	17.00

2003–04 SRI LANKA v AUSTRALIA

AUSTRALIAN TEST SQUAD

Ricky Ponting (captain) Tas, Adam Gilchrist (vice-captain) WA, Jason Gillespie SA, Matthew Hayden Qld, Michael Kasprowicz Qld, Simon Katich NSW, Justin Langer WA, Darren Lehmann SA, Stuart MacGiill NSW, Damien Martyn WA, Wade Seccombe Qld, Andrew Symonds Qld, Shane Warne Vic, Brad Williams WA. Brett Lee NSW replaced on March 11 by Shaun Tait SA due to injury.

AUSTRALIAN INTERNATIONAL LIMITED SQUAD

Ricky Ponting (captain) Tas, Adam Gilchrist (vice-captain) WA, Michael Bevan NSW, Michael Clarke NSW, Jason Gillespie SA, Brad Haddin NSW, Ian Harvey Vic, Matthew Hayden Qld, Brad Hogg WA, Michael Kasprowicz Qld, Simon Katich NSW, Brett Lee NSW, Damien Martyn WA, Andrew Symonds Qld, Brad Williams WA.

Team Management: John Buchanan (Coach), Steve Bernard (Team Manager), Tim Nielsen (Performance Analyst/Assistant), Alex Kountouri (Physiotherapist), Lucy Frostick (Masseur), Jock Campbell (Physical Performance Manager), Jonathan Rose (Media Manager).

AUSTRALIAN TOUR RESULTS
Test matches – Played 3: Won 3, Lost 0.
First-class matches – Played 4, Won 4, Lost 0.
Wins – Sri Lanka (3), Sri Lanka Cricket President's XI.
International limited overs – Played 5: Won 3, Lost 2.

SRI LANKA CRICKET PRESIDENT'S XI v AUSTRALIANS at De Zoysa Stadium, Moratuwa, February 17, 2004. Australians won by five wickets. 8 for 283 (WS Jayantha 50, J Mubarak 56, RP Arnold 35, WMG Ramyakumara 33*; GB Hogg 2/46). Australian XI 2 for 284 (AC Gilchrist 43, ML Hayden 35, RT Ponting 57, DR Martyn 41, A Symonds 47).

INTERNATIONAL LIMITED OVERS GAME 1

SRI LANKA v AUSTRALIA
Rangiri Dambulla International Stadium, Dambulla. February 20, 2004.
Toss: Australia. Australia won by 84 runs.

AUSTRALIA	
AC Gilchrist (+) c Atapattu b Chandana	66
ML Hayden run out (Atapattu)	40
RT Ponting (c) c Dilshan b Jayasuriya	58
DR Martyn c and b Chandana	27
MG Bevan st Kaluwitharana b Muralitharan	21
A Symonds not out	37
MJ Clarke lbw b Muralitharan	0
GB Hogg not out	2
B Lee	
JN Gillespie	
BA Williams	
EXTRAS (LB 5, W 5, NB 1)	11
TOTAL	6 for 262

FOW: 104 114 189 207 239 239

Bowling: Vaas 3–0–19–0, Kulasekara 3–0–18–0, Dharmasena 10–0–49–0, Dilshan 5–0–28–0, Muralitharan 10–2–30–2, Chandana 10–0–47–2, Jayasuriya 9–0–66–1.

SRI LANKA	
ST Jayasuriya run out (Lee/Gilchrist)	8
RS Kaluwitharana (+) run out (Ponting)	2
MS Atapattu (c) b Gillespie	1
KC Sangakkara c Gilchrist b Lee	58
DPM Jayawardene b Symonds	61
TM Dilshan not out	18
UDU Chandana lbw b Hogg	9
WPUJC Vaas c Hayden b Hogg	0
HDPK Dharmasena st Gilchrist b Hogg	0
KMDN Kulasekara b Hogg	1
M Muralitharan c Lee b Hogg	0
EXTRAS (B 1, LB 2, W 13, NB 4)	20
TOTAL	178

FOW: 12 13 24 145 147 166 170 170 178 178

Bowling: Gillespie 6–2–14–1, Lee 8–1–31–1, Williams 5–0–28–0, Hogg 9.3–1–41–5, Clarke 5–0–21–0, Symonds 10–0–40–1.

Umpires: BF Bowden & EAR De Silva (TV Umpire – PT Manuel)

INTERNATIONAL LIMITED OVERS GAME 2

SRI LANKA v AUSTRALIA
Rangiri Dambulla International Stadium, Dambulla. February 22, 2004.
Toss: Sri Lanka. Sri Lanka won by one run.

SRI LANKA	
MS Atapattu (c) run out (Ponting)	47
ST Jayasuriya lbw b Symonds	55
KC Sangakkara c Bevan b Harvey	39
DPM Jayawardene c Ponting b Clarke	38
TM Dilshan b Clarke	11
RS Kaluwitharana (+) run out (Hayden/Gilchrist)	0
UDU Chandana c Gilchrist b Clarke	4
RP Arnold lbw b Clarke	10
WPUJC Vaas c Lee b Clarke	5
HDPK Dharmasena run out (Ponting/Harvey)	2
M Muralitharan not out	2
EXTRAS (B 1, LB 16, W 8, NB 7)	32
TOTAL	245

FOW: 121 122 192 216 220 225 226 236 242 245

Bowling: Gillespie 7–0–36–0, Lee 6–0–39–0, Harvey 9–0–38–1, Symonds 10–0–45–1, Hogg 10–1–35–0, Clarke 7.5–0–35–5.

AUSTRALIA	
MJ Clarke c Chandana b Vaas	0
ML Hayden c Jayawardene b Dharmasena	93
RT Ponting (c) c Vaas b Chandana	69
DR Martyn c Atapattu b Vaas	5
A Symonds not out	36
AC Gilchrist (+) c and b Vaas	0
MG Bevan not out	24
IJ Harvey	
GB Hogg	
B Lee	
JN Gillespie	
EXTRAS (B 1, LB 7, W 9)	17
TOTAL	5 for 244

FOW: 0 148 170 190 192

Bowling: Vaas 10–0–48–3, Dilshan 6–0–32–0, Dharmasena 10–0–40–1, Muralitharan 10–0–49–0, Chandana 9–0–40–1, Arnold 2–0–9–0, Jayasuriya 3–0–18–0.

Umpires: BF Bowden & PT Manuel (TV Umpire – MG Silva)

INTERNATIONAL LIMITED OVERS GAME 3

SRI LANKA v AUSTRALIA
R Premadasa Stadium, Colombo. February 25, 2004.
Toss: Sri Lanka. Australia won by five wickets.

SRI LANKA	
MS Atapattu (c) b Gillespie	3
ST Jayasuriya c Clarke b Gillespie	0
KC Sangakkara (+) c Hayden b Gillespie	15
DPM Jayawardene run out (Hogg/Gilchrist)	80
RP Arnold c Clarke b Hogg	4
TM Dilshan c Gilchrist b Symonds	30
UDU Chandana run out (Hogg/Symonds)	34
WPUJC Vaas c Hogg b Kasprowicz	24
HDPK Dharmasena not out	24
DNT Zoysa not out	0
M Muralitharan	
EXTRAS (B 1, LB 8, W 3)	12
TOTAL	8 for 226

FOW: 1 10 34 54 112 170 182 218

Bowling: Gillespie 10–1–36–3, Kasprowicz 10–2–37–1, Harvey 6–0–29–0, Hogg 10–0–41–1, Clarke 5–0–26–0, Symonds 9–0–48–1.

AUSTRALIA	
AC Gilchrist (+) c Jayawardene b Vaas	0
ML Hayden c Muralitharan b Vaas	3
RT Ponting (c) b Vaas	63
DR Martyn run out (Jayasuriya)	62
A Symonds not out	45
MG Bevan run out (Jayawardene/Jayasuriya)	10
MJ Clarke not out	31
IJ Harvey	
GB Hogg	
MS Kasprowicz	
JN Gillespie	
EXTRAS (LB 4, W 8, NB 1)	13
TOTAL	5 for 227

FOW: 3 4 133 136 159

Bowling: Vaas 9–2–34–3, Zoysa 7.1–0–37–0, Dharmasena 6.5–0–31–0, Muralitharan 10–0–43–0, Chandana 7–0–36–0, Jayasuriya 8–0–40–0, Dilshan 0.3–0–2–0.

Umpires: BF Bowden & EAR De Silva (TV Umpire – MG Silva)

INTERNATIONAL LIMITED OVERS GAME 4

SRI LANKA v AUSTRALIA
R Premadasa Stadium, Colombo. February 27, 2004.
Toss: Australia. Australia won by 40 runs.

AUSTRALIA	
AC Gilchrist (+) c Sangakkara b Zoysa	14
ML Hayden c Zoysa b Vaas	15
RT Ponting (c) lbw b Muralitharan	67
DR Martyn c Zoysa b Lokuarachchi	1
A Symonds c Jayantha b Muralitharan	53
MG Bevan c and b Muralitharan	14
MJ Clarke c Dilshan b Chandana	36
IJ Harvey run out (Atapattu/Muralitharan)	4
GB Hogg lbw b Chandana	0
MS Kasprowicz c Sangakkara b Chandana	0
JN Gillespie not out	8
EXTRAS (LB 3, W 12, NB 6)	21
TOTAL	233

FOW: 28 42 62 136 177 201 205 205 206 233

Bowling: Vaas 10–0–45–1, Zoysa 8–0–40–1, Lokuarachchi 8–0–40–1, Muralitharan 10–0–44–3, Jayasuriya 4–0–24–0, Chandana 7.4–0–37–3.

SRI LANKA	
MS Atapattu (c) c Bevan b Hogg	19
ST Jayasuriya c Gilchrist b Kasprowicz	0
KC Sangakkara (+) c Gilchrist b Kasprowicz	101
DPM Jayawardene c Gilchrist b Gillespie	25
WS Jayantha c Gilchrist b Harvey	1
TM Dilshan run out (Symonds/Ponting)	9
UDU Chandana c Gilchrist b Kasprowicz	13
KS Lokuarachchi lbw b Kasprowicz	18
WPUJC Vaas c Gilchrist b Kasprowicz	0
DNT Zoysa lbw b Hogg	1
M Muralitharan not out	2
EXTRAS (LB 2, W 2)	4
TOTAL	193

FOW: 0 78 143 148 150 158 189 189 190 193

Bowling: Gillespie 8–2–20–1, Kasprowicz 9–1–45–5, Harvey 7–0–34–1, Symonds 10–1–47–0, Hogg 6.4–0–32–2, Clarke 3–0–13–0.

Umpires: BF Bowden & TH Wijewardene (TV Umpire – PE Manuel)

INTERNATIONAL LIMITED OVERS GAME 5

SRI LANKA v AUSTRALIA
Sinhalese Sports Club Ground, Colombo. February 29, 2004.
Toss: Australia. Sri Lanka won by three wickets.

AUSTRALIA	
AC Gilchrist (c+) lbw b Zoysa	18
BJ Haddin c Jayasuriya b Zoysa	9
MJ Clarke c Dilshan b Muralitharan	16
SM Katich run out (Zoysa/Sangakkara)	13
DR Martyn b Chandana	38
MG Bevan c Jayawardene b Muralitharan	14
A Symonds c Arnold b Zoysa	40
GB Hogg not out	35
B Lee not out	1
MS Kasprowicz	
BA Williams	
EXTRAS (LB 6, W 7, NB 1)	14
TOTAL	7 for 198

FOW: 23 34 55 86 117 120 196

Bowling: Zoysa 10–3–34–3, Kulasekara 10–0–50–0, Chandana 8–0–38–1, Dilshan 3–0–11–0, Jayasuriya 10–1–24–0, Muralitharan 9–0–35–2.

SRI LANKA	
MS Atapattu (c) b Kasprowicz	0
ST Jayasuriya c Williams b Lee	13
KC Sangakkara (+) b Hogg	37
DPM Jayawardene c Clarke b Williams	21
WS Jayantha b Kasprowicz	23
TM Dilshan b Symonds	15
RP Arnold not out	23
UDU Chandana c Katich b Symonds	4
DNT Zoysa not out	47
KMDN Kulasekara	
M Muralitharan	
EXTRAS (LB 6, W 11, NB 2)	19
TOTAL	7 for 202

FOW: 2 25 85 91 117 126 136

Bowling: Lee 9–1–52–1, Kasprowicz 9–2–20–2, Williams 9–1–29–1, Hogg 7–0–44–1, Clarke 4–0–17–0, Symonds 9.5–2–34–2.

Umpires: BF Bowden & EAR De Silva (TV Umpire – TH Wijewardene)

SRI LANKA CRICKET PRESIDENT'S XI v AUSTRALIANS at Bloomfield Cricket & Athletic Club, Colombo, March 2, 3, 4, 2004. Australians won by 245 runs. Australian XI 7 dec 484 (JL Langer 35, RT Ponting 116, SM Katich 116, DS Lehmann 134, A Symonds 45*; HMRKB Herath 3/132, SI Fernando 2/15). Sri Lanka President's XI 166 (DA Gunawardene 70; B Lee 4/29, MS Kasprowicz 2/46, SCG MacGill 3/34). Australian XI 4 dec 250 (JL Langer 63, A Symonds 119*, SK Warne 31; KS Lokuarachchi 2/51). Sri Lanka President's XI 323 (WS Jayantha 45, TT Samaraweera 50, SKL De Silva 92, WMG Ramyakumara 67; SK Warne 2/79, SCG MacGill 3/57).

FIRST TEST

SRI LANKA v AUSTRALIA

Galle International Stadium, Galle. March 8, 9, 10, 11, 12 2004.
Toss: Australia. Australia won by 197 runs.

AUSTRALIA			
JL Langer c Sangakkara b Dharmasena	12	lbw b Jayasuriya	32
ML Hayden c Chandana b Muralitharan	41	c Jayawardene b Muralitharan	130
RT Ponting (c) st Sangakkara b Chandana	21	run out (Chandana/Sangakkara)	28
DR Martyn c Jayawardene b Dharmasena	42	c (sub) KS Lokuarachchi b Muralitharan	110
DS Lehmann b Muralitharan	63	c and b Muralitharan	129
A Symonds c Jayawardene b Muralitharan	0	st Sangakkara b Muralitharan	24
AC Gilchrist (+) c Dharmasena b Muralitharan	4	lbw b Chandana	0
SK Warne c Sangakkara b Vaas	23	st Sangakkara b Muralitharan	0
JN Gillespie not out	4	not out	11
MS Kasprowicz b Muralitharan	1	not out	3
SCG MacGill lbw b Muralitharan	0		
EXTRAS (LB 9)	9	(B 15, LB 28, NB 2)	45
TOTAL	220		8 dec 512

FOW 1st Inns: 31 62 76 148 153 163 215 219 220 220
FOW 2nd Inns: 91 175 245 451 480 498 498 498

Bowling: First Innings: Vaas 12–2–39–1, Dharmasena 20–4–52–2, Muralitharan 21.3–5–59–6, Chandana 14–1–59–1, Jayasuriya 1–0–2–0. Second Innings: Vaas 27–3–67–0, Dharmasena 24–1–100–0, Muralitharan 56–9–153–5, Dilshan 6–3–9–0, Jayasuriya 14.3–2–38–1, Chandana 24.3–2–102–1.

SRI LANKA				
MS Atapattu b Gillespie	47		c Hayden b Warne	16
ST Jayasuriya lbw b Warne	35	(5)	c Hayden b MacGill	5
KC Sangakkara (+) c and b Kasprowicz	22	(2)	lbw b Kasprowicz	7
DPM Jayawardene c Hayden b Symonds	68	(3)	c Hayden b Warne	21

SRI LANKA *continued*				
TM Dilshan c Langer b Kasprowicz	104	(4)	lbw b Warne	6
HP Tillakaratne (c) lbw b Warne	33		c Symonds b Warne	25
TT Samaraweera not out	36		b MacGill	15
UDU Chandana c Gilchrist b Warne	27		c Langer b MacGill	43
WPUJC Vaas c Hayden b MacGill	0		not out	10
HDPK Dharmasena c Hayden b Warne	6		c Hayden b Warne	0
M Muralitharan c and b Warne	0		st Gilchrist b MacGill	0
EXTRAS (B 2, NB 1)	3		(B 4, W 1, NB 1)	6
TOTAL	381			154

FOW 1st Inns: 53 92 123 198 298 323 369 372 381 381
FOW 2nd Inns: 14 41 49 56 56 89 119 153 153 154

Bowling: First Innings: Gillespie 28–9–61–1, Kasprowicz 23–3–56–2, Warne 42.4–9–116–5, Symonds 19–3–68–1, MacGill 22–4–69–1, Lehmann 2–0–9–0.
Second Innings: Warne 15–5–43–5, Gillespie 9–2–20–0, Kasprowicz 5–1–13–1, MacGill 16.2–2–74–4.

Umpires: RE Koertzen & DR Shepherd (TV Umpire – MG Silva)

SECOND TEST

SRI LANKA v AUSTRALIA
Asgiriya Stadium, Kandy. March 16, 17, 18, 19, 20, 2004.
Toss: Australia. Australia won by 27 runs.

AUSTRALIA				
JL Langer lbw b Zoysa	3	c	Sangakkara b Zoysa	9
ML Hayden lbw b Muralitharan	54		c and b Vaas	5
RT Ponting (c) lbw b Vaas	10	(6)	c Sangakkara b Vaas	27
DR Martyn lbw b Muralitharan	1		st Sangakkara b Muralitharan	161
DS Lehmann b Zoysa	8		lbw b Vaas	21
A Symonds c Tillakaratne b Zoysa	6	(7)	lbw b Muralitharan	23
AC Gilchrist (+) c Sangakkara b Zoysa	0	(3)	lbw b Muralitharan	144
SK Warne c Muralitharan b Vaas	18		c Zoysa b Muralitharan	6
JN Gillespie c Jayawardene b Muralitharan	8		c Atapattu b Muralitharan	11
MS Kasprowicz b Muralitharan	0		c Jayawardene b Zoysa	8

AUSTRALIA *continued*				
SCG MacGill not out	8		not out	17
EXTRAS (B 1, LB 3)	4		(B 2, LB 7, NB 1)	10
TOTAL	120			442

FOW 1st Inns: 25 47 50 60 84 84 86 100 106 120
FOW 2nd Inns: 11 26 226 255 304 360 376 393 408 442

Bowling: First Innings: Vaas 11.2–5–14–2, Zoysa 16–3–54–4, Muralitharan 15–4–48–4. Second Innings: Vaas 33–6–103–3, Muralitharan 50.3–8–173–5, Zoysa 33–11–102–2, Lokuarachchi 12–2–33–0, Jayasuriya 5–0–16–0, Dilshan 1–0–6–0.

SRI LANKA				
MS Atapattu c Gilchrist b Kasprowicz	9		lbw b Gillespie	8
ST Jayasuriya lbw b Kasprowicz	1		c Gilchrist b Gillespie	131
DA Gunawardene lbw b Kasprowicz	13		lbw b Kasprowicz	9
KC Sangakkara (+) c Symonds b Gillespie	5		c and b Warne	29
DPM Jayawardene c Symonds b Warne	17		c Gilchrist b Gillespie	13
HP Tillakaratne (c) c Gilchrist b Warne	16	(7)	c Ponting b Warne	7
TM Dilshan lbw b Warne	0	(6)	b Warne	43
WPUJC Vaas not out	68		c Langer b Warne	45
DNT Zoysa c Gilchrist b Kasprowicz	4	(10)	c Gilchrist b Gillespie	0
KS Lokuarachchi c Kasprowicz b Warne	15	(9)	lbw b Warne	16
M Muralitharan c Symonds b Warne	43		not out	4
EXTRAS (B 8, LB 9, NB 3)	20		(B 4, LB 14, NB 1)	19
TOTAL	211			324

FOW 1st Inns: 6 34 39 49 67 67 88 111 132 211
FOW 2nd Inns: 17 36 98 174 218 239 274 319 320 324

Bowling: First Innings: Gillespie 12–4–25–1, Kasprowicz 24–5–83–4, Warne 20.1–3–65–5, Symonds 2–1–1–0, MacGill 5–1–20–0. Second Innings: Kasprowicz 17–1–55–1, Gillespie 20–1–76–4, Warne 21.1–2–90–5, Symonds 3–0–16–0, MacGill 12–0–69–0.

Umpires: SA Bucknor & DL Orchard (TV Umpire – TH Wijewardene)

THIRD TEST

SRI LANKA v AUSTRALIA
Sinhalese Sports Club Ground, Colombo. March 24, 25, 26, 27, 28, 2004.
Toss: Australia. Australia won by 121 runs.

AUSTRALIA				
JL Langer c Dilshan b Vaas	19		b Vaas	166
ML Hayden c (sub) Chandana b Samaraweera	25		lbw b Vaas	28
RT Ponting (c) c Muralitharan b Vaas	92		c Samaraweera b Herath	20
DR Martyn c Sangakkara b Vaas	14	(5)	lbw b Herath	5
DS Lehmann c Jayasuriya b Muralitharan	153	(6)	c Sangakkara b Muralitharan	1
SM Katich c and b Muralitharan	14	(7)	lbw b Muralitharan	86
AC Gilchrist (+) c Jayasuriya b Muralitharan	22	(8)	not out	31
SK Warne lbw b Muralitharan	32	(9)	c Samaraweera b Herath	0
JN Gillespie c Tillakaratne b Muralitharan	0	(4)	c Jayawardene b Muralitharan	1
MS Kasprowicz b Jayasuriya	4		run out (Jayasuriya)	3
BA Williams not out	0		c and b Herath	2
EXTRAS (B 13, LB 9, NB 4)	26		(B 11, LB 11, W 4, NB 6)	32
TOTAL	401			375

FOW 1st Inns: 43 60 96 217 244 299 376 380 387 401
FOW 2nd Inns: 40 79 80 89 98 316 341 346 368 375

Bowling: First Innings: Vaas 26–3–93–3, Zoysa 3.3–1–23–0, Samaraweera 14.3–1–37–1, Muralitharan 37.1–6–123–5, Herath 23–4–76–0, Jayasuriya 11–1–27–1. Second Innings: Vaas 21–3–61–2, Zoysa 12–0–54–0, Muralitharan 29–5–93–3, Herath 24.2–1–92–4, Samaraweera 15–4–40–0, Jayasuriya 4–0–13–0, Dilshan 1–1–0–0.

SRI LANKA				
MS Atapattu b Kasprowicz	118		b Kasprowicz	14
ST Jayasuriya c Gillespie b Lehmann	71		c Katich b Lehmann	51
KC Sangakkara (+) c Gilchrist b Lehmann	22	(5)	b Warne	27
DPM Jayawardene c Gilchrist b Gillespie	29		c Gilchrist b Lehmann	37

SRI LANKA *continued*				
TM Dilshan b Gillespie	0	(6)	c Martyn b Warne	31
HP Tillakaratne (c) not out	74		lbw b Gillespie	17
TT Samaraweera c Gilchrist b Gillespie	41	(3)	st Gilchrist b Lehmann	53
WPUJC Vaas b Warne	24		lbw b Warne	9
DNT Zoysa st Gilchrist b Lehmann	3		b Warne	1
HMRKB Herath c Martyn b Warne	3		lbw b Kasprowicz	0
M Muralitharan c Warne b Kasprowicz	8		not out	0
EXTRAS (B 4, LB 7, W 1, NB 2)	14		(B 4, LB 1, W 1, NB 2)	8
TOTAL	407			248

FOW 1st Inns: 134 175 240 240 256 327 378 381 390 407
FOW 2nd Inns: 45 92 156 181 191 231 245 247 248 248

Bowling: First Innings: Gillespie 23–4–96–3, Kasprowicz 22.1–5–58–2, Williams 19–5–48–0, Warne 36–7–115–2, Lehmann 19–2–50–3, Katich 8–0–29–0. Second Innings: Gillespie 18–6–38–1, Kasprowicz 16.4–5–37–2, Warne 33–11–92–4, Williams 5–0–19–0, Lehmann 17–2–42–3, Katich 4–1–15–0.

Umpires: SA Bucknor & DL Orchard (TV Umpire – PT Manuel)

2003–04 SRI LANKA-AUSTRALIA TEST AVERAGES

Batting	Team	M	Inn	NO	Runs	HS	50	100	Avrge	Ct/St
DS Lehmann	Aus	3	6	–	375	153	1	2	62.50	0
DR Martyn	Aus	3	6	–	333	161	–	2	55.50	2
SM Katich	Aus	1	2	–	100	86	1	–	50.00	1
ST Jayasuriya	SL	3	6	–	294	131	2	1	49.00	2
TT Samaraweera	SL	2	4	1	145	53	1	–	48.33	2
ML Hayden	Aus	3	6	–	283	130	1	1	47.17	7
AC Gilchrist	Aus	3	6	1	201	144	–	1	40.20	11/3
JL Langer	Aus	3	6	–	241	166	–	1	40.17	3
WPUJC Vaas	SL	3	6	2	156	68*	1	–	39.00	1
MS Atapattu	SL	3	6	–	212	118	–	1	35.33	1
UDU Chandana	SL	1	2	–	70	43	–	–	35.00	1
HP Tillakaratne	SL	3	6	1	172	74*	1	–	34.40	2
RT Ponting	Aus	3	6	–	198	92	1	–	33.00	1
DPM Jayawardene	SL	3	6	–	185	68	1	–	30.83	6

continued

Batting	Team	M	Inn	NO	Runs	HS	50	100	Avrge	Ct/St
TM Dilshan	SL	3	6	–	184	104	–	1	30.67	1
SCG MacGill	Aus	2	3	2	25	17*	–	–	25.00	0
KC Sangakkara	SL	3	6	–	112	29	–	–	18.67	7/4
KS Lokuarachchi	SL	1	2	–	31	16	–	–	15.50	0
M Muralitharan	SL	3	6	2	55	43	–	–	13.75	4
A Symonds	Aus	2	4	–	53	24	–	–	13.25	4
SK Warne	Aus	3	6	–	79	32	–	–	13.17	3
DA Gunawardene	SL	1	2	–	22	13	–	–	11.00	0
JN Gillespie	Aus	3	6	2	35	11*	–	–	8.75	1
MS Kasprowicz	Aus	3	6	1	19	8	–	–	3.80	2
HDPK Dharmasena	SL	1	2	–	6	6	–	–	3.00	1
BA Williams	Aus	1	2	1	2	2	–	–	2.00	0
DNT Zoysa	SL	2	4	–	8	4	–	–	2.00	1
HMRKB Herath	SL	1	2	–	3	3	–	–	1.50	1

Bowling	Team	Overs	Mds	Runs	Wkts	Avrge	5wi	10wm	Best
SK Warne	Aus	168.0	37	521	26	20.04	4	2	5/43
M Muralitharan	SL	209.1	37	649	28	23.18	4	1	6/59
DS Lehmann	Aus	38.0	4	101	6	16.83	–	–	3/42
MS Kasprowicz	Aus	107.5	20	302	12	25.17	–	–	4/83
JN Gillespie	Aus	110.0	26	316	10	31.60	–	–	4/76
WPUJC Vaas	SL	130.2	22	377	11	34.27	–	–	3/93
DNT Zoysa	SL	64.3	15	233	6	38.83	–	–	4/54
HMRKB Herath	SL	47.2	6	167	4	41.75	–	–	4/92
SCG MacGill	Aus	55.2	7	232	5	46.40	–	–	4/74
ST Jayasuriya	SL	35.3	3	96	2	48.00	–	–	1/27
HDPK Dharmasena	SL	44.0	5	152	2	76.00	–	–	2/52
TT Samaraweera	SL	29.3	5	78	1	78.00	–	–	1/38
UDU Chandana	SL	38.3	3	161	2	80.50	–	–	1/59
A Symonds	Aus	24.0	4	85	1	85.00	–	–	1/68
TM Dilshan	SL	8.0	4	15	0	–	–	–	–
SM Katich	Aus	12.0	1	44	0	–	–	–	–
KS Lokuarachchi	SL	12.0	2	33	0	–	–	–	–
BA Williams	Aus	24.0	5	67	0	–	–	–	–

2003–04 SRI LANKA–AUSTRALIA INTERNATIONAL LIMITED OVERS

Batting	Team	M	Inn	NO	Runs	HS	50	100	Avrge	Ct/St	Stk-Rt
RT Ponting	Aus	4	4	–	257	69	4	–	64.25	1	78.35
KC Sangakkara	SL	5	5	–	250	101	1	1	50.00	2	75.76
DPM Jayawardene	SL	5	5	–	225	80	2	–	45.00	3	66.77
A Symonds	Aus	5	5	3	211	53	1	–	105.50	–	85.08
ML Hayden	Aus	4	4	–	151	93	1	–	37.75	2	75.88
DR Martyn	Aus	5	5	–	133	62	1	–	26.60	–	61.29
AC Gilchrist	Aus	5	5	–	98	66	1	–	19.60	9/1	83.05
MG Bevan	Aus	5	5	1	83	24*	–	–	20.75	2	60.58
MJ Clarke	Aus	5	5	1	83	36	–	–	20.75	3	68.60
TM Dilshan	SL	5	5	1	83	30	–	–	20.75	3	62.88
ST Jayasuriya	SL	5	5	–	76	55	1	–	15.20	1	78.35
MS Atapattu	SL	5	5	–	70	47	–	–	14.00	2	47.62
UDU Chandana	SL	5	5	–	64	34	–	–	12.80	2	64.65
DNT Zoysa	SL	3	3	2	48	47*	–	–	48.00	2	101.91
RP Arnold	SL	3	3	1	37	23*	–	–	18.50	1	35.92
GB Hogg	Aus	5	3	2	37	35*	–	–	37.00	1	67.27
WPUJC Vaas	SL	4	4	–	29	24	–	–	7.25	2	80.56
HDPK Dharmasena	SL	3	3	1	26	24*	–	–	13.00	–	118.18
WS Jayantha	SL	2	2	–	24	23	–	–	12.00	1	77.42
KS Lokuarachchi	SL	1	1	–	18	18	–	–	18.00	–	94.74
SM Katich	Aus	1	1	–	13	13	–	–	13.00	1	86.67
BJ Haddin	Aus	1	1	–	9	9	–	–	9.00	–	42.86
JN Gillespie	Aus	4	1	1	8	8*	–	–	–	–	53.33
IJ Harvey	Aus	3	1	–	4	4	–	–	4.00	–	100.00
M Muralitharan	SL	5	3	2	4	2*	–	–	4.00	2	80.00
RS Kaluwitharana	SL	2	2	–	2	2	–	–	1.00	–/1	18.18
KMDN Kulasekara	SL	2	1	–	1	1	–	–	1.00	–	33.33
B Lee	Aus	3	1	1	1	1*	–	–	–	2	100.00
MS Kasprowicz	Aus	3	1	–	0	0	–	–	0.00	–	0.00
BA Williams	Aus	2	–	–	–	–	–	–	–	1	–

Bowling	Team	Overs	Mds	Runs	Wkts	Avrge	5wi	Best	RPO
GB Hogg	Aus	43.1	2	193	9	21.44	1	5/41	4.47
MS Kasprowicz	Aus	28.0	5	102	8	12.75	1	5/45	3.64
UDU Chandana	SL	41.4	–	198	7	28.29	–	3/37	4.75
M Muralitharan	SL	49.0	2	201	7	28.71	–	3/44	4.10
WPUJC Vaas	SL	32.0	2	146	7	20.86	–	3/34	4.56
MJ Clarke	Aus	24.5	–	112	5	22.40	1	5/35	4.51
JN Gillespie	Aus	31.0	5	106	5	21.20	–	3/36	3.42
A Symonds	Aus	48.5	3	214	5	42.80	–	2/34	4.38
DNT Zoysa	SL	25.1	3	111	4	27.75	–	3/34	4.41
IJ Harvey	Aus	22.0	–	101	2	50.50	–	1/34	4.59
B Lee	Aus	23.0	2	122	2	61.00	–	1/31	5.30
HDPK Dharmasena	SL	26.5	–	120	1	120.00	–	1/40	4.47
ST Jayasuriya	SL	34.0	1	172	1	172.00	–	1/66	5.06
KS Lokuarachchi	SL	8.0	–	40	1	40.00	–	1/40	5.00
BA Williams	Aus	14.0	1	57	1	57.00	–	1/29	4.07
RP Arnold	SL	2.0	–	9	0	–	–	–	4.50
TM Dilshan	SL	14.3	–	73	0	–	–	–	5.03
KMDN Kulasekara	SL	13.0	–	68	0	–	–	–	5.23

2003–04 ZIMBABWE v AUSTRALIA

AUSTRALIAN TEST SQUAD

Ricky Ponting (captain) Tas, Adam Gilchrist (vice-captain) WA, Jason Gillespie SA, Matthew Hayden Qld, Michael Kasprowicz Qld, Simon Katich NSW, Justin Langer WA, Darren Lehmann SA, Stuart MacGill NSW, Damien Martyn WA, Wade Seccombe Qld, Andrew Symonds Qld, Shane Warne Vic, Brad Williams WA. Brett Lee NSW replaced on March 11 by Shaun Tait SA due to injury.

AUSTRALIAN INTERNATIONAL LIMITED SQUAD

Ricky Ponting (captain) Tas, Adam Gilchrist (vice-captain) WA, Michael Bevan NSW, Michael Clarke NSW, Jason Gillespie SA, Brad Haddin NSW, Ian Harvey Vic, Matthew Hayden Qld, Brad Hogg WA, Michael Kasprowicz Qld, Simon Katich NSW, Brett Lee NSW, Damien Martyn WA, Andrew Symonds Qld, Brad Williams WA.

Team Management: John Buchanan (Coach), Steve Bernard (Team Manager), Alex Kountouri (Physiotherapist), Lucy Frostick (Masseur), Jock Campbell (Physical Performance Manager), Ben Romalus (Physical Performance Manager), Jonathan Rose (Media Manager).

INTERNATIONAL LIMITED OVERS GAME 1

ZIMBABWE v AUSTRALIA
Harare Sports Club Ground, Harare. May 25, 2004.
Toss: Zimbabwe. Australia won by seven wickets.

ZIMBABWE	
S Matsikenyeri c Gilchrist b Gillespie	8
BRM Taylor c Ponting b Lehmann	59
V Sibanda b McGrath	18
DD Ebrahim b Williams	8
T Taibu (c+) c Ponting b Kasprowicz	57
MA Vermeulen c Ponting b Kasprowicz	20
A Maregwede c Clarke b Gillespie	5
ML Nkala run out (Kasprowicz)	0
T Panyangara not out	14
T Mupariwa run out (Symonds)	3
DT Hondo not out	0
EXTRAS (B 2, LB 5, W 4, NB 2)	13
TOTAL	9 for 205

FOW: 9 46 64 125 172 184 184 188 204

Bowling: McGrath 10–1–35–1, Gillespie 10–4–21–2, Kasprowicz 10–2–26–2, Williams 5–0–31–1, Lehmann 6–0–32–1, Symonds 9–0–53–0.

AUSTRALIA	
AC Gilchrist (+) c Sibanda b Hondo	26
ML Hayden c Mupariwa b Panyangara	0
RT Ponting (c) c Sibanda b Panyangara	91
DR Martyn not out	74
MJ Clarke not out	5
DS Lehmann	
A Symonds	
JN Gillespie	
MS Kasprowicz	
BA Williams	
GD McGrath	
EXTRAS (LB 4, W 7)	11
TOTAL	3 for 207

FOW: 1 53 197

Bowling: Hondo 7–0–40–1, Panyangara 9.4–1–48–2, Nkala 5–1–24–0, Mupariwa 10–1–47–0, Matsikenyeri 6–0–31–0, Sibanda 2–0–13–0.

Umpires: KC Barbour & SA Bucknor (TV Umpire – RB Tiffin)

INTERNATIONAL LIMITED OVERS GAME 2

ZIMBABWE v AUSTRALIA
Harare Sports Club Ground, Harare. May 27, 2004.
Toss: Zimbabwe. Australia won by 139 runs.

AUSTRALIA	
AC Gilchrist (+) c Mwayenga b Hondo	20
ML Hayden c Taylor b Mupariwa	87
MJ Clarke b Panyangara	16
DS Lehmann b Matsikenyeri	67
IJ Harvey c Mupariwa b Matsikenyeri	22
GB Hogg c Matsikenyeri b Taylor	26
DR Martyn c Panyangara b Mupariwa	20
RT Ponting (c) st Taibu b Mwayenga	10
JN Gillespie not out	33
MS Kasprowicz not out	2
GD McGrath	
EXTRAS (B 1, LB 7, W 9, NB 3)	20
TOTAL	8 for 323

FOW: 25 43 180 219 233 274 276 314

Bowling: Hondo 9.3–1–47–1, Panyangara 6–0–34–1, Mwayenga 9–1–61–1, Mupariwa 8.3–0–64–2, Matsikenyeri 10–0–43–2, Sibanda 2–0–24–0, Taylor 5–0–42–1.

ZIMBABWE	
S Matsikenyeri c Hayden b Kasprowicz	27
BRM Taylor c Gillespie b Hogg	65
V Sibanda c Lehmann b Kasprowicz	23
MA Vermeulen c McGrath b Lehmann	25
T Taibu (c+) run out (McGrath/Lehmann)	1
A Maregwede not out	18
DD Ebrahim lbw b Hogg	1
T Panyangara c and b Lehmann	1
T Mupariwa c McGrath b Lehmann	0
W Mwayenga c McGrath b Lehmann	0
DT Hondo	
EXTRAS (B 4, LB 8, W 10, NB 1)	23
TOTAL	9 for 184

FOW: 48 108 163 164 164 168 179 180 184

Bowling: McGrath 8–1–24–0, Gillespie 8–0–37–0, Harvey 5–0–25–0, Kasprowicz 9–1–23–2, Hogg 10–1–56–2, Lehmann 4.3–1–7–4.

Umpires: SA Bucknor & ID Robinson (TV Umpire – KC Barbour)

INTERNATIONAL LIMITED OVERS GAME 3

ZIMBABWE v AUSTRALIA
Harare Sports Club Ground, Harare. May 29, 2004.
Toss: Zimbabwe. Australia won by eight wickets.

ZIMBABWE	
S Matsikenyeri c Watson b Gillespie	4
BRM Taylor lbw b Gillespie	1
V Sibanda c Gilchrist b Gillespie	2
T Taibu (c+) lbw b Kasprowicz	27
MA Vermeulen c and b Gillespie	17
A Maregwede b Gillespie	1
E Chigumbura b Hogg	77
ML Nkala b Hogg	47
T Mupariwa run out (Harvey/Gilchrist)	4
W Mwayenga lbw b Hogg	1
EC Rainsford not out	1
EXTRAS (LB 5, W 8, NB 1)	14
TOTAL	196

FOW: 4 9 10 42 50 61 175 194 195 196

Bowling: Gillespie 10–2–32–5, Kasprowicz 10–1–27–1, McGrath 8–1–28–0, Watson 8–0–38–0, Hogg 6.5–0–37–3, Symonds 6–0–29–0.

AUSTRALIA	
AC Gilchrist (+) b Mupariwa	44
MJ Clarke not out	105
A Symonds c Mwayenga b Mupariwa	20
SR Watson not out	18
RT Ponting (c)	
DR Martyn	
IJ Harvey	
GB Hogg	
JN Gillespie	
MS Kasprowicz	
GD McGrath	
EXTRAS (LB 4, W 8)	12
TOTAL	2 for 199

FOW: 68 115

Bowling: Nkala 5–0–27–0, Mwayenga 3–1–22–0, Mupariwa 8–0–48–2, Rainsford 7–0–36–0, Matsikenyeri 5–0–35–0, Chigumbura 2.4–0–27–0.

Umpires: SA Bucknor & ID Robinson (TV Umpire – RB Tiffin)

2003–04 ZIMBABWE–AUSTRALIA INTERNATIONAL LIMITED OVERS

Batting	Team	M	Inn	NO	Runs	HS	50	100	Avrge	Ct/St	Stk-Rt
MJ Clarke	Aus	3	3	2	126	105*	–	1	126.00	1	96.18
BRM Taylor	Zim	3	3	–	125	65	2	–	41.67	1	63.45
RT Ponting	Aus	3	2	–	101	91	1	–	50.50	3	98.06
DR Martyn	Aus	3	2	1	94	74*	1	–	94.00	–	80.34
AC Gilchrist	Aus	3	3	–	90	44	–	–	30.00	2	113.92
ML Hayden	Aus	2	2	–	87	87	1	–	43.50	1	85.29
T Taibu	Zim	3	3	–	85	57	1	–	28.33	–/1	63.91
E Chigumbura	Zim	1	1	–	77	77	1	–	77.00	–	85.56
DS Lehmann	Aus	2	1	–	67	67	1	–	67.00	2	97.10
MA Vermeulen	Zim	3	3	–	62	25	–	–	20.67	–	112.73
ML Nkala	Zim	2	2	–	47	47	–	–	23.50	–	58.02
V Sibanda	Zim	3	3	–	43	23	–	–	14.33	2	39.45
S Matsikenyeri	Zim	3	3	–	39	27	–	–	13.00	1	46.99
JN Gillespie	Aus	3	1	1	33	33*	–	–	–	2	206.25
GB Hogg	Aus	2	1	–	26	26	–	–	26.00	–	96.30
A Maregwede	Zim	3	3	1	24	18*	–	–	12.00	–	58.54
IJ Harvey	Aus	2	1	–	22	22	–	–	22.00	–	100.00
A Symonds	Aus	2	1	–	20	20	–	–	20.00	–	90.91
SR Watson	Aus	1	1	1	18	18*	–	–	–	1	54.55
T Panyangara	Zim	2	2	1	15	14*	–	–	15.00	1	78.95
DD Ebrahim	Zim	2	2	–	9	8	–	–	4.50	–	45.00
T Mupariwa	Zim	3	3	–	7	4	–	–	2.33	2	29.17
MS Kasprowicz	Aus	3	1	1	2	2*	–	–	–	–	66.67
EC Rainsford	Zim	1	1	1	1	1*	–	–	–	–	100.00
W Mwayenga	Zim	2	2	–	1	1	–	–	0.50	2	9.09
DT Hondo	Zim	2	1	1	0	0*	–	–	–	–	0.00
GD McGrath	Aus	3	–	–	–	–	–	–	–	3	–
BA Williams	Aus	1	–	–	–	–	–	–	–	–	–

Bowling	Team	Overs	Mds	Runs	Wkts	Avrge	5wi	Best	RPO
JN Gillespie	Aus	28.0	6	90	7	12.86	1	5/32	3.21
GB Hogg	Aus	16.5	1	93	5	18.60	–	3/37	5.52
MS Kasprowicz	Aus	29.0	4	76	5	15.20	–	2/23	2.62
DS Lehmann	Aus	10.3	1	39	5	7.80	–	4/7	3.71
T Mupariwa	Zim	26.3	1	159	4	39.75	–	2/48	6.00
T Panyangara	Zim	15.4	1	82	3	27.33	–	2/48	5.23
DT Hondo	Zim	16.3	1	87	2	43.50	–	1/40	5.27
S Matsikenyeri	Zim	21.0	–	109	2	54.50	–	2/43	5.19
GD McGrath	Aus	26.0	3	87	1	87.00	–	1/35	3.35
W Mwayenga	Zim	12.0	2	83	1	83.00	–	1/61	6.92
BRM Taylor	Zim	5.0	–	42	1	42.00	–	1/42	8.40
BA Williams	Aus	5.0	–	31	1	31.00	–	1/31	6.20
E Chigumbura	Zim	2.4	–	27	0	–	–	–	10.13
IJ Harvey	Aus	5.0	–	25	0	–	–	–	5.00
ML Nkala	Zim	10.0	1	51	0	–	–	–	5.10
EC Rainsford	Zim	7.0	–	36	0	–	–	–	5.14
V Sibanda	Zim	4.0	–	37	0	–	–	–	9.25
A Symonds	Aus	15.0	–	82	0	–	–	–	5.47
SR Watson	Aus	8.0	–	38	0	–	–	–	4.75

AUSTRALIAN TEST AVERAGES

Batting	M	Inn	NO	Runs	HS	50	100	Avrge	Ct/St
RT Ponting	14	24	3	1755	257	5	6	83.57	9
SR Waugh	12	15	4	888	156*	4	3	80.73	4
ML Hayden	15	27	4	1675	380	5	6	72.83	28
DS Lehmann	10	16	1	1045	177	3	5	69.67	3
SM Katich	6	9	1	505	125	4	1	63.13	5
DR Martyn	9	15	1	672	161	2	2	48.00	6
JL Langer	15	27	1	1201	166	4	5	46.19	12
ML Love	3	4	1	138	100*	0	1	46.00	3
AC Gilchrist	15	20	3	755	144	2	3	44.41	51/9
AJ Bichel	8	8	0	180	71	1	0	22.50	9

continued

Batting	M	Inn	NO	Runs	HS	50	100	Avrge	Ct/St
JN Gillespie		13	16	6	197	48*	0	0	19.704
GD McGrath	4	2	1	19	14	0	0	19.00	0
GB Hogg	3	3	1	33	17*	0	0	16.50	0
B Lee	10	8	1	95	23	0	0	13.57	6
A Symonds	2	4	0	53	24	0	0	13.25	4
SK Warne	3	6	0	79	32	0	0	13.17	3
BA Williams	4	6	3	23	10*	0	0	7.67	4
NW Bracken	3	3	1	9	6*	0	0	4.50	1
SCG MacGill	13	12	4	33	17*	0	0	4.13	4
MS Kasprowicz	3	6	1	19	8	0	0	3.80	2

Bowling	Overs	Mds	Runs	Wkts	Avrge	5wi	10wm	Best
SK Warne	168.0	37	521	26	20.04	4	2	5/43
SCG MacGill	549.0	102	1904	58	32.83	4	1	5/56
DS Lehmann	95.2	23	225	11	20.45	–	–	3/42
JN Gillespie	508.0	143	1274	53	24.04	1	–	5/39
MS Kasprowicz	107.5	20	302	12	25.17	–	–	4/83
SM Katich	95.5	9	349	11	31.73	1	–	6/65
AJ Bichel	266.2	61	896	27	33.19	–	–	4/63
GD McGrath	133.1	44	282	8	35.25	–	–	3/20
B Lee	367.4	77	1379	37	37.27	–	–	4/63
BA Williams	142.0	43	406	9	45.11	–	–	4/53
GB Hogg	112.0	23	383	8	47.88	–	–	2/40
NW Bracken	128.0	38	351	6	58.50	–	–	2/12
A Symonds	24.0	4	85	1	85.00	–	–	1/68
SR Waugh	77.0	15	205	1	205.00	–	–	1/35
DR Martyn	25.0	7	70	0	–	–	–	–
RT Ponting	8.0	1	25	0	–	–	–	–

AUSTRALIA INTERNATIONAL LIMITED OVERS

Batting	M	Inn	NO	Runs	HS	50	100	Avrge	Ct/St	Stk-Rt
RT Ponting	33	31	3	1260	108*	10	2	45.00	17	80.20
AC Gilchrist	31	30	0	1243	172	6	2	41.43	50/2	103.76
ML Hayden	30	29	2	1080	126	6	2	40.00	14	77.47
A Symonds	33	29	6	976	88	6	–	42.43	15	83.92
DR Martyn	28	27	7	779	100	6	1	38.95	3	83.49
MJ Clarke	27	25	7	745	105*	4	1	41.39	12	87.65
MG Bevan	27	23	7	736	84*	5	–	46.00	4	76.75
DS Lehmann	7	4	–	272	107	2	1	68.00	3	85.80
IJ Harvey	24	14	1	220	48*	–	–	16.92	4	97.78
GB Hogg	23	13	6	165	53	1	–	23.57	6	77.79
AJ Bichel	21	11	4	124	41	–	–	17.71	6	88.57
JP Maher	5	4	–	60	21	–	–	15.00	5	48.78
JN Gillespie	22	7	6	57	33*	–	–	57.00	3	107.34
BJ Haddin	3	3	–	55	32	–	–	18.33	1/1	65.48
B Lee	19	8	3	52	14	–	–	10.40	9	69.33
SM Katich	5	4	2	44	18*	–	–	22.00	1	73.33
NM Hauritz	3	2	1	22	20*	–	–	22.00	–	122.22
SR Watson	1	1	1	18	18*	–	–	–	1	54.55
MEK Hussey	1	1	1	17	17*	–	–	–	1	73.91
BA Williams	19	5	3	14	11*	–	–	7.00	4	58.09
NW Bracken	6	1	1	7	7*	–	–	–	2	70.00
GD McGrath	9	1	1	3	3*	–	–	–	4	60.00
MS Kasprowicz	8	2	1	2	2*	–	–	2.00	1	22.22

Bowling	Overs	Mds	Runs	Wkts	Avrge	5wi	Best	RPO
JN Gillespie	202.0	28	758	32	23.69	1	5/32	3.75
IJ Harvey	164.5	8	794	30	26.47	–	4/16	4.82
B Lee	154.4	16	702	29	24.21	–	4/25	4.54
BA Williams	143.3	13	605	28	21.61	2	5/22	4.22
A Symonds	211.5	8	1054	26	40.54	–	3/42	4.98
GB Hogg	184.2	8	769	25	30.76	1	5/41	4.17
AJ Bichel	157.0	5	789	18	43.83	–	2/24	5.03
MJ Clarke	89.5	1	472	16	29.50	1	5/35	5.25
MS Kasprowicz	75.0	9	243	15	16.20	1	5/45	3.24
NW Bracken	54.3	8	195	14	13.93	–	4/29	3.58
DS Lehmann	17.1	1	93	9	10.33	–	4/7	5.42
GD McGrath	77.0	7	283	8	35.38	–	4/31	3.68
NM Hauritz	21.0	1	123	2	61.50	–	2/50	5.86
MEK Hussey	3.0	–	15	0	–	–	–	5.00
SR Watson	8.0	–	38	0	–	–	–	4.75

PLAYERS' INTERNATIONAL PERFORMANCES

Bevan, Michael Gwyl

Start Date	Opp	Venue	How Out	Runs	O	M	R	W	Ct	St
17/05/03	WI	Kingston	not out	43*	–	–	–	–	–	–
18/05/03	WI	Kingston		–	–	–	–	–	–	–
21/05/03	WI	Gros Islet	not out	32*	–	–	–	–	–	–
24/05/03	WI	Port of Spain	c BC Lara b VC Drakes	21	–	–	–	–	–	–
25/05/03	WI	Port of Spain	c MN Samuels b M Dillon	31	–	–	–	–	–	–
02/08/03	Ban	Cairns		–	–	–	–	–	–	–
03/08/03	Ban	Cairns	not out	40*	–	–	–	–	2	–
06/08/03	Ban	Darwin	b Mashrafe Bin Mortaza	57	–	–	–	–	–	–
26/10/03	Ind	Gwalior	b V Sehwag	18	–	–	–	–	–	–
29/10/03	NZ	Faridabad		–	–	–	–	–	–	–
01/11/03	Ind	Mumbai	c M Kaif b AB Agarkar	42	–	–	–	–	–	–
03/11/03	NZ	Pune	c CZ Harris b CL Cairns	50	–	–	–	–	–	–
09/11/03	NZ	Guwahati	not out	84*	–	–	–	–	–	–
12/11/03	Ind	Bangalore		–	–	–	–	–	–	–
18/11/03	Ind	Kolkata	not out	40*	–	–	–	–	–	–
09/01/04	Ind	Melbourne	c SC Ganguly b V Sehwag	1	–	–	–	–	–	–
11/01/04	Zim	Sydney	c GW Flower b GW Flower	3	–	–	–	–	–	–
16/01/04	Zim	Hobart	c HH Streak b SM Ervine	7	–	–	–	–	–	–
18/01/04	Ind	Brisbane	not out	41*	–	–	–	–	–	–
22/01/04	Ind	Sydney	b SC Ganguly	12	–	–	–	–	–	–
26/01/04	Zim	Adelaide	c SM Ervine b DT Hondo	75	–	–	–	–	–	–
29/01/04	Zim	Melbourne	run out (Blignaut/Taibu)	56	–	–	–	–	–	–
20/02/04	SL	Dambulla	st RS Kaluwitharana b M Muralitharan	21	–	–	–	–	–	–
22/02/04	SL	Dambulla	not out	24*	–	–	–	–	1	–
25/02/04	SL	Colombo	run out (Jayawardene/Jayasuriya)	10	–	–	–	–	–	–

continued

Start Date	Opp	Venue	How Out	Runs	O	M	R	W	Ct	St
27/02/04	SL	Colombo	c and b M Muralitharan	14	–	–	–	–	1	–
29/02/04	SL	Colombo	c DPM Jayawardene b M Muralitharan	14	–	–	–	–	–	–

Bichel, Andrew John

Start Date	Opp	Venue	How Out	Runs	O	M	R	W	Ct	St
09/05/03	WI	St John's	c (sub) MN Samuels b JJC Lawson	34	14.0	4	53	3	1	–
			c DS Smith b M Dillon	0	15.0	3	49	–	–	–
17/05/03	WI	Kingston		–	7.0	1	38	–	–	–
18/05/03	WI	Kingston		–	5.0	–	27	2	–	–
21/05/03	WI	Gros Islet		–	10.0	1	44	1	–	–
25/05/03	WI	Port of Spain	b MN Samuels	7	10.0	–	67	2	–	–
30/05/03	WI	St George's	c BC Lara b CH Gayle	41	10.0	–	52	1	–	–
18/07/03	Ban	Darwin		–	–	–	–	–	–	–
25/07/03	Ban	Cairns		–	–	–	–	–	–	–
02/08/03	Ban	Cairns		–	5.0	–	24	2	–	–
03/08/03	Ban	Cairns		–	10.0	–	29	1	1	–
06/08/03	Ban	Darwin		–	10.0	1	35	1	–	–
09/10/03	Zim	Perth		–	21.0	2	62	2	–	–
				–	28.2	15	63	4	–	–
17/10/03	Zim	Sydney	c CB Wishart b AM Blignaut	5	24.2	7	66	4	–	–
				–	19.0	5	64	–	–	–
26/10/03	Ind	Gwalior	c M Kaif b Zaheer Khan	14	7.0	–	39	–	–	–
29/10/03	NZ	Faridabad		–	7.0	–	29	1	1	–
01/11/03	Ind	Mumbai	b AB Agarkar	1	6.0	–	31	1	1	–
03/11/03	NZ	Pune	c BB McCullum b DL Vettori	9	9.0	–	59	1	–	–
09/11/03	NZ	Guwahati	not out	15*	7.0	–	21	1	–	–
12/11/03	Ind	Bangalore		–	9.0	–	46	–	1	–
18/11/03	Ind	Kolkata		–	8.0	–	51	1	–	–
04/12/03	Ind	Brisbane	c VVS Laxman b AB Agarkar	11	28.0	6	130	1	1	–
				–	3.0	–	12	–	–	–

continued

Start Date	Opp	Venue	How Out	Runs	O	M	R	W	Ct	St
12/12/03	Ind	Adelaide	c A Chopra b AR Kumble	19	28.0	3	118	4	2	–
			b AB Agarkar	1	11.4	2	35	1	1	–
26/12/03	Ind	Melbourne		–	–	–	–	–	–	–
09/01/04	Ind	Melbourne	run out (Balaji)	1	6.0	–	38	–	–	–
11/01/04	Zim	Sydney	not out	11*	6.0	2	24	–	–	–
16/01/04	Zim	Hobart	b HH Streak	0	9.0	–	31	1	1	–
22/01/04	Ind	Sydney	not out	2*	9.0	–	60	1	–	–
29/01/04	Zim	Melbourne	not out	23*	–	–	–	–	–	–
01/02/04	Ind	Perth		–	7.0	–	44	1	1	–

Bracken, Nathan Wade

Start Date	Opp	Venue	How Out	Runs	O	M	R	W	Ct	St
17/10/03	Zim	Sydney		–	–	–	–	–	–	–
26/10/03	Ind	Gwalior	not out	7*	10.0	–	53	3	–	–
29/10/03	NZ	Faridabad		–	9.0	2	25	3	–	–
01/11/03	Ind	Mumbai		–	10.0	2	29	4	1	–
03/11/03	NZ	Pune		–	10.0	3	39	–	–	–
09/11/03	NZ	Guwahati		–	7.3	–	34	3	–	–
18/11/03	Ind	Kolkata		–	8.0	1	15	1	1	–
04/12/03	Ind	Brisbane	not out	6*	26.0	5	90	1	–	–
				–	4.0	1	12	2	–	–
12/12/03	Ind	Adelaide		–	–	–	–	–	–	–
26/12/03	Ind	Melbourne	c and b SR Tendulkar	1	28.0	6	71	1	1	–
				–	25.0	13	45	2	–	–
02/01/04	Ind	Sydney	c AB Agarkar b AR Kumble	2	37.0	13	97	–	–	–
				–	8.0	–	36	–	–	–

Clarke, Michael John

Start Date	Opp	Venue	How Out	Runs	O	M	R	W	Ct	St
21/05/03	WI	Gros Islet	not out	75*	–	–	–	–	3	–
24/05/03	WI	Port of Spain	not out	55*	–	–	–	–	–	–
25/05/03	WI	Port of Spain	c BC Lara b M Dillon	39	4.0	–	25	–	–	–

continued

Start Date	Opp	Venue	How Out	Runs	O	M	R	W	Ct	St
01/06/03	WI	St George's	st RD Jacobs b CH Gayle	1	–	–	–	–	–	–
01/11/03	Ind	Mumbai	run out (Tendular/Agarkar)	2	10.0	–	42	4	1	–
03/11/03	NZ	Pune	b DR Tuffey	70	2.0	–	14	–	–	–
09/11/03	NZ	Guwahati	c CD McMillan b DL Vettori	2	5.0	–	21	–	–	–
12/11/03	Ind	Bangalore		–	4.0	–	36	1	–	–
18/11/03	Ind	Kolkata	not out	44*	7.0	1	36	2	–	–
09/01/04	Ind	Melbourne	c VVS Laxman b AR Kumble	63	4.0	–	22	1	4	–
11/01/04	Zim	Sydney	c V Sibanda b SM Ervine	40	5.0	–	14	1	–	–
16/01/04	Zim	Hobart	c MA Vermeulen b HH Streak	0	3.0	–	16	–	–	–
18/01/04	Ind	Brisbane	cwk RS Dravid b IK Pathan	42	4.0	–	26	–	–	–
22/01/04	Ind	Sydney	c HK Badani b SC Ganguly	21	5.0	–	29	–	–	–
26/01/04	Zim	Adelaide	run out (Flower/Taibu)	36	7.0	–	57	1	–	–
29/01/04	Zim	Melbourne	b NB Mahwire	11	–	–	–	–	–	–
01/02/04	Ind	Perth	c V Sehwag b L Balaji	2	2.0	–	4	–	–	–
06/02/04	Ind	Melbourne		–	3.0	–	18	1	–	–
08/02/04	Ind	Sydney	not out	33*	–	–	–	–	–	–
20/02/04	SL	Dambulla	lbw b M Muralitharan	0	5.0	–	21	–	–	–
22/02/04	SL	Dambulla	c UDU Chandana b WPUJC Vaas	0	7.5	–	35	5	–	–
25/02/04	SL	Colombo	not out	31*	5.0	–	26	–	2	–
27/02/04	SL	Colombo	c TM Dilshan b UDU Chandana	36	3.0	–	13	–	–	–
29/02/04	SL	Colombo	c TM Dilshan	16	4.0	–	17	–	1	–
25/05/04	Zim	Harare	not out	5*	–	–	–	–	1	–
27/05/04	Zim	Harare	b T Panyangara	16	–	–	–	–	–	–
29/05/04	Zim	Harare	not out	105*	–	–	–	–	–	–

Gilchrist, Adam Craig

Start Date	Opp	Venue	How Out	Runs	O	M	R	W	Ct	St
09/05/03	WI	St John's	c S Chanderpaul b M Dillon	33	–	–	–	–	2	–
			c (sub) MN Samuels b OAC Banks	6	–	–	–	–	3	–
17/05/03	WI	Kingston	c MN Samuels b M Dillon	21	–	–	–	–	3	–
18/05/03	WI	Kingston	c MN Samuels b CD Collymore	27	–	–	–	–	4	–
24/05/03	WI	Port of Spain	b RO Hurley	84	–	–	–	–	–	–
25/05/03	WI	Port of Spain	c WW Hinds b CD Collymore	11	–	–	–	–	3	–
30/05/03	WI	St George's	c BC Lara b MN Samuels	64	–	–	–	–	1	–
01/06/03	WI	St George's	b MN Samuels	5	–	–	–	–	–	–
18/07/03	Ban	Darwin	b Manjural Islam	43	–	–	–	–	3	–
				–	–	–	–	–	3	–
25/07/03	Ban	Cairns		–	–	–	–	–	3	–
				–	–	–	–	–	–	–
02/08/03	Ban	Cairns	cwk Hannan Sarkar b Mashrafe Bin Morta	18	–	–	–	–	4	–
03/08/03	Ban	Cairns		–	–	–	–	–	2	–
06/08/03	Ban	Darwin	cwk Hannan Sarkar b Mohammad Rafiq	31	–	–	–	–	–	–
09/10/03	Zim	Perth	not out	113*	–	–	–	–	1	–
				–	–	–	–	–	3	1
17/10/03	Zim	Sydney	b HH Streak	20	–	–	–	–	4	–
				–	–	–	–	–	1	1
26/10/03	Ind	Gwalior	b Zaheer Khan	83	–	–	–	–	1	–
29/10/03	NZ	Faridabad	c and b JDP Oram	29	–	–	–	–	2	–
01/11/03	Ind	Mumbai	c M Kaif b Harbhajan Singh	41	–	–	–	–	3	–
03/11/03	NZ	Pune	c DL Vettori b DR Tuffey	25	–	–	–	–	–	–
12/11/03	Ind	Bangalore	c Zaheer Khan b AR Kumble	111	–	–	–	–	–	–
18/11/03	Ind	Kolkata	b AB Agarkar	7	–	–	–	–	–	–
04/12/03	Ind	Brisbane	c VVS Laxman b Zaheer Khan	0	–	–	–	–	–	–
				–	–	–	–	–	–	–

continued

Start Date	Opp	Venue	How Out	Runs	O	M	R	W	Ct	St
12/12/03	Ind	Adelaide	c V Sehwag b AB Agarkar	29	–	–	–	–	2	–
			b AR Kumble	43	–	–	–	–	–	1
26/12/03	Ind	Melbourne	c A Nehra b AR Kumble	14	–	–	–	–	3	–
				–	–	–	–	–	3	–
02/01/04	Ind	Sydney	b IK Pathan	6	–	–	–	–	2	–
			st PA Patel b AR Kumble	4	–	–	–	–	–	–
09/01/04	Ind	Melbourne	c IK Pathan b AB Agarkar	34	–	–	–	–	–	–
11/01/04	Zim	Sydney	cwk T Taibu b AM Blignaut	34	–	–	–	–	2	1
16/01/04	Zim	Hobart	b SM Ervine	172	–	–	–	–	3	–
18/01/04	Ind	Brisbane	c L Balaji b IK Pathan	21	–	–	–	–	–	–
22/01/04	Ind	Sydney	c and b M Kartik	95	–	–	–	–	3	–
01/02/04	Ind	Perth	c L Balaji b IK Pathan	75	–	–	–	–	3	–
06/0204	Ind	Melbourne	c SR Tendulkar b L Balaji	38	–	–	–	–	3	–
08/02/04	Ind	Sydney	c SC Ganguly b A Nehra	29	–	–	–	–	2	–
20/02/04	SL	Dambulla	c MS Atapattu b UDU Chandana	66	–	–	–	–	1	1
22/02/04	SL	Dambulla	c and b WPUJC Vaas	0	–	–	–	–	1	–
25/02/04	SL	Colombo	c DPM Jayawardene b WPUJC Vaas	0	–	–	–	–	1	–
27/02/04	SL	Colombo	cwk KC Sangakkara b DNT Zoysa	14	–	–	–	–	6	–
29/02/04	SL	Colombo	lbw b DNT Zoysa	18	–	–	–	–	–	–
08/03/04	SL	Galle	c HDPK Dharmasena b M Muralitharan	4	–	–	–	–	1	–
			lbw b UDU Chandana	0	–	–	–	–	–	1
16/03/04	SL	Kandy	cwk KC Sangakkara b DNT Zoysa	0	–	–	–	–	3	–
			lbw b M Muralitharan	144	–	–	–	–	3	–
24/03/04	SL	Colombo	c ST Jayasuriya b M Muralitharan	22	–	–	–	–	3	1
			not out	31*	–	–	–	–	1	1

continued

Start Date	Opp	Venue	How Out	Runs	O	M	R	W	Ct	St
25/05/04	Zim	Harare	c V Sibanda b DT Hondo	26	–	–	–	–	1	–
27/05/04	Zim	Harare	c W Mwayenga b DT Hondo	20	–	–	–	–	–	–
29/05/04	Zim	Harare	b T Mupariwa	44	–	–	–	–	1	–

Gillespie, Jason Neil

Start Date	Opp	Venue	How Out	Runs	O	M	R	W	Ct	St
09/05/03	WI	St John's	cwk RD Jacobs b JJC Lawson	6	17.0	3	56	–	–	–
			c BC Lara b VC Drakes	5	25.0	10	64	1	–	–
18/05/03	WI	Kingston		–	9.0	–	28	1	–	–
21/05/03	WI	Gros Islet		–	10.0	1	48	2	1	–
24/05/03	WI	Port of Spain		–	8.0	–	30	2	–	–
30/05/03	WI	St George's	not out	1*	9.0	2	33	1	–	–
01/06/03	WI	St George's	not out	0*	10.0	1	41	–	–	–
18/07/03	Ban	Darwin	not out	16*	8.0	1	27	2	1	–
				–	16.0	3	48	2	–	–
25/07/03	Ban	Cairns		–	25.0	7	57	3	–	–
				–	12.4	3	38	4	–	–
02/08/03	Ban	Cairns		–	10.0	3	23	3	–	–
06/08/03	Ban	Darwin		–	10.0	6	16	1	–	–
09/10/03	Zim	Perth		–	25.3	9	52	3	–	–
				–	3.0	–	6	2	–	–
04/12/03	Ind	Brisbane	run out (Harbhajan/Agarkar)	8	31.0	12	65	4	1	–
				–	5.0	1	17	–	–	–
12/12/03	Ind	Adelaide	not out	48*	40.5	13	106	1	–	–
			cwk PA Patel b AB Agarkar	3	10.2	2	22	1	–	–
02/01/04	Ind	Sydney	st PA Patel b AR Kumble	47	45.0	11	135	3	–	–
			not out	4*	7.0	2	32	1	1	–
09/01/04	Ind	Melbourne	not out	8*	10.0	1	50	1	–	–
11/01/04	Zim	Sydney	not out	1*	8.0	–	21	2	–	–
18/01/04	Ind	Brisbane	c IK Pathan b L Balaji	6	10.0	–	40	–	–	–

continued

Start Date	Opp	Venue	How Out	Runs	O	M	R	W	Ct	St
22/01/04	Ind	Sydney		–	10.0	–	50	1	–	–
26/01/04	Zim	Adelaide		–	10.0	2	40	1	–	–
01/02/04	Ind	Perth		–	10.0	–	51	1	–	–
06/02/04	Ind	Melbourne		–	10.0	–	39	2	–	–
08/02/04	Ind	Sydney		–	9.0	1	52	2	–	–
20/02/04	SL	Dambulla		–	6.0	2	14	1	–	–
22/02/04	SL	Dambulla		–	7.0	–	36	–	–	–
25/02/04	SL	Colombo		–	10.0	1	36	3	–	–
27/02/04	SL	Colombo	not out	8*	8.0	2	20	1	–	–
08/03/04	SL	Galle	not out	4*	28.0	9	61	1	–	–
			not out	11*	9.0	2	20	–	–	–
16/03/04	SL	Kandy	c DPM Jayawardene b M Muralitharan	8	12.0	4	25	1	–	–
			c MS Atapattu b M Muralitharan	11	20.0	1	76	4	–	–
24/03/04	SL	Colombo	c HP Tillakaratne b M Muralitharan	0	23.0	4	96	3	1	–
			c DPM Jayawardene b M Muralitharan	1	18.0	6	38	1	–	–
25/05/04	Zim	Harare		–	10.0	4	21	2	–	–
27/05/04	Zim	Harare	not out	33*	8.0	–	37	–	1	–
29/05/04	Zim	Harare		–	10.0	2	32	5	1	–

Haddin, Bradley James

Start Date	Opp	Venue	How Out	Runs	O	M	R	W	Ct	St
26/01/04	Zim	Adelaide	lbw b HH Streak	14	–	–	–	–	1	1
29/01/04	Zim	Melbourne	b HH Streak	32	–	–	–	–	–	–
29/02/04	SL	Colombo	c ST Jayasuriya b DNT Zoysa	9	–	–	–	–	–	–

Harvey, Ian Joseph

Start Date	Opp	Venue	How Out	Runs	O	M	R	W	Ct	St
17/05/03	WI	Kingston	not out	48*	7.0	–	37	3	–	–
24/05/03	WI	Port of Spain		–	9.3	–	58	2	–	–
25/05/03	WI	Port of Spain	b CH Gayle	2	10.0	1	46	–	–	–
01/06/03	WI	St George's	run out (Lara)	4	5.0	–	31	–	–	–

continued

Start Date	Opp	Venue	How Out	Runs	O	M	R	W	Ct	St
02/08/03	Ban	Cairns		–	–	–	–	–	–	–
03/08/03	Ban	Cairns		–	7.0	1	21	1	–	–
06/08/03	Ban	Darwin	c Mohammad Rafiq b Mashrafe Bin Mortaz	5	6.3	–	16	4	–	–
26/10/03	Ind	Gwalior	b SR Tendulkar	4	8.0	–	46	–	–	–
29/10/03	NZ	Faridabad		–	8.0	2	9	2	–	–
03/11/03	NZ	Pune	c SB Styris b DL Vettori	19	9.0	1	33	1	2	–
09/11/03	NZ	Guwahati	c CJ Nevin b DR Tuffey	25	4.0	–	14	1	1	–
12/11/03	Ind	Bangalore		–	10.0	–	71	2	–	–
18/11/03	Ind	Kolkata		–	4.5	–	21	4	–	–
09/01/04	Ind	Melbourne	c SR Tendulkar b AB Agarkar	28	10.0	1	52	3	1	–
11/01/04	Zim	Sydney	c SM Ervine b SM Ervine	22	4.0	–	14	–	–	–
16/01/04	Zim	Hobart		–	–	–	–	–	–	–
18/01/04	Ind	Brisbane	c RS Gavaskar b A Nehra	13	10.0	–	61	1	–	–
22/01/04	Ind	Sydney	run out (Agarkar/Ganguly)	1	10.0	–	68	–	–	–
26/01/04	Zim	Adelaide		–	–	–	–	–	–	–
29/01/04	Zim	Melbourne	run out (Blignaut/Taibu)	23	–	–	–	–	–	–
01/02/04	Ind	Perth		–	–	–	–	–	–	–
06/02/04	Ind	Melbourne		–	10.0	–	40	2	–	–
08/02/04	Ind	Sydney		–	5.0	2	30	2	–	–
22/02/04	SL	Dambulla		–	9.0	–	38	1	–	–
25/02/04	SL	Colombo		–	6.0	–	29	–	–	–
27/02/04	SL	Colombo	run out (Atapattu/Muralitharan)	4	7.0	–	34	1	–	–
29/02/04	SL	Colombo		–	–	–	–	–	–	–
27/05/04	Zim	Harare	c T Mupariwa b S Matsikenyeri	22	5.0	–	25	–	–	–
29/05/04	Zim	Harare		–	–	–	–	–	–	–

Hauritz, Nathan Michael

Start Date	Opp	Venue	How Out	Runs	O	M	R	W	Ct	St
21/05/03	WI	Gros Islet		–	10.0	1	50	2	–	–
25/05/03	WI	Port of Spain	not out	20*	6.0	–	38	–	–	–
30/05/03	WI	St George's	run out (Bernard)	2	5.0	–	35	–	–	–

Hayden, Matthew Lawrence

Start Date	Opp	Venue	How Out	Runs	O	M	R	W	Ct	St
09/05/03	WI	St John's	c VC Drakes b JJC Lawson	14	–	–	–	–	–	–
			run out (sub) CS Baugh	177	–	–	–	–	–	–
17/05/03	WI	Kingston	c CH Gayle b M Dillon	7	–	–	–	–	–	–
18/05/03	WI	Kingston	c CD Collymore b OAC Banks	51	–	–	–	–	1	–
21/05/03	WI	Gros Islet	cwk CS Baugh b M Dillon	20	–	–	–	–	–	–
24/05/03	WI	Port of Spain	c RO Hurley b VC Drakes	44	–	–	–	–	1	–
30/05/03	WI	St George's	c WW Hinds b CD Collymore	29	–	–	–	–	–	–
01/06/03	WI	St George's	c DE Bernard b M Dillon	8	–	–	–	–	–	–
18/07/03	Ban	Darwin	b Mashrafe Bin Mortaza	11	–	–	–	–	–	–
				–	–	–	–	–	–	–
25/07/03	Ban	Cairns	b Sanwar Hossain	50	–	–	–	–	–	–
				–	–	–	–	–	1	–
02/08/03	Ban	Cairns	not out	46*	–	–	–	–	1	–
03/08/03	Ban	Cairns		–	–	–	–	–	–	–
06/08/03	Ban	Darwin	c and b Mohammad Rafiq	42	–	–	–	–	–	–
09/10/03	Zim	Perth	c SV Carlisle b TR Gripper	380	–	–	–	–	2	–
				–	–	–	–	–	1	–
17/10/03	Zim	Sydney	c SV Carlisle b AM Blignaut	20	–	–	–	–	–	–
			not out	101*	–	–	–	–	1	–
26/10/03	Ind	Gwalior	st PA Patel b AR Kumble	47	–	–	–	–	1	–

continued

Start Date	Opp	Venue	How Out	Runs	O	M	R	W	Ct	St
29/10/03	NZ	Faridabad	not out	51*	–	–	–	–	1	–
01/11/03	Ind	Mumbai	c Yuvraj Singh b Zaheer Khan	0	–	–	–	–	–	–
03/11/03	NZ	Pune	c SB Styris b DR Tuffey	9	–	–	–	–	–	–
12/11/03	Ind	Bangalore	run out (Ganguly/Dravid)	44	–	–	–	–	–	–
18/11/03	Ind	Kolkata	c VVS Laxman b Zaheer Khan	19	–	–	–	–	1	–
04/12/03	Ind	Brisbane	c VVS Laxman b Zaheer Khan	37	–	–	–	–	4	–
			c V Sehwag b Harbhajan Singh	99	–	–	–	–	–	–
12/12/03	Ind	Adelaide	cwk PA Patel b IK Pathan	12	–	–	–	–	1	–
			c V Sehwag b A Nehra	17	–	–	–	–	–	–
26/12/03	Ind	Melbourne	lbw b AR Kumble	136	–	–	–	–	1	–
			not out	53*	–	–	–	–	3	–
02/01/04	Ind	Sydney	c SC Ganguly b AR Kumble	67	–	–	–	–	–	–
			c RS Dravid b AR Kumble	30	–	–	–	–	–	–
09/01/04	Ind	Melbourne	c Yuvraj Singh b AB Agarkar	20	–	–	–	–	1	–
11/01/04	Zim	Sydney	b HH Streak	14	–	–	–	–	1	–
16/01/04	Zim	Hobart	c V Sibanda b HH Streak	63	–	–	–	–	1	–
18/01/04	Ind	Brisbane	cwk RS Dravid b IK Pathan	109	–	–	–	–	–	–
26/01/04	Zim	Adelaide	c DD Ebrahim b AM Blignaut	20	–	–	–	–	–	–
29/01/04	Zim	Melbourne	b DT Hondo	23	–	–	–	–	–	–
01/02/04	Ind	Perth	c RS Gavaskar b AB Agarkar	0	–	–	–	–	1	–
06/02/04	Ind	Melbourne	c and b L Balaji	50	–	–	–	–	1	–
08/02/04	Ind	Sydney	b SR Tendulkar	126	–	–	–	–	–	–
20/02/04	SL	Dambulla	run out (Atapattu)	40	–	–	–	–	1	–
22/02/04	SL	Dambulla	c DPM Jayawardene b HDPK Dharmasena	93	–	–	–	–	–	–
25/02/04	SL	Colombo	c M Muralitharan b WPUJC Vaas	3	–	–	–	–	1	–

continued

Start Date	Opp	Venue	How Out	Runs	O	M	R	W	Ct	St
27/02/04	SL	Colombo	c DNT Zoysa b WPUJC Vaas	15	–	–	–	–	–	–
08/03/04	SL	Galle	c UDU Chandana b M Muralitharan	41	–	–	–	–	3	–
			c DPM Jayawardene b M Muralitharan	130	–	–	–	–	4	–
16/03/04	SL	Kandy	lbw b M Muralitharan	54	–	–	–	–	–	–
			c and b WPUJC Vaas	5	–	–	–	–	–	–
24/03/04	SL	Colombo	c (sub) UDUChandanab TT Samaraweera	25	–	–	–	–	–	–
			lbw b WPUJC Vaas	28	–	–	–	–	–	–
25/05/04	Zim	Harare	c T Mupariwa b T Panyangara	0	–	–	–	–	–	–
27/05/04	Zim	Harare	c BRM Taylor b T Mupariwa	87	–	–	–	–	1	–
29/05/04	Zim	Harare		–	–	–	–	–	–	–

Hogg, George Bradley

Start Date	Opp	Venue	How Out	Runs	O	M	R	W	Ct	St
09/05/03	WI	St John's		–	–	–	–	–	–	–
17/05/03	WI	Kingston		–	–	–	–	–	1	–
18/05/03	WI	Kingston		–	10.0	3	27	1	–	–
21/05/03	WI	Gros Islet		–	10.0	–	53	–	–	–
24/05/03	WI	Port of Spain		–	9.0	1	41	–	1	–
30/05/03	WI	St George's	c CH Gayle b MN Samuels	0	10.0	1	35	–	–	–
01/06/03	WI	St George's	b CH Gayle	53	10.0	–	47	–	–	–
02/08/03	Ban	Cairns		–	10.0	–	27	–	–	–
03/08/03	Ban	Cairns		–	10.0	–	31	3	–	–
06/08/03	Ban	Darwin	not out	4*	10.0	–	32	2	2	–
17/10/03	Zim	Sydney	c DD Ebrahim b RW Price	13	23.0	8	49	2	–	–
				–	31.0	9	70	1	–	–
26/10/03	Ind	Gwalior	st PA Patel b Harbhajan Singh	29	10.0	–	47	–	–	–
29/10/03	NZ	Faridabad		–	–	–	–	–	–	–
01/11/03	Ind	Mumbai	not out	0*	5.2	–	28	1	–	–

continued

Start Date	Opp	Venue	How Out	Runs	O	M	R	W	Ct	St
09/11/03	NZ	Guwahati	c SB Styris b CZ Harris	9	10.0	–	39	2	1	–
09/01/04	Ind	Melbourne		–	–	–	–	–	–	–
11/01/04	Zim	Sydney		–	–	–	–	–	–	–
16/01/04	Zim	Hobart	not out	6*	10.0	–	36	1	–	–
18/01/04	Ind	Brisbane		–	–	–	–	–	–	–
22/01/04	Ind	Sydney		–	–	–	–	–	–	–
26/01/04	Zim	Adelaide	not out	1*	10.0	–	40	1	–	–
29/01/04	Zim	Melbourne	run out (Streak)	0	–	–	–	–	–	–
06/02/04	Ind	Melbourne		–	–	–	–	–	–	–
08/02/04	Ind	Sydney		–	–	–	–	–	–	–
20/02/04	SL	Dambulla	not out	2*	9.3	1	41	5	–	–
22/02/04	SL	Dambulla		–	10.0	1	35	–	–	–
25/02/04	SL	Colombo		–	10.0	–	41	1	1	–
27/02/04	SL	Colombo	lbw b UDU Chandana	0	6.4	–	32	2	–	–
29/02/04	SL	Colombo	not out	35*	7.0	–	44	1	–	–
25/05/04	Zim	Harare		–	–	–	–	–	–	–
27/05/04	Zim	Harare	c S Matsikenyeri b BRM Taylor	26	10.0	1	56	2	–	–
29/05/04	Zim	Harare		–	6.5	–	37	3	–	–

Hussey, Michael Edward Killeen

Start Date	Opp	Venue	How Out	Runs	O	M	R	W	Ct	St
01/02/04	Ind	Perth	not out	17*	3.0	–	15	–	1	–

Kasprowicz, Michael Scott

Start Date	Opp	Venue	How Out	Runs	O	M	R	W	Ct	St
09/11/03	NZ	Guwahati		–	8.0	–	28	1	–	–
12/11/03	Ind	Bangalore		–	10.0	–	37	1	1	–
25/02/04	SL	Colombo		–	10.0	2	37	1	–	–
27/02/04	SL	Colombo	cwk KC Sangakkara b UDU Chandana	0	9.0	1	45	5	–	–
29/02/04	SL	Colombo		–	9.0	2	20	2	–	–
08/03/04	SL	Galle	b M Muralitharan	1	23.0	3	56	2	1	–
			not out	3*	5.0	1	13	1	–	–

continued

Start Date	Opp	Venue	How Out	Runs	O	M	R	W	Ct	St
16/03/04	SL	Kandy	b M Muralitharan	0	24.0	5	83	4	1	–
			c DPM Jayawardene b DNT Zoysa	8	17.0	1	55	1	–	–
24/03/04	SL	Colombo	b ST Jayasuriya	4	22.1	5	58	2	–	–
			run out (Jayasuriya)	3	16.4	5	37	2	–	–
25/05/04	Zim	Harare		–	10.0	2	26	2	–	–
27/05/04	Zim	Harare	not out	2*	9.0	1	23	2	–	–
29/05/04	Zim	Harare		–	10.0	1	27	1	–	–

Katich, Simon Matthew

Start Date	Opp	Venue	How Out	Runs	O	M	R	W	Ct	St
17/10/03	Zim	Sydney	b RW Price	52	7.0	–	25	–	–	–
				–	25.5	3	65	6	1	–
04/12/03	Ind	Brisbane	cwk PA Patel b Zaheer Khan	16	2.0	–	16	–	1	–
				–	–	–	–	–	–	–
12/12/03	Ind	Adelaide	c V Sehwag b AB Agarkar	75	16.0	3	59	2	–	–
			c A Nehra b AB Agarkar	31	8.0	1	22	2	1	–
26/12/03	Ind	Melbourne	c A Chopra b AR Kumble	29	4.0	–	18	1	1	–
				–	4.0	–	16	–	–	–
02/01/04	Ind	Sydney	c V Sehwag b AR Kumble	125	17.0	1	84	–	–	–
			not out	77*	–	–	–	–	–	–
22/01/04	Ind	Sydney	c SC Ganguly b IK Pathan	2	–	–	–	–	–	–
01/02/04	Ind	Perth	not out	18*	–	–	–	–	–	–
06/02/04	Ind	Melbourne		–	–	–	–	–	–	–
08/02/04	Ind	Sydney	not out	11*	–	–	–	–	–	–
20/02/04	SL	Dambulla		–	–	–	–	–	–	–
22/02/04	SL	Dambulla		–	–	–	–	–	–	–
25/02/04	SL	Colombo		–	–	–	–	–	–	–
27/02/04	SL	Colombo		–	–	–	–	–	–	–
29/02/04	SL	Colombo	run out (Zoysa/Sangakkara)	13	–	–	–	–	1	–
08/03/04	SL	Galle		–	–	–	–	–	–	–
16/03/04	SL	Kandy		–	–	–	–	–	–	–

continued

Start Date	Opp	Venue	How Out	Runs	O	M	R	W	Ct	St
24/03/04	SL	Colombo	c and b M Muralitharan	14	8.0	–	29	–	–	–
			lbw b M Muralitharan	86	4.0	1	15	–	1	–

Langer, Justin Lee

Start Date	Opp	Venue	How Out	Runs	O	M	R	W	Ct	St
09/05/03	WI	St John's	c OAC Banks b JJC Lawson	42	–	–	–	–	1	–
			c BC Lara b CH Gayle	111	–	–	–	–	–	–
18/07/03	Ban	Darwin	lbw b Alok Kapali	71	–	–	–	–	1	–
				–	–	–	–	–	–	–
25/07/03	Ban	Cairns	c Javed Omar b Mashrafe Bin Mortaza	1	–	–	–	–	–	–
				–	–	–	–	–	2	–
09/10/03	Zim	Perth	b SM Ervine	26	–	–	–	–	–	–
				–	–	–	–	–	–	–
17/10/03	Zim	Sydney	c HH Streak x b Mashrafe Bin Mortaza	2	–	–	–	–	–	–
			cwk T Taibu b HH Streak	8	–	–	–	–	–	–
04/12/03	Ind	Brisbane	lbw b AB Agarkar	121	–	–	–	–	–	–
			cwk PA Patel b AB Agarkar	0	–	–	–	–	1	–
12/12/03	Ind	Adelaide	c V Sehwag b AR Kumble	58	–	–	–	–	–	–
			lbw b AB Agarkar	10	–	–	–	–	–	–
26/12/03	Ind	Melbourne	c SR Tendulkar b AB Agarkar	14	–	–	–	–	2	–
			lbw b AB Agarkar	2	–	–	–	–	–	–
02/01/04	Ind	Sydney	cwk PA Patel b AR Kumble	117	–	–	–	–	–	–
			c V Sehwag b M Kartik	47	–	–	–	–	–	–
08/03/04	SL	Galle	cwk KC Sangakkara b HDPK Dharmasena	12	–	–	–	–	1	–
			lbw b ST Jayasuriya	32	–	–	–	–	1	–
16/03/04	SL	Kandy	lbw b DNT Zoysa	3	–	–	–	–	–	–
			cwk KC Sangakkara b DNT Zoysa	9	–	–	–	–	1	–
24/03/04	SL	Colombo	c TM Dilshan b WPUJC Vaas	19	–	–	–	–	–	–
			b WPUJC Vaas	166	–	–	–	–	–	–

Lee, Brett

Start Date	Opp	Venue	How Out	Runs	O	M	R	W	Ct	St
09/05/03	WI	St John's	cwk RD Jacobs b JJC Lawson	9	15.0	2	72	3	–	–
			c (sub) SC Joseph b M Dillon	18	23.0	4	63	4	1	–
17/05/03	WI	Kingston		–	8.0	2	52	2	–	–
18/05/03	WI	Kingston		–	7.0	–	22	2	1	–
24/05/03	WI	Port of Spain		–	8.0	1	30	1	–	–
25/05/03	WI	Port of Spain	c CH Gayle b RR Sarwan	6	10.0	2	56	3	–	–
30/05/03	WI	St George's	c RL Powell b CD Collymore	14	9.4	2	50	3	–	–
01/06/03	WI	St George's	c MN Samuels b CH Gayle	4	6.0	–	36	–	–	–
18/07/03	Ban	Darwin	run out (Tapash Baisya)	23	8.2	2	23	3	–	–
				–	12.0	5	34	1	–	–
25/07/03	Ban	Cairns		–	18.0	1	88	1	1	–
				–	11.0	2	45	1	1	–
02/08/03	Ban	Cairns		–	8.0	1	25	4	–	–
03/08/03	Ban	Cairns		–	9.0	2	24	–	–	–
09/10/03	Zim	Perth		–	15.0	4	48	3	–	–
				–	35.0	8	96	1	–	–
17/10/03	Zim	Sydney	not out	6*	23.0	5	78	2	–	–
26/12/03	Ind	Melbourne	c VVS Laxman b AR Kumble	8	27.0	7	103	2	–	–
				–	22.0	3	97	2	–	–
02/01/04	Ind	Sydney	c A Chopra b AR Kumble	0	39.3	5	201	4	–	–
				–	12.2	2	75	–	–	–
16/01/04	Zim	Hobart		–	10.0	1	29	1	–	–
18/01/04	Ind	Brisbane	c AR Kumble b L Balaji	6	10.0	–	83	1	–	–
22/01/04	Ind	Sydney	not out	12*	9.0	–	46	2	–	–
26/01/04	Zim	Adelaide	not out	6*	8.0	–	32	1	1	–
29/01/04	Zim	Melbourne	c AM Blignaut b SM Ervine	3	–	–	–	–	–	–
01/02/04	Ind	Perth		–	10.0	2	22	3	1	–
06/02/04	Ind	Melbourne		–	9.0	–	34	2	1	–

continued

Start Date	Opp	Venue	How Out	Runs	O	M	R	W	Ct	St
08/02/04	Ind	Sydney		–	10.0	1	39	2	3	–
20/02/04	SL	Dambulla		–	8.0	1	31	1	1	–
22/02/04	SL	Dambulla		–	6.0	–	39	–	1	–
29/02/04	SL	Colombo	not out	1*	9.0	1	52	1	–	–

Lehmann, Darren Scott

Start Date	Opp	Venue	How Out	Runs	O	M	R	W	Ct	St
09/05/03	WI	St John's	cwk RD Jacobs b JJC Lawson	7	–	–	–	–	–	–
			b M Dillon	14	–	–	–	–	–	–
17/05/03	WI	Kingston	c RL Powell b OAC Banks	55	–	–	–	–	–	–
30/05/03	WI	St George's	c and b CH Gayle	43	1.0	–	11	1	1	–
01/06/03	WI	St George's	c MN Samuels b CH Gayle	107	1.3	–	27	–	–	–
18/07/03	Ban	Darwin	c Javed Omar b Mashrafe Bin Mortaza	110	–	–	–	–	–	–
				–	–	–	–	–	–	–
25/07/03	Ban	Cairns	c Mohammad Ashraful b Tapash Baisya	177	3.0	1	4	–	–	–
				–	–	–	–	–	–	–
02/08/03	Ban	Cairns		–	–	–	–	–	–	–
03/08/03	Ban	Cairns		–	4.1	–	16	3	–	–
06/08/03	Ban	Darwin		–	–	–	–	–	–	–
09/10/03	Zim	Perth	c and b SM Ervine	30	2.0	1	3	–	1	–
				–	31.2	15	61	3	–	–
08/03/04	SL	Galle	b M Muralitharan	63	2.0	–	9	–	–	–
			c and b M Muralitharan	129	–	–	–	–	–	–
16/03/04	SL	Kandy	b DNT Zoysa	8	–	–	–	–	–	–
			lbw b WPUJC Vaas	21	–	–	–	–	–	–
24/03/04	SL	Colombo	c ST Jayasuriya b M Muralitharan	153	19.0	2	50	3	–	–
			cwk KC Sangakkara b M Muralitharan	1	17.0	2	42	3	–	–
25/05/04	Zim	Harare		–	6.0	–	32	1	–	–
27/05/04	Zim	Harare	b S Matsikenyeri	67	4.3	1	7	4	2	–

Love, Martin Lloyd

Start Date	Opp	Venue	How Out	Runs	O	M	R	W	Ct	St
09/05/03	WI	St John's	b OAC Banks	36	–	–	–	–	1	–
			c (sub) MN Samuels b OAC Banks	2	–	–	–	–	–	–
18/07/03	Ban	Darwin	b Mashrafe Bin Mortaza	0	–	–	–	–	–	–
				–	–	–	–	–	–	–
25/07/03	Ban	Cairns	not out	100*	–	–	–	–	2	–
				–	–	–	–	–	–	–

MacGill, Stuart Charles Glyndwr

Start Date	Opp	Venue	How Out	Runs	O	M	R	W	Ct	St
09/05/03	WI	St John's	c RR Sarwan b JJC Lawson	2	2.3	–	7	1	–	–
			c BC Lara b M Dillon	0	35.5	8	149	1	–	–
18/07/03	Ban	Darwin		–	13.0	4	21	2	–	–
				–	13.1	1	65	5	1	–
25/07/03	Ban	Cairns		–	24.0	9	77	5	1	–
				–	20.0	3	56	5	–	–
09/10/03	Zim	Perth		–	21.0	4	54	2	–	–
				–	3.4	1	10	–	–	–
04/12/03	Ind	Brisbane	c A Chopra b AB Agarkar	1	26.1	4	86	4	–	–
				–	4.0	–	32	–	–	–
12/12/03	Ind	Adelaide	lbw b AR Kumble	0	44.0	8	143	2	2	–
			b AB Agarkar	1	24.4	3	101	2	–	–
26/12/03	Ind	Melbourne	lbw b AB Agarkar	0	15.0	3	70	3	–	–
				–	26.5	5	68	2	–	–
02/01/04	Ind	Sydney	not out	0*	38.0	5	146	–	–	–
				–	16.0	1	65	1	–	–
08/03/04	SL	Galle	lbw b M Muralitharan	0	22.0	4	69	1	–	–
				–	16.2	2	74	4	–	–
16/03/04	SL	Kandy	not out	8*	5.0	1	20	–	–	–
			not out	17*	12.0	–	69	–	–	–

Maher, James Patrick

Start Date	Opp	Venue	How Out	Runs	O	M	R	W	Ct	St
18/05/03	WI	Kingston		–	–	–	–	–	–	–
21/05/03	WI	Gros Islet	c DS Smith b OAC Banks	17	–	–	–	–	1	–
25/05/03	WI	Port of Spain	c RO Hurley b CD Collymore	21	–	–	–	–	–	–
30/05/03	WI	St George's	c and b CH Gayle	19	–	–	–	–	1	–
09/11/03	NZ	Guwahati	lbw b DR Tuffey	3	–	–	–	–	3	–

Martyn, Damien Richard

Start Date	Opp	Venue	How Out	Runs	O	M	R	W	Ct	St
02/08/03	Ban	Cairns	not out	0*	–	–	–	–	–	–
03/08/03	Ban	Cairns	not out	92*	–	–	–	–	2	–
06/08/03	Ban	Darwin	b Alok Kapali	1	–	–	–	–	–	–
09/10/03	Zim	Perth	c CB Wishart b TR Gripper	53	–	–	–	–	–	–
				–	13.0	5	34	–	–	–
17/10/03	Zim	Sydney	lbw b RW Price	32	3.0	1	9	–	1	–
				–	–	–	–	–	–	–
26/10/03	Ind	Gwalior	b V Sehwag	16	–	–	–	–	–	–
29/10/03	NZ	Faridabad	not out	2*	–	–	–	–	1	–
01/11/03	Ind	Mumbai	b AB Agarkar	100	–	–	–	–	–	–
03/11/03	NZ	Pune	b DR Tuffey	10	–	–	–	–	–	–
09/11/03	NZ	Guwahati	cwk BB McCullum b KD Mills	0	–	–	–	–	–	–
12/11/03	Ind	Bangalore	not out	61*	–	–	–	–	–	–
18/11/03	Ind	Kolkata	c Yuvraj Singh b V Sehwag	61	–	–	–	–	–	–
04/12/03	Ind	Brisbane	run out (Harbhjan/ Patel/Ganguly)	42	–	–	–	–	–	–
			not out	66*	–	–	–	–	1	–
12/12/03	Ind	Adelaide	c VVS Laxman b A Nehra	30	–	–	–	–	–	–
			c RS Dravid b SR Tendulkar	38	–	–	–	–	–	–
26/12/03	Ind	Melbourne	cwk PA Patel b AB Agarkar	31	–	–	–	–	1	–
				–	–	–	–	–	–	–

continued

Start Date	Opp	Venue	How Out	Runs	O	M	R	W	Ct	St
02/01/04	Ind	Sydney	c and b AR Kumble	7	9.0	1	27	–	–	–
			c (sub)Yuvraj Singh b AR Kumble	40	–	–	–	–	1	–
09/01/04	Ind	Melbourne	c L Balaji b AB Agarkar	0	–	–	–	–	–	–
11/01/04	Zim	Sydney	c and b GW Flower	21	–	–	–	–	–	–
16/01/04	Zim	Hobart	not out	47*	–	–	–	–	–	–
18/01/04	Ind	Brisbane	c Yuvraj Singh b L Balaji	1	–	–	–	–	–	–
22/01/04	Ind	Sydney	cwk PA Patel b IK Pathan	0	–	–	–	–	–	–
26/01/04	Zim	Adelaide	c DD Ebrahim b HH Streak	9	–	–	–	–	–	–
29/01/04	Zim	Melbourne	lbw b HH Streak	42	–	–	–	–	–	–
01/02/04	Ind	Perth	c VVS Laxman b AB Agarkar	2	–	–	–	–	–	–
06/02/04	Ind	Melbourne	not out	20*	–	–	–	–	–	–
08/02/04	Ind	Sydney	c HK Badani b IK Pathan	67	–	–	–	–	–	–
20/02/04	SL	Dambulla	c and b UDU Chandana	27	–	–	–	–	–	–
22/02/04	SL	Dambulla	c MS Atapattu b WPUJC Vaas	5	–	–	–	–	–	–
25/02/04	SL	Colombo	run out (Jayasuriya)	62	–	–	–	–	–	–
27/02/04	SL	Colombo	c DNT Zoysa b KS Lokuarachchi	1	–	–	–	–	–	–
29/02/04	SL	Colombo	b UDU Chandana	38	–	–	–	–	–	–
08/03/04	SL	Galle	c DPM Jayawardene b HDPK Dharmasena	42	–	–	–	–	–	–
			c (sub) KS Lokuarachchi b M Muralitharan	110	–	–	–	–	–	–
16/03/04	SL	Kandy	lbw b M Muralitharan	1	–	–	–	–	–	–
			st KC Sangakkara b M Muralitharan	161	–	–	–	–	–	–
24/03/04	SL	Colombo	cwk KC Sangakkara b WPUJC Vaas	14	–	–	–	–	1	–
			lbw b HMRKB Herath	5	–	–	–	–	1	–
25/05/04	Zim	Harare	not out	74*	–	–	–	–	–	–

continued

Start Date	Opp	Venue	How Out	Runs	O	M	R	W	Ct	St
27/05/04	Zim	Harare	c T Panyangara b T Mupariwa	20	–	–	–	–	–	–
29/05/04	Zim	Harare		–	–	–	–	–	–	–

McGrath, Glenn Donald

Start Date	Opp	Venue	How Out	Runs	O	M	R	W	Ct	St
09/05/03	WI	St John's	not out	5*	17.0	6	44	2	–	–
			c D Ganga b VC Drakes	14	25.0	10	50	1	–	–
17/05/03	WI	Kingston		–	8.0	1	34	1	–	–
18/05/03	WI	Kingston		–	10.0	2	31	4	1	–
21/05/03	WI	Gros Islet		–	10.0	1	35	1	–	–
24/05/03	WI	Port of Spain		–	7.0	–	21	1	–	–
25/05/03	WI	Port of Spain	not out	3*	10.0	–	46	–	–	–
01/06/03	WI	St George's		–	6.0	–	29	–	–	–
18/07/03	Ban	Darwin		–	13.0	6	20	3	–	–
				–	10.0	–	25	1	–	–
25/07/03	Ban	Cairns		–	17.1	2	57	1	–	–
				–	15.0	9	22	–	–	–
25/05/04	Zim	Harare		–	10.0	1	35	1	–	–
27/05/04	Zim	Harare		–	8.0	1	24	–	3	–
29/05/04	Zim	Harare		–	8.0	1	28	–	–	–

Ponting, Ricky Thomas

Start Date	Opp	Venue	How Out	Runs	O	M	R	W	Ct	St
17/05/03	WI	Kingston	c CD Collymore b CH Gayle	59	–	–	–	–	–	–
18/05/03	WI	Kingston	not out	57*	–	–	–	–	–	–
21/05/03	WI	Gros Islet	run out (Collymore)	32	–	–	–	–	–	–
24/05/03	WI	Port of Spain	c RO Hurley b RL Powell	38	–	–	–	–	1	–
25/05/03	WI	Port of Spain	c WW Hinds b M Dillon	10	–	–	–	–	–	–
30/05/03	WI	St George's	run out (Lara/Samuels)	2	–	–	–	–	–	–

continued

Start Date	Opp	Venue	How Out	Runs	O	M	R	W	Ct	St
01/06/03	WI	St George's	not out	2*	–	–	–	–	–	–
18/07/03	Ban	Darwin	c Javed Omar b Tapash Baisya	10	–	–	–	–	–	–
				–	–	–	–	–	–	–
25/07/03	Ban	Cairns	c Mohammad Ashraful b Sanwar Hossain	59	–	–	–	–	–	–
				–	–	–	–	–	2	–
02/08/03	Ban	Cairns	b Mohammad Rafiq	29	–	–	–	–	1	–
03/08/03	Ban	Cairns		–	–	–	–	–	1	–
06/08/03	Ban	Darwin	c Tushar Imran b Tapash Baisya	101	–	–	–	–	2	–
09/10/03	Zim	Perth	lbw b SM Ervine	37	–	–	–	–	–	–
				–	5.0	1	15	–	–	–
17/10/03	Zim	Sydney	b RW Price	169	–	–	–	–	1	–
			not out	53*	–	–	–	–	1	–
26/10/03	Ind	Gwalior	c and b AR Kumble	2	–	–	–	–	–	–
29/10/03	NZ	Faridabad	cwk BB McCullum b DR Tuffey	12	–	–	–	–	1	–
01/11/03	Ind	Mumbai	lbw b AB Agarkar	31	–	–	–	–	–	–
03/11/03	NZ	Pune	b SB Styris	16	–	–	–	–	1	–
09/11/03	NZ	Guwahati	c CD McMillan b DL Vettori	52	–	–	–	–	2	–
12/11/03	Ind	Bangalore	not out	108*	–	–	–	–	–	–
18/11/03	Ind	Kolkata	c VVS Laxman b M Kartik	36	–	–	–	–	–	–
04/12/03	Ind	Brisbane	cwk PA Patel b Zaheer Khan	54	–	–	–	–	–	–
			c V Sehwag b A Nehra	50	–	–	–	–	–	–
12/12/03	Ind	Adelaide	c RS Dravid b AR Kumble	242	1.0	–	4	–	1	–
			c A Chopra b AB Agarkar	0	–	–	–	–	–	–
26/12/03	Ind	Melbourne	st PA Patel b AR Kumble	257	–	–	–	–	–	–
			not out	31*	–	–	–	–	–	–
02/01/04	Ind	Sydney	lbw b AR Kumble	25	–	–	–	–	–	–
			c and b IK Pathan	47	–	–	–	–	–	–
09/01/04	Ind	Melbourne	c and b L Balaji	18	–	–	–	–	2	–
11/01/04	Zim	Sydney	c SV Carlisle b AM Blignaut	21	–	–	–	–	2	–

continued

Start Date	Opp	Venue	How Out	Runs	O	M	R	W	Ct	St
16/01/04	Zim	Hobart	c S Matsikenyeri b GW Flower	37	–	–	–	–	–	–
18/01/04	Ind	Brisbane	c VVS Laxman b L Balaji	7	–	–	–	–	–	–
22/01/04	Ind	Sydney	cwk PA Patel b IK Pathan	42	–	–	–	–	–	–
26/01/04	Zim	Adelaide	run out (Blignaut/Taibu)	63	–	–	–	–	–	–
29/01/04	Zim	Melbourne	c NB Mahwire b RW Price	35	–	–	–	–	–	–
06/02/04	Ind	Melbourne	cwk RS Dravid b L Balaji	88	–	–	–	–	–	–
08/02/04	Ind	Sydney	cwk RS Dravid b IK Pathan	4	–	–	–	–	–	–
20/02/04	SL	Dambulla	c TM Dilshan b ST Jayasuriya	58	–	–	–	–	–	–
22/02/04	SL	Dambulla	c WPUJC Vaas b UDU Chandana	69	–	–	–	–	1	–
25/02/04	SL	Colombo	b WPUJC Vaas	63	–	–	–	–	–	–
27/02/04	SL	Colombo	lbw b M Muralitharan	67	–	–	–	–	–	–
08/03/04	SL	Galle	st KC Sangakkara b UDU Chandana	21	–	–	–	–	–	–
			run out (Chandana/ Sangakkara)	28	–	–	–	–	–	–
16/03/04	SL	Kandy	lbw b WPUJC Vaas	10	–	–	–	–	–	–
			cwk KC Sangakkara b WPUJC Vaas	27	–	–	–	–	1	–
24/03/04	SL	Colombo	c M Muralitharan b WPUJC Vaas	92	–	–	–	–	–	–
			c TT Samaraweera b HMRKB Herath	20	–	–	–	–	–	–
25/05/04	Zim	Harare	c V Sibanda b T Panyangara	91	–	–	–	–	3	–
27/05/04	Zim	Harare	st T Taibu b W Mwayenga	10	–	–	–	–	–	–
29/05/04	Zim	Harare	–	–	–	–	–	–	–	–

Symonds, Andrew

Start Date	Opp	Venue	How Out	Runs	O	M	R	W	Ct	St
17/05/03	WI	Kingston	c M Dillon b OAC Banks	18	7.0	–	42	1	1	–
18/05/03	WI	Kingston	not out	17*	8.0	–	22	–	–	–
21/05/03	WI	Gros Islet	b CH Gayle	75	–	–	–	–	–	–
24/05/03	WI	Port of Spain	b CD Collymore	24	4.0	–	31	1	–	–
25/05/03	WI	Port of Spain	b MN Samuels	77	–	–	–	–	–	–
30/05/03	WI	St George's	c BC Lara b RR Sarwan	16	4.0	–	19	1	2	–
01/06/03	WI	St George's	c WW Hinds b CH Gayle	48	5.0	–	36	1	–	–
02/08/03	Ban	Cairns		–	1.0	–	5	–	1	–
03/08/03	Ban	Cairns	c Sanwar Hossain b HasibulHassan	7	5.0	–	24	1	1	–
06/08/03	Ban	Darwin	run out (Sanwar/Sarkar)	0	1.0	1	0	–	–	–
26/10/03	Ind	Gwalior	lbw b Zaheer Khan	1	5.0	–	24	–	2	–
29/10/03	NZ	Faridabad		–	–	–	–	–	–	–
01/11/03	Ind	Mumbai	c Harbhajan Singh b Yuvraj Singh	48	10.0	–	57	–	1	–
03/11/03	NZ	Pune	not out	37*	10.0	2	56	2	–	–
09/11/03	NZ	Guwahati	cwk BB McCullum b KD Mills	18	4.0	–	14	–	–	–
12/11/03	Ind	Bangalore		–	9.0	–	42	3	1	–
18/11/03	Ind	Kolkata	c HK Badani b Harbhajan Singh	10	7.0	–	36	1	2	–
09/01/04	Ind	Melbourne	c AR Kumble b AB Agarkar	88	10.0	–	47	2	–	–
11/01/04	Zim	Sydney	c DT Hondo b SM Ervine	42	6.0	1	24	2	–	–
16/01/04	Zim	Hobart	run out (Matsikenyeri/Ervine)	0	10.0	–	48	1	–	–
18/01/04	Ind	Brisbane	c and b RS Gavaskar	20	8.0	–	47	1	1	–
22/01/04	Ind	Sydney	c AB Agarkar b SC Ganguly	16	7.0	–	42	–	–	–
26/01/04	Zim	Adelaide	c DT Hondo b HH Streak	34	7.0	–	47	2	1	–
29/01/04	Zim	Melbourne		–	–	–	–	–	–	–

continued

Start Date	Opp	Venue	How Out	Runs	O	M	R	W	Ct	St
01/02/04	Ind	Perth	c VVS Laxman b IK Pathan	73	10.0	–	37	2	–	–
06/02/04	Ind	Melbourne	not out	10*	7.0	–	47	–	1	–
08/02/04	Ind	Sydney	b A Nehra	66	3.0	1	11	–	1	–
20/02/04	SL	Dambulla	not out	37*	10.0	–	40	1	–	–
22/02/04	SL	Dambulla	not out	36*	10.0	–	45	1	–	–
25/02/04	SL	Colombo	not out	45*	9.0	–	48	1	–	–
27/02/04	SL	Colombo	c WS Jayantha b M Muralitharan	53	10.0	1	47	–	–	–
29/02/04	SL	Colombo	c RP Arnold b DNT Zoysa	40	9.5	2	34	2	–	–
08/03/04	SL	Galle	c DPM Jayawardene b M Muralitharan	0	19.0	3	68	1	–	–
			st KC Sangakkara b M Muralitharan	24	–	–	–	–	1	–
16/03/04	SL	Kandy	c HP Tillakaratne b DNT Zoysa	6	2.0	1	1	–	3	–
			lbw b M Muralitharan	23	3.0	–	16	–	–	–
25/05/04	Zim	Harare		–	9.0	–	53	–	–	–
27/05/04	Zim	Harare		–	–	–	–	–	–	–
29/05/04	Zim	Harare	c W Mwayenga b T Mupariwa	20	6.0	–	29	–	–	–

Warne, Shane Keith

Start Date	Opp	Venue	How Out	Runs	O	M	R	W	Ct	St
08/03/04	SL	Galle	cwk KC Sangakkara b WPUJC Vaas	23	42.4	9	116	5	1	–
			st KC Sangakkara b M Muralitharan	0	15.0	5	43	5	–	–
16/03/04	SL	Kandy	c M Muralitharan b WPUJC Vaas	18	20.1	3	65	5	–	–
			c DNT Zoysa b M Muralitharan	6	21.1	2	90	5	1	–
24/03/04	SL	Colombo	lbw b M Muralitharan	32	36.0	7	115	2	1	–
			c TT Samaraweera b HMRKB Herath	0	33.0	11	92	4	–	–

Watson, Shane Robert

Start Date	Opp	Venue	How Out	Runs	O	M	R	W	Ct	St
29/05/04	Zim	Harare	not out	18*	8.0	–	38	–	1	–

Waugh, Stephen Rodger

Start Date	Opp	Venue	How Out	Runs	O	M	R	W	Ct	St
09/05/03	WI	St John's	c RD Jacobs b M Dillon	41	–	–	–	–	–	–
			not out	45*	5.0	–	25	–	1	–
18/07/03	Ban	Darwin	not out	100*	–	–	–	–	–	–
				–	–	–	–	–	–	–
25/07/03	Ban	Cairns	not out	156*	5.0	3	4	–	–	–
				–	–	–	–	–	–	–
09/10/03	Zim	Perth	c and b SM Ervine	78	5.0	1	10	–	1	–
				–	8.0	2	26	–	1	–
17/10/03	Zim	Sydney	c SV Carlisle b RW Price	61	4.0	–	7	–	–	–
				–	–	–	–	–	1	–
04/12/03	Ind	Brisbane	hit wicket b Zaheer Khan	0	7.0	3	16	–	–	–
			not out	56*	–	–	–	–	–	–
12/12/03	Ind	Adelaide	b A Nehra	30	9.0	2	15	–	–	–
			c RS Dravid b SR Tendulkar	42	4.0	–	10	–	–	–
26/12/03	Ind	Melbourne	lbw b AR Kumble	19	9.0	–	35	1	–	–
				–	–	–	–	–	–	–
02/01/04	Ind	Sydney	cwk PA Patel b IK Pathan	40	2.0	–	6	–	–	–
			c SR Tendulkar b AR Kumble	80	–	–	–	–	–	–

Williams, Bradley Andrew

Start Date	Opp	Venue	How Out	Runs	O	M	R	W	Ct	St
03/08/03	Ban	Cairns		–	–	–	–	–	–	–
06/08/03	Ban	Darwin		–	10.0	2	32	–	–	–
09/10/03	Zim	Perth		–	–	–	–	–	–	–
17/10/03	Zim	Sydney	c and b RW Price	7	23.0	6	58	2	1	–
				–	16.0	8	56	2	2	–
26/10/03	Ind	Gwalior	not out	11*	10.0	–	67	1	–	–
29/10/03	NZ	Faridabad		–	9.4	1	22	4	–	–

continued

Start Date	Opp	Venue	How Out	Runs	O	M	R	W	Ct	St
01/11/03	Ind	Mumbai		–	5.0	–	20	–	–	–
03/11/03	NZ	Pune	not out	3*	10.0	1	53	5	–	–
12/11/03	Ind	Bangalore		–	8.0	–	43	–	–	–
18/11/03	Ind	Kolkata		–	7.0	1	30	1	–	–
04/12/03	Ind	Brisbane		–	–	–	–	–	–	–
12/12/03	Ind	Adelaide	b AR Kumble	0	23.0	7	72	–	–	–
			not out	4*	14.0	6	34	–	–	–
26/12/03	Ind	Melbourne	not out	10*	20.0	6	66	1	–	–
				–	22.0	5	53	4	1	–
02/01/04	Ind	Sydney		–	–	–	–	–	–	–
09/01/04	Ind	Melbourne	c Yuvraj Singh b AB Agarkar	0	9.0	–	52	2	–	–
11/01/04	Zim	Sydney		–	8.3	2	22	5	1	–
16/01/04	Zim	Hobart		–	8.0	–	25	1	–	–
18/01/04	Ind	Brisbane	run out (Dravid)	0	8.0	–	40	1	2	–
26/01/04	Zim	Adelaide		–	8.0	1	38	2	–	–
29/01/04	Zim	Melbourne	not out	0*	–	–	–	–	–	–
01/02/04	Ind	Perth		–	7.0	2	23	1	–	–
06/02/04	Ind	Melbourne		–	10.0	1	38	1	–	–
08/02/04	Ind	Sydney		–	6.2	1	12	2	–	–
20/02/04	SL	Dambulla		–	5.0	–	28	–	–	–
29/02/04	SL	Colombo		–	9.0	1	29	1	1	–
24/03/04	SL	Colombo	not out	0*	19.0	5	48	–	–	–
			c and b HMRKB Herath	2	5.0	–	19	–	–	–
25/05/04	Zim	Harare		–	5.0	–	31	1	–	–